Overview

Contents

Quick Reference

Peter's Principles

Performance

Troubleshooting

Acknowledgments

Thanks to my wife, Rebecca, for working with me to get this book completed. I really don't know what I would have done without her help in researching and compiling some of the information that appears in this book. She also did a fine job of proofreading my rough draft.

Don Doherty deserves special thanks for his invaluable input, especially in Chapter 24.

John Goodman graciously did a thorough tech edit of Chapters 17, 22, and 23, and he also helped with the final author review of these chapters. Thanks also to Ned Snell for tech editing Chapter 24.

I would like to thank Scott Clark for his help and direction. His input was instrumental in helping this book achieve the depth of information it required.

Matt Wagner, my agent, deserves credit for helping me get the contract in the first place and taking care of all the details that most authors don't really think about.

The technical support staff at Microsoft (especially those on CompuServe) deserve credit for answering the questions that helped fill in the blanks and made the Windows 95 learning experience go faster.

Finally, I would like to thank Sunthar Visuvalingam and Gayle Johnson of Sams for their assistance in bringing this book to print.

Introduction

Windows 95 represents a major leap in technology from the Windows 3.x days. It provides many of the features that DOS and Windows users have been asking for. You'll find new features such as long filenames and better utilities for maintaining your system. The new Explorer interface will make a lot of people happy as well.

When I was writing this book, I took the opportunity to really look at Windows 95. Not only did I look at the user interface, but I also looked at the architectural changes that Microsoft made. I appreciated the differences you can't readily see. The 32-bit components really speed things along. Windows 95 handles many tasks differently as well. You'll find that it's a lot more stable than Windows 3.x.

Whether you like the changes you can see—or those that you can't—everyone will agree that Windows 95 is a superior operating system for the user. That's right—I said the user. If you're looking for a server, you're in the wrong place. Windows NT is the superior operating system.

As you read this book, you'll learn about all the new things Windows 95 has to offer. I'll also spend some time telling you about the features that haven't changed, those that need a bit more work, and some of the unexpected ways that you can use the new features that do work well.

Who Should Read This Book?

This book's intended audience is intermediate to advanced Windows 95 users who need to get the last ounce of computing power from their machines. I'll provide you with tips and techniques to make Windows 95 easier to use, enhance overall system performance, and improve system stability. Of course, every Windows 95 user can gain something from this book, even if only a better understanding of how Windows 95 works. We'll also spend some time looking at the internal workings of Windows 95. Not only will you learn about where Windows 95 is today, but I'll also help you understand how Windows 95 differs from its predecessor and how these differences will help you become more productive. If you want the most detailed description of Windows 95 available, this is the book for you.

What You Will Learn

Here are some of the more important topics I cover in this book:

- Installation tips that everyone can use
- Architectural details—how things work under the hood
- Exploiting the new utilities that Windows 95 provides

- Taking advantage of the Accessibility features
- The purpose of the files in the \SYSTEM folder
- Windows 95 fonts and ways to make them easier to use
- Creating your own setup script files
- MSDOS.SYS features that can make your system harder to break into
- The truth about the DOS-Windows connection
- Performance tips to turn your machine into a speed demon
- Using Microsoft Exchange for all your communication needs
- OLE architecture and how to use OLE in your applications
- Navigating the new Explorer interface
- The new object-oriented approach to using resources on your machine
- How plug and play makes it easier to install new devices
- Compatibility tips about what works and what doesn't under Windows 95
- The objects available on the context menu and how you can modify it to meet your needs
- Modifying your system setup to fully meet your needs
- Work-arounds for potential Windows 95 problems

We'll also spend some time learning about some of the fun parts of computing. For example, Appendix A deals exclusively with the features provided by both the Microsoft Network (MSN) and CompuServe. I'll even provide a few tips that should help you decide which one to subscribe to. This appendix also includes some important information you need to know about WUGNET (Windows Users Group Network)—an organization that every Windows user needs to know about.

I spend a great deal of time talking about the Windows 95 architecture in various chapters. There are two reasons for this extensive exposure. First, you, as a user, really do need to know how the operating system works—or at least get an overview—so that you can maximize the way you use its features. Second, you need to know what Windows 95 provides that Windows 3.x didn't. Exploring the architecture is one of the best ways to meet this goal.

How This Book Is Organized

This book divides Windows 95 into functional and task-oriented areas. These parts of the book break each piece of Windows 95 apart to see how it ticks and what you can use it for. Of course, many chapters help you understand what's going on under the hood too. Without this information, it would be difficult at best to make full use of the new features that Windows 95 offers.

I'd like to offer one final piece of advice. Windows 95 is a very user- and data-oriented operating system. It's probably the most user-tuned product available right now for the PC. This doesn't mean that Windows 95 is perfect, nor does it mean that everything is as it seems. Sometimes you'll find something that's so difficult to use that you'll wonder why Microsoft did it that way. For example, I found the registry really difficult to work with until I discovered all the tools that Microsoft provides to make the job easier. You should take the time to really explore this product and figure out which techniques work best for you. Windows 95 offers more than one way to do every task. You need to find the one that's best for you.

Next Stop—Windows 95!

Before you start a journey, it always helps to know where you are and where you're going. Chapter 1 tells you where we are now. It also gives you a little history on why we're here. Chapter 2 tells you where we're going. These chapters work together to help you put Windows 95 into context. We'll look at important issues such as how Windows 95 compares to past versions of Windows and what you can expect from it. I also spend a little time predicting where we might go in the future.

Power Primers

This section of the book has three chapters. The first deals with tuning tips. Getting the best performance and highest reliability is the concern of everyone who's just starting to use a new operating system. Windows 95 offers many ways to tune your system. It would seem that all these controls could help you get a tuned system with a very minimal amount of effort. Actually, the exact opposite is true. All these controls interact—and you have to take these interactions into account as you change settings. Optimizing one area usually means detuning another area by an equal amount.

This section of the book will help you determine what type of tuning you need to perform and how that tuning will affect your system. A little turn here and a bump there can really make a big difference in how your system performs. The idea is to tune each area of Windows 95 in moderation. You also need to take your special needs into account. Even the type of network you use will affect the way you tune your system.

One thing is certain: Windows 95 offers more in the way of reliability and performance features than Windows 3.x did. Your job now is to decide how to use those features to your benefit. Getting that high-performance system together is the first goal you'll want to achieve under Windows 95. After that, the data-centric approach to managing your system should make operating it a breeze.

The second and third chapters of this section include setup tips (in Chapter 4) and startup shortcuts (in Chapter 5). There are a number of ways to set up Windows 95. The Microsoft documentation tells you most of the mechanical information you need but provides very little in the way of trade-offs. What do you have to give up in order to use a Server setup? How does a floppy setup differ from a CD-ROM? These are some of the questions we'll look at in this section.

Of course, I'll also offer a few tips on actually getting the installation done based on real-world experience rather than what should theoretically happen. Sometimes you'll want to do the opposite of what the Microsoft documentation says to do, just to get a more efficient setup. This section of the book looks at some of the tips and techniques I've accumulated over months of beta testing Windows 95.

The Windows 95 Anatomy

Learning to use an operating system often means learning a bit about how it works inside. For some people, a quick overview of Windows 95's internals will be enough, especially if you only plan to use Windows 95 in a single-user mode and really don't need to get every ounce of power from your machine.

But if you do have to manage a large number of machines or need to really get inside and learn how things work from a programmer's point of view, you'll really appreciate this section of the book. I don't go into a bits-and-bytes blow-by-blow description, but this section blows the lid off all the architectural aspects of Windows 95. We'll examine every major component of Windows 95, from the file system to the API.

Understanding and Using Windows 95

Some people learn to use a computer but never learn to use it well. The problem, in many cases, is that they lack knowledge of some of the hidden features that a product provides. In other cases, a lack of system optimization is to blame. Still other people have problems understanding the documentation that comes with the product.

This section of the book is filled with tips and techniques that are so often missing from the vendor documentation. There's a big difference between the way things should work and the way they really do. Use this section of the book to gain the real-world information you'll need to really use Windows 95 to its full potential.

Troubleshooting Windows 95

Have you ever installed something and gotten it to work right the first time? That's what I thought. I usually have some problems too. Unlike the Macintosh, the PC is made up of parts that come from a myriad of vendors. All these parts are supposed to work together, but sometimes they don't.

A lot of hardware and software installation-related problems have nothing to do with hidden agendas or vendor ineptitude. Some problems occur because of a poorly written specification. One vendor interprets a specification one way, and another uses a very different interpretation. The result is hardware and software that really don't work together. Each one follows the "standard," and each one follows it differently.

Other times, a user will shoot himself in the foot. How many times have you thought that you did something according to the instructions, only to find out that you really didn't? It happens to everyone. Even a bad keystroke can kill an installation. Take the Windows registry. It's all too easy to take a misstep when editing it and end up with an operating system that won't boot.

Even if you do manage to get a fully functional system the first time through and you keep from shooting yourself in the foot, what are the chances that the installation will stay stable forever? It's pretty unlikely. Your system configuration changes on a daily basis as you optimize applications and perform various tasks.

As you can see, the typical computer has a lot of failure points, so it's no wonder that things fall apart from time to time. This section of the book will help you quickly diagnose and fix most of the major problems you'll run into with Windows 95. We'll even look at a few undocumented ways to determine what's going on and how to interpret the information you get.

Microsoft Plus!

Sometimes it's nice to end a book on a fun note. Chapter 24 does just that. Sure, Microsoft Plus! provides some important aids, such as advanced disk compression and Dial-Up Networking, but it also provides some fun things, such as Desktop Themes. We'll take a look at everything you can expect from this Windows 95 add-on package. Once you get a good look at what it offers, you can decide whether this package will enhance your system or not.

Conventions Used in This Book

I've used the following conventions in this book:

File | Open	Menus and the selections on them are separated by a vertical bar. "File | Open" means "Access the File menu and choose Open."
Program Files | Plus! | Themes	The names of folders are separated by a vertical bar.
HKEY_CLASSES_ROOT | CLSID	The names of keys are separated by a vertical bar.
`monospace`	It's important to differentiate the text that you use in a macro or that you type at the command line from the text that explains it. I've used monospace type to make this differentiation. Whenever you see something in monospace, you'll know that this information will

appear in a macro, within a system file such as
CONFIG.SYS or AUTOEXEC.BAT, or as something
you'll type at the command line. You'll even see the
switches used with Windows commands in monospace.

italic monospace

Sometimes you need to supply a value for a Windows or
DOS command. For example, when you use the DIR
command, you might need to supply a filename. It's
convenient to use a variable name—essentially a
placeholder—to describe the kind of value you need to
supply. The same holds true for any other kind of entry,
from macro commands to dialog box fields. Whenever
you see a word in italic monospace, you know that the
word is a placeholder that you'll need to replace with a
value. The placeholder simply tells you what kind of
value you need to provide.

`<Filename>`

A variable name between angle brackets is a value that
you need to replace with something else. The variable
name I use usually provides a clue as to what kind of
information you need to supply. In this case, I'm asking
for a filename. Never type the angle brackets when you
type the value.

`[<Filename>]`

When you see square brackets around a value, switch, or
command, it means that this is an optional component.
You don't have to include it as part of the command line
or dialog field unless you want the additional functionality that the value, switch, or command provides.

italic

I use italic wherever the actual value of something is
unknown. I also use italic where more than one value
might be correct. For example, you might see FILExxxx
in text. This means that the value could be anywhere
between FILE0000 and FILE9999. Italic is also used to
introduce new terms in text.

ALL CAPS

Commands use all capital letters. Some registry entries
also use all caps even though they aren't commands.
Normally you'll type a command at the DOS prompt,
within a PIF file field, or within the Run dialog field. If
you see all caps somewhere else, it's safe to assume that
the item is a case-sensitive registry entry or some other
value. Filenames also appear in all caps.

➡ The code continuation character is used when one line of code is too long to fit on one line of the book. Here's an example:

```
{DDE-EXECUTE "[InsertObject .IconNumber = 0, .FileName = ""D:\WIN95\LEAVES.BMP"",
➡.Link = 1, .DisplayIcon = 0, .Tab = ""1"", .Class = ""Paint.Picture"",
➡.IconFilename = """", .Caption = ""LEAVES.BMP""]"}
```

When typing these lines, you would type them as one long line without the continuation character.

Icons

This book contains many icons that help you identify certain types of information. The following paragraphs describe the purpose of each icon.

Note: Notes tell you about interesting facts that don't necessarily affect your ability to use the other information in the book. I use note boxes to give you bits of information that I've picked up while using Windows 95.

Tip: Everyone likes tips, because they tell you new ways of doing things that you might not have thought about before. Tip boxes also provide an alternative way of doing something that you might like better than the first approach I provided.

Warning: This means watch out! Warnings almost always tell you about some kind of system or data damage that will occur if you perform a certain action (or fail to perform others). Make sure you understand a warning thoroughly before you follow any instructions that come after it.

Peter's Principle: I usually include a Peter's Principle to tell you how to manage your Windows environment more efficiently. Boxes with this icon might also include ideas on where to find additional information or even telephone numbers that you can call. You'll also find the names of shareware and freeware utility programs here.

Looking Ahead: It's always good to know what you'll find along the road. Whenever you see a Looking Ahead box, I'm providing a road sign that tells you where we're headed. That way, you can follow the path of a particular subject as I provide more detailed information throughout the book.

Gaining good access to the features provided by Windows 95 is important for everyone—especially to those who are physically challenged. I applaud Microsoft's efforts in taking this first step toward making Windows 95 the operating system that everyone can use. You'll see the Accessibility icon wherever I talk about these special features. Don't be surprised at how many of them you can use to get your work done faster or more efficiently, even if you're not physically challenged.

Knowing how something works inside is important to some people but not so important to others. Whenever you see the Architecture icon, I'm talking about the internal workings of Windows 95. Knowing how Windows 95 performs its job can help you determine why things don't work as they should.

You can't survive in the modern business world without spending some time talking to other people. Whether you spend that time on the phone or with an online service such as CompuServe or Microsoft Network, the result is the same. It's the exchange of information that drives business—at least in part. Whenever you see the Communications icon, you know that I'm describing some way of using Windows 95 to better communicate with those around you.

Whenever you change something as important as your operating system, there will be problems with older devices and applications that were designed for the older version. The Compatibility icon clues you in to tips, techniques, and notes that will help you get over the compatibility hurdle.

DOS is still with us and will continue to be for the foreseeable future. Microsoft at least provides better support for DOS applications under Windows 95. Whenever you see the DOS icon, I provide you with a tip, technique, or note about a way to make DOS applications and Windows coexist.

Before Windows 95 even appeared on the market, Microsoft was working on a way to enhance it. Microsoft Plus! is an add-on package for Windows 95 that enhances its built-in capabilities. Whenever you see the Microsoft Plus! icon, I'm talking about some enhancement that Microsoft Plus! provides to the standard Windows 95 environment. Of course, this product is covered in detail in Chapter 24.

Even home users need to worry about networking these days. It's no surprise, then, that this book provides a wealth of networking tips and techniques that everyone can use. Expect to find one of these tidbits of knowledge wherever you see the Networking icon.

I use the Performance icon to designate a performance-related tip. There are many throughout this book, and they cover a variety of optimization techniques. You'll need to read them carefully and decide which ones suit your needs. Not every performance tip is for everyone. Most of them require a trade-off of some kind, which I'll mention.

Your printer is probably the most used, yet most frustrating, part of your computer. I include the Printer icon to tell you when a tip or technique will help you keep your printer under control and make it work more efficiently.

Square pegs that had to fit in round holes—that's what some products were in the past. Recent standards efforts have helped reduce the number of square pegs on the market. I think it's important to know what these standards are so that you can make the best buying decisions possible. Getting a square peg at a discount rate isn't such a good deal if you end up spending hours making it round. Every time you see the Standards icon, you know that I'm talking about some standard that defines a product that will fit into that round hole with relative ease.

Technical details can really help you localize a problem or decide precisely what you need in order to get a job done. They can also help improve your overall knowledge of a product. Sometimes they're just fun to learn. However, sometimes you just need an overview of how something works; learning the details would slow you down. I use the Technical Note icon to tell you when a piece of information is a detail. You can bypass this information if you need only an overview of a Windows 95 process or feature. This icon also gives you clues as to where you can look for additional information.

Everyone encounters problems from time to time. It doesn't matter if the problem is hardware- or software-related if it's keeping you from getting your work done. Every time you see the Troubleshooting icon, I'm providing you with a tool you'll need to find a problem.

It's helpful to compare the benefits of using one operating system over another. I already gave you some tips in this regard earlier. You'll find a lot of other notes throughout this book. Every time I provide some insight into a comparison of Windows NT versus Windows 95, I use the Windows NT icon.

The predecessor of Windows 95 left a lot of people wondering whether Windows would ever completely meet their needs. The Windows 3.1 icon tells you about a note that compares Windows 95 and Windows 3.1. These notes will help you understand what you can expect to gain (and, in some cases, lose) by using Windows 95 rather than its predecessor.

I

Next Stop—
Windows 95!

1

A Decade Spent with Windows

The last 10 years have marked a major change in the way we view computing. PCs started out as mere playthings that had character-mode screens, a little memory, a few small applications, and not much more. Today we use computer systems crammed with megabytes of RAM, huge hard drives, impressive displays, and applications that provide an ease of use that early computer users wouldn't have dreamed possible. All this new activity centers around the graphical user interface (GUI) rather than the text-mode interface of yesterday. At least part of the reason for that change is Microsoft Windows. Of course, Microsoft would have you believe that Windows is the entire reason, but frankly, it isn't. Windows is only part of the GUI picture—albeit a large one.

If someone had told me 10 years ago that today I would be spending the majority of my time using Windows, I would have thought him crazy. The Windows of 10 years ago hardly merited a first look, much less a second. When Windows was first developed, it was competing with an entrenched GUI environment—the Macintosh—and the first few releases of Windows simply weren't designed as well as Apple computers. Besides, not many applications made use of the Windows interface. You could run programs in Windows, but there was little benefit. Besides, I could do everything I needed to do faster, and with a lot less effort, under DOS. My favorite quote back then was "I don't do Windows."

Ever since Windows 3.0 hit the streets in late spring of 1990, many software vendors have announced products to support this GUI. The release of Windows 3.1, which includes many enhancements, has further fueled the growth of Windows-based applications. Windows for Workgroups and Windows NT added networking and other refinements to the Windows environment, further increasing its appeal to corporate America. (An interim release of Windows for Workgroups, version 3.11, takes care of some reliability and speed problems found in earlier versions.) Unfortunately, some people view Windows for Workgroups as too little because it doesn't provide a robust multitasking environment for some tasks, and Windows NT as too much because of its stringent hardware requirements. Enter Windows 95, Microsoft's latest entry in the Windows market. Now there are windowing environments for beginning, intermediate, and advanced users from the same source and with much the same interface.

Why has Windows become so popular? Windows-based programs simply are easier—*much* easier—to learn and use than conventional DOS applications. And, as most mainstream products (the ones most PC users already know and love) have joined the Windows ranks, the real power of computing is being made available to people who couldn't use it before. In fact, some Windows versions of products such as WordPerfect are so popular that their vendors don't plan to release a new DOS version of the product, except to fix bugs.

Looking Ahead: This chapter presents a historical view of Windows: What did we start with, and where did Windows go from there? It's always important to examine where you've been in order to fully appreciate where you are now. Windows 95 is far from perfect. In fact, I doubt it will really be ready for prime time when Microsoft releases it. Hidden bugs in the release version of Windows 95 will certainly appear and provide lots of gossip for the industry. For example, the current problems with some device drivers and many older DOS programs, especially games, have caused some beta testers more than a few problems. The important thing to remember with this release is how much Windows really has improved over the years. This chapter gives you that historical view and helps you understand how Windows 95 adds to the Windows legacy.

We'll also take a quick look at some of the new Windows 95 features that differentiate it from the previous versions of Windows. I won't really take a detailed look at them until later. The sole purpose of this chapter is to help you see the big picture. Future chapters take a detailed look at each feature.

A Historical View of Windows

The history of Windows is dotted with a number of successes and an equal number of failures. First we'll discuss the failures. Windows started out as little more than a task-switching environment. The initial 1985 release of version 1.0 left a lot to be desired, and its reception by the industry as a whole was, frankly, rather dismal.

There were many problems with the initial Windows release. Many of these problems stemmed from the hardware available at the time. An underpowered Intel processor, low-resolution graphics adapters, a lack of memory, and a lack of mice made the PC a graphics-hostile computer. Other problems occurred because of a lack of support from software vendors. However, I believe one of the biggest hurdles was the user. The earliest computer users were technical types who understood hardware and software design. They took to cryptic procedures and arcane commands easily.

As computer power became available to a wider audience, however, users struggled with "computerese" and sought ways to ease access to applications. The Apple Macintosh, introduced in 1984, was the first successful business-oriented product to provide a natural, picture-oriented interface for the computer. (Many people remember the ill-fated Lisa, the Macintosh's predecessor. Even though the Macintosh eventually included many of the Lisa's features, it was a total failure before Apple even started.) The Macintosh operating system and other features were designed from the beginning with this GUI in mind. Microsoft recognized the Macintosh as the wave of the future, and Windows was the result of its development efforts.

The following sections look at the four major Windows releases that preceded Windows 95. (We'll skip version 1.0, which was a total failure.) Hopefully you will see the progress that each version made toward the product we use today. Equally important is that you note which failures are still with us as Microsoft strives to provide backward compatibility as it moves forward. Should we give up some compatibility in order to get an improved operating system? Corporate America says no, but the typical user says yes. Who do you think Microsoft will listen to?

Windows 2.x

Microsoft's second attempt at a GUI wasn't much better than its first. Windows 2.0, which appeared in 1987, didn't offer the Program Manager interface that people associate with Windows today. In fact, it didn't even use the icons that most people associate with a GUI. This version of Windows provided a list of applications in text and not much more. In fact, it didn't offer much more than a menuing system. This was due in part to the memory restrictions and lack of horsepower provided by the 8086 processor. However, it still made DOS easier to use and enabled the user to start more than one task at a time—as long as the multiple tasks would fit in available memory. Windows 2.0 was a small but important step away from DOS. This version, like its predecessor, did poorly in the marketplace.

Intel introduced two new chips prior to the release of Windows 2.0. The 80286 appeared on the scene in 1983, and the 80386 appeared in 1985. Both processors offered features that made them far superior to the 8088. You might wonder why Microsoft even bothered to introduce a version of Windows for the 8088. The answer is simple—marketing. The majority of PC owners still owned 8088 machines when Windows 2.0 became available, so that's the market they developed for.

Microsoft introduced two other versions of Windows that allowed people to use the power of Intel's newer chips. 80286 users could use all of their extended memory for applications by getting the Windows/286 version. Like its counterpart, this version offered task switching, not multitasking. Task switching allows you to run several applications, but not simultaneously. Only the foreground application does any work. Background applications are suspended until you bring them to the foreground. Multitasking allows both foreground and background applications to execute. The Windows/386 version, released in 1988, at least allowed the user to multitask applications. This wasn't the preemptive multitasking that provides a smooth transition from application to application that most people think about, but a cooperative multitasking that allowed one application to grab all the system resources if it wanted to. Think of cooperative multitasking as an honor-system method of managing applications (and we all know how well the honor system works). Preemptive multitasking leaves Windows in charge, ensuring that all the applications work together fairly. In other words, this version of Windows was a step in the right direction, but it was still a far cry from what Windows is today.

Here is the short take on Windows 2.0: None of its incarnations was very successful. All three versions suffered from the same problem. They didn't deliver the type of interface that people needed and wanted. Reliability was also a problem, but people really never got past the interface to find this out. (Throughout this book we'll look at some of the reliability problems previous versions of Windows had and see how Windows 95 fixes some, but not all, of them.) A GUI without graphics isn't really a GUI at all.

Windows 3.x

Windows 3.0, introduced on May 22, 1990, really got the ball rolling. This was the first version that offered users a real reason for switching from DOS-based applications. Not only did Windows 3.0 offer enhanced memory support so that applications could do more, but it also offered an attractive interface as well. (See Figure 1.1.) This was the first version to make extensive use of icons. It also offered the Program Manager interface that most people associate with Windows. Most important of all, you could run more than one task simultaneously under Windows 3.0, a feat impossible with DOS alone. Of course, Microsoft had to make a few concessions to gain the support that version 3.0 enjoyed. For example, version 3.0 was the last version you could use on an 8088.

Figure 1.1.
Windows versions 3.0 and above offer one of the things that users need to use a computer efficiently: a graphical user interface (GUI).

Even though the marketplace welcomed Windows 3.0 with open arms, users soon discovered problems. Most of the negative aspects of version 3.0 revolved around the concessions Microsoft had to make for backward compatibility. For one thing, running Windows 3.0 in real mode meant that Microsoft couldn't make the system as reliable as they wanted it to be. (We'll look at what real mode is and see its impact on the system in Chapter 6.) An operating system that runs in protected mode can intercept and deal with maverick applications that cause the system to crash. Using real-mode drivers in some areas meant that the Windows 3.0 safety net was pretty thin—or nonexistent. One faulty application could cause a data-killing system crash. The biggest complaint that people had about this version, however, was its own inherent instability.

Another problem was the infamous UAE (unrecoverable application error). Although Windows itself was responsible for some of these errors, they often had nothing to do with Windows itself, but with the applications it ran. An application could try to grab a file handle to a nonexistent file—or some other system resource—and crash the system as a result.

Undaunted by these problems, Microsoft introduced yet another version of Windows. Version 3.1 offered the user even more, but it's the hidden details that set this version apart from version 3.0. The UAE disappeared in this version because Microsoft added methods for validating system requests. Every time an application wanted to look at a disk file or perform some other task, Windows made sure that task could succeed before it gave the go-ahead. This forced a lot of vendors to rewrite their software to actually look for potential problems before the software requested a system service. Unfortunately, even with all these checks, some applications still violated system integrity. The result was a general protection fault (GPF). From a user point of view, the GPF didn't look much different than the UAE did; both could cause the machine to freeze. However, Windows usually recovered better from a GPF. In addition, users saw many fewer GPFs than UAEs. The GPF also showed that Windows at least recognized an error before the machine froze; the UAE always resulted from a failure to recognize a symptom. This difference meant that Windows could now provide more information to a vendor in an effort to find and fix the source of a GPF. (This is why Windows 3.1 included the Dr. Watson utility, which records the set of conditions that Windows detected right before a system failure.) Suffice it to say that version 3.1 added a lot under the hood and forced developers to rethink their Windows programming strategy.

Microsoft also decided to provide a fully enhanced memory environment for Windows 3.1. For example, no longer did the user have to pay as much attention to the amount of actual system memory available for running applications. Windows 3.1 could use virtual memory, a method of using part of the hard drive to simulate RAM. (I discuss this in detail later.) Microsoft used part of this additional memory to provide enhanced driver support. A user could no longer run Windows on an 8088 by starting it in real mode, because the 16-bit drivers needed to run in protected mode. In addition, the extra memory allowed Microsoft to improve driver performance and the overall reliability of Windows. (We'll look at real mode versus protected mode in Chapter 6.) Needless to say, running everything in protected mode enabled you to utilize all that memory sitting above the 1 MB conventional memory boundary. Using protected mode also made Windows 3.1 a little more stable than its predecessor. However, this version still had to call on DOS to perform some tasks.

Windows for Workgroups 3.11

Now that Windows is entrenched in the corporate environment, certain failings have come to light. The biggest failure was the lack of good network support. I'm not talking about the big-mainframe-to-PC connection, but the small, intimate, Local Area Network (LAN) connections required for workgroup computing. These small groups of users don't have the monetary resources required to create a big network. What they really need is something that allows them to share a few devices and some files. Windows for Workgroups solved this problem. A user can now create very inexpensive connections for a small group of people by installing a network card and some cable. This version of Windows also provides some simple network-related utilities such as a meeting scheduler and an e-mail system. A peer-to-peer network that uses Windows for Workgroups might not provide the robust environment needed for enterprise computing, but it will work for a small organization.

This version of Windows also provides better reliability than its predecessor. For one thing, Microsoft provided many bug fixes to Windows-specific features. As a result of these bug fixes and the enhanced support provided by Windows for Workgroups, many pundits in the trade presses recommended that people switch to Windows for Workgroups, even on stand-alone machines. Other than that, Windows for Workgroups provides essentially the same feature set as Windows 3.1.

Windows 3.11

As soon as Windows for Workgroups 3.11 arrived on the scene, users of Windows 3.1 wanted the increased reliability of those same bug fixes. Microsoft offered a free upgrade disk to existing Windows users and replaced unsold copies of Windows 3.1 with the completely new version, 3.11. No other feature set changes or technical changes were made in this version. Essentially, Windows 3.11 is Windows for Workgroups 3.11 with no networking support.

Windows NT

Some people use Windows for mission-critical applications. They want more reliability from Windows than either the 3.1 or Workgroups versions can offer. For example, the reliability problems presented by the current Windows setup make it unfeasible as a database server. What if the server went down in the middle of a transaction? The results could be devastating, even in a workgroup setting. Windows NT solves this problem by getting rid of DOS altogether. It provides a totally new Windows environment that looks like the old one but runs completely in protected mode. Windows NT provides many other features as well. For one thing, it isn't restricted to the Intel family of processors. The initial version of Windows NT came out with support for the DEC Alpha processor as well.

Unfortunately, this new and improved version of Windows comes with a big price tag. Microsoft really designed NT as a server-based operating system. As a result, there's no way to run Windows NT with less than 8 MB of RAM and a fast processor. Many users complain that the high hardware price tag just isn't worth the additional security that Windows NT provides. Enter Windows 95. This version of Windows doesn't rely on DOS for Windows application needs; all the Windows DLLs and supporting code run in protected mode. (Windows 95 does rely on DOS to run DOS applications, to provide some low-level BIOS support on non-plug and play machines, and to support antiquated devices that use real-mode drivers.) It also uses a subset of the Windows NT 32-bit programming interface and runs completely in protected mode (except for real-mode drivers). Not only does Windows 95 perform better, faster, and more reliably, but it also sports a new interface. (See Figure 1.2.) Windows 95 represents a halfway point between Windows for Workgroups and

Windows NT. It also represents the future of Windows. For example, Windows 95 is the first version of Windows to include plug and play as an integral part of the operating system.

Figure 1.2.
Windows 95 sports a new interface that should make life a lot easier for the novice user.

Windows 95 Improvements

Now that we have some idea of where we've been, let's get an overview of where we are. Windows 95 is the new version of Windows that Microsoft hopes will appear on every workstation sometime in the near future. Not only is it less expensive than Windows NT, but it's more robust than Windows 3.1 as well. The new interface and other design considerations make Windows 95 a lot better than any of its predecessors.

Tip: Even though Windows 95 provides a vast improvement in speed, reliability, and interface over Windows 3.x and Windows for Workgroups 3.x, it isn't the platform to use as a server. If you need a server, you'll need the additional reliability provided by Windows NT. On the other hand, if you want an inexpensive replacement for your current workstation operating system that provides a lot of added functionality, Windows 95 is the product you've been looking for.

Improvements Over Windows 3.11

There's no doubt that Windows 3.11 made a lot of headway in the bug department. Remember the GPFs I told you about? Some of them were Microsoft's fault (even though Microsoft would have you believe that Windows is the perfect product and that the third-party vendors are really to blame). There were situations in which Windows simply didn't work as advertised. Windows 3.11 fixed many of these problem areas, especially the crippling memory allocation problems that plagued earlier versions. Of course, Windows 3.11 still isn't perfect, or we'd be using it in place of Windows 95. Some of the memory problems aren't in the code, but in the architecture. Microsoft didn't deal with any memory-related architectural issues in the 3.11 release.

Many people noticed that Windows 3.11 (and Windows for Workgroups 3.11) still has many problems. For one thing, GPFs are still common, although less common than before. Even though the 3.11 versions do fix a few architectural problems by providing features such as 32-bit disk access, they didn't—*couldn't*—fix all of them. Some of the problems in Windows 3.x—such as disk-related failures—are a result of using DOS for disk access. When you base your protected-mode, multitasking operating environment on a real-mode, single-tasking operating system, it's not too difficult to understand why there are problems. Any real-mode access leaves Windows open for attack from any application. As a result, even though Windows 3.11 and Windows for Workgroups 3.11 offer 32-bit disk access and other reliability additions, they aren't enough. Microsoft had to get rid of the underlying problem—DOS. Windows 95 does just that. (We'll see later that DOS isn't completely gone, but it's far enough away now that its impact is minimal.)

> **Looking Ahead:** Chapter 6 provides the details of the Windows 95 architecture. It will help you understand not only why Windows 95 is more robust than Windows 3.x, but also why it's less robust than Windows NT. Read Chapter 6 if you want to find out more about the specific improvements that Microsoft has made to enhance Windows 95 reliability. If you want to know more about the Windows 95 file system and how it compares to previous versions, read Chapter 8, which compares the various forms of disk access used by previous versions.

Other problems occur when application writers misuse or misunderstand the Windows API (application programming interface). Anyone who's tried to figure out the Windows API in order to write an application knows what I mean. The problems aren't even limited to C programmers, as you might think. Microsoft Visual Basic, Microsoft Access, CA-Visual Objects, Borland Delphi, and a wealth of other "high-end" application development languages give the programmer access to Windows functionality through the API. In fact, you might be surprised at the level of access provided by some application programs such as Microsoft Word for Windows through its Word Basic "macro" language. Many API functions are so counterintuitive that Houdini himself couldn't untie the knot. Combining these counterintuitive commands with a programmer who might have very limited programming skills is a recipe for application disaster.

Windows 95 can't fix these API-related problems for you—at least, it can't fix the 16-bit API problems. However, Microsoft did take the opportunity to change the API and make it more intuitive when it developed WIN32s. Since programmers will probably use this 32-bit API in place of the old one to develop new applications, they should reap the benefit of using an API that is at least a little easier to understand. With understanding should come some level of enhanced stability.

Some users shot themselves in the foot while installing previous versions of Windows. You had to know quite a bit about DOS and Windows to get a decent installation on some machines. This meant looking up every IRQ and port address that your system was using. Windows 95 eliminates this problem to a certain degree. It includes dialog boxes that tell you what resources each device in your system is using. In addition, it tells you which resources you can't use when it's time to reconfigure a device. Is the Windows 95 installation foolproof? No. You can still shoot yourself in the foot in certain circumstances. However, Windows 95's new installation features can greatly reduce your chances of getting a bad installation due to device configuration conflicts.

Improvements Over Windows for Workgroups 3.11

One of the biggest reasons that people use Windows for Workgroups is the networking features it provides. Not only does it include the network operating system itself, but it provides several utility programs as well. A small workgroup can easily get by using the features provided by Microsoft Mail for e-mail and Schedule+ to manage everyone's appointments. It's also easy to use WFW, as long as you already know how to use the stand-alone product. You can build a small peer-to-peer network for your local workgroup in a matter of hours.

Just like everything else with Windows, getting everything right the first time is nearly impossible. For example, what if you want a small workgroup setup and still have access to your NetWare or NT file server? WFW is ill-equipped to provide this level of functionality. The problem is twofold. Not only do you have to battle Windows 3.x-specific networking problems, but you also have to deal with the local peer-to-peer network. Many a network administrator spends sleepless nights trying to get everything to work together.

Windows 95, on the other hand, comes with dual network protocol support built right in. Theoretically, all you need to do is select both networks in the Network Configuration dialog box. After doing a few additional setups, you should have a local peer-to-peer network that also connects to the company's main network on the file server.

Looking Ahead: The networking support that Windows 95 provides might sound like a dream come true, but reality is a bit different. Although Windows 95 does make dual networks a reality and does reduce the amount of work required by an order of magnitude, it doesn't work completely. Chapter 19 helps you understand what Windows 95 does and doesn't do for networking.

We can all be thankful that Microsoft took a first step by offering the user WFW for simple networking needs. However, most people will leave WFW behind and never look back once they see the networking capabilities provided by Windows 95. These features might not be perfect, but they do go a long way toward providing the user the capabilities needed to build an efficient networking solution.

Along with the better networking features that Windows 95 provides, it is also faster than WFW. Using 32-bit code to perform much of the work, coupled with preemptive multitasking, makes Windows 95 run much faster using the same hardware as a WFW machine. However, faster isn't always better. Inefficient use of speed can rob a system of the power it should have. For example, if you spend time waiting for a print job to spool to the hard drive, you aren't using the speed your system can provide efficiently. Another example is when two applications require system resources and one ends up grabbing the entire resource. Windows 95 comes out ahead in this regard as well. The Windows 3.x tasking system just isn't as efficient as the one used by Windows 95. The use of threads for 32-bit applications under Windows 95 only serves to increase the efficiency of an already improved system. As with everything else, though, Windows 95 will probably need a little tweaking before all these new performance-enhancing features really do the job they're supposed to do.

Improvements Over Windows NT

No one should ever confuse Windows NT with a workstation operating system. It requires too many resources. Can you really justify a 486 or Pentium baseline machine with a minimum of 16 MB just to start the operating system as a word processing workstation? Windows NT needs a lot of resources to perform well—there's just no way around it. The strange thing is that some people upgraded their workstations just so that they could gain the additional reliability that Windows NT provides.

There are many problems with using Windows NT as a workstation. For one thing, anyone who's ever tried to run certain older DOS applications, such as games, has been very disappointed with NT. The reason is simple. Windows NT is designed without any flexibility in mind. The only thing it knows is that the application you're trying to run just violated system integrity. As a result, the application gets squashed. Microsoft wrote this operating system to run as reliably as possible, which means that it can't bend to the needs of an application that thinks it needs to run alone.

Windows 95 will never be as stable as Windows NT. It will bend as much as possible to allow that old application to run. Because of this added flexibility, Windows 95 will run most—if not all—of your DOS applications with a little tinkering. Microsoft even provided a special startup mode for applications that don't run well in either a full-screen or windowed DOS session. With all this additional assistance, you might even find that these old applications run better under Windows 95 than they used to from the DOS prompt. The tradeoff is that you don't get the same level of reliability. And, of course, it's always possible that your particular DOS-based application—particularly vertical-market applications—might not run at all under Windows 95 without being upgraded.

Note: The one new feature that Windows 95 provides is its interface. Windows NT still uses Program Manager. (The 3.51 version will use the new Explorer interface.) Right now, you might be wondering how you will ever get used to the new interface. The longer you've used Program Manager, the more likely it is that you'll ask this question. You might even insist on hanging on to that old interface.

It's OK. Microsoft still provides Program Manager for those who are leery of trying something new. I took advantage of this alternative during the first few months I used Windows 95. I think it made the transition a bit easier since I didn't need to worry about learning a new interface and new operating system features at the same time. However, after a few months, I did try the new interface, and now I don't think I'll ever go back. Using the Explorer interface is so much faster than Program Manager that you'll wonder how you ever got work done using it.

An Overview of Windows 95's Major Features

Stability, speed, and better networking aren't the only ways in which Windows 95 distinguishes itself from its predecessors. This new version of Windows is packed with so many new features that you might think Microsoft started from scratch. Actually, they didn't. They took some of Windows 3.x, added a bit of Windows NT, mixed them together, and added some new features. It's all there if you look hard.

The bottom line is that the combination of a new 32-bit environment and new features gives Windows 95 that new operating system look and feel. The fact that it borrows some of the time-tested code from previous versions means that it should be more stable than a completely new operating system. Here are the major new features:

- A new interface: Explorer
- Configuration management: The registry
- Distributed applications: Remote procedure calls
- Printer support
- DDE/OLE support
- Connectivity: Going online
- Special-needs support: Accessibility Options
- File system update: Long filenames

In the next few sections we'll look at the new features that Windows 95 provides. You'll get an overview of just how much these features will help you in your day-to-day work. You'll see more details of these features as the book goes on. Right now, just sit back and think about the big picture. Windows 95 provides a new panorama of welcome changes that you're sure to like.

> **Tip:** Unlike with previous versions of Windows, it's easy to add features to and remove features from Windows 95. If you really want to fully explore the capabilities of this new operating system, perform a full installation. Check out all the new applications and see which ones work well for you. Once you have time to really check things out, remove the applications you don't need. We'll go into the specifics of how to do this in Chapter 4.

Explorer

Explorer is the new Windows 95 interface that replaces both Program Manager and File Manager. It provides the functionality of both, but in one package. Of course, if that's all Explorer had to offer, you might be well advised to keep your current programs in place. After all, you already know how to use them, so why bother to learn something new?

Several features make Explorer an interface that you will want to learn how to use. Figure 1.3 shows one of the myriad of reasons that you'll want to switch to this product. It shows what appears to be two completely different utility windows, yet both are Explorer. This utility allows you to configure the Windows interface to suit your needs; it doesn't force you into a certain way of thinking.

Figure 1.3.

Explorer offers both a one-pane and a two-pane interface that you can use to look at your hard drive. It doesn't require you to conform to one way of seeing the information you have available on your system.

Note: Windows 95 provides you with a new term—*folder*. It uses this term to describe any kind of container. A folder can hold files, applications, or other folders. Even the Desktop is a folder. Whenever you see the term *folder*, you'll probably think of a directory. A folder isn't exactly the same as a directory, however. Think of it as a directory (real or imagined) with intelligence. We'll look at this concept in detail in Chapter 8.

The one- and two-pane look isn't the only way in which Explorer differentiates itself. Figure 1.4 shows another reason you'll want to make the change. There are four different ways to display the information on your hard drive: large icon, small icon, list, and details. I find that I'm most comfortable with the details view when I really need to know everything there is to know about a file and the large icon view when I'm just working with some data. You will likely find your own set of preferences. You might switch from view to view as I do. This is an important leap. Windows 3.x tended to stifle any kind of creative environment management. Windows 95 does everything it can to encourage this process.

Figure 1.4.
Explorer provides a variety of ways to display the information on your system. You can choose from large icons, small icons, list, or details displays.

There is actually a third form of Explorer, but you'll see only one copy of it installed on the system. It's better known as the Taskbar. You'll probably see it at the bottom of the Windows 95 display unless you specifically asked Windows 95 to move it. Figure 1.5 shows a typical Taskbar with some open applications.

Figure 1.5.
*The Taskbar is really just
another form of Explorer. It
allows you to keep track of
any open applications and
start new ones.*

Taskbar —

The Taskbar is probably one of the most versatile ways of keeping your system in check. Not only does it maintain a list of all your applications, but it helps you manage the open ones too. Ever try to find an application buried beneath all the other windows you have open? It's a real pain trying to figure out which window is which. Taskbar displays all your applications in an easy-to-reach format. To select an open application, just click on its button.

Starting a new application is easy too. All you need to do is click on the Start button and select from the menu the application you want to use. The Taskbar uses what is known as *sticky menus*. A sticky menu doesn't go away immediately. It stays in place until you're done using it. You have to actually tell Windows 95 to get rid of the menu if you decide not to select something from it. This means that you don't have to work very hard to find something. Just point your way through the menu to find what you need.

At the right end of the Taskbar you will see one or more icons. In most cases you'll see a clock. If your system has some type of sound board, the volume icon will appear there as well. Notebook computers usually display a battery icon in this area. International users might see an international icon at the end of the Taskbar. We'll cover all these features in detail in Chapter 5.

The Registry

The Windows 3.x registry was so simple that most people never gave it a second thought. About the only thing it contained were some file associations and a few OLE settings. You might have found a few bits and pieces of other information in there as well, but for the most part, even Windows ignored the registry.

Along came Windows NT. This product contains a registry that is so complex that you need a four-year degree just to figure out the basics. The Windows NT registry contains every piece of information about everything that the operating system needs to know. This includes equipment settings, software configuration, network setup, and all the DLLs it needs to run applications.

Windows 95 uses a Windows NT-style registry. However, because Windows 95 is designed for work-station use and not as a file server, its registry is a bit less complex. You'll still see all the file associations that you did with Windows 3.x. The Windows 95 registry also contains all your equipment settings, software configuration information, and a list of DLLs to load. In essence, the registry has become the central repository of information for the Windows 95 operating system.

The Windows 95 registry also replaces two files that had bad reputations under Windows 3.x. Anyone who has spent time working with Windows 3.x knows about the fun of working with the SYSTEM.INI and WIN.INI files. The WIN.INI file holds Windows environment settings; it changes the way Windows interacts with the user. The SYSTEM.INI file contains hardware and device-driver configuration information; it changes the way Windows configures itself during startup. Of course, the distinction between these two files is somewhat blurred. For example, WIN.INI holds the serial port and printer configuration information.

These two poorly organized, cryptic files hold the vast majority of configuration information for the Windows 3.1 system. Every time the user adds an application to Windows 3.1, the application adds yet another heading or two and some additional entries to both files. On the other hand, when the user gets rid of an application, the entries don't go with it. They just sort of hang around and slow system performance. Some entries can even cause error messages or, in extreme circumstances, a system crash. Windows 95 still supports these rather archaic and difficult-to-understand files, but it prefers that applications use the new registry.

Note: Windows 95 copies the contents of SYSTEM.INI and WIN.INI into the registry whenever possible. The only reason that these two files exist is to meet the needs of Windows 3.x applications. You could remove both files from your hard drive if you didn't have any older applications to run. Of course, in reality, it'll be quite a while before you can get rid of either file.

You use the RegEdit utility to view and change the contents of the registry. It displays the registry in the format shown in Figure 1.6. Windows 95 uses two hidden files, USER.DAT and SYSTEM.DAT, to store the registry information, but RegEdit displays them as one contiguous file. Even though the RegEdit display might seem a bit difficult to understand at first, it's really not. The big difference between the registry and the Windows 3.1 alternative of SYSTEM.INI and WIN.INI is that the registry uses a hierarchical organization and plain English descriptions that you will find easy to edit and maintain. Every application you add will add entries to this file, but the file's organization makes it easy for an application to remove the entries when you uninstall it. Even if you install an older application that doesn't understand the registry, you can still remove its entries with ease.

Figure 1.6.

A typical RegEdit opening screen. Each HKEY key controls a different part of the Windows setup.

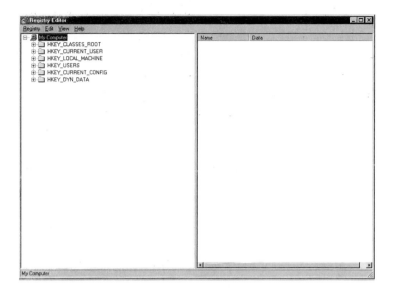

The Windows 95 registry uses two types of entries to maintain its organization: keys and values. *Keys* are a RegEdit topic. Think of a key as the heading that tells you what a particular section contains. Looking at all the keys provides an outline for a particular topic. The topics could range from the setup of each drive in the system to the file associations needed to configure the machine. The key at the top of the hierarchy usually contains generic information. Each subkey provides a little more detail about that particular topic. Keys always appear on the left side of the RegEdit window.

Values are the definition of a RegEdit topic; they describe the key in some way. Think of a value as the text that fills out the heading provided by a key. Values are like the text in this book, while keys are the headings that organize the text. A value can contain just about anything. For example, the value for a file association key can tell you which application Windows 95 will start when you double-click on a file that has that extension in Explorer. A value could tell you which interrupt and I/O port settings a piece of hardware uses as well. Suffice it to say that you'll find the value you need using the keys, but you'll find the actual information you need by reading the values.

There are three types of values: binary, string, and DWORD. Usually, only applications use the binary and DWORD value types. Values usually store configuration data in a format that can't be understood by humans. Some applications use DWORD or binary values to store data. For example, you might find the score from your last game of FreeCell here. String values provide a lot of information about the application and how it's configured. Hardware usually uses string values as well for interrupt and port information. Values always appear on the right side of the RegEdit window.

Key entries also have a superset. I differentiate these particular keys from the rest because they are the major headings in the registry. During the rest of this discussion I refer to these special keys as *categories*. Think of categories as the chapter titles in a book. You need to go to the right chapter before you can find the right type of information. Information in one category might appear in the same order and at the same level in another category. The difference between the two is when Windows 95 uses the entries in one category versus another.

Categories are the six main keys under the My Computer key. Categories divide the registry into six main areas:

```
HKEY_CLASSES_ROOT
HKEY_CURRENT_USER
HKEY_LOCAL_MACHINE
HKEY_USERS
HKEY_CURRENT_CONFIG
HKEY_DYN_DATA
```

Each category contains a specific type of information. As you can see, the Windows 95 registry is much enhanced from its Windows 3.1 counterpart. Even though Windows 95 still has to use the infamous SYSTEM.INI and WIN.INI files for antiquated applications, the use of the registry for all other purposes does reduce the user's workload. Eventually, all applications will use the registry to store their configuration data. The following paragraphs provide an overview of the registry's categories.

Looking Ahead: This part of the book provides you with a quick overview of the registry. Chapter 6 provides an in-depth view of this very important aspect of Windows 95. The registry allows you to mold Windows 95 into the configuration you need. As a result, learning everything you can about the registry and how to modify it allows you to configure your system for optimum results. In addition, troubleshooting the registry can often help you find problem areas that other tools might miss.

HKEY_CLASSES_ROOT

There are two types of entries in the HKEY_CLASSES_ROOT category. The first key type (remember, a key is a RegEdit topic) is a file extension. Think of all the three-letter extensions you've used, such as .DOC and .TXT. Windows 95 still uses them to differentiate one file type from another. It also uses them to associate that file type with a specific action. For example, even though you can't do anything with a file that uses the .DLL extension, it appears in this list because Windows 95 needs to associate DLLs with an executable file type. The second entry type is the association itself. The file extension entries normally associate a data file with an application or an executable file with a specific Windows 95 function. Below the association key are entries for the menus you see when you right-click on an entry in the Explorer. It also contains keys that determine what type of icon to display and other parameters associated with a particular file type. Figure 1.7 shows the typical HKEY_CLASSES_ROOT organization.

Figure 1.7.
A typical
HKEY_CLASSES_ROOT
display. Notice the distinct
difference between file
extension and file association
keys.

HKEY_CURRENT_USER

The HKEY_CURRENT_USER category contains a lot of "soft" settings for your machine. These soft settings tell how to configure the Desktop and the keyboard. It also contains color settings and the configuration of the Start menu. All user-specific settings appear in this category.

The HKEY_CURRENT_USER category is slaved to the settings for the current user, the one who is logged into the machine at the time. This is differentiated from all the user configuration entries in other parts of the registry. This is a dynamic setting category; the other user-related categories contain static information. The registry copies the contents of one of the user entries in the HKEY_USERS category into this category and updates HKEY_USERS when you shut down.

This is the area where Windows 95 obtains new setting information and places any changes you make. As you can see from Figure 1.8, the keys within the HKEY_CURRENT_USER category are pretty self-explanatory in most cases. All the entries adjust some type of user-specific setting, nothing that affects a global element such as a device driver.

Figure 1.8.

The HKEY_CURRENT_USER category contains all user-specific settings.

HKEY_LOCAL_MACHINE

The HKEY_LOCAL_MACHINE category centers its attention on the machine hardware. This includes the drivers and configuration information required to run the hardware. Every piece of hardware appears somewhere in this section of the registry, even if that hardware uses real-mode drivers. If a piece of hardware doesn't appear here, Windows 95 can't use it.

A lot of subtle information about your hardware is stored in this category. For example, this category contains all the plug and play information about your machine. It also provides a complete listing of the device drivers and their revision level. This section might even contain the revision information for the hardware itself. For example, there's a distinct difference between a Pro Audio Spectrum 16+ Revision C sound board and a Revision D version of that same board. Windows 95 stores that difference in the registry.

This category does contain some software-specific information of a global nature. For example, a 32-bit application will store the location of its Setup and Format Table (SFT) here. This is a file that the application uses during installation. Some applications also use it during a setup modification. Applications such as Word for Windows NT store all their setup information in SFT tables. The only application information that does appear here is global-configuration-specific like the SFT. Figure 1.9 shows a typical HKEY_LOCAL_MACHINE category setup.

Figure 1.9.

The HKEY_LOCAL_MACHINE category contains all the hardware and device-driver-specific information about your machine. It also contains the global application setup information.

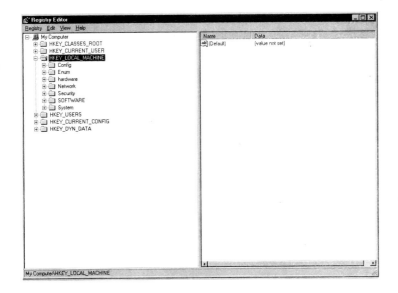

HKEY_USERS

The HKEY_USERS category contains a static listing of all the users of this particular registry file. It never pays to edit any of the information you find in this category. However, you can use this category for reference purposes. The reason for this hands-off policy is simple: None of the entries here will take effect until the next time the user logs into Windows 95, so you really don't know what effect they'll have until you reboot the machine. In addition, changing the settings for the current user is a waste of time since Windows 95 will overwrite the new data with the data contained in HKEY_CURRENT_USER during log out or shutdown.

One other problem is associated with using this category as your sole source of information. Windows 95 actually maintains multiple registries in a multiuser configuration—in some cases, one for each user who logs into the system. Because of this, you never quite know where you'll find the information for a particular user. Windows 95 tracks this information, but it really is a pain for the administrator to have to do it as well. Besides, Microsoft thoughtfully provided a utility that helps the network administrator maintain the various registries. The Policy Editor utility enables the network administrator to maintain static user information with ease. Using the Policy Editor lets the network administrator bridge the various registry files on the system when each user provides his or her own Desktop configuration.

Figure 1.10 shows a setup that includes the default key. If this system were set up for multiple Desktops, each user would have a separate entry in this section. Each entry would contain precisely the same keys, but the values might differ from user to user. When a user logs into the network, Windows 95 copies all the information in his profile to the HKEY_CURRENT_USER area of the registry. When he logs out or shuts down, Windows 95 updates the information in his specific section from the HKEY_CURRENT_USER category.

Figure 1.10.
Windows 95 creates one entry in the HKEY_USERS category for each user who logs into the machine.

HKEY_CURRENT_CONFIG

The HKEY_CURRENT_CONFIG category is the simplest part of the registry. It contains two major keys: Display and System. Essentially, these entries are used by the GDI API (described later) to configure the display and printer.

The Display key provides two subkeys: Fonts and Settings. The Fonts subkey determines which fonts Windows 95 uses for general display purposes. These are the raster (non-TrueType) fonts that it displays when you get a choice of which font to use for icons or other purposes. Raster fonts are essentially bitmaps or pictures of the characters. We'll take a more detailed look at fonts in Chapter 14.

The Settings subkey contains the current display resolution and number of bits per pixel. The bits per pixel value determines the number of colors available. For example, 4 bits per pixel provides 16 colors, and 8 bits per pixel provides 256 colors. The three fonts listed as values under this key are the default fonts used for icons and application menus. You can change all the settings under this key using the Settings tab of the Properties for Display dialog box found in Control Panel.

The System key looks like a convoluted mess. However, only one of the subkeys under this key has any meaning for the user. The Printers subkey contains a list of the printers attached to the machine. It does not include printers accessed through a network connection. Figure 1.11 shows the major keys in this category.

Figure 1.11.
The HKEY_CURRENT_CONFIG category echoes the settings under the Config key of the HKEY_LOCAL_MACHINE category.

HKEY_DYN_DATA

The final category, HKEY_DYN_DATA, contains two subkeys: Config Manager and PerfStats. You can monitor the status of the Dynamic key using the Device Manager. The PerfStats key values appear as statistics in the System Monitor utility display. Figure 1.12 shows these two main keys and their subkeys.

Figure 1.12.
HKEY_DYN_DATA contains registry entries for current events. The values in these keys reflect the current, or dynamic, state of the computer.

RPCs

Imagine, if you will, that your machine is part of a vast network of interconnected machines. Everyone on the network uses the same set of applications, including one fairly complex database program. In the old days, management would have simply gone out and bought a jumbo economy-sized mainframe to take care of the job. However, we're living in the days of distributed processing, where LANs abound and mainframes are somewhat passé. How do you make this big clunker of a database application work?

Remote procedure calls (RPCs) provide at least part of the answer to this puzzle. Everyone knows that Windows uses something called a DLL (dynamic link library). What you might not realize is that these are mini-applications of a sort. Your application might need the functions contained in a DLL. It asks Windows 95 to load that DLL, and then it loads and executes the required code that the DLL contains.

Old versions of Windows required that DLLs appear on your machine. You couldn't use a DLL that appeared on someone else's machine. Windows 95 changes all that. It allows you to call a DLL that is on someone else's machine.

RPCs are a lot more than just a better way to find code that an application might need to run, though. They provide an extra bit of functionality that will literally change the way people compute. What would you do if you could install a second processor in your machine at a moment's notice, and then get rid of it when it was no longer needed? This is the second part of an RPC. The code that you ask it to execute actually executes on the machine where the DLL resides. In effect, you get to load a second processor for a while, and you can get rid of it when it's no longer needed.

This is a very brief description of a complex process. The level of support you can expect from Windows 95 for RPCs varies as a factor of the network protocol you use. There are other environmental factors that you need to consider as well. Of course, your application has to make use of RPCs before you will see any benefit from them. In most cases, this means writing a custom application.

Looking Ahead: Chapters 11 and 19 help you understand what kind of RPC support you can expect from Windows 95. In most cases, it's a lot less than you might think because this technology is still in its infancy.

Printer Support

How often have you heard people say that they disabled Print Manager under Windows 3.x for one reason or another? It's all too common, I'm afraid. There are several reasons that people do it. First and foremost, people feel that Print Manager is too slow to meet their needs. Lack of adequate DOS and interprocess support is another reason that people cite. Even the Print Manager interface receives its share of criticism.

Windows 95 fixes all these problems and more. Not only is the Printer dialog easier to use in Windows 95, but it also provides far more options in the way you configure you printer. Figure 1.13 shows a typical display. Your dialog might differ due to differences in printer capabilities. Network printing receives special emphasis in Windows 95 as well. Finally, you can now print from multiple applications—you can even mix a few DOS applications in for good measure—and never fear that the output from your printer will be a confused mess.

Figure 1.13.

Printing under Windows 95 is a lot easier and more flexible than it was under Windows 3.x.

Looking Ahead: Chapter 14 contains the majority of the printer-specific information for this book. However, you'll find little nuggets of printer information throughout the book. For example, Chapter 9 describes printer configuration for the Desktop. Chapter 13 gives you some ideas on how to fully exploit your printer hardware, and Chapter 17 looks at printer connections in general. Finally, Chapter 19 talks about some of the choices you need to make when using a printer in a network setting.

DDE/OLE Support

Windows 95 provides several new features, especially in the area of OLE (object linking and embedding) support. One of the biggest aids that Windows 95 provides is installed support for OLE 2. Windows 3.x came with OLE 1 support. If you've installed an application that provided OLE 2 support, you're in luck.

The differences between OLE 2 and OLE 1 are significant. For example, OLE 2 provides the means to embed objects within objects. It also provides methods of allowing the server application to change the menus and toolbar of the client application. As far as the user is concerned, he's using the same application. The window doesn't change; only the tools change to meet the current requirements.

Windows 95 provides a few additional features as well. For example, OLE now use 32-bit drivers whenever possible. This change will dramatically increase the speed of either linking or embedding objects in applications. It will also help reduce the memory burden of using OLE.

DDE support under Windows 95 hasn't changed much in theory from Windows 3.x. However, we'll look at some of the ways that Windows 95 does make it easier to use DDE.

Looking Ahead: Chapter 11 concentrates on both OLE and DDE support under Windows 95. Not only will we examine some of the architectural requirements for both, but we'll also spend some hands-on time with these two important features. Have you ever been able to figure out the Object Packager? This chapter will tell you how to use it to your advantage.

Going Online

Connectivity is the name of the game under Windows 95. Older versions of Windows provided only the most rudimentary communication facilities. Windows 95 provides Microsoft Exchange—a centralized location for all your communication needs. It doesn't really matter where a message needs to go—online or network. All you need to do is specify a recipient, and Microsoft Exchange will make sure it gets to where it needs to go.

Figure 1.14 shows Microsoft Exchange. As you can see, it consists of an in box, out box, and sent messages box. A fourth box allows you to recover messages deleted by accident. Overall, this represents one of the easiest ways to manage all your e-mail if you get it from more than one source. It also represents an efficient method of sharing that information with other people, even if they aren't connected to the same services you are.

Of course, there are always a few problems with something as complex as this. We might eventually have a single package that provides every bit of support you'll need to access all your e-mail, but you won't see it today. Microsoft Exchange currently provides limited support for only some of the online services. In addition, you'll still need a separate communication program if you plan to "explore" these online services much. Even though Microsoft Exchange provides a platform for total coverage, it doesn't currently provide all the modules needed to do so. Microsoft Exchange is excellent at managing your e-mail, but not much more.

Figure 1.14.
*Windows 95 provides
extensive connectivity
features using Microsoft
Exchange. This centralized
approach to managing all
your e-mail presents some
very definite advantages.*

Looking Ahead: Chapter 17 helps you understand some of the hardware requirements for using the communication features that Windows 95 provides. Once you get the hardware working, look at Chapter 18 for full details on using the software. Connectivity has become a major need for most users. It doesn't matter what line of work you're in or precisely how you use your computer. Somewhere along the way, you'll need to communicate with someone.

Accessibility

Windows 95 addresses the needs of people who have special computing requirements. The Accessibility dialog, shown in Figure 1.15, provides everyone with features that make the computer easier to use. Features such as sticky keys and the ability of the computer to ignore too many repeated keystrokes really help those who can't easily use a computer.

Peter's Principle: Always Check the Tools at Hand

A common misconception about the accessibility tools supplied with Windows 95 is that they're useful only if you have a handicap. Nothing could be further from the truth. It always pays to explore all the tools at hand, whether you think you can use them or not.

Many people turn on the ToggleKeys feature on the Keyboard tab of the Accessibility dialog. This feature makes an audible noise when you press the Caps Lock, Num Lock, or Scroll Lock keys. It's a really handy feature for touch typists who might be paying more attention to the paper they're typing from than the screen they're typing to.

I personally find the MouseKeys feature a bonus. It allows you to use the arrow keys to move the mouse cursor. This is a real bonus when you're using a drawing program and need a little extra control over the size and position of drawing elements.

Still other people find that the High Contrast Display feature is a nice way to give their eyes a break after a difficult day. You don't have to leave it on all the time, just when your eyes get tired.

Windows 95 is filled with little hidden tools. I discuss the majority of them in this book, but only you can decide to use them. Always use the tools at hand whenever possible to improve your productivity—especially when that tool is provided free of charge.

Figure 1.15.
The Accessibility features that Windows 95 provides are for everyone, not just those with special needs.

There are four major tabs within the Accessibility Options dialog (plus one general tab that configures the dialog itself):

- Mouse: MouseKeys lets you use the arrow keys to move the mouse pointer. Of course, any peripheral device that acts the same way that the arrow keys do will also move the mouse pointer, so you have a variety of options at your disposal. For example, some people use an external keypad that acts like the arrow keys. Using MouseKeys would allow you to use this external keypad to move the on-screen mouse pointer.

- Keyboard: There are actually three aids in this area. StickyKeys lets you send a Ctrl, Shift, or Alt key in combination with a second key to the computer. The FilterKeys option prevents Windows 95 from misinterpreting mistaken keystrokes. Essentially, it delays the repeating keystroke feature of most keyboards. The keyboard still sends the repeating keystrokes, but Windows 95 ignores them for a specific period of time. The additional keystrokes end up in the "bit bucket" instead of on your display. Finally, ToggleKeys causes Windows 95 to output a sound whenever you press the Caps Lock, Num Lock, or Scroll Lock keys.

- Display: The Use High Contrast option provided on this tab is fairly self-explanatory. It causes Windows 95 to use colors and fonts that are easily seen. This high-contrast display feature makes it very easy to see everything on the display without eye strain.
- Sound: The SoundSentry feature displays a visual cue every time your computer makes a sound. The ShowSounds feature displays a dialog every time your system makes a sound. The caption tells you what sound the computer made.

Each of these features helps people who have special considerations when using a computer. The solutions aren't perfect, but they're a step in the right direction.

Looking Ahead: Chapter 15 takes a look at two of the most important aspects of the Accessibility dialog—mice and keyboards. These two components represent a major challenge to a lot of people out there, but Windows 95 does a good job of making them more user-friendly. You'll find some additional information about the Accessibility Options in Chapter 16. This chapter shows how you can use the display adapter features to reduce eye strain by making the display much more readable. Finally, Chapter 13 will help you understand some of the limited sound options provided by the Accessibility dialog.

Long Filenames

Macintosh users have long thumbed their noses at PC users for a variety of reasons. Some of these reasons are right on the mark. Take long filenames, for example. Macintosh users have long had this very valuable resource at their disposal while PC users have been stuck with filenames that are limited to eight characters and a three-character extension.

Trying to think of descriptive filenames while limiting yourself to eight characters is pretty difficult. You can end up with some very strange combinations if you're not careful. Also, these filenames almost always fail to help you much when it's time to figure out what the file contains. For example, consider a spreadsheet that contains the fourth quarter report on southeastern sales for 1994. How do you condense this idea into eight short characters? You'd probably end up with something like 4QSES94.WKS. Isn't that easy to remember?

Windows 95 fixes this problem. Filenames can now be up to 255 characters long. This means that you should be able to get as descriptive as necessary and that no one will ever again spend days searching through your files looking for the annual report.

Peter's Principle: Sometimes Long is Too Long

Windows 95 finally provides one feature that Macintosh folks have had for a long time—long filenames. You could create a filename that contained 255 characters if you so desired, but that would be counterproductive for three reasons. First, a long filename should be descriptive, but making a filename too descriptive mires the meaning in a cloud of details. Second, making a filename too long makes it difficult to type from the command line if you need to. Third, extremely long filenames consume a great amount of space on-screen and reward you with very little additional information.

Use a simple but descriptive filename such as Letter to Sally at Accounting. You might even want to include a little more detail, such as Letter to Sally at Accounting About Pay Raise. The point where you cross the line between a filename that is descriptive and one that is too long is when you use one such as Letter to Sally Jones at the Accounting Department That Asks About the Pay Raise I Requested in 1994 But Got Turned Down by the Boss for Reasons Unknown. See my point?

Microsoft did have to make a concession with long filenames. A lot of old applications on the market can read only 8.3 filenames. Microsoft had to come up with some way to allow these old applications to work with the new file system. Suppose you have a file with the name Fourth Quarter Report On Southeastern Sales For 1994.WKS. Windows 95 will display this as FOURTH~1.WKS to a DOS application. It takes the first six letters of the filename as a starting point. Then it looks to see if any other files start with the same six letters. If not, it adds ~1 to the filename. If so, it adds a ~ with the next number in line. Assuming that there are three other FOURTH files in that directory, Windows 95 would name the fourth file FOURTH~4.WKS. If you create more than 9—or 99, or 999, and so on—files with the same first six letters, the tilde will move to the left, replacing one letter at a time and making room for another power-of-ten's worth of numbers. Numbers, if necessary, will automatically be split across the extension dot. It's not a perfect solution, but it works.

Tip: You won't always work with people who have access to Windows 95 long filename support. Therefore, it almost always pays to begin your long filename in a way that translates well into the old 8.3 filenaming technique. Remember that because of the way Windows 95 creates an 8.3 filename, you will get only six characters for the name itself.

Use a name such as FY 94 Accounting Support Data to name a spreadsheet file. This will translate to FY94AC~1.WKS or something similar. (Windows 95 automatically removes spaces from a long filename when creating a short filename equivalent.) You get the convenience of using a long filename without inconveniencing your coworkers.

I was a little amazed by something else Microsoft decided to do. The new file system used by Windows 95 isn't compatible with Windows NT. This means that anyone using Windows NT will still see the 8.3 filenames of yesterday when looking at your machine, even though Windows NT supports long filenames. You'd think that people could have gotten together to ensure compatibility across product lines for something as simple as a filename.

On Your Own

Open the System Properties dialog for your computer by right-clicking on My Computer and selecting Properties from the context menu. Click on the Performance tab. Do all the indicators show that your machine is fully optimized?

If your machine is completely optimized from Windows' point of view, look at the File System and Virtual Memory dialogs by clicking on their respective pushbuttons. Does your system make optimum use of both settings? Make sure that you check your CD-ROM settings, because Windows 95 will not automatically detect your CD-ROM drive. Does the CD-ROM setting reflect the speed of your drive? Are you using the largest cache that your machine can support?

Install and load the Resource Meter and System Monitor utilities. Check your system performance over the course of a week or so. Then, try to optimize your settings and see if you can improve system performance. Fully tuning your system could take a while, but it's well worth the effort.

2

Introducing Windows 95

Learning to use a new product almost always involves some painful decisions on the part of the user. You always need to decide what to keep and what to throw away. For example, when I started making the move from DOS to Windows, I had to make a painful decision about my word processor. I was still using DOS enough that it would have been nice to have a word processor available there. Yet trying to make my DOS word processor work from within Windows was an exercise in frustration. Besides the problems of using my old word processor, making the move also meant converting all those files to the new format. Talk about a nightmare! I eventually decided to use the Windows version exclusively and rely on a small text editor for taking notes while working in DOS. It actually worked out to my advantage, because the text editor was a TSR that allowed me to take all my notes without ever leaving the main application I was working with.

Moving from Windows 3.x to Windows 95 involves similar decisions on the part of the user—albeit for different reasons. My current word processor works just fine under Windows 95. I won't have to replace it anytime soon to make it do what I need it to. However, it's a pain having to translate any long filenames that I run across before I know which file to load. In other words, I might have several chapters for a book with a long filename such as Chapter 1 - Introducing a New Topic. This title ends up looking like CHAPTE~3.DOC when I go to open it under the Windows 3.x version of Word for Windows. Of course, using the filenaming technique I introduced in Chapter 1 helps, but it doesn't do much in situations where people send me files with filenames that aren't recognizable in the 8.3 format.

You need to consider other things when making the move as well. For example, will that old Windows 3.x version of a product give you the same performance as a new Windows 95 version? In many respects it will, but checking out the differences between Word for Windows (a 16-bit application) and Word for Windows NT (a 32-bit application) shows that the NT version will always perform some tasks better. For example, I send a lot of long documents to the printer. NT actually returns control to me a lot faster than its Windows 3.x counterpart, and I seldom notice any slowing while the print cycle proceeds. The reason for this improved performance is simple: Windows 95 allows you to use applications that provide 32-bit support. In addition, these applications normally hand off tasks such as printing and background pagination to a lower-priority thread. The application doesn't worry about the task again until it's complete. We'll discuss threads later. For now, all you need to know is that they enhance your system's performance in a variety of ways by organizing its use of resources better.

Tip: Many products from Microsoft and other vendors were made available in Windows 95-specific versions on the same day as Windows 95's release. These included the entire Microsoft Office suite of applications and the Norton software products. However, you don't have to wait until vendors get around to actually writing Windows 95-specific applications. Many Windows NT applications run just fine under Windows 95. For example, Word for Windows NT works, as does Microsoft Excel. I've also tested 32-bit products such as Texam Project. Don't try to use Windows NT disk utilities under Windows 95, though; you could damage your system. The only other criteria that you need to worry about is whether the product supports the WIN32s standard. Even if an application doesn't use the full Windows NT API, it will likely run under Windows 95. Of course, it always pays to check the return policy of the software you buy—especially when you're not 100 percent certain that it will work. Using Windows NT applications today means that you won't have to wait for a vendor to release a new version of their product tomorrow.

Some of your decisions will even affect the Microsoft-supplied utilities you use. For example, the version of Microsoft Paintbrush supplied with Windows 3.x provides support for both .BMP and .PCX files. This is a very handy feature to have available, because you can use this program to make quick transitions from the Windows format to the more common .PCX format that many applications support. The version of Microsoft Paint provided with Windows 95 supports only .BMP files. You no longer have the option of using .PCX files. This is a real loss in some situations. Unfortunately, the differences don't end here. Paintbrush provides only OLE 1 support, while Paint provides OLE 2 support (and 32-bit support at that). It's a no-win situation unless you keep both Paintbrush and Paint handy, which really doesn't make sense either. The bottom line is that every transition involves compromise. You will likely find this true for the transition from Windows 3.x to Windows 95 as well.

Note: Microsoft might or might not fix the problems associated with using the OLE 2 features of Paint in the released version of the product. Currently, you can't use the Copy and Paste Special method of inserting an object into a compound document using Paint. You must use the newer "Insert Object" method of inserting the object from the client application. (We'll cover the differences between these two methods in Chapter 11.) This could seriously affect how people use this handy utility. I often grabbed a piece of a .PCX file and used it in another document. Paint doesn't allow me to do this very easily.

This chapter continues where we left off in Chapter 1. It gives you a bird's-eye view of what you can expect from Windows 95. This includes the new utilities as well as a quick look at the internal workings of Windows 95. Of course, we'll cover more specific details of some of these items in later chapters. Right now, just sit back and enjoy the view of a new operating system.

Explorer: The New Interface

The first thing that every Windows 95 user will notice is the new interface. Windows 95 enjoys a new and cleaner look that every user will come to enjoy using. In fact, I'm often surprised at just how cumbersome Windows 3.x feels when I need to use someone else's machine. Explorer is the replacement for Program Manager that many users wanted from the very beginning. (The fact that Program Manager was a poorly designed interface was highlighted by the proliferation of alternative Desktop products on the market.) It offers something for everyone, and in a way that makes it simultaneously powerful and easy to use.

Note: You can probably use your current Windows 3.x alternative interface under Windows 95, but you'll want to update it when a Windows 95-specific version becomes available. Most Windows 3.x interfaces can't offer the full support they provided under the old version because they don't know how to work with Windows 95. In addition, you won't receive Windows 95-specific benefits such as long filenames.

In the last chapter, we took a quick look at Explorer and some of the data views that it offers. Viewing information is only the tip of the interface iceberg. To really use an interface, you need to get inside and work with it. Your data has to be accessible at all times and yet not get in the way.

Let's begin our tour of Explorer by examining how it's organized. Figure 2.1 shows the two-pane configuration of Explorer and the large icons view. On the left side of the display is the directory tree. You need to make note of several features of this directory tree for future reference. The first thing you'll notice is that the tree doesn't represent a single drive or even the contents of all the drives; it's more of a "machine tree" than anything else. This "machine tree" is divided into three elements:

- The drive section: This is the area where the contents of all your data drives get displayed. This includes any network drives you're connected to.

- The configuration section: This area contains two icons in our sample display. You might see other icons here as well. Control Panel provides access to every machine configuration component that Windows 95 has to offer. It includes both hardware and software configuration. We'll take a much more detailed look at this particular component later in the book. Windows 95 also provides a Printers icon. You could access this icon from within Control Panel, but putting it here makes access a lot more convenient.

- The ancillary section: The ancillary section could contain any number of icons. Our sample in Figure 2.1 contains several, including the Recycle Bin icon. The Recycle Bin is where any documents that you erase using the Delete key in Explorer end up. We'll cover this feature in greater detail later. This is the only icon that will always appear. It performs the same function as the Recycle Bin on your Desktop. The Network Neighborhood icon appears when you have a network installed on your machine. It allows you to attach to network resources and view network data. The Network Neighborhood is a very handy way to discover what types of information you have at your fingertips.

Figure 2.1.
The Explorer display is easier
to understand when you
break it into its components.

Looking Ahead: We'll look at other aspects of Explorer in future chapters. Read Chapter 5 if you want some additional tips on optimizing your work environment using Explorer. Chapter 9 provides some advanced tips on ways to configure Explorer.

Now that you have some idea of what the left pane contains, let's look at the right pane. Clicking on any of the objects in the left pane displays its contents in the right pane. If you click on a drive icon, you will see the folders and files that the drive contains in the right pane. Click on Network Neighborhood and you'll get a view of all the machines attached to the network. You can also use the icons in the right pane to open a file or folder. Double-click on a folder and you'll see what it contains. Double-click on a file and you'll perform the default action associated with that file.

There are a number of ways to use Explorer to organize your data. Each tool provides a different method of viewing and working with your data. Let's begin with one of the first tools you'll need to use under Windows 95—the context menu.

Every object you use in Windows 95 provides a context menu. If you have a doubt as to what something is, how to configure it, or just about anything else you can do with that object, a simple right click will answer your question. Figure 2.2 shows a typical context menu. Don't let its simplicity fool you. There's a lot more here than meets the eye.

Figure 2.2.
*The context menu is one
way to discover exactly what
you can do with an object.
In most cases it also tells you
enough about the object that
you can determine its
purpose.*

Every context menu for a file or folder contains five or six major sections. Each section tells you
something about the object associated with that menu. The following paragraphs outline each section and its purpose.

- Actions: The very first section of the context menu tells you what kinds of actions you can
  perform with the object. The default action—normally Open—appears in bold print. We'll
  see in Chapter 5 how you can change the default action to meet your needs. Besides the
  Open action, you'll likely see a print data file action. Folders normally include an Explore
  and a Find action. One new feature of Windows 95 is the ability to view specific file types.
  This action appears on the context menu when available. Using a viewer allows you to see
  what a file contains without actually opening it for editing. A viewer also consumes less
  memory. We'll explore how View works a little later in this chapter. You'll see one other
  type of entry in the context menu. If the file extension doesn't appear in the registry,
  Windows 95 won't know what to do with it. In this case, you'll see an Open With... entry
  in place of the usual ones.

- Network: This is an optional section that normally contains a single entry—Sharing. Some
  objects support sharing and others don't. It all depends on how you have your network set
  up. Normally, peer-to-peer networks enable this option only for folders. Larger networks—
  such as those from Novell—provide this entry for both files and folders.

- Send To: Use this special entry if you want to send the folder or file to a floppy drive or
  other location. We'll see later that you can modify the destinations listed in this entry to
  include just about anything you might need. Windows 95 comes installed to support any
  floppies connected to your system and the Briefcase as destinations. I'll describe the
  Briefcase in detail in Chapter 21.

Tip: It's often handy to create additional destinations such as the Desktop, project folders, and network drives for this section of the context menu. Always make these destinations practical. In other words, don't add another directory listing to this rather important list. All you need to do is add destinations that you use on a daily basis.

- Editing: Believe it or not, you can edit an object just like everything else under Windows 95. This section contains entries for Cut, Copy, and Paste. You can place a copy of the object on the Clipboard, then paste as many copies as needed onto other objects. These are full-fledged copies, not the shortcuts (object links) we will examine in the next section. If you cut an object, Windows 95 doesn't remove the icon from the display. It grays the icon and waits until you paste the object somewhere else before removing it permanently. This prevents you from accidentally erasing objects. Cutting a new object before you paste the first one leaves the first object in its original location.

- Manipulation: This section usually contains three entries, but it can contain more. The Create Shortcut option allows you to place a link to a file or folder somewhere else. We'll see in Chapter 5 how you can use this feature to make your Desktop a friendlier place. The Delete option sends the file to the Recycle Bin. You can still recover it later if necessary. The Rename option allows you to change the long filename associated with the file. Remember that Windows 95 automatically determines the 8.3 filename based on the specific formula we looked at in Chapter 1.

Tip: You don't have to send objects to the Recycle Bin if you don't want to. Simply select the object you want to delete, and then press Shift-Delete to erase it permanently (as far as Windows is concerned). Even if an object does get erased by accident, you can usually unerase it using the Norton Utilities for some length of time after you permanently erase it. (The time interval varies by the amount of empty space on your drive and the amount of use that drive gets.) Since the Recycle Bin's space is limited, you'll always want to reserve it for objects you might need later. (If you do want to send an object to the Recycle Bin, select the object and press Delete without the Shift key.)

- Properties: Every object—it doesn't matter what—contains a Properties entry on its context menu. Clicking on this entry always displays a dialog box that allows you to view and configure the properties of that particular object. Figure 2.3 shows the Properties dialog for a file. As you can see, the Properties dialog for a file shows the full filename, any attributes associated with the file, and some statistical information. Folders usually contain about the same information as files but provide some additional statistics as well. Disks, on the other hand, contain a wealth of information about the drive as a whole. This Properties dialog even provides access to the three maintenance tools that Windows 95 provides to manage disk drives. You'll find that the Properties dialog for other objects, such as the

Desktop, contains a wealth of information too. For example, the Desktop Properties dialog allows you to change the system colors and display resolution. You can even use it to change your wallpaper.

Figure 2.3.

Every object in Windows 95 has a Properties dialog. The contents of this dialog vary by object. This dialog shows the properties of a file.

Peter's Principle: Learning by Doing: A Fun Way to Increase Your Windows 95 Knowledge

You'll want to spend some time right-clicking various objects on your system to see what type of context menu options they provide. It also pays to spend a little time looking at the Properties dialogs for various objects, even if you don't use certain objects very much. Windows 95 provides a variety of methods to access each of the configuration dialogs on your system, and most of them appear in these context menus or within the Properties dialog. If you think—as I do—that changing common configuration items using Control Panel is a waste of time, see if Windows 95 provides a faster method of doing so.

There are two things to remember when you experiment with your system. First, always click on Cancel instead of OK when backing out of a Properties dialog to avoid making inadvertent changes to your system. Second, clicking outside of a context menu closes it without performing any action. In most cases, the safest place to click is the Desktop.

Some objects on your system include some very specialized context menu entries. For example, if you right-click on the Recycle Bin, you'll see an option to empty it. Right-clicking on the Desktop provides a New option that you can use to create new files. (You see the same menu option if you right-click on a blank area of Explorer.)

The context menu isn't the only new tool that Windows 95 provides. You'll also enjoy the capabilities provided by other parts of this application. The toolbar, shown in Figure 2.4, is one feature I use quite a bit. With a single click, it allows me to change the view I get. The following paragraphs describe the various toolbar features.

Figure 2.4.
*The Explorer toolbar
contains controls that
perform a variety of tasks.*

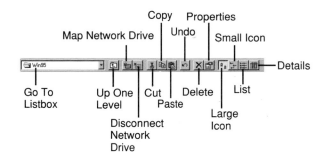

- The Go to a Different Folder listbox: The Go to a Different Folder listbox contains a list of drives and other upper-level objects. It also contains the tree used to access the current folder, as shown in Figure 2.5. You can use this listbox to quickly move from one area of your machine to another.

Figure 2.5.
*The Go to a Different Folder
listbox allows you to quickly
move between major areas of
your machine. It also shows
the directory tree leading to
the currently selected object.*

- Up One Level: Use this tool to move up one level in the directory tree. This tool isn't quite as handy in this view of Explorer as it is in others. The Up One Level tool is especially helpful when you're moving between levels in the single-pane view of Explorer.

- Map Network Drive: Explorer displays this tool only if you're connected to a network. It displays a dialog box that allows you to map one of your drives to a network drive (see Figure 2.6). Of course, you can still access the drive using Network Neighborhood even if you don't map it.

Figure 2.6.
*The Map Network Drive
dialog allows you to map a
local drive to a network
location. Note the Reconnect
at logon box, which remaps
the drives automatically each
time you log onto the system.*

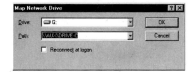

- Disconnect Network Drive: This tool becomes active only when you install a network and map some network drives to your local drives. Clicking on this tool displays the dialog shown in Figure 2.7. You can use it to disconnect from any network drive. Of course, the drives remain accessible using Network Neighborhood even after you disconnect.

Figure 2.7.
*Use the Disconnect Network
Drive tool to remove one or
more drive maps.*

- Cut: Allows you to cut one or more objects.

- Copy: Allows you to copy one or more objects.

- Paste: This tool allows you to paste any object in the Clipboard to the currently selected object in Explorer.

- Undo: The Undo tool allows you to undo your previous action. This comes in handy if you send a file to the Recycle Bin and discover that you really intended to delete something else. The Undo tool doesn't work for some types of actions. For example, you can't undo a permanent erase.

- Delete: The Delete tool sends the currently selected objects to the Recycle Bin. It doesn't delete them permanently. You need to perform the second step of emptying the Recycle Bin to remove things permanently.

- Properties: This tool displays the Properties dialog for the currently selected object. Nothing happens if you don't select an object.

- Large Icon: Displays the objects in the right pane using the large icon format.

- Small Icon: Displays the objects in the right pane using the small icon format.

- List: Uses the list format to display objects in the right pane. This doesn't include any details about these objects.

- Details: This tool displays the objects in a list format and includes all the details about that object, including file size, type, and date last modified.

- Update All: Used with the Briefcase to update all the links it contains. See Chapter 21 for more details.

- Update Selection: Used with the Briefcase to update just the link for the selected (highlighted) files. See Chapter 21 for more details.

This gives you a quick overview of using Explorer. It doesn't show you everything, but we'll revisit this tool later on. The important thing to remember for now is that you can do just about anything within Windows 95 just by knowing how to perform these few simple acts with Explorer.

New Windows 95 Applications

Windows 95 has a lot more to offer than just Explorer. A whole new group of utility programs are available to make life a lot easier for the user. In the past, most of these applications were supplied by third parties, but today you get them as part of the operating system package.

The next few paragraphs highlight these new utility programs. We'll take a close look at them in future chapters, but the information that follows should provide you with what you need to get started.

> **Looking Ahead:** The following paragraphs provide only highlights of the new utilities. They all appear in other, product-specific areas of this book. For example, you'll find out more about the remote access utilities in Chapter 19. Microsoft Exchange also appears in several other chapters, including Chapter 18. You'll want to visit Chapter 10 to find out more about all the Windows 95 applets.

Microsoft Exchange

In days past, you had to use one program to access your company e-mail and another to get your online e-mail. In fact, depending on your online services, you might have ended up working with three or four applications just to maintain contact. Once you got past the contact hurdle, you had to figure out how to get everything to work together.

Microsoft Exchange, shown in Figure 2.8, acts as a central repository for all your e-mail, no matter where it comes from. Of course, this product has its limitations. For one thing, it supports only Microsoft Mail, Microsoft Network, and CompuServe right now. You can access the Internet through Microsoft Network, so that's not too much of a problem. However, you do start running into problems if you use online services other than these.

Figure 2.8.

Microsoft Exchange might offer a centralized communication capability, but it falls short of actually providing it.

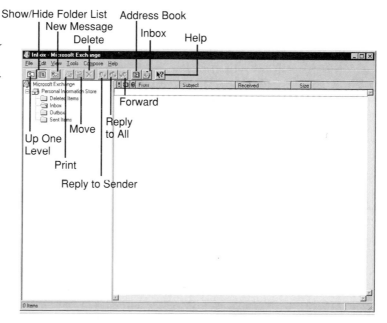

The Exchange interface is fairly simple. It looks a bit like the Explorer interface (as do a great many things under Windows 95). You access Exchange using the Inbox icon on the Desktop. The left panel contains what looks like a directory tree. However, this tree uses the Microsoft Exchange icon as the root object. Below this object is the Personal Information Store folder, which contains four folders. These four folders include Deleted Items, Inbox, Outbox, and Sent Items. Their purposes are fairly straightforward.

The toolbar contains all the tools you'll need in most circumstances. It includes the following tools:

- Up One Level: Use this tool to move up one level in the directory tree. This serves the same purpose as the equivalent tool in Explorer.

- Show/Hide Folder List: Some people might find the dual-pane look of Microsoft Exchange less useful than the single-pane view. You can use this button to turn off the directory tree shown in this left pane.

- New Message: This button always creates a new message. It doesn't matter where you are in the directory tree. The new message can go to your company e-mail or an online service. Microsoft exchange always uses the address to determine where a message gets sent. In fact, you can send a single message to a combination of local and online addresses if you wish.

- Print: Select this tool to print one or more messages.

- Move Item: Use this tool to move the selected messages from one folder to another. I find this particular tool handy for resending messages that never got to the intended person.

- Delete: Moves the selected messages to the Deleted Items folder. If you delete messages in the Deleted Items folder, Exchange removes them completely. Exchange doesn't send messages to the Recycle Bin, so if you remove them from the Deleted folder, you can't undelete them later.

- Reply to Sender: This feature allows you to send a reply to the originator of a message.

- Reply to All: Use this feature if you want to send a reply to the originator of a message and all the other recipients. This works well in group-discussion-type e-mails.

- Forward: Allows you to send to a third party a copy of the message plus any comments you might want to make.

- Address Book: Select this tool to gain access to your personal address book or any other accessible address book. You can use this tool when you need to add a new address or edit an existing one.

- Inbox: Clicking on this tool takes you to your inbox without going through the directory tree.

- Help: Provides online help for Exchange.

In addition to the toolbar, you might notice that the individual column headings provide some functionality. If you move the mouse pointer between two headings, it turns into a double-headed arrow. This allows you to resize the column heading as needed. Right-clicking on a column heading displays a context menu. The context menu allows you to sort the list of messages in either ascending or descending order by that column. For example, you would right-click on the Sent column to sort your e-mail by date. Exchange places an up or down arrow in the column you select for sorting.

Remote Access

There are two tools you can use for remote access. The first is Dial-Up Networking, shown in Figure 2.9. Interestingly enough, the interface for this application looks very similar to the single-pane Explorer interface that appears when you open a folder. Most of the controls operate the same way as well, so I won't discuss them here.

Figure 2.9.
Dial-Up Networking allows you to connect your machine to another machine through a modem.

Dial-Up Networking allows you to connect to another computer much as you would with any peer-to-peer connection. The big difference is that you use a modem instead of a NIC (network interface card) to make the connection. You could use this application to dial into a terminal connected to the company network using your notebook. It would also come in handy for off-site employees who needed to check in for their e-mail.

The second utility is Direct Cable Connection. Figure 2.10 shows the host dialog box. Essentially, this utility replaces the Interserver application provided with DOS 6.x. It allows the client machine to access the host machine's drives and other resources. I find that I normally use it to move data from my notebook computer to the Desktop machine. As you can see, there are no controls to worry about with this application.

Figure 2.10.
The Direct Cable Connection interface shows that its only purpose is to allow temporary data transfer between two machines.

Tip: Always use a parallel connection if at all possible when using the Direct Cable Connection utility. Doing so will greatly increase throughput. You can at least triple the amount of information moved per second by using a parallel cable. A machine-to-machine parallel cable might prove a little difficult to find. If so, you can modify a standard 25-pin serial cable by adding a gender changer to each end. Most electronics stores carry both serial cables and gender changers. The one advantage to this approach is that you can use the same cable for both serial and parallel connections.

Accessories

Windows 95 doesn't add very much when it comes to accessory applications. The multimedia offerings are much the same as you got with Windows 3.x. They consist of a multimedia player (media player), (sound) recorder, mixer (volume control), and CD player.

Windows 95 also includes some of the other familiar utilities from previous versions of Windows, including the calculator and WinPopUp. Conspicuously absent, though, are Cardfile and Calendar. Early beta releases of Windows 95 contained a replacement named WinPad, but it disappeared in later releases. As of this writing, it isn't certain what Microsoft plans to do to replace the lost functionality.

You'll really like two of the new utilities. The first one allows you to configure the various international settings. The second allows you to monitor system resources. Windows 95 doesn't automatically install either one of these features; you need to install them separately using the Add/Remove Programs utility. Icons for both applications appear on the Taskbar, as shown in Figure 2.11.

Figure 2.11.
Icons for two of the new Windows 95 utilities, Resource Monitor and International Settings, appear on the Taskbar.

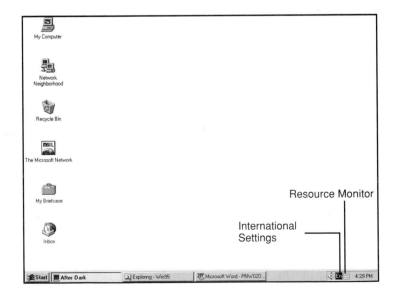

Figure 2.12 shows the Resource Meter dialog. You can display it by double-clicking on the Resource Meter icon. Placing the mouse cursor over the icon for a few seconds displays a quick readout of all the various levels. All this display tells you is the status of the three memory-related areas of the system:

- System resources: This tells you the amount of memory you have left in the smaller of the two 64 KB memory pools used for windows, icons, dialog boxes, and other system objects.

- User resources: This level tells you how much memory Windows 95 is using for interface-related objects such as windows and dialog boxes.

- GDI resources: All icon and other graphical device interface object memory usage appears in this level. This level always pertains to graphic system elements rather than an interface element such as a pushbutton or window.

Figure 2.12.
The Resource Monitor helps you keep track of system memory usage.

There are a number of ways to use the International Settings utility. The first way is to click on the Taskbar icon to display a list of installed languages. You can select which language you want to use from the list. This makes it easy to switch from language to language as needed.

The second way to use the International Settings utility is to right-click on the International icon and select the Properties option. This displays the Keyboard Properties dialog, shown in Figure 2.13. As you can see, this dialog allows you to change the currently selected language. It also allows you to add support for additional languages.

Figure 2.13.
Use the International Settings properties option to gain quick access to the Keyboard Properties dialog box.

Tip: Even if you don't use more than one language, adding the International Settings utility to your Startup folder can make you more productive. I use it to gain quick access to the Keyboard Properties dialog without going through Control Panel. The Speed tab of this dialog contains settings I can change as needed to make the system more comfortable to use.

A Quick Look Inside

Learning about a new operating system usually includes knowing a bit about the components that comprise it. You don't start learning about DOS by knowing that there are two hidden files (MSDOS.SYS and IO.SYS) and one visible file (COMMAND.COM) that make up its core, but you do learn about them later. It doesn't take too long for most people to figure out some of the things that take place under DOS as well. An in-depth knowledge of interrupts and vector tables isn't required, but a basic knowledge of what takes place is. Just about every user spends some time learning about ancillary system files as well. Everyone knows about the DOS configuration files— AUTOEXEC.BAT and CONFIG.SYS—because you can't do much without them.

With this in mind, let's take a look at the Windows 95 architecture and some of the components that comprise it. We won't go into bits and bytes during this discussion. In fact, we'll barely scratch the surface of what Windows 95 contains. Still, you'll gain an appreciation of what goes on under the hood of this operating system. Having that knowledge can make it a lot easier to both configure and use Windows 95 effectively.

Architecture

Several elements make up the Windows 95 architecture, as shown in Figure 2.14. Each element takes care of one part of the Windows environment. For example, the Windows API (Application Programming Interface) layer lets applications communicate with Windows internals such as the file management system. You couldn't write a Windows application without the API layer. I describe each of these main components in detail in the following sections.

The System Virtual Machine (VM) component of Windows 95 contains three main elements: 32-bit Windows applications, the shell, and 16-bit Windows applications. Essentially, the System VM component provides most of the Windows 95 user-specific functionality. Without it, you couldn't run any applications. Note that I don't include DOS applications here. This is because Windows uses an entirely different set of capabilities to run DOS applications. It even runs them in a different processor mode.

Figure 2.14.
Windows contains several major elements. Each element provides a different service to the user and other applications running under Windows.

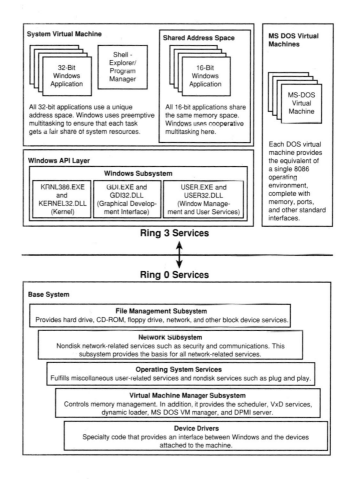

Two Windows APIs are included with Windows 95. The first API is exactly like the old one supplied with Windows 3.1. It provides all the 16-bit services that the old Windows had to provide for applications. An older 16-bit application will use this API when it runs. The other API is the new Win32 API used by Windows NT. It provides a subset of the features that all 32-bit applications running under Windows NT can access. The 32-bit API provides about the same feature set as the 16-bit API, but it's more robust. We'll discuss both of these APIs as part of the system file discussion in the next section.

The Base System component of Windows 95 contains all the operating system-specific services. This is the core of Windows 95, the part that has to be operating in order for Windows to perform its work. The following list describes each part of the Base System in detail:

- File Management Subsystem: This particular part of Windows 95 is examined in detail in the section "A Historical View of Windows" in Chapter 1. Essentially, this part of the Base System provides an interface to all the block devices connected to your machine. It doesn't matter how the connection is made—physically or through a network. All that matters is that your machine can access the device. The main thing to remember about the File Management Subsystem is that Windows 95 no longer relies on DOS to manage files.

- Network subsystem: Windows for Workgroups was the first version of Windows to address the networking needs of the workgroup. It even incorporated networking as part of the operating system rather than as a third-party add-on product. Windows 95 extends this capability. Not only can you run a Microsoft peer-to-peer network, but Windows 95 also provides protected-mode hooks for most major LAN products. In fact, you can keep more than one network active at a time. The modular nature of the Network Subsystem enables other vendors to add to Windows 95-inherent capabilities through the use of VxDs.

- Operating system services: This is the part of the operating system that deals with features such as plug and play. It also fulfills miscellaneous user and operating system requests. For example, every time the user asks Windows 95 for the time of day, he is requesting a service from this Windows 95 component.

- Virtual Machine Manager: Ever wonder where the exact center of Windows 95 is? This is it; this is the component that holds everything else together. The Virtual Machine Manager takes care of task scheduling, and it starts and stops every application on the system (including any DOS applications that you might run). This operating system component manages virtual memory on your machine as well. Of course, your application uses the Windows API to make the request instead of talking with this part of the system directly. Since the Virtual Machine Manager handles all memory allocations, it also has to act as a DPMI (DOS Protected Mode Interface) server for DOS applications that run in protected mode. When a DOS application makes a memory request, it's actually calling routines in this component of Windows. As with Windows applications, DOS applications can't directly access this component of Windows. The DOS application uses a DOS extender API to make its call. Finally, the Virtual Machine Manager is responsible for intertask communication. All this means is that all DDE and OLE requests filter through this section of the operating system.

- Device drivers: Windows would never know what to do with your system if it weren't for the lowly device driver. This bit of specialty code acts as an interpreter. It takes Windows requests and provides them to the device in a format it can understand. Windows 95 supports two forms of device driver. The first type is the real-mode device driver that you used with Windows 3.1. The problem with using this type of driver is that Windows has to keep switching between real and protected mode to use it. Windows 95 also provides the VxD, or virtual device driver, which lets Windows talk to the devices on your system without switching to real mode. There are three reasons to use VxDs over standard real-mode device drivers: Your system remains more stable, runs faster, and recovers from errors better.

I've separated the DOS Virtual Machine component of Windows from the other components for several reasons. DOS applications have formed the basis for using the PC for a long time. In fact, for many years, nothing else was available. Yet most of these applications were written at a time when the standard PC ran one application and one application only. That one application had total control of the entire machine.

Windows 95 deals with DOS applications differently than it deals with the Windows-specific applications on your machine. Each DOS application runs on what Intel terms a *virtual machine*. Essentially, the processor fools the application into thinking that it is the only application running on your machine at the moment. Each virtual machine has its own memory space and access to devices on the system. The amazing thing is that you can have many virtual machines running on your one physical machine at a time. We'll take a more detailed look at the DOS Virtual Machine later. Suffice it to say that Windows 95 has to literally perform backflips to make this whole concept work properly, especially when you consider Windows-hostile applications such as games.

Looking Ahead: If you want an in-depth look at the Windows 95 architecture, check out Chapter 6. We'll blow the covers off every area of Windows 95, including the registry and some of the deep, dark secrets that Microsoft doesn't want you to know.

The System Files

DOS programmers know you're supposed to gain access to the operating system using an interrupt service routine. These interrupts ask the operating system to perform a specific task. All the code for the interrupt routines appears in the system files. This old method worked well in the DOS single-tasking environment, where the application was in control. Under Windows, the user is in control, and the old system won't work properly. Every Windows application gains access to the operating system using an API. Essentially, an API call does the same thing as an interrupt: It asks the operating system to perform a task. The code for the API appears in the system files, just like it does for DOS. Of course, this is a very simplified view of the API. An API is written using protected-mode code, unlike DOS, which is written in real-mode code. In addition, API code is reentrant, but DOS code isn't. A reentrant piece of code allows Windows 95 to process more than one call at a time. Under DOS, you couldn't reenter a piece of code—you had to complete one call at a time. There are other differences as well, but the only people who really need to know about them are programmers. As we discussed in the preceding section, Windows 95 actually uses two APIs—one 16-bit and one 32-bit.

The big news under Windows 95 is the 32-bit API. Not only are 32-bit system calls a lot more logical from a programmer's point of view (Windows 3.x was a programmer's nightmare; Windows 95 is merely an inconvenience), but they also provide many more features as well. In addition, a 32-bit application enjoys the benefits that this environment provides. Of course, the biggest benefit that you'll hear most programmers talk about is the flat memory address space. Every application running under Windows has had to spend time working with Intel's segmented address scheme—until now. A 32-bit application doesn't need to worry about segmentation anymore. Every call is a near call; every call is in a single segment.

No matter which API you use, your application will address three basic components. The 16-bit versions of these files are GDI.EXE, USER.EXE, and KRNL386.EXE. The 32-bit versions of these files are GDI32.DLL, USER32.DLL, and KERNEL32.DLL. The following paragraphs describe these three components in detail:

- Windows Kernel (KRNL386.EXE or KERNEL32.DLL): This part of Windows 95 provides support for the lower-level functions that an application needs to run. For example, every time your application needs memory, it runs to the Windows Kernel to get it. This component doesn't deal with either the interface or devices; it interacts only with Windows itself.

- Graphical Device Interface (GDI.EXE or GDI32.DLL): Every time an application writes to the screen, it uses a GDI service. This Windows component takes care of fonts, printer services, the display, color management, and every other artistic aspect of Windows that users can see as they use your application.

- User (USER.EXE or USER32.DLL): Windows is all about just that—windows. It needs a manager to keep track of all the windows that applications create to display various types of information. However, User only begins there. Every time your application displays an icon or pushbutton, it's using some type of User component function. It's easier to think of the User component of the Windows API as a work manager; it helps you organize things and keep them straight.

There is actually one more piece to the Windows API, but it's a small piece that your application will never use. Windows 95 still starts out as a 16-bit application so that it can implement plug and play. The plug and play BIOS contains separate sections for real-mode and 16-bit protected-mode calls. If Windows 95 started out in 32-bit mode, it couldn't call the plug and play BIOS to set up all your devices without a lot of overhead. (See the section "Getting 16-Bit and 32-Bit Applications to Work Together" in Chapter 6 to understand why.) All device configuration has to occur before Windows actually starts the GUI.

However, 16-bit mode operations end very soon after you start Windows 95. The user shell is a 32-bit application. As soon as the 16-bit kernel sees the call for the shell, it loads an application called VWIN32.386. This little program loads the three 32-bit DLLs that form the Win32 API. Once it completes this task, VWIN32.386 returns control to the 16-bit kernel, which in turn calls the 32-bit kernel. Windows runs in 32-bit mode from that point on.

The Plug and Play BIOS

Plug and play (PNP) is big news for Windows 95. The first misconception that I want to clear up is that this is some new piece of "magic" that Microsoft pulled from its bag of tricks. PNP isn't magic, nor is it even all that new. The only thing that Windows 95 does differently is actually use the capabilities provided by PNP hardware.

Let's go back a bit. The very first MCA (microchannel architecture) machine produced by IBM contained everything needed by PNP except one thing—an operating system. The same can be said of many EISA machines.

The problem wasn't simply a matter of adding some capabilities to an operating system. You have to build this feature into every aspect of the operating system; it can't be added on. In addition, you need routines that will handle problems between the various pieces of hardware vying for a particular port address or interrupt. Finally, the BIOS itself has to provide a standardized interface, and these earlier offerings were anything but standard.

PNP is actually the work of three system components: hardware, BIOS, and operating system. The BIOS queries all the system components during startup. It activates essential system components such as the disk drive and display adapter. Everything else waits on the sidelines until the operating system boots. During the boot process, the operating system finishes the task of assigning interrupts and port addresses to every system component. It also asks the BIOS to provide a list of previous assignments so that it won't use them again.

The EISA and MCA BIOS weren't prepared for this kind of interaction with the operating system. Enter the PNP BIOS. This isn't the work of Microsoft, but of Compaq Computer Corporation, Phoenix Technologies Ltd., and Intel Corporation.

In addition to cooperating with the operating system, the PNP BIOS provides something very important that the EISA and MCA BIOS don't—protected-mode routines. The current BIOS specification only requires vendors to provide 16-bit protected-mode routines. That is why Windows 95 still starts in 16-bit mode instead of 32-bit mode. In addition, that is one of the reasons why a real-mode DOS stub (a functional subset of the DOS that you're familiar with) is part of the picture. (The version of real-mode DOS provided with Windows 95 also executes the AUTOEXEC.BAT and CONFIG.SYS, but we'll look into that aspect later.) You can't use the protected-mode routines without first gathering the information that the BIOS needs in real mode. The real-mode DOS stub performs this function for the BIOS.

Note: A few "used car salesman" type of people out there will try to convince you that their systems are fully PNP-compatible. If you look inside, you'll see shiny new components, all of which are indeed PNP-compatible. But, unbeknownst to you, something is missing. A lot of folks find out too late that their system lacks a PNP BIOS. So how can you avoid the same fate?

Intel, inspired by the PNP BIOS problems, created a test utility to check your PNP BIOS. You can download a copy of this BIOS test program from the plug and play forum (GO PLUGPLAY) on CompuServe. Look in Library 6 for BIOTST.ZIP. You might want to check out BIO10A.DOC (BIO1A.ZIP) while you're at it. This specification talks about the capabilities of the plug and play BIOS. It also provides some information about the peripheral board setup.

When looking at a PNP-compatible system, you should see a lot more than just three different entities cooperating to provide automatic system configuration. PNP wouldn't be worth all the hubbub if that's all it provided. The following paragraphs provide a list of additional features that you get as part of a PNP system.

- Identify installed devices: Windows 95 automatically detects all of the plug and play components attached to your system. This means that you need to provide a minimum of information during installation and nothing at all during subsequent reboots. Contrast this with the almost continuous flow of information needed under Windows 3.1.

- Determine device resource needs: Every device on your computer needs resources in the form of processor cycles, input/output ports, DMA channels, memory, and interrupts. Windows 95 works with the BIOS and peripheral devices to meet these needs without any intervention.

- Automatic system configuration updates and resource conflict detection: All of this communication between peripheral devices, the BIOS, and the operating system allows Windows 95 to create a system configuration without any user intervention. The Device Manager configuration blocks are grayed out because the user doesn't need to supply this information anymore. The enhanced level of communication also allows Windows 95 to poll the peripherals for alternative port and interrupt settings when a conflict with another device occurs.

- Device driver loading and unloading: CONFIG.SYS and AUTOEXEC.BAT used to contain line after line of device driver and TSR statements. This is because the system had to bring these devices online before it loaded the command processor and Windows 3.1. Windows 95 can actually maintain or even enhance the performance of a plug-and-play-compatible system without using an AUTOEXEC.BAT or CONFIG.SYS. Plug and play compatibility allows Windows 95 to load and unload any device drivers that your system needs dynamically.

- Configuration change notification: Plug and play might make system configuration changes automatic, but that doesn't mean that Windows 95 leaves you in the dark. Every time the system configuration changes, Windows 95 notifies you by displaying a dialog box on-screen. Essentially, this dialog box tells you what changed. This capability provides an additional side benefit. Windows 95 also notifies you whenever your equipment experiences some kind of failure. When a piece of equipment fails, Windows 95 notices that it is no longer online. Plug and play requires three-way communication, and a defective device usually fails to communicate. Instead of your finding out that you no longer have access to a drive or other device when you need it most, Windows 95 notifies you of the change immediately after it takes place.

What's Next?

Windows is a moving target. Looking through Chapter 1 will tell you that. What you see today is only a shadow of what you will get tomorrow. It's always fun to look back a bit and then see what you have today and use it as a basis for what you could have tomorrow. That's what most science-fiction writers have to do to ply their trade.

I'm often reminded of *Star Trek*. Back when the series was first designed, Gene Roddenberry did his best to think about the future. Not the far-off future, but a realistic near future (as the timeline of history goes, anyway). When *Star Trek* was still a gleam in his eye, the computers and other futuristic machinery of the *Enterprise* seemed like a far-away dream. What seemed so far away then was in reality very close. I was struck by a recent article that showed that much of the technology that seemed so futuristic in 1966 is almost a reality today. In fact, I often look at those shows with just a little awe and a tad of amusement when I think that what was the future yesterday is the present now.

It's little wonder that science-fiction writers have a difficult time coming up with ideas futuristic enough that they won't become reality until at least tomorrow. This is especially true of computers. Just think about how far we've traveled with the PC since its introduction. A few short years ago we were using machines that would be considered nonfunctional today. Text-based displays and 64 KB of RAM today wouldn't even make it in most embedded equipment (discussed later), much less a personal computer. Take with me a step into the future of Windows—at least the way I see it.

Windows at Work

Reading the trade papers a few days ago turned out to be a worthwhile venture. Microsoft had released some new information about the future direction of OLE and how it will affect computers. Just yesterday, OLE was a simple method of connecting two applications. Today, a server application can actually make a client application change its appearance to meet a user's needs. Tomorrow, that same application will allow you to connect to anything on a network without really knowing where the connection leads. All you'll really need to know is what you want. The computer will find the information for you.

Connectivity isn't the only way that Windows will change the way you work. Consider the business trip. How many of us really like to get up early on a Sunday, trudge down to the airport, spend the day traveling, and then sleep in a bed not our own? It's a pain, but also a necessity of modern business. Windows might change all that. An article in the same trade paper talked about modems that allow both voice and data transfer using one telephone wire. Think about it: This technology is available right now. It's not in the future; you can have it today. How will this new technology affect business travel? I think we'll all spend a lot less time traveling. It doesn't take a college education to figure out that a telephone call, even a five- or six-hour telephone call, is a lot less expensive than sending someone halfway around the country.

Windows 95 also presents some new technology that I think will become the future of all communication. You can use Microsoft Exchange to manage your company and online e-mail. In fact, you don't even have to pay much attention to the source of the e-mail; Exchange will route it to the right place automatically. What does this mean to the user? It means that you can spend less time worrying about the details of communicating and more time about the substance.

This whole idea of spending less time worrying about your environment relates to the general design of Windows 95. How much time did you spend under Windows 3.x worrying about which application to use and what types of data that application supports? Configuration details were a matter of a computer user's daily existence in that old environment. Windows 95 isn't perfect by a long shot, but the new data-centric approach that it provides takes users and places them in the driver's seat. Windows 95 enforces the idea that it's the data, not the application, that is your main concern. For example, I just stick all the files related to a particular project in a folder on my Desktop and let Windows 95 worry about which application to start when I double-click on one of them. You'll find that this approach allows you to organize and use your data just like its paper equivalent—a feature that Windows 3.x lacked.

As you can see, Windows 95 is not the future. It is today. Tomorrow will provide much more in the way of a user-friendly environment. Tomorrow's version of Windows will still have bugs—those won't go away—but you should be able to get a lot more work done in a lot less time despite the problems with whatever direction Windows takes.

Embedded APIs

There's been a lot of talk about sticking Windows into embedded-systems technology. What are embedded systems? Think of the computer in your car or the alarm that protects your house. A computer in your television set provides automatic channel programming and other features. Of course, this is a personal view of embedded systems.

The industry view of embedded systems takes a slightly different route. Have you ever seen the robotic arms that put your car together? They contain embedded systems. What about the device that automatically machines the flywheel for that car? The number of embedded systems in industry is amazing.

Now, what do most of these embedded systems have in common? They almost always have size constraints that make it nearly impossible for them to contain what we would call a modern computer. Up to a few years ago, it wasn't uncommon to find embedded-systems programmers using hexadecimal to program older systems. Some of the newer systems actually allowed them to use assembler or perhaps C.

All that is changing. Embedded systems are slowly coming up to the level of modern computers thanks to the constant miniaturization taking place. The same technology that put a Pentium in your notebook is putting it into embedded systems as well.

It's not unlikely that we might see a form of Windows in embedded systems tomorrow. This won't be the Windows that you use today. It will be something slightly different, something designed to provide for the special needs of embedded systems.

How will Microsoft enable you to use Windows for both your car and your work? Through the use of embedded APIs. We currently use several different APIs to make various parts of Windows work. (We'll discuss these APIs in detail later.) It's not too much of a leap to add some additional APIs that will work with nonstandard computers such as those used in embedded systems.

Windows APIs in Your Toaster?

What these embedded APIs mean to you as a user is that you'll eventually be able to control many household appliances with your computer. Your VCR will no longer be a challenge to program because it won't use an archaic text interface. It will probably use an interface that looks very familiar, perhaps even as familiar as the version of Windows running on your computer.

Have you ever watched futuristic movies and envied the person who walked into his house and talked to it? All of a sudden, the house began doing some of the more mundane tasks of living while the person worked on something creative. It's not too unrealistic to think that this technology is just around the corner.

Voice technology is already becoming a reality. Even though Windows 95 currently doesn't implement what I would consider a viable voice technology, it is on the drawing boards right now. Sound-card vendors such as Creative Technologies and Media Vision are already marketing Windows-compatible voice systems that can execute commands for you. If Windows becomes a part of embedded systems, it's only one more step before the emerging voice technology actually lets you talk to your house.

At Work Fax

Let's get back to reality. One of the things that Windows 95 should allow you to do today is share a fax. It doesn't sound like a big deal until you start to think about the logistics of people sharing one fax connected to a communications server. Outgoing faxes don't present much of a problem. It's the incoming faxes that you have to worry about.

How do you determine where to send an incoming fax? That's one of the things that this new version of Windows should help you resolve (but doesn't). Another problem is what format to provide for the incoming fax. Does the person receiving it want a text or graphic format? Text format would allow him to import the fax into a word processor. A graphic format would allow him to print faxes containing pictures and other nontext information. You need to choose that part of the equation almost immediately to make the fax software work properly.

Even though Windows 95 does come with fax software, it needs a lot of help before it will be truly useful. For one thing, a lot of people are having trouble making it work at all on a network. Routing is only one part of the problem that they seem to have. Another problem is getting the fax software to spool properly. I think it will be a while before Microsoft will get this one worked out.

At least the fax software provided with Windows 95 works well on a local machine. Of course, you need a standard fax/modem, or you'll run into other problems. Remember the fax/modems of about three years ago? I've yet to see one of them work with Windows 95. The problem is simple. Most faxes use nonstandard port assignments and might not even work properly with the attached modem.

At Work Xerox

Since fax and scanner software are here today, it's not too surprising to think that we might be looking at Windows-controlled Xerox machines in the future. However, these won't be ordinary Xerox machines. What would happen if you could make copies of a company memo and distribute it through the company e-mail, through the Internet, or over CompuServe with equal ease? Not only would the recipient receive a copy faster, but she would receive it without wasting paper or postage. Sure, it costs a little bit to send some types of information over the online services, but in most cases that cost is far less than using the postal system.

There are no Windows-controlled Xerox machines today, but it's only a matter of time. More and more office equipment comes with a built-in Ethernet connection, and recent events would seem to point to an eventual connection to every piece of office equipment, including the Xerox machine. Just think, a few years ago an Ethernet-equipped printer was an unheard-of luxury. Today it is standard equipment.

On Your Own

Explorer is one of the cornerstones of the new Windows 95 interface. It allows you to move around your machine—and the network, for that matter—in a way that was impossible under Windows 3.x. Spend some time getting used to the interface and trying out the various display modes. Click on the column headings in the Detail view to see how Explorer rearranges the filenames.

Context menus are also an important part of Windows 95. Try right-clicking on all the objects you see. See how the context menus vary from object to object. Don't forget that even the Desktop is an object with a context menu. Make sure you click on the Desktop to close its context menu without selecting anything.

Download a copy of BIOTST.ZIP from CompuServe if you own a plug-and-play-compatible machine. See if your BIOS really does support plug and play features by running this test program.

Thinking about the future can be a lot of fun. What kinds of future applications do you see for Windows based on the material in this chapter? It might be fun to make a list and see which items are actually available five or 10 years from now.

II

Power
Primers

3

Performance Primer

Tuning or optimizing a machine for optimum performance is one of the first things that many people think about when they install a new operating system. After they get all their applications installed and check out some of the new utilities, they want to see just how much they can get out of their new toy. The first thing you need to consider when reading this chapter is what *tuning* means. Getting every last ounce of power out of a system to perform a specific task represents one type of tuning. Allowing a system to perform a variety of specific tasks simultaneously (multitasking) is another. General tuning to provide the best performance in a variety of situations is yet another. I could go on. The fact of the matter is that there is no default configuration and no standard machine. Everyone has different needs and different hardware that they need to use to get the job done. Any form of worthwhile optimization will take your specific needs into account.

I won't tell you how to tune your specific machine in this chapter. There's no way I can provide step-by-step tuning instructions for anyone without knowing his or her situation. What I will provide you with are some guidelines and tips you can use to create your own solution. You'll need to decide which tips you should implement and which you should ignore. I plan to provide tips for a variety of machine configurations, and your machine will appear somewhere in the list.

So, do you start reading right this second and hope to find the tips you need the first time through? You probably won't. It takes a bit of time and patience to really tune a system for optimum performance. To get some idea of what I'm talking about, consider race car drivers. A race car gets tuned to fit its particular "personality." The mechanic and driver work together to come up with the best configuration for that particular car. In addition, the car gets tuned to fit the track that it will race on and even the weather conditions. Tuning the car is probably the easy part of the process. Planning how to tune it requires a bit more effort.

You won't need to worry about the weather when tuning your system, but many other principles do apply. Planning how you need to tune your system is always a good idea. Just like any other worthwhile endeavor, tuning your system requires that you create a few goals and take a few potholes into account. Your machine contains hardware from a variety of sources. It probably contains a combination of components that are unique within your company. You need to consider how that hardware will react. Your applications are unique. Even if your job isn't unique, your way of doing that job probably is. A system that's perfectly tuned for the way I work probably won't do a lot for you.

Looking Ahead: This chapter takes a look at the physical tuning of your system. We'll look at other aspects—such as tuning your Desktop—in other chapters. Physically tuning your system is an important first step. Once you complete it, read the rest of this book (especially Chapter 9) for additional ideas on ways you can improve the efficiency of actually using your computer.

Keeping these personal needs in mind, let's look at some of the things you should consider before you start tuning up for the big race. The following list provides criteria you must consider before you start to tune your system. Of course, the time and effort you expend in this effort is directly proportional to the amount of performance you can expect to receive.

- Memory: The amount of real memory your system contains is a big factor in how well Windows 95 will operate. You shouldn't consider starting to tune until you have a minimum of 8 MB of real RAM. You'll need to tailor this number to meet the demands of the applications you plan to run. For example, a spreadsheet requires a lot of memory, a database even more, but a word processor is relatively light when it comes to memory consumption. You might find that a graphics application requires a moderate amount of memory but takes a heavy toll on both the processor and graphics adapter. The number of simultaneous applications you plan to run also affects the point at which you should start to tune your system. I equipped my system with 24 MB of RAM because I often run a word processor, spreadsheet, and communications program simultaneously. Virtual memory helps take up the slack between real memory and what you need, but you can't count on it to assume the full burden.

- Hard disk size: Windows 95 runs best when you give it a large swap area to work with. In addition, you need space for the application itself and some space for data files. The one factor many people underestimate is the size of their data files. I was quite surprised the other day when I translated a small Word for Windows file from 1.0 format to 6.0. The file consumed almost twice as much space even though the amount of data hadn't changed one iota. Of course, the 6.0 format file provides many features the 1.0 file doesn't. The extra space used by the 6.0 format bought me added functionality—an important trade-off to consider. The general rule of thumb I use for figuring out the amount of hard disk space I need is to add up the space required for installed configurations of my applications and triple it. This is a very coarse calculation, but it works for me.

- Hard disk speed: Older operating systems were a lot less disk-intensive than Windows 95 is. Not only do you have the swap file that Windows 95 creates, but applications also make greater use of the hard drive today for temporary storage. To see what I mean, open just about any application and check for the number of .TMP files on your drive. You might be surprised by what you see. All this disk access means just one thing: You have to have a fast drive to make Windows 95 jump through the hoops that you want it to. Drive speed isn't the cure-all for every problem, but it has become a much bigger part of the overall picture.

- Processor speed: Your processor speed affects the way your computer runs. No other factor so greatly affects your system once you meet the basic storage requirements. Herein lies the rub. Many people opt for a high-speed processor, then choke it with limited memory and hard drive space. Remember, the processor makes a big impact on system throughput only after you meet the basic storage requirements. A thrashing hard drive can eat up every bit of extra speed you might add to a system.

- Motherboard features: Items such as the size of the motherboard's SRAM cache might seem a bit on the technical side, but these features aren't just for technicians. An optimized system starts with an optimized motherboard. Get a motherboard that offers plenty of room to grow and the ability to tune. For example, I just upgraded one of my systems from a 486-33 to a 486-66 with a simple processor change that took just 15 minutes from start to finish.

- Peripheral devices: I/O has always been a bottleneck in the PC. That was true yesterday, and it's even more true today. The two peripherals you need to concentrate on the most are your disk controller and display adapter. Think about the way Windows is designed for a second, and you'll understand why. Windows is a GUI; it consumes huge amounts of time simply drawing all those pretty images you see on the display. A display adapter that uses processor cycles efficiently (or even unloads some processing tasks) can greatly affect the perceived speed of your system. The less time Windows spends drawing icons and other graphics, the more time it will have to service your application. Likewise, a slow controller will make even a fast hard disk look slow. It's the controller that becomes a bottleneck with many systems today. The short take on peripherals? Always get 32-bit peripherals whenever possible and make certain that they are fully compatible with Windows 95. (Using real mode or 16-bit Windows device drivers is also a major source of speed and reliability problems on many systems.)

- Bus speed: You might not think very much about the little connectors that you stick cards into, but the system does. The system bus has been a source of major concern for a great number of years, and I don't see this changing anytime soon. What good is a fast peripheral if you can't access it at full speed? There's a slew of 32-bit bus architectures on the market. Everything from EISA to VL and the MCA bus has tried to solve the problem with bottlenecks. Suffice it to say that the speed of your bus is yet another factor in how your system will perform.

- Network interface card (NIC): If you spend a lot of time working on the network, you'll most certainly want a high-capacity NIC. The minimum you should settle for is a 16-bit Ethernet card. Anything less is a waste of perfectly good network bandwidth. People who share graphics or other very large files across the system should consider getting 32-bit NICs for their machine. Some NICs also come equipped with an expandable cache. Using a larger cache can buy you some additional network speed in some cases, especially under Windows 95.

Peter's Principle: Stretching Your Hard Drive

Making your hard drive hold more has become a major topic in the wake of today's mega application. (Doesn't it always seem to come down to the size of your hard drive and/or system memory?) Talk to just about anyone, and the first way they'll suggest making your hard drive hold more information is disk compression. That's a good idea in some circumstances, but in others it could prove problematic. Some systems just don't compress all that well because of conflicts with the hard drive or controller. Other people worry about the reliability of disk compression, so they don't use it. Still another problem is the type of data your machine contains; application code doesn't compress all that well. If you store your data on the network, your machine probably won't make the best candidate for compression.

Several other ways you can extend your hard drive cost a bit but provide long-term benefits. The first is to buy a good CD-ROM. I'm not talking about an older double-speed model, but a high-end quadruple- or sextuple- (6X) speed drive. (NEC just introduced its new 6X drive; other vendors are sure to follow.) Make sure it gets connected to a good controller and that you have a separate hard drive extension. A few controllers actually limit throughput to the speed of the slowest device in the chain. Placing the CD-ROM on a separate chain ensures that you won't adversely affect the speed of higher-speed devices. Many vendors such as Corel Systems and Microsoft are making their applications so that you can copy a few files to the hard drive but run the application from the CD-ROM. Not only does this save hard drive space, but it also allows you to install the full capabilities of a product. You'll pay a performance penalty for using this type of installation, so you'll want to reserve it for applications you don't use on a daily basis.

Another disk space saver is to use compressed file formats whenever possible. This is especially true in the multimedia and graphics areas. For example, a CorelDRAW! file that consumes a mere 60 KB in its native format could consume 1 MB or more in AI (Adobe Illustrator) format. Another example is the PCX format. Storing a 1024 × 768 16-color image requires 90 KB. That same image requires 200 KB if you increase the number of colors to 256. Storing the same 256-color image in TIF format (using LZW compression) uses 136 KB and only 124 KB in GIF format. As you can see, something as simple as a file format can make a big impact on the amount of space available on your hard drive.

Once you get your hardware configuration out of the way, it's time to consider your software configuration. Windows 95 does a much better job of managing resources than Windows 3.x did, but it's by no means perfect. Windows 3.x's infamous system resources problem is still with us. You still have the same problem with the 64 KB USER and GDI areas. Filling these areas with icons, windows, and other graphical elements still results in a system that runs out of memory before physical memory is exhausted. (We'll see later there's a lot more than meets the eye to the whole topic of system resources under Windows 95. Microsoft has tuned this operating system to make many of the problems you suffered under Windows 3.x disappear.) However, the way Microsoft configures and uses memory now really reduces the drag you will see as system requirements increase.

Under Windows 3.x, I'd start to run out of resources after loading my word processor, spreadsheet, communications program, and one or two small utility programs such as a screen saver or Notepad. I usually consider closing an application or two when I get to the 35 percent system resources level, which is about where I was with this configuration. Windows 95 still has 78 percent of its resources free when using the same configuration. This means that I can usually open two or three more applications on top of my usual configuration.

Of course, system resources are only one memory factor. There's the actual level of RAM to take into consideration as well. Under Windows 3.x, you would start to notice a fairly large performance penalty when you got to the point where the swap file was as large as real memory. Under Windows 95, this doesn't seem to be as much of a problem, but it's still very noticeable. The bottom line is that if your swap file starts approaching the size of your installed memory, it's time for an upgrade.

You need to take into consideration the combination of system resources and system memory when thinking about your software situation. A memory-constrained system always lacks enough memory to perform the job you need it to. It's a subjective type of measurement based on how you actually use your system. You should load the Resource Monitor (discussed in Chapter 2) and, over a few days, track both the size of your swap file and the number of resources you have available. If you start to see a pattern of low memory, read the next section. You might even find that the problem isn't the amount of installed memory on your machine, but the way you use that memory.

By now you can see what all this preliminary checking is leading to. A mechanic would never consider tuning a car before checking it over for the first time. Likewise, you should never consider tuning your system before you know what type of system you have and how you use it. It's not enough to say that you have 24 MB of RAM installed. The way you use that RAM determines whether it's sufficient or not. A 1 GB hard drive might sound impressive—unless you're trying to create a lot of multimedia presentations with it. Then this will sound like a rather paltry amount. (I've seen some multimedia systems that have 4 GB of storage, although that's by no means standard.)

Top Performance Tips for Memory-Constrained Systems

Memory would seem to be the biggest problem most people face on a system, but it really shouldn't be. I recently looked at memory prices at my local parts store and found that I could buy an 8 MB SIMM for a mere $320. I'm almost positive that isn't the cheapest price in town, either. Although memory isn't free, it certainly isn't the most expensive upgrade you can make to your system. Few new items can provide as much potential for a noticeable increase in system performance as memory.

Microsoft will try to tell you that you can get by with as little as 4 MB of RAM when running Windows 95. I wouldn't believe this if I were you. The minimum I recommend is 8 MB, and that's if you intend to run only one application at a time. A more reasonable system will contain 16 MB of RAM. Even with 24 MB of RAM, I find my system a tad constraining at times. Of course, the opposite extreme exists as well. Few people I've talked to report any noticeable improvement in system performance after they exceed 32 MB. At the present time, a system with 32 MB would probably be the maximum you would need.

But let's say for the moment that your boss absolutely won't buy any additional memory for your machine and you're stuck at that 8 MB level. What can you do to improve the situation? How can you stretch 8 MB of RAM enough to make your single-tasking system (from a memory perspective) work as a multitasking system?

Tip: The generic optimization techniques in this section work equally well with Windows NT, WFW 3.x, and Windows 3.x workstations. If you're using Windows 95 in a peer-to-peer LAN environment, it's very likely that you'll use a Windows NT workstation as your file server. You also might have some older machines that still use WFW 3.x connected to the network. Whatever your setup, these generic tips can help just about any workstation make better use of the memory it contains.

General Tuning Tips for Windows

There are a few quick and easy methods that I recommend you start with. Anyone can use these methods, but using them always involves some level of compromise that you might or might not be willing to make. The following list shows my quick fixes to memory problems.

- Wallpaper: Did you know it costs you a little memory and some processing time to keep wallpaper on your system? If you have a memory-constrained system and can do without some bells and whistles, here's one item to get rid of. Don't think you'll save much by using smaller wallpaper or restricting yourself to patterns. Both items chew up some memory.

- Colors: The number of colors you use for your display directly affects the amount of memory it uses. A 16-color display uses roughly half the memory of a 256-color display. Although a 16-color display doesn't look as appealing as its 256-color or 32 KB color counterpart, using one does help you save memory. You probably won't notice that much of a difference in appearance if the programs on your machine are word processing and spreadsheets.

- Screen resolution: The resolution you set your display at affects processing speed and, to a much smaller degree, memory. Of course, the problem with changing your display resolution is fairly simple to figure out. You can probably get by with fewer colors, but fewer pixels is a whole different matter. You'll probably want to save changing the screen resolution as a last-ditch effort to get that last bit of needed performance.

- Doodads: I put a whole realm of utility programs into the "doodad" category. For example, if you run one of the fancier screen savers rather than the built-in Windows counterpart, you're wasting memory. The new screen saver might look pretty, but it'll really cost you in terms of performance. Some people also keep a small game program such as Solitaire running. These small applications might provide a few seconds of pleasure here and there, but you really don't need to keep them active all the time. If you insist on using that screen saver, run it right before you leave the room for a while and then exit it when you return. The same holds true with a game program—keep it open when you play it, and then close it before you get back to work.

• Icons and other graphics: Every icon displayed on your Desktop consumes memory. The same holds true for any other form of graphic image or window. At least Windows 95 doesn't penalize you for opening a folder like Windows 3.x did. You can actually recover the memory by closing the folder. The simple way of looking at this is to organize your data into folders and open only the folders that you need at any given time.

• Leaky applications: Some programs leak when it comes to memory. They allocate memory from Windows but never give it back, even after they terminate. After a while you might find that you don't have enough memory to run programs even though you should. This problem was severe under Windows 3.x. It's less so under Windows 95 and Windows NT. However, the Windows 95 data-centric interface does tend to accelerate the rate at which memory seems to dissipate if you open and close an application for each data file you want to edit. You can alleviate this situation somewhat by keeping leaky applications open until you know for certain you won't need them again later. You can find a leaky application by checking system resources and memory before you open it, opening and closing the application a few times (make sure you also open some documents while inside), and then checking the amount of memory again after the last time you close it. If you find you have less memory—I mean a measurable amount, not a few bytes—the application is leaky.

• Extra drivers: Windows 95 and Windows NT do a fairly good job of cleaning old drivers out of the registry. Windows 3.x, on the other hand, doesn't do any cleaning at all. No matter which version of Windows you use, you'll want to take the time to see if all the drivers got removed from the system after you remove an application. This isn't such a big deal for newer applications that are specifically designed for Windows 95 or Windows NT. Both of these newer operating systems provide a special installation utility that removes newer applications from the system—including the files they stick in the SYSTEM directory and any references to them in the system files. What I'm talking about are those old Windows 3.x applications that don't remove anything.

• DOS applications: Nothing grabs memory and holds it like a DOS application under Windows. Unlike other applications, Windows normally can't move the memory used by a DOS application around to free space. This means that you might have a lot of memory on your system, but Windows won't be able to use it because it's all too fragmented. If your system is so constricted on memory that it can't tolerate even the smallest amount of memory fragmentation, you'll probably want to avoid using DOS applications.

Windows 95-Specific Tuning Tips

Now that we've gotten past the generic tips, let's look at a few Windows 95-specific ways to en-hance overall system performance and the amount of memory you have available. Unfortunately, none of these tips will work for Windows 3.x systems. Even though a few might work with Windows NT, you'll want to give them a long test before making them permanent.

- 386 versus 486 or Pentium processors: Windows 3.x didn't care about the processor you used, only the processing speed. The facts are plain: Windows 3.x used 16-bit code that ran equally well on any processor 386 or above. There's a big difference in performance when using different processor types under Windows 95 because it uses 32-bit code. A 486 processor is better optimized to take advantage of 32-bit code. The Pentium is better still. Theoretically, you should notice a fairly substantial improvement in processing capability between a machine equipped with a 486 versus a 386 machine of the same processor speed. In reality, the difference is noticeable, but not that noticeable. You'll want to get the extra performance if possible, but don't worry about it until you take care of other problems, such as upgrading your memory.

- CONFIG.SYS and AUTOEXEC.BAT: In most cases, you're better off without any form of AUTOEXEC.BAT or CONFIG.SYS. If all you have in your CONFIG.SYS is a memory manager, get rid of it, because Windows 95 supplies its own. Adding a memory manager to CONFIG.SYS will reduce the amount of flexibility Windows 95 has in configuring your system. The only time you should keep CONFIG.SYS around is if you have to load real-mode drivers. It's also a good idea to get rid of AUTOEXEC.BAT in most circumstances, but it isn't always possible. There's a problem with old 16-bit Windows applications under Windows 95—they need some of the entries in AUTOEXEC.BAT. The most common requirement is the addition of entries to the PATH statement. You can open a DOS window and add a PATH statement to a batch file to set the path. However, you don't have the same privilege for Windows applications. You have to set the path before you enter Windows in order for the application to work right.

- Real-mode drivers: There are all kinds of penalties for using real-mode drivers under Windows 95. The penalties are so severe that you should consider getting rid of real-mode drivers at all costs. As far as optimizing your system is concerned, real-mode drivers cost you in both performance and system reliability. We'll examine this topic in greater detail in Chapter 6, but suffice it to say that the penalty is very real. The short explanation is that real-mode drivers force Windows 95 to make a transition between protected and real mode every time an application requires access to the device. Not only does this transition waste precious processor time, it also makes it possible for a maverick application to cause system failure. Real-mode drivers might also reduce the amount of memory available in some circumstances, but this really isn't the major consideration.

- 16-bit drivers and DLLs: Windows 95 is essentially a 32-bit operating system with some 16-bit compatibility components and a few items left over from Windows 3.x. It runs every 32-bit application in a separate session. Doing this allows Windows 95 to perform some very intense memory management on the resources needed by that application. 16-bit applications all share one session. The amount of management Windows 95 can perform on this one session is a lot less than what it can do for the individual 32-bit sessions because it can't make certain assumptions about how that memory is getting used. In addition, the 32-bit memory space is flat (every call is a near call), reducing the number of clock cycles required to make a function call or look at something in memory. On the other hand, the segmented address space used by 16-bit components requires two to three times the number of clock cycles to process because every call is a far call.

- Using Explorer in place of folders: Folders are more efficient to use than Explorer. This might seem like a contradiction in terms, because folders use the Explorer interface, but it's not. Opening a copy of Explorer will eat a lot more system resources than opening a folder. Actually, you might think this is a foregone conclusion—opening any application will eat system resources. Here's the memory saver for you. Place all your data in folders, and then place a shortcut to those folders on the Desktop. You can still get to all your important files without opening a copy of Explorer. The cost in memory will be a lot less than keeping Explorer running all the time. Use Explorer to actually explore your system, not as a substitute for File Manager.

- Use context menus in place of Control Panel: I find I occasionally need to adjust the properties of various system elements during a session. Windows 3.x always forced me to open Control Panel to make these adjustments. Old habits die hard. It took me a while to adjust to the new Windows 95 way of dealing with this situation. Chapter 2 talked a lot about the context menu attached to every object. Using that context menu is not only more efficient from a keystroke perspective, but it uses less memory as well. This is something to consider if you need to keep an Object Properties dialog open for any length of time.

- Reset your printer for RAW printing: Windows 95 automatically installs support for Enhanced Metafile Format (EMF) printing on systems it thinks will support it. This feature allows Windows 95 to print faster by translating the output to generic commands in the foreground, then creating printer-specific output in the background. Creating generic commands requires a lot less processing time than writing printer-specific output. Changing the setting of the Spool Data Format field of the Spool Settings dialog to RAW forces Windows 95 to create a printer-specific output in the first pass. (You can access this dialog by opening the Details tab of the Printer Properties dialog and clicking on the Spool Settings pushbutton.) Using the RAW setting means that less operating system code is maintained in memory during the print process. Some memory-constrained systems receive a large benefit by using this print mode. Of course, the trade-off is longer foreground print times.

- Keep your disk defragmented: Older versions of Windows allowed you to create a permanent swap file. Using a permanent swap file improved performance by reducing hard disk head movement to read swap file data. It didn't matter how fragmented your drive got after you set up the swap file, because the swap file always resided in the same contiguous disk sectors. Windows 95 doesn't provide the permanent swap file option. It always uses a temporary file. However, Microsoft has improved the access algorithms and reduced the penalty for using a temporary swap file. Of course, the system doesn't work perfectly. You can still get a highly fragmented drive that reduces system performance as Windows moves from area to area in an attempt to read the swap file. Defragmenting your drive will reduce the possibility that the swap file will become too fragmented. Most people find that a weekly maintenance session takes care of this requirement.

Looking Ahead: System Agent, a scheduling program supplied with Microsoft Plus!, can automatically run Disk Defragmenter and help maintain your system in the background while you work or sleep. See Chapter 24 for details on how to use this and other tools that allow you to automate much of the system maintenance drudgery.

- Place your swap file on the fastest drive: Windows 95 usually chooses the drive with the largest amount of available memory for the swap file. (There are other occasions in which the exact criteria Windows used to select a swap-file location eludes me—it seems to use hit-and-miss tactics from time to time.) In most cases, the drive it chooses doesn't make that big of a difference. However, if you have a system with one large, slow drive and a second small, fast drive, you'll probably want to change the virtual memory settings. See the section titled "Using Windows 95 Automatic Tuning Features" for details.

- Get rid of nonessentials: You'll find that some parts of Windows 95 will make you slightly more efficient, but at a fairly large cost in memory. For example, enabling the International Settings feature (described in Chapter 2) will make you more efficient if you work with several languages, but that enhancement will cost you some memory. Unfortunately, once you activate this feature, you can't get rid of it until you reboot the machine—the memory is gone for good. The same holds true for the Resource Monitor and many of the other icons that appear on the Taskbar near the clock. All these features are nice to have, but not essential. For example, the Accessibility Options are a nice enhancement to have, but you might want to get rid of them on a memory-constrained system unless you actually use them. Even though it doesn't display an icon on the Taskbar, installing this feature consumes some memory every time you start Windows 95.

Peter's Principle: Efficiency of Actions Versus Memory Usage
Something I'm discovering under Windows 95 is that efficiency in action is sometimes accompanied by some decrease in memory usage. The Windows 95 interface seems to be

designed to make every movement as easy as possible (although some users still find it difficult to use).

Using features such as a context menu might not seem like a very big deal—you save only two or three mouse clicks in most cases—but they also result in memory savings. Windows 95 provides other speed-enhancing features that save you memory. For example, using the automatic settings for most of the system parameters such as virtual memory will improve performance and enhance memory usage.

Some Windows 95 features aren't only extremely efficient, but also save you a considerable amount of time. For example, you'll find that using Explorer costs you a lot less memory compared to using Program Manager. (A comparison on my machine shows system resources at 98 percent when using Explorer but only 87 percent when using Program Manager in the same configuration.) You can check this out on your machine by changing the `shell=Explorer.exe` line in SYSTEM.INI to `shell=Progman.exe` and then shutting down and rebooting your system. Using the Explorer interface is so much more efficient that I would think twice about going back to Program Manager.

Using Windows 95 Automatic Tuning Features

Besides user-related activities, Windows 95 provides some additional features for making automated changes to your configuration. In most cases, you can determine at a glance whether all these automated features are in effect. All you need to do is display the Performance tab of the System Properties dialog. Simply right-click the My Computer icon and select Properties from the context menu to display it. You should see a display similar to the one in Figure 3.1 if your system is completely tuned. Windows 95 will provide some suggestions on things you can do to improve system performance. In most cases, this means enabling an automatic feature to provide additional memory, reduce the system's reliance on out-of-date drivers, or allow some additional flexibility. If your system isn't completely tuned, Windows 95 will provide tips on what you can do to make the automatic tuning features work properly.

Note the three buttons near the bottom. Clicking on the first one displays a dialog similar to the one shown in Figure 3.2. The General tab of the File System Properties dialog box allows you to change the way Windows 95 reacts to certain requests for information and allocates memory for the file system without really changing its overall management strategy. The following paragraphs describe each field in this dialog.

- Typical role of this machine: This field has three settings. The way you should use this field is pretty self-explanatory. Select the role that best describes your computer. In most cases, you will select either Desktop Computer or Mobile or Docking System. If your machine acts as a file server on a peer-to-peer network, select the Network Server setting. There's one way in which you can use this setting to improve performance. I found that the Network Server setting actually seems to speed some tasks that perform small data reads, such as database managers. It also seems to enhance performance in a multitasking environment.

Figure 3.1.
The Performance tab of the System Properties dialog box.

Figure 3.2.
The General tab of the File System Properties dialog.

- Supplemental cache size: This is one field where you can save about 1 MB on a memory-starved system. Of course, you'll trade performance for that savings. Since this setting affects only the CD-ROM cache, you might not notice much of a difference if you use your CD-ROM on an occasional basis. Don't shortchange this area if you regularly use your CD-ROM to run applications, though, because the loss in cache size will become very noticeable after a while. Using a large cache means you set aside 1,238 KB of RAM for a cache. The small cache uses a mere 214 KB.

- Optimize access pattern for: Set this field to reflect the speed of your CD-ROM drive. Windows 95 uses a different timing formula for each drive type. You can play with this field to see if there is any performance benefit to changing it from the default. I actually found one double-speed Toshiba CD-ROM drive that worked better at the triple-speed setting. It's pretty rare to get any kind of increase by doing this, but you never know.

The Troubleshooting tab (see Figure 3.3) is where you can really help or really damage your system's memory management strategy. The key term here is troubleshooting. Microsoft originally included this tab for the sole purpose of troubleshooting. However, on certain rare occasions you can use these items as part of your tuning strategy. Each of the checkboxes allows you to change a part of the Windows 95 file system management strategy. Be careful when changing these settings, or you might find yourself troubleshooting a nonfunctional system. The following paragraphs describe each of these options in detail.

Figure 3.3.
The Troubleshooting tab of the File System Properties dialog box.

- Disable new file sharing and locking semantics: Windows 95 uses new drivers to maintain file locks for networks. The new setup uses a 32-bit protected-mode driver. The old setup uses a 16-bit driver similar to the VSHARE.386 driver provided by WFW 3.x. The only reason to check this box is if you experience network-related file-locking problems. In some cases, file locking will work either way, but checking this block will reduce the number of failed attempts. The time differential is quite noticeable with applications such as database managers that require many locks during any given session.

- Disable long name preservation for old programs: Checking this block will help you maintain compatibility with existing DOS machines. It forces Windows 95 to use the 8.3 filenaming scheme everyone has used from the earliest days of DOS. Of course, you will lose the benefits of long filenames, and you won't garner even one byte of additional RAM for your system. Companies that use a mixed group of workstations on the network, however, will gain a benefit from consistent filenaming. In most cases, you'll want to leave this box unchecked.

- Disable protect-mode hard disk interrupt handling: Some applications won't work properly using the new Windows 95 interrupt handlers. You can check this box in order to install the old real-mode handlers. One note of caution: Make sure you don't use non-Windows 95 disk defragmenters or other low-level file management utility programs, because they don't support long filenames and other Windows 95 features. These old programs probably will require to you disable the protected-mode handlers.

- Disable all 32 bit protected-mode disk drivers: A few hard drives and controllers won't work properly with the Windows 32-bit drivers. Chapter 6 takes a detailed look at the architectural aspects of these drivers. The important consideration right now is that these drivers might not cause a total drive failure; they might simply cause the drive to slow down. If you notice that your drive's performance isn't what it used to be, you might want to see if disabling 32-bit support brings it back to normal.

• Disable write-behind caching for all drives: Data loss on network drives is a major headache for most administrators at one time or another. Windows 95 uses a write-behind caching scheme to improve workstation performance. This same feature can actually cause data loss, especially with networked database managers. If you find you have records that don't get written or other forms of data loss, you might want to check this box. Even though checking this box will most certainly reduce local workstation performance, it might improve overall network performance by forcing the workstation to write shared data faster. This is especially true in situations where many people share relatively few records in the database—for example, a reservation or scheduling system.

The Advanced Graphics Settings dialog box, shown in Figure 3.4, provides a single slider control. The new protected-mode drivers provided with Windows 95 accelerate writes to the display adapter. The slider controls the amount of acceleration you receive. Most adapters work fine at the highest setting. However, if you find that your adapter performs only partial screen writes, or if you see other types of corruption, you might need to use a lower setting.

Figure 3.4.
The Advanced Graphics Settings dialog box.

Figure 3.5 shows the Virtual Memory dialog box, which provides one way to enhance system performance when the automatic method selects the wrong drive for your swap file. In most cases, it pays to let Windows manage the virtual memory settings. However, there are a few cases where you'll want to manually adjust the virtual memory settings. Windows 95 normally selects the drive with the largest amount of free disk space as the virtual memory drive. However, this might not be the fastest drive on your system. In this case, it would make sense to manually adjust the virtual memory drive to be the fastest one on your machine.

Warning: Never disable virtual memory. The Virtual Memory dialog provides this setting for troubleshooting purposes only. Disabling virtual memory can (and probably will) result in some type of system failure. Such a failure could prevent Windows 95 from writing everything in disk cache to the drive. This could corrupt the registry or other system files and prevent you from rebooting the operating system.

Figure 3.5.
The Virtual Memory dialog box.

There are other ways to configure the swap file. For example, what if the fastest drive on your machine doesn't contain enough space for the size of swap file you need? Windows 95 allows you to individually configure the swap file for each drive on your system. If you don't want a swap file on a particular drive, set its minimum and maximum sizes to 0.

You also can create a pseudo-permanent drive using the manual parameters. Setting the minimum size for a drive to something other than 0 always reserves that amount of disk space for the swap file. If you defragment the drive on a regular basis, you could end up with what will look like a permanent swap file. Of course, if Windows needs to increase the file beyond this minimal setting, the new data could end up in a fragmented area of the drive.

Finding Unneeded Hidden Drivers

Sometimes Windows 95 does a less-than-perfect job of setting up your machine. Earlier I mentioned that you should remove any unneeded drivers. What would happen if you had some "hidden" drivers you really didn't need installed on your system? Figure 3.6 shows a dialog that illustrates this point perfectly. I installed Windows on a machine in a peer-to-peer networking environment. The installation program even asked about the level of support I wanted when I got to that point in the installation. However, it assumes that not everyone knows what they're talking about, so it installed both Microsoft and Novell support on my system. The Novell support goes to waste because this is a peer-to-peer network that doesn't connect to a NetWare file server. I have a Windows NT server, a Windows 95 workstation, and a WFW 3.x machine all connected and sharing resources.

There are three things you need to look at in this particular situation. First, eliminate additional network support. You need to install support for only one network if you're using a peer-to-peer setup. In most cases, this means that you'll retain the Microsoft network and discard NetWare support. Likewise, if you don't plan to set up a peer-to-peer network, remove the Microsoft network support in a NetWare environment.

Tip: LANtastic users will want to consider moving to a Microsoft network for three reasons. First, LANtastic currently requires you to load real-mode drivers that introduce a certain level of instability into your system. Second, Windows 95 doesn't provide all the services that a LANtastic network requires. For example, the network drives won't show up in Network Neighborhood. Finally, you can't run a dual network environment when using LANtastic. This means that you can't run a peer-to-peer network and connect to a NetWare file server at the same time.

If you do decide to use a LANtastic network, be certain you don't install either a network adapter or a protocol. Installing either of these items will produce some very strange results. In some cases, your network won't work at all. You'll also want to install version 5.x or above. Older LANtastic versions won't run properly under Windows 95. Finally, you won't be able to use Artisoft Exchange until Artisoft comes out with a Windows 95-specific version.

Figure 3.6.
Sometimes Windows 95 installs too much support. You can reduce your memory footprint and improve performance by getting rid of this additional support.

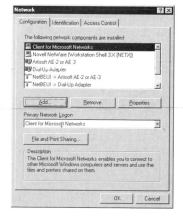

You'll also want to reduce the number of protocols you have installed. I typically maintain NetBEUI support for a peer-to-peer setup if at all possible. Of course, the protocol you choose must reflect the capabilities of the network you install.

Tip: If you remove one of the protocols from your workstation and find that you can't connect to the other workstations, make sure that all of the workstations are using the same protocol. Many people find that working networks suddenly fail when they try to optimize their setup. This simple fix repairs the vast majority of "broken" installations.

Installing the fewest possible network services is the third step I take. For example, installing sharing support for a floppy drive is a waste of memory because it's unlikely that someone will need it. If someone does need it, you can always add the support later. Try starting out with the lowest level of support possible. You'll also want to think about which workstation printers you really want to share.

If a workstation has an older printer attached, you probably won't want to install print sharing support for it.

Top Performance Tips for DOS Applications

DOS applications represent a big challenge under Windows 3.x. I'd love to say that Windows 95 will run every DOS application you ever owned without any major configuration problems, but that wouldn't be very accurate. You will encounter problems when running certain DOS applications, and you need to tune your system to avoid them.

The good news is that you can make all the required changes using the application's Properties dialog. Windows 95 supports all the old configuration features provided by Windows 3.x and adds quite a few of its own. (You'll find that Windows 95 provides far superior support for DOS applications than even Windows NT. Microsoft made some design decisions that we'll explore in Chapter 6 to make this level of support possible.) This means that you can make the required changes by right-clicking on the object and selecting Properties from the context menu. The first thing you'll see is a Diskcopy Properties dialog similar to the one shown in Figure 3.7. Everything you need to run DOS applications efficiently under Windows 95 appears in this dialog. It replaces the PIF editor used in previous versions of Windows.

Figure 3.7.
The Diskcopy Properties dialog box.

There are many similarities between the entries you'll find in the Properties dialog and those in the PIF files of previous versions of Windows. Don't be fooled. Windows 95 provides much the same functionality as those previous versions; it just makes it a bit easier to change the settings. Fortunately, the Properties dialog does add some much-needed fields and a new mode or two.

Tip: Some Windows 95 users will find it very easy to set all their DOS applications to run in MS-DOS mode since this mode provides the most familiar configuration options. However, running your applications in this mode means you'll have to forego any DOS-to-Windows interaction. It also means you won't be able to use any Windows 95 features. Finally, since running an application in MS-DOS mode unloads all the Windows 95 drivers, you'll actually lose the benefits of 32-bit driver support. The application might actually run slower than if you ran it under Windows 95 directly.

Looking Ahead: This chapter looks at the Properties dialog settings that affect DOS application performance. We'll cover the rest of the settings in Chapter 12.

Several tabs directly affect the way a DOS application behaves under Windows 95. The first one we'll look at appears in Figure 3.8. The visible part of the Program tab contains some fields that tell Windows 95 what application to run and where to run it. This includes the application name and its working directory. The area of concern for this chapter is the Advanced Settings pushbutton near the bottom of the dialog. Clicking on that pushbutton displays the Advanced Program Settings dialog, shown in Figure 3.9, which contains some of the DOS-specific settings that affect how Windows 95 will react.

Figure 3.8.
The Program tab of the Diskcopy Properties dialog box.

The checkbox I like the most on this dialog box is Prevent MS-DOS-based programs from detecting Windows. I had several applications that wouldn't work under Windows 3.x simply because the application looked for the Windows signature before it ran. Even if the application could run, it wouldn't. This checkbox allows you to fool those applications into thinking that they're all alone on the machine. In many cases, this is all you need to get an application to cooperate with Windows.

Figure 3.9.
*The Advanced Program
Settings dialog box.*

Many applications will still experience problems when running under Windows 95. The next checkbox provides a diagnostic mode of sorts. The Suggest MS-DOS mode as necessary field is another automatic tuning aid that you can turn on. If you run an application that really does have to be run in MS-DOS mode, Windows 95 displays a dialog that suggests you do so. Unfortunately, Windows doesn't check this box for you automatically, so you'll need to check it yourself.

The final checkbox is a real performance buster in every situation, according to Microsoft. The fact is that using MS-DOS mode will slow the majority of your applications at least a little. I'd be a lot more concerned about the loss in functionality you'll experience when using this mode. However, there are at least two categories of applications in which you'll probably experience a performance gain, not a loss. The first one is game programs. Many of these applications will run correctly under Windows 95; many more won't. Your only choice in this case is to run the program in MS-DOS mode.

The other category—strangely enough—is older graphics applications. For some reason, they actually perform better in MS-DOS mode. For example, the old copy of Harvard Graphics I had lying around performed almost twice as fast in MS-DOS mode as it did under Windows 95. After a bit of research, I concluded it was a combination of factors such as direct-screen writing and other rule-breaking behaviors that make these applications run faster in MS-DOS mode. I'd still say this is the exception to the rule. The best idea is to check out an application both ways and see which way it runs faster. Better yet, replace it with a Windows 95-specific product if at all possible.

After you place a check in the MS-DOS mode checkbox, you'll get several more options. The first checkbox asks if you want Windows 95 to warn you before it enters MS-DOS mode. Keep this one checked as a precaution. You wouldn't want to accidentally leave some other application in an uncertain state. This checkbox provides a sort of safety valve to ensure that you don't start something you'll regret later.

The two radio buttons allow you to choose between the default DOS setup and a custom setup for this particular application. Since Windows 95 gives you the choice, I'd recommend a custom configuration whenever possible. If the application you want to run is having problems with Windows 95, it probably will also have special needs when running in MS-DOS mode. I have several custom configurations on my hard drive right now. One works fine for games that need expanded memory but don't use the CD-ROM drive. Another helps my old copy of Harvard Graphics squeeze that last ounce of performance out of the system. You don't necessarily need a separate CONFIG.SYS and AUTOEXEC.BAT for each application, but it does help to have separate configurations for each group of applications.

> **Tip:** An easy way to take care of the various configuration needs you might have for MS-DOS mode applications is to specify the CONFIG.DOS and AUTOEXEC.DOS files as special configuration files. If the application worked with your old DOS setup, there's no reason why the same configuration won't work under Windows 95.

The Memory tab, shown in Figure 3.10, can also help you obtain the best possible setup for your application. In most cases, you'll want to stick to the Auto setting. However, I have several applications that require more environment space than the Auto setting provides. All you need to do is adjust the setting of the dropdown listbox as required. The same thing holds true for any other memory settings you might need to adjust.

Figure 3.10.
The Memory tab allows you to customize the DOS application's memory settings.

There's one thing you should always keep in mind with this tab. Setting any memory entries you don't need to None will save system memory and allow Windows 95 to provide better services to the rest of the applications on your machine. Windows 95 always assumes a worst-case scenario with DOS applications; setting the various memory options gives it a little more information to work with.

The Protected checkbox in the Conventional memory group is a two-edged sword. Setting it will allow some applications to run. It will also prevent Windows 95 from moving applications around in memory. Some applications that access memory directly need this kind of protection. The downside of checking this box is that a fixed session in memory always increases memory fragmentation and the chance that you'll artificially run out of memory.

The last tab we'll look at from a performance perspective is the Screen tab, shown in Figure 3.11. We'll talk about only two checkboxes in this chapter—the rest will get covered in Chapter 12. Not surprisingly, both appear in the Performance group near the bottom of the dialog box.

Figure 3.11.
The Screen tab provides two performance settings.

The Dynamic memory allocation checkbox is the important one here. As with the Protected checkbox in the Memory tab, this checkbox determines whether Windows 95 can move memory around. Here's the problem. Many graphics applications resort to using direct screen writes to get the performance they need. Those same graphics applications won't work under Windows 95 if you keep this box checked, because Windows might move the "virtual" screen that the application is actually writing to somewhere else. The warning sign you need to look for on a graphics application is some type of distortion. Most applications display vertical bars or some type of striation. You might see part of the display shift or what appears to be cursor trails on-screen. All these types of distortion tell you that you need to uncheck the Dynamic memory allocation checkbox.

Another group of applications somewhere (I've yet to find it in my office) needs to directly access the ROM routines. The Fast ROM emulation checkbox tells Windows 95 to emulate the display ROM in fast protected-mode RAM. However, if your application is looking for the system ROM in conventional memory, it won't find the emulated version. One way to tell if your application needs to have this box unchecked is if you get unexplainable system crashes that you can't pinpoint to another cause. These crashes could be caused when the application looks for ROM code at a certain address and doesn't find it.

Top Performance Tips for Multitasking Systems

Getting more than one application to run on a system at the same time usually involves making some compromises. You can tune a single-tasking system to provide the best performance for that one application. For example, you could tune your system in such a way that a disk-intensive application gets everything it needs in order to get the job done quickly. But what happens if you run one application that's disk-intensive and another that's CPU-intensive? Do you starve the resources of one to get better performance from the other?

We've already looked at most of the generic ways to provide additional memory. This is one area you'll need to concentrate on if you plan to multitask. Running more than one application at once always consumes a lot of memory. What you might not realize is that your performance levels might become artificially low because of the way Windows 95 handles memory management.

Disk swapping, the same feature that provides so much virtual memory for your applications, can also wreak havoc in a multitasking environment. Two big clues tell you when disk swapping has become a problem and not a cure. First, you'll notice a dramatic increase in your system's disk activity. This isn't always a bad thing under Windows 95, but it *is* an indicator. Windows 95 uses a very aggressive disk-writing algorithm to make the most of system idle time. You might see what seems like a lot of disk activity, when all Windows 95 is doing is writing some of the data from memory to disk.

The second clue will tell you just how bad the memory situation is. Look at the size of your swap file. If your swap file is about the same size as your real memory, your system is memory-starved, and you really can't run the number of applications you're trying to run. Windows 95 will try its best to provide a satisfactory level of performance, but the truth is that you just won't see it.

There are far more scientific ways to precisely measure system performance, and we'll look at them in the next section. The two clues we just discussed provide you with a very quick idea of what your system performance is like right this minute without wasting a lot of your time trying to define it completely. Of course, using System Monitor to display your actual system performance for your boss could get you the memory upgrade you've been wanting.

You'll also want to take into account the needs of the LAN as a whole if your system doubles as a file server. A peer-to-peer network depends on the resources of one or more workstations to act as file and print servers. This doubling of tasks is really another form of multitasking. You might run only one or two tasks on your machine, but it'll run very slowly if you don't take into account the needs of other people who are using your system. In this case, however, a simple look at the swap file and disk activity probably won't provide you with enough information. You'll have to monitor the network statistics using the System Monitor program.

Windows 95 also provides another utility that will come in handy here. The Net Watcher utility (described in Chapter 19) provides information about who's logged in and what type of resource they're using. You can combine this information with that obtained from System Monitor to create a clear picture of how your machine is being used in the network environment. Figure 3.12 shows a typical example of the type of information you can expect. Making a correlation between who's using which resource and what the level of activity is might seem like a difficult task, but after a while you'll notice certain patterns emerging. You can use those patterns as a basis for tuning your system.

Figure 3.12.
Net Watcher allows you to monitor who is sharing your computer and which resources they're using.

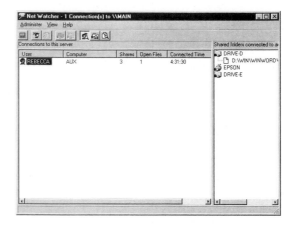

Load balancing was a term I thought I'd never have to apply to a PC, but here it is. You can get better performance out of your system if you balance the types of tasks it performs. Scheduling all your disk-intensive tasks to run at the same time is one sure way to bring your system to its knees. Likewise, scheduling all your CPU-intensive tasks at the same time will garner the same results—only faster. If you're working on a spreadsheet in the foreground, that might be a good time to compile an application or perform some database-related task in the background. Of course, the opposite is true as well. You can always perform that really intense spreadsheet recalculation in the background while performing data entry in the foreground.

> **Tip:** Unlike previous versions of Windows, Windows 95 actually does a reasonable job of downloading files and performing other forms of online communication in the background. I recently spent almost eight hours downloading a new copy of Windows 95 from the Internet at 9600 baud while working on articles and my spreadsheet in the foreground. I never did miss a file or experience any form of corruption. Under Windows 3.x, I would've had to give up my system for the day in similar circumstances. One rule of thumb you need to follow is to keep resource-hogging 16-bit applications to a minimum. Windows 95 does a good job of handling short delays without losing characters. However, some older applications grab the system for so long that background communications are impossible, even with the improved features that Windows 95 provides.

There's one final consideration you need to make when you want to get the most out of your multitasking environment. Using 16-bit applications under Windows 95 means you must suffer the consequences of cooperative multitasking. In essence, a program can be a bad sport and grab the system for however long it wants to. 32-bit applications don't get this kind of treatment. Ready or not, they have to turn control of the system back over to Windows 95 at specific intervals. The difference between multitasking 16-bit and 32-bit applications will absolutely amaze you. If multitasking is the name of the game, 32-bit applications are what you need to make it work smoothly.

Monitoring the Results of Performance Enhancements

There are three different ways I monitor the results of any optimization changes I make. The first is by looking at the Resource Monitor. Checking how much system resource memory you have left after an optimization is one way to see if the change was effective. I also monitor the size of the swap file. Even though this isn't a precise measure of the state of system memory, it does provide an overall indicator of system memory. Windows 95 increases the size of the swap file as it needs more memory, so checking on the size of the swap file is one way to see how much memory Windows 95 needs over the physical memory available on the system.

The third method is an actual monitoring tool. System Monitor is an optional utility that you can install—and it's a very worthwhile tool. It allows you to track a variety of system statistics, including CPU usage and actual memory allocation. Monitoring these statistics will tell you if a certain optimization strategy was successful or not. System Monitor also provides a means of detecting performance-robbing hardware and software errors on the system. Figure 3.13 shows a typical System Monitor display.

Figure 3.13.
System Monitor.

When you start System Monitor for the very first time, it always displays the current Kernel Processor Usage. Figure 3.13 shows one way to display this information. You can use the View | Bar Chart or the View | Numeric Chart commands to change the presentation. I find that the bar chart presentation (see Figure 3.14) is the most helpful when I need to monitor system performance over a long interval, and the numeric chart (see Figure 3.15) is handy when I need to troubleshoot a particular problem area. Notice the line displayed somewhere along the length of the bar. This line tells you the maximum usage level for that particular statistic. Of course, the bar itself shows the current usage level. You can also select any of the three chart types by clicking on the correct tool-bar icon.

Figure 3.14.
The bar graph presentation allows you to easily monitor events over the long term.

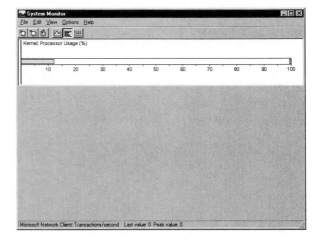

Figure 3.15.
You can use the numeric chart presentation to get a quick look at the current machine statistics.

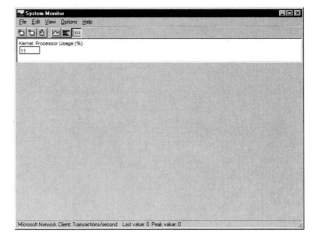

System Monitor uses a default monitoring period of 5 seconds. This might not be fast enough in certain situations. If you're troubleshooting a bad NIC or you want instant feedback on a configuration change, you'll want to change this setting to a lower value. Likewise, if you're performing long-term monitoring, you might want to set it high. Use the Options | Chart command to change this setting. Figure 3.16 shows the dialog box that changes the interval.

The first three toolbar buttons allow you to change the items that System Monitor displays. Use the add button to add new items to the list. You can use the edit button to change the way System Monitor displays a particular value. For example, you might want to display something in green rather than blue. You can also change the upper limit of some values to provide a consistent range of values for particular items. Finally, the remove button allows you to remove an item from the monitoring list. Remember that the more items you display on-screen, the less screen area each item will receive. This in turn limits the accuracy of the readings you'll take. Make sure you monitor only the essentials. For that matter, you might want to break the items into groups and monitor a single group at a time.

Figure 3.16.
Short intervals aid trouble-shooting efforts; long intervals help you monitor your machine's performance more accurately.

What types of things will System Monitor track for you? Tables 3.1 through 3.7 provide a complete list grouped by functional area. Of course, there's no limit to the ways you can arrange the items you want to track.

Table 3.1. File system items.

Item	Function
Bytes Read per Second	This item tells you how many bytes the file system reads each second. It helps you understand how much data the file system is reading.
Bytes Written per Second	This item tells you how many bytes the file system writes each second. It helps you understand how much data the file system is writing to disk.
Dirty Data	This number tells you how much data is stored in memory instead of on disk. A high level can indicate when a system is overloaded, because Windows 95 usually waits until system idle time to write data to disk.
Reads per Second	Use this number to determine how many reads the system makes per second. If you divide the Bytes Read per Second value by this value, you'll get the average read size. This value can help you tune your system for either large or small reads.
Writes per Second	Use this number to determine how many writes the system makes per second. If you divide the Bytes Written per Second value by this value, you'll get the average write size. This value can help you tune your system for either large or small writes.

Table 3.2. IPX/SPX-compatible protocol items.

Item	Function
IPX Packets Lost per Second	This number tells you how many IPX packets the workstation ignored due to a lack of resources or other problems. A high number here indicates an overloaded system in some cases.
IPX Packets Received per Second	Use this number to determine the total number of IPX packets the workstation received. This includes the packets the workstation ignored.
IPX Packets Sent per Second	This item records how many IPX packets the workstation sends per second. A high value tells you that the workstation makes heavy use of the network and that you might want to concentrate on optimizing network resources.
Open Sockets	The number of free sockets.
Routing Table Entries	Use this entry to determine the number of internetworking routes the workstation knows about. It can help you find some types of network communication problems.
SAP Table Entries	Use this entry to determine the number of service advertisements the workstation knows about. It can help you find some types of network communication problems.
SPX Packets Received Per Second	This item records how many SPX packets the workstation receives per second.
SPX Packets Sent Per Second	This item records how many SPX packets the workstation sends per second. A high value tells you that the workstation makes heavy use of the network and that you might want to concentrate on optimizing network resources.

Table 3.3. Kernel items.

Item	Function
Processor Usage (%)	Use this number to determine how much of the time the processor is busy. A high number doesn't necessarily mean you need a better processor. Check to make sure you have enough memory and that the other system settings are correct before you get a new processor.
Threads	Each 32-bit application under Windows 95 can create a thread (subprogram). For example, a word processor might create a print thread to output a document to the printer in the background. This item monitors the number of active threads.

Item	Function
Virtual Machines	This item allows you to track the number of virtual machines that are currently active on your system. It's one way to measure the amount of multitasking you're performing. Remember that this number includes system virtual machines as well as those used by any applications.

Table 3.4. Memory Manager (VMM32) items.

Item	Function
Allocated memory	Use this item to determine the total amount of memory allocated in the system. This includes all your application needs as well as any memory used by the operating system itself. You can check this entry to see the effect of any memory conservation steps you take.
Discards	This item tells you how much page swapping Windows has to do to provide enough resources for all your applications. This is the number of pages Windows can remove from memory without writing them to the swap file. In most cases, this is application code that's no longer needed. A high value indicates that you don't have enough RAM in your system and really should upgrade.
Disk Cache Size	The current size of the disk cache in bytes. This item tells you how much memory Windows has set aside to speed disk access.
Free Memory	If you add physical memory and swap file memory together, then subtract the amount of memory in use for a variety of purposes, you'll arrive at this value. Essentially, this item tells you how much memory is left over after Windows satisfies every system need.
Instance Faults	This item tells you how many instance faults Windows experiences. In most cases, you really don't need to worry about this value.
Locked Memory	An application locks memory when it needs to maintain access to it and keep Windows from moving the block around. There's no cut-and-dried answer as to how much locked memory is too much. However, a high percentage of locked memory when compared to the overall allocated memory might indicate that your application is hogging system resources. It also means that

continues

Table 3.4. continued

Item	Function
	Windows can't do as good a job of maintaining large blocks of accessible memory. (In other words, the memory is still available, but it might be fragmented.)
Maximum Disk Cache Size	This number tells you the largest disk cache that Windows will allocate to speed disk access.
Minimum Disk Cache Size	This number tells you the smallest disk cache that Windows will allocate to speed disk access.
Other Memory	Use this entry to determine the amount of allocated memory that's not stored in the swap file. For example, memory-mapped files, nonpageable memory, and disk cache pages all provide specific types of nonswap file memory used by your application.
Page Faults	This item tells you how much page swapping Windows has to do in order to provide enough resources for all your applications. This is the number of pages Windows writes to the swap file. A high value indicates that you don't have enough RAM in your system and that you really should upgrade.
Page-ins	This item tells you how much page swapping Windows has to do in order to provide enough resources for all your applications. This is the number of pages that Windows reads from the swap file. A high value indicates that you don't have enough RAM in your system and that you really should upgrade.
Page-outs	This item tells you how much page swapping Windows has to do in order to provide enough resources for all your applications. This is the number of pages Windows discards per second by either writing them to disk or simply overwriting them with new data. A high value indicates that you don't have enough RAM in your system and that you really should upgrade.
Swapfile Defective	You'll want to monitor this number carefully, because it indicates the number of bytes in the swap file that are bad due to media defects. What this really tells you is that there's a bad spot on the hard drive and that you need to maintain the hard drive. Windows allocates page frame file segments in 4,000-byte blocks, so even a small media defect can look huge.
Swapfile In Use	Windows normally makes the swap file a lot bigger than necessary. This value tells you just how much of the current swap file is in use. It gives you a more accurate picture of the memory situation than the swap file size would.

Item	Function
Swapfile Size	Use this item to monitor the size of the swap file on your hard drive.
Swappable Memory	This item tells you how much of the swap file memory is actually allocated for some purpose. This includes all allocation types, including locked memory.

Table 3.5. Microsoft Client for NetWare Networks items.

Item	Function
Burst Packets Dropped	This entry tells you the number of burst packets lost in transit. A high number could indicate an overloaded system, an inoperative NIC, or bad cabling. In some cases, it also reflects a lack of memory needed to process requests.
Burst Receive Gap Time	This item tells you how long Windows will wait (in microseconds) between packets before it sends another packet. This wait allows the previous packet to circulate throughout the network.
Burst Send Gap Time	This item tells you how long Windows must wait (in microseconds) between packets before it can receive another packet. The wait represents the time it takes for Windows to recover from processing the previous packet.
Bytes in Cache	The redirector acts as a buffer (container) to hold incoming data until Windows can process it. It also holds data waiting for transmission to other machines. This value represents how much information the buffer contains.
Bytes Read per Second	This item tells you how much data Windows reads from the redirector per second.
Bytes Written per Second	This item tells you how much data Windows writes to the redirector per second.
Dirty Bytes in Cache	Use this item with the Bytes in Cache value. It contains the amount of data in the redirector that Windows needs to write. A high value here indicates an overloaded system. This isn't a memory-related problem. It usually indicates some type of throughput restriction such as a bus or an underpowered processor.

continues

Table 3.5. continued

Item	Function
NCP Packets Dropped	This entry tells you the number of NCP packets lost in transit. A high number could indicate an overloaded system, an inoperative NIC, or bad cabling. In some cases, it also reflects a lack of memory needed to process requests.
Requests Pending	This value tells you how many requests the server needs to fulfill. A high number normally indicates an overloaded system or a lack of system resources. If additional memory won't bring this value down, you'll probably need to upgrade the server or not allow anyone to use it as a workstation. (If the server is currently a workstation and you need to dedicate it as a server, you might want to upgrade it to Windows NT as well.)

Table 3.6. Microsoft Network Client (Client for Microsoft Networks) items.

Item	Function
Bytes Read per Second	This item tells you how much data Windows reads from the redirector per second.
Bytes Written per Second	This item tells you how much data Windows writes to the redirector per second.
Number of Nets	This value tells you how many networks are running. In most cases, you'll see a value ranging from 1 to 3. A dial-up network counts as a separate network in this category.
Open Files	Use this value to determine how many files are open on the network. This value could help you determine how users are actually using the network.
Resources	This number tells you the number of resources in use.
Sessions	Use this number to determine how many people are logged into your machine. Each login counts as one. (If the same person logs in from multiple locations, Windows updates the number to reflect each login separately.)
Transactions Per Second	This value indicates the level of redirector activity as the number of SMB transactions per second.

Table 3.7. Microsoft Network Server (File and Printer Sharing for Microsoft Networks) items.

Item	Function
Buffers	A buffer stores one unit of data. DOS uses buffers to hold data read from the disk. A Windows server does essentially the same thing: It uses buffers to hold the data it receives from the local hard drive. This value tells you how many buffers the system needed to allocate in order to handle network data requests. A high number might indicate an overloaded system. It could just as easily reflect a network with a high usage rate, so you will need to verify this number using other sources.
Bytes Read	This item tells you how many bytes the server reads from disk in a given period of time.
Bytes Written	This item tells you how many bytes the server writes to disk in a given period of time.
Memory	Use this item to determine the amount of memory used by the server. It doesn't include any memory used by the workstation. This means you can determine the memory cost of using a workstation as a server.
NBs	Like the Buffers item, this item tells you about the server's data storage requirements. This value tells you how many buffers the system needed to allocate in order to handle network requests. A high number might indicate an overloaded system. It could just as easily reflect a network with a high usage rate, so you'll need to verify this number using other sources.
Server Threads	Like applications, the server can offload some tasks as separate "mini-applications" called *threads*. This item indicates the current number of threads used by the server.
Bytes/Second	This value tells you how many bytes the server is writing to and reading from the local hard drive per second. A high value indicates a large amount of network activity. It doesn't necessarily reflect any type of resource problem.

As you can see from the tables, the System Monitor utility can provide a wealth of information. The trick is to leverage that information in a way that you can really use it. For example, you'd want to look at all server-related items as a group. In addition, you wouldn't want to look at the current number of server threads if resource allocation was your major concern. There's no hard-and-fast rule as to what you should and shouldn't monitor in a given circumstance. However, you should strive to keep the number of items to a minimum.

On Your Own

Practice creating long filenames that a DOS or Windows 3.x user can understand. Use Explorer to create a new file in a temporary folder, and give it a long filename. Then open the DOS prompt and view that same filename. Does the name make sense in both contexts? If not, you'll need to spend a little more time working on this. Remember that you're effectively reduced to six characters for the filename because of the way that Windows 95 differentiates between different files with similar long filenames.

4

Setup Primer

I'm often surprised at just how little emphasis some people put on the installation of their software. Many people—including me—got the idea somewhere along the way that you should be able to stick a floppy in the drive, type a command (or double-click on an icon), and then forget about anything other than shuffling the rest of the floppies in the stack. This is the way software installation should work for the most part, but it doesn't.

Reality is somewhat different from the theory of software installation. I recently spent half an hour configuring a piece of software for installation and another 15 minutes installing it from the CD. The amount of time it took to configure this piece of software was staggering when compared to the relatively short time required to actually install it. Software now comes with so many different configuration options because some people want bells and whistles and others don't. (Of course, the fact that vendors are trying to create applications that are all things to all people doesn't help matters much. What happened to the good old days when you got a word processor to perform just that task?)

Today's software often reminds me of the proverbial Chinese menu in which you have to select one from Column A and two from Column B. I don't mind having a few choices, but some software has become ridiculous. You could easily get lost in the sea of choices that some software offers.

Imagine you're a network administrator (perhaps you don't need to try too hard, because you *are* one). How many weeks would you spend installing the same piece of software I did on the company network of about 100 machines (assuming, of course, that the installation on each machine went perfectly)? You're looking at a minimum of two and a half weeks—just for one application! Now imagine you have to install all the applications required by each machine in addition to a copy of Windows 95. This is one of the major reasons many people think the move from Windows 3.x to Windows 95 will be a very slow one. To its credit, Windows 95 does provide some methods to automate the installation process, but the transition will still take a lot of time for most network administrators. (We'll talk about automation methods later in this chapter.)

If Windows did free us in any way, it was from having to tell every one of our applications what hardware had been installed every time we installed it. That's one of my pet peeves with DOS software: You have to know everything about your machine to get any and every application installed. Of course, this ease of installation doesn't extend to Windows 3.x itself. To install the operating system, you still have to know a lot about the machine you are installing it to. For most people, this means dragging out every piece of paperwork you can find about the machine to answer the myriad of questions Windows 3.x presents.

My previous installation experience was still fresh in my mind as I tore open my beta copy of Windows 95. Would the installation cost me as many hours as OS/2 did the first few times I tried it out? Worse still, would I have to spend endless hours trying to configure the software after installation as I did with Windows NT? Thankfully, the answer to both questions was no. Windows 95 is about as easy to install as Windows 3.x in most cases, and perhaps a tad easier in others.

Before we go much further, let's get a few important items out of the way. If you're installing the upgrade version of Windows 95 to your system, you'll need to install one of the following operating systems first. Windows 95 looks for these operating systems as a prerequisite to starting the installation process:

- Windows 3.x
- Windows for Workgroups 3.1x
- Dual-boot OS/2 (with MS-DOS)
- Dual-boot Windows NT (with MS-DOS)

You'll also need to do a quick check on your hardware. Microsoft has one set of hardware specifications, but I don't think you'll want to use them. (Microsoft played the same game when creating the system requirements for Windows NT.) The problem is the "minimum" system that the specifications describe is too minimal to get any kind of performance. If you want a system that will really work with Windows 95, use the following parameters:

- 80486SX or higher processor: You can try to use one of the faster 80386 systems, but the performance you receive won't be all that useful.

Note: You must have an 80486SX or higher to use Microsoft Plus!. It simply won't run on anything less. You really should have a fast 80486DX, preferably a 100 MHz or Pentium machine, to use it. See Chapter 24 to learn more about Microsoft Plus!.

- 8 MB memory minimum: I would really think about increasing your memory to 16 MB as soon as possible, but an 8 MB system will perform adequately.

- 80 MB of free hard disk space: The Microsoft minimum of 30 MB just isn't realistic unless you want to install a stripped version of Windows 95 with no room to run any applications. If you plan to upgrade from Windows 3.x, you can decrease this amount by 10 MB. Likewise, a Windows for Workgroups (WFW) 3.x upgrader can reduce this requirement by 20 MB.

Note: If you're squeezed for disk space, you probably shouldn't install Microsoft Plus!. Much of it is for desktop beautification, a luxury you might not be able to afford. On the other hand, you could take advantage of its very useful tools, such as System Agent, the program scheduler, and its enhanced disk compression tools. See Chapter 24 for more details on Microsoft Plus!.

- High density 3-1/2 floppy drive: Everyone who installs Windows 95 will want to create an emergency boot disk. You need a high-density floppy to store the emergency files. Windows 95 can automatically create this disk for you during installation. You can also create or update the disk later from the Startup Disk page of the Add/Remove Programs Properties dialog.

- SVGA (800 × 600) or higher display adapter: You can get by using a VGA display with Windows 95, but that doesn't really provide enough space to get any work done. The Explorer interface does clear a lot more room than you had under Windows 3.x. But, let's face it, was a VGA display really adequate under Windows 3.x either?

Note: If you're using Microsoft Plus!, you'll want to consider your display adapter's ability to display colors along with its resolution. Most modern adapters display at least 256 colors at all resolutions. However, you might have an adapter that displays only 16 colors, especially at higher resolutions. Most of Microsoft Plus! demands at least 256 colors. If you stick to maintenance utility programs, you don't need to worry about the number of colors you can display with your adapter. However, if you want to use Desktop Themes to make your Desktop interesting, exciting, or at least attractive, you'll want a display adapter that can handle at least 256 colors at the resolution you plan to use. Ideally, your adapter should be able to handle high color. See Chapter 24 for a detailed discussion of Microsoft Plus!.

- Mouse: Someone will try to tell you that you can work efficiently under Windows 95 using the keyboard. You can get around; there's no doubt about it. But a mouse makes Windows 95 so much more efficient that I can't understand why anyone would want to go without one.

- Optional devices: You can also install any number of optional peripheral devices. I strongly recommend that you install a modem and a CD-ROM drive as a minimum. Windows 95 provides much better multimedia capabilities as well. You'll probably want to install a sound board somewhere along the way. Now is as good a time as any.

Note: You must have a CD-ROM drive in order to install Microsoft Plus!. As of this writing, there are no plans to make it available on floppy disk. Also, although it's not required, you should have a sound board to fully appreciate the Desktop Themes and 3D Pinball. See Chapter 24 for more details on Microsoft Plus!.

Note: Windows 95 won't install at all on machines that use the B-step 80386 processor. Intel introduced the B-step processor early in the 80386 production cycle to fix some minor problems. Think of it as a .1 revision of an application software package, and you'll have the right idea. This processor has an ID of 0303. If you have any doubt as to whether you have a B-step processor, contact the vendor before you start the Windows 95 installation.

The one feature that will stick out in your mind is the way Windows 95 automatically detects the majority of your hardware. I installed the product on a variety of machines using all the methods mentioned here and met with a variety of successes in that regard, but at least Windows 95 provides a starting point for future efforts. I also like the way that the software led me by the hand in getting things configured. Again, there were choices to make, but the way they were laid out made it a lot easier to figure out what I wanted to do. In addition, unlike previous versions of Windows, the online help for this installation routine actually told me a little bit about what I was installing.

Is the new installation for Windows 95 perfect? Not by a long shot. I experienced some truly weird problems during installation—from hardware that was detected fine during one installation but not during another to utility programs that installed even when I asked Windows 95 not to install them (more about that later). Some of the worst failings of the installation routine in one way were the highlights in another. For example, during one installation I found it nearly impossible to get through the installation procedure and end up with the correct sound card installed in my machine. (I finally figured out a surefire method of getting an accurate detection from Windows 95. I'll explain it later in this chapter.)

Installing Windows 95

You might want to spend a little time preparing for your Windows 95 installation, especially if you're the ill-fated network administrator who will spend the next few weeks getting it installed on all 100 network workstations. Of course, the first piece of preparation is to make a complete backup of each system before you start the installation. Trying to back out of a failed installation can prove to be quite a problem in some situations. In fact, if you have the upgrade version of Windows 95, you might find recovering from a failed installation quite impossible without reinstalling your old software first.

Peter's Principle: Boot Disks: The Cheap Form of Insurance

You just started an installation and it goes south for the winter. The machine is frozen and you can't get back to the DOS prompt. What do you do?

If you're like me, you stick your boot disk into the A drive and reboot the machine. I never start anything as involved as an operating system installation without making a boot disk first. In fact, I usually make a boot disk for all my installations, even if I think the software will install without a hitch.

Just what does a boot disk contain? It has to contain the operating system; otherwise, you can't use it to boot the system. I usually include renamed copies of my CONFIG.SYS and AUTOEXEC.BAT files as well. You don't want to use the original files to boot the machine because they contain entries that you probably won't need. If I'm performing some type of Windows installation, I always include copies of my WIN.INI and

SYSTEM.INI files as well. In fact, for shaky installations, I make a copy of all my .INI files on a separate disk.

A boot disk really needs some utility programs too. I usually include FDisk and Format. Debug normally makes an appearance also. The disk has to include any files required to activate your disk compression—if the drive is compressed. A disk editor usually comes in handy, as does a small text editor. You'll probably want to include a disk scanning program such as ChkDsk or its equivalent as well, because a disk crash will require the services of such a diagnostic program.

You'll also need a DOS backup program that can read the backup of the workstation you created. There are two fatal assumptions that some people make when they make their workstation backup. First, you can't assume that you'll have network access after a failed workstation installation. That's why I make a local backup of the machine instead of using network resources. Second, because you're booting DOS, you need a DOS application that can read your backup. I once ran into someone who thoughtfully made a backup of his hard drive but used a Windows program to do it. His only choice after the system failed was to reinstall Windows and all the software required to gain access to the tape drive. It cost him almost three hours to restore the drive. Using a DOS backup program means nearly instantaneous access to the data you need to restore after a failed installation attempt.

Don't be afraid to make up a two- or three-disk package to ensure that you'll have everything you need in order to diagnose problems with the machine. Just because this is a software installation, you can't assume that the hard drive will be accessible. Those trips back and forth to the office to pick up this utility or that can get to be quite time consuming. A little preparation goes a long way toward making what looks like a difficult problem easier to fix.

Tip: When you partition your hard drive, it's always a good idea to keep this principle in mind: Don't compress your boot drive. The reason is simple. You can't access a compressed drive very easily in an emergency. I always set aside a 30 MB to 40 MB partition that I won't compress. A partition this large is just big enough to accommodate my copy of DOS, any files required to boot the machine in its normal configuration, a few utility programs, and some diagnostic aids. Compressing your boot drive is just another way to play Russian Roulette. Somewhere along the line you'll shoot yourself, and it won't be in the foot.

Getting all the required equipment together to perform the installation is only the first step. You need to do other things before you actually perform the installation. The following sections give you the inside scoop on all the pre-installation steps you should take. Then you will see several different installation methods.

Check Your Hardware

Remember that stack of hardware brochures I talked about earlier? You can probably put some of them away, but not until you've checked a few details. Windows 95 automatically detects the vast majority of hardware out there. It even includes information files (discussed near the end of this chapter), which allow it to detect older hardware. However, the detection capabilities that Windows 95 currently provides are less than perfect, so you'll want to spend a little time checking your system hardware for potential problems.

Microsoft groups all Windows 95 autodetection capabilities under plug and play. Even if your hardware isn't plug and play-compatible, Windows 95 will try to treat it as such for installation purposes. We'll look at plug and play from an installation perspective later in this chapter. Suffice it to say right now that Windows 95 won't do a perfect job of installing your hardware if you don't have a 100 percent plug and play-compatible machine.

There are certain types of hardware that I can almost guarantee you'll run into problems with under Windows 95. If you have hardware with the following characteristics, you might want to take a second look at it before you install Windows 95. Of course, you can always try to install it, but I've run into more than my share of problems with these hardware types:

- Older disk controllers that don't provide their own BIOS: A lot of old MFM controllers fall into this category. Windows 95 depends on the contents of the peripheral BIOS as one of the means to detect it. Every vendor writes their company name (or at least someone else's name) into the BIOS. Looking for this company name is one way to determine who made the device. The first step in reducing the number of checks required to detect a piece of hardware is knowing the vendor. If you have a peripheral that lacks a BIOS and other characteristic "electronic" signatures, Windows 95 won't be able to detect it. Because Windows 95 requires a working disk controller and display adapter to get the installation started, you can see what would happen if it couldn't detect your disk controller.

- Machines that use a clone BIOS: Some older machines use what I call a clone BIOS. These are the machines that boot with some strange logo from a company you've never heard of before. A machine containing a BIOS from one of the mainstream companies such as AMI or Phoenix is almost always a better bet than a clone BIOS machine. Of course, machines containing an IBM or other major hardware vendor BIOS are the safest bet. You might be able to replace the BIOS on a motherboard containing a clone BIOS, but replacing that dinosaur is probably the easiest way to fix the problem.

- Nonstandard peripheral devices: Developers who latch onto new technology early in the game are often applauded by everyone when they first introduce an item. Later, the same people who applauded these developers wonder why they would ever buy such a nonstandard piece of equipment. Standards evolve as users and companies gain knowledge about a particular area of technology. Unfortunate as it might seem, some of the hardware that appeared before the standard was introduced just isn't compatible with it. Without a standard way to access the hardware, it's very difficult to talk to it and determine what capabilities it provides. Windows 95 easily detects standard devices, but it might have problems with older peripherals that do not adhere to the standards.

- Peripherals that almost emulate something else: IBM and other vendors are to blame for this problem. They started placing their company name in the BIOS of some types of hardware. When someone would try to use some piece of generic software developed by these companies, the first thing the software would do is check the BIOS for the correct company name. Clone makers aren't stupid, so they started putting the IBM (or other) company name where needed in their BIOS chips too. That isn't a problem as long as the device in question completely emulates the hardware it replaces. The problems begin when the clone vendor adds some additional "features" that render this emulation incompatible with the original. Because Windows 95 has no way to recognize the clone from the real McCoy, you could end up installing the wrong kind of support during installation.

There's also some marginal hardware out there that you can fix after the initial installation is over. Sound boards are one big item that falls into this category. Windows 95 does a pretty good job of detecting them, considering that one sound board is designed to emulate the qualities of another. Just about every sound board out there claims some sort of Sound Blaster emulation mode. Trying to detect this hardware is a nightmare. In some cases, you'll just have to manually install the hardware later. You'll see the procedure for performing a manual installation later in this chapter.

A final "difficult to install" hardware category is the older stuff that depends on a real-mode driver for support. I had an old Hitachi 1503S CD-ROM drive that fell into this category. Believe it or not, it worked just fine under Windows 95, even though I had to use real-mode drivers. The downside is that I couldn't seem to share it on the network, and the stability and performance problems it introduced into the system just weren't worth the effort of keeping it around. I finally replaced the drive with something a little less archaic and haven't looked back since.

Peter's Principle: Replacing Old Hardware to Save Money

Sometimes you'll actually save money right now by spending a little on new hardware. Whenever you choose to keep an old piece of hardware to save money, but introduce some type of instability into your system as a result, you're actually wasting more money than you're saving.

Windows 95 provides an opportunity to rid your system of all the old hardware that makes it inefficient. Not only will you get your work done faster, but you'll get it done with fewer problems. Think about the last time you spent days trying to find a problem with your system only to discover that it was a bad driver or some other hardware-related problem. The hardware still works, so it's very difficult to give it up. But doing so when you upgrade might mean that you spend a few less hours trying to find those mysterious problems related to the real-mode drivers that the hardware requires to work.

Looking Ahead: Just because you have a few pieces of older or incompatible hardware in your system is no reason to roll over and give up any idea of installing Windows 95. Chapter 23 takes a detailed look at hardware troubleshooting techniques—especially tough-to-install hardware. In some cases, you might find that Windows 95 even provides protected-mode drivers you can use with the old stuff.

When you figure out whether you're going to have any potential problems with your hardware, you'll want to create an inventory of what you have. Some hardware, such as the newer sound boards, use a real-mode driver that accepts configuration parameters as part of the device driver command line. If Windows supports the device, you can normally REM the driver out of CONFIG.SYS before you start your Windows 95 installation. (Make sure you also take care of any AUTOEXEC.BAT entries when you do this.) There are exceptions to this rule. You wouldn't want to get rid of any drivers needed for your CD-ROM drive (if you plan to use it for installation purposes) or your hard drive controller. Any essential drivers should stay in place; any nonessential drivers should get REMed out.

Some hardware still uses jumpers for configuration purposes. The one main item that just about everyone will need to consider is NICs (network interface cards). NICs usually have one or more address settings and an IRQ setting. You need to write down the settings of any boards that use jumpers before you start your Windows 95 installation. This list will come in handy later as you try to resolve any IRQ or address conflicts that arise during installation. Changing a "soft" setting is easy; changing jumpers is a lot more difficult.

When you get to this point, you have just about every piece of hardware information you need. It doesn't seem like such a big deal to take care of this step prior to installation if you're doing it on your personal machine. Gathering all this information before you leave the office to work on a remote machine is essential if you want to do it with any level of efficiency.

There is one final piece of information that you should check for machines that use file compression. Windows 95 will supposedly work with the following list of drive compression software:

- Microsoft DriveSpace and DoubleSpace
- Stacker versions 3.0 and 4.x
- AddStor SuperStor

A few people I've talked with say they had problems getting Windows 95 to work properly with their disk compression software. In most cases, it turned out to be some kind of interaction between the compression software, the drive controller, and Windows 95. Almost everyone will use their disk compression software without any problem under Windows 95. However, if you want to make absolutely certain that there aren't any problems, decompress the drive prior to installation and recompress it using the Windows 95-specific disk compression software.

Inside Setup Information Files

Network administrators will really like one of the new features of Windows 95. There's a method of automating the responses required during setup. The rest of this section looks at the script writing program provided with the CD-ROM version of Windows 95. The floppy disk version does not include this utility.

Look on your CD-ROM in the \ADMIN95\NETTOOLS\NETSETUP directory. You should see a utility named NetSetup. Even if you installed Windows using the complete installation option, you won't see that utility on your hard drive. (For that matter, all of the network-related tools require a separate installation.)

The following procedure takes you through the automated portion of creating a network setup directory and a batch file. It's pretty easy to do, and creating a network installation directory will make that 100-user setup a lot easier to complete in most cases. The next section of this chapter will show you how to edit the default batch file to meet your special requirements.

1. Double-click on the NetSetup icon. You'll see a display similar to the one in Figure 4.1, with options for installing a server version of Windows 95, creating a home directory for users who use the server to start Windows 95, and automated script writing.

Figure 4.1.
The main NetSetup dialog.

2. Click on the Set Path pushbutton. You will see the dialog shown in Figure 4.2. Type the drive and path you want to use to install the server software. It's important to choose a drive with a lot of space because you'll need to create home directories for each user later.

Figure 4.2.
One of the first server installation steps is to select the destination path all users will use to install their copy of Windows 95.

3. Click on OK. If the path does not exist, NetSetup asks whether you want to create it.

4. Click on the Install pushbutton. NetSetup displays the Source Path dialog, shown in Figure 4.3. The Server setting creates an installation script that leaves most of the files on the file server. The installation program places a limited number of files on the user's local hard drive. This option optimizes hard disk usage. The Local hard drive option places all the files on the user's hard drive. It provides the best performance on machines that provide enough space. The final option, User's choice, gives the user the option of where to install the files.

Figure 4.3.
The Source Path dialog allows you to select the method used to install Windows 95 on the workstations.

5. Fill in the source and destination path fields (if required). Select the desired installation choice and click on OK to start the installation. NetSetup will display the Create Default dialog, shown in Figure 4.4.

Figure 4.4.
The Create Default dialog provides one method of creating the installation script that Setup will use later to install the software on the workstations.

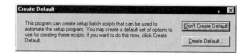

6. Click on the Create Default pushbutton. NetSetup displays the Default Properties dialog, shown in Figure 4.5. Notice that this dialog looks like the Policy Editor display. It uses the same interface. Table 4.1 outlines all the options you can modify within the display. The dialog uses a hierarchical format; just keep clicking plus signs until you reach the option that you want to modify.

7. When you finish modifying all the options on the Default Properties dialog, click on OK. NetSetup displays the Copying Files dialog, shown in Figure 4.6, until it completes the copying process.

Figure 4.5.
The Default Properties dialog is a powerful tool. It allows you to define the majority of the installation options that the user will have.

Figure 4.6.
You can use the Copying Files dialog to monitor the server software installation process.

8. Follow the remaining prompts until you get the Server Setup dialog box saying that Windows 95 completed the installation successfully.

This procedure took you through the process of creating a server installation and an automatic script. You use the script by entering SETUP *<Script Name>* at the run prompt within Windows or at the DOS prompt. You can define many options using this automated script capability. Table 4.1 describes all the options, leaving them in hierarchical format to make it easier to figure out which ones you actually need. Words that appear within angle brackets describe a value that you should supply. Do not add the angle brackets when you type the entry in the script file. Likewise, values that appear within square brackets provide you with a list of entries you can select from. Don't type other values or the square brackets when adding this entry to a script file. Each of the headings will contain the heading name as you see it in NetSetup in the first column and the name of the heading it affects within the script file in the second column.

Table 4.1. Server-based setup options for custom scripts.

Option	Script Parameter	Meaning
Setup Options:	**[Setup]**	
Automated Install	Express=[0 ¦ 1]	A setting of 1 allows you to bypass the Safe Setup screen after a failed install. It also forces Setup to use only the values in MSBATCH.INF

Option	Script Parameter	Meaning
		(or another batch file). Because this option disables a significant portion of the user interface, you will need to test the batch file before enabling it.
Setup Mode	`InstallType=` `[0 ¦ 1 ¦ 2 ¦ 3]`	Selects the installation type: compact (0), typical (1), portable (2), or custom (3).
Create an Emergency Boot Disk	`EBD=[0 ¦ 1]`	Determines whether Setup creates an emergency boot disk (0 means no).
Install Verification	`Verify=[0 ¦ 1]`	Setting this value to 0 bypasses install verification. This setting allows Setup to check the integrity of the files already installed in the system directory.
Enable Pen Windows Warning	`PenWinWarning=[0 ¦ 1]`	Setting this value to 0 bypasses the Pen Windows Warning dialog. This dialog tells the user if there is an unknown version of Pen Windows installed in the destination directory.
Installation Location:	**`[Setup]`**	
Install Directory	`InstallDir=<path>`	This setting allows you to install Windows 95 in a directory other than the default.
Server-based Setup	`[Network]`	Checking this option creates the network header entry in the script file. It doesn't actually select an option.
Name and Organization:	**`[NameAndOrg]`**	
Display name and organization page	`Display=[0 ¦ 1]`	A value of 0 in this entry bypasses the Name and Organization dialog box.
Name	`Name=<Name>`	You can use this entry to enter the user name automatically.

continues

Table 4.1. continued

Option	Script Parameter	Meaning
Organization	`Organization=` `<Organization>`	You can use this entry to enter the organization name automatically.
Network Options:	`[Network]`	
Display network screens during custom setup	`Display=[0 ¦ 1]`	A value of 0 here bypasses the network dialog box when using a custom installation.
Clients to Install	`Clients=<client list>`	The NETCLI.INF and NETCLI3.INF files contain the values you can enter here. The default setting is in NETDEF.INF. This entry allows you to define which network clients get installed.
Hard Disk Boot (for shared installations)	`HDBoot=[0 ¦ 1]`	Setting this value to 1 allows the user to boot from a local hard drive. Setting this value to 0 and `RPLSetup` to 0 forces the user to boot from a local floppy.
Remoteboot (RPL) Setup	`RPLSetup=[0 ¦ 1]`	Setting this value to 1 allows the user to boot from a server drive. (You must set up the appropriate boot image to make this feature work.)
Workstation Setup	`WorkstationSetup=[0 ¦ 1]`	Setting this value to 0 forces the user to install Windows 95 on his or her local hard drive rather than use the server copy. Setting this value to 1 and `DisplayWorkstationSetup` to 1 allows the user to choose between a local or file server setup.
Display Workstation Setup	`DisplayWorkstationSetup` `=[0 ¦ 1]`	Setting this value to 0 bypasses the Workstation setup dialog (which gives the user a choice of where to install Windows 95).

Option	Script Parameter	Meaning
Client for Microsoft Networks:	**[VReDir]**	
Validated Logon	`ValidatedLogon=[0 ¦ 1]`	Setting this value to 1 forces the user to provide a password.
Logon Domain	`LogonDomain=<domain name>`	This entry contains a string that automatically defines the workstation domain.
Client for NetWare Networks:	**[Nwredir]**	
Preferred Server	`PreferredServer= <server name>`	Use this entry to define a default server name.
First Network Drive	`FirstNetDrive= <drive letter>`	This entry allows you to define the first network drive letter (usually F).
Search Mode	`SearchMode=[0 - 7]`	This entry contains one of the search mode values that appear in NET.CFG.
Protocols:	**[Network]**	
Protocols to Install	`Protocols=<protocol list>`	This entry tells Setup which network protocol to install. See the NETTRANS.INF file for a list of appropriate numbers. The NETDEF.INF file contains the default settings.
IPX/SPX-compatible protocol:	**[Nwlink]**	
Frame Type	`FrameType=[0 ¦ 1 ¦ 2 ¦ 3 ¦ 4 ¦ 5 ¦ 6]`	This entry allows you to select from one of the following frame types: 0 = 802.3, 1 = 802.2, 2 = Ethernet II, 3 = SNAP, 4 = Auto, 5 = Token Ring, and 6 = Token Ring SNAP. The default setting is 4.
NetBIOS support	`NetBIOS=[0 ¦ 1]`	Setting this value to 1 installs IPX/SPX NetBIOS support.

continues

Table 4.1. continued

Option	Script Parameter	Meaning
Microsoft TCP/IP:	`[Mstcp]`	
DHCP	`DHCP=[0 ¦ 1]`	A value of 1 tells Setup that TCP/IP is configured to use DHCP for dynamic TCP/IP configuration.
IP Address	`IPAddress=<IP address>`	Sets the computer's IP address if you do not enable DHCP.
Subnet Mask	`SubnetMask=<IP address>`	Sets the computer's subnet IP address if you do not enable DHCP.
WINS	`WINS=[0 ¦ 1 ¦ DHCP]`	Setting this entry to 1 enables WINS resolution. Setting it to DHCP enables WINS but gets the parameters from the DHCP server.
Primary WINS	`PrimaryWINS=<IP address>`	Use this entry to set the address of the primary WINS name server.
Secondary WINS	`SecondaryWINS=` `<IP address>`	Use this entry to set the address of the secondary WINS name server.
Scope ID	`ScopeID=` `<scope ID string>`	This entry contains the scope ID.
Enable DNS	`DNS=[0 ¦ 1]`	You can enable DNS name resolution by setting this value to 1.
Hostname	`Hostname=` `<hostname string>`	Contains the DNS host name for this computer. (Usually the same value as the computer name.)
Domain	`Domain=<domain string>`	Use this entry to specify the DNS domain name for this computer.
DNS Server search order	`DNSServers=` `<list of servers>`	This entry contains a list of comma-delimited DNS server names.
Domain search order	`DomainOrder=` `<list of domains>`	This entry contains a list of command-delimited domain names used for host name resolution.
LMHOST Path	`LMHostPath=` `<LMHOST file path>`	Sets the path for the LMHOST file.

Option	Script Parameter	Meaning
Gateways	`Gateways=` `<IP address list>`	Use this entry to specify a list of IP gateway (router) addresses. Enter them in the same order that you want them used.
Network adapters:		
Network adapters to install	`Netcards=` `<list of adapters>`	This entry contains the ID number of the NIC you want to install. See the appropriate vendor-specific .INF file for the correct number.
Services:		
Services to install	`Services=` `<list of services>`	Use this entry to define which file, print, and other network-related services to install. See the appropriate vendor-specific .INF file for a list of identifiers.
File and Printer Sharing for NetWare Networks:	`[Nwserver]`	
SAP Browsing	`SAPBrowse=[0 ¦ 1]`	This entry contains 1 if a computer that provides file and print sharing for NetWare uses Server Advertising Protocol (SAP) browsing. A SAP-enabled computer does not appear in Network Neighborhood, but any NetWare client can see it.
Browse Master	`BrowseMaster=` `[0 ¦ 1 ¦ 2]`	This entry determines whether a computer that provides file and print sharing is the preferred browse master (2), can be a browse master (1), or is ineligible to be the browse master (0).
File and Printer Sharing for Microsoft Networks:	`[VServer]`	
LMAnnounce	`Announce=[0 ¦ 1]`	A setting of 1 announces VSERVER to the network.

continues

Table 4.1. continued

Option	Script Parameter	Meaning
Browse Master	BrowseMaster=[0 ¦ 1]	A setting of 1 allows the computer to become the browse master.
Identification:	**[Network]**	
Computer Name	ComputerName= <name string>	Contains the name of the computer for network purposes. The default setting uses the first eight characters of the user name minus any spaces.
Workgroup	Workgroup= <workgroup string>	Contains the name of the workgroup that this computer belongs to. The default setting uses the first 15 characters of the organization name minus any spaces.
Description	Description= <description string>	Contains a string that provides a plain-English description of the computer for other users. The default setting is the user name.
Access Control	[Network]	Checking this option creates the network header entry in the script file. It doesn't actually select an option.
Security Type	UserSecurity=[share ¦ domain ¦ msserver ¦ nwserver]	Defines the types of security used. share is share-level security, domain is user-level security passing to a Windows NT domain, msserver is user-level security passing to a Windows NT server, and nwserver is user-level security passing to a NetWare server.
Pass-through Agent	PassThroughAgent= <server> or <domain>	This entry defines the passthrough agent used for security purposes. It is ignored if you specify share-level security. NetWare servers always use the preferred server as a passthrough agent.

Option	Script Parameter	Meaning
System Components:	**[System]**	**This section contains references to the default drivers you want to use. The device must already exist as a class entry in the specified .INF file section.**
Power Management	Power= *<Inf section name>*	Determines the .INF file section used to install this feature.
Locale	Locale= *<Inf section name>*	Determines the .INF file section used to install this feature.
Machine	Machine= *<Inf section name>*	Determines the .INF file section used to install this feature.
Pen Windows	PenWindows= *<Inf section name>*	Determines the .INF file section used to install this feature.
Tablet	Tablet= *<Inf section name>*	Determines the .INF file section used to install this feature.
Keyboard	Keyboard= *<Inf section name>*	Determines the .INF file section used to install this feature.
Monitor	Monitor= *<Inf section name>*	Determines the .INF file section used to install this feature.
Display	Display= *<Inf section name>*	Determines the .INF file section used to install this feature.
Mouse	Mouse= *<Inf section name>*	Determines the .INF file section used to install this feature.
Most Recently Used Paths:	**[InstallLocationsMRU]**	
UNC name for path to Windows 95 source files	MRU1=*<install path>*	This entry is a string containing the installation file path. You can provide more than one default path for the user to choose by adding MRU*<number>*= entries on separate lines. Each MRU is numbered in order of preference.

The initial installation doesn't represent the only time you can modify the script. At the bottom of Figure 4.1 is a pushbutton called Make Script. You can also use this pushbutton to modify an existing script. Clicking on this pushbutton presents a dialog that asks for an .INF filename. All you need to do is select an existing script or type in the name of a new one. After you accept the new filename, NetSetup displays a dialog exactly like the one shown in Figure 4.5. When you accept the options you select, NetSetup creates a new script for you.

Peter's Principle: Keeping Your .INF Files Straight

You might think all .INF files are the same, but they aren't. At least three different kinds of .INF files are used under Windows 95, and they're all incompatible. The first type is the OEMSETUP.INF file Windows 3.x used to configure devices. This file might work under Windows 95, but in most cases it won't work correctly. You'll probably want to get Windows 95-specific drivers from the vendor anyway, so don't take a chance using this old file. The second type is the MSBATCH.INF we just created as a script file for Setup. Table 4.1 shows you that its format varies from the third type of .INF file, which we'll explore later. The third type of .INF file contains hardware and software configuration information for Windows 95. It's a superset of the OEMSETUP.INF file.

The best thing you can do to avoid confusing one .INF file with another is to keep them totally separate. This is actually very easy to do with only a little work from you. The Windows 95 hardware and software configuration .INF files always appear in the \WIN95\INF folder. If you only use that folder to hold those files (and nothing else), you already have part of the problem solved. I always see the OEMSETUP.INF files in my \WIN95\SETUP folder or on a floppy disk, but some vendor probably stuck them in other places as well. If you see any .INF files in the SYSTEM folder, it's a good bet that they are leftovers from Windows 3.x. I always keep my setup scripts in a separate folder. If you place them in the \WIN95\SCRIPTS folder on the server, you have a pretty good chance of keeping them separate as well.

Of course, the problem with finding an .INF file anywhere else on your system is that you will never be sure just what kind of an .INF it is. I always begin by checking the date. If it's older than sometime in 1995, you know that the file is probably something left over from Windows 3.x. The Windows 95 hardware and software configuration files follow a very specific format that you can see by just looking at them with a text editor. I usually check for this kind of file next. Finally, if I just can't figure out where that .INF is supposed to go, I move it to a special directory and keep it there until an application asks for it. If it sits there too long, it's probably time to recycle it.

The very last item you need to look at is creating a home directory for any users who'll use the server files instead of placing Windows 95 on their local hard drive. The following procedure will help you through this process. It assumes that you have already started NetSetup.

1. Click on the Add pushbutton in the Server Based Setup dialog, shown in Figure 4.1. NetSetup displays the Set Up Machine dialog, shown in Figure 4.7. Notice that there are

two different ways to tackle the task of creating home directories. In most cases, setting up one machine is less error-prone and provides more flexibility. Use the multiple machine method only if you have a lot of machines to set up and after you gain some experience using Windows 95.

Figure 4.7.
The Set Up Machine dialog allows you to create the home directory required by users who will use the server copy of Windows 95 instead of running it from a local hard drive.

2. Click on OK to add the new user. NetSetup returns you to the main screen.

You might have noticed that a script was automatically generated for the new user. This script will help set up Windows 95 for file server use (if the user chooses that option or you selected it as a forced option). You can modify the default script by entering the same machine and user name in the Set Up Machine dialog, shown in Figure 4.7, and then clicking on the Edit Script pushbutton.

Customizing Setup

Creating a default installation for Windows 95 is relatively easy. The preceding section showed you how to do it in eight easy steps. You can use the information contained in Table 4.1 to further customize the setup file. Simply make a copy of MSBATCH.INF (the default installation script) and make any required changes using a text editor.

There are several advantages to this approach. The biggest advantage is that a properly configured script allows you to add the setup routine to the network login script. The next time the user logs into the network, he will automatically install Windows 95 on his machine. Of course, a successful installation requires a bit of work on your part to get the script just right. In addition, you should still expect the occasional glitch that will keep the automated installation from working. In theory, automated installs sound wonderful. In practice, they require a lot of work, a little luck, and a very thorough understanding of the network on the part of the administrator. The problem is very simple: You need to set up each user's script to take into account the quirks of his or her machine or the setup will fail.

Manually editing the setup script allows you to modify or add some parameters not supported by the automatic script creation utility. Some of these items fall into the "nice to have" category, but others are essential if you plan to create a script that will allow the users on your network to automatically install Windows 95. In fact, some of them will come in handy even if you perform all the installations using the network by yourself. Table 4.2 contains a complete list of these items. Assume that all the values appear under the [Setup] heading of the file unless the comments tell you otherwise.

Table 4.2. Custom setup script options.

Option	Comments
ChangeDir=[0 ¦ 1]	A value of 0 allows you to bypass the Change Directory dialog that appears if you decide to install Windows 95 into a directory other than the default. Using the automatic script generator automatically inserts this value.
Customize=[0 ¦ 1]	Use this option to specify whether the user can customize the setup process.
Detection=[0 ¦ 1]	This entry allows you to skip all or part of the hardware detection process. A value of 0 bypasses the entire detection process.
Devicepath=[0 ¦ 1]	Contains the 0 if you want to use the normal method of installing new device support. A value of 1 allows the network administrator to place updated .INF files in one location. The user configuration is updated automatically the next time the user checks into the network. This parameter only works for server installations.
IgnoreDetectedNetCards=[0 ¦ 1]	Use this entry to tell Setup whether you want to detect any installed network adapters. A problem exists if you decide to install a network that does not provide protected-mode support for the NIC (LANtastic 6.x, for example). If you don't provide this entry, Windows 95 automatically assumes that you want to install an MS Network in many cases. Installing two sets of NIC drivers (one Windows 95 and the one real-mode) will cause conflicts with your installed real-mode network. This setting appears under the [Network] heading.
LogonDomain=<String>	This setting appears under the [VReDir] heading. It allows you to specify a Windows NT logon domain to use for password validation. You can set this value even if you set ValidatedLogon to 0.

Option	Comments
`Network=0`	Adding this entry allows you to define which network components are selected (see Table 4.1 for a complete description of the network section entries). A value of 0 bypasses the entire network installation process.
`[OptionalComponents]`	This is an actual section within the batch file. You create the header as shown and then add entries below it—one for each optional component you want to either install or not install. The entries take the format `"<Optional Component>"=[0 ¦ 1]`, where `<Optional Component>` is the name of an option enclosed in quotes. A value of 1 installs that option. Windows 95 provides a default installation status for each optional component based on the type of installation you perform (see Table 4.4 for details). Here is a list of the optional components that you can install:

Accessories options include the following: Accessories, Accessibility Options, Briefcase, Calculator, Character Map, Clipboard Viewer, Desktop Wallpaper, Document Templates, Extra Cursors, Games, Multi-Language Support, Net Watcher, Object Packager, Online User's Guide, Paint, Quick View, Screen Savers, Scrolling Marquee, Blank Screen, Curves and Colors, Mystify Your Mind, Flying Through Space, System Monitor, Windows 95 Tour, and WordPad.

Communications options include the following: Communications, Dial-Up Networking, Direct Cable Connection, HyperTerminal, and Phone Dialer.

Disk Tools options include the following: Disk Tools, Backup, Defrag (disk defragmenter), and Disk Compression Tools.

Microsoft Exchange options include the following: Microsoft Exchange, CompuServe Mail Services, Internet Mail, and Microsoft Fax.

continues

Table 4.2. continued

Option	Comments
	Multimedia options include the following: Multimedia, Audio Compression, CD Player, Media Player, Musica Sound Scheme, Nature Sound Scheme, Robotz Sound Scheme, Sound and Video Clips, Sound Recorder, Utopia Sound Scheme, Video Compression, and Volume Control.
	The Microsoft Network options include the Microsoft Network.
ProductID=<*String*>	This entry allows you to add the product identification found on the Windows 95 installation disks. In most cases, you will want to use the default setting.
RemoveBinding=<*DevID*>,<*DevID*>	This option allows you to unbind one device from another. You can use it to tune bindings in a setup script. This setting appears under the [Network] heading.
ValidateNetCardResources=[0 ¦ 1]	Setting this entry to 1 displays a configuration wizard if Setup detects a network card IRQ or address conflict with another device. This setting appears under the [Network] heading.
ValidatedLogon=[0 ¦ 1]	This setting appears under the [VReDir] heading. A setting of 1 forces a validation of the user password when logging into a Windows NT domain.

Besides all the installation parameters you can place in a script file, you can also add an [Install] header. This heading allows you to install optional programs or even Windows components such as the network administrator's tools. It is especially handy for automatically entering all the "run once" installation routines such as setting the time zone. The key to making the [Install] section work is adding the proper macro instructions. We'll explore this process of hardware and software configuration later in this chapter. You can also use the files in the \WIN95\INF directory on your machine. In most cases, you'll find that the files follow the same general format, but that there are subtle differences you'll need to observe. Be sure to look at a file that installs a component just like the one you want to install. That way, you can get all the details correct the first time. The run once install entries consist of a combination of DelReg= and AddReg= macro commands. You delete the old registry entry using the DelReg= command, and then add the new entry using the AddReg= command.

Getting Ready to Install

When you get to this point in the chapter, you should have created a boot disk and inventoried your hardware. Network administrators will have created an MSBATCH.INF file to make installation easier. You should've also removed many of the device drivers from CONFIG.SYS and AUTOEXEC.BAT. Before you begin the setup process, you might want to make a few additional changes to these two files. It might seem like a pain to have to pre-setup your machine to provide the best possible environment for an operating system installation, but you really will get better results this way.

The first thing you'll want to do is REM out any unneeded TSRs from your AUTOEXEC.BAT. I even took out the little utility programs such as DOSKey. You'll also want to REM out ANSI.SYS (or a vendor-specific alternative) because you won't need it under Windows 95. If you use a real-mode network such as LANtastic, you'll want to disable it for the time being—at least as a server. Windows 95 has problems with LANtastic (and other peer-to-peer real-mode network software) when you try to install it with the server running. In addition, you'll need to disable any drive mappings, or Setup will run into problems trying to identify your boot drive.

Tip: The Windows 95 Setup program will overwrite or replace some of the files in your DOS directory. If you have any intention of uninstalling Windows 95 later, it's a good idea to make a copy of this directory before you start the installation. That way you can easily restore it later.

After you complete these final modifications, reboot your system. You should now have a completely clean environment in which to install Windows 95. One last check using the MEM /C command to verify that memory is as clean as possible is always a good idea.

Tip: When you start the setup process, the first thing Windows 95 does is scan your drives for errors. You might want to save yourself a bit of time by doing this check in advance. That way you can fix any errors and prevent the Windows 95 Setup program from stopping before it even gets started.

Let's look at some of the Setup command-line switches. They'll help you get around any problems you might experience while installing Windows 95. For example, some computers might freeze when Setup tries to perform a disk scan, so you can use the /IQ or /IS switch to get around the problem. The following is a complete list of these switches. There's one thing you need to know about the way I present this information. When you see something between angle brackets, it means you have to supply a value of some kind. The description will tell you what to provide. Don't type the angle brackets when you type the switch.

- **/?:** Use this switch to display a list of currently documented command-line switches. As of this writing there are two: `/T:<Temporary Directory>` and `<Batch>`.

- **/D:** The `/D` switch helps you get around situations in which one or more of your Windows 3.x or WFW 3.1x support files are missing or corrupted and Setup won't run properly. It tells Setup not to use the existing copy of Windows for the initial phase of the setup. As soon as the new Windows 95 support files get copied to your drive, Setup switches back to a Windows interface.

- **/ID:** Setup doesn't check for the required disk space when you use this switch. I can't think of any time when you'd want to use it. If your system is that short on hard disk space, you should consider clearing additional space before you try to install Windows 95.

- **/IQ:** Use this switch to bypass ScanDisk as the first step of the installation process when performing the installation from DOS. It's not a good idea to skip this step unless your system experiences some kind of problem running ScanDisk with Setup running. Make sure you do a separate scan of your drives if you use this switch.

- **/IS:** Use this switch to bypass ScanDisk as the first step of the installation process when performing the installation from Windows. It's not a good idea to skip this step unless your system experiences some kind of problem running ScanDisk with Setup running. Make sure you do a separate scan of your drives if you use this switch.

- **/NOSTART:** The `/NOSTART` switch allows you to copy to the hard drive the minimum number of Windows 3.x DLLs that the Windows 95 Setup program requires to start. Setup then exits to the DOS prompt. You can use this feature to replace or repair any missing or damaged Windows 3.x or WFW 3.1x support files prior to starting an installation.

- **/T:<Temporary Directory>:** This switch allows you to tell Windows 95 which drive to use as a temporary directory. It normally tries to use the drive you are using for installation. However, if the drive you choose is a little short on space, you can use this switch to redirect installation-specific items to another drive.

- **<Batch>:** This option was discussed in detail in the preceding two sections. The MSBATCH.INF (or other) batch file contains custom installation instructions.

Believe it or not, you're finally ready to install Windows 95. The very last thing you need to do before you start Setup is to choose what type of installation you want. (My personal choice is the Custom Setup option because it gives you the most control over the final appearance of the installation.) You can perform four types of installations:

- Typical Setup: This is the default setup that Windows 95 provides. It will allow you to install a standard set of options for your machine (the table that follows shows the features this method includes). Because this is the default setting, the only questions Setup will ask is where you want to put the Windows 95 files and whether you want to create an emergency disk.

- Portable Setup: Use this setup if you are using a portable computer. It installs a minimal set of standard utility programs—the same set included with the Compact Setup option. This installation also includes all the special utilities that Windows 95 provides for portable computers, such as the Briefcase and Direct Cable Connection.

- Compact Setup: This is the option to use if you're really tight on hard disk space. It only installs the bare essentials—perhaps a little too bare for many users. The nice thing about using this particular option is that you can get a minimal system started and then add other features as you need them. That way you never end up with more than you'll actually use on your computer. Of course, this option also presents very little opportunity for the user who wants to explore what Windows 95 has to offer.

- Custom Setup: The custom option provides the most flexibility of all the Setup options we've looked at. It also requires the greatest amount of time to set up. This is the perfect option for those who already have a good idea of what they do and don't want out of Windows 95. It's also a good option for a network administrator who uses a batch file to install Windows 95 on workstations. The administrator gets the maximum flexibility, yet the batch file hides any details from the user.

Note: As of this writing, you must use the portable installation option if you want the installation program to place the power management utilities on your system. You can manually install these utilities using the Expand utility later. However, Microsoft (for whatever strange reason) decided not to include this option on the Windows Setup page of the Add/Remove Programs Properties dialog.

The decision of which installation route you want to use is partly based on which files you need to use. The one thing you'll want to remember is that you can always add or remove features later on. A mistake right now doesn't mean you'll have to start the installation from scratch later. With that in mind, Table 4.3 contains a list of the various files that Windows 95 installs using the four installation options. (All four options obviously install the entire core system.)

Table 4.3. Optional features installed by various setup options.

Feature	Typical	Portable	Compact	Custom
Accessories	Yes			Yes
Audio Compression Codecs	Yes	Yes		Yes
Backup	Yes			Yes
Briefcase		Yes		
Desktop Bitmaps	Yes	Yes		Yes

continues

Table 4.3. continued

Feature	Typical	Portable	Compact	Custom
Dial-Up Networking	Yes	Yes		Yes
Direct Cable Connection	Yes	Yes		Yes
Disk Compression Tools	Yes	Yes	Yes	Yes
Disk Maintenance and Repair Tools	Yes	Yes	Yes	Yes
Document Templates	Yes			Yes
Games	Yes			Yes
Hyper Terminal	Yes	Yes		Yes
Internet Mail Service				
Microsoft Exchange				
Microsoft Fax				
Multimedia Applications	Yes	Yes		Yes
Multimedia Sound and Video Clips	Yes	Yes		Yes
Musica Sound Scheme	Yes	Yes		Yes
Network Administration Tools				
Online User's Guide				
Paint	Yes			Yes
Quick View	Yes	Yes		Yes
Screen Savers	Yes	Yes		Yes
The Microsoft Network				
Video Compression Codecs	Yes	Yes		Yes
Windows 95 Tour	Yes			Yes
WordPad	Yes			Yes

Installing Windows 95 from Disks

Installing Windows 95 from a floppy is just as simple as the same installation was for Windows 3.x. All you need to do is start DOS or Windows and type Setup. Microsoft suggests that you install Windows 95 from an existing copy of Windows 3.x, and it's true that this particular installation provides you with a better interface. However, beyond the interface issue, both installation methods (character-mode or GUI) are the same. The following paragraphs walk you through the installation procedure.

1. Type Setup at the Run prompt and press Enter. You should see a display similar to the one shown in Figure 4.8.

Figure 4.8.
The initial Windows 95 screen starts like most Microsoft installation programs.

2. Click on Continue. You'll see a dialog box similar to the one shown in Figure 4.9. Windows 95 checks your hard drive for errors before it starts the actual install. When it gets past this point, Setup displays a message saying it's installing the Windows 95 Setup Wizard. About halfway through this process, it asks you to insert disk 2.

Figure 4.9.
The Windows 95 Setup program scans your drive before it starts the actual installation.

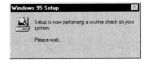

3. Insert disk 2 and click on OK. When the Setup Wizard installation is complete, Setup displays the licensing agreement shown in Figure 4.10 and asks you to agree to the terms of the licensing agreement. If you decide that you don't like the terms, Setup exits.

Figure 4.10.
When the Setup Wizard installation is complete, Setup asks you to agree to the terms of the licensing agreement.

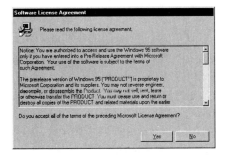

4. Signal your agreement to the licensing terms by clicking Yes. Setup makes some checks at this point. For one thing, it checks to make sure that it's the only application running. If it finds any other applications running, Setup displays a dialog telling you to use Alt-Tab to access the applications and exit them. It provides similar dialogs for any other problems that it finds. You should see a Setup Wizard dialog similar to the one shown in Figure 4.11 at this point. This is the entry point for the main part of the Windows 95 installation.

Figure 4.11.
The Setup Wizard helps you
get the rest of the operating
system configured and
installed on your machine.

5. Click on the Next button to get to the next dialog box. At this point, Setup asks where you want to install Windows 95, as shown in Figure 4.12. It suggests a default directory, or you can choose another location. Setup always suggests your current Windows directory if it detects a prior installation. If you plan to keep Windows 95 on your machine, this is the right way to go because you'll preserve all your current settings and application configurations. However, if you think you might want to return to your previous setup, select a new directory. You'll have to reinstall all your applications, but at least it will be easy to return your system to its previous condition.

Figure 4.12.
This dialog allows you to
choose a location for
Windows 95.

6. Select a directory option and click on Next. If you chose a new directory, Windows 95 asks you to enter it in the next screen and click on Next. Setup then displays a message saying that you'll have to reinstall your applications if you install Windows 95 in a new directory. Click on OK to get past this dialog. Either directory selection will take you to the dialog shown in Figure 4.13. If you don't have enough disk space, Setup provides some additional dialogs to help you find enough space on the hard drive or recommends some other corrective action. When Setup finishes checking for installed components and the amount of required disk space, it presents the dialog box shown in Figure 4.14.

7. Select one of the four installation types. These options were discussed at length in the preceding section. Most users should select either the Typical or Custom installation type.

Figure 4.13.
Windows 95 begins the installation by checking for installed components and the correct amount of disk space.

Figure 4.14.
Now that Setup is ready to go, you must select an installation type.

8. After you select an installation type, click on Next to get to the display shown in Figure 4.15.

Figure 4.15.
Setup assumes that you want all your hardware automatically detected except for a few special devices such as the CD-ROM.

Note: If you select the Custom installation, Windows 95 asks whether you want it to autodetect the devices installed on your machine. The other configurations don't get this option. If you choose to modify the hardware configuration list, Windows 95 displays a dialog containing all the various types of hardware available on your machine. You'll need to select which types you want to automatically detect.

Tip: Users of LANtastic and other real-mode peer-to-peer networking systems should select the Custom installation option. This allows you to tell Windows 95 not to automatically detect your network adapter. Automatic detection assumes that you want to install a Microsoft network when using these networks.

9. Click on Next to start the hardware detection phase. Setup displays a dialog similar to the one shown in Figure 4.16. The hardware detection phase can take quite a while—especially on older machines. The one constant I've noticed is that when disk activity stops for more than five minutes, it's a pretty safe bet that the machine is frozen. As long as you hear disk activity during this phase, you can assume that hardware detection is still taking place. (The hardware detection indicator doesn't move at a steady pace. It appears to take more time as it nears the end.) When Setup finishes this process, it displays the Get Connected dialog, shown in Figure 4.17.

Figure 4.16.
The hardware detection phase is one of the few areas where Setup could freeze.

Figure 4.17.
The Get Connected dialog box is where you select your connection options.

10. Check the connection options you think you'll need and then click on Next to continue. Windows 95 presents one of two dialog boxes at this point. The Custom option allows you to select individual components using the dialog shown in Figure 4.18. The other three installation methods only allow you to select between no optional components or the most

common components for that installation type. See Table 4.3 for a list of common components. I also provided an overview of these accessories in Chapter 2.

Figure 4.18.
Using the Custom installation option gives you the most flexibility when it comes time to select Windows 95 features to install.

11. If you're using the Custom installation feature, use the dialog to select the components you want to install. If you're using one of the other three installation options, select either no optional components or the common components radio button. Click on Next to display the Network Configuration dialog, shown in Figure 4.19, which is the most confusing step for new users. Most network administrators will want to provide a script to get users through this part of the installation automatically.

Figure 4.19.
The Network Configuration dialog is the most confusing step for new users.

12. After you select the network installation options, Setup takes you through a series of screens to configure that network. Each network has different requirements, so the installation screens will vary. You'll see various network options later in this book. If you find that you can't answer the questions here, you might want to skip ahead to those networking chapters for a few answers. It's also important that you read the manuals that come with your networking software. In many cases, they will provide the answers you need.

13. Complete the network configuration dialogs one at a time. Click on Next to move from screen to screen. Some networks, such as Microsoft networks, require a single screen.

Others might require more screens depending on the options you select. The last time you click on Next, Setup displays a dialog similar to the one shown in Figure 4.20. This dialog contains all the settings for your machine.

Figure 4.20.

You need to check the Computer Settings dialog thoroughly to make certain that Setup Wizard detected all your hardware correctly.

14. Check all your hardware settings completely by scrolling through the list. Sometimes the Setup Wizard fails to detect a piece of hardware. Worse still, it might incorrectly detect a piece of hardware. There are techniques you can use to make this process a little less error-prone. These techniques are discussed in the plug and play section that follows. If this list doesn't reflect your computer, change the settings in this dialog using the Change pushbutton.

Note: This dialog doesn't display every hardware and software installation choice that the Setup Wizard made. You'll have to check all the settings for your hardware after Setup completes. See Chapter 23 for tips and techniques that you can use to troubleshoot hardware-related problems.

15. After you complete any required changes to your hardware setup, click on Next. The Setup Wizard will ask whether you want to create a startup disk (see Figure 4.21).

Figure 4.21.

The Startup Disk dialog is one place where you shouldn't take the quick way out. Always create a startup disk for your machine.

> **Tip:** There's never a good reason to avoid making a startup disk. This is the most automatic method at your disposal for ensuring that you'll always have a way to boot your machine. In fact, you can run this procedure from within the Add/Remove Programs Properties dialog. You should keep the startup disk up to date by creating a new one whenever your system configuration changes (even a little).

16. Always select Yes and click on Next. The next display tells you that the configuration portion of the installation is complete. Remember that disk swapping exercise I talked about at the beginning of this chapter? You're about to start doing just that. Setup now starts to copy files to the hard drive. All you need to do is click on Next and follow the prompts. Sometime during the copying phase, Setup will ask you to provide a blank formatted floppy for the startup disk.

As you can see, Windows 95 requires a lot more configuration than its predecessors. I think it makes this process much easier, though, by organizing the configuration dialogs better and asking for the information in a more logical sequence. Of course, a higher quality of online help doesn't hurt either.

Installing Windows 95 from a CD-ROM

The only difference between installing Windows 95 from floppy disks and from a CD-ROM is that you use a different drive. The CD-ROM installation doesn't require you to change disks either. It automatically knows all the information required to install Windows 95 is on that one disk.

> **Note:** You will need to retain any drivers and TSRs required to access your CD-ROM drive in the DOS startup files in order to install Windows 95 from a CD. Remember to REM out any unneeded drivers as soon as the Windows 95 installation is complete.

The CD-ROM version of the installation program does contain some added features. First, it includes all the network administrator tools and help files. The floppy disk version doesn't provide these tools because it's designed for the single-user machine. The CD-ROM also contains a copy of the Windows Resource Kit in Windows help format. The CD-ROM contains a few additional goodies as well. You'll find a game called Hover and a few video demonstrations in the \FUNSTUFF folder. The \PRODUCTS folder contains a summary of many Microsoft products that you can access from the Autoplay dialog that comes up when you insert the CD into the drive. There are other features as well, all of which we'll cover throughout the rest of this book.

Installing Windows 95 from a Server

A server installation can differ from the floppy disk version in quite a few ways. You could install the entire operating system without telling the user much, if anything, about what you're doing (believe me when I say that this isn't a good idea). You might not choose to provide any automation at all, in which case the user would see the same thing you did for the floppy disk installation in the preceding section. Reality will probably fit somewhere in between these two extremes. As a network administrator, you should provide some level of automation to protect the user from the ambiguities of installing network support. However, whether you install Windows 95 from a server, a CD-ROM, or a floppy, the same sequence of events must take place. The only factor is the way you choose to smooth the way for the users on the system.

Earlier we looked at all the automation you could provide using an MSBATCH.INF file. The level of automation that you, as a network administrator, provide is the one random element in the server installation. As I said earlier, as a minimum you should hide the network installation details from the user. My personal preference, though, is to allow the user as much freedom as possible when it comes to installing optional components. I can't really give you a play-by-play look at a server installation. Each server installation will differ because each network and company has different needs. You'll determine how the install program looks to the user.

The one other thing you will need to determine for a server installation is the location of the operating system. Forcing users to use Windows 95 from the server is certainly more secure than allowing them to install it on a local workstation. It also allows you to maintain a firmer grip on the licenses. Finally, keeping the files on the server reduces the amount of hard disk space that Windows 95 consumes across the network. (You have to provide room for the one copy of the operating system on the network and a home directory for user-specific files.)

The advantages of a local hard disk install are few but very important. A local install will definitely increase performance. That's going to be a big factor for many people who are already looking for ways to get the last ounce of performance out of a machine. Using the local install option also reduces network activity. Some networks already suffer from a lack of bandwidth, and installing Windows 95 on the server will only make a bad situation worse. Finally, a local hard disk installation allows you to keep the server clear of user files and open for data files. The distinction is important. A user configuration file only helps that particular user, while a data file helps the company as a whole. Keeping user data on the file server might add a lot of clutter and make it more difficult for people to find the data files that they need to interact with.

Plug and Play Installation Tips

I am a great fan of automation that works. Anything that will make my job easier or faster is a good idea in my book. Using plug and play to automatically install the hardware it recognizes is one form of that kind of automation. It makes sense that a computer could figure out a set of port and interrupt settings faster and with greater accuracy than the average human. Windows 3.x didn't provide any form of plug and play. Even if it did, it couldn't have dealt with the problems of supporting older, non-plug and play hardware. One of the reasons that this is possible under Windows 95 is that the computer does have all the statistics it needs to do the job. The majority of this information is contained in the on-board BIOS that plug and play hardware uses to communicate with the rest of the machine.

Of course, the BIOS only takes care of one part of the equation. Plug and play is an example of a good idea—but one whose time hasn't come yet. Windows 95 does a fairly good job of detecting non-plug and play hardware, even when it gets mixed with plug and play-compatible hardware. All the configuration information for the hardware that Windows 95 supports is stored on the hard disk. In fact, if you look in the \WIN95\INF directory, you'll see some of these files (they all have an .INF extension). Besides storing the required configuration information on disk, Windows 95 gives older hardware first choice of ports and interrupts. This allows older hardware to work most of the time.

Problems start to arise when the system doesn't or can't recognize one or more components in your system. The problem is so bad on some systems that I've heard people refer to the new Windows 95 hardware detection scheme as "plug and pray." Usually, the unrecognized hardware refuses to work properly, if at all. The second this happens, Windows 95 has the unfortunate tendency of either going to pieces or ignoring the problem. Unrecognized hardware falls into two categories. There's the difficult-to-recognize piece of hardware, which emulates something else so well that the computer has a hard time telling exactly what it is. The second category is older hardware that lacks Windows 95-specific drivers.

So now that you have some idea of what the problem is, let's take a quick look at ways you can fix it. This list isn't exhaustive, but it will help you with the majority of the problems you're likely to run into.

Looking Ahead: If you didn't find a technique that helped you here, take a look at the end of this book. Chapter 23 takes a detailed look at hardware troubleshooting techniques—especially tough-to-install hardware. In some cases, you might find that Windows 95 even provides protected-mode drivers that you can use with the old stuff.

- Avoid interrupt and port address conflicts whenever possible. This is probably the number one reason that Windows 95 will fail to recognize the board. If two devices use the same address, there's no way that Windows 95 can test for the presence of the second board.

- Plug all your older boards into the slots next to the power supply whenever possible. The BIOS checks the slots in order during POST. Placing these older boards first, followed by the plug and play boards, ensures that the BIOS will see the older ones first.

- Try different board configurations to see whether Windows 95 will recognize one of them. There are situations in which the .INF files that Windows 95 uses to check for the older boards contain only the default board settings. A good rule of thumb is to try the best setting first and then the default setting if that doesn't work.

- Check the .INF files to see whether they contain all the settings for your boards. There's an .INF directory directly below the main Windows 95 directory. It contains ASCII text files that Windows 95 uses to search for these older boards. Modifying these files is a tricky proposition, but it could help Windows 95 find the peripherals in your machine.

Installation with Real-Mode Drivers Intact

If the quick help in the preceding section didn't help much, you can always try some back-door techniques that I've discovered. Some devices—especially those that rely on software configuration instead of jumpers—don't provide enough information for autodetection until you turn them on. Normally, this means that the user has to install any required real-mode drivers in CONFIG.SYS. These drivers perform the setups required to make the device visible to Windows 95. The following procedure will help Windows 95 "discover" these hidden boards in most cases.

1. After you install these drivers, reboot the machine. When Windows 95 starts, use the Start | Settings | Control Panel command to open Control Panel.

2. Double-click on the Add New Hardware icon. You should see the dialog shown in Figure 4.22.

Figure 4.22.
The Hardware Installation Wizard allows you to install new hardware with a minimum of effort.

3. Click on the Next pushbutton. You should see the dialog box shown in Figure 4.23. Using automatic hardware detection reduces the amount of work the user needs to perform, and it can reduce the possibility of hardware conflicts because Windows 95 performs some additional detection steps. Notice that the Yes (Recommended) radio button is selected. When you select this radio button, you tell Windows to automatically detect your hardware.

4. Click on the Next pushbutton on this dialog and again on the next dialog. Windows 95 displays the dialog shown in Figure 4.24 during the detection process.

Figure 4.23.
Using automatic hardware detection reduces the amount of work the user needs to perform.

Figure 4.24.
Windows 95 displays this detection progress indicator while it searches the machine for new devices.

Note: The hardware detection phase can take quite a while—especially on older machines. The one constant I noticed is that when disk activity stops for more than five minutes, it's a pretty safe bet that the machine is frozen. As long as you hear disk activity during this phase, you can assume that hardware detection is still taking place. (The hardware detection indicator does not move at a steady pace; it appears to take more time as it nears the end.)

5. Click on the Details pushbutton to determine whether Windows 95 successfully detected the new hardware, as shown in Figure 4.25.

Figure 4.25.
The Detected field of the final Installation Wizard dialog tells you whether Windows 95 detected the new hardware correctly.

6. If Windows 95 successfully detected the new hardware, click on the Finish pushbutton to complete the installation process. Windows 95 might ask you to supply some setting information if this is a non-plug and play device. In most cases, it provides default settings that match your current real-mode setup. Windows 95 copies all the required drivers to disk. It also displays some messages about the new hardware it found and perhaps a driver database building message. In some cases, Windows 95 asks you to reboot when you complete this step. Even if it doesn't ask you to reboot, you must do so to make this procedure work properly. The real-mode drivers that you installed to aid in detection will destabilize the system if you leave them in place.

7. Make sure you remove the real-mode drivers from CONFIG.SYS before you shut down and reboot the machine. If Windows 95 didn't detect the new hardware, remove the real-mode drivers from CONFIG.SYS, shut down and reboot the system, and then perform the manual installation procedure in the next section.

Manual Installation

It always seems to come down to the same old procedure. You finally get everything working using the automated procedures, except that old CD-ROM drive or an especially difficult sound card. There are a few situations in which you'll have to help Windows 95 install an older device in your machine. Usually, something else you installed—probably a plug and play device—is using some resource that the older device needs. The following example shows how to install a CD-ROM drive; the same principles apply to any manual installation. However, let me warn you ahead of time that simply installing the device might not make it work. You might have to perform some troubleshooting to get this older device to work (see Chapter 23). At the very least, you'll have to shuffle some IRQ and address settings around.

1. Use the Start | Settings | Control Panel command to open Control Panel. Double-click on the Add New Hardware icon (see Figure 4.22). Click on the Next pushbutton (see Figure 4.23).

2. Click on the No radio button and then click on Next. Highlight the CD-ROM Controller entry of the Install Specific Hardware field and then click on the Next pushbutton. You should see the dialog box shown in Figure 4.26. The manufacturers and models list in this dialog allows you to scroll with ease through the list of devices supported by Windows 95. If the device installed on the current machine does not appear on the list, the dialog also affords the opportunity to use a third-party disk.

3. This dialog appears every time you select a device from the previous dialog. The manufacturer list changes to match the particular device type. Normally you would select the device connected to your machine. In this case, leave the default device highlighted and click on the Next pushbutton.

Figure 4.26.
The manufacturers and models list in this dialog allows you to scroll with ease through the list of devices supported by Windows 95.

4. Click on the Details pushbutton. Windows 95 displays a dialog containing the interrupt and address settings for this particular device, as shown in Figure 4.27. Windows 95 chooses a device setting based on all available information; it chooses the best setting that won't interfere with other devices in the system (if possible).

Figure 4.27.
Windows 95 always tells the user what interrupts and addresses it uses for the devices it installs.

Tip: A special "Unknown hardware" device type allows you to view all the devices supported by Windows 95 on one screen. This comes in handy for two purposes. First, Microsoft doesn't always place devices in the category where you expect them to be. Searching through this list provides one final check if you don't find a device where you expect to see it. Second, you can use this list when researching a new product. It allows you to choose a device that Windows 95 will definitely support. I'm not saying other products are incompatible, just that these products received a little more attention than some of the others you might find.

5. Clicking the Next pushbutton again installs the device drivers required for this device. Normally, you would take this action. Windows 95 might prompt you for a disk if the driver did not appear on the hard drive and the appropriate disk did not appear in the CD-ROM drive. It would display a dialog showing the progress of the file copy process. However, because you don't want to install this particular device, click on the Cancel pushbutton. Windows 95 exits the Hardware Installation Wizard without installing the new device.

Adding Your Own Devices

Now that you have Windows 95 installed, let's take some of the magic out of the new Windows 95 detection capability. If you take a look in your \WIN95\INF directory, you'll see a new type of file there. The .INF file is part of the database of information that Windows 95 uses to recognize hardware that isn't plug and play-compatible. These files are enhanced versions of the OEMSETUP.INF files that used to appear on the vendor-supplied installation disks under Windows 3.x. They contain a description of the hardware—the same type of information that the plug and play BIOS would normally provide when Windows 95 scanned it.

There are two main differences between these .INF files and the Windows 3.x version. First, the Windows 95 version contains a lot more information. It provides detailed configuration and detection information to the system. Under Windows 3.x, the same file would only provide general operating parameters. Second, Windows 95 has constant access to these .INF files. It can scan them any time you install new hardware or reconfigure the existing hardware. Under Windows 3.x, this file tended to stay on the OEM disk that you got with your display adapter or other hardware. Even if the vendor did write this file to the \WIN\SYSTEM directory, the next vendor installing a product would overwrite the file. Under Windows 3.x, every setup disk contained an OEMSETUP.INF file. Using the same filename prevented you from saving these settings for future use (at least it prevented you from doing so in a convenient way).

As good as these new .INF files are, there might be times when you want to modify them. For example, what if you have a piece of hardware that provides interrupt and port address settings in addition to those found in the .INF file? Modifying the .INF file to reflect these additional capabilities could help you install a piece of hardware in some cases.

> **Tip:** Microsoft is devoted to making the .INF file format a standard way to configure future versions of Windows to support non-plug and play hardware. However, the contents of that file are a moving target at the moment because Microsoft is still trying to work out bugs in the detection scheme. You can obtain your own copy of the .INF file specification from the CompuServe Plug and Play forum (GO PLUGPLAY). Just download INFWHITE1.DOC or INFWHT.ZIP. You also get a copy with the Windows 95 DDK (Driver Development Kit). This file contains a lot more information than the average user will need; however, it can help a system administrator find a way to incorporate some devices into the Windows 95 environment.

Let's look at some of the general characteristics that every .INF file shares. You might find all or only some of these sections in the file; it really depends on what kind of hardware the .INF file is trying to define. An .INF file only needs to contain the information required to fully define the characteristics of the hardware. For example, a display adapter would need to define the resolutions that it supports. A multiscanning monitor, such as the NEC MultiSync series, would need to define the precise frequency ranges that it supports. This includes the refresh rate, an important specification for the new ergonomic display adapters. Table 4.4 shows these generic sections and tells you what they mean. You might even want to open one of the .INF files and see whether you can identify each section. (Just make certain that you don't save the file or change its contents in any way.)

Table 4.4. .INF file generic sections.

Heading	Description
Version	This section provides version-specific information such as the operating system, vendor name, and the device class supported by the .INF file. It also provides the name of the general setup file. The general setup file contains the definitions common to all the devices of that type. You might see some additional entries in this section. One special entry allows the vendor to link a new .INF file into the list of files for a specific device type. Never change the contents of this section.
Manufacturer	The manufacturer section contains a list of all the manufacturers for devices of this class. Not every .INF file contains this section. For example, this section appears in the MONITOR.INF file but not the MSPORTS.INF file. The only time you need to change this section is if you want to add a new vendor. The list might seem incomplete if there is more than one .INF file required to describe a specific class of device. There are four monitor files, and each one contains only the vendors that appear in that particular file. You need to check all of the .INF files for a particular device class before you resort to adding a new vendor. Make sure that you add the new vendor in alphabetical order to the correct .INF file (you'll see an example later in this chapter). There is a subsection after this one that provides specifics about each device supported by that vendor. If the vendor already appears in the manufacturer list, adding a new device consists of adding an entry here, in the Install section, and in the Strings section.
Install	This is the most important section of the file. It describes all the characteristics of the hardware and the device drivers needed to activate it. It also contains macro commands that perform the actual installation of support in the registry. Follow the example of other entries in this section when adding a new device. Only change physical characteristics such as port address and interrupt when modifying an existing entry.

continues

Table 4.4. continued

Heading	Description
Miscellaneous Control	A vendor can use this section to describe how a device works with the Windows 95 interface. If you see this section, you need to use other entries as an example for creating your own entries. Most .INF files do not contain this section.
Strings	You'll see how to add a new device to Windows 95 using the Add New Hardware dialog later in this chapter. When you use this dialog, you'll see some descriptive strings that tell you about the hardware. This is the section that contains those user-friendly strings. It identifies the device in human-readable form.

I was looking through my list of available displays the other day and noticed that one of my displays—a Samsung CQ-4551 VGA monitor—wasn't supported. It's a fairly easy matter to add support for this new device to the .INF file, so I made a copy and placed it in a backup folder right below the .INF folder. That way I wouldn't erase the original file by accident. We can go through this exercise together to make the process of adding a new device a little clearer. Before we begin, though, I'll outline a few guidelines that I used during the modification process.

- Always print a copy of the original .INF file. This way you can scan through the listing quickly as you make a new entry. Some entries depend on the contents of other entries in the file. A mistyped or misinterpreted entry will make the .INF file useless.

- Use the other entries in the file as a guideline for your new entries. Windows 95 performs a very strict interpretation of the contents of the .INF file. Adding your own "enhancements" to what seems like an inadequate entry will make the .INF file unusable. Remember, some of the .INF file entries appear in one or more generic files that appear in the Version section of the file.

- Follow punctuation marks, spelling, and capitalization carefully when making a new entry. Windows 95 is extremely sensitive when it comes to how you format the entries in an .INF file.

- Never change the Version section of the file. Yes, it's very tempting to fiddle with what looks like an interesting file section, but don't do it in this case.

- Make your entries to an existing file. You might be tempted to create your own unique .INF file. Don't do it! Always add new devices to existing files. That way you can be absolutely sure that your entries look like the other entries in the file.

Warning: Always modify the original copy of an .INF file after making a backup. Place the copy in a backup directory using a different extension than the original file. Your modified

> version of the original file must appear in the .INF directory in order for Windows 95 to recognize it. Keeping a copy of the original version in a temporary directory allows you to restore the file later.

Now that you have a better idea of what an .INF file contains, let's go through the procedure for modifying one. You can use the same set of steps to modify any of the files in the .INF folder. The only thing that changes from file to file is the precise format of the entries themselves and the sections that the file supports.

1. Use WordPad to open MONITOR2.INF. There are four sections in the .INF file that you need to change. These sections were discussed in Table 4.4. The first section we'll modify contains the manufacturer information. Because I wanted to add an entry for a Samsung monitor, I used WordPad's Find command to see whether I could find the vendor name. Samsung is already in the vendor list, so I didn't need to add it. However, if you decide to add a new vendor, all you need to do is follow the format of the other vendor entries in the first manufacturer section. After I found the vendor name entry, I searched for the device subsection that would contain the list of devices from that vendor that Windows 95 supports. I added the following text (shown in bold) to this section so that Windows 95 would know to add a new device.

```
[Samsung]
%CQ-4551%=CQ-4551.Install
%CT-4581%=CT-4581.Install
```

2. As you can see, I formatted my entry to look exactly like the existing entry. This is a very important part of the process of adding an unsupported device to Windows 95. This entry tells Windows 95 that Samsung produces a model CQ-4551 monitor and that it can find further details about that monitor in the CQ-4551.Install section of the .INF file. Now use the Find command to locate the second CT-4581 entry (it's the Samsung model that appears directly below our new entry). This entry appears in the install section of the .INF file. I added the following bold text to tell Windows 95 how to install this new monitor. Notice that these instructions look a lot like the macros you might have created with applications in the past—which they should, because that's exactly what this section contains.

```
[KDM-2066.Install]
DelReg=DEL_CURRENT_REG
AddReg=KDM-2066.AddReg, 1280

[CQ-4551.Install]
DelReg=DEL_CURRENT_REG
AddReg=CQ-4551.AddReg, 640

[CT-4581.Install]
DelReg=DEL_CURRENT_REG
AddReg=CT-4581.AddReg, 800
```

3. I started by adding a heading that identifies the macro code that follows as the Samsung model CQ-4551 installation procedure. An .INF file always encloses its headings between a left and right bracket, just like WIN.INI and SYSTEM.INI do for their headers. I also added two macro entries to the section. The first one tells Windows 95 to delete the current registry entry. You need to delete the old entry so that Windows 95 won't get confused when it tries to configure the display adapter to match the monitor. The second entry tells Windows 95 to add a new registry entry following the instructions located in the `CQ-4551.AddReg` section of the .INF file. Note the `640` after the add registry command. This tells Windows 95 to use the 640 display mode as a default. Use the Find command to find the `CT-4581` entry in the next section of the file. I added the following bold text to tell Windows 95 how to modify the registry to support this new monitor. We're still in the Installation section of the file.

```
[KDM-2066.AddReg]
HKR,"MODES\1280,1024",Mode1,,"30.0-67.0,40.0-120.0,+,+"

[CQ-4551.AddReg]
HKR,"MODES\640,480",Mode1,,"31.5,60.0-70.0,-,-"

[CT-4581.AddReg]
HKR,"MODES\800,600",Mode1,,"15.0-38.0,47.0-73.0,+,+"
```

4. The registry entry section of any .INF file requires some detective work on your part. I always look at the registry itself as a starting point (see Chapter 6 for a complete description of the registry). Knowing how the existing device modified the registry can help you determine how to add support for a new device. You should also check the specification sheet that comes with the device for "common" characteristics. Any change you make to an .INF file will ultimately require this type of detective work. In this case, the first important component is `"MODES\640,480"`. This describes the operational resolution for that monitor mode. The second component, `Mode1`, tells Windows 95 that this is the first mode supported by the monitor. Looking at other entries in this .INF file shows that some monitors support multiple modes. The final component, `"31.5,60.0-70.0,-,-"`, looks a bit mysterious until you check a monitor manual. The first number, `31.5`, is the horizontal scanning frequency. You could supply a numeric range here as well. The second numeric range, `60.0-70.0`, is the vertical scanning frequency. The two minus signs tell you that this is not a multiscanning monitor. I figured this out by checking the other entries in the file. After looking at a few monitor models that I recognized, it was pretty evident that the ones with multiscanning capabilities used plus signs in place of the minus signs. Let's get to the final section of the .INF file—the Strings section. This is where you'll describe the monitor in terms that the user can understand. To do this, use the Find command to search for the next (and last) occurrence of the `CT-4581` string. When I found this entry, I added this bold text:

```
CQ-4551="Samsung, Inc. CQ-4551"
CT-4581="Samsung, Inc. CT-4581"
```

That's all there is to it. After you get the hang of it, you can add support for just about any unsupported device to Windows 95. Of course, that won't solve some problems such as the lack of protected-mode drivers and some of the incompatibilities you'll experience with some older devices. But it will make it easier to install an older device. If you want to see how the new entry looks, save the MONITOR2.INF file and close WordPad. Right-click on the desktop and select Properties from the Context menu to display the Display Properties dialog, shown in Figure 4.28. You can use this quick procedure to display the monitor entries.

Figure 4.28.
Right-clicking the Desktop and selecting Properties from the Context menu displays the Display Properties dialog.

1. Click on the Settings tab to display the Display Properties dialog box, shown in Figure 4.29.

Figure 4.29.
The Display Properties dialog allows you to change the current monitor settings.

2. Click on the Change Display Type pushbutton to see the Change Display Type dialog, shown in Figure 4.30.

3. Click on the Change command in the Monitor group to display the Select Device dialog. Windows 95 displays an update dialog while it adds the new monitor to the list.

Figure 4.30.
*The Change Display Type
dialog allows you to modify
either the display adapter or
monitor settings.*

4. Scroll through the list of vendors until you find Samsung, Inc. (there might be a Samsung entry right before this one). You should see the new monitor selection, as shown in Figure 4.31.

Figure 4.31.
*Modifications to the
MONITOR2.INF file
appear in the Select Device
dialog.*

5. Click on Cancel three times to exit the Display Settings dialog without changing the monitor type. Adding a new device to an .INF file can prove time-consuming and even frustrating at times. However, the benefits in reduced maintenance time are well worth the effort.

This is a quick tour of adding new devices to Windows 95. You might find that some devices are so complex that you'll end up downloading the full .INF file specification (see the tip earlier in this chapter) to really understand how to make the change. The worst thing you can do is try to tackle a complex device addition as your first project. Look for something fairly easy, such as a monitor, as your first project so that you can get a better idea of what the modification will require.

Uninstalling Windows 95

As of this writing, Microsoft hasn't decided to include an uninstall feature with Windows 95. You can install it on your system, but you won't get it back off very easily—that is, unless you took my advice earlier in this chapter.

It wasn't too difficult to figure out that there wasn't going to be an easy way to get rid of Windows 95 once I installed it if it overwrote all my system files and changed quite a few others. Even if I did manage to get my old operating system to boot, I'd have to spend a lot of time reinstalling applications.

There is an easier way. The following procedure assumes that you did three things. First, it assumes that you made a boot disk like the one I mentioned at the beginning of this chapter. Second, it assumes that you made a copy of your DOS directory. Finally, it assumes that you installed Windows 95 to a clean directory. If you didn't follow one of those three steps, you won't have the resources to put your system back together.

1. The first step in this process is to get DOS to boot again. Use your boot disk to reboot your machine from the floppy. (Make sure you shut down Windows 95 properly first.)

2. Use the SYS command to restore the system files. Then, copy COMMAND.COM and an original copy of AUTOEXEC.BAT and CONFIG.SYS from your floppy to the hard drive.

3. Copy the contents of the DOS directory backup that you made to the DOS directory.

4. Take the floppy out of the drive and reboot your system. You should now get to a DOS prompt.

5. Carefully erase all the Windows 95-specific files. Make absolutely certain that you look for all the hidden files that Microsoft thoughtfully stored in your root directory. You can find them by using the DIR /AH /S command. The /AH switch displays every file that has a hidden attribute. The /S command tells DIR to look in any subdirectories as well as the root directory. Don't erase any DOS-specific files such as IO.SYS and MSDOS.SYS. The date stamp on the file should give you a clue as to which files belong to DOS and which belong to Windows 95. When in doubt, leave the file in place rather than removing it and making your system nonoperational. It will take a little effort to find all the entries. In fact, this is where a good disk editor will come into play.

6. Reboot your machine one more time to make sure everything works correctly.

That's it. This isn't the fanciest uninstall method in the world, but it works. You'll probably find bits and pieces of Windows 95 lying around on your system for a few weeks. If you were careful when you installed it, the pieces should appear in the root directory of all your drives. Of course, the first directory you'll erase is the \WIN95 directory. Make sure you get all the Recycle Bin directories (one on each drive) and the program directory that contained Microsoft Network and other accessory applications.

On Your Own

Create your own boot disk that contains the items I mentioned earlier in this chapter. Make sure you test it before you install Windows 95. You'll also want to create a Windows 95-specific startup disk during installation. Label both disks and keep them until you're certain that your Windows 95 installation is stable. When it's stable, create a new startup disk using the Startup Disk page of the Add/Remove Programs Properties dialog.

Make a list of all the equipment you think you might have problems with. Include all the items that Windows 95 doesn't provide entries for in the existing .INF files. Do you see any entries that you can fix using the procedures I provided in this chapter? Are there any ways to eliminate some of the real-mode drivers that you might need to use in order to keep older equipment running? Develop a comprehensive strategy for handling any problem areas before you begin the installation process.

5

Startup Shortcuts

An efficient machine is only as fast as the operator using it. If you can't use all the speed your machine provides, part of that speed is lost, and you might as well not look for anything faster. I've found that Windows 3.x users—like me—have developed some terrible habits because of that operating system's inefficiencies. For example, do you automatically assume that the machine is going to be tied up every time you use the modem? I know that's what I thought when I started using Windows 95.

As an experiment, a while back I tried performing a background download with one additional task—my word processor—running. The download completed in the background at 9600 baud without a single missed character while I worked in the foreground. The next day I decided to add another task. This time I compiled a program in one background session, downloaded a few files in another, and typed away in a third. I was ecstatic, to say the least. Everything went perfectly. So, I tried a third task, but Windows 95 just wasn't up to it. Everything bombed.

So what's the moral of this story? I don't think any operating system will ever be able to perform every task there is to perform and simultaneously communicate in the background. You need to have the required resources if you want to get the job done. In my case, two tasks in addition to the background download are about all my machine can handle.

I did learn something important, though. Using Windows 95 allowed me to get three times the amount of work done that I would have under Windows 3.x in this particular instance. I want to emphasize that point because the new and exciting methods Windows 95 introduces can become very inefficient, too.

Peter's Principle: Discovering Your Maximum Load—Without the Pain of Failure

Windows 3.x provided so many visual cues, I almost always knew when it was time to stop adding tasks by the way it acted. That old-shoe feel doesn't come with Windows 95, because you really haven't had a chance to break it in yet. Until you do start learning the little quirks that tell you when it's time to stop adding new tasks, you can do a few things to keep your system from crashing.

Unlike Windows 3.x, Windows 95 actually comes with some easy-to-use tools that keep track of your system resources. For example, I keep a copy of Resource Meter loaded all the time. (This isn't the Resource Monitor application I described earlier. Resource Meter is a small utility designed to track system resources.) A quick check of the Taskbar tells me just how low I'm getting on system resources. (For more information about this utility, see Chapter 3.) I also run Resource Monitor as needed to keep track of how certain tasks load the processor and disk subsystems. As a result, I'm learning to use Windows 95's capabilities more efficiently.

Now that we have a user-friendly operating system that can actually run more than a couple of tasks at a time without dying, we need to learn how to use it efficiently. Task loading is a new technique that all of us old hands will have to learn.

This chapter looks at some of the ways you can make yourself a little more efficient so that you can get the full benefits of using Windows 95 as an operating system. This means everything from the way you start your applications to the way you arrange your Desktop. Windows 95 provides many new tools you can use to make each step a little faster.

The Windows 95 Shortcut and OLE

Chapter 11 spends a lot of time discussing OLE from a user perspective. The programmer's point of view appears in Chapter 6. Let's take some time now to look at one unique way that Windows 95 uses OLE.

Every shortcut you create is a form of OLE. It's an actual link to another object on your machine. Windows 95 provides some special handling for these objects.

Unlike an application that can create compound documents to hold all the linking information, Windows 95 has to store that information someplace on the drive. After all, the drive is the container that Windows 95 uses to store information. The .LNK file is Windows 95's answer to this problem. It contains all the linking information needed to keep the shortcuts on your Desktop current with the real object.

You can easily test this by creating a shortcut of a folder on your Desktop. Every change you make to the real folder will appear in the linked copy. Likewise, every change you make in the linked copy will appear in the real thing. OLE and the Desktop are a part of Windows 95—a new part that will take time to get used to.

Faster Startups

Starting an application might not seem like a big deal. It wasn't a big deal under Windows 3.x. After all, how many ways can you double-click on an application icon sitting in a folder in Program Manager? Windows 95 provides more than just one or two ways to start your applications. In fact, here's a whole list of ways:

- Right-click on the application's icon while in Explorer, and then click on Open in the context menu.
- Double-click on the application's icon while in Explorer or File Manager.
- Double-click on a data file associated with the application while in Explorer. (This requires that you create a file association or that the application create it for you.)
- Select Start | Run, and then type the application's path and filename. Click on OK to start the application.
- Select Start | Run, and then drag and drop the application's icon into the Run dialog box. Click on OK to start the application.

- Select the application's entry from the Start menu.
- Create a shortcut icon on the Desktop. You can start the application by right-clicking or double-clicking on the icon.
- Assign a shortcut key to the application, and then start it using the keyboard shortcut. (You must create a .LNK file to do this. We'll look at the process for doing this later.)
- Use the Windows 3.x Program Manager (provided in the \WIN95 directory) to run the application.
- Place the application's icon or associated data file in the Startup folder in the Start menu to run it automatically the next time you start Windows. Placing a data file in the Startup folder automatically opens it for you.
- Use the Find dialog to find your application, and then right- or double-click on it.
- Embed or link the application's data in an OLE compound document. The user can start the application by double-clicking on the object embedded in the document. (The application must support OLE in order for this to work.)

Because I grew up using DOS, I really hated having to use the mouse just to start an application, so I didn't. Few users knew that you can make Windows 3.x somewhat keyboard-friendly by installing shortcut keys. Windows 95 provides this same feature.

If all Windows 95 provided were this particular shortcut, I could stop right here and let you read some material on Windows 3.x. Even though Windows 95 uses the same type of shortcut method, the implementation is a lot better. We'll also look at some "undocumented" ways of using the keyboard.

There are times where you really do need to use the mouse—if for no other reason than the fact your hand is resting on it at that particular moment. Like many people, I spend my share of time mousing around. CorelDRAW! and other drawing programs come in handy for some of the work I do. Using the mouse is nothing new for most people.

Windows 95 provides a lot of neat ways to use the mouse with your applications. You'll find that you can do a lot of things you couldn't do before with a simple mouse click. We'll look at some of these mouse techniques in this section.

Startups from the Keyboard

Nothing beat the keyboard if DOS was your home before you moved to Windows 95. But a quick look at the Windows 95 GUI tells you that most of your keyboard techniques won't work here. Some people figure that there's no way to use any of the old techniques. But nothing could be further from the truth.

Some shortcut keys come installed with Windows 95. I find that many of them are attached to the Accessibility Options, but you can change all that with just a little effort (we look at this later in this section). Table 5.1 provides a list of keystrokes and the actions they perform. You're probably familiar with most of them, but others are new to Windows 95.

> **Note:** Windows 95 doesn't provide any way to get to the control (system) menu using just the keyboard. This means that you'll have to use the MouseKeys feature of the Accessibility Options to move windows and perform other control menu-related functions when using the keyboard instead of the mouse.

Table 5.1. Windows 95 shortcut keys.

Key or Key Combination	Purpose
Alt-F4	Ends the current application. You can also use this key combination to end Windows if you're at the Desktop.
Alt-Shift-Tab	Switches to the previous window.
Alt-Tab	Switches to the next window.
Ctrl-Esc	Opens the Start menu on the Taskbar. You can then use the arrow keys to select an application. Pressing Enter starts the application you selected.
Esc	Cancels the last action in most cases. However, you can't back out of some actions.
F1	Displays online help. In most cases, this help is general in nature but is application-specific.
F2	Pressing this while an icon is highlighted allows you to change the object name.
F3	Unless your application uses this key for something else, you can press it to access the Find dialog. In most cases, you'll get better results if you press F3 while at the Desktop. You can also use this key at the Taskbar and the Start menu.
Left Alt-Left Shift-Num Lock	Holding these three keys down turns on the MouseKeys feature of the Accessibility Options.
Left Alt-Left Shift-Print Screen	Holding these three keys down turns on the High Contrast feature of the Accessibility Options.

continues

Table 5.1. continued

Key or Key Combination	Purpose
Num Lock	Holding the Num Lock key down for five seconds turns on the ToggleKeys feature of the Accessibility Options.
Right Shift	Holding the Right Shift key down for eight seconds turns on the FilterKeys feature of the Accessibility Options.
Shift five times	Pressing the Shift key five times turns on the StickyKeys feature of the Accessibility Options.
Shift-F1	Displays context-sensitive help when the application supports it. The Windows 95 Desktop doesn't appear to support this option.
Shift-F10	You must select an object before you use this key combination. It displays the context menu. Considering the number of options on the context menu, this key combination allows you to do almost anything with the object.
Tab	Use this key while at the Desktop to switch between the Desktop, Taskbar, and Start menu. You also can use Ctrl-Esc to bring up the Start menu and then press Tab to switch between applications.

Tip: Combining the various keystrokes makes them much more powerful. For example, what if you have a lot of applications open and need to quickly get to the Desktop? Use Ctrl-Esc to display the Start menu, Esc to close the menu itself, Tab to get to the Taskbar, and Shift-F10 to display the context menu. All you need to do now is select Minimize All Windows and press Enter. Pressing Tab one more time will take you to the Desktop.

Windows 95 provides two additional methods of using the keyboard to start applications. You can use the Windows 3.x method of assigning a shortcut key to the application. There are also automated methods of starting some applications.

Undocumented Parameters

The first program you need to learn about in order to use this section of the book is START. It's a new program you'll find in your \WIN95\COMMAND directory. At first, I couldn't figure out what use this program would really be. Then I started playing with it and figured out a few ways you could use this program if you learned about the undocumented parameters that most Windows applications provide. First, though, let's look at some documented parameters that START provides.

Chapter 5 • Startup Shortcuts 155

- /MAX: Use this to run a maximized application in the background.
- /M: This switch allows you to run the application in the background minimized.
- /R: The default setting for START is to run the program in the foreground. You can still switch back to the DOS prompt, but you'll take a quick trip to Windows first.
- /W: Use this switch if you want to start a Windows application, work with it for a while, and return to the DOS prompt when you're done.
- <Program Name>: This is the name of the program you want to run and any parameters it needs in order to execute.

All this is fine if you want to run a Windows application from DOS. However, this information doesn't really become useful until you can get some work done in Windows without leaving the DOS prompt. What would happen if you wanted to gain the advantage of Windows background printing while performing other work at the DOS prompt? You could switch back to Windows, start Notepad or some other appropriate application, load your file, and print, but that would disrupt what you were doing. The following line shows an easier, faster, and much better method:

```
START /M NOTEPAD /P SOMEFILE.TXT
```

There are a few things here you really need to take a look at. The first is the /P parameter right after NOTEPAD. Where did I get it? It isn't documented anywhere. All you have to do is look in Explorer.

Let's take a look at this now. Open Explorer. It doesn't matter what directory you're looking at or how it's configured. Use the View | Options command to display the Options dialog. Click on the File Types tab. Scroll through the file types until you come across an entry for Text Document. Highlight it and click on Edit. Click on Print and then Edit. You should see a display similar to the one in Figure 5.1.

Figure 5.1.
Windows 95 hides a wealth of information. Explorer is just one of the gold mines. It's a treasure hunt; make sure you spend enough time digging.

Now you can see where I came up with the /P parameter. Press Cancel three times to get back to the main Explorer display. Every other registered application will provide the same types of information. Some of them will be a little too complex to use from the DOS prompt, but you could use them if you wanted to. The whole idea of this shortcut is that you get to stay at the DOS prompt and still use the new features that Windows provides.

> **Tip:** Just about every Windows application provides undocumented command-line switches. Even though you can only guess at what those switches are in most cases, you can usually count on them supporting one or two switches. The /P parameter almost always allows you to print using that application. Some applications also provide a /W parameter that suppresses the display of any opening screens. Looking through the Explorer file listings will provide you with additional ideas.

There are a few other caveats you need to consider. Notice how I formatted my command line. You have to place the START program command-line switches first, and then the application name, the application switches, and any filenames. If you change this order, the application will usually start, but it will report some type of error in opening your file. I've even had some applications insist that the file isn't present on my drive.

Shortcut Keys

After you spend some time with Windows 95, you'll discover that it's a lot more user-friendly than Windows 3.x. I find that I spend a lot less time at the DOS prompt now because I can get just about everything accomplished without it. However, that still doesn't make me happy about moving my hand from the keyboard to the mouse to start a new application.

Do you remember the first section of this chapter, where I talked about the Desktop and OLE? This is one of those times when that fact comes into play. To really make use of the shortcuts Windows 95 provides, you have to create a shortcut. It doesn't matter where the shortcut is, but it does matter that it's a shortcut.

> **Tip:** Every entry on the Start menu is a shortcut. If your application appears on the Start menu, you already have a shortcut to use. If it doesn't appear on the Start menu, you'll want to add it there or to the Desktop.

To get the ball rolling, let's look at the Notepad shortcut on the Start menu. All you need to do is open the Start menu (press Ctrl-Esc, then Esc), open the context menu (Shift-F10), and select Explore. Use a combination of the arrow keys and Enter to get to the Notepad shortcut. Press Shift-F10 to display Notepad's context menu. Select Properties and press Enter. You'll need to select the Shortcut tab. You should see a display similar to the one in Figure 5.2.

Figure 5.2.
The Shortcut tab of the Properties dialog allows you to add a shortcut key to an application or to another shortcut.

The Shortcut field of this dialog is where you enter the shortcut key combination you want to use. To save the setting, just close the dialog as normal. The next time you press that key combination, Windows 95 will open the application for you.

Startups from the Desktop

Windows 95 comes installed with several applications already on the Desktop. If you decide to install Exchange, you'll find it on the Desktop. The Microsoft Network icon is also connected to an application. Just like the Start menu, none of these icons represents the actual application. You create a shortcut to the application, just like you would for the Start menu.

Of course, the big question is why you would even consider adding an application shortcut to the Desktop. The big reason is convenience: It's faster to grab an application on the Desktop than to burrow through several layers of menu to find it. Of course, your Desktop has only so much space, so placing all your applications here would lead to a cluttered environment very quickly.

However, placing on the Desktop the one or two applications you use regularly could mean an increase in efficiency. Just think how nice it would be if your word processor or communications program were just a double-click away. You could open them as needed and close them immediately after you finished using them. This would mean that the applications you used most would still be handy, but they would be out of the way and wouldn't use up precious memory.

Tip: Keyboard users will probably get the same response time by using shortcut keys instead of placing their applications on the Desktop. Not only will this give you a neater-looking Desktop, but it will reduce the number of redundant links your computer has to maintain.

Placing a shortcut to your application on the Desktop might provide an increase in efficiency, but double-clicking isn't the only way to open an application. The next few sections describe other ways you can access your applications faster by placing shortcuts to them on the Desktop. We'll also look

at something new for Windows 95 in the section "The Data-Oriented Approach to Applications."
You really owe it to yourself to get out of the application-centric mode and take the new data-
centric approach.

Click Starts

Right-clicking is new to Windows 95. We took a quick look at the context menu in previous chapters. However, it's such an important concept that I felt we needed to take a special look at right-
clicking for applications. Figure 5.3 shows the context menu for an application.

Figure 5.3.
Right-clicking on an
application shortcut produces
this context menu.

To start an application this way, all you need to do is select the Open option. This has the same
effect as double-clicking, but it might be more convenient if you have slower fingers. Some people
really do have a hard time getting the double-click to work. This new method of starting an application has the advantage of requiring only a single click.

I was kind of curious about the Quick View option on this menu. If you select it, you'll see a dialog
similar to the one in Figure 5.4. The majority of the information here is stuff that only a programmer
could love. At first glance, you do see some useful information, such as the name of the program and
the version of Windows that it expects to find on your machine. You might even be able to use some
of the information here to determine the amount of memory that your application needs to run.

Figure 5.4.
The View option for
executable files provides
some interesting information
that you can use to learn
more about how the
application works.

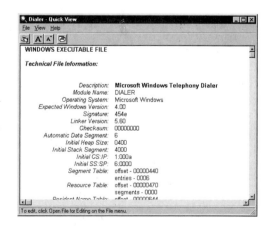

In reality, this isn't the information you want to see, because you can determine most of it using other methods. This view provides some special information that makes it easier for you to figure out which files to remove the next time you need to get rid of an old application. If you scroll down a bit, you'll notice a heading that says Imported-Name Table (Link-Time Imports), as shown in Figure 5.5.

Figure 5.5.
The Imported-Name Table heading is the one you really want to look at in this view.

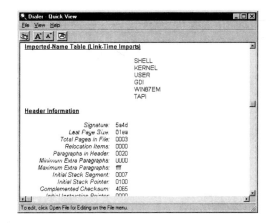

Look at the list of files underneath this heading. All of them are somewhere on your drive—usually in the application folder or the \WIN95\SYSTEM folder. Unlike Windows 3.1, where it took some major tinkering to discover the files you needed to run an application, Windows 95 makes this information easy to find.

Use this information when it comes time to remove an application from your system. This view will help you come up with a list of files you need to delete. Of course, you don't want to delete any files that another application needs, so you'll have to carefully prune this list so that it reflects only the files that are unique to a particular application. There's another problem with this list as well: It provides only one level of import file support. If one of the support files calls yet another group of files, you won't see that file here. Fortunately, you can also get to this view using other types of Windows executables. Make sure you look through the entire hierarchy before you consider your list of files complete.

This isn't the end of the story. There's another way to use this information to your advantage. Have you ever had an application that refused to start? It gave you a really cryptic message that looked like it was written in Klingon, then killed itself and perhaps a few other applications. Once you got past this point, Windows displayed that really helpful message about not finding one of the components needed to run the application. The Quick View dialog can help you get past this situation. Coming up with a list of DLLs and other support files needed by the application is the first step in getting it to run. Next, check the application and the \WIN95\SYSTEM directory. As soon as you find which one of the files is missing, replace it and, voilà, no more mystery message.

Auto Starts

If you used Windows 3.x, you probably used the Startup folder to run specific applications every time you started your machine. Windows 95 provides the same feature. All you need to do is add an application to the Startup folder to allow it to run automatically. I always start a copy of Explorer this way so that my machine is ready for use the instant Windows completes the boot process.

Windows 95 can do something that Windows 3.x couldn't. I usually drag the data files I'm going to be working on for the next few days into my Startup folder. The reason is simple: Not only do I automatically start the application associated with that data file, but I also automatically load the file itself. This makes morning startups extremely efficient. When I get back to Windows after starting it, my machine is completely set up for use. Every application I need is already loaded with the files I want to edit.

Peter's Principle: Becoming Too Efficient for Your Own Good

Have you ever seen the "ransom note" effect produced by someone who has just discovered the joy of using multiple fonts in a document? To that person, it looks like the most incredible document he has ever produced. The rest of us think the document is pretty incredible too, but not for the same reason.

You can get into the same kind of habit with Windows 95 and its advanced features. Consider the Startup folder. It would be very easy for people to load every document they think they'll use for the entire week in there so that the documents would be ready when they booted the machine the next morning.

The best way to use this feature is to think about what you plan to do first thing the next morning or perhaps for the majority of the day. Don't open more than two or perhaps three documents unless they all use the same application. Someone who works on the same document, such as a writer, can really benefit from this feature. People who create presentations or work on other documents for long periods of time can also benefit. However, if you work a little bit on one document and then a little bit on another one, you might be better off starting the main application you use and letting it go at that.

So, how do you add entries to the Startup folder? Just as you would with any other folder. The following procedure shows you a quick way to do it using some of the new features that Windows 95 provides.

1. Right-click the Taskbar to display the context menu. Select the Properties option. Click on the Start Menu Programs tab. You should see the Taskbar Properties dialog, shown in Figure 5.6.

2. Click on the Add pushbutton. You should see the Create Shortcut dialog, shown in Figure 5.7.

Figure 5.6.

The Taskbar Properties dialog allows you to add new programs to the Start menu using a menu-driven interface.

Figure 5.7.

The Create Shortcut dialog is where you provide the name of the application or file that you want to add to the Startup folder (or another folder).

3. Click on the Browse pushbutton to look for the file you want to add. As an alternative, you can type the full path and filename right into the Command line field of this dialog. Click on Next. You should see the Select Program Folder dialog, shown in Figure 5.8. This dialog allows you to select the location of the shortcut in the Start menu. In this case, we'll select the Startup folder, but you could just as easily select something else. Notice that you can add a new folder as well.

Figure 5.8.

The Select Program Folder dialog box.

4. Scroll through the list of folders and highlight the Startup folder. Click on Next. You should see the Select a Title for the Program dialog, shown in Figure 5.9. This is the final dialog of the process. It allows you to change the name of the shortcut. Using a name you

can remember is the best idea. Changing the name here won't change the name of the file, only the shortcut.

Figure 5.9.
The Select a Title for the Program dialog box.

5. Type the name you want associated with this file. This is the entry as it will appear in the Startup folder. This won't affect the actual name of the file.

6. Click on Finish to complete the task, and then click on OK to close the Taskbar Properties dialog.

Once you complete this task, the application or data file you added to the Startup folder will load automatically each time you start Windows 95. Getting your system set up efficiently means that you can do a little extra reading or perform some other task while you wait for everything to load. Of course, adding a file to the load sequence won't make it load faster, but it will give you a bigger block of time.

Controlled Starts

We won't spend a lot of time on this category of starting your application because you're already familiar with most of what you can do here. Everyone is familiar with double-clicking on an application to start it. The fact that Windows 95 provides so many places to double-click doesn't really change the mechanics one iota. It might be useful, though, to take a quick look at the number of ways you can double-click to start an application. The following list does just that.

-   Explorer: You can double-click on an application or its associated data file. This interface also supports DDE, something I had trouble with when using File Manager. Of course, Program Manager doesn't support DDE at all.

-   Program Manager: Like Explorer, you can double-click on any application.

-   File Manager: Like Explorer, you can double-click on any application or its associated data file. However, the interface isn't quite as flexible as that provided by Explorer. You'll find that DDE is hard to implement.

-   Find: The Find dialog comes in very handy. You can look for a data file and then double-click on it to bring up the application associated with it. I've also used this dialog as a quick method of finding the program I need.

- Desktop: Any data file or application sitting on the Desktop follows the same rules as Explorer does.
- Network Neighborhood: You can double-click on any application or file sitting on someone else's machine.

Tip: Double-clicking under Windows 3.x always meant that you started the application. There's no such limitation under Windows 95. You can assign other default actions to an application or its data folder. For example, instead of unzipping when I double-click on a .ZIP file, I view its contents instead. You could make opening and printing the default action for a word processing file instead of just opening. The actual number of ways you can use this feature is fairly unlimited.

Well, that's the long and short of double-clicking. You can always use the old controlled start (double-click) method we all know and love to start an application. I hope this section provided some food for thought on other—perhaps better—ways of using the Windows 95 interface.

The Data-Oriented Approach to Applications

Windows 95 really shines when it comes to data. In fact, the whole interface is oriented toward data-centric access. You can force it to work the older Windows 3.x way, but Windows 95 will give you a lot less grief and a lot more efficiency if you start thinking about your data first and your application second. The next few sections discuss some of the tools that Windows 95 provides to make a data-oriented approach a lot easier.

Using Explorer to Get the Job Done

We've taken a long, hard look at Explorer in several of the sections of this book already. However, we haven't really taken a good look at one important feature. No longer are you tied to one specific action when it comes to data on your machine. If you've looked at the various context menus I presented in this and other sections, you'll notice that there's always more than one thing you can do to a particular file.

What you might not have realized is that the actions you saw are all under your control. You don't have to do things the Windows 95 way; you can do them any way that feels comfortable and allows you to get your work done faster. This is a nice change from the rather rigid tools Windows 3.x provided. Let's take a look at how you can add a new file extension and then define a set of actions associated with that file.

> **Tip:** The first time you double-click on a file that lacks a file association, Windows 95 will ask which application you want to use to open it. You can choose an application that is already on the list or use the browse feature to find a new one. Windows 95 defines only one action for this new association—open. Always take the time to modify that file association and add options for all the ways you plan to work with it. That way, the context menu associated with it will be completely set up the next time you right-click on the file or any like it.

1. Open a copy of Explorer.
2. Use the View | Options command to open the Options dialog. Click on the File Types tab. You should see a dialog similar to the one shown in Figure 5.10.

Figure 5.10.

The File Types tab of the Options dialog allows you to add, remove, and modify file associations.

3. Click on New Type to display the New Type dialog.
4. Fill in the first two fields as shown in Figure 5.11. The first field describes what kind of file it is. This is the text you'll see in various list boxes. The second field contains the exact file extension.

Figure 5.11.

The Add New File Type dialog contains several fields that you use to describe a file's association to an application.

Tip: One problem you might run into is thinking about file extensions in the DOS/ Windows 3.x format. Remember that Windows 95 supports long filenames, including long file extensions, as shown in Figure 5.11. You can define new file extensions that are more than three characters long. Windows 95 even allows some alternative characters in this format. For example, you could have a file extension of Word_Document if you wanted to. One character you need to avoid is the period (for obvious reasons).

5. Now we need to define some actions for this association. Click on the New pushbutton. Fill out the information as shown in Figure 5.12. This is just one way to fill out this dialog. Wordpad uses a command-line interface, so all you need to do is fill out the Application used to perform action section of the dialog. Click on OK.

6. Create the same kind of entry for Notepad. Make sure you substitute NOTEPAD.EXE for the location and change the path as necessary. Also change the Action to read Open with Notepad.

Figure 5.12.
This dialog shows one type of file association entry. It uses command-line parameters.

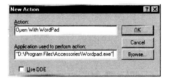

7. Click on the New pushbutton. Fill out the information as shown in Figure 5.13. This second type of association might look overly complicated, but it really isn't. It's the DDE format of a file association and an extremely powerful way to manage your data files. The DDE instructions form what equates to macros. They actually force the application to perform the same types of tasks that you would accomplish using a menu or the product's built-in macro capability. We'll discuss this topic at greater length in Chapter 11. Right now, suffice it to say that if your application provides DDE support, you really owe it to yourself to use it. Click on OK.

Figure 5.13.
This dialog shows the second type of association you can create. This DDE entry allows you to include macro-like instructions that control the way the application opens or works with the file.

8. Create the DDE dialog shown in Figure 5.14 to add some additional support for this new file association. This DDE macro allows you to print the file using Microsoft Word. The DDE Application Not Running field is incomplete in the figure because it was too long to fit in the area provided. Here is the complete entry: `[FileOpen(""%1"")][FilePrint.Background = 0][FileExit(2)]`. After you finish this entry, click on OK. Your Add New File Type dialog should now look like the one shown in Figure 5.15. Notice the two checkboxes near the bottom of the dialog. The second allows you to display the file extension at all times. Normally you would leave this off to make it easier to rename files in Explorer without accidentally changing their extensions. Since this is an ASCII file, you would probably turn on the first checkbox, Enable Quick View. This will allow you to use the Quick View utility provided with Windows 95.

Figure 5.14.
The previous DDE File showed you how to open the file. This one shows you how to print it using the same type of macro commands.

Figure 5.15.
Here are the completed entries for this Add New File Type dialog box.

9. Highlight Open With NotePad and click on Set Default. This sets the double-click action for the file type. You can right-click to display the full context menu and use a different application to open the file, but this is the default action. You might also want to change the icon. I used the Notepad icon, but you could use any of those provided by the applications in this group or within an icon file. Click on Close to complete the process. Click on Close to close the Options dialog.

10. Create a new file with an extension of .ASCII. I placed my copy on the Desktop for sample purposes, but you could put your copy anywhere.

11. Right-click on the file. You should see a list of opening options similar to the ones shown in Figure 5.16. Notice that Open With NotePad is highlighted, indicating that this entry is the default setting.

Figure 5.16.
The final result of our new file association is an extended context menu that allows any one of three applications to open the file.

There are a few additional things you could do to really extend this new file association. Chapter 6 will tell you all about the registry and the file association entries there. Pay special attention to the section "Special Extension Subkeys." Since we just added a new text file entry to the list of file associations, you could use the registry to add a ShellX entry to it as well. That way, when you right-clicked on the Desktop or within Explorer, you would see the new file extension as one of the files you could create using the New option of the context menu. In most cases, there won't be a convenient method to add this support, but you should use it whenever possible.

This example also shows you something else. Productivity under Windows 95 is as much a matter of how you configure the Desktop and the file associations as it is anything else. Being able to really use your machine's speed is what this data-centric approach to computing is all about.

Folders: A Real Organizational Tool

I really hate it when someone creates a new name for something I've been using for a long time. It's like throwing out a perfectly useable set of clothes because fashion has changed or giving someone a new title in order to be politically correct. That's how I used to feel about the use of the term *folder* under Windows 95. As far as I was concerned, it was a new name for directories.

Nothing could be further from the truth. Folders are not directories. They might look similar and provide about the same functionality when viewed from a certain perspective, but folders really do provide some features that directories don't. I'm still not as happy as I could be about the name switch, but at least it makes sense.

So, how do folders help you work efficiently? Figure 5.17 shows one way. Folders support a context menu. Like most of the objects in Windows 95, you can open and explore them. This isn't really all that surprising by now. I *was* a little surprised, however, when I saw that you could copy and paste folders just like any other object. Putting a group of files in a folder allows you to move an entire project from place to place or make a copy of the data for someone else to use. It's actually faster to use folders than it is to type the required commands at the DOS prompt—something I thought I would never see.

Figure 5.17.
*The Folder context menu
tells it all when it comes to
the intelligence that this new
form of directory possesses.*

The Sharing option of the context menu allows you to share the folder with other folks on the network. I'll cover this feature in greater detail in Chapter 19.

You'll find the Send To option very useful. This option allows you to place the folder somewhere
else. Default locations include the floppy drives and your Briefcase. You can even send the folder to
Microsoft Exchange. Imagine using e-mail to send the folder to a partner or coworker who needs to
see the information you've put together so far. Unlike past experiences in which I had to get all the
files together and zip them up, this option is fairly convenient and really makes the work flow
smoother.

I use the Create Shortcut option to create a link to the existing file. Then I move the shortcut to my
Desktop or some other convenient place. Each shortcut uses 1 KB of memory, a small price to pay
for the convenience they provide.

We'll cover the Properties option in greater detail in Chapters 9 and 19. For right now, suffice it to
say that files and folders share many of the same characteristics. The Properties dialog will reflect
this fact.

Desktop Tips and Techniques

I've gone to a totally data-centric approach on my Desktop when it comes to projects. All I do is
create a folder, give it a project name, and then gather shortcuts to everything I need for that project
in that folder. It doesn't matter anymore where the data resides or what application I need to use to
open the file. The only important element is that I have a data file that needs editing, so I open the
project folder and double-click on its icon.

This data-centric approach is very important for managers. Think about the time you'll save by putting
one folder together, then mailing that folder to all the people who have to work on it. You control

the location of the data and the type of access these people have to it. They need to know only that the data exists and that they can access it as needed. All the other information that you needed when working under DOS or Windows 3.x is no longer important.

Of course, like everything else under Windows 95, all is not perfect with the total data-centric approach. Even Microsoft agrees with me on this issue. They placed your InBox, Recycle Bin, My Computer, and Network Neighborhood on the Desktop for a reason. There are times when you need to open an application instead of a piece of data.

I keep my communications program handy on the Desktop. I can't really access any of its data from outside the application. My database manager sits on the Desktop too, but that's for a different reason. I use Access to design databases more often than I use it for data entry, so, for me, it's really more important to work with the application.

You'll probably run into situations in which the application is more important than the data. The bottom line is that you should try to work with the data first. If this proves to be an inconvenient solution, the data-centric approach probably isn't correct for that situation. The following is a list of some of the types of data I work with using the project folder approach I just described. You'll probably have some of these applications too.

- Word processing: Every word processor is designed to primarily work with data, so it makes a perfect candidate for the data-centric approach. Microsoft Word even appears on the New submenu of the context menu, so there isn't any problem with creating new files without entering the word processor first. There's one minor inconvenience here: Word always creates a new document using the Normal stylesheet. This means that if I use the context menu to create a new file, I'll probably have to change the template after I open the file. It's a minor flaw, but an irritating one all the same.

- Spreadsheet: I very seldom open just one spreadsheet. If I open one at all, I'm in there for hours. Therefore, I stick all my major files into a folder and place it on my Desktop. That way, I can at least open a data file that will stay open throughout most of the editing session. I usually end up opening the other files I need in the usual way—using File | Open.

- Graphics: I work with quite a few different types of graphics, each of which requires its own application. Keeping the graphics files in a folder and opening them that way makes perfect sense. In fact, it's actually one of the application types that really made me see the value of a data-centric approach. By the way, this is one place where you'll really want to enable the Quick View option if you haven't already. Most graphics files are time-consuming to load. Having Quick View handy for the files that it supports can really save you time.

On Your Own

Try adding a shortcut to the Startup folder on your Desktop. Place any work that you'll need to do tomorrow there tonight. Watch what happens when you start your machine tomorrow morning. You should get a Desktop that has all the work you need to do loaded automatically.

Start separating your work into projects if possible. Place each project in a separate folder on the Desktop. Use separate folders if necessary to make it easier to find a particular kind of data. For example, you might need to place your graphics files in one subfolder to keep them from crowding the text files.

Look through your drives for data files that Windows 95 can't associate with a particular application. Add any new file extensions that you might need to Explorer using the procedure discussed earlier. Check out each new association as you add it. Does the new addition work as anticipated? Evaluate the results you get after a few weeks to see if you need to add more options to the data file's context menu.

III

The
Windows 95
Anatomy

6

The
Windows 95
Architecture

Windows 95 uses an architecture that borrows from the past while embracing the future. Many of the components you've come to know and hate in Windows 3.x are still present in Windows 95. Some people think DOS has gone completely away, but it's still there under the covers. The 16-bit interface that gave us so much grief under Windows 3.x is still there, too.

That's the bad news. The good news is the problems that plagued users in the past are a lot less noticeable under Windows 95. DOS isn't present at every turn—Windows 95 actually uses it very little once you start it up (depending on some very specific conditions that I'll explain later). The 16-bit interface is augmented by new 32-bit underpinnings. You can actually get some decent performance from Windows 95 and a moderate level of application protection as well. All these new features make Windows 95 better than Windows 3.x, but it's still far from the perfect operating system if reliability is your main concern.

Windows NT is the operating system that provides the entirely new way of doing things—few people would say it shares the same stability problems that have made Windows 3.x almost unusable in mission-critical situations—but it falls short on one count. It just isn't as compatible as the average user needs it to be. Just try to play a DOS game using Windows NT, and you'll see what I mean. The types of security required to make Windows NT or any other operating system stable also prevent it from running some types of ill-behaved applications. Windows 95 represents a halfway point—you get some added stability and a new 32-bit capability and still keep the compatibility that most people need to make Windows really work on a workstation.

We'll examine the details of all these architectural wonders in the following sections. I'll show you the great and the not-so-great components that make Windows 95 better than Windows 3.x ever thought of being, but a lot less than it could be. This chapter will also provide a few additional glimpses of what Windows could become in the future. It's important to realize that even with all its flaws, Windows 95 is a step in the right direction. It really does show how workstation operating systems will evolve in the future.

Windows 95 Compatibility Configuration Files

There's no doubt about it: Windows 95 starts by booting DOS. You can even gain access to this "raw" DOS (as Microsoft calls it) using a variety of methods—some sanctioned, some not. Microsoft had to provide the four compatibility files that older applications need in order to run. Some of these files are easy to bypass; others won't go away until you get rid of all those applications. Part of the reason DOS is still hanging around is because of these compatibility files. Windows 95 has to boot using real mode so that it can read and process both CONFIG.SYS and AUTOEXEC.BAT. There are other reasons that Windows 95 boots into real mode, and we'll examine them later in this chapter.

The following sections take an in-depth look at the four compatibility files: AUTOEXEC.BAT, CONFIG.SYS, SYSTEM.INI, and WIN.INI. I'll show you that even though Microsoft doesn't want to admit it, Windows 95 still needs at least one of these files to work properly. Fortunately, you really only need this one compatibility file—SYSTEM.INI—to run Windows 95. The other files are there for compatibility purposes only.

Note: You could probably boot Windows 95 without keeping any of the four compatibility files and expect it to work sometimes. The majority of your 16-bit applications wouldn't run because they couldn't find the information stored in the compatibility files. A lot of Windows applications also require that the path statement contain an entry that points to their files. Even if you avoid running any 16-bit applications, it's unlikely that you'll keep Windows 95 running for very long without SYSTEM.INI. For reasons I don't understand, there are still system settings that Microsoft chose to store there. These system settings are important to Windows 95, no matter which applications you decide to run.

AUTOEXEC.BAT

This is the one file you could get rid of if you didn't have any 16-bit Windows applications that required a path statement. Windows 95 provides the means for defining a path and a prompt and loading any TSRs that a DOS application might require to run. The most efficient way to use Windows 95 is to not load anything a DOS application would need here.

Use AUTOEXEC.BAT only for settings you need on a global basis or as part of the requirement for running an older Windows application. Some 16-bit Windows applications require SET and PATH entries to run. This is especially true of compilers and advanced applications.

Looking Ahead: We'll look at how you can replace both CONFIG.SYS and AUTOEXEC.BAT for DOS applications in Chapter 12. If your only reason for keeping these two files around is so you can run DOS applications, consider the faster alternative presented here.

The following list contains a few things you should never run from AUTOEXEC.BAT. Most of these items consume memory before you load Windows—memory you can't retrieve later. Using this technique might cost you a little conventional memory for your DOS applications, but you'll still have about the same or perhaps even more than you had available under Windows 3.x. The reason for this is simple: You don't have to load a bunch of drivers in CONFIG.SYS to make Windows 95 run.

- TSRs: Try to avoid running any TSRs from AUTOEXEC.BAT. A small utility such as DOSKey might not appear to consume much memory, but why run it from AUTOEXEC.BAT at all? You can easily customize the settings for your DOS applications. Those that will never use DOSKey don't need to give up the memory required to install it. In essence, loading a TSR in AUTOEXEC.BAT penalizes the applications that can't use it.

- DOS application environment variables: If you have a DOS application that requires a path entry or other environmental variables, load them as part of its special configuration rather than as part of AUTOEXEC.BAT. You can individually adjust the size of the environment for each DOS application you run.

- DOS applications with Windows counterparts: I used to run CHKDSK as part of every startup cycle. A lot of other people do the same thing. Running some DOS applications before you enter Windows doesn't harm the amount of memory you have available one iota. Running other applications can consume memory. For example, if you run MODE to change your screen size to 43 lines before you enter Windows, every DOS program you load will consume 43 lines worth of memory (more if you ask for a larger screen in the custom settings). You can reduce the memory required for each DOS session by using the application's custom screen settings.

- Disk or printer caching software: You'll find that Windows 95's disk and print caching services are far superior to those provided with Windows 3.x. The memory allocated to these services is dynamic—Windows 95 can increase and decrease the amount of memory used as needed—as long as you use the Windows 95-specific capability. When you load disk or print caching software in AUTOEXEC.BAT, you lose the ability to control the size of that cache within Windows (in most cases). Even if you could change the size of the cache, it's unlikely that Windows 95 could use it unless the caching program is specially designed to communicate with Windows.

CONFIG.SYS

Unless you're still playing Russian roulette with those real-mode drivers on your system, you can get rid of CONFIG.SYS. Windows 95 provides its own extended memory manager (EMM), so it doesn't need one loaded like Windows 3.x did. Windows 95 also takes care of the BUFFERS, LASTDRIVE, and STACKS entries for you. In other words, CONFIG.SYS is out of a job unless you give it one.

I recently threw caution to the wind and tried booting my system for several days with a pared-down AUTOEXEC.BAT and no CONFIG.SYS. Not only did I notice a speed increase when loading Windows, but I also had far greater control over the settings for each individual DOS setting. Windows also could provide much better memory control than before. (I used the Monitor utility described in Chapter 3 to check all this out.)

I had to deal with a few negatives, however. Getting rid of CONFIG.SYS lost me about 5 KB of conventional memory. I still have 600 KB of RAM available in a DOS window, though, so the memory loss is pretty minimal. I could probably get even more available memory by decreasing the environment size and not loading DOSKey as part of my custom settings. It also cost me some time to set each of my DOS applications up. The greater flexibility and better memory management came at the cost of increased complexity. Even though there were negative elements, I'd still say it was worth the effort.

Tip: In the past, users with large hard drives usually resorted to using special drivers such as those from OnTrack Systems to access their entire drive using one partition. You can still do this under Windows 95 with relative success. However, such an action will destabilize your system. The reason is clear. Whenever Windows needs to access the drive, it must switch to real mode in order to access the real-mode driver. It's probably a better idea to partition your drive into more manageable partition sizes and get rid of the real-mode drivers if at all possible.

WIN.INI

Windows 95 can get along just fine without WIN.INI. However, before you get rid of your file, you might want to check it out first. A few applications, especially screen savers, load themselves using the LOAD= or RUN= lines of this file. You can get around this limitation by adding the filenames to your Startup folder and changing the application settings as needed.

Many applications also store their file association information here. Windows 95 applications don't need these entries, because they already appear in the registry. Any new 32-bit applications will know to look in the registry for file association information, but some older 16-bit applications won't. You might want to check for problems by saving a copy of WIN.INI under a different name and then editing out the [Extensions] section. If all your applications seem to work properly, you might be able to remove this section for good.

Note: Windows 95 always checks for new entries in both WIN.INI and SYSTEM.INI. It automatically adds any new entries that it finds to the appropriate section of the registry. This is why you can get rid of these two files if you have a stable system and none of the 16-bit applications that you use relies on them. Of course, that's a big if, and you still have the mysterious Windows 95 problem with SYSTEM.INI to deal with. In reality, you'll probably need to wait until you've gotten rid of all your 16-bit applications before you can get rid of these two files.

If you look through the Windows 95 version of WIN.INI, you'll notice that it's a lot slimmer. Microsoft moved all the Windows-specific information that this file contained into the registry. Windows 95 doesn't use it at all. In fact, if you compare the contents of the registry to a Windows 3.x version of WIN.INI, you'll find every entry that the old file contained.

SYSTEM.INI

Getting rid of SYSTEM.INI will take a major miracle. Just about every application on my machine sticks something in there. Even Microsoft still uses this file—though they swear they don't. Most of these settings have become so standard that other applications read the file in anticipation of finding out about the environment.

Of course, this is one source of the problem. Getting rid of SYSTEM.INI or even excluding some of the settings would break a lot of applications out there. Part of the goal of Windows 95 is to provide the compatibility people need out of a workstation. Windows NT is the place to go if you need reliability and stability. Microsoft probably made the right call by keeping SYSTEM.INI in place and up-to-date.

Note: Microsoft is spending a great deal of time telling programmers not to place anything in SYSTEM.INI anymore. The registry is the new way to store all of these settings. A quick look at SYSTEM.INI, though, shows some Windows 95-specific information there. For example, look near the bottom of the file and you'll see entries for passwords and VCache. These two entries don't appear in Windows 3.x-specific versions of the file.

The Registry: The New Method of Configuration

We started to take a look at the registry in Chapter 1. That section covered just some of the main topics. This chapter will get into the meat of the registry—the low-level tips and techniques you can use to really check your system out. Hopefully you read and understood the overview I presented. If not, you might want to take this opportunity to read it again.

The registry is a complex piece of software. Windows 95 can't boot without a clean registry. Any corruption in this file will cause a host of problems even if Windows 95 does manage to boot. Of course, the fact that you can't edit this file at the DOS prompt is another potential problem. (The other side of the coin is that the Windows 95 registry editor is a lot easier to use than the old Windows 3.x combination of WIN.INI and SYSTEM.INI.)

Tip: Windows 95 stores the previous copy of your registry in the USER.DA0 and SYSTEM.DA0 files. If you make a mistake in editing the registry, exit immediately, shut Windows 95 down, and boot into DOS mode. Change directories to your Windows 95 main directory. Use the ATTRIB utility to make the SYSTEM.DA0, SYSTEM.DAT, USER.DA0, and USER.DAT files visible by using the -R, -H, and -S switches. Now copy the backup of your registry to the two original files (that is, SYSTEM.DA0 to SYSTEM.DAT and USER.DA0 to USER.DAT). This will restore your registry to its pre-edit state. Make sure you restore the previous file attribute state by using the +R, +H, and +S switches of the ATTRIB utility.

I presented an overview of the nuts and bolts of the registry in Chapter 1, but I never really said anything about what it could do for you. When you look at the registry, you're seeing a complete definition of Windows 95 as it relates to your specific machine. Not only does the registry contain hardware and application settings, but it also contains every other piece of information you can imagine about your machine. You can learn a lot about Windows by simply looking at the information presented by this application. For example, did you know you can use multiple Desktops in Windows 95? Of course, that leads to another problem: maintaining those separate Desktops. The hierarchical format presented by the registry editor helps the administrator compare the differences between the various Desktops. It also allows the administrator to configure them with ease. Best of all, editing the registry doesn't involve a session with a text editor. Windows provides a GUI editor that the administrator can use to change the settings in the registry.

Knowing that the registry contains a lot of information and is easy to edit still doesn't tell you what it can do for you. When was the last time you used the Explorer to check out your hard drive? I use it a lot because it provides an easy way to find what I need. The registry can help you make Explorer easier to use. One of my favorite ways to use it for Explorer modifications is to create multiple associations for the same file type. Suppose you want to associate a graphics editor with .PCX and .BMP files. This isn't too difficult. However, what if each file type requires a different set of command-line switches? Now you get into an area where using the registry can really help. Using the registry to edit these entries can help you customize file access.

Note: You should add the registry editor, RegEdit, to your Start menu before proceeding. It helps to look at the actual registry entries as you read about them. I'll also present some exercises that will help you understand the inner workings of the registry better. See Chapter 9 if you need information about adding new applications to the Start menu.

A Centralized Database of Setup Information

It's time to take a look at how the registry is organized. To start the registry editor, simply open RegEdit as you would any other application on the Start menu. You'll probably get a lot more out of the detailed discussion that follows if you actually open the registry editor now. Using the registry editor to see how Windows 95 arranges the various entries can make using it a lot easier in an emergency.

I always step lightly when it comes to the registry. You might want to follow the same procedure I use to back up the registry before you go much further. The big advantage of this method is that it produces a text file that you can view with any text editor. (The file is huge, so Notepad won't handle it, but Wordpad will.) You can use this backup file to restore the registry later if you run into difficulty. Unfortunately, this method won't help much if you permanently destroy the registry and reboot the machine. Windows 95 needs a clean registry to boot. To preserve a clean, bootable copy of the registry, you need to copy the USER.DAT and SYSTEM.DAT files to a safe location.

Warning: RegEdit is an application designed to assist experienced users in changing Windows 95 and associated application behavior. Although it will allow you to enhance system performance and make applications easier to use, it can cause unexpected results when misused. Never edit an entry unless you know what that entry is for. Failure to observe this precaution can result in data loss and even prevent your system from booting the next time you start Windows 95.

1. Highlight the My Computer entry of the registry. Select Registry | Export Registry File, as shown in Figure 6.1.

Figure 6.1.
The Registry menu allows you to import and export registry settings.

2. You should see an Export Registry File dialog box similar to the one shown in Figure 6.2. Notice that the File name field already contains a name. You can use any name you wish. I selected OLDENTRY to designate a pre-edited registry. Notice that the All radio button is selected in the Export Range group.

Figure 6.2.
*The Export Registry File
dialog allows you to save
your current registry settings.*

3. Click on the Save button to place a copy of the registry on disk. The OLDENTRY.REG file in your main Windows 95 directory now contains a complete copy of your original registry.

HKEY_CLASSES_ROOT

I introduced this category in Chapter 1. It's the one you will probably change the most often. Don't let the deceptively simple appearance of this category fool you. To refresh your memory, there are two types of entries in this category. The first key type (remember, a key is a RegEdit topic) is a file extension. The second key type is the file association. These are the two obvious key types. We'll explore a third key type a bit later.

Tip: You should always change your application file entries to make your working environment as efficient as possible. However, you should never change an executable file association. Changing an executable file extension such as .DLL could make it hard for Windows 95 to start your applications or could even crash the system. We'll look at the procedure for changing an application file association in the "Modifying File Associations" section of this chapter.

Special Extension Subkeys

Some file extensions such as .TXT provide a ShellX subkey (see Figure 6.3). In the case of .TXT and .DOC, the standard subkey is ShellNew (the most common key). The term ShellX means "shell extension." I like to think of it as an automated method of extending the functionality of Windows as a whole. When you right-click on the Desktop and look at the New option on the context menu, all the types of files you can create are the result of shell extensions. Even though ShellNew is the most common type of shell extension, a variety of other shell extensions are available. The actual number is limited only by your application vendor. For example, Microsoft Excel provides no less than three different shell extension entries for the .XLS file extension.

Figure 6.3.

The shell extension is a pow-
erful OLE 2 feature that few
applications implement.

A shell extension is an OLE hook into Windows 95. Only an application that supports OLE 2 extensions can place a ShellX key into the registry; don't add one of these keys on your own. When you see this key, you know that the application provides some type of extended OLE-related functionality. For example, if you double-click on a shortcut to a data file that no longer exists, an application with the ShellNew shell extension will ask if you want to create a new file of the same type. (If you look at the values associated with ShellNew, there's always a NullFile entry that tells the shell extension what type of file to create.)

Tip: Sometimes a file type won't appear on the context menu even though the application provides support for it. Most of the time it happens with 16-bit applications that don't install correctly. You can use the shell extension behavior to create new files as if the context menu entry did exist. All you need to do is create a temporary file, place a shortcut to it on your Desktop, and erase the temporary file. (Make certain that the application provides a ShellNew shell extension before you do this.) Whenever you double-click on the shortcut, your application will create a new file for you. This behavior also works if you place the file shortcut in the Start menu folder.

There are other, more generic, shell extensions as well. For example, the * extension has a generic Shellex subkey. Below this you'll see a PropertySheetHandler key and a 128-digit key that looks like some kind of secret code. Actually, the 128-digit value *is* a secret code. It's a reference identifier for the DLL (a type of application) that takes care of the * extension. You'll find this key under the CLSID key. (CLSID stands for "class identifier.") The secret code is for the OLE Docfile Property

Page. Looking at the value of the next key will tell you it exists in DOCPROP.DLL. This DLL provides the dialog that asks which application you want to use to open a file when no registry entry is associated with that extension.

As you can see, shell extensions are a powerful addition to the Windows 95 registry. Suffice it to say that you shouldn't change or delete shell extensions; let the application take care of them for you.

OLE 1 and OLE 2 Registry Entries

Windows 95 provides both OLE 1 and OLE 2 support; so do many of the applications. To show you just how organized the registry is, the OLE 1 and OLE 2 entries appear in different areas. You can always tell what kind of OLE support an application provides by checking its registry entries. If you see registry entries in one area of the registry, you know that the application provides OLE 1 support. Registry entries in a second area of the registry show that the application provides OLE 2 support. In fact, the registry will often tell you more than the application's documentation does. You might find by looking at the registry that the application supports certain verbs. A verb in OLE is like a verb in a sentence: It represents a type of action that you can perform using the application's OLE capabilities. I'll tell you more about verbs later. Windows always places OLE 1 support information in the file association area. (I'll show you where OLE 2 support appears in the registry after we look at OLE 1.) Figure 6.4 shows a typical setup, but the actual setup varies between applications. Table 6.1 describes the various entries in this area (plus a few not supported by this particular application). The OLE support provided by each application on your machine will probably differ from that shown in Figure 6.4. This is only a sample for you to look at right now. Table 6.1 talks about all the potential OLE 1 entries you might find. I don't think any application uses them all.

Figure 6.4.
Windows places OLE 1 support in the file association area of the registry.

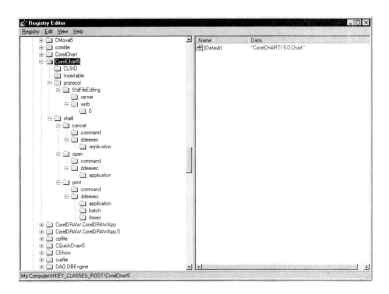

Table 6.1. OLE 1 entries in the Windows registry.

Entry	Description
CLSID	This is actually part of the OLE 2 entry even though it appears in the OLE 1 section. It's a pointer to an entry in the CLSID section of the category. C programmers use a special application to generate this 128-digit "magic number." If you look for this number under the CLSID key (as we'll do in just a bit), you'll find the OLE 2 entries for this file association.
Insertable	Normally you won't see any value associated with this key. A blank value means that Windows can place this file association in the Insert Object (or equivalent) dialog provided by many applications, such as Word for Windows. Some OLE 1 objects aren't insertable for a variety of reasons.
Protocol	This is a header key. Underneath it you'll find all the standard actions that this OLE 1 application can perform. The only supported function in most cases is a standard file edit.
StdFileEditing	This key is another header. In this case it's the heading for all the keys that will define a particular action—standard file editing.
Server	You'll find the name of the application Windows will call to service any OLE 1 calls for this file association. The string always includes the application's name, extension, and path. If you ever run into a situation in which your OLE links worked yesterday but won't work today, check this value to make certain the path matches the actual application location.
Verb	Several verbs are associated with an OLE 1 object. Each verb defines a specific action that the server will perform. This key doesn't have a value associated with it; its sole purpose is to organize actual verb entries. A client application can use only the verbs that are defined for a specific server.
	−3 = Hide, 0, 1 This verb allows the client application to hide the server window. The first number following the verb is a menu flag. The second number is the verb flag. As a user, you don't need to worry about either value as long as you supply the values shown here (or use the settings provided by the vendor).

Entry	Description
	−2 = Open, 0, 1 This verb allows the client to open the server in a separate window rather than allow it to take over the client window.
	−1 = Show, 0, 1 A client would use this verb to display the server window in its preferred state. The whole idea of a state can get to be quite complex. Think of it as the way the window looks, and you'll have a pretty good idea of what to expect from a user's point of view.
	0 = &Edit, 0, 2 Every server provides this verb. It allows the client to call the server to edit the object.
	1 = &Play, 0, 3 The only time you'll see this verb is when you're looking at some form of multimedia object.
RequestDataFormats	This entry allows the server to define what data formats it supports for retrieval purposes.
SetDataFormats	This entry allows the server to define what data formats it supports for storage purposes.

While you're still looking at this OLE 1 entry, you'll notice that I didn't cover anything under the Shell key. Each of these entries defines an action you can perform on the file using Explorer. The shell key is a refinement of the same entry used for file associations by File Manager. The entries defined here will appear on the context menu for each file of that type. We looked at the actual process of defining a file association with Explorer in Chapter 5. We'll also cover a registry-specific technique later in this chapter.

Now it's time to look at the OLE 2 part of the registry. You'll find these entries under the HKEY_CLASSES_ROOT | CLSID key. Each 128-digit number here represents a specific class (a programmer's term for a specific type of object) of information. Not all of the entries under the HKEY_CLASSES_ROOT | CLSID key are OLE 2 entries, but some of them are. You'll also find that not every application supports OLE 2. Your first clue that CorelChart supports it is the CLSID entry in the OLE 1 section. (We talked about the HKEY_CLASSES_ROOT | CorelChart5 | CLSID key in Table 6.1, and you saw it in Figure 6.4.) The HKEY_CLASSES_ROOT | CorelChart5 | CLSID entry is a pointer to the OLE 2 entry under the CLSID key. Figure 6.5 shows this key for CorelChart—the same application I used to describe an OLE 1 registry entry. Table 6.2 describes these entries in detail. An application doesn't necessarily need to provide every entry that I describe in Table 6.2 in the registry. It depends on what OLE 2 features the application vendor decided to support. You can use these registry entries to determine the capabilities of your application, just like you can with OLE 1.

Figure 6.5.

Windows places OLE 2
support in the file association
area of the registry.

Table 6.2. OLE 2 entries in the Windows registry.

Entry	Description
AuxUserType	This key is a heading for all the user type keys that follow.
2	The 2 AuxUserType always contains the short name for the application. A client can use this name in a list box to identify the object's owner.
3	This key contains the full name of the application that created the object. Like the 2 key, a client could use the 3 key value to provide an English application name for the object.
DataFormats	This key is a heading for all the data format keys that follow.
GetSet	This key is a subheading for all the data formats the server can store and retrieve. For example, an OLE server such as Word for Windows would support a DOC, RTF, and standard text format. Its OLE 2 entries would reflect this fact. Each entry below this one defines a specific format type:

Entry	Description
n = format, aspect, medium, flag	Each of the sequentially numbered keys contains a different format. Format contains the type of format as a string. You might find some as easy to understand as "Rich TextFormat" or as cryptic as "Embed Source." In every case, this string tells you the name of the format that the application supports. The client displays this string (for get formats) in the dialog box where you select the format you want to use when performing a Paste Special command. Aspect tells the client what display orientation the object supports. This usually means portrait and/or landscape. You'll usually find a value of 1 here for portrait. Medium contains the supported format as a computer-readable number. Flag tells the client whether this is a get, set, or both format. A value of 1 is get, a value of 2 is set, and a value of 3 is both.
DefaultFile	This entry works much like GetSet, except it identifies the default file format for this particular object.
DefaultIcon	The value of this key tells the client which application icon to use when displaying the object as an icon.
InProcHandler	This key contains the name of the in process handler. In most cases, this is OLE2.DLL unless the application provides its own OLE 2 handler. (A handler is a special program that helps two programs communicate.)
Insertable	Normally you won't see any value associated with this key. A blank value means that Windows can place this file association in the Insert Object (or equivalent) dialog provided by many applications such as Word for Windows. Some OLE 1 objects aren't insertable for a variety of reasons.
LocalServer	Every OLE 2 object must have a server. This key contains the name of the server on the local machine. Since OLE 2 doesn't support RPCs (remote procedure calls), you'll always need a local server.
MiscStatus	This key contains the default value for all data format aspects.

continues

Table 6.2. continued

Entry	Description
ProgID	The program identifier is a pointer back to the file association that this class identifier belongs to. The file association is always a character string of some sort. It's the same string you look for when you try to find the file association that goes with a file extension in the HKEY_CLASSES_ROOT category. For example, if you looked at the ProgID value for Corel Chart, you would see CorelChart5. That's the same value you see in Figure 6.4 as the first key for the file association.
Verb	Several verbs are associated with an OLE 2 object. Each verb defines a specific action that the server will perform. This key doesn't have a value associated with it; its sole purpose is to organize actual verb entries. A client application can use only the verbs that are defined for a specific server. See Table 6.1 for a list of verbs and their meanings.
InProcServer	This is a special form of OLE server. Instead of calling the application that created the object, the client calls a DLL to handle any necessary display or editing functions. This has the advantage of speed; a DLL is faster than calling the executable. However, the programmer has to do a lot more coding to make this kind of interface work.
TreatAs	When this key is present, it contains the CLSID for another file format. The client can treat the current file format like the specified file format. For example, if you looked at the Paintbrush Picture OLE 2 entry, you would find a TreatAs value with the same 128-digit value as a Bitmap Image. This tells you that Windows 95 uses the same application to service Paintbrush Picture files as it does for Bitmap Image files. A little more research would tell you that the OLE 2 server for Paintbrush Pictures is Microsoft Paint.
AutoTreatAs	This key forces the client to treat the current file format the same way it would treat the file format specified by the CLSID. From a user perspective, it works just like TreatAs.

Entry	Description
AutoConvert	Some objects' context menus contain a Convert option. This key allows you to automatically convert the current file format to the one identified by CLSID. For example, Word for Windows allows you to convert many types of data to a format that it specifically supports. This conversion process changes the embedded or linked object into a Word for Windows object. In other words, it changes the data into something that Word might have created itself.
Convertible	There are two levels of subkeys below this one. The first level contains two keys, Readable and Writeable. Below them are keys that contain a list of readable or writeable file formats that you can convert this file format to. For example, you will find that Word for Windows supports several formats, including Word Document. The number of entries in this area usually varies by the number of file filters you install for the application. For example, if you install Word Perfect file support for Word for Windows, you'll likely find an entry for it here. Remember, though, that these are OLE 2 entries. Even if an application supports another application's file format as part of a Save As option, it still might not support it for OLE purposes.
Interfaces	This key contains a list of interfaces supported by the server. The value for this key will eventually contain the names of other ways of accessing the OLE server (other than from the local machine), but no applications support it right now. For example, this entry could contain the types of network protocols that the application supports.

Looking Ahead: This chapter only tells you about the registry portion of the OLE picture. Chapter 11 provides detailed information about OLE from a user level.

HKEY_CURRENT_USER

Our earlier discussion of the HKEY_CURRENT_USER category centered on the fact that it's slaved to the current user settings. These settings get copied to the HKEY_USERS category when you shut down. In other words, this particular category is a scratch pad of sorts. It's very useful to remember this fact. If you make a mistake, you can always use the settings in HKEY_USERS to reset the values to their previous settings. The following sections describe each of the HKEY_CURRENT_USER keys in detail.

> **Note:** Using a common setup for all users means that HKEY_CURRENT_USER settings automatically reflect the default setting in HKEY_USERS. (Click on the first radio button in the User Profiles tab of the Passwords selection in Control Panel.) See the "HKEY_USERS" section for more details on these settings.

AppEvents

Everyone likes to add a few sounds to their system to make it through the day. This key defines these sounds in a number of ways. Take a look at Figure 6.6 to see what the AppEvents subkeys look like. There are two subkeys under this one: EventLabels and Schemes. The EventLabels key holds a list of events. Each event key contains the long name of a sound event. For example, the EmptyRecycleBin event uses "Empty Recycle Bin" as a long name. This is what Windows displays in the dialog box you use to set the sound value.

Figure 6.6.
The AppEvents key controls the sounds you hear for various system events. It also contains the strings used to display these event names in the Sounds Properties dialog.

Tip: This registry provides the only way you can change the strings displayed in the Sounds Properties dialog. You might want to use this option after changing the name of the Recycle Bin or other Windows components.

The Schemes key is the one you'll probably want to explore. There are two subkeys below this one. The first one we'll look at is the Names key. The subkeys hold the full names of the various sound schemes you might have defined. The Apps key contains major subkeys for each kind of application that defines special sounds. The default sounds are the beeps and other general Windows noises you hear on a daily basis. If you looked at the values for each of the minor keys, you'd see the name of a sound file.

Control Panel

This is probably the most familiar registry key. Figure 6.7 shows all the subkeys that this key contains. As you can see, the Control Panel key doesn't contain subkeys for each icon in the control, but it does contain keys for all the icons that control user-specific settings. The following list describes these subkeys in more detail.

- Accessibility: This subkey contains all the settings for the accessibility features such as sticky keys and high contrast monitor. You can find a complete description of these features in Chapter 2.

Figure 6.7.
The Control Panel key contains subkeys for every user-specific feature on Control Panel.

- Appearance: The Appearance key contains the current display's color settings. It includes both a text description and the custom colors. This value doesn't include the actual color values. Below this key is the Schemes subkey. It contains the text description and actual color value for all the color schemes you've defined.

Tip: If you want to share your color schemes with someone else, you can export this key using the same procedure we used to save the registry. Instead of saving the entire registry, save just the Schemes branch. When the other person imports your .REG file, he'll have the same color schemes you do.

- Colors: This subkey contains a list of object types and their associated colors. Windows 95 uses these settings to present everything on your display.

Tip: The Color key settings provide a level of flexibility that you can't get using the standard Display Properties dialog. For example, clicking on the pushbutton displays the 3D object settings. These settings don't provide the same precise control as the Button values in this key.

- Cursors: This subkey contains a list of cursor types and their associated cursor files. Below this key is the Schemes subkey. It contains a list of all the cursor schemes you have defined and their associated settings.
- Desktop: All your Desktop settings appear in the values of this key. It includes the current wallpaper, background, and screen saver settings. Below this key is the ResourceLocale subkey, which contains the current country code. The WindowMetrics subkey defines all the icon spacing and other graphic specifications for the Desktop.
- International: The International key contains the current country code.
- Mouse: This key contains the standard mouse settings, not the Accessibility mouse settings. It determines how the mouse reacts when you're using a standard setup.

Environment

This key contains the DOS environment settings. Windows stores them in hexadecimal instead of plain English. It uses these values when you start a DOS session. Windows applications can request this information as well.

InstallLocationsMRU

This registry key contains the most recently used locations of installation files. This doesn't pertain to the location of software installation files, but to device or service-related installation files. For example, installing a new set of network drivers would place an entry here, but installing a new word processor wouldn't. Notice that there's a special value called MRUList. This value controls the order in which Windows displays the filenames that appear in the list. If you do add an entry to the list, you also have to add it to the MRUList value.

Keyboard Layout

This registry key provides information about the keyboard currently attached to the machine. It doesn't really change from user to user unless one user needs to use a different language or keyboard layout than another. The Preload key under the Keyboard section reflects the different languages in use. The Substitutes key reflects the keyboard layout. For example, you could use English (United States) as a language and English (Dvorak) as a layout. The Toggle key tells you which control key combination you can use to switch between languages.

Peter's Principle: Using Two Keyboard Layouts

I ran into an interesting situation the other day. Two friends were using the same machine. One uses the Dvorak layout, and the other uses the standard layout. Windows 95 will allow you to install multiple languages and switch between them using the International icon on the Taskbar, but not different layouts of the same language. So how do you get around this?

Start by installing two languages using the standard keyboard dialog. Make certain that the languages are at least compatible. To make life simple, I installed English (United States) using the standard layout and English (British) using the Dvorak layout. If you look at the HKEY_CURRENT_USER | Keyboard Layout | Preload key, you'll notice two subkeys. The value for one is 00000409 (United States), and the value for the other is 00000809 (British).

Look at the Substitutes key. You'll see a subkey for 00000809. The value in this key says 00020409. If you look this value up in the HKEY_LOCAL_MACHINE | System | CurrentControlSet | Control | Keyboard Layouts | 00020409 key, you'll see that we're using the standard Dvorak keyboard KBD driver. Our language is English, and the keyboard layout matches what the second person needs.

The only thing left to do is change the International icon list so that it matches what the machine actually has installed. If you look at it right now, it says that you have an English

(United States) and an English (British) keyboard setup installed. What you really have is an English (Dvorak) keyboard installed. We need to look at the `HKEY_LOCAL_MACHINE` | System | CurrentControlSet | Control | NLS | Locale key. Find the 00000809 value and change it from British to Dvorak. Close the Registry Editor to make sure the change gets recorded. Now, open the Keyboard Properties dialog in Control Panel. Make a simple change and then change it back. Click on Apply. The International icon will now show a United States and a Dvorak keyboard, making it simple for you to switch back and forth.

Network

Unfortunately, most of this key's contents are network-specific. Essentially, it provides the user-specific network information your machine needs. One key remains constant across networks—the Recent key. This key contains one subkey for each of the network drives you've recently accessed. Windows 95 updates it only on a session basis, so you probably won't find current information here if you maintain your network connection for a long time between sessions. Each subkey uses the full network access path for a drive. For example, if you have a Microsoft network installed and you connect to the C drive of a machine named AUX, one of the subkeys might look like this: //AUX/DRIVE-C.

RemoteAccess

You may or may not find this key in your registry. It depends on what features you choose to install. Within the key itself is an area code value and a `DWORD` configuration value for the Make New Connection Wizard.

Below this key you'll find one subkey that holds the addresses you define. There's one binary value for each address you define. These values include all the configuration information for that address. Obviously, you won't want to edit this value outside the Dial-Up Networking application.

Software

This registry key should contain plenty of configuration information for your software. However, until you upgrade to 32-bit versions of your applications, it will probably contain a few default entries for Windows 95-specific applications. The SSC section contains information related to the viewers. The Microsoft section contains keys for a variety of applications, whether you have them installed or not.

The registry provides this section to replace all those entries you used to have in WIN.INI and SYSTEM.INI. The hierarchical structure of this key makes it very easy to remove application-specific information from your Windows 95 installation. There's one subkey of particular interest. The MS Setup (ACME) | User Info key, shown in Figure 6.8, contains the user's name and company information. Applications will look at this entry during installation. This is the only place you can change this information in Windows 95. If you need to change the user name for software installation purposes, this is the place to do it.

Figure 6.8.
Many 32-bit programs use the information in the User Info key as a default during installation for burning the user information into the application.

HKEY_LOCAL_MACHINE

The HKEY_LOCAL_MACHINE category centers its attention on the machine hardware. This includes the drivers and configuration information required to run the hardware. A lot of subtle information about your hardware is stored under this category. For example, it contains all the plug and play information about your machine. It also provides a complete listing of the device drivers and their revision level.

This category does contain some software-specific information. For example, a 32-bit application will store the location of its setup table here. The application uses this table during installation. Some applications also use it during a setup modification. Applications such as Word for Windows NT store all their setup information in SFT tables. Figure 6.9 shows a typical HKEY_LOCAL_MACHINE category setup. The following sections describe each key in detail.

Figure 6.9.

The HKEY_LOCAL_MACHINE *category contains all the hardware and device driver-specific information about your machine, as well as the global application setup information.*

Config

The Config key provides specific information needed to set up the machine during boot. The two main references are the display and the printer. The printer settings appear under the System key. In most cases, the only printer configuration information you'll see is the specific name of the printer attached to the current machine. This key doesn't provide any network-specific information.

Note: Windows 95 copies the contents of the Config key to the HKEY_CURRENT_CONFIG category. It will overwrite any changes you make to the values in this key during logout or shutdown. Make any required changes to the HKEY_CURRENT_CONFIG values. Fortunately, having a backup copy of the configuration under the HKEY_LOCAL_MACHINE | Config key means that you can easily correct editing mistakes in the HKEY_CURRENT_CONFIG key values.

The Display settings include the resolution and fonts. It's a lot more detailed than the printer settings. There are two subkeys under the main Display key. The Fonts key provides a list of default font requirements and the name of the font file that satisfies that need. In most cases, you can change these settings using the Display utility in Control Panel. The Settings key provides information on the current number of colors (as bits per pixel) and the display resolution. It also provides the names of the default display fonts.

Enum

This registry key enumerates the hardware connected to your machine. Figure 6.9 shows a typical installation. Some hardware receives special attention through the use of separate keys. For example, an IDE hard drive and the floppy drives fall into this category. Other hardware falls into the plug and play category. The actual plug and play hardware listing appears under the root key. The subkeys under the root key also appear in the Device Manager listing. Figure 6.10 shows a typical set of values for the COM ports.

Figure 6.10.
A typical plug and play registry entry doesn't provide much information. However, it does provide important clues for the network troubleshooter. One of the most important pieces of information is the location of the .INF file associated with the device.

As you can see, the Device Manager display is much easier to read. However, the registry display does provide one important piece of troubleshooting information. It provides the name of the .INF file that holds the COM port configuration information (MSPORTS.INF). These .INF files provide a wealth of information about the default port interrupts. They also provide information about the DLLs and VxDs used to support them. You can also modify the .INF files for any device to provide support for nonstandard devices or additional port/interrupt configurations. Think of an .INF file as an .INI file for devices.

Hardware

In most cases, you can ignore the Hardware registry key. Its only function is to list the communication ports and any floating-point processors attached to the machine. This key doesn't contain any actual configuration information.

Network

This key contains some network-specific security information. The only entry most users will find here is what parameters—their user and machine name—they use to log onto a network. This key also contains some configuration information, such as whether Windows needs to process a login script or not.

Security

This registry key is network-specific. Refer to your network manuals for additional information. As a general rule, it contains pointers to files holding account and other network security-specific information. In some cases (usually with peer-to-peer networks), you won't see anything here, even if you have a network connected to your machine. It's also interesting to see some information placed here when you enable multiple Desktop configurations.

SOFTWARE

The SOFTWARE registry key contains device driver and global application information. Most applications store their specific configuration information under the Application key and any global information under another, common, key. Figure 6.9 shows a typical setup. Notice that the subkeys include a variety of vendor-specific information.

One of the interesting subkeys is Classes. Opening this key reveals a list of file extensions and associations just like the one in HKEY_CLASSES_ROOT. The purpose behind this set of keys is totally different, though. Windows 95 uses this list to locate application- or device driver-specific files instead of creating links for Explorer or providing OLE configuration information. Changing any of these keys won't affect your Explorer display. Unfortunately, it might affect how some of your applications work. The bottom line is, don't change any of these settings unless you have a good reason to do so and know exactly how the change will affect your setup.

The Description key also provides some interesting information. A default setup always contains the Microsoft remote procedure call (RPC) listing. However, a network could use this section to describe other links between machines as well. An RPC allows your machine to use the resources found on another machine. This is an automatic feature. The application and operating system must support RPCs. In addition, the resource has to be available—you can't steal someone's resource if he's already using it. RPCs can include all kinds of resources, but they normally refer to code. For example, you could borrow someone else's DLL if that DLL didn't appear on your machine. The unique aspect of RPCs is that the code for that DLL would execute on the other person's machine, not your machine. You would, in effect, borrow not only his code, but his processor as well. Notice that this section doesn't define any light remote procedure call (LRPC) information. An LRPC is the same as an RPC, except that it deals with very specific types of resources, and it always deals with code. You could borrow another person's DLL, but the code for that DLL would execute on your machine, not his machine. These statistics always appear as part of the OLE configuration information or within the RPC keys.

Unless you have a Microsoft mouse, there's a good chance that you'll have a mouse-specific entry—even if your mouse doesn't provide Windows 95-specific software. The Logitech key shown in Figure 6.9 provides mouse setup information as well as the driver version. For example, under the MouseMan | 0000 key are values that determine which buttons become assigned to various mouse functions.

> **Tip:** Using the registry to edit a hardware configuration setting is almost always more flexible than using the Control Panel settings. For example, what if you wanted to gain some additional control over your three-button Logitech mouse? The default setup program allows you to assign a left- or a right-handed setup to the mouse. What if you wanted to exchange the right and middle button functions, essentially creating a two-button mouse? You could do so by transposing the MappingButton2 and MappingButton3 registry values even though the configuration utility doesn't provide the means to do so.

The Microsoft section of the SOFTWARE key provides some useful information as well. One of these keys is the New Users Settings key. Most 32-bit applications and some 16-bit applications can provide an entry in this area. A new user inherits these settings when you set up a new login on the machine. In essence, this key contains the global settings that everyone uses with this application (at least until they customize their setup). This key also provides the location of shared tools and any global network settings required to make the application work.

If you install any applications that support open database connectivity (ODBC), all those settings will appear under this key. ODBC is Microsoft's new method of allowing you to access information in foreign data formats. Its main purpose is to allow access to mainframe databases, but you'll find it used to access other sources of information, including those commonly found on a PC. You'll also see the 32-bit ODBC settings here as well. The strange thing is that they aren't identified using separate keys, even though the 32-bit settings appear as a separate icon in Control Panel. Every ODBC connection and its configuration appears under the ODBC | ODBCINST.INI key. The two important values are the name of the ODBC driver and its version. Most 32-bit drivers include a 32 somewhere in the filename. This fact allows you to separate the 32-bit drivers from the 16-bit drivers in this area.

The SCC key contains information about the viewers if you installed them. At first glance, you might not think that there is anything worthwhile to look at. There are two keys at the bottom of the hierarchy, and both use descriptive value entry names such as Element 1. However, if you double-click on one of these entries, you will find the name of the DLL that controls it embedded in the binary data that each value contains.

System

The last registry key in this category is also the most destructive when edited incorrectly. A bad entry in any value under this key can kill your installation. Figure 6.11 shows the subkeys associated with the System key.

Figure 6.11.
The System key provides much information and many opportunities for system optimization.

Microsoft split these keys into two categories: control and services. The Control key contains all the subkeys that change the way the user reacts to the system.

> **Warning:** Exploring this part of the registry is somewhat risky. Some settings won't harm your system much—they might just change the text in a listbox or under an icon. However, other settings will damage your Windows 95 installation beyond repair, and still others will prevent access to your system. Wandering through this section and seeing what will happen when you change a setting is one sure way to make your system unusable. Always make a backup of your registry before you make any change to this section.

One of the keys you'll see here is the NLS (national language support) key. Remember the keyboard setting we looked at before? This is where all the language settings come from. If you had the correct driver, you could add support for Martian by changing the value of one of these keys. The network administration-specific keys appear here as well. One of the first keys you'll see is the computer name used to log onto the network.

Several subkeys give the advanced user an opportunity to tune system performance. One of the most interesting keys to look at is the Known16DLLs key under the SessionManager key. The values in this key tell you where you can optimize the system. A 16-bit DLL doesn't perform as well as its 32-bit counterpart. Finding 32-bit DLLs to replace the 16-bit DLLs in this section will improve your system performance without requiring you to buy any new hardware.

> **Tip:** Not every 16-bit DLL is bad. You pay a price in program size when you use a 32-bit DLL. This translates to larger code size and actually means a decrease in performance. However, most 32-bit DLLs offset this performance hit by offering more efficient code. In addition, 32-bit DLLs are more stable because of how Windows manages them. You should always base the decision to try and get rid of a specific 16-bit DLL on known performance improvement. Hoping you'll get something in return is like gambling: You never quite know if you'll win.

One of the more dangerous keys in this section is the PwdProvider key. It tells Windows 95 the location of any password or user account files. This key also contains the name of any DLLs or VxDs required to implement system security. You can't log into the network if this key becomes deleted. The problem is you can't get into Windows because the key doesn't exist, and you can't add it back in because you can't use the registry editor without Windows. You can't even access the registry from another machine because Windows must be online in order to enable remote registry support. The bottom line is that you should get those backup disks out and hope you have a DOS-based backup program that can read them. You're going to need a good copy of the registry to get back into Windows.

The System Monitor utility (installed during network installation) gets some of its input here as well. Look under the PerfStats | Enum key. Here are all the statistics that you can choose from in the System Monitor utility. Each subkey in this section contains a description, a differentiate flag, and a name. Theoretically, you could add a performance monitor statistic here and it would show up in the System Monitor utility. Of course, you wouldn't get any useful information out of it unless you happened to find an undocumented statistic. Other registry entries are required, and you'd need to write the supporting software. However, you could remove statistics from here to prevent network users from monitoring areas that you don't want them to touch. You could also change the name or description of a statistic to meet your needs.

On to the second part of the System key, Services. This group of keys does just the opposite of what the Control key section does: It allows the user to change the way the system reacts. There are a few keys in this group that you should never touch. They include Arbitrators, Unknown, and Nodriver.

The majority of the Class key subkeys provide useful information. For example, the CDROM key can tell you about the drivers associated with the CD-ROM drive. In some cases, it might provide clues about why the CD-ROM drive fails to play music or interface with the system in some other way.

The Display key contains several subkeys related to the display adapter. This includes specifics about resolution and color combinations that the driver supports. (In one case, I was actually able to change this entry and provide 256-color support at 1024 × 768 resolution on one machine even though the driver originally showed that it didn't support this combination.) Of course, as with any other keys in this group, editing the values for these keys can result in a boot failure or other unforeseen occurrences.

Besides these keys, you might find some network-related information in this section as well. For example, anyone using the Microsoft Network support provided with Windows 95 will see an MSNP32 key. The values under this key contain information about the user setup and logon information.

HKEY_USERS

We discussed the major aspects of this category in Chapter 1. All it contains is one profile for each user who logs into a particular workstation when you enable multiple Desktops using the User Profiles tab of the Password Properties dialog.

So where does the original information for each user come from? The registry contains one entry called .Default. (Notice the period in front of the keyname. Default without a period is an actual user name.) Windows 95 takes the information in this key and copies it to a user-specific key when the user logs in for the first time. Each profile will look precisely the same as the one provided for the .Default key. The user can't add new keys for his configuration.

Each subkey and value under the .Default key is echoed in the HKEY_CURRENT_USER category, so I won't go into the settings again here. (The initial login does more work than create a simple registry entry, but we won't cover that in this chapter.) You should follow a few registry-related tips when setting up your network:

- Always configure the workstation for the minimum possible access rights for the .Default user. This allows you to create new users without the risk of circumventing network security.

- Consider renaming the .Default user entry so that other people can't log in without a password. (Windows 95 will come to a screeching halt if it can't find the default user.)

- Use the System Policy Editor in place of the Registry Editor whenever possible to make changes to the network setup.

- Make a backup of both the USER.DAT and SYSTEM.DAT files before you set the network up. Failure to take this step means you'll have to reinstall Windows 95 from scratch if the network setup fails.

Tip: You can save at least 100 KB (each user profile on my machine ate 300 KB) for each user who logs onto a particular machine by using the same profile for all users. Unless you need the security or Desktop setup flexibility that such a setup provides, the additional hard disk space is wasted. Never enable multiple Desktops for a single user setup; use the shortcuts we talked about in Chapter 5 instead.

HKEY_CURRENT_CONFIG

The HKEY_CURRENT_CONFIG category is the simplest part of the registry. It's so simple that I covered it completely in Chapter 1. There aren't any hidden secrets here—nothing for you to exploit. Overall, it's probably the most boring part of the registry.

HKEY_DYN_DATA

The final category, HKEY_DYN_DATA, contains two subkeys, Config Manager and PerfStats. We took a generic look at this key in Chapter 1, but let's take a more detailed look now. Figure 6.12 shows a detailed view of this particular category.

Figure 6.12.

HKEY_DYN_DATA contains registry entries for current events. The values in these keys reflect the current, or dynamic, state of the computer.

The Enum key contains subkeys for every device attached to the computer. Each one of the subkeys contains the same four values. The Allocation value shows which process has control of the device. The HardwareKey value contains an entry that matches the plug and play values we talked about for the HKEY_LOCAL_MACHINE | Enum | Root key. Essentially, this value identifies the device. For example, a plug and play value of 0500 matches the first serial port. The Problem value should equal 0 in most cases (unless the hardware experiences a fault). This value always contains an error number during a hardware failure. The final key, Status, contains a value of 4F 4A 00 00 when the hardware is error-free.

The PerfStats key contains five subkeys. The first two subkeys control the starting time for gathering server and statistical data. The last two control the stopping time. These four keys probably won't tell you too much about your machine or anything to improve its performance. The only interesting key in this group is the StatData key. It contains the current usage level data for each of the categories that the System Monitor utility tracks. In fact, if you press F5 to refresh the registry data, you can watch the data values change. (You must start the System Monitor utility to see any change, because it's this utility that tracks the data values and places them in the registry.) Keeping the System Monitor utility window and the Registry Editor window on-screen at the same time will show you how these numbers track the information you see in the utility.

Modifying File Associations

Explorer is the Windows 95 alternative to the Windows 3.x File Manager. It goes a long way toward making Windows 95 truly usable. However, as with any other tool, you'll probably want to customize this one to meet your needs. One of the first things you'll want to do is change the file associations.

The problem with Explorer is that you can't add new extensions to an existing file type. This means that if you want to extend the ability of Word for Windows to open file types other than the default types, you can't do it with the tools that Explorer provides. However, you can still get the job done using the Registry Editor. This simple procedure will allow you to add new extensions to an existing entry. (We'll approach it from an exercise point of view to make the illustration clearer. Just substitute the values you need in place of the ones I provide here.)

Tip: Always use the right tool for the job. It might be tempting to use the Registry Editor to make all your file association changes. However, the Explorer interface is a lot faster, simpler, and less error-prone than making the modifications by hand. The only time you should need to use the Registry Editor on a file extension is when you need to extend an existing association.

1. Open a copy of the Registry Editor.

2. Click on the plus sign next to the HKEY_CLASSES_ROOT key. Click on the .DOC entry. You should see "Word.Document.6" or something similar as a value for this key. We'll use this value as the basis for adding a new value to Word. Note the use of periods. Formatting is very important in the registry, as are punctuation marks.

Note: If you already have an .ASC extension in your registry, choose another extension for right now.

3. Click on the HKEY_CLASSES_ROOT key. Use the Edit | New | Key command to add a new key named .ASC. Make sure you type a period before ASC.

4. Double-click on the Default value and type Word.Document.6 as a value. You should see a display similar to the one shown in Figure 6.13.

Figure 6.13.

Adding a new key to extend the linkages supported by an application is relatively easy when using the Registry Editor.

5. Close the Registry Editor.

6. Open a copy of Explorer.

7. Use the View | Options command to display the Options dialog. Click on the File Types tab. Highlight the Microsoft Word 6.0 Document entry. You'll see the new Word file association shown in Figure 6.14.

Figure 6.14.
Word used to provide just
three file associations. It now
provides four, including the
new .ASC extension.

Using Find to Change Strings

One of the things that really annoyed me when I started using Windows 95 was that Microsoft prevented me from changing some names—and for no real reason. One of these was the name of the Recycle Bin. I'd prefer just about any name to that (and so would a lot of other people I've talked to).

You don't have to live with any names you really don't want under Windows 95. The vast majority of the titles that appear under icons and, in some cases, even the items you'll see in a listbox are all in the registry. This simple procedure will use the Find command to help you locate the offending string and change it.

> **Warning:** Windows 95 relies on the contents of some strings to perform specific work. For example, you might change your network name, and it will work fine. Then again, in other cases it won't because your network embedded that name in a file. Changing a string without knowing how it will affect your computer is never a good idea. Only change the strings that contain names you can see. Icons and some listboxes are good candidates.

As with the preceding section, we'll approach this from an exercise perspective. I've kept things as simple as possible so that you can use this procedure to modify other names you might not like.

1. Open a copy of the Registry Editor.
2. Use the Edit | Find command to open the Find dialog. Type `Recycle Bin` in the Find What dialog. Click on Find Next. The registry might take a little while to find the first occurrence of "Recycle Bin," so be patient. There's very little chance your machine will freeze during the search.

3. Double-click on the value that holds the words "Recycle Bin" (usually Default). You should see the Edit String dialog. Type anything you want (within reason, of course). This will be the new name of your Recycle Bin. Your new entry should look similar to the one shown in Figure 6.15.

Figure 6.15.
Changing the name of the Recycle Bin consists of changing the value of the strings that define it.

4. Press F3 to find the next occurrence of the string.

5. Repeat steps 3 and 4 for every occurrence of the string. Be sure you find every occurrence and replace it with exactly the same value in every instance. Otherwise, you could end up confusing Windows 95 when it goes to look for that value later.

6. Close the Registry Editor and reboot the machine. This will allow the change to take effect.

That's all there is to it. You can use this procedure for a variety of tasks, including changing names you don't like. The same word of caution applies here as it does everywhere else. If you do decide to change the registry, be sure to make a backup first. Trying to restore a failed registry is pretty much impossible under Windows 95.

Importing and Exporting Registry Data

One of the problems with using a registry for everything is that you have to put the configuration data into a form that the registry can accept. Quite a few mainstream applications create a .REG file that you can import into the registry. Even the .REG files created with 16-bit applications are compatible with the Windows 95 registry.

Importing Data

You can use several techniques to import your current registry information into the registry. First, you can open a copy of Explorer and find the registry file you want to import. Figure 6.16 shows a typical example.

Figure 6.16.
A typical registry file entry. This one is for Word for Windows 6.0.

All you need to do is double-click on the REG icon (which appears as Winword6.reg in Figure 6.16), and RegEdit automatically enters it into the registry. Notice that the REG file icon looks like the Registry Editor icon with a document behind it. After the registry enters the new configuration information for your application, it displays the dialog shown in Figure 6.17.

Figure 6.17.
The registry signals a successful configuration data entry for Word for Windows 6.0.

A second technique comes in handy when you have the Registry Editor open. Simply select Registry | Import Registry File. The Registry Editor will display a dialog box similar to the one shown in Figure 6.18.

Figure 6.18.
You can use menu commands to import configuration into the registry when RegEdit is open.

Click on the Open pushbutton to complete the task. You should see the same dialog box shown in Figure 6.17 when RegEdit completes the task.

Exporting Data

What happens when you want to save some configuration changes you made in the past? For example, what if you added a new file extension to the registry and wanted to save those entries for future use? How about the custom color combinations that you create? Wouldn't it be nice to save them before installing a new version of Windows 95? You can export either all or part of the registry by using the Registry | Export Registry File command in the Registry Editor. Figure 6.19 shows the Export Registry File dialog box.

Figure 6.19.
The registry provides the means to export configuration data into a pure ASCII text file. You can edit this data using a standard text editor such as Notepad.

Notice that this dialog box has the All radio button selected. This option saves the entire registry to a text file. Use this option when you want to save the registry before you start editing it. It's also easy to save a branch (or section) of the registry. When you click on the Selected branch radio button, you can either highlight the branch you want to save before you open the Export Registry File dialog box or type the path in later.

All you need to do to complete the process is click on the Save pushbutton. RegEdit doesn't provide any kind of feedback once it exports the registry to disk. You'll probably want to view the saved file before you make any changes to the registry.

Viewing the Contents of an Exported Registry Entry

Exported registry data files contain pure ASCII text. They don't contain any control characters that you need to worry about. You normally need to use Wordpad to view a save of the entire registry. (A full registry export file normally takes between 400 KB and 500 KB of storage.) Notepad will probably do the job if you want to look at a saved branch.

Figure 6.20 shows a typical saved registry branch. Notice that this file has three lines. The first line contains REGEDIT4, which identifies the version of the Registry Editor that created the file. It also prevents you from importing the file into an older version of the registry. Application .REG files normally don't contain any version numbers as part of the REGEDIT entry. This allows you to import them using any version of REGEDIT.

Figure 6.20.
This saved registry branch contains a mere four lines of data. Each line serves a specific purpose during the import process.

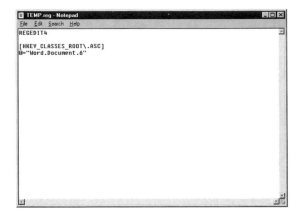

The real second line of the file contains a blank. RegEdit uses this blank line as a delimiter between registry key entries. The second line of text (the third line of the file) contains the registry key. Notice that it looks like a hard disk directory listing. Each backslash tells RegEdit to create a new key level.

The final line of text contains the actual key value. The @ symbol at the beginning of the line tells RegEdit that this is the default entry. Any other value begins with a value name. The double quotes around the value itself tell RegEdit that this is a string value. Binary values begin with the word *hex* followed by a colon, and DWORD values begin with the word *dword* followed by a colon.

Tip: You might find that you need to add the keys from one branch to another branch in the registry. For example, you might want to use some of the OLE information from one file association when creating a new one. It seems like RegEdit should provide some type of cut and paste capability to take care of this task, but it doesn't. The fastest, most efficient way to add the contents of one branch to another is to export the registry, use a text editor to cut and paste the values you need, and import the modified registry file. Of course, you could find yourself with a machine that won't boot using this method. Make sure you keep an unmodified copy of the registry handy just in case.

A Look at the Windows 95 Boot Sequence

Getting your machine up and running after you turn the power on is called the boot process. It includes everything from the time that the power on startup test (POST) routines begin until the time you can start to use the machine. Under DOS, this boot process was relatively straightforward. Windows 95 requires something a bit more exotic because we expect it to do more.

We'll look at the boot process from a user's perspective in the next few sections. This means you won't get a blow-by-blow "this bit does this and that byte does that" explanation. We'll just look at the highlights of the boot process.

> **Tip:** If you ever do want to see a blow-by-blow description of the entire boot process, look at BOOTLOG.TXT in the root directory of your boot drive. This file records every action that Windows 95 performs during the boot process. However, it doesn't include a few of the initial actions such as loading IO.SYS. At most, three or four actions take place before the log starts, though, so your chances of missing anything important are almost nonexistent.

Starting at the DOS Prompt

Windows 95 doesn't, as some people think, start the boot process in protected mode. It actually starts up a copy of DOS. The difference is that the copy of DOS it uses isn't the same as the one you used in the past. Even the system files are different.

The whole reason for starting DOS (at least the one that Microsoft will sort of admit to) is for compatibility purposes. All those machines with older hardware will still need to run device drivers and the like from CONFIG.SYS and AUTOEXEC.BAT. Something has to read those files and act on their contents in a way that the drivers can understand.

Your system starts just like it always has. Installing Windows 95 does not stop the system from performing POST. Once the ROM-BIOS determines that your machine is working correctly, it takes care of any required hardware initialization and builds a vector table in lower memory. The vector table contains pointers to all the BIOS routines so that DOS can use them later as part of its boot process. Once this initialization phase is over, the BIOS looks for a bootable drive. A bootable drive will contain an operating system loader. In the case of both DOS and Windows 95, that loader will look for a file called IO.SYS.

Up to this point, the workings of DOS and Windows 95 are precisely the same. However, unlike the old version of DOS, everything that the new version needs in the way of code appears in the IO.SYS file. The old MSDOS.SYS file is no longer required. Microsoft combined the contents of the two files that used to appear in your root directory into one. By now you're looking at your drive and noticing that there's still an MSDOS.SYS file.

The MSDOS.SYS file now contains important boot configuration information. You can include a lot of different configuration switches here. Most of them aren't essential, but some are. Figure 6.21 shows the shortest MSDOS.SYS that most people can get by with. Notice that there is a special section that contains what looks like junk. Actually, it *is* junk. MSDOS.SYS must contain more than 1,024 bytes for compatibility reasons.

Figure 6.21.
MSDOS.SYS doesn't have to contain a lot of information, but what it does contain is very important. These "switches" help configure Windows 95 during the DOS portion of the boot process.

Note: MSDOS.SYS is a hidden, read-only file on your boot drive. You can use the ATTRIB command to remove these attributes and edit the file from the DOS prompt. An easier way is to right-click on the file from Explorer, use the Properties dialog to remove the file attributes, and edit it using Notepad.

Figuring out what these entries mean is pretty straightforward in most cases. The main thing to remember is that they all affect how your system boots. If you remember this, you won't have too many problems. The minimalistic MSDOS.SYS shown in Figure 6.21 doesn't give you any idea of the types of things you do with it, though. Table 6.3 provides you with a complete description of all the entries you can put in it.

Table 6.3. Configuration switches for MSDOS.SYS.

Switch	Description
	[Paths] Section
HostWinBootDrv=C	This switch tells Windows 95 where to find the host (Windows 95) boot drive. This isn't the same as the physical boot drive; it's the drive that contains the Windows 95 files. The default is drive C.
WinBootDir=C:\WIN95	All the Windows 95 executable files appear in the directory you provide here. Setup automatically places the installation drive here. If you ever move Windows 95 to a different directory, you will need to change this setting.
WinDir=C:\WIN95	Use this switch to define the Windows 95 directory. It should be the same as the WinBootDir setting.
	[Options] Section
BootDelay=2	Windows 95 provides a dual boot capability that allows you to use your old setup if you want to. All you need to do is press F4 when you see that POST is finished. Pressing F8 during this time will display the Safe Boot options. We'll examine this feature later. This setting changes the delay that Windows 95 provides for pressing either of these two function keys. The default setting is 2 seconds. You may add an entry of 0 if you want to disable the delay.
BootFailSafe=0	This switch allows you to bypass the Save Boot option screen unless you really need it after a failed boot. Normally you'll want to boot Windows in a regular mode. However, if you write software or need to fully control how Windows loads for some reason, you can set this value to 1.
BootGUI=1	If you'd rather boot to DOS 7.0 (or raw DOS, as Microsoft calls it), set this switch to 0. You can still start Windows by typing WIN as before.
BootKeys=1	System administrators will really like this switch. Setting it to 0 disables all the startup keys such as F8 that a user could use to bypass your security measures. However, this isn't a perfect solution. The user can still get past security with a boot disk and an editor, but at least this adds a little extra protection.
BootMenu=0	Set this switch to 1 if you want to see the Windows 95 boot menu. Essentially, this is the same menu you get when you press F8.

continues

Table 6.3. continued

Switch	Description
BootMenuDefault=1 or BootMenuDefault=3	This switch changes the default boot menu option. It normally defaults to 1. If your system experienced a failure of some kind, the boot menu defaults to 3.
BootMenuDelay=30	Use this switch to change the number of seconds that Windows 95 displays the boot menu before it executes the default option. The default setting is 30.
BootMulti=0	Setup normally doesn't include this switch in MSDOS.SYS. It allows you to add dual boot capabilities to your system. Pressing F4 at the Starting Windows prompt (right after POST is finished) allows you to boot your previous version of DOS if it's still intact.
BootWarn=1	This switch enables the Safe Mode startup warning and menu.
BootWin=1	If you use DOS 5 or 6 as your primary operating system and you want to use Windows 95 only on an experimental basis for now, this switch is a must. It allows you to boot your old operating system instead of Windows 95 as a default.
DblSpace=1	You can disable automatic loading of DBLSPACE.BIN by setting this switch to 0.
DoubleBuffer=0	This switch tells Windows 95 whether a SCSI controller needs a double-buffering driver loaded. Setting this value to 1 enables double buffering.
DrvSpace=1	You can disable automatic loading of DRVSPACE.BIN by setting this switch to 0.
LoadTop=1	Use this switch to tell Windows 95 whether you want to load COMMAND.COM or DRVSPACE.BIN at the top of 640 KB memory. The default setting does load these items at the top of memory. However, you might need to set the switch to 0 if you experience network-related problems. This is especially true for Novell NetWare.
Logo=1	If you aren't all that thrilled with the logo that Windows 95 displays during the boot process, you can set this switch to 0. This also keeps Windows 95 from grabbing some interrupts that might cause conflicts with some memory managers.
Network=0	Setting this switch to 0 tells Windows 95 not to install any network components. Use a value of 1 to enable the Safe Mode with Networking menu option.

IO.SYS reads the contents of MSDOS.SYS as part of the pre-booting cycle. Think of MSDOS.SYS as a configuration file for the boot process, because that's exactly what it is. After IO.SYS configures itself using the contents of MSDOS.SYS, it reads the contents of CONFIG.SYS (if there is one). There's no longer a need for CONFIG.SYS, because IO.SYS has several features added to it. The following list tells you everything you need to know about these new settings.

- `DOS=HIGH,UMB`: IO.SYS always loads DOS high unless you override this setting in CONFIG.SYS.

- `HIMEM.SYS`: IO.SYS always loads a copy of the real-mode memory manager. It doesn't load EMM386.EXE. You'll need to load this from CONFIG.SYS if you plan to run an application that requires expanded memory without going into Windows first.

- `IFSHLP.SYS` (installable file system helper): Loading this device driver also loads several others. It gives you full access to the file system.

- `SETVER.EXE`: Some of your older applications might require a specific version of DOS. This program fools them into thinking that the version of DOS provided with Windows 95 is the one they need.

- `FILES=60`: Windows 95 doesn't require this setting. It's provided for any MS-DOS applications you might run. Some older applications require more than 60 file handles, but this setting should work for the majority of installations.

- `LASTDRIVE=Z`: This sets the last drive letter you can use for your DOS applications. As with the FILES setting, Windows 95 does not require a `LASTDRIVE` setting.

- `BUFFERS=30`: The `BUFFERS` setting affects the number of file buffers that IO.SYS provides. Windows 95 uses its own file management system and is unaffected by this setting.

- `STACKS=9,256`: IO.SYS sets up a specific number of stack frames using this entry. Each stack frame is the same size.

- `SHELL=COMMAND.COM /P`: If you don't specify another command processor in CONFIG.SYS, IO.SYS defaults to using COMMAND.COM, just as it always has. The `/P` parameter makes the command processor permanent.

- `FCBS=4`: Ancient programs used file control blocks. These programs are so old that I really can't believe anyone would still have them lying around. You can provide additional FCBS by overriding this setting in CONFIG.SYS.

As you can see, IO.SYS comes with a fairly complete CONFIG.SYS built in. Once IO.SYS loads the command processor, its job is finished for the time being. The command processor takes over and reads the contents of AUTOEXEC.BAT. Right at this point you're running DOS. You might not see a DOS prompt, but that's because Microsoft hides it behind a logo.

Loading the 16-Bit Core

After the command processor completes its work, a new phase in the boot process begins. You might wonder why Windows 95, a 32-bit operating system, would even think about starting in 16-bit mode. There are several interesting reasons.

One reason has to do with the way the plug and play BIOS specification is written. The current specification requires a vendor to provide a 16-bit protected-mode interface. This allows an operating system vendor such as Microsoft to check the plug and play hardware without switching to real mode. The result is a much more stable operating system that (supposedly) always runs in protected mode.

The very first thing Windows has to do once you start it is to check the status of all the hardware. It calls on the plug and play BIOS to provide it with a list of all the installed equipment. Windows uses this information to configure the system. Of course, it also has to take any non-plug and play peripherals into account as well. Once it comes up with a configuration list, Windows 95 starts to load all the 16-bit VxDs required to support that hardware.

What precisely is a VxD? It's a virtual device driver, the protected-mode version of the device drivers you used under DOS. However, it's more than that since a device can be a lot more than just a piece of hardware under Windows 95. To avoid getting into the bits and bytes of device management, let's just say that Windows uses virtual device drivers to manage all its low-level functions.

Once it completes this step, Windows initializes all those drivers. It starts with the system drivers first—all the drivers required to make the low-level functions in Windows work (such as the file system). The device drivers come next.

At this point, Windows 95 loads the three 16-bit shell components: USER.EXE, GDI.EXE, and KRNL386.EXE. It also loads some additional drivers and a few other components such as fonts. Now Windows 95 is completely up and running in 16-bit mode. It doesn't have an interface yet, but every other component is present.

Loading the 32-Bit Core

The preceding section ended with a copy of Windows running in 16-bit mode without any form of user interface. 16-bit mode operations end very soon after you start Windows 95. The user shell, Explorer, is a 32-bit application. As soon as the 16-bit kernel sees the call for the shell, it loads an application called VWIN32.386. This little program loads the three 32-bit DLLs that form the Win32 API: USER32.DLL, GDI32.DLL, and KERNEL32.DLL. Once it completes this task, VWIN32.386 returns control to the 16-bit kernel, which in turn calls the 32-bit kernel. Windows runs in 32-bit mode from that point on.

Now that it's operating in 32-bit mode, the operating system loads and initializes all the 32-bit drivers. This is the same process the 16-bit part of the operating system performed, so I won't discuss it again here.

Somewhere in all this, Windows 95 asks the user to provide some input in the form of a name and password. It checks this against the contents of the appropriate .PWL file. If the password checks out, Windows 95 completes the boot process.

Finally, Windows gets the Explorer interface up and running (it was loaded before but wasn't running). It displays all the required objects on the Desktop and initializes the Taskbar. This is the point where it also looks at your Startup folder to see which applications you want to start automatically. You're set up and ready to compute.

Addressing Memory

If you think memory management under Windows 95 is a simple matter, think again. Windows has many ways of looking at this critical resource, and it's important to understand how they differ. We'll look at the two different memory models that Windows must use to manage the memory on your system: segmented and flat. Of the two, flat is more efficient, but Windows needs to maintain both for compatibility reasons. The following paragraphs explain why.

The Windows 3.1 Segmented Memory Model

The preceding section briefly presented the two Windows memory models and explained how they differ. I told you that segmented memory mode is a lot harder for a programmer to use than the flat memory model used with Windows NT. Of course, the first question that comes to mind is why Microsoft would even bother using the segmented memory model for enhanced-mode Windows 3.1. After all, enhanced mode is designed for the 80386, and we already know it supports the flat memory model. There are two good reasons. First, the 80286 processor doesn't provide flat memory model support. If Microsoft had decided to use the flat memory model, they would have had to include a double set of files for every aspect of Windows 3.1. The second reason is equally simple. Windows 3.1 rides on top of DOS, and DOS uses 16-bit code. Windows 3.x already performs quite a juggling act in talking with DOS, and keeping a 32-bit ball up in the air as well would have been a little too much. So, we ended up with a 16-bit operating environment called Windows 3.1.

Now that you have a feel for why segmentation is still around, let's look at how it works. A segmented memory model uses two 16-bit registers to hold an address. In real mode, the processor uses a segment and an offset. Think of the segment as the street number and the offset as a specific house on that street. The processor combines the segment with the offset to create a 20-bit address for the 8086 or a 24-bit address for the 80286. Just how does it do this? The processor shifts the segment register's contents 4 bits to the right to make the transition. A 20-bit address yields the 1 MB of address space that you've come to know and love when using DOS. Of course, the bottom line for the application is that the application, not the operating system, has control over the memory it uses.

Windows doesn't operate in real mode; it uses protected mode. The theory behind the protected-mode segmented memory model is slightly different than with real mode. Look at Figure 6.22, which shows a simplified version of the protected-mode segmented memory model. Notice that we no longer use a segment:offset pair, but a selector:offset pair. There's a big difference between a segment and a selector. A segment represents an actual location in memory, and a selector represents a position in a descriptor table. The table contains the actual location in memory. (It also contains a variety of other information that I won't cover here.)

Figure 6.22.

Windows 3.x uses the segmented memory model shown here. Windows 95 also uses this model for 16-bit applications.

So how does this look-up table work? When Windows grants an application access to a specific range of memory, it gives that application a key to it. That key is the selector. The application sends two values to the processor when it needs to access memory. The first value is the key (selector) that the processor needs to unlock the memory. The second value is the exact location (offset) within that range. Using selectors gives the operating system control over the entire range of memory on the system. Since an application must use a key to unlock its memory, and only the processor knows the physical location of that memory, the system should be fairly secure.

In fact, the selector does provide some security information to the operating system. Bits 0 and 1 of the selector tell the operating system its privilege level. This equates the rings of protection that I discuss later. Suffice it to say that 0 (00b) provides the most privileged access and 3 (11b) provides the least privileged. All applications run at privilege level 3 under Windows; only the operating system runs at privilege level 0. Bit 2 contains the number of the table that Windows should use to access the memory. There are two descriptor tables: the global descriptor table (GDT) and the local descriptor table (LDT). A value of 1 selects the LDT. Windows uses the GDT for all common data. There is only one GDT for the entire system. Each application also has its own LDT for private data. Finally, bits 3 through 15 contain the actual index into the table.

Rather than get mired in a wealth of bits at this point, let's just say that Windows verifies that the application's security level is high enough to access the data it wants to see. It then takes the base address value (the protected-mode version of a segment) that it finds at the specified location in the descriptor table and combines it with the offset to find the physical location of the requested data in memory.

The segmented memory model has several problems. The biggest one (if you're a programmer) is that you can allocate memory only in 64 KB chunks. Remember, the address is made of a selector and an offset. Since the offset register is only 16 bits, it can handle only 64 KB of memory. This means that the programmer has to write an application that manages a bunch of selectors, each pointing to a different 64 KB chunk of memory. The chance of corrupting one of these selectors increases as the application uses more and more memory. It isn't too difficult to understand why a 16-bit Windows application could get confused and end up writing to the wrong section of memory. The results are usually catastrophic and end in a frozen machine.

Of course, there's a limitation here for the user as well. Have you ever wondered where all those "out of memory" messages come from? Many users have experienced the problem of Windows reporting that it has all kinds of memory available, then deciding for no reason that it doesn't. Well, here's one culprit. Every icon, every dialog box, every menu, and every other resource you can imagine has to go somewhere in memory in order for Windows to use it. When Microsoft originally designed Windows 3.0, they decided that all those resources had to go into what programmers call the near heap—a 64 KB chunk of global memory that Windows 3.0 sets aside for resources. Using the near heap increases execution speed, especially for time-consuming screen redraws, since the operating system isn't constantly manipulating selectors to access multiple 64 KB chunks of memory. Needless to say, when you consider that just one icon is 766 bytes, it doesn't take too many of them to fill that 64 KB heap.

After many user complaints about strange memory problems, Microsoft set aside two heaps in Windows 3.1. The first heap, the GDI heap, contains icons and other graphic resources. The other heap, the USER heap, contains nongraphic resources such as dialog boxes. Even with two 64 KB heaps, Windows 3.1 users still ran out of memory. There's an easy way to determine if you're about to run out of space in one of these two heaps. If you look at Program Manager's About dialog, you'll notice a value that tells you the percentage of system resources—the amount of that 64 KB chunk of memory that's left in the smallest heap. In other words, if the GDI heap has 20 percent of its space left and the USER heap has 30 percent, Windows will report a value of 20 percent (12.8 KB) for system resources.

The Windows NT Flat Memory Model

When Microsoft designed Windows NT, they decided to use a different memory model supported by 80386 and above processors—the flat memory model. When the operating system places the processor in this mode, it essentially says that everything will use the same segment. The processor hasn't done away with segmentation, but the operating system chooses to ignore this capability. Eliminating segmentation greatly simplifies life for the programmer. No longer does the programmer need to worry about the segment registers; only the address is important.

Finding an Address

You might wonder how the operating system maintains control of memory using the flat addressing scheme. Under the segmented scheme, the processor maintained control through a table of selectors. The application used a selector as a key to open up to a 64 KB chunk of memory. The flat addressing mode has a protection scheme as well. In fact, this scheme provides even more flexibility than the segmented model. Figure 6.23 shows the flat memory model.

Each 32-bit address has three fields. Each field corresponds to one level of protection enforced by the processor under the flat memory model. Even though the programmer doesn't have to worry about these fields when writing an application, the operating system and processor do. The first field resides in bits 31 through 22 of the address. It points to an entry in the page table directory. Just like the segmented memory model, the flat model gives the application a key to a specific piece of memory, not its actual location. Locating the right page table is the first step in finding the address.

Let's take a moment to look at what a page table really is. Remember that in the segmented memory model, an application would have to allocate memory in 64 KB chunks. If it needed a larger allocation, the application would have to ask for multiple chunks. A page table gets rid of this problem; the application simply asks for the total amount of memory that it needs, and Windows provides it. The number of pages in this table corresponds to the number of 4 KB pages that the application allocates. If an application asked for 400 KB of RAM, the table would contain 100 entries. As you can see, the flat address model is already more flexible than the segmented model.

Figure 6.23.
The flat address model doesn't use a selector:offset pair to address memory. Each register contains a 32-bit address that is split into three fields.

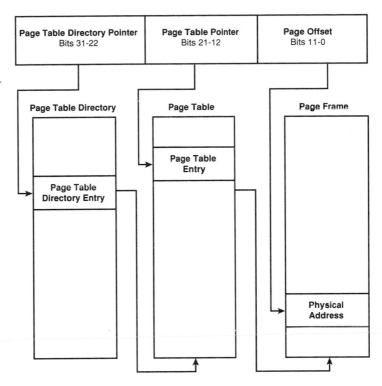

Once Windows finds a specific page table, it uses the value in bits 21 through 12 of the address to find a specific page. Think back to what I told you about an application's memory limit. Every application can use up to 4 GB of memory. Now, look at the number of bits set aside for pages under Windows. There are 10. There are also 10 bits set aside for page table directory entries. If you take 2^{10} page table directory entries × 2^{10} page table entries × 4 KB pages, you get 4 GB.

After Windows finds a specific page within a specific page table, it takes the address it finds there and adds it to the offset in bits 11 through 0 of the address. These 12 bits allow an application to select any byte within the 4 KB page.

Sleight-of-Hand Memory Management

Using 4 KB pages provides a number of benefits when it comes to memory management. Remember in the preceding section when I talked about the page table directory and the page table? Each entry in these tables contains 32 bits of data, yet the actual pointers consume a lot less than that. So what does the processor use the additional space for? I don't want to go into a blow-by-blow description of 80386 memory management. However, it might be useful to look at what some of these extra entries do. Fortunately, both tables use the same format, so we'll cover them at the same time.

Of course, the main purpose of using these tables in the first place is to point to something. That's what bits 31 through 12 do. In the page table directory, they point to a page table. In the page table, they contain the physical address that gets combined with the offset in the original address. Bit 6 contains the D (dirty) bit. Whenever an application changes the contents of a page of memory, Windows changes the dirty bit. This reminds the processor that it hasn't written the change to disk. If the processor wants to use this page of physical memory for some other purpose, it needs to write the existing page to the Windows swap file.

Bit 5 contains the A (accessed) bit. Whenever an application reads, writes, or executes a 4 KB page of memory, Windows changes the status of this bit. Windows can use this bit to determine whether or not it should remove the page from memory to make room for something else.

Bit 2 contains the U/S (user/supervisor) bit. This is part of the 80386 protection scheme. If the bit is set to 0, it contains a supervisor page. Applications can never access supervisor pages, because they belong to the operating system. On the other hand, setting the bit to 1 means that it's a user page. Applications can access any user page that belongs to them.

Bit 1 contains the R/W (read/write) bit. You wouldn't want an application to overwrite the code in a page. Setting this bit to 0 prevents an application from doing so. Data pages are set to 1; code pages are set to 0.

Bit 0 contains the P (present) bit. Windows needs to know whether or not a page is in physical memory. The application can't use a page of memory that's sitting on disk in the swap file. The page must reside in physical memory. If the application asks for access to a page of memory that is on disk, the processor raises an exception (basically an alarm). This exception tells Windows that it needs to retrieve the page from its swap file on disk so that the application can access it.

As you can see, these table entries help Windows perform memory management sleight of hand. It can move 4 KB pages from physical memory to disk as needed. Other bits protect operating system-specific memory from prying application eyes. Still other bits help protect your application from itself by preventing it from overwriting precious application code.

Virtual 86 Mode

Up to this point, you've seen how Windows manages memory for its own applications. What happens when you open a DOS box and run an application? The first thing you need to realize is that Windows takes a snapshot of your DOS environment before it completely boots. It creates a "phantom" DOS environment and holds on to it until needed. When you open a DOS box, Windows creates what is known as a virtual machine. This isn't a physical machine that you can touch, but it has all the capabilities of a standard 8086. After Windows creates this virtual machine, it copies the phantom DOS environment to it, and you have a DOS box. This DOS box has all the same device drivers and TSRs as the DOS environment you left when booting Windows.

But what differentiates a virtual DOS machine from the rest of the Windows environment? The 80386 processor introduced a new mode called virtual 86 mode (V86 for short) in which Windows can create multiple 8086s. Each of these virtual machines thinks it's the only machine running. On the other hand, Windows applications run in protected mode. Windows has to switch between protected mode (to run Windows applications) and V86 mode (to run DOS applications). I won't go into the actual intricacies of how the processor switches between protected and V86 here; only a heavy-duty chip designer would enjoy that conversation. Suffice it to say that each machine is totally separate and that V86 mode is a third mode that emulates real mode but doesn't actually run there.

Cooperative Versus Preemptive Multitasking

Multitasking is one of those nebulous words that everyone uses but no one takes the time to define. The first thing you need to do before you can understand multitasking is to define the word *task*. A task is essentially an application that is running. When you start Windows, you might think that nothing is running, but there are already several applications getting work done on your machine. For example, Explorer (or Program Manager) is considered a task. Any network connections or print spoolers are considered tasks. A screen saver is yet another task. There are numerous system-related tasks as well. The Windows kernel is considered a task. Industry uses two terms to refer to a running application or thread: process and task. I prefer *task* since it's a little less nebulous than *process*. However, you will probably see a mixture of both in the documentation you read.

When talking about Windows 3.1, you can associate every task with a single application. The definition of *task* doesn't really stop here for Windows 95 and Windows NT. Some 32-bit applications use a technique called *multithreading*, which enables them to perform more than one task at a time. For example, you could recalculate your spreadsheet and print at the same time if the application supports multithreading. What happens is the spreadsheet starts another task (called a *thread*) to take care of printing. It might even start a second thread to do the recalculation so that you can continue to enter data. One way to look at threads is as a subtask under the application that is running.

Now that you understand what a task is, it's time to look at the definition of multitasking. Everyone assumes that multitasking is just that—several tasks (or processes) running simultaneously on one machine. This is a good start for a definition, but it doesn't end there. An important consideration is how the operating system allocates time between tasks. When talking about Windows, it becomes very important to actually define the method used to manage tasks and to differentiate between different kinds of multitasking. Windows 95 supports two kinds of multitasking: cooperative and preemptive.

Windows 3.0 introduced a feature called *cooperative multitasking*. This is how it was supposed to work: Application A would run for a little while, just long enough to get one component of a task finished. It would then turn control of the system back over to Windows so that Windows could take care of any housekeeping chores and allow application B to run for a while. This cycle continued in a round-robin fashion between all the tasks running at any given time.

What really happened is that some applications followed the rules but others didn't. Under cooperative multitasking, the operating system gave up too much control; an application could hog all the system resources if it wanted to. Some applications do just that. The result is that cooperative multitasking doesn't really work all that well. Most of the time the user spends looking at the hourglass is really time in which Windows has temporarily lost control of the system to an application that doesn't want to share with anyone else.

All the legacy applications that run under Windows 95—the 16-bit applications that you moved from Windows 3.x—still have to run in a cooperative multitasking mode. However, Windows 95 minimizes the impact of these applications by running them in one shared address space. All the 16-bit applications have to cooperate with each other, but they don't affect any 32-bit applications running on your machine. This includes Explorer and any other Windows 95-specific tools. (And, of course, you will upgrade most of your commonly-used 16-bit applications, such as your word processor and spreadsheet, to Windows 95 versions.)

When Microsoft designed Windows NT, they wanted something better than cooperative multitasking, so they designed an operating system that uses preemptive multitasking. Windows 95 supports preemptive multitasking for any 32-bit application you run. Think of it this way: Preemptive multitasking works like a traffic light. Traffic goes one way for a while, but then the light changes and traffic goes the other way. The actual amount of time each task gets is weighed by the user and the operating system to meet some criteria, but this access is supposed to be fair. Every application is supposed to get its fair share of processor time, and preemptive multitasking enforces this principle. Windows 95 monitors each application and interrupts it when its time is up. It doesn't matter if the application wants to give up control over the system or not. Windows 95 doesn't give it a choice.

There's another, more important, difference in the way the system reacts under preemptive multitasking. Under Windows 3.1, an hourglass means that the system is tied up. You can't do anything else until the hourglass goes away. On the other hand, an hourglass under Windows 95 only means that the current task is tied up. You can always start another task or switch to an existing task. If that task isn't busy, you can perform some work with it while you wait for the initial task to complete its work. You know when the original application has finished because the hourglass goes away when you place your cursor over the task's window. The bottom line? Preemptive multitasking means that the user doesn't have to wait for the system.

Finally, cooperative multitasking has a serious flaw. Because Windows lost control when some applications took over, there was no way to clear that application if the machine froze. Since

Windows 95 maintains constant control of the machine, you no longer need to worry about the machine freezing in the middle of a task. Even if one application does hang, you only need to end that task, not reboot the entire machine. As with Windows 3.1, pressing Ctrl-Alt-Delete doesn't automatically reboot the machine. However, unlike Windows 3.1, Windows 95 displays a list of applications, and you get to choose which one to terminate. See Figure 6.24.

Figure 6.24.
Preemptive multitasking means that Windows 95 never loses control of the machine. It also means that you can recover from an application error with ease.

You might wonder why Microsoft (or any other vendor) would use cooperative multitasking if preemptive multitasking is so much better. There are a few good reasons. First, DOS is nonreentrant. This means you have to allow DOS to complete one task before you give it another one. If you disturb DOS in the middle of a task, the entire system could (and will) freeze. Since Windows 3.x runs on top of DOS, it can't use preemptive multitasking for any services that interact with DOS. Unfortunately, one of those services is the disk subsystem. Do you see now why it would be fairly difficult to use preemptive multitasking on any system that runs on top of DOS?

The second problem with preemptive multitasking is really a two-part scenario. Both relate to ease of designing the operating system. When an operating system provides preemptive multitasking, it also has to include some kind of method for monitoring devices. What if two applications decided that they needed to use the COM port at the same time? With cooperative multitasking, the application that started to use the COM port would gain control of it and lock the other application out. In a preemptive multitasking situation, the first application could get halfway through the allocation process and get stopped, and then the second application could start the allocation process. What happens if the first application is reactivated by the system? You have two applications that think they have access to one device. In reality, both applications have access, and you have a mess. Windows 95 handles this problem by using a programming construct called a critical section. (I'll discuss this feature more in a moment.)

Preemptive multitasking also needs some type of priority system to ensure that critical tasks get a larger share of the processor's time than noncritical tasks. Remember, a task can no longer dictate how long it needs system resources; that's all in the hands of the operating system. Theoretically, you should be able to rely on the users to tell the operating system how they want their applications prioritized, and then allow the operating system to take care of the rest. What really happens is that a low-priority task could run into a fault situation and need system resources immediately to resolve it. A static priority system can't handle that situation. In addition, that low-priority task could end up getting little or no system resources when a group of high-priority tasks starts to run. The priority system Windows 95 uses provides a dynamic means of changing a task's priority. When a high-priority task runs, Windows 95 lowers its priority. When a low-priority task gets passed over in favor of a high-priority task, Windows 95 increases its priority. As you can see, the dynamic priority system enforces the idea that some tasks should get more system resources than others, yet ensures that every task gets at least some system resources.

There's a final consideration when looking at preemptive multitasking. Even if you use the best dynamic priority system in the world and every piece of the operating system works just the way it should, you'll run into situations where a task has to complete a sequence of events without getting disturbed. For example, the application might need to make certain that a database transaction gets written to disk before it hands control of the system back to the operating system. If another task tried to do something related to that transaction before the first task completed, you could end up with invalid or damaged data in the database. Programmers call a piece of code that performs this task a *critical section*. Normally a critical section occurs with system-related tasks such as memory allocation, but it also can happen with application-related tasks such as writing information to a file. Cooperative multitasking systems don't have to worry as much about critical sections, because the task decides when the operating system regains control of the system. On the other hand, a preemptive multitasking system needs some way for a task to communicate the need to complete a critical section of code. Under Windows 95, a task tells the operating system that it needs to perform a critical section of code using a semaphore (a flag). If a hardware interrupt or some other application were to ask to perform a task that didn't interfere with any part of the critical section, Windows 95 could allow it to proceed. All a critical section guarantees is that the task and its environment will remain undisturbed until the task completes its work.

Windows 95 Internals

I provided an overview of Windows 95's internal architecture in Chapter 2. This chapter assumes that you've read that overview and are ready to move on to bigger and better things. The following paragraphs start where that discussion left off and show you some of the deeper and darker secrets of Windows 95.

Before I begin a discussion of individual Windows architectural components, I'd like to direct your attention to the "rings" of protection that the 80386 (and above) processor provides. There are four security rings within the Intel protection scheme, but most operating systems use only two (or sometimes three) of them. The inner security ring is ring 0. This is where the operating system proper is. The outermost ring is 3. That's where the applications reside. Sometimes an operating system gives device drivers better access to some operating system features than an application gets by running them at ring 1 or 2. Windows doesn't make any concessions; device drivers run at ring 0 or 3, depending on their purpose.

Windows uses these protection rings to make certain that only operating system components can access the inner workings of Windows, that an application can't change settings that might cause the entire system to crash. For example, Windows reserves the right to allocate memory from the global pool; therefore, the capabilities needed to perform this task rest at ring 0. On the other hand, applications need to access memory assigned to them. That's why Windows assigns local memory a protection value of 3.

Think of each ring as a security perimeter. Before you can enter that perimeter, you have to know the secret password. Windows gives the password only to applications that it knows it can trust; everyone else has to stay out. Whenever an application does try to circumvent security, the processor raises an exception. Think of an exception as a security alarm. The exception sends the Windows police (better known as an exception handler) after the offending application. After its arrest and trial, Windows calmly terminates the offending application. Of course, it notifies the user before performing this task, but the user usually doesn't have much of a choice in the matter.

Figure 2.14 gives you a pretty good idea of exactly who Windows trusts. Applications and device drivers running at ring 3 have very few capabilities outside their own resources. In fact, Windows even curtails these capabilities somewhat. Some of the activities that a DOS application could get by with, such as directly manipulating video memory, aren't allowed here. The reason is simple: Video memory is a shared resource. Whenever another application would need to share something, you can be certain that your application wouldn't be able to access it directly.

Now, on to the various components that actually make up Windows. The following sections break the Windows components into main areas. Each of these general groups contains descriptions of the individual components and what tasks they perform. Remember that this is only a general discussion. Windows is much more complex than it might first appear. The deeper you get as a programmer, the more you'll see the actual complexity of this operating system.

System Virtual Machine

The System Virtual Machine (VM) component of Windows 95 contains three main elements: 32-bit Windows applications, the shell, and 16-bit Windows applications. Essentially, the System VM component provides most of the Windows 95 user-specific functionality. Without it, you couldn't run any applications. Notice that I don't include DOS applications here. This is because Windows uses an entirely different set of capabilities to run DOS applications. It even runs them in a different processor mode.

Theoretically, the System VM also provides support for the various Windows API layer components. However, since these components provide a different sort of service, I chose to discuss them in a separate area. Even though applications use the API and users interact with applications, you really don't think about the API until it comes time to write an application. Therefore, I always think of the API as a programmer-specific service rather than something that the user really needs to worry about. The following list describes the System VM components in detail:

- 32-bit Windows applications: These are the new Win32-specific applications that use a subset of the Windows NT API. In fact, many Windows NT applications, such as Word for Windows NT, will run just fine under Windows 95. A 32-bit application usually provides better multitasking capabilities than its 16-bit counterpart. In addition, many 32-bit applications support new Windows features such as long filenames, while most 16-bit applications do not. 32-bit applications provide two additional features. The more important one is the use of preemptive versus cooperative multitasking. This makes your work flow more smoothly and forces the system to wait for you as necessary, rather than the other way around. The second one is the use of a flat memory address space. This feature really makes a difference in how much memory an application gets and how well it uses it. In addition, an application that uses a flat address space should run slightly faster since it no longer has to spend time working with Intel's memory segmentation scheme.

- The shell: Two shells are supplied with Windows 95, and you can choose either. The newer shell, Explorer, provides full 32-bit capabilities. It also sports the new interface shown in Figure 1.2. Explorer combines all the features you used to find in Program Manager, Print Manager, and File Manager. You can also use the older Program Manager interface with Windows 95 (see Figure 1.1). It doesn't provide all the bells and whistles that Explorer does, but it will certainly ease the transition for some users who learned the Program Manager interface. Switching between shells is easy. All you need to do is change the Shell= entry in the [Boot] section of SYSTEM.INI. Of course, Windows 95 also lets you choose which shell you want to use when you install it.

- 16-bit Windows applications: All your older applications—the ones you own right now— are 16-bit applications unless you bought them for use with Windows NT. Windows 95 runs all these applications in one shared address space. Essentially, Windows 95 groups all these 16-bit applications into one area and treats them as if they were one task. You really won't notice any performance hit as a result, but it does make it easier for Windows 95 to recover from application errors. With it, Windows 95 can mix 16-bit and 32-bit applications on one system.

The Windows API Layer

Two Windows APIs are included with Windows 95. The first is exactly like the one supplied with Windows 3.1. It provides all the 16-bit services that the old Windows had to provide for applications. This is the API that an older application will use when it runs.

The other API is the new Win32 API used by Windows NT. It provides a subset of the features that all 32-bit applications running under Windows NT can access. The 32-bit API provides about the same feature set as the 16-bit API, but it's more robust. In addition, a 32-bit application enjoys the benefits that this environment provides. Check out the section "The System Files" in Chapter 2 for more details about the system files and the Windows 95 API.

Getting 16-Bit and 32-Bit Applications to Work Together

Windows 95 consists of a combination of 16-bit and 32-bit applications. All those older applications and device drivers you use now have to work within the same environment as the new 32-bit drivers and applications that Windows 95 provides. You already know how Windows takes care of separating the two by using different memory schemes. The 16-bit applications work within their own virtual machine area. It would be nice if things ended there, but they can't.

There are times when 16-bit and 32-bit applications have to talk to each other. This doesn't just apply to programs the user uses to perform work, but to device drivers and other types of Windows applications as well. Most Windows applications use a memory structure called the *stack* to transfer information from one application to another. Think of the stack as a database of variables. Each record in this database is a fixed length so that every application knows how to grab information from it. Here's where the problems start. The stack for 32-bit applications is 32 bits wide. That makes sense. It makes equal sense that the stack for 16-bit applications should be 16 bits wide. See the problem?

Of course, the problems are only beginning. What happens when you need to send a 32-bit value from a 16-bit application to a 32-bit application? The 32-bit application will expect to see the whole value in the EAX register. On the other hand, the 16-bit application expects to see the value in a combination of the DX and AX registers. This same problem translates to pointers as well. A 32-bit application, for example, will use the SS:ESP register pair to point to the stack.

But wait, there's more! Remember that 16-bit applications use a segmented address space. An address consists of a selector and an offset. A 16-bit application combines these two pieces to form a complete address. On the other hand, 32-bit applications use a flat address space. They wouldn't know what to do with a selector if you gave them one. All they want is the actual address within the total realm of available memory. So how do you send the address of a string from a 16-bit to a 32-bit application?

By now you're probably wondering how Windows keeps 16-bit and 32-bit applications working together. After all, there are a number of inconsistencies and incompatibilities to deal with. The stack is only the tip of the incompatibility iceberg. It's easy to envision a method of converting 16-bit data to a 32-bit format. All you really need to do is pad the front end of the variable with zeros. But how does a 32-bit application send data to a 16-bit application? If the 32-bit application just dumps a wide variable onto the stack, the 16-bit application will never know what do to with the information it receives. Clearly the data needs to go through some type of conversion. Windows uses something called the *thunk layer* to allow 16-bit and 32-bit applications to communicate. Figure 6.25 shows the interaction of 16-bit and 32-bit applications through the thunk layer.

Figure 6.25.

The thunk layer makes it possible for 16-bit and 32-bit applications to coexist peacefully under Windows.

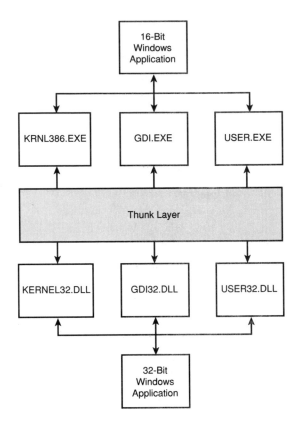

As you can see, the three components of the API layer provide translation services in addition to the other services they perform. Each API component translates the data and addresses within its area of expertise. For example, the two GDI components translate all graphics data between 16-bit and 32-bit applications.

Most thunking is pretty straightforward. For example, Windows simply moves register data to the appropriate register. The thunk layer builds a new stack to meet the needs of the application receiving it. Address translation takes a little more work. In addition, address translation is very expensive timewise. Every time Windows has to translate an address, it must perform several selector loads. The processor has to verify every selector load, so these translations can get cumbersome. Fortunately, you as an application programmer won't have to worry too much about the actual thunk process. What you do need to worry about is making certain that the process actually takes place when calling a piece of code that needs it.

Windows and DLLs

Under DOS, an application must contain every component it needs in order to execute. The programmer links in library support for graphics, low-level utilities, and a variety of other needs. Of course, this whole scenario is based on the fact that the application is the only thing running under DOS.

Windows is a different kind of environment. There's always more than one task running under Windows. Somewhere along the way, someone figured out that if you have multiple applications running, there might be some duplicate code out there as well. For example, the display routines used by one application are probably the same as the display routines used by another application at some particular level. The same person probably figured out that you could reduce the overall memory requirements of a system if you allowed all the applications to share these redundant pieces of code instead of loading them from scratch for each application.

The DLL (dynamic link library) is the culmination of just such an idea. There are two forms of linking under Windows (or OS/2 or UNIX, for that matter). The first link combines all the object modules required to create a unique application. That link cycle happens right after the programmer finishes compiling the code. The second link cycle happens when the user goes to load the application. This is where the DLL comes in.

Every Windows application has unresolved references to functions. Microsoft calls them import library calls. What these calls do is load a DLL containing the code required to satisfy that function call. If the DLL happens to be in memory when Windows calls it, Windows increments the DLL's usage level to indicate that more than one application is using the DLL. When an application stops using a DLL, Windows decrements its usage level. When the DLL's usage count goes to 0, Windows can unload it from memory. In effect, using DLLs can save quite a bit of memory when you're loading multiple applications.

So what does this have to do with the API? The Windows API starts with three files, as just described. However, these three files call other files—DLLs, to be exact. Rather than create three huge files, Microsoft chose to reduce the size of the Windows kernel by using DLLs.

This capability also makes Windows more flexible. Consider printer support. All you need to do to add printer support for a new printer is copy some files to disk. At least one of those files will be a DLL. Every printer DLL contains the same entry points (function names), so Windows doesn't need to learn anything new to support the printer. The only thing it has to do is install a new DLL. Your application performs the same task when you tell it to print. It looks at the DLLs currently installed for the system. The application doesn't have to care whether the printer is a dot matrix or a laser. All it needs to know how to do is tell the printer to print; the DLL takes care of the rest.

The Base System

Windows 95 uses the base system component to take care of any system-specific services. We covered this particular component in detail in the section "Architecture" in Chapter 2. Refer to that discussion if you want to know the details of the base system.

The DOS Virtual Machine

The PC revolution started with the DOS application. It's not too surprising, then, that a number of DOS applications are still floating around. I told you in the "Architecture" section of Chapter 2 that each DOS application runs in a virtual machine. Let's look at this topic in a little more detail.

The word *virtual* gets severely overused in the Windows environment. We have virtual memory, virtual system machines, and every other kind of virtual device you can think of. I wanted to make sure that you understand that the DOS virtual machine is a different kind of virtual than all these other virtuals on the system. A virtual DOS machine runs in the virtual 8086 mode of the processor. All the other virtual machines in Windows run in protected mode. Virtual 8086 mode creates multiple 1 MB 8086 machines in protected memory. Each machine has its own copy of DOS, device drivers, I/O space, and everything else that an 8086 would have. About the only thing missing is the hardware itself, and that's why this machine is known as a virtual machine. You can't touch it, but it does exist. As far as the application is concerned, there's no difference between this machine and any real machine it could run on.

The virtual machine hasn't changed much since the days when Quarterdeck first introduced QEMM. Except for a few new features designed to enhance the performance of applications running under the Windows virtual machine, this aspect of Windows hasn't really changed much from version 3.1. However, there is one exception to this rule. Some DOS applications use DPMI-compatible extenders that allow them to run in protected mode. Under Windows 3.1, these applications would still run under the processor's virtual 8086 mode. Windows 95 improves system performance by allowing these applications to run in protected mode.

On Your Own

Use the Registry Editor to create a copy of your registry using the procedure found in this chapter. Make sure you store this text copy of the registry in a safe place.

The registry is a central part of Windows 95. You can't do anything without it. Explore the registry using the Registry Editor. What do the values associated with each of the keys tell you about your system's configuration? Make sure you exit the Registry Editor without making any changes to any of the keys.

Open MSDOS.SYS using Notepad or another text editor. Identify all the switches in your current configuration using Table 6.3. Are there any switches you could add to this file to improve system performance? If so, follow this procedure to modify MSDOS.SYS:

1. Right-click on MSDOS.SYS and select Properties from the context menu.
2. Uncheck the Hidden and Read-only attributes on the General page. Close the Properties dialog by clicking on OK.
3. Use an editor such as Notepad to make the required changes. Save the changes and exit the editor.
4. Open the MSDOS.SYS Properties dialog again. This time, check both the Read-only and Hidden attributes. Click on OK to close the dialog.

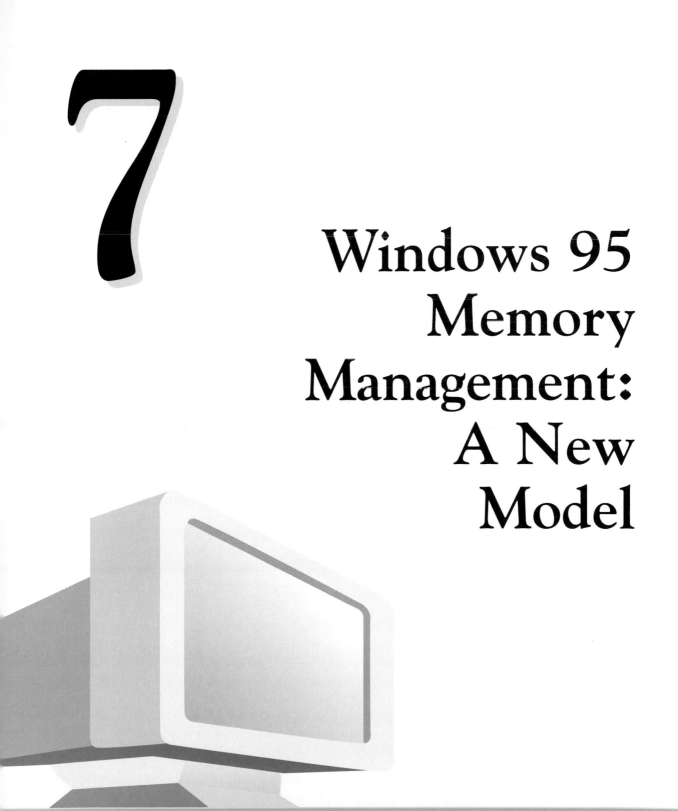

7

Windows 95 Memory Management: A New Model

I hear so much about managing this and that today that I often wonder how anyone gets any work done. Management tools abound to help people perform the complex task of making the most out of the resources they have available, whether it's people, equipment, or even components of that equipment. In this respect, using Windows 95 is no different than any other aspect of life. You have to manage your resources carefully to get the biggest payback from your investment. However, if you spend all your time managing your resources, you won't get any return, because you will have spent everything before you start. Therein lies the challenge of managing time without wasting it.

So what are the resources you have to be so careful about? Memory and hard disk space are the two major concerns that come to mind. Of course, processor cycles are in there somewhere as well. However, you might not think about some resources right away. For example, how valuable is your time? Trading some memory or processor cycles for a big increase in your personal productivity can mean having more resources available for other people to use in the long run. For right now, let's take a close look at managing memory. We'll pursue the other topics later.

Looking Ahead: We'll look at managing your hard drive in Chapter 8. Personal time management appears in Chapter 9. Reading the "Exploring Explorer" section of Chapter 9 will help you learn to use Explorer in the most efficient manner possible. Learning to use Explorer well is just one of the time management principles you'll learn in this chapter. Chapter 9 also presents other time management aids, such as how to use the Startup Folder to reduce the time you spend configuring your machine by hand. Looking at Chapters 7, 8, and 9 together will give you the total management picture for Windows 95. The trick is to balance them as needed. (I'll talk about that in Chapter 9 as well.)

Managing memory was always a problem under Windows 3.x. The problem wasn't so much a matter of lack of memory, but a lack of the tools required to adequately manage memory. The first thing you need to understand is that there are two different kinds of memory to worry about when you're working with Windows applications. You need enough system memory to load the application and any data files. Windows also needs enough system resources to load things such as the windows, dialog boxes, and icons your application uses.

System memory is very difficult to pin down under Windows 3.x. For example, when you look at the About box in Program Manager and see that you have 15 MB of RAM and 55 percent of system resources left, what does that really tell you? There are a few problems here. First, Windows 3.x always includes the amount of virtual memory it creates on disk in the number it provides for RAM. This means that you could have almost no physical memory left, and all your RAM is really on disk. A lack of physical memory under Windows 3.x always leads to disk thrashing—Windows spends more time swapping things to disk than it does taking care of your application's needs. This is just one example of an improperly managed system.

What about the system resources number? Does it really tell you what kind of system resource? Windows 3.x actually has two system resources to worry about: user and GDI (graphics device interface). The first one contains all your windows and other user presentation elements. The second one contains all the graphic elements that make Windows a joy to use. A lack of one resource means closing some applications. A lack of the other might be cured by removing your wallpaper for a while. The difference is important. Wallpaper isn't a productivity enhancer; you can get by without it for a while. The same can't be said of an important application you might need to run.

Here's the problem: Windows 3.x never gives you enough information to manage those system resources. The About box tells you about the system resource with the least amount of memory left. Of course, this doesn't tell you which resource the number refers to or what is left of the other resource. So now what do you do? I usually got rid of my wallpaper long enough to see if I had enough system resources to get the job done. If that didn't work, one of my applications had to bite the dust. This productive way of managing system resources usually cost me a lot more than it saved. With such wonderful tools available to the average user, it's no wonder that no one could manage their system resources under Windows 3.x without buying a third-party product.

Windows 95 doesn't follow the example of its predecessor. It provides a lot of tools to manage your system resources. We looked at some of these new tools in Chapter 3. The short view of this is that Microsoft has finally provided at least a minimal set of tools to manage your memory (and other system resources). Those tools aren't automatic by any definition, and they don't provide the most detailed information, but at least they're available and they can get the job done. It's definitely a step in the right direction.

Peter's Principle: Management Versus Micro-Management

A good manager will often provide a little input and see what happens. If more input is required, fine. Otherwise, the manager leaves his employees alone to get their jobs done in whatever way works for them. This is the kind of person everyone likes to work for, and he still manages to amaze his superiors with the amount of work he can accomplish. There isn't much of a secret to his success. Spending your time getting your work done instead of doing someone else's work is always more productive.

There's another kind of manager: the micro-manager. He's the one you see following behind an employee at every step of every task. There's only one way to get the job done: his way. It might not be efficient—it might even be counterproductive for that particular employee—but at least he can always tell his superiors what the people under him are doing. This fellow will always fail to impress everyone.

You might become a micro-manager under Windows 95 if you're not careful. There are a lot more tools at your disposal, and it's easy to suppose that they are there for a reason. The truth of the matter is that even though you have more tools when using Windows 95, the operating system is actually better at managing its memory without any help from you. The tools are there so that you can better determine what kind of "little input" Windows 95 needs.

When working with Windows 95, the best principle is to provide a little input and see what happens. If more input is required, fine. If not, you've got a fully tuned system that will get the job done for you. Let the system do the work it's designed to do until you see a good reason to provide that little bit of input.

The problems with Windows 3.x don't stop at a lack of tools. I find myself constantly fighting to get enough of the type of memory I need at any given time. If I manage to get enough memory together to run a program that requires expanded memory and a page frame in a DOS window, I don't have enough conventional memory because my device drivers won't load high. (A page frame consumes a memory-killing 64 KB of upper memory, more than enough to load one or two drivers.) It always seems that Windows 3.x can't provide the kinds of memory that I need.

The bottom-line reason for all these memory problems under Windows 3.x is all the real-mode drivers and TSRs you have to load just to get your system running. My CONFIG.SYS and AUTOEXEC.BAT are filled with all kinds of entries, many of which are essential to configuring the machine the way I need to. For example, there's no way I can get by without loading the drivers for my CD-ROM, yet these drivers consume about 62 KB of RAM. My sound card consumes another memory-clogging 37 KB—and don't forget about all those handy utilities that most people load. All these drivers mean that I need some form of advanced memory management to load some of it high. The alternative is to give up running some of my DOS applications—all of which assume I have at least 512 KB of conventional memory free.

You can force Windows 95 to have this same kind of problem. Installing a memory manager is about the worst thing you can do if you don't have real-mode drivers to load. Letting Windows 95 manage memory for you will provide better—or at least more consistent—results. Before we get into a heavy-duty discussion of specific memory-tuning techniques, let's look at the types of memory that Windows 95 provides and how it affects you from a user standpoint. We'll also take a quick look at the various Windows operating modes and how they affect memory.

Memory Types

Windows uses a variety of memory types to accomplish a variety of tasks. Some of them relate to Windows itself; others relate to the applications that Windows supports. The following paragraphs will help you understand these memory types.

- Conventional: This is the original 640 KB of memory that IBM set aside for DOS applications. Every DOS application needs conventional memory in order to run. Windows always uses a small piece of conventional memory as well, even if there's enough upper memory for it to load. Even though the processor can access that upper memory, DOS can't. In order for Windows to activate itself, it has to load a section of itself where DOS can call it. Figures 8.1 through 8.3 in Chapter 8 show how Windows and DOS interact for file transfers. This interaction is why Windows has to load part of itself low. DOS calls this "stub" to get Windows' attention.

- Upper: IBM set aside 384 KB of the 8086 address space for ROMs and video memory. In most cases, a system never uses all of that memory. A memory manager can fill this area with RAM, allowing you to load some of your device drivers high and free conventional memory for applications. Part of Windows 3.x has to load in either conventional or upper memory in order to support the file system and other DOS-related functions. The more upper memory Windows has to use, the more conventional memory you'll have free to run DOS applications.

- High: This is a magic 64 KB block that actually appears above the 1,024 KB address limit. Remember the discussion of segmentation in Chapter 6? Well, special segmentation techniques make it possible for the processor to address this memory in real mode. Most users place DOS in this area to free more conventional memory.

- Extended: This is where Windows spends most of its time. A machine has to run in protected mode in order to access extended memory. This is the area beyond the addressing capability of the 8086.

- Expanded: Many game and some older business applications require expanded memory. At one time, you needed a special EMS card to create expanded memory. Now, memory managers can convert extended memory to expanded memory on-the-fly. There are a number of ways to convert extended memory to expanded memory under Windows. The easiest way, of course, is to simply specify the amount of expanded memory you need in a PIF.

Conventional Memory

Let's talk for a few minutes about conventional memory and Windows 95. Except for a few system calls, Windows 95 never even moves to real mode anymore, so you don't really need any conventional memory to run it. However, just about everyone has some DOS applications that they need to run, and every DOS application needs conventional memory. You could easily get mired in a lot of details when running DOS applications under Windows 95, but here's the short view: Don't use a memory manager to increase the amount of conventional memory you have unless you really have to clear some space in order to get an important application to run.

Tip: A lot of people think that MS DOS mode is a "bad" way to run your applications. In reality, there's nothing bad about using MS DOS mode at all. If you find that you have one application that requires more conventional memory than your standard setup will support, running it in MS DOS mode might be the way to go. The whole idea of MS DOS mode is to provide the flexibility you need in order to run demanding applications without giving up the overall efficiency of a hands-off setup. This doesn't just apply to applications that won't cooperate with Windows 95; it applies to applications with special needs too. If you have an application with special conventional memory needs, MS DOS mode might be the way to go.

As I prepared to write this chapter, I decided it might be fun to run a few different setups to see what kind of memory configurations I could get on my machine. Figure 7.1 shows the results I got. The goal was to see how much conventional memory I could get without seriously impairing my machine. After several attempts, I finally got 386MAX to install. (The beta product has some significant problems with this particular memory manager, and I don't think they'll be fixed by the time Microsoft releases Windows 95.) The 386MAX configuration netted me a machine with 613 KB at the DOS prompt. Of course, my system crashed more often after the installation because the real-mode memory manager kept fighting against Windows 95, but this setup did give me the biggest conventional memory boost.

Figure 7.1.
Using no memory manager will cost you some conventional memory but results in a flexible setup with greater stability.

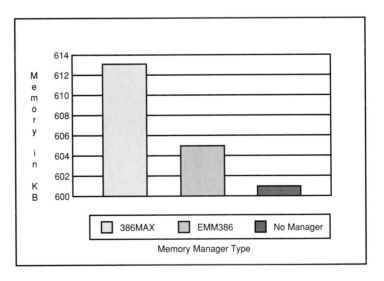

Next, I tried to use EMM386. It worked fine, and I didn't suffer as many debilitating crashes as I did when using 386MAX. Unfortunately, I was now down to 605 KB using the same DOS prompt setup as before. Still, a loss of 8 KB isn't very significant. I don't have any applications that require that much conventional memory, anyway; all of them require 600 KB or less (including my games). The big difference between the two setups seems to be the way that 386MAX loads DOS high. I noticed that it had a smaller footprint than the EMM386 setup seemed to have.

Finally, I tried getting rid of CONFIG.SYS altogether. None of my peripherals require a real-mode device driver, so getting rid of CONFIG.SYS made sense since I didn't plan to use a memory manager. The same DOS prompt I had used for the previous two tests now showed 601 KB. That's a total loss of 12 KB from my 386MAX setup. I admit some applications could really use that 12 KB to run, but how many do you own that fall into that category? A hands-off approach to memory management won't give you the ultimate conventional memory setup. Any set of tests will tell you that. However, I consider the gain in stability and flexibility well worth the loss of 12 KB of conventional memory.

> **Note:** It's extremely important to remember that Windows 95 provides its own memory manager. The only reason to load an additional driver is if you have a lot of real-mode device drivers or TSRs to load. Otherwise, all your DOS applications will work fine from a window or by using MS DOS mode.

We'll cover the use of the Program Properties dialog later in this chapter; this is where you should work on creating the perfect environment for your application. In most cases, the 600+ KB of conventional memory that you can achieve using the automatic Windows 95 settings will provide more-than-sufficient memory for your applications.

Upper Memory

The first thing you need to know about upper memory is what it is. There are six 64 KB segments between 640 KB and 1 MB. Originally, IBM called this area "reserved memory." They had reserved it for add-on peripherals and BIOS extensions. The current term for this area of real-mode addressable memory is the *upper memory block* (UMB). Microsoft invented the term UMB when programmers learned how to circumvent IBM's original plan. Faced with a demand for more conventional memory, programmers from Quarterdeck Office Systems figured out how to use the "reserved" area as additional space for user programs. Microsoft eventually incorporated some of these techniques into the DOS operating system (starting with version 5.0).

You will have to use a memory manager if you need UMBs under Windows 95. Of course, you can only access these UMBs before you run the operating system to load device drivers or TSRs high. (You can also use them within an MS DOS session, but this is the same as working without Windows loaded.) The problem with using UMBs under Windows 95 is the real-mode memory manager. Using Windows 95's built-in capabilities is always the best solution. You get the most flexibility and the least number of stability problems.

Tip: Never run a TSR before you load Windows 95 unless you have to. For example, I used to run DOSKey before I got into Windows so that every DOS box would contain a copy of this very handy TSR. Now I run all my utility commands from a batch file when I open the DOS box to save memory. The same holds true for environment settings. Use the smallest environment possible, and then set the size of your environment as needed when you open the DOS box. Optimizing each DOS box to meet the needs of the application you're running is the best way to use the flexibility that Windows 95 provides. This type of optimization also reduces your need to rely on UMBs.

There are situations in which UMBs do come in handy. For example, what if you have a device that uses a real-mode driver, and it's very unlikely that the vendor will ever produce a Windows 95-specific version? Suppose you have a data-collection device that uses a DOS data manager, and the manager needs every bit of conventional memory it can get. This is one situation in which you need the UMB to load the device driver. Loading the device driver high frees the conventional memory you need to load the data manager that uses it. I follow one of three routes in such situations. The following list shows them in order of preference from a system reliability point of view. You'll have to choose the route you want to use based on personal needs and system requirements.

- MS DOS mode: If you can get by with using the driver by itself, run it in MS DOS mode. (Later I'll show you how to create custom setups for applications and devices that need it.) This solution has the advantage of allowing you to load a device driver and run its associated application whenever you need to. The downside is that you can't access any of your Windows applications while using the device.

- Multiple-boot configuration: When interaction between the device, a real-mode application, and Windows is absolutely essential, you can still reduce the effect by using a multiple-boot configuration. All you do is set up the boot menu the way you used to under DOS. Use the memory manager setup when you need to load the device driver. Otherwise, boot into an empty configuration that doesn't do anything. The benefit of this setup is obvious: You don't lose access to Windows while running the real-mode device driver and its associated application. The downside is that you have to reboot every time you want to restore your configuration to a default state.

- Use a memory manager: This is the setup that I would encourage you to avoid. You'll definitely run into problems using a real-mode memory manager under Windows 95. If you do have to go this route, try to use the copy of EMM386 that comes with Windows 95 as your memory manager—at least until Windows 95-specific versions of any third-party memory managers arrive on the scene. The downside of this setup is that you'll have stability problems. The benefit of this solution is that you'll always have access to the device and its associated application.

Expanded Memory

Anyone who has been computing very long will run into the need for expanded memory (EMS) at some point. EMS first appeared in 1985 as a means to bypass the DOS address limitations. It seems that spreadsheet users were complaining that they didn't have enough memory to run those gargantuan worksheets anymore. These were the same folks who kept expanding the memory envelope throughout most of the PC's early history. This initial version allowed you to place data in the expanded memory area, but not code. The spreadsheet and, to a larger degree, database users were happy for a while, but not forever.

In 1985, the buying public put considerable pressure on software vendors to find more memory for spreadsheet and database applications. This meant running code in the expanded memory area. Remember, there wasn't any extended memory yet for most users. The 80386 had just appeared on the scene, and the 80286 wasn't what you would call a good extended-memory candidate. The alternative was to handle large files by swapping information to the hard disk, a slow and unwieldy procedure. If the user paged down in a spreadsheet or address list, the application would pause to read the next page from disk.

Adding to this already-bad situation was the proliferation of TSR utilities that popped up over the user's display. Every one of these programs had to load in conventional memory because UMBs didn't exist yet. It's hard to remember sometimes just how crunched memory could get under those old versions of DOS. Let's take a quick stroll down memory lane and look at the history of EMS before we get into the Windows 95 specifics.

EMS Version 3.0

Lotus and Intel announced EMS version 3.0 at the spring Comdex convention in 1985. This specification was designed to head off the rapid demise of 8088/8086 machines. However, this specification was short-lived because Microsoft almost immediately announced it would support EMS in the fall of 1985. Microsoft further promised to enhance Windows to use the memory made available by EMS hardware and software.

LIM EMS Version 3.2

The LIM expanded-memory standard, version 3.2, was a joint effort of three companies: Lotus, Intel, and Microsoft. LIM 3.2 memory allowed 1-2-3, Symphony, dBASE III, and Framework to keep relatively large data files in memory. Before expanded memory was introduced, the only way to manipulate large spreadsheets was to swap portions to and from disk. Under LIM 3.2, the user could add memory cards containing from 64 KB to 8 MB of RAM using expansion slots on the PC's bus. Only the expanded memory manager (EMM) could address all the memory; DOS looked at a 64 KB window (called a *page frame*) supplied by the EMM in the upper memory area. The page frame was placed in reserved memory between 640 KB and 1 MB. Normally this page frame appeared at segment D000h, but other page frame segments were used as well. All PCs (including 8088 machines) could use LIM 3.2 memory to ferry information to applications from the expanded memory card.

Note: As out-of-date as this specification might seem, many applications still use it because this is the version of EMS many programmers understand best. If you've ever tried to run an application that requires EMS under Windows 3.x and have gotten the message that it couldn't find any EMS (even though you know that the memory is present), you've seen the effect of this old specification. The newer 4.0 specification doesn't require a page frame. An old application that's looking for a page frame under 4.0 might not find it. As a result, you can run the DOS MEM program and see that EMS is available, but you won't be able to use it with some applications unless you allocate a page frame. Herein lies the rub. If you use an external memory manager with Windows 95 and don't allocate an EMS page frame, you won't be able to allocate one once Windows 95 starts (Windows 3.x had the same limitation). This is just one more area in which not using an external memory manager with Windows 95 provides greater flexibility. The built-in Windows 95 EMM automatically allocates a page frame for every application that needs it.

The LIM 3.2 EMM could tag and stash 16 KB chunks of data, shipping them to the "warehouse" of extra RAM on the expanded memory card. When an application claimed the data, the EMM placed it back into the page frame 16 KB at a time. Storing data in expanded memory was similar to storing it on a RAM disk: Applications could retrieve the information without time-consuming hard-disk access. Figure 7.2 illustrates how the LIM 3.2 EMM ferries data between expanded memory and DOS using the EMS page frame.

EEMS

The LIM EMS 3.2 standard was fine for storing data such as spreadsheets, but PC users wanted even more power from their machines. Utilities that performed background processing, such as Print and Sidekick, whetted the PC user's appetite for multitasking. However, even the most sophisticated TSR left a lot to be desired when compared to the features of a full-fledged application. Users wanted memory to multitask DOS applications.

Unfortunately, LIM EMS 3.2 provided neither the hardware basis nor the software interface to multitask applications. An application couldn't use LIM EMS 3.2 memory to run program code. This annoying limitation of LIM EMS 3.2 was tied to the fact that DOS couldn't directly access the expanded memory hardware; only the EMM was allowed to do that. In addition, the memory-mapping hardware limited the size and location of each page in the page frame.

Figure 7.2.
LIM EMS 3.2 used 4 to 16 KB pages to store data required by any application running under DOS.

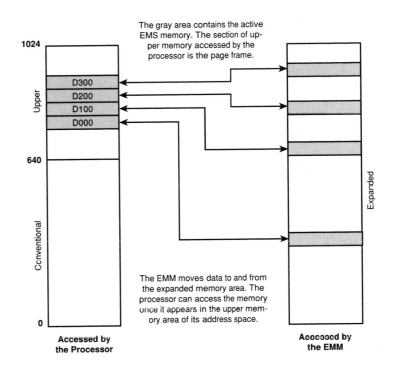

The gray area contains the active EMS memory. The section of upper memory accessed by the processor is the page frame.

The EMM moves data to and from the expanded memory area. The processor can access the memory once it appears in the upper memory area of its address space.

Accessed by the Processor

Accessed by the EMM

In 1986, AST Research Corporation, QUADRAM Corporation, and Ashton-Tate added some enhancements to the Lotus-Intel-Microsoft specification. Their improved standard, Enhanced Expanded Memory Specification, was a breakthrough in the PC industry.

EEMS revised the hardware functions of memory cards to improve the software standard. With EEMS, areas larger than 64 KB could be used as a page frame. The page frame could be mapped below 640 KB as well as between 640 KB and 1 MB. This permitted entire programs to run in enhanced expanded memory.

When AST Research's EEMS cards were combined with Quarterdeck's DESQview, PCs had the capability to multitask a number of applications exceeding 640 KB. A communication program could download files while a spreadsheet was recalculated. The user could type a document in a word processor and format a floppy disk concurrently.

LIM EMS Version 4.0

Lotus, Intel, and Microsoft eventually recognized the superiority of EEMS to LIM 3.2. In 1987, the LIM partners collaborated with AST Research, QUADRAM, and Ashton-Tate to define a new joint standard called LIM EMS version 4.0. EMS 4.0 superseded AST's EEMS by allowing the memory manager to control 32 MB of expanded memory instead of 8. It incorporated many, but not all, of the features provided by EEMS. Improvements of EMS 4.0 over EMS 3.2 included the following:

- The capability to hold larger spreadsheets and databases in memory
- The capability to address more than 64 KB at a time (although the page frame was still 64 KB)
- The capability to map memory both above and below 640 KB

How EMS 4.0 Works

There are many differences between EMS 4.0 and its predecessors. Under EMS 4.0, allocated expanded memory may be mapped as conventional memory. The memory is usually divided into 16 KB segments called *standard pages*. However, a program may use pages other than the standard 16 KB size. These pages are called *raw pages*. Obviously, determining the number of pages of memory available is no longer a matter of simply knowing how many 16 KB segments are installed, so EMS 4.0 also provides methods of determining the number of raw and standard pages.

Instead of only providing access to expanded memory through the page frame (as LIM 3.2 memory does), any number of standard or raw pages can be mapped between conventional memory and the RAM set aside for EMS. In addition, EMS 4.0 provides methods of moving memory regions between conventional and expanded memory. This makes it possible to execute multiple programs up to the full 640 KB address range. The same EMM addresses both the conventional and expanded memory storage areas. To perform this task, the EMM marks a block of EMS memory for each program and assigns it an EMS handle. An EMS handle works and acts much like a DOS file handle, so programmers can easily make the transition in terms of understanding how the process works.

Other, more subtle differences include handle management. Under EMS 3.2, there was no standard technique for managing handles. EMS 4.0 provides the means to get, set, and search for handle names. This enables an application to determine not only what memory is in use, but also who owns it.

Even with these changes, however, it would be impossible to run specific types of programs without another capability added to EMS 4.0. Some programs perform direct memory access (DMA) transfers. For example, many backup programs and some telecommunication programs do this. It would take too long to transfer information one byte at a time through the processor, so the program creates a direct link between one storage device and another. Unlike EMS 3.2, EMS 4.0 allows specific types of DMA transfers to occur. This is made possible through the use of alternative register sets, part of the hardware (or hardware emulation). Alternative register sets also allow a whole range of other unique and powerful software management routines, many of which are at the operating system level.

One of the most unique differences between the two versions is that EMS 4.0 provides the means to allow the contents of expanded memory to survive a warm boot. DESQview uses this capability to allow you to reboot a hung window without affecting any other windows. Of course, should the errant application affect the memory containing the EMM, your only recourse is the big red switch. Figure 7.3 depicts some of the differences between EMS 3.2 and EMS 4.0.

Figure 7.3.

Differences in the way that LIM EMS 3.2 and 4.0 get the job done.

VCPI Versus DPMI

You might be tempted to say that everything DOS needs to multitask is provided by EMS 4.0. Nothing could be further from the truth. The Extended Memory Specification (XMS) doesn't really do the job either. Both of these specifications talk about the availability of memory, not necessarily how to control it. Think of the memory provided by EMS or XMS as being similar to a city street. Your application is a car traveling on that street. It needs the street to get from point A to point B. If you started running more than one application, there would be one car for each application, and the street would begin to fill with traffic. What would happen if there were no traffic lights? Cars could still move around on the streets, but they would crash into each other because there wouldn't be any way to control their movement.

Applications need traffic lights to multitask successfully. An 80386 multitasks DOS applications in virtual 8086 mode. DOS extenders operate in protected mode. To avoid conflicts between programs using virtual 8086 mode and programs running in protected mode, a standard was devised by Quarterdeck, Rational Systems, Phar Lap, and other companies. The Virtual Control Program Interface (VCPI) is the standard that allows DOS extended programs to coexist in an 80386 multitasking environment. In other words, VCPI adds traffic lights to city streets and keeps applications from crashing into each other. Under VCPI, users of DESQview can run protected-mode AutoCAD, 1-2-3, or Paradox side by side with other DOS applications.

Curiously, IBM and Microsoft didn't choose to actively support VCPI. Perhaps in 1988 and 1989 they expected that OS/2 would soon replace DOS, so it wasn't worth the trouble. In 1990, Microsoft premiered its own—independent—protected-mode standard called the DOS Protected-Mode Interface (DPMI). This is the function of the HIMEM.SYS entry in CONFIG.SYS. Microsoft developed DPMI specifically for Windows version 3.0, and we've been using it ever since (even Windows 95 automatically loads it as part of IO.SYS). Like VCPI, DPMI provides mode switching and extended memory management to client programs.

Unfortunately, Microsoft's DPMI standard for Windows is incompatible with the VCPI DOS extender software. In most cases, users can't run the old 386 versions of Paradox, AutoCAD, and so on as DOS tasks under Windows. Microsoft eventually agreed to participate in a committee that included representatives from Quarterdeck, Intel, Lotus, Phar Lap, and Rational Systems. The committee's goal was to develop a more generic version of DPMI. The resultant standard, DPMI version 1.0, is fully VCPI-compatible, but to date, Microsoft hasn't implemented DPMI version 1.0 in Windows. Version 3.x of Windows still uses Microsoft's older DPMI version 0.9, the version that's incompatible with VCPI DOS extenders.

The thinking in 1991 was that if Microsoft wouldn't go to the mountain, other companies would accommodate Microsoft. In July of 1991, Rational Systems introduced a series of 32-bit DOS extenders designed to be Windows 3.x-compatible, even under the older standard. However, even these extenders failed to make the grade. The result, of course, was that the world is using DPMI now. Programs that use VCPI are probably sitting on a shelf somewhere. Of course, now that no one's using VCPI, Microsoft graciously decided to add VCPI support to EMM386. There's probably a profound moral to this entire story, but I've yet to see it. Suffice it to say that you can run those old moth-eaten VCPI applications if you really want to, but a new Windows version of the application would probably give you a lot more in the way of features and stability.

Using EMS with Windows 95

The simple way to get expanded memory under Windows 95 is to load Windows without a memory manager and select the appropriate settings in the Programs Properties dialog. We'll look at this dialog in detail in Chapter 12. For right now, the important thing to remember is that Windows 95 requires a different EMS strategy than previous versions.

Tip: Many TSRs provide some method of loading them into either expanded or extended memory. The TSR normally leaves a small 1 KB to 2 KB footprint in conventional memory but loads the rest of itself where your DOS application can't see it. I always create DOS boxes with the automatic maximum amount of both expanded and extended memory. That way, both types are available whenever I need them to load a TSR out of reach. Using this method allows you to load the TSR high without killing your conventional memory settings or loading the TSR before you start Windows 95.

You can also load an EMM prior to running Windows 95. Follow the instructions provided with your EMM to do this. (Use the copy of EMM386 provided with Windows 95 if possible.) There are several very limiting problems with using an EMM under Windows 95:

- The real-mode EMM will limit the amount of EMS available to your applications to the amount of memory you set aside in the CONFIG.SYS entry. Of course, this amount of memory will always be less than the total amount available on your machine, because there's no way you can run Windows 95 without setting some extended memory aside. Each of my DOS windows under Windows 95 has a total of 24 MB of EMS (16 MB of which is available), because I don't use an external EMM. This is the same amount of memory I have installed on the machine.

- The real-mode device driver will affect your machine's stability. Even the copy of EMM386 produces a noticeable result on my machine. I invariably have to reboot more often whenever there's any real-mode driver around to trash the system memory.

- If you don't allocate enough memory when you boot the machine, you can't adjust it later on. The same holds true if you allocate too much EMS. The extra memory will go to waste. You can adjust the amount set aside in CONFIG.SYS and then reboot, but this runs counter to the other ease-of-use features provided by Windows 95.

Extended Memory

Microsoft's Extended Memory Specification (XMS) got its start from the discovery of a Quarterdeck programmer in 1986. At the time, Quarterdeck was looking for any means possible to reduce the conventional memory overhead of DESQview, its multitasking product. Here is a quick view of what they discovered.

A standard PC breaks the first megabyte of memory into 16 64 KB address segments. To produce an address, the processor combines this 16-bit segment with a 16-bit offset. The result of combining these two numbers is a 20-bit address. Each of these 20 bits controls an address-line gate circuit. The address lines are numbered A0 through A19. Each address line can contain a 1 or a 0, resulting in 2^{20}, or 1,048,576, memory locations (1 MB).

The A20 gate circuit (the 21st address line) isn't present in the original 8088 version of the PC. Therefore, when an address exceeds the amount addressable by 20 address lines, it simply wraps to low memory. For example, if you have segment FFFFh and offset 0010h, the resulting address is 100000h. However, the original PC simply lops the 1 off the left and ends up with address 00000h. Instead of ending up near the very end of memory, you're at the very beginning.

What the Quarterdeck programmer discovered was that turning on the A20 gate of an 80286/80386/80486 chip also turned off the wrap-around. Since these chips do have a 21st address line (actually, the 80286 has 24 and the 80386 and 80486 have 32), you can address the additional memory as if it were conventional memory. If a program were instructed to load code between 960 KB and 1024 KB, up to 64 KB of code could spill over into the first segment beyond 1024 KB. DOS could actually address code placed in the first segment of extended memory. Since the last segment of DOS memory isn't normally contiguous with conventional memory, programs can't use it automatically. But the last segment of DOS memory can be specially programmed to hold up to 64 KB of a single device driver or application program.

This bug (or feature) of the 80286 and above architecture prompted Quarterdeck to develop its QEXT.SYS device driver to reduce the conventional memory overhead of DESQview. In 1987, Microsoft formalized this quirk by issuing its own driver, HIMEM.SYS, and by naming the first segment above 1 MB the High Memory Area (HMA). By publishing instructions on how to use the HMA, Microsoft allowed other third-party vendors to reduce the conventional overhead of their programs. Xerox was one of the first to recognize the HMA with Ventura Publisher. Microsoft's popularization of the HMA with HIMEM.SYS was the beginning of its Extended Memory Specification.

In 1990, Microsoft revised its HIMEM.SYS driver with the release of Windows version 3.0. The scope of XMS memory was increased to include all of extended memory. The new release of Windows could use all of extended memory to multitask Windows applications. Disk caches, print spoolers, and RAM disks could now access extended memory through Microsoft's device driver. Formerly, any driver using extended memory had to provide its own scheme for switching in and out of protected mode. Microsoft established new terminology for all memory above 640 KB:

- UMB (Upper Memory Blocks): This became the term for the memory area above the 640 KB boundary and below the 1 MB boundary.

- HMA (High Memory Area): This term refers to the 64 KB block of memory starting at the 1 MB boundary (1024 KB). This is the beginning of extended memory on 80286 and 80386 systems.

- EMB (Extended Memory Blocks): This term refers to the remaining extended memory (above the HMA) available to an XMS driver.

Tip: TSRs almost always run faster in expanded memory than they do in extended memory. Try the TSR both ways to see which works best for you. For example, I found that Collage (a screen-capture program) actually works faster when you load it into extended memory.

As with expanded memory, Windows 95 provides the means to precisely control how much extended memory you give an application. Of course, you can always give it as much as it could possibly want by using the automatic settings. My system currently offers 23 MB of extended memory to each DOS application if I use the automatic settings and the Windows 95 memory manager. There is absolutely no reason to load an external XMS driver if an application needs it. IO.SYS automatically loads HIMEM.SYS as part of the boot process.

Virtual Memory

In Chapter 6 we looked at the actual process of addressing memory. This included a detailed description of how virtual memory works under Windows 95, so I won't address that issue again. However, knowing the theory behind how something works, and actually using that theory to do something useful, are two different things.

I've spent a lot of time in this chapter telling you how great the automated features of Windows 95 are and how they will make your life a lot easier and provide much more flexibility. I've even gone so far as to say you'd be better off leaving them completely alone. Of course, you knew that wasn't going to last, didn't you? Yes, it's true that Windows 95 does provide all those things, but we're still talking about a piece of software that can't think independently the way you and I can. The problem with Windows 95 is it only looks for a "convenient" drive when it creates your swap file. It doesn't look at the speed of that drive or how you use it. That kind of thought process is something only you and I can accomplish. It's also the reason why you might want to manually adjust your machine's virtual memory settings in some cases.

Let's take my machine as a case in point. I have a small, fast drive and a larger, slow drive. The small drive contains some boot information, my DOS files, and a few other things I need to get my machine up and running or to figure out why it won't work. There's more than enough space left on that drive for a swap file. The faster speed of this drive and the fact that I very seldom change anything on it makes this drive the perfect location for a swap file. Of course, Windows 95 is absolutely determined to use the slower, fragmented drive.

Tip: You can get a speed boost from your machine by hand-tuning the virtual memory setup in some cases. Generally, you'll want to allow Windows 95 to choose the drive and the size of the swap files. However, there are times when Windows 95 will choose the slowest drive on your machine. You can override this selection and choose the fastest drive. This means that you'll trade some extra speed for a little bit of flexibility. As soon as you turn off the automatic settings, you become responsible for adjusting the size of the swap file as required. (Of course, if Windows 95 runs out of swap file space before you adjust it, you could experience a system crash. At the very minimum, you'll get an error message when you try to run another application).

Let's take a look at the process for changing your virtual memory setup. If you cut your teeth on Windows 3.x, you'll recognize this dialog even though it looks a bit different under Windows 95.

1. Right click on My Computer and select the Properties option.

2. Click on the Performance tab. You should see the System Properties dialog, shown in Figure 7.4.

Figure 7.4.
The Performance page of the System Properties dialog provides access to the virtual memory settings for your machine.

3. Click the Virtual Memory pushbutton. You should see the dialog shown in Figure 7.5.

Figure 7.5.
The Virtual Memory dialog allows you to hand-tune your machine's virtual memory settings.

4. Select the drive you want to use, then the amount you want to allocate for virtual memory.

> **Tip:** Another way to get a little bit of a speed boost out of your virtual memory setup is to create a pseudo-permanent swap file. Under Windows 3.x, you could defragment your drive and then allocate a permanent swap file. Using this arrangement would provide a notice-able speed boost, because Windows could read from contiguous disk sectors instead of looking all over the drive for various pieces of the swap file. Microsoft claims that this is no longer necessary, but you can still get a speed boost by optimizing your drive and manually changing the virtual memory settings. All you need to do is select your fastest drive and set the minimum virtual memory setting to something other than 0. If you set the minimum and maximum size to the same value, you'll experience a lot less disk fragmentation and get a slight speed boost. Of course, you'll give up some flexibility to get this boost.

I would be remiss in my duty to you as a writer if I didn't mention the Disable virtual memory checkbox near the bottom of the dialog. When Microsoft recommends that you not check it, they really mean it. I used to run Windows 3.x without any virtual memory management (VMM) because my system was actually faster without it. Under Windows 95, this has all changed. Microsoft really did tune the VMM algorithms to a certain extent. You can't run Windows 95 safely without a swap file. It depends on that swap file a lot more than Windows 3.x ever did, and it uses that swap file much more efficiently. Unless someone at Microsoft tells you to turn off the VMM for some type of maintenance check, leave it on.

Well, that's about all there is to the VMM. It's not like Windows 3.x, where you could spend weeks just trying to figure out the best settings for a particular task. The only thing you need to worry about with Windows 95 is choosing the fastest drive and making sure it has enough space for the swap file. Making sure that the drive stays defragmented is one way to ensure that you always get the best performance. I also included a couple of tips in this section that you can use to get the optimum performance from your setup. VMM still isn't perfect under Windows 95, but it's a lot closer. The amount of tuning you'll actually need to do is a lot less under this new operating system. Of course, it would be nicer if you didn't have to tune the system at all. Maybe the next version of Windows will take us there.

Windows Modes and Memory

Any discussion of Windows and its evolution has to include the modes of operation that Windows supports. Previous versions of Windows supported three modes: real, standard, and 386 enhanced. Real mode went out with the 8088 and Windows 3.0. It's just too limited to perform any useful work, so I won't waste time talking about it here. Suffice it to say that real mode is limited to a mere 1 MB of memory, hardly enough to load Windows, much less applications. The following sections provide an overview of the other two modes of operation.

Windows Applications in Standard Mode

The only reason for the existence of standard mode is the 80286. This mode enables Windows to run on a chip that provides access to only 16 MB of RAM as a maximum and doesn't provide all the features that the 80386 does. The important feature that the 80286 lacks is the capability to create virtual machines. Think of a virtual machine as a way of separating tasks so that they can't interfere with each other. Every application thinks it's running on its own machine, but each virtual machine is really part of the "real" machine you can see.

Standard mode has some important limitations. For one thing, you can't multitask. Windows only task-switches in this mode. Essentially, this means that you can open as many applications as memory will permit, but only the foreground task will actually do anything.

Another important limitation of standard mode is the lack of virtual memory support. Without this support, the user is limited to the physical memory provided by the machine. Since 80286 machines were never known for their surplus of memory, most users will run out of memory long before they run out of applications to run.

Note: The only version of Windows that still supports standard mode is Windows 3.1. You access it using the /s switch at the command line. The new versions of Windows—including Windows for Workgroups 3.11—support only 386 enhanced mode.

DOS Applications in Standard Mode

I'm not going to beat around the bush with this topic: Standard mode is dead, and for good reason, if you need to run DOS applications under Windows. Like their Windows application counterparts, you can only task-switch between DOS and Windows applications in standard mode. There is no multitasking in standard mode. The big surprise is that you can have only one active DOS application running at a time in this mode. That's one of the reasons this mode is such a waste of time. Most people who used it opened a DOS window and started one application at a time, just like they would at the command prompt. The thing I wonder about is why they even bothered.

Windows also provides very limited memory in this mode since you can't create a virtual machine. What you got at the DOS prompt was what you had before you entered Windows, minus a lot of memory for Windows itself. Often, the amount of memory left just wouldn't do the job. Many people who used standard mode did so only for their Windows applications because memory was at such a premium at the DOS prompt.

The combination of a lack of memory and the inability to multitask is a significant problem if you need to run more than one application at a time. Just think, even though it used to be difficult to run a communications program in the background under Windows 3.x in enhanced mode, you couldn't do it at all in standard mode. Suffice it to say that since Windows 95 no longer supports this mode of operation, you can always multitask as many DOS applications as you need to.

Windows in 386 Enhanced Mode

You need to have an 80386 or above processor to use 386 enhanced mode. This is the default mode that Windows 3.1 and above uses to get the most out of your machine. It offers all the features people normally associate with Windows now. Even though someone out there might be trying to run Windows in standard mode, most people switched to 80386 machines long ago. Several important features differentiate enhanced mode from standard mode:

- Multitasking: Using 386 enhanced mode enables Windows to perform more than one task simultaneously. There are various forms of multitasking. I cover them in the section "Cooperative Versus Preemptive Multitasking" in Chapter 6.

- Virtual Memory: Have you ever used a machine that has enough memory? Most of us haven't. Applications always seem to require 1 MB more RAM than you have installed. Virtual memory enables Windows to get past this problem so that you don't have to worry about whether your application will run.

- VxD Support: Virtual device drivers make Windows a much safer environment to work in. (VxD stands for "Virtual Anything Driver.") Not only are VxDs safer, but they're faster as well. Standard mode never supported the 32-bit enhanced disk services or any of the extended functionality that 386 enhanced mode can.

It's not too difficult to imagine why 386 enhanced mode is the way to go if you have an 80386 machine to run Windows on. In fact, I often wonder how people could expect to run Windows on an 80286 in the first place. Frankly, as I said in a column I wrote for *PC Week* many years ago, I wonder why anyone ever *bought* an 80286, but that's another story entirely. It's one of those "hindsight is 20/20" situations, I guess.

DOS Applications on Virtual Machines

Enhanced mode is the name of the game if you want to multitask DOS applications under Windows. As I stated earlier, this is the only mode you get with Windows versions 3.11 and above (including Windows 95). The underlying reason you can run more than one application is that they no longer load on the physical machine, but on a virtual machine instead. I have only one physical machine, so if I use it to run an application, there's nothing left to run something else. Virtual machines are different. Windows can continue to create new virtual machines as long as I have the memory to do so. Each virtual machine can run one DOS application. The capability to create multiple virtual machines means that you can always run more than one application.

What exactly is a virtual machine? We looked at many of the ramifications from an architectural point of view in Chapter 6. Essentially, a virtual machine is a memory structure that acts like a physical machine. There used to be big gaps in this technology under Windows 3.x, but Microsoft has greatly improved the virtual machine under Windows 95. Of course, Windows 95 is still far from perfect. In fact, there will be situations in which Windows 95 just can't cope. Thankfully, Microsoft includes the ability to run your DOS application on the physical machine under Windows 95 using DOS mode. Of course, this means you lose the ability to use the machine for any other purpose.

From a memory standpoint, Windows 95 creates each virtual machine from extended memory. Once it sets the memory aside, it loads a copy of DOS from the phantom copy Windows 95 keeps around just for this purpose. It then loads and runs your DOS application. As far as the DOS application is concerned, it's running on its own 8088 machine. Of course, this application can still request expanded and extended memory. It can even use Windows DPMI services to switch to protected mode and run itself as a protected-mode application.

Warning: DOS applications that use DPMI services to load themselves into protected memory can cause a lot of problems under Windows 95. These applications essentially reside outside the watchful eye of the Windows 95 memory manager. The fact that they switch back and forth between protected mode and real mode only complicates matters. You can, and probably will, experience memory corruption from time to time if you load an application of this type. Checking the Protected checkbox (located on the Memory page of the Application Properties dialog) will slow the application down slightly but will help Windows catch some errant applications before any memory corruption occurs. The best way to prevent this problem, though, is to update to 32-bit applications as quickly as possible.

Once you exit your DOS application, Windows destroys the virtual machine it used. It returns the memory used by the virtual machine to the system memory pool. Windows might or might not decrease the size of your swap file (depending on your virtual memory settings and the current system load). Each DOS application you load gets a new virtual machine to operate in. Windows simply creates and destroys them as needed.

Which Mode Do You Need?

There's only one mode for any modern user of Windows—enhanced mode. A standard-mode machine is so limited and the cost for upgrading so small in comparison to the speed you'll gain that I really don't think anyone has an excuse for running one of these dinosaurs. The 80286 was braindead before it even appeared in the first PC. It's time to bury this relic for good. If you aren't using enhanced mode, you really need to ask yourself why you use Windows at all.

Memory Tuning and Optimization

I have gone through most of the following material in other chapters. However, this is a good place to summarize the various tips and techniques that I have presented (or will present in Chapter 12). Here are my top 10 tips and techniques for tuning your system to make the best use of memory.

Note: You might ask yourself how much memory you need in order to obtain optimum performance. An operating system such as Windows 95 doesn't have any theoretical limits as far as memory goes—at least, not that any of the current crop of Desktop machines can achieve. However, from a practical point of view, you'll see performance top off at 32 MB of RAM for most installations since everything should be loaded in memory at that point. Depending on your processor, you might actually see a performance drop-off starting at 64 MB as Windows 95 spends more time managing memory than using it. Your actual performance curve will vary, depending on a lot of factors, including processor type and the number and size of applications you run.

1. Always use the built-in memory manager if possible. We've looked at quite a few of the ways you can use the extra flexibility in this chapter. I'll present a few more in future chapters as well.

2. Use your fastest drive for the swap file, but don't starve Windows in the process. A fast drive will improve performance in one respect. A small swap file could kill that performance gain by reducing system stability and introducing some memory thrashing. Always choose the fastest drive that contains enough memory to hold the entire swap file.

3. Manage your system, but don't micro-manage it. I can already see that this will be a major problem area for some users. Tune the individual files for the performance you need. Tell Windows what you need to do, but don't worry too much about how it gets the job done. I wouldn't have said this under Windows 3.x, but leaving Windows 95 alone to do its work is about the best performance enhancement you can provide. (Of course, a little monitoring from time to time as your computing habits change wouldn't hurt either.)

4. Never load real-mode device drivers or TSRs you don't need. The old approach of loading everything before you start Windows is a dead end under Windows 95. Make each environment unique—custom-made to perform the job you need it to do.

5. Use the automatic memory settings whenever possible. There are times when you'll have to step in and adjust them manually if you have an application that starts by grabbing everything available. In most cases, though, you'll get ahead if you let Windows manage the memory for you. Letting Windows manage your memory provides a much greater degree of flexibility for you in the long run. That flexibility usually translates into increased efficiency and performance.

6. Avoid MS DOS mode, but use it if you must. Windows 95 has come a long way in providing the level of support that Microsoft has promised for years. It still isn't perfect, but neither are the applications that run under it. If you do find an application that simply won't run using the default Windows memory setup, try creating an optimized environment for it in MS DOS mode. (I'll show the procedure for doing this in Chapter 12.)

7. Enhance your memory usage by getting rid of the frills. Wallpaper, excess icons, screen savers, and other doodads consume memory without giving you much in return. Entertainment is always nice, but not at the cost of efficiency. The question you should always ask yourself is whether something relieves fatigue or merely consumes resources.

8. Increase your level of physical RAM as needed. Windows 95 can literally make as much RAM as you need from your hard drive, but there's a limit to how much performance you can get by doing this. I always follow a simple rule. When the size of my swap file equals the amount of RAM in my machine on a consistent basis, it's time to buy more RAM.

9. Get a faster hard drive. Swap files are a fact of life under Windows 95, and that means you're at least partially dependent on its speed for overall system performance—even when it comes to memory. I find that a drive with a higher level of throughput is a better choice than one with faster access time when it comes to memory management. Windows tends to read from the swap file in small, contiguous blocks. A drive with a higher throughput can deliver that data faster.

10. Kill those old applications. If you're still using a lot of DOS applications, it's time to upgrade. Get rid of those old moth-eaten remnants. The only thing that old DOS applications will do for you is slow the system down and cause reliability problems. Of course, 16-bit Windows applications aren't much better for the most part. Upgrading to the newer 32-bit applications will help you use memory efficiently and usually will provide a speed benefit as well. Remember that you can use many Windows NT applications under Windows 95 until the official Windows 95 products hit the streets.

On Your Own

Open a DOS box and use the MEM command to see what kinds of memory you have available. Also note the amount of each type of memory you have available. If you don't see that both expanded and extended memory are available, try to discover the reason that one or the other is absent.

If you're using a memory manager, try booting your machine without it. What differences do you see in the amount of Windows 95 memory available? What about the memory available in a DOS box? You'll want to use the information you get as part of your criteria for determining whether to get rid of the memory manager.

Explore the list of memory tuning techniques in the preceding section. Can you use any of these tips to improve your machine's performance? Try different ways of implementing these changes to see what works best with your configuration. Windows 95 is a new operating system, so you need to explore its weaknesses and strengths to see what you can do to improve your machine's capabilities. I think you'll find that many of the old techniques you used no longer work properly.

8

The
Windows 95
File System

One of the big news items for Windows 95 is its use of long filenames. From a user's perspective, it's one of the more noticeable changes in the operating system (besides the interface and a few new utilities). Although many of the inner changes will go unnoticed—mainly because they work—this is one feature you are fairly certain not to miss.

Long filename support also ends one of the main criticisms that really irked me when talking with a Macintosh user. Flat memory address space and long filenames were just two of the things the Macintosh had that the PC just couldn't seem to get a grip on. Now that we have those two items, I can stop worrying about every Mac user who comes toward me at a convention.

Of course, every time you change the file system, you have to change the utilities to manage that file system. Fortunately, Windows 95 still uses a version of the FAT (file allocation table) file system. This means a lot of your old utilities will still work, albeit a little less than they did before. Actually, the new and improved file system looks and works a lot like the old one did. Microsoft merely used some of the space in the directory table they didn't use in the past.

> **Warning:** Using an old disk management utility with Windows 95 might mean a loss of your long filenames since these old utilities don't know to move everything needed to support them. Windows 95 actually provides support for two filenames—an older DOS version and a newer long filename. They are stored in separate areas and require different DOS and Windows operating system calls in order for you to use them. These old utilities know how to use the DOS 8.3 filename, but they know nothing about long filenames and invariably destroy them. The next time you try to view a long filename with Windows 95, there is nothing to view, because the long filename got destroyed by the old utility. This might seem like an inconvenience only until you realize that loss of the long filenames will also mean a loss of the "Start Menu" and other Windows 95-specific long filenames. Windows 95 might not even restart in certain cases if you lose the long filenames it requires. Use the LFNBACK utility (located on the CD-ROM in the \WIN95\OTHER\ LFNBACK folder) to create a backup of all your long filenames prior to using any utility you're not absolutely certain about. Unfortunately, the Add/Remove Programs dialog doesn't provide an entry for this useful utility, so you'll need to install it manually. I'll go into more detail later in this chapter.

This chapter will take you on a tour of the Windows 95 file system from a user perspective. We'll even take a brief look at the architecture and put on our programmer's hat for a while. The Windows 95 VFAT (virtual file allocation table) file system might look and act like an enhanced version of the old system, but I think you'll be surprised at all the new features under the hood.

File Structures

There's a proliferation of file systems on my hard drives. Right now I can boot Windows, Windows 95, Windows NT, and OS/2. Each of these operating systems supports the FAT file system. The last three also support their own file systems. Of the three, only the VFAT file system used by Windows 95 looks familiar. The other two are enhanced file systems that started from scratch because no one thought the FAT file system could ever be repaired. (We'll look at a few of the remaining problems with VFAT in the following paragraphs.)

So, what do you do with a system that is literally bogged down with incompatible file systems? You could take the easy way out—the way I originally took when I started working with OS/2. If you stick with the FAT file system, you'll certainly get everybody talking to each other and run into the very minimum of problems.

There's only one problem with this solution: If you stick with the FAT file system, you'll have compatibility, but you'll also miss out on the special features each of the other file systems has to offer. Both NTFS (Windows NT file system) and HPFS (high-performance file system) offer improved reliability and a higher access speed than the old FAT file system. The battle is still raging over which one is better, HPFS or NTFS. My personal favorite is NTFS, but that's another story.

Peter's Principle: A Method of Dealing with Multiple File Systems

After a lot of thought, I finally came up with a middle-ground solution to the problem of dealing with multiple file systems on one computer. It offers the maximum in compatibility, yet lets me make the most out of what the other file systems have to offer.

The first thing I did was partition my drives. I set aside one partition for each of the operating systems installed on my machine. I had to do that anyway to get everything to boot correctly. Each operating system's specific partition uses the special file format it provides. This way, the operating system and its utility programs can benefit from the improved performance and reliability that the new file system has to offer. I also stick any operating system-specific applications in these partitions.

Once I figured out where each operating system would go, I installed them. Each installation required a bit of time and patience, but I got through it. It's important to test the ability to boot each operating system after you install a new one. Both Windows NT and Windows 95 like to overwrite the bootable partition marker. This means that whatever boot manager you have installed won't boot until you use a disk editor to set the active partition back to its original position.

After I installed the operating systems and tested the boot sequence, I had one large partition left (actually, I set the whole second drive aside). I labeled the partition on this drive COMMON and placed all my data and common applications there. It uses the FAT file system so everyone can access it. In some cases, I had to install each application once for each operating system. However, if you're careful, you can determine which files to copy from your Windows \SYSTEM directory into each of the other \SYSTEM directories. (DLLs and VxDs need to appear in the \SYSTEM directory in most cases or Windows won't be able to find them.) Is this a perfect solution? Not by a long shot. However, it is a solution that works.

So, why did I go through this entire rundown of my system configuration? I think you might find yourself in the same dilemma I was in. You have to test all (or at least many) of the solutions available today, which means keeping multiple operating systems on your machine. This solution might be just what the doctor ordered when it comes time to test an OS/2 or a Windows NT solution that the entire company might adopt. If you don't test the advanced file system that comes with the operating system, can you really say you tested everything when the time comes to make a decision?

FAT Versus VFAT

Now that we have some preliminaries out of the way, let's look at the new VFAT file system provided with Windows 95. As I said in an earlier chapter, one of the reasons for Windows 3.0's success was that the user could upgrade DOS to use it. In other words, the user could make the transition slowly without having to give up a comfortable environment. Windows 95 continues this line of reasoning, even to maintaining a level of compatibility with the old FAT file system. However, people weren't satisfied with the old 8.3 filenames. They wanted long filenames, and the FAT file system can't provide this feature. The VFAT file system represents an effort on the part of Microsoft to give people what they want and still maintain a level of compatibility with previous versions of DOS (and more importantly, the applications that ran under it).

The following sections provide you with a bit of history and then a current look at the way Windows handles file access. It's important to start at the beginning to see what you have gained with various versions of Windows. Even more important, this historical view will help you understand certain constraints that faced Microsoft programmers when they designed Windows 95. It's easy to start out with a new product and design all the features that people want today. It's another story altogether to start with something that was fine yesterday and redesign it to meet today's needs. Windows 95 isn't a completely new operating system; it's the next generation of Windows 3.x from a compatibility point of view. In other words, even though much of Windows 3.x is gone, Windows 95 still has to work as if Windows 3.x were still present.

A Look at Windows Under DOS

Everyone who has worked with DOS and Windows 3.x knows that they have at least one thing in common: the FAT file system. That relationship between DOS and Windows 3.x also causes some problems for the user. Consider the speed issue many people bring up when you talk about using Windows. Since this older version of Windows rides on top of DOS, it must use some DOS services to access the hardware. The hard disk drive falls into this category. DOS provides all the file services Windows 3.x uses. In fact, this is about the only DOS service Windows 3.1 does use.

What using DOS to provide file services means to the user is that the system has to slow down every time Windows wants to access the hard drive. To see what I mean, look at Figure 8.1. Every time Windows wants to access the hard drive, it has to create a request in a format that DOS will understand, switch over to real mode so that it can access DOS, and then wait for DOS to get the job done. Meanwhile, all those applications that are supposed to do something in the background get suspended. Remember, the Intel processor can't multitask in real mode; it can do that only in protected mode. Once DOS finds the bit of information Windows needs, Windows has to copy that information out of the conventional memory space into an area it can reach in protected mode. It must then switch the processor from real mode back into protected mode.

Figure 8.1.
Windows 3.1 needs to switch from protected mode to real mode to access the hard drive through DOS. Not only does this waste time, but it also opens the door for a system crash if a rampant application decides to do something unexpected.

This is only where the problem starts, not where it ends. Every time Windows has to make the switch from protected mode to real mode, it becomes vulnerable to attack from a maverick application. When the processor is in real mode, the operating system can no longer track system activity. The processor won't alert the operating system when an application creates a memory fault. As a result, an application could crash the system before Windows 3.x even knows what is going on.

32-Bit Access Under Windows 3.1

Windows 3.1 provides a new feature called 32-bit access. This feature reduces the opportunity for system crashes and enhances overall system speed. However, before I talk about how 32-bit access affects your computing environment, you need to understand what it is.

If you tried to figure out what 32-bit access is by its name, you might suspect that it's some new technique for accessing the data on your drive 32 bits at a time. What 32-bit access actually provides is a little more complex.

Every time an application requests data from the hard drive, Windows intercepts the request to see if it can be fulfilled using data in protected memory. Usually this request asks to open a file or to read specific byte ranges of data. Once Windows determines that it can't fulfill the request, it switches to real mode and passes the request to the DOS interrupt 21h handler. This handler looks at the request and starts to take care of it by issuing interrupt 13h requests. You can look at interrupt 21h as the manager and interrupt 13h as the worker. Interrupt 21h gets the whole problem in one big chunk. It breaks the problem up into small pieces interrupt 13h can handle. As a result, each interrupt 21h call can result in a lot of interrupt 13h calls.

Of course, since Windows is monitoring everything, the system doesn't just stay in real mode and take care of the entire disk request at one time. Windows intercepts each interrupt 13h call the DOS interrupt 21h handler makes and sees if it can fulfill the request using data in protected memory. If not, Windows switches back to real mode and the BIOS handles the call. The BIOS performs the work required to fulfill the call and passes the information back to Windows, which passes it back to DOS, which passes it back to Windows, which finally passes it back to the application. This might seem like a lot of work just to read a few bytes of data from the disk, and it is.

Figure 8.2 shows the new 32-bit access method used by Windows 3.1x. Notice the BIOS is completely cut out of the picture. That's because FastDisk (a 32-bit protected-mode driver) emulates the BIOS using protected-mode code. This means not only that Windows eliminates two mode transitions for every interrupt 13h call, but also that it can effectively multitask during more of the disk access cycle. You lose only the DOS processing time instead of both DOS and BIOS processing time. This improvement accounts for part of the noticeable speed-up in Windows 3.1. It also accounts for some of the improved stability that people experience.

Windows 3.11 and Windows for Workgroups 3.11 add even more. In addition to 32-bit disk access, these versions add 32-bit file access. These versions of Windows use the DOS file access features to search for files and to perform other file-specific activities. (This differentiates a file access from a disk access, which deals with reading and writing sections of data.) This means even fewer transitions to DOS, because the file system no longer keeps the BIOS in the picture. The result is an overall improvement in system speed and reliability.

Figure 8.2.
*Windows 3.11 provides a
32-bit access feature that
reduces the opportunities for
a system crash and enhances
system throughput.*

The Windows 95 Alternative to 32-Bit Access

Windows 95 gets around the entire real-mode access problem by incorporating all operating system functions into a 32-bit architecture. Microsoft has named this technique the VFAT interface. Its full name is the Protected-Mode FAT File System. Figure 8.3 shows how this disk management system differs from the one used under Windows 3.x. Using protected-mode drivers means there's less chance that a random application will cause a system failure, because Windows 95 is never unprotected long enough. It always runs in protected mode. (The only exception to this rule is if you install real-mode drivers in CONFIG.SYS to support an antiquated device such as a CD-ROM drive. Windows 95 does switch to Virtual 86 mode when accessing a device that uses a real-mode driver.) Using protected mode means the operating system constantly monitors every event taking place on the machine. It has the final say before a particular event takes place. This new system runs totally in protected memory, reducing the chance of system crashes due to disk-related problems to nearly zero and greatly enhancing disk access speed.

As Figure 8.3 shows, there are several discrete components in the Windows 95 file system. Actually, Microsoft refers to these components as layers. There are 32 possible layers in the Windows 95 file system, starting at the I/O subsystem. (The current configuration doesn't use all 32 layers.) Layer 0 is closest to the I/O subsystem, while layer 31 is closest to the hardware. The current version of Windows 95 requires only a few of these layers (normally 12) to get the job done. The other layers are placeholders for future use. Each layer provides hooks for third-party software used to support custom file systems and devices. For example, adding a network driver to the file system layer enables you to access drives on other machines. Unlike with previous versions of Windows, a vendor can retrofit the Windows 95 file system to provide additional capabilities with relative ease. Each of these components performs a different task.

Figure 8.3.
*Windows 95 uses a totally
different system than its
predecessors to access this
disk.*

- Installable File System (IFS) Manager: This is the highest layer in the file system. The IFS is a VxD that provides the interface to applications. It doesn't matter whether the application uses the Interrupt 21h interface or either the 16- or 32-bit Windows interface, this is the component that receives application requests. It's the responsibility of the IFS to transfer control to the appropriate file system driver (FSD). The VFAT FSD component appears in Figure 8.3, but Windows 95 also includes network and CD FSDs as well.

- File System Driver (FSD) layer: The most common file system driver layer component is the VFAT FSD. This is the VxD that takes care of all local hard drive requests. It provides the long filename support and protected-mode stability that makes Windows 95 better than its predecessors. Your machine might have several other FSDs, depending on the type of equipment you have installed. For example, Windows 95 installs a network file system handler if you install any form of a LAN. All of the FSDs talk with the IFS manager. They also send requests to the layers that directly communicate with the hardware.

- I/O Subsystem (IOS) layer: This is the highest level of the block device layer. What do I mean by a block device? Any device that sends information in blocks (such as a hard drive does) is called a block device. A hard drive usually uses some multiple of 512 bytes as its block size. Other devices might use a different block size. Network devices, tape drives, and CD-ROM drives all fall into the block device category. The IOS provides general device services to the FSDs. For example, it routes requests from the FSDs to various device-specific drivers. It also sends status information from the device-specific drivers to the FSDs.

- Volume Tracking Driver (VTD) layer: Windows 95 might or might not install this driver. It handles any removable devices attached to your system. For example, if you have a floppy or CD-ROM drive, Windows 95 will install this component. On the other hand, if you use a diskless workstation or rely on local and network hard drives alone, Windows 95 won't need to install this component. The VTD performs one, and only one, basic function. It monitors the status of all removable media drives and reports any change in media. This is the component that will complain if you remove a floppy prematurely (usually in the middle of a write).

- Type-Specific Driver (TSD) layer: Every type of device needs a driver that understands its peculiar needs. For example, the hard disk drive driver wouldn't understand the needs of a floppy drive very well. This layer deals with logical device types rather than specific devices. For example, one TSD handles all the hard drives on your system, while another TSD handles all the floppy drives. A third TSD would handle all network drives.

- Vendor-Supplied Driver (VSD) layer: This is where a vendor would install support for a proprietary bus CD-ROM, or a removable media device, such as a floptical drive. Every specific device type needs a driver that can translate its requests for Windows. This is the layer that performs those services. The VSD knows things such as the number of heads a disk has or the amount of time it needs to wait for a floppy to get up to speed.

- Port Driver (PD) layer: The PD performs the actual task of communicating with the device through an adapter. It's the last stage before a message leaves Windows and the first stage when a message arrives from the device. The PD is usually adapter-specific. For example, you would have one VSD for each hard drive and one PD for each hard drive adapter. If your system uses an IDE hard drive, Windows would load the IDE PD to talk to the IDE adapter.

- SCSIzer: Don't let the strange-looking name for this layer fool you. It deals with SCSI command language. Think of the command language as the method the computer uses to tell a SCSI device to perform a task. It isn't the data the SCSI device handles; rather, it's the act the SCSI device will perform. Windows 95 has one SCSIzer for each SCSI device.

- SCSI Manager: Windows NT introduced something called the miniport driver. With Windows 95, you can use the Windows NT miniport binaries. However, before you can actually do this, Windows 95 has to translate its commands to a format the miniport driver will understand. The SCSI Manager performs this service.

- Miniport Driver: This is a device driver that provides support for a specific SCSI device. No other device uses the miniport driver. The miniport driver works with the SCSI manager to perform the same task as a PD. Both Windows NT and Windows 95 use the same miniport drivers.

- Protected-Mode Mapper: This layer performs a very special task. It enables you to use your DOS drivers under Windows 95. Without the support of this VxD, Windows 95 couldn't support legacy devices that lack Windows 95-specific drivers. Essentially, the protected-mode mapper disguises a real-mode driver to look like a Windows 95 protected-mode driver.

- Real-Mode Driver: It is almost certain that some vendors won't supply drivers for every device they ever made. In reality, they have no reason to do so. The older device that still does the job for you is probably so far out of date, you're the only one still using it. Still, like a really comfortable pair of shoes, you hate to give that old device up. (I personally have a proprietary bus Hitachi CD-ROM hanging around; it still does the job, so I'm not going to give it up just yet.) One of the goals of the Windows 95 development team was to allow you to keep that old legacy device hanging around until you are ready to give it up. It's going to cost some system speed to keep it, but that real-mode driver will work just fine under Windows 95.

Gaining Access to VFAT from DOS

You can access the VFAT interface in a DOS application. Microsoft incorporated a new set of services into the Interrupt 21h handler. Table 8.1 shows the various calls you can make to this new interface. Notice that the AL part of the service call corresponds to the current disk service call numbers. The contents of the other registers correspond to the old DOS register setups as well. If you know how to use the current set of Interrupt 21h disk routines, using the new ones means a simple change in the contents of the AX register (in most cases). Microsoft recommends you use the Get Volume Information (71A0h) to detect if the current system supports long filenames. Set the carry flag before making the call. If the machine doesn't support long filenames, the carry flag will be unchanged on return, and DOS will clear the AL register. Never use the long filename calls on a system that doesn't support them. Remember that all of these service numbers go into the AX register and that the values are in hexadecimal.

Table 8.1. VFAT interface interrupt 21h functions.

AX Code	Function Name
7139h	Create Directory
713Ah	Remove Directory
713Bh	Set Current Directory
7141h	Delete File
7143h	Get/Set File Attributes
7147h	Get Current Directory
714Eh	Find First File
714Fh	Find Next File
7156h	Move or Rename File
716Ch	Extended Open/Create File
71A0h	Get Volume Information
71A1h	Find Close

VCache

Did you ever play with the size of the cache you provided for SmartDRV under Windows 3.x? If you ever spent as much time doing it as I did, you were pretty frustrated with the results. The problem was simple: If you allocated enough memory to cover every situation that the cache might encounter, you didn't have enough left to run all those applications you needed.

You might have encountered other problems as well. Until the latest release of DOS, SmartDRV didn't support CD-ROM drives. This wasn't a problem a few years ago when CD-ROM drives were still less than common. Today, however, CD-ROM drives are very common. I wouldn't say that every machine has one, but it won't be very long before a CD-ROM drive is standard equipment on every machine sold. It makes sense, then, that later versions of the drive cache support a CD-ROM drive.

One thing SmartDRV still doesn't support is network access, even when that access is through a Microsoft network. How many PCs in your company are still used in stand-alone mode? In a few more years I doubt that there'll be many stand-alone machines to be found in corporate America or even small companies for that matter. I know of some home users who network their machines. If you fall into the "networked" category in any way, you know the frustration of waiting for your machine to load data from the server. A cache that could keep track of some of the most recently used data would be a big help in speeding network access.

The VCache VxD found in Windows 95 is a 32-bit protected-mode replacement for SmartDRV that does all the things I just mentioned and more. It automatically supports network and CD-ROM drives, in addition to the standard local hard drive support. Plus, you'll find even more here than meets the eye.

VCache creates a separate cache for each type of drive. It also balances the total cache size with the memory requirements of your system. The result is a dynamically sized cache that's optimized to meet the needs of the particular kind of access you're performing most often right now. If you are loading a lot of data from the network, VCache increases the size of your network cache. Loading a new application from the CD-ROM drive allocates more space for the CD-ROM cache. Likewise, local drive access will change the size of that cache.

When I say that VCache does all this work, I don't mean it does the work by itself. The CDFS (compact disk file system) that I described earlier as part of the miniport driver discussion comes into play for CD-ROM drives. CDFS cooperates with VCache to create a part of the drive cache picture. Likewise, the network redirector (depending on which network you install) works with VCache. Windows 95 automatically changes the configuration of both drivers as the configuration of your system changes. For example, it won't add network redirector support on systems that don't have access to a network. The same holds true for CD-ROM drive support on non-CD-equipped systems.

Peter's Principle: Real-Mode and 16-Bit Windows Drivers: Just Say No

Everything that VCache provides will work as I just described if you use 32-bit drivers for all your drives. However, what if you use an older CD-ROM drive that needs a real-mode or 16-bit driver? Then you will lose part of the dynamic caching that VCache provides. MSCDEX uses a static cache that VCache will not override. It needs the cooperation of CDFS to provide support for CD-ROM drives.

Likewise, if your network uses real-mode drivers (as the current version of LANtastic does), VCache can't provide network drive cache support. The network will run just as sluggishly as it did before. You won't see any of the anticipated speed boost because Windows 95 can't override those real-mode drivers. It has to have a 32-bit substitute before it can remove the old drivers.

The fact is that the entire Windows 95 drive system relies on the new 32-bit drivers to provide a complete package. Replace an element with a real-mode or 16-bit Windows driver and you remove a piece of the picture. Getting the most out of VCache means that your network and CD-ROM drive have to use the 32-bit drivers.

What is the bottom line? If you want maximum reliability and performance, don't use old drivers. A piece of equipment that requires a real-mode or 16-bit Windows driver is a disaster waiting to happen. Do you really want to play Russian Roulette with your data? If the answer is no, replace that old equipment.

We looked at how you could change the way that VCache looks at the CD-ROM drive in Chapter 3, when we discussed the Supplemental Drive Cache and other CD-ROM drive caches. Essentially, this is all the tuning you need to do; everything else is optimized dynamically to meet system file access and memory requirements.

VCache also supports a feature you might want to get by without. Lazy writes allow Windows 95 to write data to the cache and then write the data from the cache to your hard drive during idle time. "Lazy write" is an industry term for a cache—especially a hard drive cache—that delays writing data from the cache to the drive until a time of low disk activity. Since writing to the cache is faster, you get a speed boost by using this feature. I keep it enabled on my system because I haven't experienced too many lockups or GPFs since I installed Windows 95. However, if you fall into the select group that does experience problems, turning off lazy writes might just save your database. Here's the way you disable lazy writes.

Right-click on the My Computer icon and select Properties. Click on the Performance page and then the File System button. Select the Troubleshooting page. You should see a display similar to the one shown in Figure 8.4. (I describe the other features of this tab in the "Using Windows 95 Automatic Tuning Features" section of Chapter 3.) This dialog allows you to disable lazy writes for all drives by checking the "Disable write behind caching for all drives" option. All you need to do now is click on OK twice to save your changes. Windows will tell you to reboot your machine in most cases to allow the change to take effect.

Figure 8.4.
*The Troubleshooting page of
the File System Properties
dialog allows you to disable
lazy writes for all drives.*

The positive side of this change is that all writes will go directly to the drive instead of the cache.
This might actually help you resolve some database problems where the program displays old or
incorrect data on another user's display after the first user changes it. The negative aspect is that
you'll lose a lot of performance by going this route. In other words, lazy writes offer a big plus in the
way of a speed boost for your system, especially for network drive access.

The main reason to disable lazy writes is if you want to avoid losing data due to a system crash. If
Windows 95 writes some data to the cache and the machine freezes before Windows has a chance to
write that data to disk, you've just experienced a data loss. It's unlikely you'll recover the data if
Windows can't get it to disk. Fortunately, this is a rare event under Windows 95 barring any major
problems with drivers, DOS applications, or older 16-bit Windows applications. Many applications
provide an autosave feature that you might want to set to a shorter interval on systems that experience many problems with machine freezes.

> **Tip:** Occasionally, Windows 95 might freeze to the point where pressing Ctrl-Alt-Delete
> won't allow you to regain control of the system. Under Windows 3.x, this would mean
> instant data loss. Windows 95 seems to recover better than its predecessor in some cases.
> You can usually reduce data loss under Windows 95 if you allow the system to go idle
> before performing a reboot after a system freeze. Wait for all data to get written to disk
> before you reboot the system. When the disk access light goes out and stays out for at least
> 30 seconds, you can reboot the system with a minimum of data loss.

HPFS and NTFS Compatibility

Windows 95 is absolutely not compatible with HPFS or NTFS. Even though it supports one of the
features of these advanced file systems—long filenames—it doesn't provide many of the other features they provide. VFAT isn't a new file system—at least it's not new from the ground up. It's probably best to look at VFAT as the remodeled version of the FAT file system—the upgrade that
Microsoft should have done long ago but didn't.

VFAT can't provide two important features that these other new file systems can: reliability and improved access speed. If either one is of higher importance than compatibility with old applications, you might want to look at Windows NT or OS/2 in place of Windows 95. The one thing Windows 95 will bring is a higher level of compatibility; you pay for it with the loss of these two features.

I could go into all the gory details of these two advanced file systems here, but the important part of this discussion is what you will miss. OS/2 definitely provides a higher level of throughput with HPFS. This file system is redesigned to get rid of one of the major flaws of the FAT file system. Every time you need to access a file under FAT, you have to go to the very beginning of the disk, look up the filename, and get the location of the first cluster of data. Then you have to move the head to the data location and read the cluster before you find out if it contains the data you need. Every access requires another trip to the directory or file allocation table (FAT). The drive head moves back and forth from one extreme to another like a pendulum. All that head movement is very time-intensive and could potentially wear out the drive sooner. HPFS takes care of this problem by moving the directory and file allocation table to the middle of the drive, where you can access them with a lot less head movement.

NTFS has the reliability part of the equation down pat. Not only does it support a much enhanced file storage system, but you can also use it directly with some of the modern data safeguard techniques such as RAID (redundant array of inexpensive disks) and data mirroring. NTFS is an advanced file system for people who can't afford to lose any data. Of course, fully using those data features will cost you a lot more than the old FAT system did in terms of drive purchase cost.

New Extensions: .LNK Files

Pointers is a term familiar to programmers when used as a computer term or familiar to everyone when talking about a directional finder. Think about .LNK files in Windows 95 as a pointer to something. They allow you to create an image of any Windows 95 object somewhere else. In most cases, the object is a file or folder.

So what good are .LNK files? Say that you're a manager and you need to get a bunch of files together for a group that will eventually put a project together. A graphics illustrator has been creating drawings for the last few weeks. A second group has worked up all the figures and statistics with Lotus 1-2-3. Still another group has worked on some text and charts to go with the other elements of the project. You're ready to get everything put together for a full-fledged presentation.

You could copy all the files to one directory and print them. After a lot of red-lining during your meeting, each group could go back and make the required changes. What a time-efficient way to spend your week! This is actually the way a lot of companies work right now, but I can't think of anything more efficient.

Of course, some groups have become more modern. They place all these files in a directory on the network so the group can work on them without making red lines. This is a bit better, but it's still not optimal because you have two copies of the files lying around. This allows too many chances to make a mistake. Besides, what happens if Mary finds another change later? Does she try to find the correct file and make the change (or worse still, try to find the correct person to make the change for her)? Using double files is OK, but it's still not the right way to go.

Windows 95 offers a new alternative. The manager can now make up a project folder containing links (or pointers) to all the project files. The folder is easy to distribute to everyone who is working on the project, even if they aren't in the same building. The links (.LNK files) make it easy for the person using the folder to access a single copy of the real file. No duplicates are needed. There's no chance for mislaid files, everyone can work on all the files as needed, and no one but the manager needs to know the physical location of the files. This is what a .LNK file can do for you. (The only downside of using .LNK files and therefore a common data file is that your application must be set up for file sharing.)

Of course, using .LNK files can help a single user manage his or her work just as easily. In fact, we'll look at some of these methods in the "Working with Desktop Objects" section of Chapter 9. (Also look at this book's color section for ideas on how you can arrange your Desktop using several different approaches.) I have found I can manage all my work as projects and not really worry about applications or the actual location of the data anymore. .LNK files are a small idea with big implications. Let's take a look at some of the details.

Your Start Menu folder contains a ton of .LNK files. If you think that any of your applications actually appear in the Start menu, you're wrong. Only the pointers to those files appear here. If you erase a Start menu entry, all you erase is a .LNK file, not the application itself.

Right-click on the Start Menu icon on the Task Bar and select the Explore option. What you should see now is a dual-pane Explorer view of your Start menu entries. You can easily recognize the .LNK files because they look like shortcuts (the icons with the arrow in the lower left corner). Right-click on any of the .LNK files and you'll see a display similar to the one in Figure 8.5. (I chose the Microsoft Exchange .LNK file, but any choice is acceptable for this discussion.)

Figure 8.5.
A .LNK file's Properties dialog provides a General page similar to that provided by other file types.

As with the General page of any file Properties dialog, you can set the file attributes: hidden, archive, and read-only. This page also tells you the short and long filename and other statistics, such as when someone last modified the file. This is all interesting information, but you'll probably bypass this page in most cases to get to the Shortcut page. Figure 8.6 shows what this page looks like.

Figure 8.6.
The Shortcut page contains all the .LNK file setup information.

The four major fields on this page are listed as follows, along with the function of each entry. Of course, the two you'll use most often are the Target and Run fields. I personally never use the Start in field, but you're likely to need it some places.

- Target: This is the name of the program you want to run. Notice this dialog doesn't provide any way to change the settings for that file. You must change the original file instead of the link. Of course, this makes sense when you think about it since each file could have multiple links pointing to it.

- Start in: Windows 95 always assumes that everything the file will need appears in its target directory. This is probably true for data files. However, you might find that some applications need to use a different "working directory" than the one they start in. The term *working directory* should be familiar if you've moved from Windows 3.x. It's the directory that Windows tells the application to look in for data files. It's the same field you used in a PIF file to control where a program started. This field does the same thing for Windows 95.

- Shortcut key: I covered this topic in Chapter 3. It allows you to assign a shortcut key combination to this particular .LNK file. Using a shortcut key can dramatically speed access to your favorite applications or data files. We'll see some other methods of speeding access to your data in the "Customizing Your Desktop" section of Chapter 9.

- Run: Windows provides three run modes for applications. You can run them in a window, minimized, or maximized. I find the default setting of window works for most of my applications. (In most cases, this is a normal window.) I start data files maximized for certain jobs. This is especially true of my word processing files since I like to get a full-screen view of them. How you set this field is solely determined by the way you work.

That's all there is to .LNK files. Chapter 5 gave you some usage tips for .LNK (or shortcut) files. You'll want to read about the various methods you can use to create shortcuts to your data files and applications. We'll revisit this topic from a Desktop point of view in the "Working with Desktop Objects" section of Chapter 9. The Desktop is where you can really benefit from using these productivity enhancers.

VxDs and DLLs

Modular programming is the way to go these days. Programmers will tell you the reason for modular programming is that it's easier to maintain and understand. Those are perfectly good reasons, but they don't really tell you much as a user. The user's view of modular programming is this: It takes a lot of code to tell your machine how to get anything done when using a GUI, such as Windows 95. More code always translates into more memory. If you replicated the common code Windows needs for tasks, such as displaying a dialog box, for every application you ran, the memory shortage you would experience would dwarf the current problems.

Windows 3.x started the DLL (dynamic link library) and VxD (virtual anything device) craze for a good reason. Creating a Windows program is a complex undertaking, and programmers needed tools to get the job done quickly. A modular approach also ensures that things such as dialog boxes look the same no matter which application you use. However, the important reason for our current discussion is memory. People were already starting to complain about the huge memory footprint of Windows. Even when applications could share some code or data, it still took a lot of memory to get anything done. A GUI will always require more memory than a character-based operating system. If Microsoft had taken a DOS view of programming when designing Windows, we would all be using OS/2 today.

A program calls a DLL or VxD to perform specific tasks. Essentially, both files contain executable code—similar to a miniapplication. When Windows sees the request, it loads the program (DLL or VxD) into memory. Of course, this sounds similar to what DOS does with external files called overlays. In theory, DLLs and VxDs do act somewhat as overlays from a code use point of view, but that's where the similarities end.

Like overlays, both file types contain entry points. Unlike overlays, any number of applications can simultaneously access the program file and use whatever parts are needed. For example, you might have noticed that the File | Open command in most applications produces the same dialog. That dialog is actually part of the COMMDLG.DLL file located in your \SYSTEM directory. An application makes a call to the COMMDLG.DLL to display a File Open dialog. Windows loads the DLL, looks for a specific function number, and then lets the DLL do its work.

Let's take a look at that file. Open Explorer and then the Windows \SYSTEM folder. Right-click on the COMMDLG.DLL file to display the context menu and select Quick View. Page down until you see the Exported Functions entry. It should look similar to the one in Figure 8.7.

Figure 8.7.
The Quick View display of
COMMDLG.DLL can tell
you a lot about the way
Windows works.

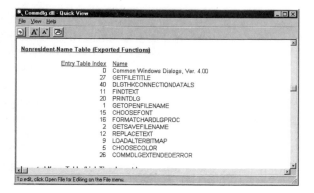

If you look at this table, you'll notice two columns. I won't take the programmer's view of this information (that could fill a book of its own), but we can take a quick look at it. The first column tells you the function number. The second column (the one that we're interested in) tells you the function name. Notice the kinds of things that a programmer can do with the COMMDLG.DLL. Especially important are function 1, which allows you to open a file; function 2, which allows you to save a file; and function 20, which displays the Print dialog.

You can check out some of the other DLLs in the \SYSTEM directory using this same method. Learning what the DLLs do for you can help when something doesn't work the way it should. For example, what would you do if the File Open dialog suddenly stopped working? It might seem to be a very unlikely prospect, but data corruption can affect any file on your system. (If you were a Windows 3.x user, you might have found out about your system files the hard way when your system would stop working unexpectedly; DLL and other system file corruption was a fairly common problem for some people.) Knowing the File Open dialog appears in the COMMDLG.DLL file could help you fix the system with just a few minutes worth of work. All you would need to do is restore a good copy of this file from your backup. (We'll cover backups later in this chapter.)

What DLLs do for software, VxDs do for hardware. When part of your system needs to access a piece of hardware, it normally calls a VxD. Of course, drivers can also work with software components, but from a different perspective than DLLs do. Drivers always provide some type of interface to a system component. For example, some types of memory allocation are performed with a VxD. This isn't a function most users would worry about, but it's one that's very important to the proper functioning of your system. One of the most used VxDs on your drive is the VMM32.VXD. It combines the functionality of a lot of the older files you found under Windows 3.x into one file. (Most of these entries appeared in the 386ENH section of SYSTEM.INI.)

Tip: If you right-click on a VxD file, you'll notice that it offers no quick view option. To view the file, make a copy and give it a .DLL extension. You can now use Quick View to see the header of this file. This same technique works with other executable file types as well. Unfortunately, about the only things the file header will tell you are the amount of memory that the VxD requires to load and some programmer-specific information, such as the size of the stack that the VxD creates. In most cases, it isn't worth your while to look at the file heading unless you're low on memory and are looking for a peripheral to unload from your system. Unloading a peripheral device can free memory that you can use for applications. (Be sure to make a backup of any drivers that you unload using the procedures near the end of this chapter.)

Viewing File Contents

We've already taken a long look at the process of viewing files in quite a few of the chapters in this book, so I won't bore you with a lot of details here. It's important to realize that Windows 95 does come with some file viewing support built in. Most of the major applications you'll use are already entered in the registry. Other levels of file support come from registry entries made by your applications during installation. Even if your applications aren't successful during installation, you can always import the .REG files they create to add support to Windows 95. We talked about all of these types of file viewing support in Chapter 6.

You can also add support to the registry for your own file extensions. We looked at one way to add it for existing files in Chapter 6. Chapter 9 will show you still other ways to add support for viewing files. The method you use to add file support isn't important. The important thing to consider here is how efficient the new support makes you. Customizing Windows 95 to the way you work is the best way to use all the added speed that this product can provide. Using your old work methods means you'll actually ignore those new features—a major problem with some people who have tried Windows 95 and have been disappointed in its performance.

Tip: OLE is a real memory hog when it comes to moving data from one major application to another. You can usually accomplish the same thing by using a small application such as NotePad, WordPad, or Microsoft Paint as the server in place of the major application you normally use. Adding multiple application support could make OLE practical on machines that normally don't have enough memory to support it. (DDE and OLE are covered in detail in Chapter 11.)

Here's a practical example of another type of file support you can add to Windows 95. I found the level of Explorer support for .DOC files didn't meet my needs, so I changed it. That's one of the first rules you'll need to learn about Windows 95. Nothing is cast in concrete as long as you have some idea of what to look for in Explorer or the registry. In this case, I simply modified an Explorer entry to suit my needs.

Figure 8.8 shows the context menu I designed for .DOC files. Of course, you could just as easily do the same thing for .PCX, or any other file extension, for that matter. Windows 95 doesn't care how you customize your system; all it cares about is interacting with you and your applications when you get through.

Figure 8.8.
There's no specific way to view data in Windows 95. Everything is configurable if you know how to use the registry and are creative.

Notice I can open .DOC files with Word for Windows or WordPad. I can also use the quick viewer to display the files when necessary. Another entry allows me to use Word for Windows to print the file without opening it first.

Now that you've seen the results, let's look at the implementation. Figure 8.9 shows the Explorer entries I made to create this context menu. You can use it as a basis for making your own changes. All I did was open the Options dialog using the View | Options command in Explorer. Then I selected the File Types page and Microsoft Word 6.0 Document. Clicking on Edit displays the dialog shown in Figure 8.9.

Figure 8.9.
Creating your own context menus for viewing files under Windows 95 is as simple as a few registry entries.

> **Tip:** It almost always pays to associate more than one application with the files you use most often because memory limitations will sometimes prevent you from opening the full-fledged application you normally use to view or print the file. Adding a second application with a smaller footprint ensures that you'll always have access to your data files.

Adding the Quick View option is simple. Just mark the Enable Quick View checkbox. Windows 95 has a problem here. It will allow you to mark this checkbox even if Quick View doesn't support your application. You'll need to check the Windows 95 documentation and any Windows 95 application documentation for application support before you check this box.

The WordPad entry is almost as simple to make. Click on New to add a new entry to the list of actions. Type the information shown in Figure 8.10. That's all there is to it. Click on OK three times to save your new entries, and you'll have a custom context menu for .DOC files.

Figure 8.10.
Adding new options to the context menu for a file extension is as simple as adding a new option to this dialog.

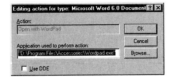

Viewing files under Windows 95 doesn't have to be the painful experience it was under Windows 3.x. I won't say that customizing your system is easy; it certainly isn't as easy as it could be. However, at least Windows 95 provides the means to do it. Maybe the next release of Windows will allow you to perform these tricks without resorting to using RegEdit.

Formatting Disks

Formatting floppy disks is one of those tasks that everyone must perform from time to time, such as taking out the garbage or doing the laundry—something you'd rather not do but end up doing anyway. I found the old File Manager interface under Windows 3.x difficult to use for any length of time because the interface just wasn't all that useable. Besides, formatting floppies in Windows 3.x was slow, and I could never get it to work right in the background. It was just faster and easier to get the job done from the DOS prompt.

I took another look at formatting floppies when I got Windows 95 installed. Windows 95 does improve on the interface problem. All you need to do is right-click on the drive you want to format from within Explorer, as shown in Figure 8.11.

Figure 8.11.

Windows 95 always displays a Format option for any drive that supports formatting.

Select the Format option and you'll see the dialog shown in Figure 8.12. This dialog should look somewhat familiar. It's actually an improved version of the same dialog that you used under Windows 3.x. I say improved because every field is self-explanatory now. There's no guessing about what this checkbox or that listbox might do.

Figure 8.12.

The Windows 95 Format dialog is an enhanced version of the File Manager dialog used with Windows 3.x.

Tip: Always use the Quick Erase option to format floppies that you know are good. This option will format the floppy in a little over a tenth of the time that a full format will take.

All you need to do now is select the options you want and click on OK. Windows 95 does offer a few nice surprises in addition to the interface. For one thing, it works very well in the background. I didn't experience a single problem with working on something else while the floppy took its time formatting. Of course, Microsoft didn't fix everything; formatting under Windows 95 is just as slow as it was under 3.x.

Tip: You can double or even triple your formatting capacity by selecting network floppies to format under Windows 95. A peer-to-peer connection will allow you to use the floppy on another machine if you have access. Two machines in close proximity in one office will double the number of disks that you can format at once.

Backup

Backing up your data is an exercise everyone hates to do. It always seems to take a long time and wastes perfectly good hours you could use for some other purpose. Of course, the day will come when your system will take a nosedive (usually after you've decided that backing up takes too much time), and you really will need that backup. Making a backup of your system is like buying insurance: No one ever sees a good reason to do it until disaster strikes, and then it's too late to do anything if you didn't prepare in advance.

Some people will try to make a backup of their system using floppy disks. That might've worked in the days of 33 MB hard drives, but with today's 300 MB to 1 GB systems, it just won't work. If you're going to back up your system, you need to invest in a tape drive of some type.

Now, here's where someone at Microsoft really wasn't thinking. Backup supports only one tape drive format—QIC. Of course, you have a nifty new DAT drive so it won't work with the Microsoft product. Hopefully the next version of Windows 95 will include a decent level of support. Until that happens, though, you'd better go out and get a third-party product if your drive isn't of the Colorado Jumbo variety. If you do have one of those SCSI or IDE drives, read the sections on maintaining your drive and rotating tapes.

Note: I won't cover the process of performing a floppy backup in this chapter for two reasons. First, a floppy backup really isn't all that practical except for the very smallest backup sessions. Second, the procedure for a floppy backup is so similar to the tape backup that you won't experience any problems going from one to the other.

Now, if you really can use Microsoft Backup, let's take a quick tour of the product. The first time you start Backup, it will create a default backup set for you that includes all the files on your drive. In most cases, you can use this backup set as a starting point to create your own custom setups. Go ahead and start Backup if you have it installed so you can take a look at this utility with me.

Once you get past the initial screen, it might take Backup a few seconds to complete the hardware detection process. Backup will automatically detect your tape drive in most cases. You can always tell if the detection was successful by the status of the Tools menu. If you see that all the tools are available, Backup successfully detected your drive. Make sure you perform the detection with a tape installed. Backup can't detect some tapes correctly if the tape isn't in place. Now you are ready to perform any of the three actions outlined in the following sections: backup, restore, and compare.

Creating a Backup

The first activity you'll perform with Backup is creating your first backup tape. Figure 8.13 shows the initial Backup window. As you can see, there are boxes next to each drive and folder on the left side of the display, and next to each folder and file on the right side of the page. (The interface works much like Explorer, in which the right pane shows a detailed view of whatever you select in the left pane.) You select the items you want to back up by clicking on the boxes. An empty box means that Backup won't send that item to tape. A gray box with a checkmark appears next to a folder or drive that you intend to partially back up. A checkmark appears next to a file, folder, or drive that you intend to completely back up.

Figure 8.13.

The initial Backup dialog allows you to select the files you want to store on tape.

You'll probably see a dialog during the file selection process. Windows 95 will continue to peel blank pages from a stack and add a checkmark to them as long as it is selecting files. (The machine froze on me several times during the selection process.) You can usually detect a problem if the pages continue to peel after the disk activity stops. Make sure you check the client machines, as well as the local machine, when backing up more than one machine on a peer-to-peer network.

> **Tip:** The first time you back your system up, Backup might find some files that it can't verify. Always check the ERROR.LOG file in the \PROGRAM FILES\ACCESSORIES\ LOG folder. This file will tell you which files Backup couldn't verify. In most cases, you'll want to exclude these files unless you have a good reason to keep them in the backup set. I've found most of these files end up being system-specific—files I would normally need to install manually before a restore.

Once you complete the selection process, it's time to select a target for the backup. Figure 8.14 shows a typical selection window. As you can see, Backup allows you to select any drive or the tape as a storage location.

Figure 8.14.
This is the window where you select the backup target. You also use it to save the backup set.

Now is the time to save your backup set. If you try to save it before this point in the process, Backup will display an error message. Notice that a target is part of the set file information. You need this information to conduct automatic backups by double-clicking on a file set icon in Explorer.

After you save the file set, click on Start Backup to begin the actual backup process. Backup will ask you to provide a set label for this particular session. A tape can contain more than one session if you want it to. I usually store an entire week's worth of backups on one tape. The amount you can store depends largely on how much storage space the tape contains and how much you need. This dialog also allows you to password protect the backup. Adding a password isn't required for on-site storage. However, if you plan to use off-site storage, a password will protect your valuable data.

Click on OK on the Backup Set Label dialog and you'll see Backup start storing the data on your machine to tape. Using this application is fairly simple, even moreso once you get the backup sets that you want to perform configured and stored on disk. All you need to do then is double-click on the set you want to use for that particular session.

I did skip past a few of Microsoft Backup's features during this quick look. Let's take a look at some of them now. All the feature dialogs appear under the Settings menu. They include File Filtering, Drag and Drop, and Options.

The File Filtering dialog appears in Figure 8.15. This dialog looks complicated but contains only two settings. The first allows you to exclude files by date range. Suppose you want to back up only files from this week. Using this entry will allow you to do that. The second allows you to select files by type. Here's another quirk of Microsoft Backup: You can exclude only registered file types. Most people don't register the file types they don't plan to use. For example, the .BAK extension rarely appears in the registry naturally. Yet, if you want to exclude that file type from your backups, you'll need to register it. Hopefully Microsoft will see fit to fix this shortcoming. All the file types you can select for exclusion appear in the upper listbox. The file types that will get excluded from this backup appear in the lower listbox.

Figure 8.15.
The File Filtering dialog
allows you to select which
files appear in the backup
set.

You control the exclusion and inclusion of file types by using four pushbuttons. Select All highlights all the files in the File Types listbox. Exclude places any highlighted file types in the Exclude File Types listbox. You can remove a file type from the Exclude File Types listbox using Delete. Finally, the Restore Default pushbutton removes all the file types from the Exclude File Types listbox.

The Drag and Drop dialog appears in Figure 8.16. Notice that this dialog contains only three entries. The first automatically keeps Microsoft Backup minimized when it starts. The second forces it to display a dialog asking your permission to start the backup. The third automatically ends the application once it completes the backup. Microsoft Backup defaults to checking all three entries. It's a good idea to leave them this way unless you have a reason for changing one or more of them. (I usually uncheck the second checkbox—Confirm operation before beginning—if I plan to be away from my desk when the backup starts.)

We'll look at two pages of the Options dialog in this section. The first page, General, contains two checkboxes, as shown in Figure 8.17. The first checkbox tells Backup to prompt you with a beep at the end of an operation. For example, if it completely fills one tape, Backup will beep and ask you to supply another. The Overwrite old status logs option, the second checkbox, prevents Backup from saving old information. This keeps your drive relatively free from extra clutter and still allows you to retain the status of the previous backup.

Figure 8.16.
The Drag and Drop dialog allows you to set the automatic settings for Microsoft Backup.

Figure 8.17.
The General page of the Options dialog allows you to select the notification and log settings.

The second page we'll look at is the Backup page, shown in Figure 8.18, which has three main sections. The first entry, a checkbox, tells Backup to exit as soon as the backup is completed.

Figure 8.18.
The Backup Page of the Options dialog contains all the parameters that affect how Microsoft performs the backup.

The second section of the Backup page contains two radio buttons. Select the first radio button if you want Backup to perform a full backup of the selected files on the drive. The second option allows you to perform a differential backup. The only files that Backup will select from the backup set are those with the archive bit set. Backup resets this bit each time it backs up your files. Whenever you change the file, Windows sets the archive bit. The status of this bit tells Backup whether you changed the file since the last time you archived it to disk. (You can see whether the archive attribute of a file is set by right-clicking on it in Explorer and selecting the Properties option. The file attributes appear on the General page of the file Properties dialog. A check in the Archive checkbox tells you that the file will get backed up.)

The third section of this dialog contains some special settings. I always check the first checkbox. Making a backup without performing a compare afterward is one sure way to end up with something unusable. I've run into several situations where the network administrator thought he had a perfect backup, only to find out the tape isn't any good. If you don't perform a compare, you don't know if the backup is any good. The other options in this group are fairly self-explanatory. You can usually count on a 2:1 ratio for a normal backup if you turn on data compression. I've gotten as high as 15:1 for graphic and sound file backups. An all-data backup usually nets a 4:1 ratio with compression turned on. You'll probably want to use the 2:1 figure for your first few backups. Once you figure out the compression ratio, use it to determine how many tapes you'll need to complete a backup.

Restoring a Backup

Restoring a backup follows a process that reverses the one you used for creating the backup in the first place. You start by specifying the original target device and the backup set that you want to use. In most cases this will be a hard or a tape drive. Then select the files from that backup set you want to restore. Finally you start the restore process.

Just as with the backup process, you can also access settings for the restore process using the Settings | Options command. Figure 8.19 shows a sample of this dialog. As you can see, it has three groups of controls, similar to the Backup dialog. The first control tells Backup to automatically exit when it completes the restore, if checked.

Figure 8.19.
The Restore page of the Options dialog allows you to set all the restore options.

The second group of controls is fairly straightforward. These options allow you to select a restore location. Normally you would choose the same directory Backup originally copied the files from. However, you can choose the second option to restore the file to an alternate location. This particular option will retain any directory structure. If you want to place all the files in a single directory, no matter where they originally appeared in the directory tree, select the third option.

The final group of controls allows you to change the way Backup restores the files. As with the Backup page, I always select the compare option here as well. If you don't compare the restored file with what appears on tape, you can't be sure you got a good restore. A momentary system glitch has corrupted more than a few files as they got restored to the hard drive from tape, even though the file was actually good. I also use the Overwrite option so I can replace corrupted files with good ones. Checking the Prompt before overwriting option still gives you the option to keep the original file. Of course, using these two options together means you'll have to sit in front of the machine during the restore to answer any questions it might have about overwriting files. Select one of the other two overwrite options if you want to perform an automatic restore.

Performing a Compare

The compare feature of Backup works much like Restore. You begin by selecting the backup device. In most cases, this will be the tape drive. As usual, you select the files, folders, and directories you want to compare. Once you make your selections, Backup compares the contents of the selected files with the files that exist on the hard drive in the same location. I find that a compare is useful when I want to check the status of a master backup. It lets me know how out-of-date the material really is.

Figure 8.20 shows the Compare page of the Options dialog. Notice it contains the same first and second group of controls that Restore did. I won't go through them here again.

Figure 8.20.
The Compare page of the Options dialog box looks very similar to the Restore page. The options let you compare the contents of the original file to your backup.

Testing and Maintaining the Backup System

I'm almost never satisfied with the thin brochures tape vendors call manuals. A quick look inside usually provides one or perhaps two pages of installation instructions. If you're lucky, you'll also get a page or two of troubleshooting instructions. Because these rather short instructions leave too much to the imagination, I came up with a few time-tested techniques for getting the most out of your backup system.

The first step, of course, is to select some hardware and software. I go by three simple rules:

1. To compute the minimum tape size you need, multiply your hard drive size (including any client machines that you plan to back up) by 1.5 for weekly backups or 3 for daily backups using the differential method I describe later in this chapter.

2. Determine the cost of the fastest tape backup system you can afford to buy. A slow backup system will only make it more difficult for you to perform the required level of maintenance. After all, who wants to hang around waiting for the tape backup to finish right before the weekend starts?

3. Add the cost of at least three backup tapes to the purchase price of your tape drive to determine the final cost. What good is a tape drive without tapes? Make sure you get enough tapes. I outline several different backup scheduling methods near the end of this chapter. You might want to look through them before deciding how many tapes you want to buy.

I always shop around for my tape drives because the prices tend to vary a lot more than for common items such as memory. You never know when you'll get the super deal of a lifetime from one of the stores that you frequent a little less often. Once you do select the hardware and software that you intend to use to back up your system, it's important to test it and maintain it. I really find it hard to believe that some people just throw the tape drive into their system and expect it to work. Testing ensures that the data you back up today will actually work when an emergency arises. Maintenance increases the longevity of the equipment you use.

It's important to take a two-phase approach to testing your new backup system: a full test today and a maintenance test tomorrow. After the initial equipment installation, you should completely test your system to make absolutely certain it works. You need to test the hardware, software, automated procedures, macros, and anything else that might stop you from getting a good backup. Test your system in stages using the procedures contained in the following section. Make sure you use techniques that fully test the hardware and software combination as well as the individual components.

Once you get things up and running, you need to continue testing your system from time to time. This will confirm that the software and hardware are still working. Remember, this is your life's work in data we're talking about here, so even a little failure is important. Some breakdowns aren't as obvious as smoking tapes or tape drives and remain undetected by the backup software.

I still remember one shop where I was called in as a consultant to solve a mystery. Someone at the shop installed a tape backup system and checked to make sure it worked. After that, they performed a backup of their system every day. The backup software always told them that they had gotten a good backup and they had no reason not to believe it. Eventually they needed to use the backup they made to restore some data. To their horror, the previous day's tape contained absolutely nothing. One by one they checked every other tape they made; the network administrator discovered that these were blank as well. The culprit of this gruesome scene? The write head had fallen off inside the tape drive with the wires still connected. As a result, the tape drive never sensed the head was dysfunctional. In fact, the tape head really worked just fine. The data it wrote simply didn't get onto the tape. Since the backup software didn't compare the contents of tape to the contents of the drive after the backup, everything appeared to work fine. The moral of this story? You can become a casualty of hardware or software errors, or you can test your system. Hardware tests aren't a convenience; they're a necessity for anyone who wants to get the most out of their system.

Let's talk about another issue that most people fail to consider—tape drive maintenance. Many network administrators delay their tape drive maintenance until it's too late. After all, who will ever see the tape drive sitting in his office? It's much better to keep the print server, which the boss can see, clean. In the preceding example, the network administrator would have found the fallen write head if he had simply maintained his tape drive. Every drive on the market requires cleaning and physical head inspection. You can use either a cotton swab and alcohol (much like the maintenance you perform on your tape system at home) or a specially designed tape cartridge to clean the drive. In addition, the vendor manual that comes with your tape drive should include some detailed maintenance procedures. (Most don't include complete instructions, so I've included the set that I use in the following sections.)

Initial Installation

I always perform a visual check of any equipment I buy before I install it. The more pieces I have to install, the closer I look before I begin. You can use the same procedure I do to make sure you get the best installation possible. First, if the vendor supplies a checklist or picture of the equipment, use it to make sure you have everything. It's not unheard of to get a package that doesn't contain everything you need. Perform the same check for your software. Make sure you have the right licenses and that the disks aren't corrupted. Also perform a virus check on any disks. Check your tape supply and make sure you have enough on hand to perform a full backup cycle. (We'll talk about this topic in the next section.) Once you have all the components required to install your tape drive, it's time to do the actual work.

Now that you've gotten the easy part out of the way, it's time to start a staged installation/test of your system. What exactly is this process? It begins with a test of the base installation and then tests each addition you make to it. As a result, you spend a lot less time troubleshooting installation problems, and you know exactly where weak areas in the system might occur. The following paragraphs provide you with the four easy steps you can follow to get a great tape drive installation. These are generic instructions, so you'll need to make some modifications of this procedure to reflect your hardware and software setup. Some companies also have a set of policies in place. Make sure you follow any company-specific regulations as well.

1. Install the hardware using any vendor-supplied instructions. Make sure you observe the proper static safeguards by grounding yourself before you begin. A standard installation usually includes attaching slides to the drive (if required) and mounting it in the system.

Once you complete that step, attach any required cables including a power cable. A lot of people skip the extra step of attaching a grounding cable to the drive. Don't do it, because the ground cable can prevent transient signals from trashing your backup.

2. Test your initial hardware installation. This usually involves an initial test of the hardware using vendor-supplied diagnostic software. Some drives, such as the Jumbo series from Colorado, don't provide any diagnostic software, so you can skip this step and move on to step 3. If your hardware fails the diagnostic test, check for interrupt conflicts, jumpers in the wrong place, or other configuration problems. Reread the diagnostic program manual to make sure you set it up correctly. If you can't correct the problem yourself, call the vendor and tell them about the symptoms you notice. Make sure you provide them with complete information about your machine. This includes the BIOS revision number and vendor, the model and vendor of all your peripheral devices and motherboard, and all the jumper settings for peripheral cards that use them. Also include the diagnostic software version number, a listing of unusual noises or odors, the failure number displayed by the diagnostic program, and any steps you took to correct the problem.

3. Check for hardware and software interaction. Once you get the hardware working, it's time to test the software. I usually begin by performing any software tests that the vendor supplies. For example, most backup software provides a speed test to make sure your hardware can perform at a given backup speed.

4. Once you complete the vendor-specific check, perform a check of your own. Back up a directory containing nonessential data and then do a compare of the tape's contents to the drive's contents (if your software supports this feature). Restore your data to a different directory if possible. Use the DOS COMPARE utility (or any other utility that will perform a detailed comparison) to compare the files in the original directory to the new directory. If you can't restore to a different directory, try restoring the files to a different drive. You could also copy your existing data to a temporary directory and restore the old data to the default directory. If either of these steps fails, check the setup of your software to make sure that all the settings are correct for your machine, tape drive controller, hard disk controller, and tape drive. Check your machine's environment to see if you have enough buffers and files allocated. Also check any network driver settings to make sure you have them set up correctly. If you still can't get a good backup from the software, call the vendor and describe the symptoms. Make sure you tell them you ran a complete diagnostic on the hardware so they don't try to place the blame on that. Provide the vendor with the version of your software as well as all the hardware specifications.

5. Create any required macros and setup files. Check each of these setups manually to make sure you set them up correctly. You'll want to verify that the backup software works by carefully executing the macros using simulated conditions. Resolve any problem areas by reviewing the procedures for setting up the macros and setup files in the vendor-supplied file. Asking a coworker to look at a printout of any handwritten macro procedures might help locate problem areas. Everyone tends to overlook obvious errors after they look at the

same piece of code for more than an hour. If you still can't get the procedures to work correctly, call the vendor. Some vendors provide a BBS that you can use to upload your setup files. This might provide faster response times than a call will, since the vendor can test the files you've created using its software.

6. Perform any required setups for the scheduling software. Make sure you take power failures and other contingencies into account. Check the scheduling software to make sure it will trigger properly. You can do this by resetting the backup workstation's system clock and seeing if the software starts at the proper time. Double-check the backup by restoring a single directory on the tape to another directory or drive, and then use the DOS COMPARE utility to compare the contents of the original directory with the new directory.

This six-step procedure should help you get up and running quickly. The most time-consuming part of the process should be writing and testing the macros required by your backup system. In most cases you should be able to get a tape drive installed and running in less than a day. Of course, it's always a good idea to prepare for the worst, just in case it happens.

Routine Maintenance

Every piece of equipment on the network requires maintenance, and the tape drive is no exception. Maintenance includes both cleaning and physical examination. It might include replacing filters and belts as well. Your vendor manual should include a set of procedures for maintaining your tape drive. Remarkably, some vendor manuals don't include these vital instructions. Somewhere along the way, a few vendors got the idea that they should sell maintenance instructions as a separate item. You might want to give your vendor a call, just to make sure it doesn't fall into this category. If you can't seem to find any vendor instructions, feel free to use the same set I do for generic tape drive maintenance. Make sure you have a flashlight, cotton swabs (the type used to clean tape drives), methyl or isopropyl alcohol, and any required filters.

1. Carefully open the tape drive door using a nonconductive material. The plastic screwdrivers included with some computer maintenance tool kits are very useful for this purpose. Use a flashlight to examine the interior of the tape drive. Penlights usually work the best.

2. You need to examine several things in the drive. Figure 8.21 provides a basic tape drive diagram as it would appear when you open the drive door. To get specific details about your drive, refer to the tape diagram in the vendor manual if the vendor supplied one. The first thing you should look at is the black rubber wheel (idler wheel) on one side of the drive carriage. If this looks shiny and has a brownish cast to it, you need to clean it using alcohol and a cotton swab. It might take a little time to get the wheel clean, but it's essential to do so.

Figure 8.21.

Anatomy of a tape drive, showing the parts you need to pay particular attention to.

3. Check the read and write heads next (see Figure 8.21). (Some tape drives use a combination read/write head so you might see only one head.) Clean them with a fresh cotton swab and some alcohol. Make sure you don't apply a lot of pressure, otherwise you might scratch the head surface. Polish the heads with a dry cotton swap using gentle pressure. Check the heads for damage such as scratches. Both heads should appear brightly polished.

4. Clean the end of the tape sensor if your tape drive has one (see Figure 8.21). This usually looks like a square or rectangular black plastic box with a tiny round light in it. The light is actually a photo sensor. You must clean the plastic covering the photo sensor so light can get through and tell the tape drive when it reaches the end of tape. Simply moisten a cotton swab with alcohol and use a rotating motion to clean the sensor. The sensor is usually recessed into the black plastic case, so rubbing back and forth only forces dirt further into the recess.

5. Close the tape drive door. If this is an internal tape drive, complete the cleaning sequence by opening your computer and vacuuming any dirt out of the inside of the case, and then proceed to step 9 of this procedure.

6. External tape drive units often come with filters. Look at the back of the tape drive unit to see if it uses a filter. If there's a filter, carefully remove the old one. The filter's usually held in place using a holder and some screws. Refer to the manual supplied with your tape drive for further details.

7. Replace the old filter with a new one if possible. Some vendors might not supply replacement filters for their systems. If this is the case, carefully wash the filter using clear water. Don't use soap, because this will actually clog the filter. Let the filter dry thoroughly. Replace the filter on the back of the tape drive unit.

8. If the tape drive provides some form of external access, open the case and carefully vacuum the inside. Never force the case open. In most cases the vendor manual will say if the case is designed to allow user access.

9. Now that you've fully cleaned your tape unit, place a blank tape in the drive and test it. Make sure that this is a test tape and not one of the tapes in your backup set. Format the tape if necessary.

10. Test your tape drive using the diagnostic program supplied by the vendor. Follow the procedures I supplied in the installation section if the tape drive doesn't work for some reason. In most cases, you'll find that you nudged a jumper or cable, so that should be the first thing you check. Also make sure you have everything back together properly.

11. Check for hardware and software interaction. Once you get the hardware working, it's time to test the software. I usually begin by performing any software tests the vendor supplies. For example, most backup software provides a speed test to make sure your hardware can perform at a given backup speed.

12. Once you complete the vendor-specific check, perform a check of your own. Back up a directory containing nonessential data and then do a compare of the tape's contents to the drive's contents (if your software supports this feature). Restore your data to a different directory if possible. Use the DOS COMPARE utility (or any other utility that will perform a detailed comparison) to compare the files in the original directory to the new directory. If you can't restore to a different directory, try restoring the files to a different drive. You could also copy your existing data to a temporary directory and restore the old data to the default directory. If either of these steps fails, check the setup of your software to make sure that all the settings are correct for your machine, tape drive controller, hard disk controller, and tape drive. Check your machine's environment to see if you have enough buffers and files allocated. Also check any network driver settings to make sure you have them set up correctly. If you still can't get a good backup from the software, call the vendor and describe the symptoms. Make sure you tell them that you ran a complete diagnostic on the hardware so they don't try to place the blame on that. Provide the vendor with the version of your software as well as all the hardware specifications.

I find that maintaining the tape drive attached to my system is a lot easier than the alternative. Never buy faulty insurance. A tape drive that isn't maintained is worse than no tape backup at all. At least if you don't have a tape backup you won't have any unexpected surprises when a hard drive fails. A good tape drive is like good insurance, it's always there when you need it. It's a good idea to perform this maintenance at least once every three months unless the vendor specifies a different maintenance cycle. You might want to perform maintenance more often if the tape drive's in a dirty or hazardous area.

You might want to take this opportunity to check your tapes as well. Tapes get old and wear out just like anything else in your system. You can use three quick steps to check a tape. First, look for any physical damage, such as a cracked case. Damage of this type might damage the tape drive as well.

Second, look at how the tape is wound on the spool (also known as the tape pack). Does it appear wavy instead of smooth? Can you see individual wraps sticking above the level of the other wraps on the spool? If so, try to re-tension the tape (unless the manufacturer doesn't recommend doing this). If re-tension doesn't give the tape a smoother appearance, the tape might contain stretched areas. Finally, remember that tape life is limited. DAT tapes last about five years, and others last about two years. If your tape is more than five years old, consider replacing it even if it looks good. You might want to consider replacing heavily used tapes more often. If you use a tape every day you should consider replacing it every two years.

> **Tip:** Some tape vendors suggest placing a label on the tape and making a hash mark every time you use it. Once you reach 40 uses, discard the tape and use a new one. Tapes will actually last much longer (remember, the people who sell tapes are the same people who tell you to buy new ones), but if you store your tapes in a warm or dirty environment, increased tape turnover might give you an added level of security.

Tape Rotation

I actually walked into a business once with a state-of-the-art file server, up-to-date workstations, and a tape backup system to boot. The only problem was that they had only one tape. A one-tape shop will always run into problems. Even if you assume that every backup will work exactly as expected, several other things could go wrong. For example, a fire could strike at any moment. A one-tape shop would come in the next morning and find its tape safely stored in the safe where it always is. Of course, it would be a ball of melted plastic, but it would still be there. Floods and theft aren't out of the question either. A lot of things can happen to your data, and if you keep it all in one place, it takes only one accident to turn your business into a disaster. Hopefully this makes my point about the need for rotating your tapes.

You can rotate tapes many different ways. The technique you use depends on the requirements of your company, the value of your data, the types of applications you use, and the number of tapes you have on-hand. Every tape rotation method has three things in common:

1. Always store at least one tape off-site. An off-site tape has a better chance of surviving the smaller disasters of life.

2. Use at least three tapes to implement what the industry terms a grandfather backup strategy. A grandfather strategy ensures that at least three generations of tape will be available at all times. Using this strategy usually reduces the probability of virus infection or other forms of data loss.

3. A good rotation strategy always includes some plan for retiring old tapes and integrating new ones.

I usually use a three-tape strategy for small businesses. My own setup uses a six-tape strategy. The following sections examine some common backup rotation techniques. Although none of these methods might exactly fit your needs, they do provide you with enough information to come up with a reliable rotation scheme of your own.

> **Tip:** Tapes are cheap when compared to the cost of the data they hold. Buying a few more tapes might rescue your data from disaster. Never let the cost of the tapes you buy interfere with a good backup strategy.

The Three-Tape Full Backup Technique

This is the method I recommend to small businesses on a very tight budget, because it represents the very least you can get by with and still maintain a safe backup strategy. Use this method for less-complex installations that use the network primarily for word processing and small spreadsheet files. For example, this technique usually meets the needs of a small four or five person company that doesn't use a complex accounting package or rely on a database management system. You might not want to use it for applications that rely heavily on shared files. The reliability of this technique greatly diminishes as the number of files you want to protect increases. Figure 8.22 illustrates this technique.

Figure 8.22.
The three-tape full backup technique works well for small businesses.

Day 1
Full Backup

Location: File Server Room/Tape Backup Area. This allows easy access to today's tape. Backing up should always be as easy as possible, without the possibility of data compromise.

Day 2
Full Backup

Location: Company Safe/Vault. This allows easy access to the previous day's backup. In some cases, you might need to access this copy if today's copy gets damaged during the backup process.

Day 3
Full Backup

Location: Off-Site Storage. Always ensure that your data is safe from fire and other hazards. Many companies specialize in off-site storage needs. Storing the two-day-old tape off-site reduces your data loss to two days.

his tape storage method is that you still maintain an off-site storage capabil-
xpands to four, five, or even six tapes. Since the tapes do rotate at a fairly
place them more often.

ape Full/Incremental Backup Technique

technique uses one dedicated tape for each day of the week, reducing the probability of virus infection or other damage that can occur when you use one tape for both full and incremental back-ups. Monday and Friday are full backup days, while Tuesday through Thursday require only incremental backups. The Friday tape alternates between the off-site storage site and on-site storage. Use this technique for moderately complex setups that rely mainly on word processing and spreadsheet applications in a nonshared environment. You can also use this technique for installations with small accounting systems or moderately complex database management systems. Figure 8.23 illustrates this technique.

The advantage to using this system is that it's more reliable than the three-tape system, yet requires less maintenance time than creating full backups each day of the week. The only disadvantage of this system is that the Monday backup represents a weak link in the backup chain. If the Monday backup becomes corrupted, the incremental backups you make from Tuesday through Thursday also become worthless. You could conceivably lose four days of work using this method. Of course, this assumes that a network crash occurs on Thursday afternoon or Friday and that you have a corrupted Monday backup. Although this sequence of events is unlikely, it could happen.

One way to expand this particular backup technique is to add additional Friday tapes to the sequence. For example, you could easily make this a nine-tape sequence, which would allow one Friday tape for each week of the month. Expandability is one of the things that I try to keep in mind when set-ting up a tape rotation scheme. It's always easy to use fewer tapes, finding a good way to use more can get to be a challenge.

The Six-Tape Full Backup Technique

I find this particular rotation scheme works best with medium-sized businesses that have very robust data storage needs (see Figure 8.24). For example, if you rely heavily on a data entry or an order entry system, this is the rotation scheme you need to look at. This technique uses one dedicated tape for each day of the week. The Friday tape alternates between the off-site storage site and on-site storage.

This rotation scheme overcomes the weakness of the Six-Tape Full/Incremental Rotation described in the preceding section by using a full backup each day of the week. Of course, this means mainte-nance time increases in proportion to the total size of your network rather than the size of the files that you change each day. On larger networks it might also mean an increase in the total number of tapes if you need more than one tape to make a full backup of the network. Unfortunately, your tapes will wear out faster because they'll receive a higher level of use with this method.

Figure 8.23.
This six-tape method works well for moderately complex setups.

	Week 1	Week 2
Monday	Full Backup	→
Tuesday	Incremental/Differential Backup	→
Wednesday	Incremental/Differential Backup	→
Thursday	Incremental/Differential Backup	→
Friday (Off-Site Storage)	Full Backup	Full Backup

The best way to expand this rotation scheme is to double the number of tapes so that you alternate sets between odd and even weeks. This will improve security and reduce tape wear. It also would allow you to maintain more tapes off-site, further reducing the chance that one tape failure would prove disastrous.

The 14-Tape Full Backup Technique

Large businesses require a more complex rotation scheme to ensure that their data remains safe. Not only is it unlikely that you'll use a single application or perhaps a simple group of applications, but it's also very unlikely that the network administrator will have as firm a grip on the inner workings of the company. (It's not that the administrator is incompetent, but administering a large setup leaves little time to understand how everyone else uses the computer.) The larger and more complex your network, the more desirable it is to provide several stages of network backup.

Figure 8.24.
This six-tape method works well for moderately complex setups that rely on data entry systems.

	Week 1	Week 2
Monday	Full Backup	→
Tuesday	Full Backup	→
Wednesday	Full Backup	→
Thursday	Full Backup	→
Friday (Off-Site Storage)	Full Backup	Full Backup

Added to these other complexities are the problems of local storage. It's improbable that all your data will appear on the network; managers will probably keep some of it on their local hard drives. Proposals and other sensitive information are likely candidates for local storage. Unfortunately, the manager could lose that data during an emergency, unless you back it up. The 14-tape full backup technique combines the best features of the six-tape method with workstation backup. Figure 8.25 illustrates this technique.

As you can see, this technique provides one backup per week for all workstations on the network, along with one tape per week for file server off-site storage. You could further expand the backup scenario to make daily full or incremental backups of the workstations. However, in most cases you should find the Friday workstation backup sufficient.

Figure 8.25.

The 14-tape rotation scheme adds workstation backup to the mix of features.

	Week 1	Week 2	Week 3	Week 4
Monday	Full Backup	→	→	→
Tuesday	Full Backup	→	→	→
Wednesday	Full Backup	→	→	→
Thursday	Full Backup	→	→	→
Friday (Off-Site Storage. Requires a 5th Tape for Months with a 5th Week)	Full Backup	Full Backup	Full Backup	Full Backup
Workstation (Requires a 5th Tape for Months with a 5th Week)	Full Backup	Full Backup	Full Backup	Full Backup

You can look at this backup method in two distinct ways. The first way is a four- or five-tape rotation. Instead of looking at tape backup on a monthly basis, you simply keep the Friday backup and workstation backup tapes in constant rotation. To implement this strategy, simply mark a calendar with the numbers one through five (or one through four) on each Friday of the year. The first Friday you use tape one, the second tape two, and so forth. On the sixth Friday of the year, you start over with tape one. Of the two methods, this is the simplest way to implement a 14-tape strategy.

The second way to look at this backup method keeps the needs of accounting firms and other month-oriented organizations in mind. Some applications perform special processing at the end of the month and the end of the quarter. They summarize the previous month's data and then get rid of the information used to create the summary. Making a backup before you do this processing ensures that you keep the old data if a problem occurs during processing but doesn't become apparent until sometime later. To implement this method always use Friday and Workstation tape number one on the first Friday of the month. Likewise, use the second tape on the second Friday of the month. Using five tapes ensures that you have enough tapes for months with five Fridays.

Off-Site Storage

You should never consider off-site storage as an *option*. It is a *mandatory* part of the backup process. Disasters strike when and where you least expect them. An unexpected electrical fire could totally wipe out your company tomorrow. Floods, earthquakes, broken pipes, and other disasters can strike at any moment.

Protecting your company's data is the main reason to create a backup. It's unlikely that a disaster will annihilate two places simultaneously, especially if those places are some distance apart. Placing your data in more than one location helps reduce the probability of tape destruction by a disaster.

Two types of off-site storage are available. The more expensive solution is to use the services of a company that specializes in providing off-site storage. These companies usually provide a fireproof vault for storage purposes. It's very unlikely that tapes stored in such a facility will get damaged in the event of an emergency. Besides the cost factor, you'll want to examine the types of service offered by the company. Some companies offer 24-hour service, but this costs significantly more than those who offer daytime-only service. Although you might save money using the latter, it's also unlikely that you could retrieve a tape on the weekend or after working hours when using this type of service. In some cases, this might prove inconvenient, but it shouldn't sway you from using these services.

The second solution is to select one or two people from management to use their homes as off-site storage sites. Make sure you get the approval of management to do this. Unless management really trusts this person, you could end up handing company secrets to someone who might try to sell them elsewhere. When using this technique, the person stores the tape at home and brings it in when it's time to replace it with the one on-site. Although this form of off-site storage is less secure than using a professional service, it's a lot less expensive as well. The downside to using this method is that the same disaster that destroys the on-site tape could destroy the off-site tape as well. The off-site tapes are also subject to theft and vandalism. Of course, one advantage of using this technique is that you'll have a good chance of retrieving a tape on the weekend or after hours.

You can also combine both techniques. Storing one tape in a vault and another at a manager's house will provide you with the advantages of both systems. In addition, you reduce at least one of the problems with using either technique alone. By storing one tape in a vault, you no longer need to worry about the same disaster destroying a tape in both the on-site and off-site storage locations. In addition, you can count on reaching the manager after hours or on the weekend to retrieve a backup tape.

Using the LFNBACK Utility

All kinds of utilities are out there, and they are all waiting to destroy the long filenames on your hard drive. Whenever you use a disk utility to perform some kind of task on your drive—whether it's a file recovery, a disk optimization, or a backup—that utility could destroy the long filenames that Windows 95 needs in order to operate correctly. You don't have to let it happen, of course. Windows 95 comes with a utility called LFNBACK that can save your long filenames to a file and restore them later. You can find it in the \WIN95\OTHER\LFNBACK folder of the Windows 95 installation CD-ROM.

This isn't a very fancy utility, and it doesn't even sport a GUI. You need to use it from the DOS prompt, without having Windows 95 loaded. I just boot into MS DOS mode and perform it from the DOS prompt. Then all I need to do is type exit, and I go right back into Windows 95.

> **Warning:** Never use LFNBACK from within Windows since you never know which files are open. If Windows has a file with a long filename opened, that filename won't appear in the LFNBK.DAT file. This means that you'll lose the filename if you perform a restore on the drive. Always use LFNBACK from the DOS prompt. Using MS DOS mode is fine, but using the DOS 7.0 prompt is probably even safer. (To get to the MS DOS prompt, press F8 at the boot message and select that mode from the menu.)

About once a week I use LFNBACK to create a backup of the long filenames on each hard drive. It's easy to do. Just type LFNBACK /B <DRIVE> at the DOS prompt. You need to do this once for each drive on your machine. The result is a file called LFNBK.DAT, which contains all the long filename information for that particular drive.

> **Peter's Principle:** LFNBACK as a Maintenance Tool
>
> Backing up your long filenames should be a regular part of your maintenance cycle. I usually back them up right before I perform a full backup of the machine. That way, the long filename backup ends up on the tape I'm using. This double backup can provide an extra measure of security when it comes to your long filenames. Remember, you could have a perfectly functional machine that won't boot because the long filenames on your drive got corrupted. Restoring them using LFNBACK could make a bad situation good again in a matter of minutes.

To restore a drive after some utility decides to eat it for lunch, just follow the reverse procedure. Make sure you run LFNBACK on a drive that has the LFNBK.DAT file on it. To perform the restoration, type LFNBACK /R <DRIVE> at the DOS prompt.

On Your Own

Spend some time looking at the file-system-related files in the Windows \SYSTEM folder. Look especially at the exported functions for DLLs such as COMMDLG.DLL. What do these entries tell you about the DLL and its purpose?

If you have a CD-ROM drive, spend some time optimizing the VCache now that you know a little more about how it works. What size of CD-ROM cache seems to use memory the most efficiently? How much of a speed difference do you notice between a large and a small cache when using applications directly from the CD-ROM drive?

Try using the LFNBACK utility to create a backup of the long filenames on your drive. Make sure you don't erase the LFNBK.DAT file; it contains all the long filename information. Keep this file handy, just in case one of your older applications removes the long filename information from your drive. Update the LFNBK.DAT file on a weekly basis to keep it current.

Write your own tape rotation plan based on the examples in this chapter. Make sure you weigh the cost of the time involved in creating the backup versus the cost of replacing lost data after a system crash. Also add times to the schedule for replacing your tapes. Don't let an old tape lull you into a false sense of security.

Determine what kind of effect disabling lazy writes has on your system from a performance perspective. Use the following procedure to disable it. (If the performance penalty is too great, you can always use this same procedure to enable lazy writes again later.)

1. Right-click on the My Computer icon and select Properties.
2. Click on the Performance page and then the File System button.
3. Select the Troubleshooting page. Click on the Disable write behind caching for all drives option.
4. Click on OK twice to save your changes. Windows will tell you to reboot your machine in most cases to allow the change to take effect.

9

The Windows 95 Desktop

I predict that the Windows 95 Desktop will be the most misunderstood part of the Windows 95 interface. People will write books and articles about optimizing it, and others will decry the lack of some feature that they thought essential. Let's face it: The Desktop is the plain fact of the Windows 95 interface, and it's up to you to dress it up.

Windows 95 makes heavy use of Explorer. We've already seen that in many ways in earlier chapters. Believe it or not, there's still more to learn about this particular utility. It's a lot more flexible and provides more features than most people will ever use. And that's the beauty of the Explorer interface: It allows you to do things your way. Windows 95 doesn't force you to do things a certain way like its predecessor did.

Once you figure out how to get Explorer to help you, giving your Desktop a face you can really use becomes a much simpler matter. It's no longer a bothersome task you're embarking on; rather, it is a voyage of discovery. You see, very few people really know how to make something work the way they do. Most of us are used to following whatever someone else tells us is the right way to go. Explorer and the Windows 95 Desktop will change all that.

The following sections will help you see how to use the Windows 95 Desktop and Explorer together to create an environment that truly reflects the way you work. It might take a little time for you to adjust to this new level of freedom, but once you do, you'll find that you work more efficiently, and you'll never view Windows the same way again.

Tip: Explorer, more than the centerpiece tool of Windows 95, is your gateway to freedom. As such, it really pays to take the time to learn how to use this key fully. Make sure you spend the time to fully optimize Explorer to your needs first, and then concentrate on the rest of Windows 95. The decisions you make in Explorer tend to snowball into other areas of Windows 95 as well. For example, in Chapter 8 we saw how the choices we made in Explorer (actually, the choices Microsoft made for us) changed the way Backup worked. A fully optimized Explorer interface includes all the objects you normally work with, including such things as backup files. Unless Windows 95 knows how to work with a particular object, you might find yourself fighting against Windows 95 instead of working with it. Optimizing Explorer is your first real step in optimizing Windows 95 from the user perspective.

Exploring Explorer

So far in this book we've looked at Explorer from many different perspectives. I doubt that you've seen a chapter so far where Explorer didn't end up in the picture in one way or another. That's how Explorer works under Windows 95. It's the Swiss army knife that you need in order to learn how to efficiently use Windows 95. Of course, once you do know how to use that tool well, everything else will fall into place.

We've already viewed Explorer as an end-user tool. However, you can perform quite a few other tasks with this utility. We'll start looking at some of these tasks in the following paragraphs. Suffice it to say that you'll probably find more things you can do with Explorer as you become more proficient in working with Windows 95.

Tip: One of the keys to fully using Explorer's capabilities is to learn the registry. Some changes to Windows 95 have to be made inside the registry; Explorer can't make them. For example, if you want to change the name of the Recycle Bin, you must do it within the registry. Some people have actually made a game of digging out all the registry's secrets. The registry and Explorer go hand-in-hand. See Chapter 6 if you want more detailed information about the registry and what it contains.

An Information Center

The most common way to look at Explorer is as your information center. It can tell you everything you need to know about your computing environment if you know where to look. Figure 9.1 shows a typical Explorer display. It's probably one of the first displays you see when working with Windows 95, and it will definitely become a constant companion. Notice that this display shows My Computer. The right pane contains all the things you'd normally see if you double-clicked on the Desktop's My Computer icon. You should note something else as well. My Computer isn't the entire universe in Explorer. Quite a few icons fall outside the My Computer purview, just like they do in real world, where my computer is only part of the network. An information center has to provide you with complete information, both inside and out. Explorer does just that.

In Chapter 1, we talked about the various ways to display data using Explorer. This chapter even included some of the elements associated with the Explorer display, such as the dual-pane display. Chapter 2 was an overview of how Explorer organizes information. For example, we looked at the way your machine is divided into drive, control, and ancillary sections. This chapter also looked at the context menu and showed what you could do with a standard setup. Finally, Chapter 5 showed you how to add new file extensions to Explorer and make it more powerful in the process. It showed you two methods for adding extensions: DDE macros and command-line interfaces.

Figure 9.1.

The now-familiar Explorer interface in dual pane with large icon view.

Now that you have all the pieces of Explorer and understand how to use them, let's put them together so that you can use Explorer as your information center. Each of the following sections describes a major element of your information center. Remember that each element is a drive, control, or ancillary unit. If you've forgotten some of the material on Explorer that you've already read, you might want to review the chapters I just mentioned.

Note: You probably won't see every one of the entries I discuss in your Explorer display. It all depends on what options you have installed and the type of equipment your machine supports. I installed the maximum number of features so that I could show you what they looked like.

Drives

We covered drives somewhat in Chapters 1, 2, and 8. However, I didn't show you everything. Windows 95 provides three different tools you can use to manage your drives. You can start them from the Start menu as you would have under Windows 3.x, or you can use the new Windows 95 method of managing your drives.

Let's look at what the drive icons have to offer. Right-click on any of your hard drives. (Floppy and CD-ROM drives provide the same type of properties, but the hard drives are easier to use for the purposes of this description.) You should see a dialog box similar the one in Figure 9.2. This is the General page of the Drive Properties dialog.

Figure 9.2.

The General page of the Drive Properties dialog tells you quite a bit about the current status of an individual drive.

There are three noteworthy items on this page. First is the drive label. Labels aren't as important for hard drives, but I do use them on my floppy disks to identify projects I'm working on.

The second item of interest is the Free space indicator. It tells the amount of drive space remaining. It appears in magenta on most machines. Likewise, the Used space indicator tells you how much space is used on the drive. In most cases, this value appears in blue. The pie chart helps you determine the current drive status at a glance.

The third item is the drive location. In this particular case, you can see that this is a local drive. You can pull up pages for network drives as well. However, you might not be able to do much, because your access rights to that drive affect what Windows 95 will allow.

The Tools page of the Drive Properties dialog, shown in Figure 9.3, can help you maintain your system. Remember the three tools I told you about before? Well, here they are. Not only are these tools present, but Windows 95 keeps track of the last time you used them. This can be a big help to folks who have trouble remembering the last time they maintained their machine.

Figure 9.3.

The Tools page of the Drive Properties dialog allows you to keep your drive in peak condition.

Peter's Principle: Disk Maintenance: A Necessity, Not an Option

Trying to perform any kind of diagnostic on your machine was a major headache in the days of DOS. I had several diagnostic utilities on my machine because none of them did everything. It was also very inconvenient to drop what I was doing and start a diagnostic cycle.

Windows 95 makes diagnostics a lot easier to perform—at least the ones on your drive system that are very important for maintaining data integrity. Even though the diagnostics are easier to access, a lot of people still don't use them because they really don't know how often they need to do so.

Chapter 8 went into the details of creating backups on your machine. It even helped you understand the need for tape rotation and provided you with some ideas on how to set up your own backup schedule. However, simply backing up the data on your machine isn't enough. Your drives require more care than that if you plan to keep them in peak condition and your data error-free.

Every day I start my machine and perform a standard disk scan in the background. That way, I can catch major structural problems before they eat an important file. Once a week, I set aside some time to perform a thorough disk scan. I make sure that every other application is closed, including the screen saver, when I do this. ScanDisk can't really vouch for the status of any files you have open, so closing all your applications is a good idea.

Defragmenting your drive isn't a big deal from a data-security standpoint. If you don't defragment your drive, the worst thing that will happen is that the drive won't work as efficiently as it could. That said, do you really want to give up any performance due to a lack of maintenance? I usually defragment my drive once a week. In fact, I usually follow a routine of scanning the drive for errors, backing it up, and defragmenting. This is the same routine I recommend for you. The disk scan will ensure that you get the best possible error-free backup. The backup itself will ensure that your data is safe if a disk failure occurs while you defragment it, and the defragmenting program will improve overall system efficiency.

Note: Would you like to tell your computer to scan your disks, defragment your drives, back up your programs on a regular, preset schedule, and do your maintenance chores? Microsoft Plus! comes with a program scheduler, System Agent, that can do all these things. In fact, when you install Microsoft Plus!, it automatically sets up System Agent to perform a regular disk scan every weekday with ScanDisk for Windows. It also runs Disk Defragmenter four times a week and scans your disks thoroughly once a week. The Microsoft Plus! setup asks you if you'd like to run these maintenance programs at night while you're sleeping or during the day in the background or while you're away from your computer. To learn more about automating maintenance routines, read Chapter 24.

The Check Now pushbutton opens ScanDisk, shown in Figure 9.4. This is the Windows form of the DOS utility you probably used sometime in the past. In essence, this utility works about the same. The difference is that you now gain the benefits of a GUI rather than a text-mode interface. (You might remember that ScanDisk replaced the old CHKDSK utility.)

Figure 9.4.
ScanDisk allows you to check the current condition of your disk drive.

Tip: None of the three utility programs described in this section limits you to one drive. I usually check all the drives on my system at once instead of opening the Properties dialog for each drive separately. Choosing to maintain your drives this way ensures that you don't miss any of them and also adds a certain level of automation to the process.

You can run two types of tests with this utility. The standard test simply checks the condition of your files and folders. All it does is check for major errors in the directory structure and the FAT. It also looks for cross-linked files and other structural problems. This test doesn't guarantee that the files are readable or that there isn't any damage to the drive media.

Use the thorough test when you want to check for more than just structural integrity. The Options button takes you to the dialog shown in Figure 9.5, where you can modify the way ScanDisk performs the thorough disk scan of your drive. The first group of options controls where ScanDisk looks for damaged media. Sometimes you might want to simply check the directory area for damage when troubleshooting your system. In most cases, you'll want to check both the system and data areas of your drive. Some people get queasy just thinking about an application writing to their drive to see if it will work. Other people don't want to take the time. The write test provides an added layer of testing integrity to your system. It actually tests to see if the media is secure by writing to it, then reading the results back. This test will help you find certain types of drive failures that a read test won't find. The write test doesn't write to every data area on your drive; that would take an enormous amount of time. It simply checks a few unused areas of the drive. Some types of system and hidden file damage can't be repaired very easily. You can check this option if you think a section of your drive contains such damage and you don't want to risk making the problem worse by "fixing" it. In most cases, though, you'll leave this checkbox unchecked because ScanDisk can handle the vast majority of hard-drive errors.

Figure 9.5.

Use the Surface Scan Options dialog to modify the way ScanDisk performs a thorough test of your hard drive.

The Automatically fix errors checkbox lets you tell ScanDisk to fix the problems without notifying you about each one in advance. This is the option I use most of the time. It doesn't matter too much what the error was, just that it's fixed now. However, sometimes I uncheck this box because I want to see if ScanDisk fixed a particular hard-disk error. For example, maybe I tried to access a file on the drive but couldn't for some reason. I would probably run ScanDisk to see if a drive error was getting in the way. Since I would be looking for a specific problem, I would want to know exactly what it was and how ScanDisk planned to fix it.

Clicking on the Advanced button at the bottom of the ScanDisk dialog displays the ScanDisk Advanced Options dialog, shown in Figure 9.6. Most of these options are self-explanatory and correspond to features provided by the DOS counterpart of this utility. I usually keep the Display summary radio button set to Only if errors found so that I can check all my drives at once. If ScanDisk doesn't find any errors, it checks all the drives without disturbing me. Using this option means I can run ScanDisk unattended in most cases.

Figure 9.6.

The ScanDisk Advanced Options dialog contains some user interface and other automatic settings.

There are two options in this dialog that you might find interesting. Both check files for invalid data in the directory area. Unchecking these two boxes might save you a modicum of time during the disk scan but could lead to disaster somewhere along the way. The first entry checks for invalid filenames. Under the old 8.3 filenaming strategy, the name you could give a file was pretty straight-forward. Under Windows 95, naming files is more complex, so scanning filenames requires a little more time. The second entry checks files for date and time data. These are the extended dates and times the new VFAT system provides. Under DOS, the only date you got was the last date a file was changed. Windows 95 provides the date on which someone created the file, as well as the date it was last accessed (but not necessarily changed or saved).

Clicking on the Backup Now pushbutton of the Drive Properties dialog brings up the standard Backup utility I described in Chapter 8. Since we've already looked at this utility in detail, I won't describe it here.

The Defragment Now pushbutton brings up the Disk Defragmenter utility. However, it acts differently when you bring it up here as opposed to simply starting it from the Start menu. Disk Defragmenter displays the current status of your drive before it offers to defragment it for you. Figure 9.7 shows this dialog.

Figure 9.7.
*Disk Defragmenter displays
the status of your drive if you
select it from the Tools page
of the Drive Properties
dialog.*

There are several pushbuttons at the bottom of this dialog. Clicking on the Select Drive pushbutton lets you select which drive you want to defragment. There's also an option to defragment all your hard drives; this is the option I normally select. The Advanced pushbutton displays the dialog shown in Figure 9.8, which allows you to change the way Disk Defragmenter performs its work. You may also choose whether to use these options once or to save them for every defragmenting session.

Figure 9.8.
*Disk Defragmenter's
Advanced Options dialog
allows you to select the
method used to defragment
your drive.*

On to the third page of the Drive Properties dialog—Sharing (see Figure 9.9). You'll normally see this page with systems that use a fully supported peer-to-peer network. Real-mode networks such as LANtastic don't add a page to this dialog because they provide their own management programs.

Figure 9.9.

The Sharing page of the Drive Properties dialog allows you to share resources with other machines.

Note: Some people won't see the Sharing page because they don't have a network installed. This page appears only under specific conditions when you're using certain types of networks.

This dialog allows you to share resources with another machine. Turning on the Not Shared radio button prevents other people from looking at your drive. If you turn on the Shared As radio button, Windows 95 will enable the other fields and buttons displayed here. The first field, Share Name, tells other machines what name to use when they access your drive. The second field, Comment, is a plain-language description of the drive that other users will see.

Tip: It's never a good idea to give someone more access to your machine than he needs. Remember that you can provide access to individual files and folders. In most cases, you'll want to reserve drive-level access to common data drives on a server rather than the entire drive on a workstation. You can always give someone more access if he needs it. Taking back access after someone compromises your network is meaningless, because the damage is already done.

After you decide on a name for your drive, you need to determine what kind of access to it other people will have. In some cases, read-only access is all that the other person will need. This means that a person can see the file and read it but can't modify it in any way. (Of course, he can copy the file to his drive and modify it there.) You could use this for drives with informational databases that you want the other person to use but not modify. Full access allows the other person to read from and write to your drive. This is the level of access most people will require if you want to share data with them. A third possibility allows you to determine the level of access the other person gets to your system by the password he enters. This option provides the most secure access and flexibility. The two fields below these radio buttons will be enabled if the access option you select enables them. You can type any standard password here to grant access to your machine to a select group of people.

Peter's Principle: Disk Access and Workgroup Activities

There are two schools of thought about the way a workgroup should use Windows 95's security features to enforce a specific way of modifying files. I find that they're both good, but for different reasons and in different circumstances.

The first method is to allow the people in the group read-only access to the master files on the leader's disk. This allows them to copy the file and make any required changes on their local drive. It also preserves the integrity of the master copy. Once a person finishes his edit, he moves the file to a temporary directory on the leader's drive. You could also create a home directory for each person and have them place the modified files there. The leader can then choose which additions and comments to incorporate into the master document. If you use a common temporary directory, each person should change the file extension or some part of the filename to include a distinctive signature. This prevents their files from accidentally overwriting the modified files that other people submit.

As an alternative to this first method, each person could keep his individual files to use as a basis for group discussion. Each member of the group would come to the meeting with a modified copy of the original document. This allows the leader to pick and choose which comments to incorporate based on the results of any group discussion. Of course, this is also the least efficient method, because you have to schedule specific meeting times, and the comments might or might not appear in electronic form.

The second method allows full access to the master document. Each member of the group uses the revision marks feature provided by the application to make changes to the document in his designated color. The advantage to this method is that everyone gets to discuss the document "online" in an interactive fashion. The group leader doesn't have to schedule a specific meeting to modify the document; changes get made on an ongoing basis. Of course, to actually implement this method, your application must support a revision marks feature that uses a different color of text for each member's modifications.

When you do allow other people access to a drive on your machine, Windows 95 adds a hand to the drive icon, as shown in Figure 9.1. This visual signal appears wherever the drive icon appears. It doesn't tell you what level of access the drive provides, however. Microsoft could have used slightly different symbols or perhaps colors to differentiate between access levels, but at least this symbol tells you to look for more information.

Note: A Compression tab appears in the Drives Properties dialog box when you install Microsoft Plus!. The Compression tab contains different information, depending on whether the drive is compressed or not. If the drive isn't compressed, the Compression tab shows you the amount of used and free space currently on your drive and how much you would have of each if you compressed the drive. It also tells the approximate size of a new drive that could be built by compressing your drive's remaining free space. This is the perfect option if you want to compress files on your boot drive but you don't want to risk having your whole boot drive compressed. Buttons on this tab allow you to compress the drive or make a new compressed drive. If your drive is compressed, the Compression tab is filled with statistics on the percentage of files compressed, with various compression types and the amount of disk space you've gained. These and other Microsoft Plus! disk compression enhancements are discussed in detail in Chapter 24.

Control Panel

A lot of people are still used to the way they accessed Control Panel under Windows 3.x. It was a pain, because you had to minimize your applications and open a specific folder to access the various configuration programs. I was surprised to see just how many different ways you can access Control Panel or its components under Windows 95. Even Explorer provides a method of access, as shown in Figure 9.10.

Figure 9.10.

You can access Control Panel or its components from many places in Windows 95, including Explorer.

Looking Ahead: We won't look at the individual Control Panel applets (Microsoft just had to change the name) here. Chapter 10 provides a full description of all the applets and what they mean to you as a user. We'll also take a look at some of the ways you can manipulate the Windows 95 Control Panel.

The number and types of icons (now called applets) you'll find here vary with the applications and equipment you've installed. Items such as the Printer folder will always appear in your Control Panel. On the other hand, you won't always see an ODBC folder or some of the other specialty items that Control Panel provides.

Printers

Using a Printer under Windows 95 is a lot easier than with previous versions of Windows, even though the actual controls look about the same (many printers have a few additional controls). The good news is that Windows 95 provides what I call "quality modes" for many older printers, and the printing speed in the standard modes is a lot faster. You'll also notice less of an impact on other applications while processing print requests in the background—a nice change from Windows 3.x, where my foreground application would actually stop at times if I got decent print speed.

I have an older Epson LQ-850. Even though this printer is capable of 360 × 360 graphics printing, I could get, at most, half of that resolution from previous versions of Windows. It was pretty frustrating when I needed the capability of a dot matrix to print multipart forms and had to give up some quality to do it. Imagine my surprise when Windows 95 offered the higher-quality print mode. The 360 × 360 resolution really makes a big difference in the appearance of graphics output from this printer.

As with just about everything else, you can control your printers from Explorer by accessing the Printer folder. It usually appears right below the Control Panel folder in the system hierarchy. Figure 9.11 shows how the Printers folder looks when accessed from Explorer.

Looking Ahead: Chapter 14 covers all the details of managing your printers. It also looks at the process of adding a new printer to your system. The second half of this chapter looks at the details of using fonts to dress up your output.

This folder shows two icons, the minimum you should see if you have any printers installed. You'll always see one icon for each printer installed on your machine. Double-clicking on that folder (or right-clicking and selecting Open) shows you any print jobs the printer is currently processing. See Figure 9.12.

Figure 9.11.
The Printer folder offers a
way to control print jobs,
configure your printer, and
add new printers, all in one
location.

Figure 9.12.
Opening a printer icon shows
the jobs that it's currently
processing.

You can also configure your existing printers in this dialog. All you need to do is right-click and select the Properties option to display the dialog shown in Figure 9.13. We'll cover this dialog in detail in Chapter 14. Suffice it to say that Windows 95 provides a lot more in the way of printer control than previous versions of Windows did.

The only nonprinter icon in this folder is the one you use to add a new printer. Windows 95 makes this process a lot easier than its predecessors did. Microsoft has gone to great effort to make this process easier than ever before. The Printer Wizard will dazzle you with its ease of use, especially if you went through any nightmare configuration sessions with previous versions of Windows. We'll explore the process of adding a new printer in Chapter 14.

Figure 9.13.
The printer Properties dialog contains everything needed to configure your printer.

Dial-Up Networking

Microsoft included a handy new utility in this version of Windows. Dial-Up Networking allows you to connect to another machine in much the same way as pcAnywhere does. It's a stripped-down dial-in client, but at least it provides the functionality many users will need. That's the good news. The bad news is that this is only a client version. Microsoft plans to follow the same method employed by Gillette: They will give away the razors (client software) and sell everyone the blades (the host). The software that turns Windows 95 into a Dial-Up Server is included in the add-on package Microsoft Plus!. You'll also be able to access Windows NT's Dial-Up Server.

The Dial-Up Networking folder will appear under the Printers folder if you install the service. Figure 9.14 shows a typical Dial-Up Networking folder view from Explorer. Notice that this folder, like the Printers folder, contains two types of icons. The first provides access to a Wizard for creating new connections. The second type is the actual connections.

> **Looking Ahead:** We'll take another look at Dial-Up Networking in several places. Chapter 17 shows you how to actually use this feature of Windows 95. We'll cover the implications of using Dial-Up Networking for the mobile user in Chapter 21.

Using the Dial-Up Networking client is easy. You double-click on a connection to open it. The program dials the phone and tries to make a connection to the host for you. Right-clicking and selecting Properties displays the dialog shown in Figure 9.15, which allows you to change the connection information and other things. We'll take a more in-depth look at the entire process in Chapter 17.

Figure 9.14.
A typical Dial-Up Network-ing folder contains one or more connection icons and access to a Wizard for creating more.

Figure 9.15.
The My Connection dialog allows you to change the Dial-Up Networking properties of each connection you create.

Network Neighborhood

Think of Network Neighborhood as a dynamic extension of Explorer for a network. Figure 9.16 shows a typical Network Neighborhood folder. As you can see, My Machine gets replaced by the Entire Network icon. No longer are we looking at the local machine, but at all the resources you can access on the network as a whole.

You might also see other entries at the same level as the Entire Network. These are machines you can access on peer-to-peer networks. You can always access your own resources, so you'll always see your machine listed here. In this case, there are two machines on the network. Notice that you can see only the shared drives for the machines, not any drive that's local. I also found it interesting that not every shared resource appears on the tree. You have to actually select the drive to see any resources beyond drives. Figure 9.17 shows a printer resource on the AUX machine in addition to the two shared drives that show up in the tree listing.

Figure 9.16.
Network Neighborhood provides a hierarchical view of the entire network and all the resources you can access on it.

Figure 9.17.
Always check the machine in question if you want to see all the resources; the directory tree shows only shared drives.

Tip: At first glance, it might seem like a waste of effort to list your machine along with everything else in Network Neighborhood. However, there's one good reason to do so. Here you can see at a glance every resource you're sharing with the rest of the network. Instead of forcing you to look through the directory tree for these elements, Microsoft thoughtfully placed them here.

You need to know a few interesting things about Network Neighborhood that make it differ from the rest of Explorer. First, you can't access the properties for the Entire Network. Unfortunately, this means that you can't disable the war and poverty settings. All joking aside, the Entire Network is simply a placeholder for Network Neighborhood; it doesn't exist as a concrete object.

Below the Entire Network are entries for each network you're currently connected to. In most cases, you'll see the actual workgroup or domain name, not the name of the network vendor or product. This list will change as your connections change. Looking here will tell you if a problem is application- or network-related. An application error, such as the inability to open a file, might look like a network error for a variety of reasons. However, if you look in the Entire Network folder and see the connection, it's very unlikely that the connection is the problem. Chapters 22 and 23 contain tips that will help you locate and fix other problems with the hardware or software on your machine.

If you attach to a peer-to-peer network, the machine names will appear before each network entry in the Network Neighborhood hierarchy. Beneath the machine entries you'll see a list of the drives you can access.

Network Neighborhood works the same as the rest of Explorer from a user perspective. Of course, you can't change the properties of network resources in most cases. All the Properties dialog will tell you is the name of the resource and what type of network it's connected to.

Recycle Bin

The Recycle Bin works the same in Explorer as it does on the Desktop. You can drop things into it, examine its contents, empty it, or restore a file that it holds to its original (or another) location. The Explorer copy of the Recycle Bin comes in handy if you see a file you want to erase and the Desktop copy is covered by another application. We partially examined this topic in Chapter 2, but let's take a complete look now. Figure 9.18 shows the Recycle Bin. As you can see, it looks just like any other folder in Windows 95.

Tip: Files in the Recycle Bin continue to take up space on the drive. Windows 95 moves deleted files to the Recycle Bin—a special folder—until you erase them for good. (The short (or old DOS) filenames are changed to allow multiple files of the same name in the Recycle Bin.) If you find that you're short on hard-drive space, you might want to see if there's anything in the Recycle Bin you can get rid of.

In most cases, your bin won't contain anything. Files in the Recycle Bin look just like files anywhere else. You can move objects in the Recycle Bin to other areas of Explorer to "unerase" them. Until you do unerase them, the Properties dialog won't tell you much except the file's name and the date you deleted it.

Figure 9.18.

Items in the Recycle Bin look just like they would anywhere else.

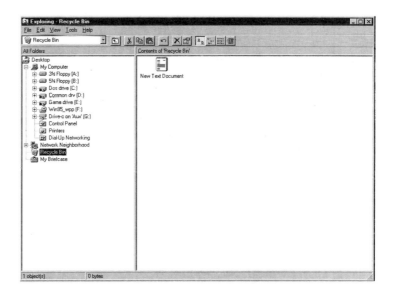

The context menu for objects in the Recycle Bin looks a little different, as shown in Figure 9.19. One of the really handy items I found on this list was Restore. You can select one or more files and then restore them by selecting this entry. Another handy option is Delete. This allows you to select just one or two Recycle Bin entries and delete them for good without disturbing the rest of the entries.

Figure 9.19.

The context menu for files in the Recycle Bin might look different, but it does contain some handy entries for managing erased files.

Briefcase

The Briefcase is one of the best Windows 95 features for mobile users. It allows you to pack everything you need for a project into one folder and then move that folder around, just like the briefcase you carry to and from work. We looked at some of the specifics of this particular part of Windows 95 in Chapter 1. Figure 9.20 shows the Explorer view of the Briefcase.

Looking Ahead: We'll take a look at how you can use Briefcase in Chapter 21. You might want to read through this material even if you aren't a mobile computer user, because I'll discuss a few techniques for using Briefcase that everyone will want to know about.

Figure 9.20.
Briefcase looks just like any other Explorer folder.

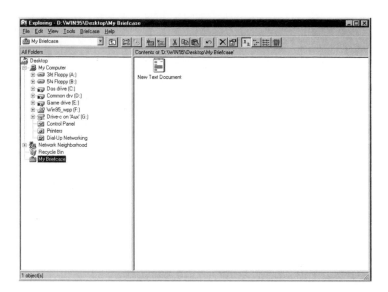

Briefcase adds one option to the context menu of items it holds. The Update option allows you to update a file from its original copy on your hard drive. This is one of the steps you need to take before packing your briefcase to go on the road. We'll cover this topic in greater depth in Chapter 21.

The Startup Folder

Windows 3.1 originated the idea of a Startup folder. It's a good idea, too. Instead of filling WIN.INI with LOAD= and RUN= entries that become a confused, tangled mess, the Startup folder allows you to maintain a certain level of order. (Of course, some applications still insist on using this antiquated method of automatically starting an application, so Windows 95 has to support it.)

Think of the Startup folder as a sort of AUTOEXEC.BAT file for your Windows applications. Windows automatically looks in this file during the boot process and launches anything it finds there. Under Windows 3.x, some types of files didn't work very well. For example, I found it difficult to automatically open any kind of data file, even when it was associated with an application. Under Windows 95, you can stick just about anything in the Startup folder and expect it to work properly.

Peter's Principle: Getting a Great Start in the Morning

A lot of people are under the impression that the Startup folder is only for loading applications. Other people feel you should place only certain classes of applications there, such as screen savers. Although putting your screen saver in the Startup folder is a good idea, using the Startup folder for this purpose alone doesn't really make full use of this resource.

Because I was used to the Windows 3.x way of doing things it never occurred to me how useful this particular folder was until I started setting up my Desktop. Placing a shortcut to the Startup folder on your Desktop is a great idea, because you can put things in there that you'll need the next morning. (Microsoft buried this folder so far in the directory tree that you'll quickly tire of trying to use it if you don't take this step.) For example, if I'm working on a proposal over the course of a few days, I'll stick a shortcut to the master file in Startup. That way, it automatically opens when I start my machine the next day.

Adding objects to the Startup folder can really boost your productivity. Instead of spending the first 15 minutes of the morning getting set up, you can start your machine, get a cup of coffee, and be ready to work when you return. Making Windows 95 more efficient is largely up to the user now. Most of the tools are there; all you need to do is use them.

Like everything else in Windows 95, you'll find the Startup folder in Explorer. Unfortunately, it's buried deep in the directory tree. If you look in the \WIN95\Start Menu\Programs folder, you'll see the Startup folder, shown in Figure 9.21. Another, faster way to access the folder is to right-click on the Start menu icon on the Taskbar and select the Explore option. This will display a two-pane version of Explorer that you can use to get to the Startup folder faster.

Figure 9.21.
The Startup folder is buried in the Windows 95 heirarchy under the Start menu.

Customizing Your Desktop

You probably don't have a "formal" desk at work. In fact, I'll bet it's customized to meet every need you have. It's a sure thing that your desk reflects the way you work. No one forced you to place the stapler in the upper-right corner.

Windows used to tell people how to set things up. It had a very formal way of arranging things that made some people feel extremely uncomfortable. In fact, it's this very formality that made some people go out and get a third-party replacement for Program Manager, the old "Desktop" in Windows 3.x.

Windows 95 doesn't force you to do things its way. Someone at Microsoft must have followed Burger King's lead by allowing people to have it their way. The Explorer interface is so flexible that I doubt any two people will ever have the same Desktop under Windows again. The Desktop, just in case you haven't figured it out yet, is the area where everything else in Windows goes. It's not like the background you used to have under Windows 3.x. The Windows 95 Desktop is an object just like everything else.

The Windows 95 Desktop has some changes that you might not think about right away. For example, remember in Chapter 1 when I told you to start right-clicking on everything? You can right-click on the Desktop. It has a context menu (see Figure 9.22), just like everything else in Windows 95. I won't go into detail about the contents of the context menu right now; all that information appears later. Suffice it to say that there are plenty of nice surprises when it comes to arranging things under Windows 95.

Figure 9.22.
The Windows 95 Desktop is an object, just like everything else. It even has its own context menu.

I'd like to briefly mention two entries—Arrange Icons and Line up Icons. Arrange Icons allows you to rearrange your Desktop in a specific order. It works just like the same entry under Explorer. (See how everything seems to have a bit of Explorer in it?) You can rearrange your icons by name, type, size, or date. Personally, I find the type and name orders the most convenient.

Some people detest all of the standard arrangements, so they just stick the icons in the order they want them. If you're not one of these people, you might find that the Line up Icons option is custom tailored for you. It allows you to keep the icons in the order you want them in but rearranges them into neat rows and columns. This option provides a sort of "grid" effect that allows you to keep your Desktop neat, but arranged in the order that you want to see it.

The following sections look at the Desktop as a whole. They are meant as a guide to things you can do to make your Desktop more usable, but I probably won't stop there. Think of this section as the most common tricks that people use to optimize their Windows 95 environment. This is the "must do" checklist you should look at when trying to get the most out of your setup.

Taskbar

A major part of the new look in Windows 95 is the Taskbar. This is the gray bar at the bottom of Figure 9.23. You could think of the Taskbar as Windows 95's replacement for Program Manager, but you'd be selling it short. The Taskbar can do a lot more for you than that. The Taskbar is the central control area for most of the things you'll do under Windows 95. It contains three major elements: a Start menu, a Task List, and a Settings area.

Figure 9.23.
This is a typical Taskbar, but don't be fooled: It can take a variety of forms.

Before giving you a full description of each of the major elements, I want to show you a few ways you can configure the Taskbar itself. The Taskbar starts out at the bottom of the display, but you don't have to leave it there. With Windows 95, you can always change your Desktop to suit your needs. Figure 9.24 shows what happens when you grab the Taskbar with the mouse pointer and move it toward the right side of the display. Windows 95 lets you place the Taskbar on any of the four sides.

Like the other objects under Windows 95, the Taskbar also provides a Properties dialog. (Simply right-click on the Taskbar and select the Properties option.) This dialog has two pages. One controls the Start menu setup, and the other controls the Taskbar itself. The four settings on the Taskbar tab enable you to change how it reacts. For example, you can remove the Taskbar from view by removing the checkmark from the Always on Top field. The Show Clock field enables you to clear more space for applications on the Taskbar by removing the clock from view. My personal favorite is the Auto Hide field. Figure 9.25 shows what happens when you select this option. The Taskbar appears as a thin gray line at the bottom of the display. The second the mouse cursor approaches it, the Taskbar resumes its normal size. This enables you to get rid of the Taskbar to clear space for application windows, yet keep it handy for when you need it.

Figure 9.24.
You can move the Taskbar. The gray box shows where the Taskbar will appear when you let go of the left mouse button.

Figure 9.25.
The Auto Hide feature of the Taskbar Properties dialog makes it possible for you to remove the Taskbar from sight until you need it.

Right-clicking on the Taskbar displays a few other object-specific options as well. All of them affect the way Windows 95 organizes the applications currently displayed on the Taskbar.

- Cascade: When you select this option, all the application windows are resized to the same size. Windows 95 arranges them diagonally, much like the display you'd normally see in a spreadsheet when opening more than one file. You can select any application out of the entire list by clicking on its title bar (the area at the top of the application window that contains the application's name).

- Tile Horizontally or Tile Vertically: Use either of these options if you want to see the window areas of all your applications at once. Windows 95 uses every available inch of Desktop space to place the applications side by side. Each application receives about the same amount of space.

- Minimize All Windows: If you ever get to the point where your screen is so cluttered that you can't tell what's opened and what's not, use this option to clean up the mess. The Minimize All Windows option minimizes every application you have running on the Desktop.

The Start Menu

The Start menu normally appears on the far-left side of the Taskbar. It contains a complete listing of all your applications, access to some system settings, and a few other things thrown in for good measure. Figure 9.26 shows how the Start menu looks. Notice that it has seven main entries. The following paragraphs describe each entry in detail.

Figure 9.26.
The Start menu replaces Program Manager as the means to start applications installed on your machine.

- Programs: This is the list of applications installed on your machine. Unlike Windows 3.x, the Explorer interface enables you to place folders within folders (programmers call this *nesting*). As Figure 9.26 shows, you can place applications several levels deep within the menu tree.

- Documents: Use this option to select a document you previously opened using Explorer. This list doesn't store the names of documents you open using your application's File | Open command. The list can contain up to 15 document names.

• Settings: Windows 95 provides you with a number of ways to change your environment. The Settings menu is just one centralized location for this information. It provides access to Control Panel, the Printers configuration dialog, and the Taskbar configuration dialog.

• Find: This option opens the same dialog you see when you use the Tools | Find command within Explorer. It enables you to find any file on your hard drive or on a network drive using a variety of search criteria. Not only can you select a file by name and location, but by modification date as well. The Advanced tab of this dialog even enables you to look for a file based on its contents or its size.

• Help: The Help option opens the main Windows 95 help file. You can use this file to search for just about any information you need to run Windows 95. Microsoft has gone a long way in improving the help files in this version of Windows. Instead of providing you with dry facts, these files actually provide procedures you can use to get the job done. As if that weren't enough, some of the help screens provide angled arrows, as shown in Figure 9.27. When you click on an angled arrow, Windows 95 starts the application relating to the help topic. For example, I opened up the Date/Time Properties dialog by clicking on the angled arrow shown in this figure.

Figure 9.27.
The Windows 95 help screens provide procedures you can use to get the job done and the ability to automatically start the applications required to do it.

Angled arrow

• Run: Remember the File | Run command under Program Manager? Well, you can still use it under Windows 95. The Run menu option opens a dialog that enables you to start an application by typing its path and name. You can also include any appropriate parameters.

• Shut Down: Windows 95 is a lot more complex than its predecessor, Windows 3.x. You saw one form of this complexity earlier in this chapter, in the discussion of the registry. This option enables you to perform an orderly shutdown of Windows 95. This includes things such as making sure that all the data gets written to disk and that the registry information gets saved.

The Taskbar Buttons

The Taskbar proper contains one icon for each application currently running on the machine. This group of buttons replaces the Task Manager found in Windows 3.x. Instead of using the Alt-Tab key combination to switch from application to application, you can now choose an application much as you would select a television station using a remote control. All you need to do is press the appropriate button.

You should be aware of a few features. For one thing, the buttons shrink in size as needed to accommodate all the running applications. You can increase the size of the Taskbar to hold two, three, or even more rows of buttons if you so desire. Placing the mouse cursor near the edge of the Taskbar produces the same double arrow you use to resize other objects under Windows 95. Of course, the buttons will only get so big, then stop growing.

Another feature is the ability to obtain more information about the application by simply placing the mouse cursor over its button. After a few seconds, Windows 95 displays a long title for the application and the foreground data file. The same principle holds true for other items on the Taskbar. For example, holding the mouse cursor over the time indicator shows today's date. In some cases, the information you receive from a button is less than awe-inspiring. For example, the Volume icon displays a single word—Volume.

The Settings Area

The Settings area of the Taskbar usually contains two or more icons. Each icon can serve multiple purposes, depending on what piece of hardware it's supposed to control. The two most common entries in this area are the Clock and Volume icons. In the preceding section, I explained how each of them reacts when you position the mouse cursor over their respective icons.

The Volume icon does a couple of things, depending on the action you take. A single click produces a master volume slider. You can use this to adjust the volume of all sounds produced by the sound board. Double-clicking on the same icon displays the Volume Control dialog, which provides detailed control of each input to your sound board. It also includes a master volume slider. Right-clicking on the icon displays the context menu. In this case, it displays only two entries. The first takes you to the Volume Control dialog; the second displays the Audio Properties dialog. We'll take a better look at the Volume controls later in this book.

The Clock icon provides similar functionality. A double-click displays the Date/Time Properties dialog. A right-click shows the context menu. Detailed information about the Clock appears later in this chapter.

Note: Several other interesting icons can appear in the Settings area. One of them enables international users to adjust their settings with ease. There's a special icon for PCMCIA-equipped machines. It displays the current bus status and the type of card plugged into the bus. Portable users will appreciate the battery indicator that appears in this area. With a quick click of the mouse, you can check your battery status before it becomes critical.

Note: Installing Microsoft Plus! usually results in adding the System Agent icon to the Taskbar's Settings area. Double-click on the icon to open System Agent, a program scheduler discussed in Chapter 24.

Passwords

Windows 95 provides an added measure of security through passwords. You can initiate password protection in several different ways. Of course, the most automatic method is to install a Microsoft (or any other) network. You'll also get a password screen if you allow users to configure their own Desktop. No matter which way you install password protection, you'll need to manage it from time to time, and that's the purpose of this section.

You get to the Passwords Properties dialog by opening Control Panel and double-clicking on the Password applet. The first page contains two pushbuttons, as shown in Figure 9.28. You use the Change Windows Password pushbutton to change the password you see when you initially log into the system. The same password is in effect whether you enable passwords through multiple user configurations or by using a Microsoft network.

Figure 9.28.
Use the Change Passwords
page of the Passwords
Properties dialog to manage
your passwords.

Tip: There's a fatal flaw in the password protection provided by Windows 95. The way Windows checks the user password is to "unlock" a decrypted file that contains the password. The filename usually corresponds to the user name and has an extension of .PWL. Windows 95 stores the .PWL file either in the main Windows folder or in the user's profile folder. Erasing this file will effectively erase the security for that particular person. A person without a .PWL file can enter Windows 95 without a password. The positive side of this is that if a user forgets her password, you can always regain access for her by erasing her security file.

However, the negative side of this is that a user could actually circumvent security given the right set of circumstances. All he would need to do is boot the computer off a floppy and erase the proper file. This change could allow him to gain access to the administrator's account so that he could change the restrictions on his own account. The bottom line is that no system is 100 percent effective; someone will always find a way to circumvent it.

The second pushbutton of the Change Passwords page allows you to change any passwords you might have for other resources or networks. For example, if you have access to a NetWare installation in addition to a peer-to-peer network, you could change that password here.

The actual process of changing your password doesn't vary much. All you need to do is select the password you want to change, and Windows will display a dialog containing three fields. (Clicking on the first pushbutton—the one you use to change your Windows password—bypasses the password selection dialog.) The first field contains your original password. This ensures that someone else won't come along and change your password without your permission. You type the new password into the second field. You need to type the new password into the third field as well so that Windows can verify it.

The Remote Administration page appears in Figure 9.29. Enabling this feature allows someone else to manage your machine from a remote location. A network administrator could make changes to every machine on a peer-to-peer network without ever leaving his desk using this option. We'll explore exactly how this works in Chapter 19. Fortunately, you can also password-protect remote administration. You type the access password into the first password field. You type it again in the second field for verification purposes.

Figure 9.29.
Remote administration is a time-saving feature for peer-to-peer network administrators with multiple servers to configure.

Windows 95 allows you to select from two different Desktop configuration methods. You can either force every user of a single machine to use the same Desktop, or you can allow multiple Desktops by selecting the correct option on the User Profiles page, shown in Figure 9.30. A single Desktop is a lot easier to maintain, reduces training costs, and enhances security. Multiple Desktops keep users happier, could make them more efficient, and provide much more flexibility. The selection you make largely depends on the needs of the people using the machine. If they all perform about the same type of work and have similar needs, a single Desktop is probably the right answer.

Figure 9.30.
A single Desktop is easy to maintain; multiple Desktops are a lot more flexible.

Tip: Multiple Desktops aren't limited to more than one user. A single user can use multiple Desktops to work more efficiently. If you find that your current Desktop gets too cluttered, it might be time to build a second one. You could keep one Desktop for each major task you perform. As an alternative, you could create a special Desktop for each project you administer. This might not be the best way to separate your work into manageable pieces, but it's one way to do so.

Once you decide to use multiple Desktops, Windows 95 gives you two additional options that determine the level of flexibility this feature offers. The first checkbox in the User Profile Settings group allows the user to configure her Desktop icons and Network Neighborhood. These user-specific settings get saved in that user's profile folder. The second checkbox allows the user to create a specialized Start menu and program groups. These settings also appear in that user's profile folder.

Enabling multiple Desktops also enables password protection. Windows 95 must know which user is using the computer so that it can open the correct profile. All it does to gather this information is display the same password dialog that the Microsoft network uses.

Desktop Settings

Everyone looks at Desktop settings in one way—as improving the appearance of their computer. For the most part, they're right. Just changing the color of something under Windows won't make it work better—at least most of the time. Configuring your Desktop for a pleasing appearance might not provide much in the way of a direct efficiency increase, but it will affect the way you view your system. A new piece of wallpaper or a change of colors can greatly affect the way you view your machine. Any positive change in attitude usually translates into improved efficiency. I find that changing my wallpaper and my display colors from time to time gives my computer that "new" feel that everyone needs occasionally.

There are other reasons for a change of configuration. In Chapter 3 we learned that wallpaper, while attractive to the eye, chews up valuable memory. You might run into a situation where memory is at a premium. Giving up your wallpaper is one way to get the memory you need in order to complete a specific task.

Eye strain is also a common problem among computer users. Let's face it: Sitting eight hours in front of what amounts to a television at close range won't do anyone's eyes much good. However, if you're like me, you probably spend more than eight hours a day staring at that screen. Somewhere along the way, you'll want to make your icons and text bigger to reduce eye fatigue. Changing your Desktop settings to improve readability is a very practical use of this feature.

> **Note:** Microsoft Plus! gives you increased control over your Desktop environment by making it easier to change all the settings discussed here and more. For more information on how to use Microsoft Plus! features such as Desktop Themes to enhance your Desktop environment, see Chapter 24.

Selecting Wallpaper

Wallpaper is one of those personal items that every computer user wants to customize. Windows 95 makes changing your wallpaper even easier than it was under Windows 3.x. All you need to do is right-click on the Desktop and choose Properties. You should see the dialog shown in Figure 9.31.

This dialog has three major sections. The first contains a monitor. Changing any of the wallpaper or pattern settings immediately affects the contents of this display. The monitor gives you a thumbnail sketch of how your background will appear.

The next section contains a listing of available patterns. You can choose one of the existing patterns or create your own. To change a pattern, click on the Edit Pattern button. Windows 95 will display a bitmap editor similar in function to those used by most paint programs.

Figure 9.31.
The Background page of the
Display Properties dialog
allows you to change your
wallpaper.

Tip: Patterns are a memory-efficient way to dress up a system. Since a pattern uses only two colors, it's a lot faster to draw and doesn't consume many system resources. If your system is short on memory, but you'd still like an interesting background, consider using patterns instead of wallpaper.

The Wallpaper listing defaults to the files found in your main Windows folder. Of course, you don't have to use these files. Click on the Browse pushbutton if you want to look in other folders on your drive. There are two ways to display wallpaper. You can center it on the background, the best choice for pictures, or tile it, the best choice for patterns.

Note: Microsoft Plus! features a wallpapering enhancement that stretches Desktop wallpaper to fit your screen. This feature is available on the Plus! page of the Display Properties dialog box. The Plus! page is available only if you've installed Microsoft Plus!. For more information, see Chapter 24.

Screen Saver

There is a very healthy third-party market for one particular item—screen savers. Some Windows users buy screen savers in bulk. You can find them in stores and on just about every BBS in existence. Unless you own an older system, using a screen saver probably isn't necessary, just fun. I own a *Star Trek* screen saver for the fun element, even though it isn't necessary.

Windows 95 also provides a screen saver feature. It isn't as fun as some of the screen savers on the market, but it gets the job done. You'll find it on the Screen Saver page of the Display Properties dialog, shown in Figure 9.32.

Figure 9.32.
The Screen Saver page of the Display Properties dialog allows you to change your screen saver and its settings.

Note: Microsoft Plus! has fun screen savers that include animation and sound. They also include advanced settings that let you set Now and Never spots on the screen. In other words, if you put your mouse pointer in one corner of the screen, the screen saver will turn on now. If you put your mouse pointer in another corner, the screen saver will never turn on.

Just like the Wallpaper selection, this dialog contains a miniature view of your monitor. You can use it as a thumbnail sketch of what the display will look like when you configure the screen saver. The Screen Saver field allows you to choose from one of the screen savers in the SYSTEM folder. If you decide to use a third-party screen saver that uses the Windows format, you need to place the file in the same directory as the others, or Windows won't see it.

Once you select a screen saver, you can use the Settings button to change its settings. In most cases, the settings affect how Windows 95 displays the screen saver. For example, it might change the number of lines you see or the number of colors.

The Wait field allows you to change the number of minutes Windows 95 will wait before it activates the screen saver. All you need to do to turn the screen saver off is move the mouse cursor or press a key.

You can also password-protect your screen saver. This allows you to leave the room without any fear that someone will use your machine while you're gone, because you have to type a password in order to turn the screen saver off and get back to what you were working on. I like the third-party screen savers that automatically restore their current condition even if you turn the machine off and reboot. Unfortunately, the Windows 95 screen saver doesn't provide this feature, so you can circumvent password protection by rebooting the machine. Of course, this does have the advantage of resetting the display so that no one knows what you were working on before they rebooted the machine. Some people might be thwarted if you also have passwords enabled on the opening Windows screen.

The final pushbutton, Preview, allows you to see what the display will look like when Windows 95 turns the screen saver on. I've used this as a quick way to hide my display when someone walks into my office and I don't want them to see what's on my display. It's a quick solution to a potential problem. Of course, you'll want to be very careful around the mouse and keyboard if you use this method. Unless you enable the password option, your display will clear if you bump the mouse or press a key.

Palette

The Appearance page of the Display Properties dialog, shown in Figure 9.33, allows you to change the actual appearance of your displays, not just the Desktop. I find that this particular dialog is a lot easier to use than its Windows 3.x counterpart was, even though the two dialogs look similar. All you need to do is click on the picture of the display to select an item.

Figure 9.33.
You can change the colors and fonts used by your display with the settings on the Appearance page.

Windows 95 does provide a feature you couldn't get under Windows 3.x. The older versions of Windows allowed you to change the font used to display text only with a great amount of fiddling with the WIN.INI file. Windows 95 moves all this information into this dialog and gives you a lot more flexibility to boot. I have several configurations with "tired eye"-sized text settings. You can individually change the size of the menu and title bar text. Everything that has text also has a setting for the font and type size here.

Changing an entry consists of making listbox selections. This dialog has six of them. The first three affect the contents of the item itself and include the item name, size, and color. The size in this case is the size of the window or another display element. For example, you could change the width of a menu bar using this option. The second three control the text used within that display element. These settings include font style, size, and color. You may select any installed font as your display font, but most people find that the MS Serif or MS Sans Serif fonts work best on displays. They were specially designed for this purpose. I occasionally use Arial and find that it works pretty well.

This dialog also contains a listbox for selecting from existing color schemes, a Delete button for removing the schemes you no longer want, and a Save As button for adding new schemes.

Resolution

Changing your display resolution under Windows 3.x was a nightmare. You had to get out of Windows, use the Setup program to make the change, and then reboot and hope that you hadn't accidentally overwritten anything important. In some cases, you even had to dig up a copy of your installation disks to supply the font Windows needed.

The Settings page of the Display Properties dialog, shown in Figure 9.34, allows you to change your display resolution, the number of colors, and the standard font with ease. Except for the system font setting, you can usually change the settings without rebooting your machine. Non-plug and play systems require a reboot if you change the system font.

Figure 9.34.
You can change your display resolution using the controls on the Settings page.

Windows 95 provides another new feature you should look at if the fonts provided by Microsoft don't quite fit the bill. You can click on the Custom button to display the dialog shown in Figure 9.35. This dialog allows you to create a custom-size system font. This is a very handy feature to have if you need a font that's either very large or very small. Normally you'll want to use the standard sizes that come with Windows.

Figure 9.35.
Windows 95 allows you to use custom font sizes to optimize your display's appearance.

There is one other button on this page, but it should be familiar from Chapter 4. We used it to check the results of adding a new monitor to our system. I won't go through this particular part of the display settings again. All they change is the monitor and display adapter type.

System Setup

You can quickly access the System Properties dialog from the Desktop by right-clicking on My Computer and selecting the Properties option. We discussed this particular dialog in detail in Chapters 2 and 3, so I won't go into its features again. You'll learn some ways to use this particular dialog to assist in fixing hardware-related problems in Chapter 23.

Clock

We took a quick look at the Clock earlier when talking about the Taskbar. Unlike the clock utility provided with Windows 3.x, this clock actually affects the way the system reacts. You can actually use it to affect the CMOS setting and, therefore, the time stamp on all your files. Of course, it will also affect any events you might schedule and anything else that relies on the clock.

The Clock properties consist of a single checkbox, Show Clock, on the Taskbar Properties dialog. The only thing this entry does is either display or not display the clock on the Taskbar. In most cases, you'll want to keep the clock displayed since there's nothing to be gained from shutting it off.

> **Tip:** When you display the Clock, it shows only the current time. You can use the mouse cursor to also display the date. Simply move the mouse cursor over the Clock icon for a few seconds, and the Clock will display the current date as well.

Double-clicking on the Clock icon displays the dialog shown in Figure 9.27. This is the same dialog that the help button activated. It contains a calendar and a clock. You use them to change the system settings.

The second page of this dialog, Time Zone, allows you to change the current area of the world (see Figure 9.36). It's the same dialog you saw when you completed the installation of Windows 95. Setting this dialog is self-explanatory. The daylight savings time checkbox allows the computer to automatically adjust the time for you.

Figure 9.36.
The Time Zone page of the Date/Time Properties dialog allows you to change the area of the world that you're located in.

Working with Desktop Objects

Making your Desktop efficient is very easy under Windows 95. The first thing you need to do, though, is throw away those outdated application-centered ideas that Windows 3.x encouraged. You need to learn to work with data—the way you should have learned to work in the first place. After all, what's more important—the tool that creates an object or the object itself? The end result is the most important goal in working with Windows.

The following sections provide you with some ideas on how to arrange your Desktop to make maximum use of the new Windows data-centric approach. This is by no means the only way to pursue the problem, but it's the way that many people are starting to work with this new product. Try this approach and then modify it to meet your needs.

We'll start by looking at the methods of moving data around. Remember that Windows 95 uses objects. Everything is an object of some sort. Objects are easy to copy, cut, and paste. You can move them around just like any object in the physical world. Once we get done looking at data-movement techniques, we'll take a quick look at the methods you can use to organize that data on your Desktop.

Making Copies

Many people use cutting and pasting to move data around. You cut the data from the place where you no longer need it and then paste it to a new location. Windows 95 supports cut and paste for objects as well. All you need to do to move a file from one location to another is cut it and then paste it. The beauty of this approach is that the copy of the file is now on the Clipboard. This means that you can make as many copies of it as you want. Of course, anything you can cut, you can copy. Copying the object means that you leave the original in place and create copies where needed. Figure 9.37 shows the context menu for a folder. Notice the copy, cut, and paste entries.

Figure 9.37.
Every object that you can copy, cut, or paste has entries for these tasks on its context menu.

Obviously you can't paste a file on top of another file. You can, however, paste a copy of a file on the Desktop or within a folder. If you take a logical, real-world approach to moving objects under Windows 95, you'll never run into problems getting objects to work.

Creating New Objects

Everywhere you can paste an existing object, you can also create a new object. The Desktop, Explorer, and most Windows 95 folders have a New option on the context menu, as shown in Figure 9.38. This menu option displays a list of file types that Windows 95 can produce automatically.

Figure 9.38.

The Desktop and other storage objects allow you to create new objects by selecting the object from a list of choices on the New menu.

Notice that one of the entries is a folder. You can always place a folder within another object normally used for storage, even another folder. Using folders will help you organize your data into more efficient units. We'll see later how you can combine these elements to make your Desktop an efficient place to work.

Using a Template

One of the problems with the New submenu of the context menu is that it always creates objects of a default type. Take Word for Windows. If you create a new Word for Windows object using the selection on the context menu, that new object will use the Normal stylesheet. What you really wanted was the Accounts stylesheet, but there isn't a fast way to create a document using the current system.

I got around this problem by placing a folder named "templates" on my Desktop. Inside are copies of each of the sample files that I use to create new documents. For example, if you write a lot of letters that use the same format, you might want to use your word processor to create a document that contains everything that normally appears in a letter. All you would need to do is place a copy of the letter template in your Templates folder. Whenever you needed to write another letter, you would right-click on the template for it in your Templates folder and drag the template to a new destination, such as a project folder. When the context menu appeared, you would select Copy to create a copy of your template. This template approach to creating new documents can greatly reduce the time you need to start a task. You can create enough copies of a template to satisfy project needs in a few seconds. Using the template also means that all your settings will be correct when you enter the document for the first time.

There are several ways you can use a template document. You can right-click, select Copy, right-click on your project folder, and select Paste from the context menu. Another method is to drag the template with the mouse key depressed. When Windows asks what you would like to do, select Copy from the menu.

Creating Work Areas

Now that you have some idea of how to move and copy data, let's look at a more efficient way to work with it. I've started using a new method of organizing information because of the way that Windows 95 works. You can follow several easy steps to get any project started:

1. Create a main project folder on the Desktop.

2. Open the folder and place one folder inside for each type of data that you plan to work with. For example, when writing this chapter, I created one folder for the word-processed document, another for the electronic research information, and a third for the graphics files.

3. Open the first data folder. Create a copy of your template, and then create as many copies as you'll need of that template within the data folder.

4. Rename the data files to match what they'll contain.

5. Close this data folder and repeat steps 3 and 4 for each of your other data folders.

6. Complete your project by filling each data folder.

Tip: Using a particular method of creating new data files for all your data might not work because of the way the application is designed. In other cases, as with the screen shots in this book, the data file gets created in a different way than normal. My screen shots are all captured from a display buffer. I don't need to create a blank file to hold them because the screen-capture program does this for me. Always use the data-creation technique that works best with the applications you use.

Figure 9.39 shows one way to arrange your projects. It contains a main folder, a few data folders, and some notes about the project. Of course, this is still only one approach to managing your data. The trick is to find the method that works best for you—one that reflects the way you get your work done.

Figure 9.39.
One way to arrange your data for easy access. Windows 95 provides almost unlimited possibilities.

By now, you're wondering why you should go this route. After all, the old method of managing your data seemed to provide just about the same results as the method I've outlined. This new technique offers several advantages that you just can't get using the application-centered approach:

- Data transmittal: Giving someone else access to a group project means sending him a folder, not a bunch of individual files. How often have you thought you had all the files for a project together, only to find you didn't send an important file? This method of organizing data prevents such problems.

- Application independence: It doesn't matter which application you need to use in order to modify a file. If everyone in your office uses the same applications, modifying a file means double-clicking on it and nothing else. You no longer need to worry about which application to open or where that application is located. All that matters is the data.

- Location: Where is your data? Do you ever find yourself searching for hours to find that small file you thought you lost somewhere? This method allows you to place all the data relating to a project in one place. Its physical location no longer matters once you get the pieces together. Of course, you still need to know where the data is when you organize the project folder. However, would you rather look for a file once or a hundred times? Using Desktop folders means that you find the data once and never worry about it again.

- Ease of storage: When I get done with a project under Windows 95, I don't worry about getting all the bits and pieces together. I send one folder to storage. When I need to work on the project again, I know that all I'll need to do is load that one folder back onto my local drive.

On Your Own

Open Explorer and check out each of the special sections we talked about in this chapter. Try to identify each section and its purpose without referring back to the discussion. Also look at some of the unique capabilities provided by your machine. For example, see if there are any special applets in Control Panel. You'll also want to check out your machine's network capabilities.

Use the tools provided on the Tools page of the Drive Properties dialog to perform maintenance on your machine. Start by scanning the disk for errors. Then perform a backup of your system to prevent devastating data loss. Finally, use the Disk Optimizer to enhance system performance.

Spend some time customizing your Desktop for optimum efficiency. See which wallpapers or other aesthetics you can change. Remove any features that might slow performance if you're using a memory-constrained system. Try out the screen saver and password options as well.

10

The Windows 95 Applets

It seems like we're always being inundated with yet another set of new words to describe something old and familiar. I was reminded of that when I started working on this chapter. Just what do you call the conglomeration of small utility programs and configuration utilities that an operating system needs in order to function? I've heard a variety of names, but it appears that Microsoft finally settled on *applet* as the term of choice. It kind of makes sense when you think about it; an applet is a small application.

We've already covered the vast majority of the utility applets in other chapters of this book. For example, I devoted quite a bit of space to the Backup applet in Chapter 8. Each of these utility applets helps you maintain, troubleshoot, or otherwise improve the system. A few even provide new features that you can use to make life easier. Since we've covered most of them, I won't bore you with another rendition of the utility applets.

There's a second group of applets: those that help you configure the machine. We also covered some of them in previous chapters, but I haven't put them together yet in an overview format. That's what this chapter is all about. We'll cover the mundane applets—the ones that you'll only use from time to time. They're always important to know about when you need to use them, but most of these applets are a one-shot deal: You'll generally use them when you install the operating system or change a piece of hardware.

What I'd like to do in this chapter is provide you with a few ideas that could expand the potential uses for this underused resource. For example, did you know that several of these applets provide full-fledged troubleshooting modules? Few people do, because they don't really take the time to see what's available here.

Configuring Windows 95 Applets

One topic we haven't covered yet is the process of installing and removing applets on your system. Part of the installation process always involves configuring the applet before you use it. For example, when you install Dial-Up Networking, Windows 95 automatically asks you for information regarding your computer setup. You can't network without a telephone number, so it makes sense that Windows 95 would ask about this information before it completes the installation process. The same reasoning holds true the first time you start Backup. Even though Windows 95 automatically takes care of the configuration, it displays a dialog telling you that it got the job done (in this case, creating a backup set of files for you). You can use the sample file as the basis for your own configuration sets. That's one of the reasons why Backup creates it for you. The other is that you can't perform a backup without at least some idea of what to do. This sample file can form the basis for someone to learn how Backup works.

The following sections outline four different methods of installing applets on your system. The standard method that I cover initially is the one you're probably most familiar with. It allows you to install or remove standard Windows 95 features. The "Special Utility Installation" section tells you how to install some of the extra utilities that Windows 95 provides. For example, you'll use this procedure to install the Policy Editor and other utilities that the standard user probably shouldn't know about. Make sure you read any text files provided with the utilities, since it's unlikely that you'll find sufficient documentation elsewhere. Windows 95 also provides printer utilities that help you manage this resource better when using certain types of printers. I tell you how to install them in the "Special Printer Installation" section. Finally, you'll find that Windows 95 provides a wealth of network management tools. You'll read about the installation procedure for them in the "Special Network Installation" section. A few of the applets you can install are so specialized that Microsoft provides a special installation method for them. I was a little surprised when I finally figured out how this works. Although I can understand Microsoft's willingness to hide a nonstandard utility from a user who might not know how to use it properly, it seems to me that there's got to be a better way. Of course, part of the reasoning behind this four-layered approach to installation is the nature of the applets themselves. They aren't all necessarily applets in the full sense of the word. You can't really execute them and expect something useful to happen. Some of them are halfway between a driver and an applet. Other types of applets work almost as TSRs, helping Windows 95 to monitor specific items of information in the background.

Make sure you scan the Windows 95 CD-ROM when you get it. All the floppy disk utilities install using the first method we will cover. The special programs appear on the CD-ROM version of Windows in a variety of folders that don't appear on the floppy version. If you want to get these utilities, you need the CD-ROM version of Windows. Most of these specialized programs appear in the Admin95 folder. Beneath this folder are three subfolders that categorize the type of applet. This makes it easy to tell which of the following methods you should use to install a specific applet.

> **Tip:** Keeping average users on your network away from some of the utilities that might damage the system could prove difficult if you give them the CD-ROM version of Windows. It doesn't take a rocket scientist to read a few text files and do some experimentation. If you really want to keep those utilities away from prying eyes, get the floppy disk version of Windows 95 for your network users. You don't actually have to use the floppies for an installation. Use the network-based installation we covered in Chapter 4 instead. Using a script file will keep the installation easy, but floppies will keep the installation from getting corrupted—at least by a stray applet.

Standard Installation and Removal

You start the standard installation in Control Panel. Simply double-click on the Add/Remove Programs applet and select the Windows Setup page, as shown in Figure 10.1. Looking through the list of applications you can install using this dialog, you'll see all the familiar utility programs Windows provides. You'll notice one thing: This list has no network administration tools. We'll take care of that deficiency a little later.

Figure 10.1.
The Add/Remove Programs applet allows you to install the standard Windows user applications.

Completing this particular installation process is easy. Simply check the items you want to install and click on OK. The Add/Remove Programs applet will take care of the rest. You might need to supply a disk or two if you aren't using the CD-ROM installation. Otherwise, the rest of the process should be fairly automated.

Note: Make sure you don't accidentally uncheck any item you want to keep. The Add/Remove Programs applet will automatically uninstall any applet you uncheck. Accidentally removing something could cause problems as you frantically try to figure out what went wrong with your system.

Most of the Windows 95 applets wait until you run them the first time to either automatically detect the required configuration information or ask you to supply it. Some of them, however, ask for this information immediately if they provide a system service. For example, installing modem support requires an immediate answer because the system never knows when it will need that information.

Special Utility Installation

The CD-ROM contains some utilities that don't appear on the Add/Remove Programs dialog box. You either need to know they exist, read about them in one of the files located on the CD-ROM, or do a little exploring like I did. It's kind of surprising to see just how many different utilities the CD-ROM contains. To check your CD-ROM, just use Explorer's Find tool to look for .INF files. You won't find any of the installation .INF files, because they're in compressed format. It's usually safe to assume that any .INF files you'll see on the CD-ROM have something to do with an applet's installation routine. Figure 10.2 shows the results of my search.

Figure 10.2.
.INF files on your CD-ROM usually provide support for some type of applet installation routine.

Tip: Many of these applets appear in the Windows 95 Resource Kit provided in the \WRK\CHAPTERS folder on your CD-ROM. Searching for the utility name using the Explorer Find tool and the Containing text field of the Advanced page will help you find the needed information quickly. Don't be surprised if you don't see the applet listed in the online help. Some of these applets are for network administrators only, so you'll need to look at the documentation provided in the applet folder instead. Using the Resource Kit and applet documentation together should help reduce any confusion over the applet's intended use.

As you can see from Figure 10.2, my list extends for quite a way. The CD-ROM has lots of .INF files, and it's pretty difficult to tell which ones you'd like to have installed on your machine. However, knowing that the file exists provides some information. A lot of .INF files contain notes about the application they're supposed to work with. The folder that holds the .INF file and the application might provide a README file as well.

Note: Hopefully, Microsoft will provide better documentation for these utilities in the future. At the time I wrote this, the documentation hadn't changed. Some of these utilities get only a single line of description in the Resource Kit (provided as part of the CD-ROM). You might need to do a little detective work before using any of these other utility programs.

After you decide that an applet will meet your need, the first thing you need to do is decide what type of installation to perform. You'll find that some of these applets are general-purpose utilities. Use the procedure described in the following paragraph to install them. Other applets require special installation. Use the section "Special Printer Installation" later in this chapter to install printer-specific applets. Likewise, use the "Special Network Installation" section for any network-related applets. Using the correct installation procedure will ensure that you get a usable utility when you finish. When in doubt, use this general-purpose installation and test the application to see if it works.

1. To perform a special utility installation, open Control Panel and double-click on the Add/Remove Programs applet just like you did before. Select the Windows Setup tab.

2. Instead of choosing an applet from the list, click on the Have Disk pushbutton. You should see a dialog similar to the one in Figure 10.3.

Figure 10.3.
The Install From Disk dialog allows you to install an applet that normally doesn't appear in the Add/Remove Program Properties dialog.

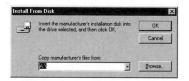

3. Click on the Browse pushbutton and use the Open dialog to find the applet's .INF file. Double-click on this file to add its name to the Copy manufacturer's files from: field of the Install From Disk dialog. Click on OK to complete the selection process. Windows 95 will display a dialog similar to the one shown in Figure 10.4.

Figure 10.4.
The Have Disk dialog displays a list of any special applets that the .INF file contains.

4. Use the Have Disk dialog to select the applets you want to install. Notice that, as usual, you make the selections using a checkbox.

Tip: If you find an .INF file that doesn't contain a list of applets, cancel the installation process immediately. Some .INF files on the CD-ROM don't contain applet-specific information. Fortunately, the installation won't proceed unless you have some boxes to check in the Have Disk dialog.

5. Click on the Install pushbutton to complete the installation. Windows 95 will copy the required files from the CD-ROM and return you to the Add/Remove Programs Properties dialog. Scrolling through the list of installed components should reveal the new applets you installed. Figure 10.5 shows an example of the applets I installed using this procedure. Unchecking a box next to one of these utilities will uninstall it. This process works exactly the same as for the standard applets. Notice that these special applets use a diamond-shaped icon to differentiate them from the standard applets in the list. You can depend on this indicator for any special applets that appear in the list.

Figure 10.5.
Any new applets you install will appear in the Add/Remove Programs Properties dialog.

Special Printer Installation

Windows 95 provides some special printer support. It would seem that you should use the standard installation methods to install these applets, but Microsoft decided to take a different path. The printer applet installation looks almost the same as a printer installation, with a few important differences.

1. To begin the installation process, open the Printers folder and double-click on the Add Printer icon. You should see the Print Wizard opening display. Click on Next to get to the next screen.

2. Select Local Printer and click on Next to get to the next screen. You should see the Add Printer Wizard dialog box, shown in Figure 10.6.

Figure 10.6.
The Add Printer Wizard dialog allows you to add a new printer or applet.

3. Click on the Have Disk pushbutton. You should see a dialog similar to the one shown in Figure 10.3.

4. Click on the Browse pushbutton and use the Open dialog to find the applet's .INF file. Double-click on this file to add its name to the Copy manufacturer's files from: field of the Install From Disk dialog. Click on OK to complete the selection process. Windows 95 will display a dialog similar to the one shown in Figure 10.7.

Figure 10.7.
Adding a printer resource using a disk is fairly easy under Windows 95.

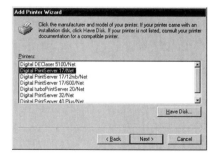

5. Use the Add Printer Wizard dialog to select the applets you want to install. Notice that the method of listing the potential resource has changed.

6. Windows 95 will copy some files to disk and then ask some additional questions based on the type of resource you want to install. Following the prompts is fairly easy and should resemble the process of adding a printer.

Special Network Installation

There are some special network administration tools on your CD-ROM as well. As with the printer-specific resources, you don't use the standard installation routine to add these applets to your system. The following procedure will help you perform a special network installation.

1. Open Control Panel and double-click on the Network icon. Click on the Add pushbutton, select Service, and click on the Add pushbutton. You should see a dialog similar to the one in Figure 10.8.

Figure 10.8.

The Select Network Service dialog allows you to install a new network resource.

2. Click on the Have Disk pushbutton. You should see a dialog similar to the one shown in Figure 10.3.

3. Click on the Browse pushbutton and use the Open dialog to find the applet's .INF file. Double-click on this file to add its name to the Copy manufacturer's files from: field of the Install From Disk dialog. Click on OK to complete the selection process. Windows 95 will display a dialog similar to the one shown in Figure 10.9.

Figure 10.9.

Use this dialog to select a special network-related resource.

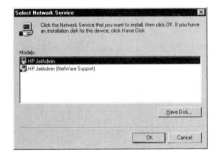

4. Use the Select Network Service dialog to select the applets you want to install. Notice that the method of listing the potential resource has changed.

5. Click on OK. Windows 95 will copy some files to disk and then display the Network dialog with a new entry added. In this case, we have added an HP LaserJet administration tool. Figure 10.10 shows the new addition.

Figure 10.10.
*Adding this new applet will
help an administrator
manage an HP LaserJet on
the network.*

Control Panel

Few people ever get comfortable with Control Panel. You access it to change a major hardware or software configuration item and then leave. You don't come back to it until your system needs adjustment again. You don't visit Control Panel on a daily basis.

The reason I brought up this point at the beginning of this discussion is simple: This lack of contact with Control Panel is probably the reason why people almost forget that it's there. I've personally spent hours trying to figure out how to change some setting in there. It's not just that Control Panel is difficult to use or illogically laid out, but too few people have experience with it.

Figure 10.11 shows a typical Control Panel setup. However, no two Control Panel setups are alike. Control Panel usually contains a set of default icons and a bunch of icons related to your particular system configuration. I still remember the Purple Logitech Mouse icon in Windows 3.x. I didn't need it with Windows 95, so you don't see it installed.

Figure 10.11.
*Control Panel is a deep, dark
secret to some people, and
none too familiar to everyone
else.*

Now might be a good time to check out some of the applets in Control Panel. Some of them will seem familiar because we've already talked about them elsewhere in the book. Others will be new because we haven't really covered them yet. The following list provides an overview of Control Panel's contents.

- Accessibility Options: We've visited this particular applet several times. It allows you to change some Windows 95 features to make them easier to use. For example, this applet allows you to enable the StickyKeys option for the keyboard.

- Add New Hardware: This applet allows you to install new hardware on your system. You can choose one of two installation methods—manual or automatic. Microsoft recommends the automatic method in most cases because it's the least error-prone (assuming that the detection program works properly).

- Add/Remove Programs: Adding and removing applications is easier in Windows 95, but probably not as easy as it could be. We've looked at some of the difficulties of using this particular applet in this chapter.

- Date/Time: Keeping the date and time current on your machine will become more important as your machine makes more connections to other resources. Older installations had to worry about the date and time only when it came to time-stamping files. New users rely on the clock to schedule automated tasks, keep track of appointments, and a host of other responsibilities.

- Display: I use this applet the most. Not only does it allow me to change my display resolution and colors with ease, but I can use it to enlarge the display fonts and change the wallpaper on the Desktop. All these features add up to an incredibly flexible and easy-to-modify display system. The big surprise is that you no longer have to reboot your machine to see the effect of a change.

- Fonts: When I started out computing with PCs, the only font available was the one that you got in the character ROM of your printer or display adapter. Now you can quickly overwhelm your system with fonts that you'll never use. One drawing package I purchased recently included more than 500 fonts. It's no wonder that people need an applet like this one to manage their font libraries.

- Joystick: Few action games would be complete without joystick support, yet older versions of Windows fail to provide this feature. Windows 95 corrects this error by providing full joystick support. Not only does Windows 95 support the joystick, but this applet includes both a calibration and a testing module. It even supports advanced joysticks such as the Thrustmaster Flight Control System.

- Keyboard: If you've ever had to do strange things such as write entire sentences using the Character Map utility under Windows 3.x, you'll really appreciate the keyboard support under Windows 95. Now you can have more than one language available as needed. A simple click on the International icon on the Taskbar allows you to choose between any of the installed keyboard layouts. This applet not only installs support for these languages, but it also provides other forms of keyboard support, such as repeat rate adjustment.

- Mail and Fax: If you have a network installed, you'll probably have some type of mail module in Control Panel. This particular applet is Microsoft network-specific, but I'm sure you'll find similar applets for NetWare and Banyan. Noticeably absent right now are any applets from real-mode networks such as LANtastic. Hopefully these vendors will provide 32-bit protected-mode drivers in the near future. The Mail and Fax applet helps you configure your online connections and even the location of your address books. It's the configuration utility for Microsoft Exchange.

- Microsoft Mail Postoffice: The difference between this applet and the preceding one is that the Microsoft Mail Postoffice is specific to the local e-mail setup. While the Mail and Fax applet helps you make the right connections, this applet deals with the intricacies of managing a postoffice. You can change security levels and add new users when using this applet. Minor conflicts with Windows for Workgroups might keep you on your toes for a while (and keep you visiting this particular applet a little more than you really wanted to).

- Modems: Online communication is a very serious business these days. It doesn't just include services such as CompuServe and America Online, but dial-up networking and a host of other forms of communication. The Modems applet allows you to configure your modem settings for optimum performance under Windows 95. It also includes a diagnostic so that you can troubleshoot any problems that the modem might experience.

- Mouse: In some respects, I miss the old Purple Logitech Mouse sitting in my Control Panel. Not only did the Logitech applet allow me to do a few things that even the Windows 95 applet wouldn't, but it looked kind of neat, too. The purpose of this applet is to help you configure the mouse. This doesn't mean just the double-click speed and other mouse-specific features; it also includes the actual pointers that the mouse uses and whether Windows 95 displays mouse trails. I find the addition of pointers to Windows 95 a welcome change. The animated icons might prove bothersome on some displays, but they show up very well on the LCDs I've checked out.

- Multimedia: This applet controls everything relating to the new sound and video features supported by Windows 95. It not only controls the actual drivers and their settings, but it helps you configure the interface as well. One thing you won't find here is a way to control the system sounds. Other than that, this applet is the one you want to check out when you have a sound or video problem.

- Network: We've viewed this particular applet several times in this book so far. It's the one that allows you to install new network components or get rid of old ones. It's also where you set your network's password policy and how the network controls access to your resources. TCP/IP users will use this applet to configure the various addresses needed to make their network functional. Overall, this is the one place you need to go to get the overall picture of your network's current setup.

- ODBC and ODBC32: Anyone who deals with database management systems for very long will understand the importance of this applet. It allows you to create new table connections and modify old ones. You also can see which drivers your system has available. Each ODBC applet is separate. There's one applet to manage 16-bit applications and a second applet for 32-bit applications. Unfortunately, I see this as another source of confusion. Make sure you use the correct applet for your application when changing its setup. I was surprised to see some of the 32-bit drivers listed in my 16-bit applet and vice versa. If I hadn't looked carefully, I could have made the changes using the wrong applet. Whenever you start creating configuration errors, there's a chance of data loss.

- Passwords: We viewed the contents of this applet at length earlier in this book. Chapter 20 will provide yet another opportunity to revisit network security. Suffice it to say that this applet provides one of the ways you can control access to the network and its resources.

- Printers: A printer is the one item no one can do without. If you don't have a printer connected directly to your machine, there's a good chance you maintain a network connection to one. The Printers applet allows you to configure existing printers or add new ones. It also allows you to maintain control over any print jobs that the printer is processing.

- Regional Settings: This applet manages all of the text-formatting information required to make the output of an application correct. It includes the actual time zone. You also use this applet to change the numeric, currency, time, date, and regional settings.

- Sounds: This is one of my favorite applets. It allows you to add a sound to just about any Windows event. I really like the fact that Windows 95 is no longer limited in the number of events it can monitor. The list of events will definitely change as you install and remove applications from your system.

- System: This applet allows you to maintain your computer as a whole. It provides access to the Device Manager. Not only is this an invaluable tool for configuring your system, but it acts as a troubleshooting aid as well. Even though you don't get specific feedback, Device Manager at least lets you know which card is bad. This applet also allows you to enhance system performance. It even displays a list of things you can do to enhance system performance.

Your setup might have more or fewer applets than mine did, but this list should give you a good idea of what the common applets do. If you have a few additional icons, the vendor documentation should tell you what types of configuration tasks you can use them for. Returning to the Logitech Mouse example, the applet associated with this device allows you to change the way the mouse behaves. More specifically, you could assign a macro to an unused key. I always used my middle mouse button for pasting and my right mouse button for cutting. Fortunately, Windows 95 has removed some of the need for this additional applet.

Warning: Some applications insist on installing a custom applet in Control Panel. In most cases, Windows 95 will ignore any incompatible applets it doesn't need to work with the hardware or software you installed. If you do get into a situation where the old driver gets loaded and affects system stability, call the vendor and see if there's an easy way to remove the applet. In most cases, you can eliminate the problem by deleting a few lines of text from SYSTEM.INI.

What other kinds of applets can you expect to see in Control Panel? This is limited only by the types of applications and hardware you install. A few examples include a digitizer pad, CAS-compliant fax, and data-capture boards. You'll probably see special applets for certain types of network connections. Most mail packages require an entry here. It's surprising to note that applications such as Lotus 1-2-3 might place an applet here to manage their data connections. (Most applications use ODBC now, so you'll see more options in the ODBC applet rather than more applets.)

Customizing Icon Displays

Some people fail to realize that Control Panel is just another form of Explorer—albeit a somewhat specialized form. You saw how to access Control Panel from Explorer in Chapter 9. The display even looked the same as the other displays. There was nothing strange about Explorer's ability to interact with Control Panel.

What that chapter really showed you was all the similarities. There are a few differences between a standard Explorer interface and Control Panel too. I think the most obvious difference is that you can't manipulate Control Panel objects the same way you can other objects. The context menu shown in Figure 10.12 reveals this fact. Notice that just about the only thing you can do with a Control Panel object is open it or create a shortcut. Even the Properties option is grayed out.

Figure 10.12.
Objects in Control Panel don't provide much flexibility through the context menu.

There are other display differences, too. A standard Explorer display provides four different methods of displaying objects. Control Panel does also. However, when it comes to arranging these objects, you have only two choices, as shown in Figure 10.13. In actuality, you'll probably never even rearrange these icons. There are so few to look at, most people leave them just the way they are.

Figure 10.13.
The methods you can use to arrange Control Panel objects are fairly limited.

Look again at Figure 10.13. Did you notice the Refresh option? Every time you add a new application or piece of hardware and want to see if it added a new Control Panel icon, you can use this command to refresh the display. Unlike with Explorer, closing Control Panel might not force it to display any new icons you add. Using this command ensures that you get an accurate picture.

If you just leave Control Panel alone, you might never see some of the nice features it provides. Use the View | Details command to change the way Control Panel icons are displayed. Normally you would see a list of files, their date of last modification, size, and so forth. Figure 10.14 tells a completely different story. As you can see, Control Panel displays a description of each of the applets instead of simply showing their statistics. This is a very handy feature if you ever see an applet you can't figure out.

I never thought I'd use Control Panel's shortcut option either, but I did. After reading the past few pages, you've probably figured out that there's no fast method to access all the applets in Control Panel. You can right-click on the Desktop and change your display settings. Right-clicking on the My Computer icon will grab the System applet for you. But what if you want to change your system sounds? You have to go to the Start menu or use some other means to bring up Control Panel and then the applet.

Placing a shortcut to the applet on the Desktop is one of the best ways to optimize your setup. Just think: Any time you needed to change your system sounds (or any other configuration item), you'd just double-click the icon on the Desktop. The problem is in how to create the shortcut. If you use the context menu entry, Windows will either ignore you or display an error message saying that it can't create the shortcut.

Figure 10.14.
Descriptive information about each applet is about the last thing you'd expect to see in a Details view, yet here it is.

To make this task a little easier, right-click on the applet and drag it to wherever you want the shortcut to appear. When you release the mouse button, Windows will display the context menu. All you need to do is select the Create Shortcut Here option.

> **Tip:** Don't get icon-happy. Crowding your Desktop with unneeded icons is one sure way to decrease efficiency. Instead of spending your time working, you'll spend it looking for the icon you need. Try to keep the number of icons on your Desktop to five or 10. Any more than that and you'll start crowding yourself out.

Accessing Control Panel from the Command Line

Trying to access Control Panel from the command line might seem like a pretty strange idea. How would you do it? That's the main question. The actual process of opening Control Panel from the command line is fairly easy. All you need to do is type is START CONTROL at the command prompt. You could also simply type CONTROL, but that seems to destabilize the system for some reason. Microsoft provided the START command to regulate access to Windows applications from DOS.

Of course, once you get to Control Panel, you can do anything you normally would and then exit to DOS. The whole idea behind this command-line access is to promote continuous work flow. Have you ever had someone come into your office and disturb you right in the middle of a thought? Trying to get that thought back can be pretty frustrating. Interruptions come in all sizes. It doesn't have to be a person who interrupts you; it could be the interface you use. When you need to stop what you're doing, think about another task, and then resume the first task later, you've experienced an interruption. Using this new technique means that you just move from one task to another without interruption. I think you'll find this new method a lot faster.

On Your Own

Open Control Panel and check its contents against the list of standard applets in this chapter. Does your Control Panel contain additional applets? Open any additional applets to see if you can figure out what purpose they serve. If there is a Help or About button, click on it to see what kind of information it provides.

Try using the START command to open Control Panel from the DOS prompt. Do you notice any differences in Control Panel's contents? Exit Control Panel and reopen the DOS session. Try using the various switches that we talked about in Chapter 5 to open Control Panel. What effect do they have?

IV

Understanding and Using Windows 95

11

DDE
and OLE

Dynamic data exchange (DDE) and object linking and embedding (OLE) are both methods for sharing data between documents. Of the two, DDE is older. There are actually two versions of OLE. Windows 95 supports the newer OLE 2 standard, but that doesn't mean your applications will. A lot of people know what the acronym means—perhaps they even use OLE from time to time—but they can't understand what all the hubbub is about. After all, it's just another form of cut and paste—or is it? The first thing you need to understand about OLE is that it's not just cut and paste. In most of the chapters in this book, I've talked about the objects that Windows 95 uses to make life simpler for the user. Would it surprise you too much to learn that these objects are a form of OLE support?

Objects (not object orientations) can really make your documents easier to use and maintain if you use them correctly. At first it will seem as if there are a lot of rules to follow, but once you learn the rules of the road, you'll find that you can create very complex documents in a lot less time, and with far better results, than before.

Let's get one of the ground rules out of the way. OLE is not the technology to use on a simple document. If the only thing you plan to do is create a word-processed memo or some other small document, you're probably right in thinking that OLE is a waste of time. However, the more complex the document becomes, the greater the benefit of using OLE.

Compound Documents: The Microsoft Strategy

We need to look at a bit of terminology before going much further. You need to speak the language of OLE to really understand it. The following list defines some of the terms you'll see in this chapter (and those that follow).

- Client: This term refers to the application that holds the linked or embedded object. For example, if you place a spreadsheet object in your word-processed document, the word processor becomes the client.

- Server: The server is the application that the client calls to manipulate an object. Embedded or linked objects are still in the native format of the application that created them. A client must call on the originating application to make any required changes to the object's content. What you really have is two applications working together to create a cohesive document.

- Compound document: This is a document that contains one or more objects. Every OLE document is considered a compound document. We'll take a better look at what this means a little later in this chapter.

- Object: An object is a piece of data that you move from one application to another in its native format. You can create objects from any data if the originating application supports

OLE. This is the big difference between an object and cutting and pasting. You can do a lot more with an object because it contains intelligence that a simple piece of text does not.

- The Object menu: We'll take another look at how to use this particular OLE menu later. Suffice it to say that this is the menu you use to change the contents of an OLE document, convert it, or perform any other operations that the object allows.

- Container: An object that holds other objects. Visualizing a folder, such as the ones used by Explorer, will give you a good idea of what a container represents. However, instead of simply holding files like a folder does, an OLE container can hold any kind of object.

Now that you have some idea of what these OLE terms mean, we can take a look at some actual examples. I used Microsoft Paint and WordPad for my example so that you could follow along if you want to. It isn't really necessary to do so; the important thing is that you understand the process.

The first thing I did was double-click on a .BMP file—Honeycomb—in the main Windows folder. Then I opened a copy of WordPad. You should see something similar to Figure 11.1. There isn't anything particularly special about these two applications, but they do both support OLE 2. This will allow me to show you some of the things you can look forward to.

Figure 11.1.

Using OLE starts with something as simple as opening two applications.

Use the Edit | Select All command in Paint to select the entire image, and then right-click on it. You should see the object menu shown in Figure 11.2. Notice that you can't drag and drop this image because Paint doesn't support that particular OLE 2 feature. If it did support drag and drop, you could simply right-click on the object and drag it where you wanted it to go in WordPad. We'll need to take a somewhat longer route.

Figure 11.2.
This object menu contains
options that allow you to
place the object on the
Clipboard.

The object menu allows you to cut or copy the image. Notice the number of other editing options this menu contains. You might want to make note of what is available and compare it to the object menu after we copy the image to WordPad. For right now, select the Copy option. Doing so will place a copy of the object on the Clipboard.

> **Note:** You could use the Edit | Paste Special command in place of the object menu when working with WordPad (or another application that provides this feature). In fact, some applications don't provide an object menu, so you have to resort to using the Edit menu. I'll demonstrate this method of linking or embedding an object later in this book.

Click on WordPad to bring it forward. Right-click anywhere within the window. You should see an object menu similar to the one in Figure 11.3. Notice how this menu differs from the one we saw in Paint. Each object menu will have features that are unique to that application. A graphics application needs menu entries to help it manipulate graphic images. A word processor needs a different set of options to manipulate text.

Figure 11.3.
The WordPad object menu
differs from the one found in
Paint because it needs to
perform different work.

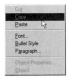

Select the Paste option from WordPad's object menu. You should see a copy of the graphic image in WordPad, as shown in Figure 11.4. The first thing you should notice is the sizing handles around the image. These handles allow you to increase or shrink the object as needed. This feature is really handy in some cases. For example, when I need to draw a logo, I usually draw it very large. That way, I can get it done quickly without worrying too much about detail. When I paste the logo into a document, I shrink it to the size I really need it to be. Voilà—instant detail. As you shrink the graphic, it actually gains some amount of detail you normally wouldn't get if you drew the image that size.

Now that the image is stored in WordPad, go ahead and close Paint. We can always open it back up if we need it later. If you right-click on the graphic object, you'll see a menu similar to the WordPad object menu that we saw earlier. Notice the two bottom options, Bitmap Image Object and Object Properties. Highlight Bitmap Image Object to display a submenu.

Figure 11.4.
The pasted object always provides sizing handles when you select it.

There are two options here: Edit and Open. The difference between them is distinct. You select Edit if you want to perform in-place editing. The Open option actually opens a copy of Paint with which you can edit the graphic. To see what I mean, select Edit now. You should see a display similar to the one in Figure 11.5. You should notice quite a few changes. For one thing, there's a hatched box around the object. This is an OLE 2 way of telling you which object you are currently editing. Also notice that the toolbar and menus changed to match those of Paint. This is what I mean by in-place editing. The window didn't change, but the tools did to meet the editing needs of the object.

Figure 11.5.
In-place editing is one of the new OLE 2 features.

You can click anywhere outside the object to restore the original WordPad menu and toolbar. This time, let's select the Open option to see what happens. You should see a display similar to the one in Figure 11.6. This figure provides you with some visual cues. The most obvious is the fact that you're editing the graphic object outside WordPad using the originating application. The method you use is largely dependent on personal taste since the end result of using either method is the same. The advantage of using the in-place method is that you remain in the same window all the time. This tends to increase efficiency and reduce the chance of losing your train of thought. The Open method has the advantage of returning you to the native editing environment. If I chose to edit one of my logos instead of opening it, I would have to perform in-place editing on a much smaller version of my original picture. Of course, I could always resize it to its original state, but that would be as inefficient as any other method—perhaps more so. Notice also that the object is hatched over in WordPad. This is another visual cue telling you which object you're editing externally.

Figure 11.6.
The Open option produces an entirely different result than Edit does.

The Open method does require one extra step. You need to tell Paint to update the copy of the graphic that's still in WordPad. Select File | Update Document, as shown in Figure 11.7. Notice how this option replaces Save. In essence, the update process does save the graphic. The only difference is where the graphic gets saved.

Figure 11.7.
Make certain you update your document before you leave the server application.

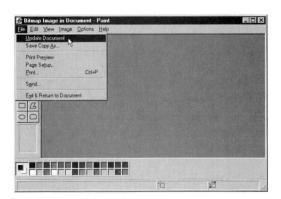

Exit Paint and return to WordPad. Notice that the Exit entry on the File menu now says Return to Document. Now it's time to see what that other object menu entry contains. Right-click on the graphics object and select the Object Properties option. You should see the Bitmap Image Properties dialog, shown in Figure 11.8. About the only interesting entry on the General page is the Convert button. Clicking on this displays another dialog with a list of conversion options. In essence, this option allows you to convert the graphic object from one file type to another. This page also displays the file size and type.

Figure 11.8.

The General page of the Bitmap Image Properties dialog provides access to the Convert dialog.

Note: Each object type provides a unique set of pages in the object dialog. It's important to remember that each dialog reflects a combination of the capabilities of the server applications and the needs of the data file format. Some file formats can't support some application features. As a result, some options might appear grayed out.

Click on the View tab. You'll see the View page of the Bitmap Image Properties dialog, shown in Figure 11.9. This page has several interesting entries. The first is the radio button that determines whether the image is displayed as a graphic or an icon. You can make your machine run faster and use less memory if you select the icon option. Using an icon means that Windows doesn't need to load the actual image or the application required to support it unless you decide to edit it. Windows will suggest a default icon, but you can use the Change Icon button to select another.

Figure 11.9.

The View page of the Bitmap Image Properties dialog allows you to change the appearance of the object.

The bottom part of this dialog is fairly interesting too, even if you can't select it at the moment. It allows you to select a precise scale to use when displaying your graphic. The .BMP format and application used to display it don't support the scaling option in this particular case. Close WordPad; we don't need it anymore for now. You don't have to save the image unless you want to.

This was a whirlwind tour of some of the things you can look forward to with OLE 2. Of course, we haven't even come close to exercising every feature yet. Now it's time to take a step back into the past to examine some of OLE's roots. The next section talks a bit about DDE before we go on with our discussion of OLE.

Data Exchange: A Static Solution

"The King is dead; long live the King!" I just had to say that. A lot of people have the mistaken idea that DDE is dead. Oh, it used to be the way to transfer data between applications, but OLE is the way to go today. There's only one thing I want to say. If DDE is so dead, why does it keep popping up in the registry? Even Explorer, an application designed for Windows 95, provides DDE capability. The fact is that every OLE application uses a little DDE to make it run. I use the term "uses" here instead of "used" because OLE 2 might actually make DDE a thing of the past, but we'll look at that later.

Now that I have your attention, let's look at DDE a bit. There are some significant problems with using DDE. The most significant of these is that it creates a static link, much like the one you get using cut and paste. The fact that it provides a stable macro language that you can use to open files and perform other fancy maneuvers from the command line doesn't change much.

DDE is a messaging protocol. It sends a message from one application to another and asks it to do something. Originally, DDE was supposed to provide the means to open another application and copy some data to the Clipboard. You could also get it to do other chores such as printing files. A DDE macro contains part DDE and part application macro language. This is another problem with using it. Not only do you need to learn the native language of the application you're using and DDE itself, but you also have to learn the macro language for the server application. Needless to say, DDE didn't get the kind of reception that Microsoft originally hoped it would. DDE is simply too hard for the average user to even consider using. In fact, even some programmers find it difficult to use (unless they use it on a regular basis).

Just to give you an idea of how difficult DDE can be to understand, here's a short macro that I created for Lotus 1-2-3. DDE is anything but user-friendly. I've seen low-level languages that provide more information than this does. All this application does is place a copy of LEAVES.BMP in a Word document. The amazing thing is that I actually got this to work. In essence, Lotus 1-2-3 is controlling Word.

```
{LAUNCH "D:\WIN\WINWORD\WINWORD"}
{DDE-OPEN "WINWORD","SYSTEM"}
{DDE-EXECUTE "[InsertObject .IconNumber = 0, .FileName = ""D:\WIN95\LEAVES.BMP"",
```

```
➥.link = 1, .DisplayIcon = 0, .Tab = ""1"", .Class = ""Paint.Picture"",
➥.IconFilename = """", .Caption = ""LEAVES.BMP""]"}
{DDE-EXECUTE "[CharLeft 1, 1]"}
{DDE-EXECUTE "[EditBookmark .Name = ""DDE_LINK1"", .SortBy = 0, .Add]"}
{SELECT A1}
{LINK-CREATE "LINK1";"Word.Document.6";"Document1";"DDE_LINK1";"Picture";"Automatic"}
{LINK-ASSIGN "LINK1";"A:A1"}
```

The first line of this mini-application launches Word for Windows. DDE sends a message to Explorer, telling it to start Word. Once Explorer completes this task, it sends a completion message back to the DDE server. The next line opens Word as a DDE server. Even though Word is running, the DDE server won't know it exists until it gets a message from your application. The third, fourth, and fifth lines are the most difficult to understand. The short version is that they tell Word to insert a copy of LEAVES.BMP into the current document. The sixth line tells Word to highlight the image, just like you would by clicking on it with the mouse. The seventh line creates a bookmark. Now, you might wonder why we would do all this just to assign a bookmark to an object we embedded in Word, but you'll find out in a second. The eighth line places the Lotus 1-2-3 cursor in the upper-left corner. The next line is very important. It assigns the object we created in Word to a link in Lotus 1-2-3. The final line makes that link a reality.

By now you're asking yourself why I would go through all that trouble just to link a .BMP file to a Lotus 1-2-3 worksheet. To answer that question, you'll have to experiment a little. I think you'll find it pretty tough to create the same kind of link that the DDE procedure performs without performing this procedure manually. Just try it sometime. OLE just doesn't provide all the features necessary to create every type of link you'll need, and it certainly doesn't allow you to create those links as part of a macro or program. (OLE automation should change that in the future, but it isn't here today.) The automatic method allows me to place logos in my worksheets with a minimum of effort. As you can see, learning DDE is a requirement if you plan to create automated links in macros and other types of programs.

You normally don't need to worry about the vagaries of DDE programming when using OLE. In fact, the first example in this chapter showed what a typical OLE session is like. The DDE section showed you what goes on in the background—the part of OLE you don't normally see. I don't want to get into all the fine points of OLE programming here. However, if you really do want to get started in OLE programming, you'll need a copy of the OLE SDK from Microsoft. The package you'll get includes a heavy-duty CD and a rather large and cumbersome book. The fine points of OLE programming are so esoteric that I really doubt anyone understands all of them completely.

Linking Versus Embedding

We saw the object part of object linking and embedding earlier. There was no doubt that what we were working with was an object, not merely a cut-and-paste example of the graphic. Now it's time to take a look at the linking and embedding part of the picture.

Peter's Principle: A Time to Link and a Time to Embed

Some people get confused as to when it's appropriate to use linking versus embedding. I break the two down into simple categories so that it's easy to determine when to use each type of OLE. The main problem is defining precisely what kind of compound document you want to create.

Embedding works best when you need to share a file with a lot of people. If the compound document is going to move around, you'll want to package it in such a way that nothing gets lost. An embedded object meets this criteria. Even though embedding is less subject to data loss, it does have a disadvantage: You can't easily share with other people the data embedded within your document.

On the other hand, linking does work well in this instance. If you plan to use the same file in more than one place, linking is the route to go. I almost always use this technique instead of embedding when working with logos.

When you link a document, you are, in essence, creating a pointer to that file on disk. Think of a link as a road sign pointing to your house. As long as you don't move the house, everyone will be able to find it, because the road sign will point them there. But what happens if you do move the house? The sign still points to where it thinks your house is, but anyone who follows the sign will find nothing but an empty foundation.

The same principle holds true for links in compound documents. The link works fine as long as you don't move the document. The second you do move the document, you break the links. Of course, you can always reestablish the links, but that's a waste of time when not moving the file in the first place would require a lot less work.

OLE 1 had a significant problem in this regard because it noted the location of the linked file in precise terms. It would be the same as using your complete address to tell someone how to get to your house. Again, if you moved, the address information would do them little good. OLE 2 takes a different approach. Instead of using a precise location, it uses a relative direction. For example, what if you told your friends that you lived two blocks south of Joe? As long as you and Joe always lived two blocks apart, and you always lived south of Joe, people would be able to find your house. (Of course, they would need to know the location of Joe's house.)

Embedding is a different process than linking. Instead of creating a pointer to your data, embedding actually places the data object within the compound document. This means that wherever the compound document goes, the data will follow. This sounds like a great fix for the problems with linking. However, embedding comes with several price tags attached. First, you'll find it very difficult to update multiple compound documents at once. For example, suppose that your company just decided to go to a different logo and they want all the letters updated to reflect that change. If you had linked the logo file to the letters, the change would be simple. You would need to change just one file. The first person who opened each document after that would see the new logo. With embedding, you'd have to change each document on an individual basis.

You'll also use a lot more disk space to store an embedded file. A link takes only a few bytes to create a pointer. An embedded object is complete. If the object is 4 KB, your compound document will grow by 4 KB to accommodate it. Unfortunately, you won't get off that easily. In addition to the size of the object, some "housekeeping" data is included as well. The server needs this information to help you maintain the object.

Now that you know the difference between linking and embedding, let's take a look at how you would implement them. Begin by opening a copy of WordPad. We're going to explore another route you can take to link and embed objects in your documents. Use the Insert | Object command to display the dialog shown in Figure 11.10. Notice that you can go two routes at this point. You can insert either a new object or an existing one.

Figure 11.10.
Use the Insert Object dialog to embed or link a new or existing object into your document.

Click on the Create from File radio button. The dialog will change to the one shown in Figure 11.11. This will allow you to embed or link an existing file. Click on the Browse pushbutton and find any .BMP file that you like. Double-click to select it. Click on the Link checkbox. If you don't check this box, Windows will automatically embed the object instead of linking it. Notice the Display As Icon checkbox in Figure 11.11. Clicking on this would display the object as an icon rather than as a full image. Displaying the image as an icon will significantly increase performance.

Figure 11.11.
The Insert Object dialog allows you to embed or link an existing file into your document.

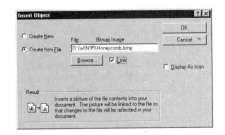

Click on OK to place a link to the object in the current document. A quick glance at this object doesn't show anything different from the last time we created a compound document. However, when you right-click on the object, you'll notice that the menu entries are slightly different. The big difference will come, though, when you try to edit the file. Instead of the in-place editing you could do after embedding the object, linking always opens the server. You must edit the object in a separate window when using linked objects in place of embedded ones. If you really dislike seeing the other application start, you might want to use embedded rather than linked objects.

I hope you now completely understand the differences between linking and embedding. These differences are important for a lot of reasons. Where there's a little overlap in functionality and it's acceptable to use either linking or embedding, select the method that appeals to you most. My favorite is embedding, because I prefer to use in-place editing when I can.

Clients and Servers

Every application that supports OLE provides one or more services. You might have noticed in all our examples I have used Paint as the server and WordPad as the client. The reason is simple: Paint can't function as a client; it offers itself only as an OLE server.

This distinction is important because it affects the way you use an application. More than that, limitations of OLE support necessarily limit an application's value for creating a finished product. Consider what would happen if you tried to use a graphics program to create a poster, but it didn't support OLE as a client. Would you simply settle for cut and paste if there were a chance that you would need to modify the chart frequently? If Paint supported OLE as a client, you could create a chart for your poster in one application, the text in another, and the graphic elements in a third, and then link them all together within Paint. The lack of client support would mean that you would have to copy the text to the Clipboard. When you pasted it into Paint, the text would become a graphic element, part of the Paint graphic image. The text wouldn't be an OLE object that you could easily manipulate later using a word processor; it would be a graphic element that you would have to erase and redo from scratch. This makes changes as small as using a different type style or font size a lot more difficult than they need to be.

Whether your application is a client or a server is an important consideration. You might find that it's less expensive from a time-investment perspective to get rid of an application with limited OLE support. You can follow some general guidelines when it comes to applications.

Any application that will serve as a central location for all the objects in a project must support OLE. In most cases, you'll want to use a word processor or presentation graphics program for this purpose. They provide the greatest amount of flexibility when it comes to formatting your data. Charts and graphs might need the services of a graphics program. Unfortunately, most low-end packages won't work as clients, so you'll need to invest in a high-end package such as CorelDRAW!. You'll definitely want a package of this sort to provide both client and server capabilities, because you'll need to use both.

You can do quick and dirty edits with low-end packages. They usually have just enough features to get the job done and don't waste a lot of precious memory. Programs of this sort usually support OLE as a server but not as a client. No one would want the output from these programs; it just doesn't look professional. Microsoft Paint and other low-end graphics packages commonly fall into this category. You might also see some note-takers here too. In some cases, all you need is the text. A note-taker (such as the Notepad utility provided with Windows 95) works fine for this purpose.

Finally, you'll never use some packages as servers because they just don't generate enough data on their own to make it worth your while to use them in that capacity. Some presentation graphics programs fall into this category. Since their output looks nice, you can use them as OLE clients without worrying about their server capabilities.

Differences Between OLE 1 and OLE 2

Microsoft introduced OLE 1 as part of Windows 3.x. It provided a basic set of linking and embedding features that users soon outgrew. One of the biggest problems was the huge amount of memory that OLE required to create more than one or two links with other applications. The lack of speed was also a major concern.

OLE 2 is supposed to remedy some of these problems and provide much more functionality to boot. The following list gives you an idea of all the improvements Microsoft made in OLE 2. Some of them are programmer-specific, but everyone benefits from something that makes a programmer's life even a little easier.

Tip: Most of these new features require that both applications support OLE 2. At the very minimum, the client must support OLE 2 in order to make any of the features work. We looked at the registry in Chapter 6. Some vendors give you an idea of how to use OLE but don't really tell you how they support it. Looking in the registry can provide important clues as to the type and level of OLE support that an application provides.

- Visual editing: One of the problems with OLE 1 was that the user's train of thought got disrupted every time he needed to make a change to an object. The reason is simple: OLE 1 loaded a copy of the server and displayed the object in the originating application's window for editing. OLE 2 allows visual (or in-place) editing. Instead of opening a new window, the host merely overlays its toolbar, menu structure, and controls with those of the client.

The user simply sees a change in tools, not a change in applications. As a result, the transition between documents is less noticeable.

- Nested objects: OLE 1 allowed you to place one object at a time in the container document. An object couldn't become a container; all the objects existed as a single layer within the container. OLE 2 treats every potential container as just that—a container. It doesn't matter how many containers you place inside a container or how many ways you stack them. To get a better idea of how nesting will help you, look at the way Windows 95 implements folders. You can treat OLE 2 container objects the same way.

- Drag and drop: You used to cut or copy an object in the server application and then place it in the client using the Paste Special command. This option still works. However, OLE 2 provides a new method of creating links to other documents. You can simply grab the object and move it wherever you want. It becomes linked wherever you decide to drop it.

- Storage-independent links: OLE 2 allows you to create links to other documents, even if they aren't physically located on the local drive. It implements this using an LRPC (Light Remote Procedure Call) mechanism. Unfortunately, this linking mechanism has limitations. For example, you'll find that it works fine with some peer-to-peer networks, but it works only marginally with other network types. The next revision of OLE is supposed to fix this problem by supporting RPCs (Remote Procedure Calls).

- Adaptable links: Many users screamed for this feature. If you moved any of the files required to create a compound document under OLE 1, all the links got destroyed, and you had to recreate them. This older version stored the full path, including drive, to the linked data. OLE 2 stores only enough path information to maintain the link. If you create links between two files in the same directory, you can move these two files anywhere on the drive, and OLE 2 can maintain the link. The only criteria for maintaining a link under OLE 2 is that the relative path remain the same.

- OLE automation: Everyone knows about Visual Basic for Applications (VBA), right? This is the new programming language that Microsoft is trying to get everyone to support. OLE automation is part of VBA. VBA defines a standard interface for talking with the server application. This allows the client application to send commands to the server that will change the contents of an object indirectly. OLE automation is the direct descendent of the DDE macro language that many applications still use. The big difference from the user's perspective is that DDE macros were difficult to write and very prone to error. VBA is the native language of the application and is consistent across platforms. The surprising thing is, even though many applications support the VBA interface right now, none of them support it as a programming language. In essence, no one has fully implemented this feature yet. This whole picture is supposed to change when the new versions of Visual Basic and Access appear. Rumor has it that the new Microsoft Office products still won't provide VBA programming support. However, the next versions of Access and Visual Basic will provide this programming capability.

- Version management: Have you ever received a document from someone, only to find that part of it wouldn't work with your software? OLE 2 can store the application name and version number as part of the link. If an application developer implements this feature correctly, a server (or client, for that matter) will detect an old version of a file and ask if you want to update it. This means that you'll never have an old file sitting around just waiting to make life difficult. Unfortunately, except for a few Microsoft applications and one or two other vendors, this feature is largely unimplemented right now. Hopefully, the Windows 95 version of products will incorporate it.

- Object conversion: Your friend uses Excel and you use Lotus 1-2-3, yet you need to share OLE documents containing spreadsheets. One of you could go through the inconvenience and expense of changing to the other person's application and document format, but OLE 2 can probably solve this problem without such a change. Object conversion allows Excel to act as a server for a compound document containing a Lotus 1-2-3 object. All you need to do is select the Convert option from the object menu. At least, that's how it's supposed to work. Real life is a bit different. Conversion will work only if the other application already supports that data format. Of course, when you think about it, this restriction makes sense.

- Optimized object storage: Remember the screaming about memory I told you about at the beginning of this section? This feature is part of the cure. It allows the linked documents to stay on disk until needed. That way, Windows doesn't need to load every application and data file required to support the compound document. In most cases, Windows uses a buffer-zone technique. A word processor might keep the applications and objects required for the preceding, current, and next page in memory. The rest of the objects stay on disk, greatly reducing the memory footprint of a compound document in some cases.

- Component object model: This is the programmer issue I was telling you about. Essentially, it means that Microsoft simplified the application programming interface (API) for OLE 2. An API is a set of tools that programmers use to create applications. Simpler tools mean programs with fewer bugs. This also means that the programmer can write at least that part of the application faster.

With all the changes to OLE 2, you might think that there would be compatibility problems. OLE 1 and OLE 2 can mix freely on your machine. Remember the two separate sets of entries we looked at in Chapter 6? Each application had a set of OLE 1 and OLE 2 entries in the registry. This is the reason for the dual set. The important thing to remember here is that OLE takes a least-common-denominator approach. Everything is tied to the application that has the fewest capabilities. This means that if you had four OLE 2 applications and one OLE 1 application, everything would be tied to the level of support provided by the OLE 1 application.

Application Interoperability

Getting two applications to work together might not always be as easy as it seems. We've already seen a lot of different ways that two applications can differ in their implementation of OLE, and this barely scratches the surface. For the most part, we've looked at the standard ways that two applications can deviate. The following list gives you some ideas of what to look for when you can't get your objects to work properly.

- Neither application is a server. Remember that you must have a server and a client to make OLE work. One application must communicate needed changes to the other. The server then makes any required changes to the object and hands it back. The whole purpose of OLE is to maintain this kind of communication.

- Data corruption has ruined one or more OLE files. This isn't very common, but it does happen. One of the reasons for this particular kind of corruption is old data files. I've seen applications overwrite newer versions of OLE files with old ones. Even though the application can use the older files, other applications might not be able to. It's usually a good idea to record the time and date stamps on your OLE files. That way, you can always check for this special form of data corruption.

- One program provides 32-bit services and the other 16-bit. This problem isn't supposed to happen. I've seen it only once or twice, and when it did occur, I couldn't get the problem to repeat after I rebooted my machine. What exactly happened is debatable. If you do find that two programs that normally talk to each other with ease are suddenly hostile toward each other, it might be time to reboot the machine and see if clearing memory helps.

- Corrupted entries in the registry prevent the application from working correctly. I covered the registry entries in detail in Chapter 6. The bottom line is that if you have so much as a punctuation mark wrong, the registry will balk and your OLE connection won't work.

- Old entries in the registry are confusing the application. Remember our discussion of the WIN.INI and SYSTEM.INI files? The registry is a lot better organized, and you'll definitely find it easier to maintain, but there are still times when you might have to remove an entry manually. Some applications get confused when they run across these old OLE entries and end up trying to use the wrong files or settings.

- Your network doesn't fully support OLE links. Some networks require the use of special software when creating OLE 2 links. LANtastic falls into this category. As long as you use Artisoft's procedures, you should maintain good OLE connections. Other networks, such as the Microsoft network supplied with Windows 95, use OLE without any additional software. A third category of network software seems to have trouble maintaining links. Banyan falls into this category. Unfortunately, all this assumes that you create exactly the same drive mappings every time you log onto the network. As an experiment, I tried a setup in which the user needed to use her old CD-ROM only occasionally. She didn't want to load the real-mode drivers every day because the driver lowered system stability. The days she didn't have the CD-ROM connected, all her OLE links worked fine. On the days it was connected, none of the OLE links would work. We finally traced the problem to changes in the drive mapping when the CD-ROM drive was active.

This is just a sample of the types of problems you could encounter with a common setup. Add to these problems a vendor who doesn't fully support the OLE 1 or OLE 2 standard. I actually ran into one piece of software that ended up providing some strange cross of support between the two standards (and I don't think this vendor was alone). These support problems only make the situation worse. If every application supported OLE perfectly, you could probably get past the other problems I listed in this section. The combination of faulty support and less-than-adequate linking mechanisms does paint a grim picture for the user. It would be easy to point a finger and say that the vendor was totally at fault. Yet anyone who has tried to read the OLE standards, much less follow them, will attest to the level of difficulty involved.

Note: Just in case curiosity has gripped you, the OLE SDK disk weighs in at 129 MB. That doesn't include all the documentation or even a compiler. (Documentation includes some white papers, a copy of the OLE 2 specification, and the complete text on OLE automation.) I also received another book with the kit that consumed another 975 pages and came with two additional floppies' worth of sample programs. Talk about a lot of information to learn! When you consider that OLE isn't the entire application—it's only a small piece of an application—would you be willing to spend the time required to go through all this material?

Before you get the idea that all is lost with OLE, let me inject a dose of reality. I wanted you to be aware of all the problems you might find. In most cases, I don't have any substantial problems with OLE that I didn't cause myself. Sure, there are times when I would like to be able to do more than the applications I'm using will allow, but these are inconveniences; they don't make OLE unusable. The best thing you can do when using OLE is to thoroughly check everything before you make a huge commitment in time and energy to a specific solution. It always pays to check for potential pitfalls, but this is especially true of a technology as new and complex as OLE.

Packaging OLE Objects

OLE wasn't the smashing success Microsoft hoped it would be, and we've already discussed some of the reasons why. Part of Microsoft's answer to the problem of a lack of OLE support was Object Packager, which comes with Windows. You can still find this utility in your main Windows directory, but you won't see it on your Start menu. I added my copy to the Start menu to make it easier to access.

Object Packager is good for only one thing: It allows you to create a package you can insert into a document. The result is similar to an object you create using the native capabilities that many programs provide today. It's still a good utility to keep around for those older applications that don't directly support OLE.

Rather than bore you with a lot of details about this particular product, let's put a package together. In fact, we'll use the same two applications we've used throughout this chapter, along with the same data file. This will allow you to see the difference between an object package and an object.

The first thing you need to do is create the object package. Open Object Packager. You should see the display shown in Figure 11.12. A lot of people claim this utility is difficult to use. Actually, they're only half-right. This utility isn't all that hard to use; it's the documentation that makes using it seem difficult.

Figure 11.12.
*Object Packager looks
simple, and it really is once
you get the hang of it.*

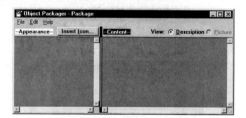

Click on the Insert Icon pushbutton. Object Packager automatically assumes that you want to use one of the icons out of Program Manager since it was designed for that interface. You can choose another icon using the Browse pushbutton, but we'll use one of the icons listed here for now. After you select an icon, click on OK to complete the task.

Use the Edit | Label command to add a label to the icon. This will identify the file we plan to use. I typed HONEYCOMB.BMP, but you could use any other identification you choose.

The Edit | Command option allows you to add the location of the file you want to edit, along with the application that will perform the editing. You need to know the command-line syntax for the application in order to do anything fancy here. In most cases, you won't use Object Packager directly with an application that registers itself, so you will probably be limited to opening the file with the application. To do that, just type the name of the program followed by the filename, just like you would at the DOS prompt. I typed MSPAINT D:\WIN95\HONEYCOMB.BMP in this case. You can modify the contents of your command to meet the needs of a particular situation. Figure 11.13 shows the results of all our edits so far. Your display might look slightly different, depending on the choices you made.

Figure 11.13.
This is the simplest form of a completed package.

Now that we have a completed package, it's time to do something with it. Use the Edit | Copy Package command to place the package on the Clipboard. Open WordPad or Word for Windows. Right-click on the edit area and select Paste from the object menu. You should see a display similar to the one in Figure 11.14.

Figure 11.14.
An object package looks and acts a lot different than its object counterpart.

There are several differences between this object package and the object we worked with before. The first difference is pretty obvious: There's no way to determine what the object looks like. This isn't the icon form of the package; it's what the package actually looks like. We can double-click on the package to bring up Paint, so at least that part of the package works satisfactorily. However, as you can see from Figure 11.15, Object Packager doesn't support in-place editing.

Figure 11.15.
Even though this object
package is embedded, it
acts as if it were linked.

You don't have to use Object Packager this way. It does support other methods of creating an object package. Some of them work with certain kinds of software. This first method works with any kind of application, even if it doesn't support OLE. The only requirement is that the application support a command-line interface.

The preceding example did leave a little to be desired as far as capability goes. Let's try one more time to make a better package. Open HONEYCOMB.BMP (or any other .BMP file) using Paint. Use the Edit | Select All command to select the graphic, and then copy it to the Clipboard using Edit | Copy.

Open Object Packager. Use the Edit | Paste command to copy the contents of the Clipboard into the package area. Figure 11.16 shows the results. Notice how different this package appears from the first one. The problem with this method is that the originating application must support OLE as a client. Fortunately, it doesn't have to provide a specific level of support.

It's time to check the results of this second attempt at creating an object package. Use the Edit | Copy Package command to place the package on the Clipboard. Open Wordpad or Word for Windows. Right-click on the edit area and select Paste from the object menu. You should see a display similar to the one in Figure 11.17.

Notice that this object looks and acts the same as the previous object did. Even though the package looked like it would support in-place editing while it was in the Object Packager, it won't support it now. I wanted to point this out because it's a limitation of Object Packager rather than Paint or

WordPad. It's a factor you need to remember whenever you resort to using Object Packager. Any objects you create using this method go from the client, through Object Packager, and to the originating application. If you want features such as in-place editing, you must use an application that supports this feature directly rather than resorting to Object Packager. Remember that Object Packager was designed to help people gain some of the benefits of OLE even when using applications that didn't support it. In most cases, you'll want to leave this dusty tool where it belongs. However, it's still nice to know it's there when you need it.

Figure 11.16.
This method of creating an object package produces a different result than the previous method.

Figure 11.17.
The new object package seems to produce the same results as before—an obvious limitation of Object Packager.

OLE Components

You'll probably see a whole group of files in your \SYSTEM directory that provide support for OLE. The following list provides some details on the tasks each file performs. You can use this list if you ever run into a problem with corruption or if you would simply like to know what level of support you can expect from a certain application. The presence or absence of these files might indicate problems with your installation as well. Missing OLE files means you won't get the kind of support needed to make your system work efficiently.

- OLE2.DLL: If you see this file, you know that some part of the Windows installation on your machine supports the OLE 2 standard. Windows 95 always installs this file. This dynamic link library (DLL) provides some "foundation" functions. (A DLL is a special Windows program.)

- OLECLI.DLL: This file contains all the basic client code your application needs. Your application uses this file as a base for building its own client features.

- OLESRV.DLL: This file contains all the basic server code your application needs. Like the client code, this DLL won't provide everything. Your application uses it as a basis for building its own set of features.

- OLE2CONV.DLL: This file provides the generic routines a program needs to convert an object to the client program's native format.

- OLE2DISP.DLL: Every OLE client application uses this program to help it display the objects it contains.

- OLE2NLS.DLL: Most versions of Windows provide National Language Support (NLS). This program helps OLE keep pace with the rest of Windows in providing support for other languages.

- OLE2.REG: You can import this registry file into your registry to install OLE 2 support. In most cases, your application will do this automatically, so you don't need to worry about it. The only time you'll need to use it is if you can't get OLE 2 to work and discover that the registry doesn't contain the correct entries.

- MCIOLE.DLL: Sounds require special handling under Windows. Unlike with most objects, you don't display a sound. This special DLL provides the support an application needs in order to handle a sound object.

- OLE32.DLL: A whole group of OLE files in the \SYSTEM directory has "32" somewhere in their names. These files provide the same services as their 16-bit counterparts to 32-bit applications.

- MFCOLEUI.DLL: C programmers need every bit of help they can get. They use something called Microsoft Foundation Classes to make their workload a little lighter. This file (and any with similar names) provides the C interface to OLE. If you see a file with "MFC" in its name, you know one of your applications uses the Microsoft Foundation Classes.

Note: The first World Wide Web browser that's also an OLE server is included in Microsoft Plus!. The Microsoft Internet Explorer allows full integration between the Internet and your Desktop using OLE. Read Chapter 24 to learn more about Microsoft Internet Explorer.

On Your Own

Test the OLE capabilities of the various applications on your machine. Which ones support OLE as a client? Which ones support it as a server? Do you see any difference between the applications that support OLE 1 and OLE 2?

Use the various techniques for inserting an object in a container that I covered in this chapter. Which methods do you find easiest to use? Why do you think some applications support one technique and others another technique?

Try making an OLE link in a large document using an OLE 1 application. Make the same link using an OLE 2 application such as WordPad. Do you see a difference in the load time of the two documents? What additional features does WordPad provide that the OLE 1 application doesn't?

Open a copy of Explorer and use it to search your SYSTEM folder. Can you find all of the OLE-specific files installed on your system? What do the names of the various files tell you about that file's purpose?

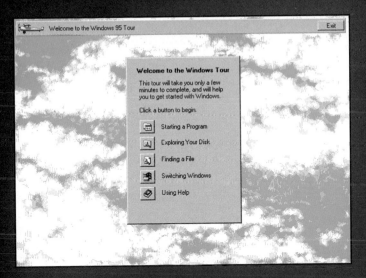

This is the initial display from Microsoft Tour. From here you can learn about some of the major Windows 95 features and at least a little about getting around. This multimedia tour is much enhanced from the tutorial provided with Windows 3.x.

The screen saver for the More Windows Desktop Theme takes whatever image is on your Desktop at the moment it was activated and turns it into a set of building blocks that the screen saver begins stacking one at a time.

The many faces of Explorer are reflected in these views of Briefcase. Pressing Shift while double-clicking produces the dual-pane view. The views clockwise from the upper-left are large icon, small icon, details, and list. The Briefcase window in the upper-left corner shows the more traditional single-pane view.

If you don't like the tiled view of applications on your Desktop, you can always use the Cascade view. Just right-click on the Taskbar and select Cascade from the context menu. This figure shows the same four Explorer views as before, but cascaded instead of tiled.

Contrast the normal view of the Desktop with that shown here. A 1024 × 768 display provides plenty of space to display the standard icons plus various projects you might be working on and still has room to spare for applications. Note that this 256-color display is the minimum that you'll want to use if color is important in your applications.

The Accessibility options can come in handy near the end of the day when your eyes are tired and a busy screen is no longer appealing. All I did to produce this display was press the High Contrast Display hot-key combination of Left Alt-Left Shift-Print Screen. It's a lot faster than changing all the settings by hand, and you don't have to reboot afterward.

You can also permanently change the display so that the fonts are a little bigger and easier on the eyes. Use the Custom Font Size dialog to change the setting. A value of 128% emulates an 800×600 view on a 1024×768 display. A value of 160% emulates a 640×480 view. Of course, using the higher resolution means that your fonts will appear smoother and your icons will appear smaller.

Yet another way to affect the readability of your display is to edit the font attributes of various display elements by hand. For example, adding bold or italics will affect the way the display looks. You'll also need to change the size of the menu and other bars when changing the font size so that the new font will fit within the required space.

The Start Menu and the Taskbar

Windows 95 allows you to nest the Start menu layers as deep as needed. Placing the items you use most often at the top of the hierarchy ensures that you can get to them as quickly as possible.

I normally hide the Taskbar, but some people prefer to have it available at all times, as shown here. You can always get the current status of an application by resting the mouse cursor on the application's button, as shown. In this case, Windows 95 is telling me that I'm editing a document called PWNINOR.DOC.

There isn't any reason why you can't move the Taskbar if it's in the way. Moving it to the right side of the display always makes the most sense to me. Moving it to the top would interfere with the menu provided by most applications. Moving it to the left would interfere with the display of the standard icons. Notice that you can make the Taskbar just about any size you need it to be.

It's not difficult to configure your Desktop to an application-centric view and still maintain all the other features that Windows 95 provides. Here I've placed shortcuts to my most common applications and devices on the Desktop. This provides quick and easy access as needed.

My personal preference for a Desktop arrangement is the document-centric approach. This one shows one way to arrange your data through the use of projects. I find that this one works best in the office.

A home office might require a different approach, like the one shown here. Notice that this arrangement is actually person-centric. Everyone who uses the file gets his or her own folder. I also provide a "common" folder that everyone can use.

There really isn't a limit to the number of ways you can rearrange your Desktop. In this case, I separated personal folders from other objects. It's especially handy when more than one person will use the machine on a consistent basis and you want to reduce the chance of doing something by mistake. Note that you'll have to disable Auto Arrange if you want to use a Desktop setup like this.

If you prefer not to clutter your Desktop, you might want to keep a copy of Explorer open by adding it to your Startup folder. You might want to start a Projects folder and place shortcuts to all your work there as well. You'll still keep your Desktop clean by using Explorer to search through the various folders for the work you need to do.

I usually use the dual-pane view of Exchange because it's simpler. However, let's look at the single-pane approach. It has two advantages. First, it always takes you to the Inbox rather than showing the entire directory structure. Second, it saves space on machines that lack the display real estate to use the dual-pane view.

When you insert a CD with an autoplay directory like the Windows 95 CD has, you'll probably see a menu containing the things you can do with that CD.

Microsoft Exposition is a nice example of how you can use multimedia under Windows 95. The Upgrade Advisor will help you determine which Microsoft products you need to round out your machine's capabilities.

The Windows 95 autoplay feature displays a dialog when it runs the AUTORUN program on the installation CD-ROM. This dialog even includes an option for adding and removing software. This is far more convenient than accessing the same feature from Control Panel. As you can see, it brings up the same dialog as the Control Panel applet does.

Games and Video

Hover is one of the games supplied with Windows 95. The idea is to capture all your enemy's flags before he captures yours. It's not quite as good as some of the games out there, but it's definitely more action-packed than Solitaire or FreeCell.

Hover isn't the only game that comes with Windows 95. You can also install the three shown here: Hearts, Minesweeper, and FreeCell. All three games allow you to fill in a few blank spots during the day with a bit of fun.

Videos are another new item supplied on your Windows 95 CD. If you own a 4X CD-ROM drive like I do, you'll find that the video looks much like you would expect to see on television or any other entertainment device. Of course, the actual size of the picture is somewhat limited.

MSN Today is always the first stop when you get online. It usually includes a list of major events happening during that day or in the near future.

Clicking on the icons in MSN Today will take you right to the topic at hand. In this case, I clicked on the Visio icon and ended up in the Visio forum.

One of the nicest features of MSN is the ability to exchange one of the things people always exchange—pictures. Doing so is quite easy. Just select what you want and click on the Download File pushbutton.

Online Treasure Hunt

You can also right-click on the picture object and simply open it, as shown here. Of course, you'll still need to wait for Exchange to download the file, but you'll reduce the number of actions required to view the graphic afterward.

You can even read a book online when using MSN. In this case, we're looking at The Big Chip, but the book selection will change periodically. Notice the detailed graphics in this and other pictures. It took my 14.4 Kbps a while to download them. Fortunately, you can interrupt the process as needed. I strongly recommend that you get a 28.8 Kbps modem if possible.

I was quite surprised at the number of photographs you can download from various theme parks. In fact, the travel section as a whole contains many photographs that people can view.

One of the more helpful sources of information that you'll get with the CD-ROM version of Windows 95 is the resource kit. It comes in two parts, as shown here. The first dialog helps you find a general area of interest, and the second dialog provides you with specific information.

One of the utilities I've really come to like is System Monitor. You can see the three different types of charts here and just a few of the many things you can monitor with it. It's important to learn how to use this tool to optimize your system.

Here you see the three utilities that Microsoft provides for maintaining your hard drives: Backup, Disk Defragmenter, and Disk Scanner. Using all three will ensure that you catch any major drive system problems quickly and that you get the maximum performance possible from your machine.

Microsoft Plus!

Time passes quickly on the travel clock animated mouse cursor that appears in the Travel Desktop Theme. Doesn't it always when you travel? You'll hear sounds of being transported to far destinations while you're working.

Private planes move through a constantly changing sky in the screen saver included with the Travel Desktop Theme.

Bugs occasionally crawl around your Desktop in the Nature Desktop Theme. You'll hear birds singing or maybe even flapping their wings. My favorite is the Recycle Bin, which is an unlit pile of campfire logs. When you drop files into the Recycle Bin, a fire ignites.

There are no sounds in the screen saver for the Nature Desktop Theme, just the quiet of nature and caterpillars crawling through the leaves.

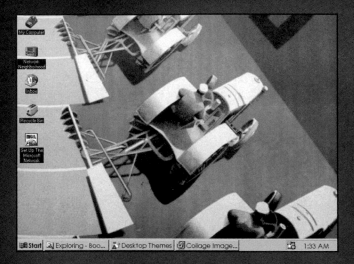

Listen to the sounds of the machine age as you work in the Golden Era Desktop Theme. A 1940s toaster is your Recycle Bin. When you drop files in, toast pops up. I particularly like the light colors and readable fonts in this theme.

The screen saver for the Golden Era Desktop Theme features communication. Watch as the man sitting in the lower-right corner taps his foot while reading the newspaper. Telephone operators and radio announcers speak as objects used for communication during the 1940s slide around your screen.

The animated mouse cursors for the Mystery Desktop Theme include footsteps and a fingerprint seen through a magnifying glass. While you work in this dark and mysterious Desktop, doors will creak and you might hear footsteps.

Bats fly around, owls contemplate, and cats prowl while the moon moves through the night sky in the screen saver for the Mystery Desktop Theme. What's that you heard? Did you see something in the window? The door creaked open and suddenly slammed shut. Who's there?

Windows 95 Takes Control

A CD-ROM spins and binary numbers scroll across a computer screen when animated mouse pointers show up on the Inside Your Computer Desktop Theme. Listen to computer sounds while you explore your Desktop.

Watch and listen as capacitors, integrated circuits, and other electronic gadgetry tumble over an integrated circuit board (your motherboard?) and give off electronic sounds in the screen saver for the Inside Your Computer Desktop Theme.

Throughout this insert, I've been showing you various wallpapers and color schemes that Windows 95 provides. Hopefully you saw a combination you liked. This final display shows one wallpaper I haven't shown you yet.

12

Exploiting Your Software

I played with a lot of titles for this chapter before I finally decided to use this one. It expresses the entire thought behind the way some people manage their systems today. In fact, it should express the way you use your system. Of course, exploiting your software could mean a lot of things, so let's take a few minutes to define what I mean.

Exploiting every possible feature of some of today's software products would be impossible for the average user. The fact that some power users have a problem doing it really says something about software bloat. Take CorelDRAW! as an example. I recently installed the latest version of this product on my system. Even if I decided not to install all the fonts, I'd still have access to a drawing program, a presentation graphics program, and a desktop publisher—and that only scratches the surface. The folks at Corel thoughtfully provided me with three CD-ROMs full of valuable information, most of which I'll never use. Obviously, exploiting your software doesn't necessarily involve using every feature it has to offer.

Note: Don't get the idea that I'm bashing anyone by saying there's a certain level of software bloat in most packages today. The computing environment has become so complex and the tasks we perform so varied that you need to expect a certain level of bloat. Even if you don't use a particular feature, some users would feel that the package wasn't complete unless the vendor provided it. Combining the requests made by the majority of customers is the reason most vendors produce the bloated packages we see on the market today. A product feature I can't use to get my work finished might make all the difference in the world to someone else.

What I mean by exploiting your software is exercising every feature you do use to its fullest potential. I use four basic criteria to measure my level of software exploitation. They're all interactive, so you'll find that changing one element will, of necessity, affect all the other elements. For me, it's kind of a game to see just how well I can get all these elements to work together. So what are these four criteria? A fully exploited piece of software will do the following things:

- Accomplish the job at hand with a minimum of effort. Everyone knows that learning to use a computer is both expensive and time-consuming. Add to that the cost of buying the equipment itself and you have a major investment before you see any kind of return. A fully exploited piece of software allows you to accomplish the same job as before, but with a lot less effort. Concentrating on the task rather than the means of performing it means that you can be a lot more creative in your work. I've always felt that computers should provide a way of removing the burden of work and leaving the "fun" parts for us to accomplish. A fully exploited piece of software can do just that.

- Produce results in a modicum of time. It wasn't too long ago that people wondered why it was faster to do something by hand than to use a computer. I personally saw this problem often. What these people were forgetting was that if you were going to use that older software to its fullest potential, you needed to set the application up only once. The computer could then automate the task for you, so it would take you less time to perform the task the second time you did it. If you didn't set your computer up for rapid duplication of rote work, you weren't exploiting it. Fortunately, the old problem of spending more time to create your original document just isn't there anymore. I can use a variety of packages to write an application in a fraction of the time it used to take. Templates and other software add-ons make it faster to produce the first copy of a document, in addition to variations of that document later. The "wizards" provided with a lot of software packages give you a built-in ease of use that was unheard of only five years ago. A fully exploited piece of software today will allow you to produce results faster than you could by hand in many cases.

- Produce output that requires the least amount of system resources. The amount of system resources you have is relative. Much of it has to do with the technology you have at your disposal. There are other considerations as well, such as the money you have to spend on upgrades, but let's concentrate on the relative aspect of this picture. A fully exploited piece of software is optimized so that it uses a minimum of system resources. We saw in Chapter 11 that there are a number of ways to embed or link an object into your document. Other chapters in this book have shown you various aspects of other forms of optimization. A fully exploited piece of software uses the least memory-intensive, yet fastest, way to accomplish a task. Optimizing the way you use the software's features will almost always result in reduced system resource requirements.

- Produce the best results possible. Optimizing your software to reduce system requirements, improving your techniques to reduce the time it takes to get the job done, and reducing the effort required to complete the task are all fine goals. However, it's the result of all this effort that everyone will see. The boss won't care that it took you half the time to get something done if the final result isn't up to par. That's a problem for many people: They look for a quick fix to a problem, and that often isn't the route they really need to pursue. The test of whether you've successfully exploited your software is in the results you produce. Using the software and hardware available today should allow you to produce an end product that's superior in every way to what you could do yesterday. If you aren't getting that result, it's time to take another look at how you're exploiting your software.

Exploiting your software also means that you use the right tool for the task you're trying to accomplish. Sure, you can use a spreadsheet as a word processor (a lot of people do), but is that really exploiting your software, or is the software exploiting you? Of course, no one can afford to buy every application on the market. There are limitations to what you can realistically use. If an inexpensive tool will do the job, that's the one you should select. It's a matter of defining the parameters of the job. Just how much work do you need to do? If I need to dig a small hole, I get a spade. A really big hole requires a backhoe.

To summarize, then, exploiting your software means you get an application that's the right size and type for the job. You optimize its operation and environment. Then you sit back and watch the application do its job in the most efficient manner possible.

If this sounds impossible, read on. A lot of things seem impossible until you take the time to analyze the situation, break it into its component parts, and solve the small problems. Trying to take an entire project and solve it with one answer isn't going to do much, if anything, to make you efficient. Of course, you probably do all this with your current business. Most successful businesses take the time to get the most out of their employees and the resources they have available. Now what you need to do is apply these same principles to your computer.

Peter's Principle: Operating System Flexibility is the Key

Windows 3.x was very inflexible in some regards. Even if you could get around some of its limitations, there were enough times when you couldn't that a total system solution was impractical. I have a lot of books and other resources sitting on my self that claim to provide the answer for Windows 3.x optimization or the inner secret that will unlock all its power. Even with all this help, I could seldom run more than three tasks at a time or fully exploit the software installed on my machine.

Using Windows 95 has shown me that it still has bugs and other limitations. This product is still inflexible in some areas. In previous chapters, we even looked at some of the strange decisions Microsoft made when putting this operating system together. However, even with all these little "gotchas," Windows 95 provides a level of flexibility that will allow you to circumvent the problem areas and (finally) use the system to its full potential. You can really exploit Windows 95. A fully optimized operating system does several things for you as the user. Besides all the obvious answers you'll probably come up with, such as improved stability, an optimized operating system allows you to fully exploit the software packages sitting on your shelf.

A flexible environment like Windows 95 provides you with the space you need to maneuver that application into the best possible setup for use. Of course, with added flexibility comes some additional responsibility for the user. Microsoft still provides you with a default setup for your Windows installation. However, if you want to fully exploit your software, you need to fully exploit the operating system as well.

Tip: Exploiting your system means that you need to tune it too. Have you ever seen a race car driver who paid more attention to his paint job than his engine? Optimizing your applications doesn't really make sense until you spend a little time under the hood optimizing Windows. Read Chapter 3 if you need some ideas on how to do this.

Using the Add/Remove Programs Utility

Have you seen the immense size of some applications today? I'm often appalled at how fast the applications I install can eat up a major piece of the 1 GB drive on my machine. Most people don't have a drive this size, so sometimes they need to remove one or more applications they don't use much to make room for the applications they use often. If you ever tried to do this under Windows 3.x, you'll know how difficult it can be to actually perform this task. You'll also be pleasantly surprised by a new Windows 95 capability. It allows you to install and remove your Windows 95 applications with ease.

Note: The Windows 95 Install/Uninstall capability doesn't extend to non-Windows 95-specific products. This includes both Windows 3.x and Windows NT products. To install and then later uninstall these products, you still need to use a third-party option. Unfortunately, there's a problem with this method as well. The Windows 95 utility ensures that the proper registry entries get made. You need to decide between the ability to easily remove the application later and performing a little more work to get the application installed correctly, or getting the best possible installation up front and doing a lot of work later to remove it. Using the correct installation utility will help you get rid of those old applications fast.

Tip: Many of the newer applications on the market provide their own uninstall program. Chances are the custom uninstall program will work better than most third-party products because the vendor can hand-tune its uninstall program. Unfortunately, this isn't always the case. I've had uninstall programs remove too many files or not enough. In some cases, they've even trashed the registry to the point where I had to reinstall some of my applications. When these native uninstall programs work, they work well. When they don't, watch out.

So what's involved in removing an application after you've installed it? Every uninstall program needs to take five things into consideration. Uninstall programs handle each criteria to a different degree.

- Application directory: Every uninstall program handles this one the same way. For that matter, it would probably take you even less time to remove the application directory when no longer needed. The problem is the application's data. Some uninstall programs leave it in place so you can recover it later; others simply remove the entire directory without giving the data it contains much thought. I prefer the first approach since it keeps me from shooting myself in the foot. The second approach is a little too thorough in my opinion.

- Windows directory: Most applications place an .INI file in the Windows directory so they can find it easily. Some applications place two or even three here. For example, when I installed LANtastic, it placed three different .INI files here. Each managed a different aspect of the product. I was surprised by the number of uninstall programs that don't take these files into account.

- Windows system file modification: It's a sure bet that Windows 95 will have the same problem that previous versions of Windows did when it comes to spurious entries in WIN.INI and SYSTEM.INI. Even though it only provides compatibility support for these files, it does read them when you boot. Suffice it to say that some of the same problems you had in the past will still crop up when you install 16-bit applications.

- SYSTEM directory: There are a ton of files in your SYSTEM directory, and there's no way of knowing which ones belong to your application. Even if an uninstall program tracks these files, it has no way of knowing how many applications use a particular file. This is especially true of DLLs. For example, an application might install a copy of VBRUN300.DLL in your SYSTEM directory. When you install another application that also requires the same file, the second application might not add the file because it sees that the file is already present. If the uninstall program removed VBRUN300.DLL along with all the other files for the first application, the second application would also cease to work. So how do you handle this situation? I don't know, and neither does your uninstall program. Some programs make a valiant effort to remove the less common files. But when it comes to removing one, you're on your own—deleting files from the SYSTEM directory by hand.

Tip: Chapter 6 contains a procedure for viewing the contents of DLLs and other system files. You can use this procedure to view the files you suspect an application uses in order to decide whether or not to delete them. Making a list of the DL_ and DLL files on the distribution disk is also very helpful. Comparing this list to the contents of the SYSTEM directory will at least provide clues on what you can remove. Be careful, though, not to remove any "common" files your SYSTEM directory might contain. Reading the heading information for the DLL will also give you clues in this regard, because common files are normally written by a compiler vendor and not the vendor of the application you're removing. (Unfortunately, this doesn't help much when it comes to Borland and Microsoft applications.)

- Common application directories: Many applications try to reduce the number of files on your hard drive by placing files that more than one application could use in a separate directory. For example, you'll find an MSAPPS directory on your machine if you use Microsoft applications. The positive side of such directories is that they do indeed reduce the load on your hard drive. The negative aspect is you really don't know which files to remove if you use multiple products from the same vendor and you want to remove only one product. In fact, I found that this common directory can actually confuse your uninstall program. Some of them remove the entire directory whether more than one application is using them or not.

As you can see, trying to remove a Windows application from your machine isn't the easy task that it was under DOS. A Windows application spreads files all over the place and makes entries in system files you might need, even if you do remove the application. (Multiple applications might need the same entry to run.) It's not too surprising, then, that Windows uninstall programs normally do a partial, not a complete, job of removing old programs from your system. Of course, a partial removal is better than nothing.

> **Tip:** Windows won't let you remove a file that's in use. Even if you close an application, Windows might not unload all its associated DLLs right away. Whenever you want to remove an application from your drive, shut everything down, reboot, and perform the uninstall routine with all applications closed. This will ensure that the uninstall program can actually remove all the files it identifies as part of the application.

A Windows 95 application gives the operating system much more information about what it installs, and why, than previous versions of Windows. That's why you can uninstall only Windows 95-specific applications with the new Install/Uninstall capability. Newer applications actually make registry entries that tell the operating system what to remove later. This also allows Windows 95 to look for common files and perform other types of analysis. When you can finally upgrade every application on your machine to a Windows 95-specific version, the Windows 95 Install/Uninstall program should work perfectly—theoretically, at least.

Now that we have all the preliminaries out of the way, let's take a look at the future. Remember that we're looking at a less-than-optimal setup here since I don't have Windows 95 applications to replace all my current applications (and neither will you for the foreseeable future). Because of this problem, you might get slightly different results than I did. The following paragraphs tell you how to use the Install/Uninstall program.

1. Open Control Panel using the Start menu or Explorer.
2. Double-click on Add/Remove Programs. You should see a dialog like the one shown in Figure 12.1.
3. Click on Install. You'll see a dialog similar to the one shown in Figure 12.2. Notice that this dialog tells you to place a floppy in one of the floppy drives or a CD-ROM in the CD-ROM drive. You don't have to do this. The Install/Uninstall program will let you search for applications on a hard drive. However, to use the automatic search features, you need to place a disk in the appropriate drive.

Figure 12.1.
The Install/Uninstall page of the Add/Remove Programs Properties dialog lets you install any application. It will uninstall only Windows 95-specific applications.

Figure 12.2.
Don't believe everything you read in this Install Program dialog.

4. Click on Next. The Install Wizard will search the A drive, B drive, and CD-ROM drive for SETUP.EXE. If you're installing a program from the hard drive, or if the setup program uses a different name, the wizard won't find it. You'll need to enter the value by hand or use the Browse dialog.

5. If the Install Wizard finds a setup program, it will type the name here for you. If not, you'll see a dialog like the one shown in Figure 12.3. Type the name of the application you want to install or use the Browse dialog to find it. To use the Browse dialog, simply click on the Browse button.

Figure 12.3.
The Run Installation Program dialog is the last time you will see the Install Wizard.

6. As soon as you complete step 5, Windows 95 will launch the setup application. Follow the vendor instructions for installing it. You won't come back to the Install Wizard when you get done. However, you might want to open the Add/Remove Programs Properties dialog again to make sure the application name appears in the list of products you can remove. Figure 12.4 shows a typical entry.

Figure 12.4.
The Install/Uninstall page containing an entry from an installed application.

Uninstalling an application is just as easy as, if not easier than, installing it using the Install Wizard. The following procedure shows you the steps you'll follow in most cases. Remember that you also have the option of using the application's uninstall utility to get this done. Of course, the trade-off is that the application might not remove all the registry entries that Windows 95 made when you installed it.

1. Open Control Panel using the Start menu or Explorer.
2. Double-click on Add/Remove Programs. You should see a dialog like the one shown in Figure 12.1.
3. Select the application you want to uninstall and click on Remove. The Install Wizard will ask if you want to remove the application, as shown in Figure 12.5.

Figure 12.5.
Windows 95 always asks permission before it removes an application.

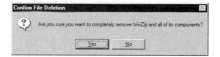

4. Click on Yes. The Install Wizard usually displays a list of everything it will remove, as shown in Figure 12.6. Notice that this list includes items such as .INI files.
5. Click on Yes. Just to make sure you really want to remove the application, Windows 95 displays yet another screen asking if you're sure. This might seem a bit extreme until you consider how many people remove applications from their machines by mistake and regret it later.

Figure 12.6.
You always get to see which
files Windows 95 will
remove before it actually
does so.

6. Click on Yes one last time. Windows 95 will attempt to remove all the application components. If it's successful, it will display a success message. Otherwise, it will display the dialog
shown in Figure 12.7. You can use the contents of this dialog to complete the uninstall
process.

Figure 12.7.
The Install Wizard displays
an error dialog if it can't
complete the uninstall.

7. Click on OK to exit the Install Wizard.

Optimizing Windows Applications

Once you get a new application installed, you need to optimize it for your use. Notice I said "for your
use." The difference between an optimized and an exploited application is simple: The optimized
application might run fast, but the exploited application is more efficient. Windows applications
provide a wealth of settings that allow you to tune the way they work. Not only do these tuning
steps affect the application's speed and memory requirements, but they also affect the user interface.
We'll look at both elements in the following sections since they're both important for fully exploiting
your applications. Make sure you read the entire section before you start tuning your applications.
Some elements are a trade-off: You need to select one over the other. I'll cover the most common
ones, but you might need to make some decisions based on your application's specific setup.

Installation Options

Installing your new application is a very important part of the tuning process. The decisions you
make here will affect the way you view the application in the future, as well as determine how the
application performs. The following list should help you make some of the hard decisions that will
come up during installation.

- Hard disk space: If hard disk space is at a premium, you might need to limit the number of
installation features you provide. For example, very few applications come without a fully
functional tutorial now. Generally, the tutorial makes use of the multimedia features

Windows provides to reduce the time it takes to learn the product. However, all these features come at a price. Learning to use the product from the manual might not seem as efficient as using the interactive tutorial—in fact, I'll tell you right out that it isn't—but the disk space you save could make room for another option you'll use long after the need for the tutorial is gone. Theoretically you could install the tutorial and remove it later, but some people invariably forget to do this, and the result is permanent loss of disk space. If you install the tutorial, make sure you remove it once it's no longer needed.

- Uninstall capability: You'll find that a lot of applications now provide an uninstall capability. More than that, they provide a feature-dependent capability. What you do is select which features you want to install by checking them off on a menu. Changing the checkbox selections will install or uninstall that particular feature. Not every application provides this feature, but you can make good use of it with the ones that do. Even if your application provides only a stock uninstall capability, you could install it fully once to learn how to use the product, uninstall it, and then install it partially a second time to get your running installation together.

- Memory: This particular selection applies to graphics programs, for the most part, since they're the biggest users of memory in this regard, but other applications are equally guilty. Have you ever noticed that some applications seem to gobble every spare bit of memory on your system? The problem might be your installation choices, not the way the application works. Graphics programs (and, to a smaller degree, other categories) often ask what types of filters and other "utility" elements you want to install. A graphics application might include a laundry list of application files that it will import from and export to. A database manager might include an autodial feature, and spreadsheets are rife with background problem solvers. It might seem like a good idea to select them all. After all, you might need them sometime. From a memory standpoint, this decision could be fatal. Some applications load all those fancy utilities and filters whenever you start them. Each filter and other add-on costs you memory you could use for some other purpose. If you need that product element, fine, but why pay for something you don't need? The bottom line is that you should install only the filters and utilities that you'll actually use later.

- Interapplication communication: I used to absolutely hate packaged applications. These suites of products normally contained things no one wanted—mini word processors with limited capabilities and a spreadsheet that could barely track your checkbook. Bundled applications suffer a lot less from this problem now and have improved in one other area as well. If you install a suite of products (such as Microsoft Office) instead of separate applications, there's a much better chance that they'll communicate seamlessly. I used to use products from different companies to get the very best that each category had to provide. With today's bloated applications, features are no longer a consideration for the most part. Unless there's a very good reason to do so, you'll probably want to go with a "one-stop shopping" solution to fulfill the better part of your application needs.

- Other support options: Some applications provide features that don't relate directly to how that product works, but how it reacts in a given situation. I just installed a new utility that gives me a thumbnail-sketch view of several files on my system. One of the installation options was to add that utility to my Startup folder. I had the memory required, so I said yes. It seems like a straightforward decision, but you still need to make it. Some of the other decisions aren't quite so straightforward. For example, one application provided the capability to track my OLE links across the network. To do this, it had to load a rather large piece of code and allow it to remain resident. Since I very seldom even think about using such a capability, I didn't install it. These other support decisions will affect the way you work, as well as the amount of memory the application uses.

 The installation process that used to seem so straightforward is no longer so simple. You need to make some hard decisions before you embark on the actual installation process. The tips I just mentioned will help you make these generic decisions, but you'll find others more difficult to resolve. For example, how do you balance workgroup and individual needs? For some products, such as Lotus Notes, this is a major concern. Using products such as these requires the administrator to make some decisions for the benefit of the group as a whole. Some users will definitely view the decisions as arbitrary and overly confining. When working with workgroup-specific applications, you'll probably need to consider some additional problems:

- Installation location: Deciding where to put a workgroup application is a major decision. Placing all the installation files on the network makes it a lot easier for the administrator to manage and maintain the application. It also reduces the chance that someone will attempt to pirate the application, since the network usually provides better security for the server than it does for the workstation. A server installation also makes it easier to add new users and reduces overall application size because not every workstation needs a copy of the common files, such as DLLs. The negative aspects of using a server installation are fairly substantial. The network will have to handle a lot more traffic as the application requests DLLs and other support files from the server. The users won't get as many configuration options as they would using a workstation installation in many cases.

- Gateway options: Many network-specific applications include gateway support. The decision of which gateways to support is fairly obvious unless your network is in a state of transition. If you're in a state of transition, it might be a good idea to wait and install the new application when the network is stable.

- Local support for network features: Many network products secretly invade the user's system and steal workstation statistics on a regular basis. This covert form of monitoring the user probably has its uses, and I don't mean to start spreading a "Big Brother" rumor. However, unless you're the sole administrator for a very large network, you have to weigh the importance of such a feature against the memory it will take from each workstation. Windows 95 is fairly memory-hungry to begin with. Adding a burden of unneeded drivers will only make things worse.

Now that we've looked at some of the things you need to consider when installing an application under Windows 95, the need to plan that installation becomes a lot clearer. Add to the installation problems the need to upgrade each user's machine and the cost of administrator time in doing so, and you'll begin to understand why some companies don't like software updates. Overall, a planned installation should provide you with a solid foundation on which to build your fully exploited application later.

Settings

Very few applications use the same settings. You'll find that applications of a particular kind (such as all word processors) might share a few of the same settings, but for the most part, you'll need to spend some time reading the user manual to figure them out. We won't discuss the actual process of changing your application's settings in this section; you'll need to read the vendor manuals later. We'll look at some general principles you can use to make life easier. These are areas you can start looking at for potential speed, memory, or efficiency gains.

Tip: Everyone's first inclination is to get into the application and complete this part of the setup immediately. That would probably be the worst mistake you could make. Software settings change as you learn how to use the application more efficiently. As your knowledge about the application increases, the feature that seemed important yesterday will appear almost foolish today. The settings I use for my applications are in an almost continuous state of flux. A little change here or a little tweak there can make a big difference in how well the application works for me. Take the time required to go through the tutorial first, and then make any setting changes you think will help. I usually keep Notepad handy to record any ideas I come up with while running the tutorial.

Changing your settings is largely a matter of personal preference. However, even a small change can make a big difference in the way you use an application. For example, you can do something as small as customize a toolbar and reap a fairly large increase in efficiency. Not using an application's autocorrect feature might allow you to run background tasks more efficiently. It's not the major changes you'll notice the most, but the little extras that you add to your computing environment. The following tips will help you get most of out of your applications.

- Toolbars: A toolbar represents one way you can greatly increase your efficiency for a very small increase in memory usage. Remember, every icon you allocate uses some additional system resources, so you'll want to maintain the minimum number required to get the job done. On the other hand, the amount of memory an icon uses is very small, usually less than 1 KB. When setting up my toolbar, I don't assume that the vendor provided something even close to optimal, so I try to track which commands I use the most. The commands that get used a lot should appear on the toolbar. It takes less time to access a command from the toolbar than it does from a menu, so placing common commands here is one way to improve your efficiency. Seven icons should appear on every toolbar: Open, Close, New, Print, Cut, Copy, and Paste. You might want to add Print Preview to this list as well. People who use OLE a lot might want to stick Paste Special here to make inserting objects faster. Be certain to remove any standard toolbar buttons that you don't use. For example, Microsoft Word usually adds links to Microsoft's other products to the toolbar. I usually remove these icons since I don't use the links in that way.

- Printer settings: Every application I own (with the exception of a few small utilities) allows me to set the printer configuration separately from the Windows general configuration. I usually set my printer configuration to match my use of that application. For example, I use my word processor for final output in most cases, so I use the best letter-quality resolution available. On the other hand, I never use one of my graphics programs for final output, so I select draft there. A draft printout might not seem very acceptable, and it isn't if you plan to send the document to someone, but it's a lot more efficient when you just want a quick look at your document. (A minor benefit of using draft output whenever possible is that you use less ink, making those expensive toner cartridges last longer.) You can also vary the print resolution. A low-resolution letter-quality printout might work fine for workgroup presentations, but you'll want to use the highest available quality when making the same presentation to a larger audience. The resolution you use will affect the amount of memory and time required to complete the printout.

- Macros: The first thing you need to know is what a macro is. I always look at a macro as "canned keystrokes." Think about the steps you take to create a letter. Every time you do so, you probably add a heading with the company name and other information. Wouldn't it be nice if you could tell the program to do this for you automatically? That's what a macro does. It replays the keystrokes you would normally make manually by recording them in a separate area of memory. A macro recorder works just like a tape recorder. It records your keystrokes and allows you to play them back later.

Macros are one area where you might find it difficult to come up with a concrete rule for settings. I almost always create macros for every repetitive task I perform with my main applications. The investment in time required to create the macro always gets paid back in improved efficiency. Let me quickly define two terms. If I perform a task manually nearly every time I use the application, that's repetitive. I really don't need to perform that task if the computer can do it equally well and in a lot less time. A main application is one that I use at least eight hours a week. Any shorter time than that, and you have to wonder when you'd have time to use the macro. Some tasks work better as macros. For example, I always set my word processing files up using one. It makes more sense for the computer to do the work than for me to do it. In fact, I use this macro so often that I attached it to my toolbar as an icon. This is another decision you'll need to make. Attaching a macro to a toolbar button is always a good idea if you use it a lot. Other tasks don't work well as macros. For example, I always thought that changing the format of a document from one form to another would make a great macro, but implementing it proved frustrating. It takes a human mind to perform some tasks.

Note: Windows 3.x provided a macro recorder that allowed you to record various Windows-related tasks and replay them later. The problem was that the macro recorder's implementation was flawed, and people complained about it. Many bugs in the macro recorder caused GPFs. It was also a little on the limited side as far as capabilities were concerned. Instead of fixing the problem, Microsoft decided to eliminate it. A macro recorder isn't provided with Windows 95.

- Stylesheets and templates: One thing you can never have too many of are custom stylesheets and templates. I always use a stylesheet for my documents if the application supports them. The reason is simple: A stylesheet doesn't take more than a few minutes to create, but it can save a lot of time later. Templates are the same. They take only a short time to create, but they will definitely reduce the time it takes to create useful output later. Templates and stylesheets also provide one other benefit: They tend to enforce uniformity in the format of your document. This is important whether you're part of a group or working as an individual. I view consistent output as one of the marks of a professional, and most other people do, too. In addition, if you spend less time worrying about how to format your document, you'll have a lot more time to work on its contents.

- Autocorrect: The autocorrect feature provided by many applications is a source of much consternation for me. On the one hand, they provide a valuable aid: autocorrecting misspelled words or other types of user input. The problem is that most of them chew up valuable memory and processor cycles—resources you could use to run a task in the background. I normally turn my autocorrect features off and rely on my spelling checker (or other tools) to find all those mistakes at one time. Whether this approach is efficient for you or not is a personal decision based on how you work.

Tip: There is an another way to use autocorrect. You can use it to substitute short phrases for long ones. For example, suppose you have to type your company name a lot—Jackson Consolidated Freight Company. You could add an acronym such as JCFC to your autocorrect dictionary. Then, every time you needed to type your company name, you could type JCFC, and your application would substitute the long name in its place.

- Autoload: This goes back to those utility and filter programs I mentioned in the "Installation Options" section. Some programs, such as Microsoft Access and Lotus 1-2-3, let you autoload some of your utilities or filters. This allows you to access them faster. There's a trade-off for the convenience of instant access, however: You have to give up some memory and perhaps a few processor cycles to do it. The middle ground is to autoload the features you know you'll use every time. It takes only a few seconds to load the other features, so you'll want to do that manually in most cases.

Peter's Principle: My Settings Won't Work on Your Machine

We're all individuals. Nowhere is this more apparent than in the way we use software. I might think the way you do something is absurd, but if it works for you, it's probably the right way to go (at least until you learn better).

There are some constants in the world of applications, and there's a wealth of tip and technique books to prove it. You can probably buy any number of tip and technique books that will help you get your application set up in a very short time with a minimum of effort. On the other hand, you need to make just as many, if not more, personal decisions. For example, I usually include the Insert Annotation command for Word for Windows on my toolbar because I use this feature a lot. I suggested the same thing to a colleague and he found it a waste of time, because he used a different technique for making annotations.

I find that the same thing holds true for just about every type of user setting, but that you might have to give up some autonomy in workgroup situations. For example, I usually use three different user dictionaries: common, computer, and jargon. This allows me to keep some words separate so that they don't contaminate my general-purpose dictionary. In a workgroup situation, you might find that everyone needs to use the same dictionary to ensure consistent results for a project. The same thing holds true for other user settings such as templates and stylesheets. A group project usually requires the individual to defer to the group's needs to enforce a certain level of consistency.

The point is that you need to work with an application long enough to build a rapport with it. Once you figure out how you want to work with the application, you can start changing some of those personal settings to meet your specific requirements. In fact, you might find that some of your settings end up working for the group as well. Experimentation is a prime ingredient in finding the settings that work best for you.

Setting up an application is a continual process. Exploiting your software is often as much a matter of using the software in the best way you know how as it is a matter of optimizing memory and speed settings. Don't give up too much personal comfort for a perceived memory or speed benefit. You have to weigh the time a specific feature will save against what it will cost. That's what you do in other business decisions; evaluating your software is no different.

Running 16-Bit Windows Applications

In Chapter 6, we looked at how 16-bit applications run. That should clue you in to some of the problems you'll encounter running them. The fact that all 16-bit applications share one address space is part of the problem. This means they have to share the system resources required to display windows, icons, and graphic elements of all sorts. A 16-bit application also faces other problems, such as cooperative multitasking, which we talked about earlier. That particular problem only gets worse under Windows 95, because 32-bit applications run in their own session.

> **Tip:** Some older Windows applications display an invalid dynalink call error message when you try to run them. This means that they're incompatible with a new Windows 95 version of a DLL. You have two choices. Upgrading the application is the best alternative, because you'll replace that old product with something that will work better with Windows 95— hopefully a 32-bit version of what you used in the past. If upgrading isn't an option, reinstall the application, reboot Windows 95, and try it again. You have to reboot in order to reload the DLL into memory. Otherwise, you'll see the same error message, because the Windows 95 version is still in place. If you still get an invalid dynalink call message, there's some incompatibility between the application and a basic Windows 95 system file. You absolutely must upgrade in this case, because you can't replace those common files to meet the needs of one program. One or more Windows 95 applications might cease to function if you do (including the operating system itself). Windows 95 always maintains a copy of its system files in the SYSBCKUP folder under the main Windows folder. You can use this copy of the file to replace the old DLL if necessary.

The same types of optimization techniques you used under Windows 3.x will probably work here as well. You'll still need to keep the cooperative multitasking aspect of 16-bit applications in mind when running certain types of applications in the background. For example, you'll probably find it difficult to run your 16-bit database and your communication program at the same time at high speed. The cooperative nature of these applications means that the database will probably take control of the system for that one second longer than the communication program can hold data in the buffer. The result is lost data. Windows 95 is a lot better in this regard than Window 3.x was, but it still isn't perfect because the applications it runs aren't perfect.

Chapter 3 looked at many ways you can tune the Windows environment by getting rid of excess icons and the like. These same tips apply to applications for the most part. Make sure you spend some time reviewing that chapter for some additional hints.

Tip: Some 16-bit applications give you a choice between storing DLL files locally or in the Windows SYSTEM directory. Choose the local option to make it easier to remove the application later. This also reduces the chance that the application's setup routine will accidentally overwrite a Windows 95 version of a file.

You should ignore a few of those old Windows 3.x optimization techniques when using Windows 95. The one I tell most people about is the use of virtual memory. If your system contained enough memory under Windows 3.x, you could get a performance boost by disabling virtual memory. Of course, this meant that you were effectively limited in the amount of system memory you could expect, but the performance gain was worth it. Don't disable virtual memory under Windows 95.

Using the Print Manager was something else a lot of people avoided when they needed to get their output fast. Windows 95 uses a much improved form of Print Manager that you'll want to use for optimum performance. I'll stop short of saying that the output will arrive at the same speed, though. If you have a heavy system load when you start the print job, you'll definitely see a decrease in print speed. However, you gain increased system performance and regain control of your application faster as a result. It's another trade-off, but I think it's a good one in this case.

Running 32-Bit Windows Applications

I tested a lot of 32-bit applications and found a few interesting facts. Overall, a 32-bit application is larger and just a tad slower (when you view a single section of code) than its 16-bit counterpart. It's larger because you're using 32 bits for everything, even structures that might not require 32 bits. In addition, 32-bit code is typically larger than its 16-bit counterpart. Does this mean that 32-bit applications are memory hogs that you shouldn't use? Not by a long shot.

Let me explain the slower part of 32-bit application performance a little better. A 32-bit application starts out a tad slower than its 16-bit equivalent but ends up faster for a number of reasons. Most of these have to do with the use of a flat address space and other architectural benefits of using a 32-bit format. Yes, it takes more time to process 32-bit code than the equivalent sections of 16-bit code because the 32-bit code is larger. However, there's still a big speed benefit in the long run because of the way a 32-bit application executes.

There are definite benefits in the way of speed when it comes to running a 32-bit application. For one thing, it supports true multitasking. I found that background repagination in the 16-bit version of Word usually meant that I had to wait until the application finished the task anyway. Under the 32-bit version, Word spawns a task that really does run in the background. I very seldom even notice that anything is going on anymore; the document just gets repaginated without my thinking about it. This is how multitasking should work from a user perspective.

Multitasking also helps you perform some tasks, such as printing, a lot faster than you could using a 16-bit application. For one thing, Windows can make better use of idle time with a 32-bit application. But this isn't the big feature that users will notice. You'll notice that you regain control of the system faster. After a 32-bit application spawns a print task, it can return control of the computer immediately. It doesn't even need to slow you down as it checks on the status of the "background" print job like a 16-bit application does.

Warning: Every time a 32-bit application spawns a new task (called a *thread*), it uses some system resources. Some applications can create so many threads that your system begins to slow to a crawl and Windows runs out of resources. The second you run completely out of resources, the machine usually freezes. Although Microsoft did increase the size of some memory areas and move others to the 32-bit area, Windows 95 still isn't perfect when it comes to managing 32-bit resources. The best thing to do is to avoid the situation altogether. Don't try to run every feature that a 32-bit application can provide at one time. Limit the number of tasks you ask an application to perform in the background to a reasonable level. Finally, run the resource monitor from time to time just to see how you're doing on system resources. You might find you need to adjust some of your techniques to compensate for limitations in the Windows 95 design.

The big performance tuning tip for Windows 95 and 32-bit applications is to use as many automatic settings as possible. The more room you give Windows 95 to compensate for changing system conditions, the better. Chapter 3 contained quite a few tips you could follow to optimize the environment. For example, we looked at the need to monitor the swap file size to ensure that you don't end up wasting processor cycles in thrashing. Once you optimize the environment for a 32-bit application, you have essentially optimized the application itself. All you need to do is check out the earlier section called "Settings" to make the application as efficient as possible during use.

Optimizing DOS Applications

It'll be a long time before we see the demise of all DOS applications. It's true that very few commercial application vendors are updating their products anymore, but that isn't the total picture. There's more to the DOS scene than just commercial applications.

One of the biggest areas where DOS will remain king for the foreseeable future is games. Why are games such a hot DOS item? Because the DOS environment gives the programmer access to more of the hardware and allows him to write a fast and visually stimulating program. Windows is notorious for grabbing too many system resources and running games at almost a snail's pace when compared to a DOS version of the same program. Microsoft is working on several strategies, including WinG, that will make Windows more attractive to game vendors, but they aren't there yet. I can usually find Windows versions of many games if I look hard enough, but the DOS versions are still selling like hotcakes, and I don't see this changing any time soon. Even if this were to change tomorrow, though, it's unlikely that users will give up their old games immediately. Some games have an amazing shelf life when you consider the technology they use. For example, I still know people who like to play the original ZORK series—a text-based DOS game with a great plot but no graphics at all.

Custom applications are another area where people are still using DOS. This time it's for a different reason. A custom application can cost thousands of dollars. The consultant who writes the program has to charge that much because the chances of his selling more than a few hundred copies are slim at best. Since custom applications usually manipulate very sensitive company data that's hard to move to another application, people are going to think twice before attempting to move that data somewhere else. Fortunately, I see this particular class of DOS application coming to an end as Windows tools become easier and faster to use. A consultant can be a lot more productive now, so the cost is less for creating a new application in some cases.

Also, old habits die hard. Some people are used to using DOS utility programs, so that's what they'll continue to use. There are perfectly acceptable substitutes for these applications in most cases— substitutes that are easier to use and that actually run faster—but some people just won't use them. This is the third group of people who will make at least some use of DOS under Windows 95.

We'll explore a variety of DOS options in the following sections. In most cases, I'll show you the best methods first and later add a few marginal methods you can use in a pinch. Of course, my advice is to move to a 32-bit Windows 95 or Windows NT application as soon as possible. DOS isn't dead, strictly speaking, but it does have one foot in the grave. Very few application vendors even support DOS anymore. It won't be long before other vendors follow as well. You'll end up with a hard disk full of old applications that no one will support.

MS-DOS 7.0 Emulation

You use MS-DOS under Windows 95 through the MS-DOS 7.0 emulation mode. What actually happens is Windows makes a copy of the phantom DOS session stored in memory, spawns a new V86 session, and places the copy it made in the new session. What you see is either a windowed or full-screen DOS session. All you need to do to open a DOS session is select MS-DOS Prompt from the Start | Programs menu option. You will also start a DOS session whenever you select a DOS application from either Explorer or the Start menu. Figure 12.8 shows a windowed session.

It isn't too difficult to see that this DOS window doesn't even come close to matching what you used in the past. Windows 95 provides about the same features, but it makes the window a lot easier to use and configure. All the controls you need immediately get displayed as part of a toolbar on the window. There are also many hidden configuration options, which we'll discuss later. Here is the list of new controls:

Figure 12.8.

The DOS window under Windows 95 sports a few new features.

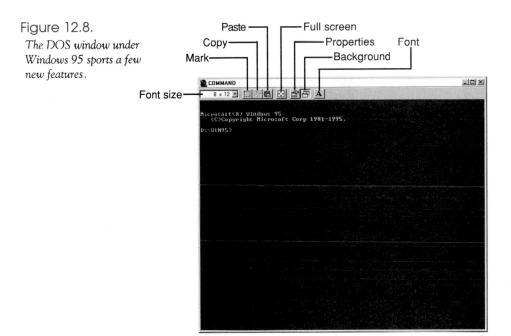

- **Font size:** This list box allows you to choose the size of font used to display information in the DOS window. It defines the number of horizontal and vertical pixels used for each character. You need to find a balance between readability and the ability to view the entire screen at once. I usually use the font size shown in Figure 12.8 because it offers the best of both worlds. Of course, the font size you choose is partially determined by the resolution of your display. A DOS window normally defaults to the Auto setting. What this means is that Windows 95 will attempt to find the proper font size based on the number of lines of text in the DOS box and the resolution of your display. For example, if you choose an 80-character × 25-line display mode and your screen provides 640 × 480 resolution, Windows 95 will select the font nearest to 8 × 19.2 pixels. To get these numbers, I divided the horizontal resolution by the number of characters (640 / 80) and the vertical resolution by the number of lines (480 / 25). In this case, Windows 95 would probably default to the 8 × 16 font listed in the Font size listbox. I usually find that the Windows 95 setting makes maximum use of the display but isn't usually the best setting for my needs. Optimizing the setting to meet your particular needs is the best way to go.

- **Mark:** Use this control to select an area of the screen for copying. Windows 95 will place the selected area on the Clipboard when you select the Copy command so that you can use it in other applications. The selected area is highlighted, as shown in Figure 12.9. You may use either the cursor keys or the mouse to select the desired area.

Figure 12.9.

You can use the Mark button to copy part of the DOS screen to the Windows Clipboard.

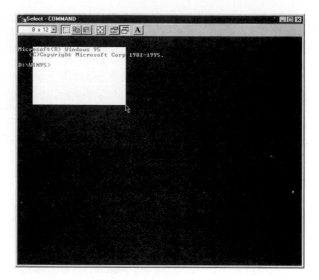

- Copy: The Copy button places the area you highlighted using the Mark button on the Clipboard.

- Paste: You can also paste information from a Windows application into the DOS box. Obviously you can't paste anything other than text unless the display is in graphics mode. Even then, your ability might be limited by the DOS application running at the time.

- Full screen: Clicking on this button will change the windowed DOS prompt into a full-screen version.

- Properties: Every DOS application has a number of properties you can set (we'll discuss these later in this chapter). Clicking on this button displays the Properties dialog for the current application.

- Background: Click on this button to run the current DOS application in the background. This comes in handy for situations in which you want to monitor the application but don't really need to interact with it.

- Font: This button performs about the same task as the font size listbox I mentioned earlier. However, instead of merely displaying a list of font sizes, it displays the Font page of the program's Properties dialog.

Once you get past the fancy new display, you'll see that DOS is unchanged. It doesn't really provide anything more than you had in the past. One feature it does provide is long filename support. Use the DIR command if you want to see what I mean. Figure 12.10 shows the results of using it to display all the .BMP files in the \WIN95 directory.

Figure 12.10.
DOS reacts differently when
you use the DIR command
under Windows 95.

Note: Long filename support is available only under Windows 95. Once you leave that environment to work in MS-DOS mode, the DIR command operates exactly as it did before. The MS-DOS mode of operation is also known as raw DOS mode. None of the Windows 95 drivers are loaded when you use this mode, including long filename support. Obviously, you must be very careful about corrupting your long filenames when in this mode.

Tip: You can also use long filenames when typing commands. The only requirement is that you use quotes to enclose the long filename or directory, like this: DIR "Some Long Directory Name".

Besides long filename support, there are a few new utility programs and changes to some old utilities. For example, you no longer need to run a copy of QBasic to use Edit. In addition, Edit now provides the capability to modify more than one file at once. We'll cover the specific changes in DOS utility support in the next section.

DOS Versus Windows 95 Commands

Microsoft must have expected people to use the DOS prompt for a while longer, or they wouldn't have improved some of the utilities that come with Windows 95. We looked at one of those utilities earlier, so I won't describe it here again. The START utility (described in the "Undocumented

Parameters" section of Chapter 5) is one new feature most people will really like. It allows you to start a Windows application from a full-screen DOS session. We really don't have room here to explore all the DOS commands, so I'm going to give you the highlights. The following list shows the changes that DOS 7.0 (running under Windows 95) provides.

- All the disk-scanning utilities from previous versions of DOS are upgraded to support long filenames. Windows 95 also replaces many of these files with batch file substitutes if you decide to maintain a dual boot capability. The renamed files include DBLSPACE.BAT, DRVSPACE.BAT, DEFRAG.BAT, and SCANDISK.BAT on my machine.

- EDIT is a stand-alone command now. It also provides the means for editing more than one file.

- Some applications, such as ScanDisk, start the Windows version of the program even when executed at the DOS prompt. There's no longer a true DOS version of the program.

 - Windows 95 includes a new NET command. You can use it to determine a wealth of information about your network from the DOS prompt. For example, typing NET VIEW will display a list of computers and other resources currently available on the network. To learn more about this command, type NET? at the DOS prompt.

Along with the new features that DOS 7.0 provides, there are a few features that you won't find. For example, DOS 7.0 doesn't include any of the following commands (although you can use them in raw DOS mode if your old DOS directory is still available):

APPEND	INTERLINK	RAMDRIVE.SYS
ASSIGN	INTERSVR	RECOVER
BACKUP	JOIN	REPLACE
COMP	MEMCARD	RESTORE
DOSSHELL	MEMMAKER	ROMDRIVE.SYS
EDLIN	MIRROR	SHARE
EGA.SYS	MSAV	SMARTMON
FASTHELP	MSBACKUP	TREE
FASTOPEN	POWER	UNDELETE
GRAFTABL	PRINT	UNFORMAT
GRAPHICS	PRINTER.SYS	VSAFE
HELP	QBASIC	

Microsoft's reason for removing the majority of these commands is that they aren't compatible with long filenames. Other programs were removed because Windows 95 supposedly makes them obsolete. I still would have liked to see Microsoft retain some of the commands. For example, an enhanced version of MEMMAKER could help a user tune a setup for an MS-DOS session. Needless to say, some users will be very unhappy about the absence of these commands and utilities.

Creating a DOS Session

You can create a DOS session using a variety of methods. Double-clicking on a DOS application from inside Explorer creates a DOS session. The session ends as soon as you end the application.

Like previous versions of Windows, Windows 95 includes a DOS prompt. All you need to do is click on the MS-DOS Prompt option found in the Programs section of the Start menu. You'll need to type exit and press Enter to end this session.

Another way to start a DOS session is to select the Restart the Computer in MS-DOS Mode entry of the Shutdown dialog. This will take you to a full-screen raw DOS session. You can perform any required tasks and then type exit and press Enter to leave. Windows 95 will automatically reload itself.

DOS Objects

As with any other object under Windows 95, right-clicking on a DOS object displays a context menu like the one shown in Figure 12.11. You can cut, copy, and paste a DOS object like any other object that Windows 95 supports. The Properties option will take you to the Properties dialog, described in the next section. This is one major area where DOS applications are treated differently than Windows applications.

Figure 12.11.
A DOS object's context menu looks much like any other context menu under Windows 95.

Settings

A DOS application's Properties dialog contains a lot more than the same dialog for a Windows application does. In fact, if you were looking for the PIF (program information file) editor, here it is. The Properties dialog shown in Figure 12.12 allows you to change every setting that the PIF editor provided and more. In fact, Windows 95 provides several new features for DOS applications that make running them a snap. The following paragraphs describe each section of the Properties dialog in detail.

Tip: Editing the Properties dialog will not perform some mysterious trick with your DOS application. It saves the settings in a PIF file just like it used to under Windows 3.x. In fact,

Windows 3.x PIF files work just fine under Windows 95. However, you won't want to try to move the PIF files the other way. Windows 95 adds a lot of information to the PIF file, making it incompatible with older versions of Windows.

Figure 12.12.
The Properties dialog replaces the old PIF editor that you used under Windows 3.x.

Program

The Program page (see Figure 12.12) allows you to change the way Windows executes the program. At the very top of the page you'll see an icon and a field containing the application's name. This is the name you will see within Explorer.

The next three fields determine what application to run. The Cmd line field contains the name of the application you want to run. It must end with an .EXE, .COM, or .BAT extension. In this case, we're running a copy of the command processor. The Working field tells Windows 95 what directory to start the application from. In most cases, you'll start the application from either its home or its data directory. The choice depends on what kind of information the application requires to start. We'll run the command processor from the \WIN95 directory. The third field, Batch file, is new to Windows 95. It allows you to designate a batch file that runs with the application. For example, in the case of the command processor, you could include a batch file that would set up the path and prompt and load any TSRs you might need.

The Shortcut key field allows you to assign a shortcut key to the program. We covered this in Chapter 5, so I won't cover it again here.

Use the Run field to determine how Windows 95 runs the application. There are three choices: Normal window, Minimized, and Maximized. The first two choices affect both windowed and full-screen sessions. The third choice starts windowed sessions maximized.

It's normally a good idea to close the DOS session as soon as you get done. Checking the Close on exit field does just that.

Clicking on the Change Icon pushbutton displays the dialog shown in Figure 12.13. It allows you to select the icon used to identify the application within Explorer and the Start menu. Windows 95 provides the same default choices as other versions of Windows. You can also choose from custom icon sets by clicking on the Browse pushbutton.

Figure 12.13.
This dialog allows you to change the icon used to identify the DOS application.

MS-DOS Mode

There's one more pushbutton left on the Program page, and I wanted to give it special attention. If you click on the Advanced pushbutton, you'll see the dialog shown in Figure 12.14.

Figure 12.14.
The Advanced Program Settings dialog is where you make the selections that enable MS-DOS mode for an application.

The first three checkboxes in this dialog control the actual implementation of MS-DOS mode. Some applications will run fine under Windows, but they look for specific Windows files when you run them. If they see Windows 95, they will quit. Checking the first checkbox will prevent the application from detecting Windows 95 in most cases. The problem with using this particular feature is that less conventional memory will be available to the application, and it will run slower as Windows works to keep itself hidden.

The second checkbox in this group keeps a detection program running with the DOS application. You can use this as a diagnostic aid when the application won't run properly under Windows 95. However, keeping this box checked after you're reasonably sure that the application doesn't require MS-DOS mode only wastes processor cycles and memory. Unfortunately, Windows 95 automatically defaults to checking this box. This means that you'll have to remember to uncheck it to gain optimum performance from your application.

The MS-DOS mode checkbox is the third one in this dialog. Checking it means that the application won't run under Windows 95. It also changes the options you have available, as shown in Figure 12.15. If you double-click on an application to start it, Windows 95 will shut down all running applications, shut itself down and unload from memory, and execute the application. You use this option as a last-ditch effort to get an application to run under Windows 95. Unfortunately, many game programs fall into this category.

Figure 12.15.
Checking the MS-DOS mode box makes some new options available but disables others.

I recommend that you always have Windows 95 warn you about entering MS-DOS mode by checking the first new checkbox in this dialog, Warn before entering MS-DOS mode. This will prevent you from entering the mode accidentally. It could prevent data loss in some rare cases where an application doesn't react properly to the Windows shutdown message.

Windows 95 usually provides default CONFIG.SYS and AUTOEXEC.BAT files for your application. I recommend against using them for one very good reason: The whole purpose of MS-DOS mode is to get your application to run. Using a set of configuration files specifically designed for it is a good first step in ensuring that not only do you get the application to run, but to run efficiently. I usually check the second radio button to enable the configuration entries, as shown in Figure 12.16.

Figure 12.16.
Always use custom configuration files if your application requires MS-DOS mode to run.

There are a number of ways to create a configuration for your application. You can even use the automated configuration method Microsoft provides using the Configuration button. However, I usually copy the appropriate sections of the CONFIG.DOS and AUTOEXEC.DOS files to these screens. (You can perform the paste by using Ctrl-V since Microsoft didn't add a Paste button to this dialog.) These files contain the old configuration that did run the application. I usually modify the entries as appropriate for this particular situation, but you won't need to do too much tuning.

As you can see, setting up an application for MS-DOS mode doesn't have to be difficult. It is very inconvenient, though, because you can't run any other applications while an MS-DOS mode application runs. Your hard drive (and associated long filenames) are also susceptible to damage from an MS-DOS mode application. You'll want to make certain that the application is relatively well behaved in regard to writing to disk before you trust it with your setup.

Font

The Font page, shown in Figure 12.17, allows you to change the appearance of the fonts used to display data in a windowed DOS application. These settings don't affect a full-screen session.

Figure 12.17.
The Font page allows you to control the way a DOS application is displayed in windowed mode.

This dialog contains four main sections. The first section controls the type of fonts you get to see in the Font size listbox. You'll normally want to use the fullest set of fonts available by selecting Both font types. The only time you might want to switch to one font type or another is if your display has problems displaying one type of font.

The second section contains the Font size listbox. It contains a list of the font sizes you have available for the DOS window. The numbers represent the number of pixels used for each character. A higher number of pixels makes the display more legible. A smaller number of pixels makes the window smaller.

The Window preview section of this dialog shows you how big the window will appear on the display. The Font preview section shows you the size of the print. You should combine the output from these two displays to determine how large a font to use. It's important to reach a setting that balances the need to see what you're doing with the need to display the entire DOS box at once.

Memory

The Memory page, shown in Figure 12.18, is the most important page in the Properties dialog from a tuning perspective. Notice that there are only five listboxes and two checkboxes, but the decisions you make here will affect how the application runs. More importantly, they will affect the way Windows runs. We discussed many of the effects this particular page has on Windows in Chapter 3, so I won't go into them here.

Figure 12.18.
The Memory page allows you to modify the way Windows allocates and manages memory for your DOS application.

 Tip: In most cases, you'll want to keep all the listboxes set to Auto and both checkboxes unmarked on the Memory page. Windows normally performs better if you allow it to manage memory. The default settings might include checking the Protected checkbox. Unchecking this box will result in better application performance.

The first group of settings affects your conventional memory. The Total field allows you to select any value up to 640 KB. You absolutely won't get more than 615 KB of conventional memory, so don't try to set the conventional memory any higher than that. Windows normally allocates a 1,024-byte environment for your DOS application. This is enough to handle most situations. However, I usually set mine to 4,096 to provide space for all those environment strings required by real-mode compilers. The Protected checkbox is another diagnostic aid. Checking it tells Windows 95 to monitor the application for memory protection errors. The only problem is that you'll suffer a performance loss when using it. If your application tends to corrupt memory, then by all means check this box to keep your environment stable. Otherwise, consider leaving it unchecked for better performance.

The second group of settings contains a single listbox that controls how much expanded memory Windows 95 allocates for your application. If you leave it on Auto, MEM will report expanded memory up to the amount of memory your machine has installed. Windows 95 will make only 16 MB of it usable if you have more RAM than that installed. The only time you should change this setting is if the application grabs every bit of expanded memory it can find. Some older DOS applications get a little greedy, so you need to provide some controls for that greed.

The third group of settings controls the amount of extended memory available to your application. The default setting allocates the full amount of RAM installed on your system. This isn't an unlimited amount of memory, but it could be fairly high—much higher than the automatic expanded memory setting. As with the expanded memory setting, I usually change this setting from Auto to some specific number if the application gets greedy or if it has problems coping with the full amount of extended memory available on my machine. I usually leave the Uses HMA checkbox blank because I normally load DOS in the high memory area. However, if you don't use the HMA, you can always choose to load all or part of an application there by checking this box.

The final group of settings allows you to determine the amount of DPMI memory available to applications. Windows 95 normally sets this to a value that reflects the current system conditions. There's little reason to change this setting from the default.

Screen

This page, shown in Figure 12.19, allows you to configure the screen settings. The first group of settings, Usage, determines the screen mode and number of display lines. You should set the number of display lines here before you set the options on the Font page of this dialog box. Otherwise, a setting that worked well at 25 lines might not work at 50.

Figure 12.19.
The Screen page allows you to adjust the size and type of display, as well as the method Windows uses to display it.

The second group of settings lets you change the window settings. It doesn't come into play if you use full-screen mode. I always set the toolbar on. This is the toolbar I described earlier in this section. It allows you to modify the font size and perform many other tasks with your application without opening the Properties dialog. The second checkbox tells Windows 95 to update the PIF to reflect any changes you made while using the toolbar. Normally the entries are good only for that session. I prefer that Windows remember my settings from session to session, so I check this box.

The third group of settings on this page affects your application's performance. I was a little surprised that this is the only section Microsoft chose to label as Performance, considering the number of other settings that affect the way your application will run. The first setting, Fast ROM emulation, acts just like shadow RAM. It allows your application to use a RAM version of your display ROM. If an application had trouble with shadow RAM under DOS, it will also have trouble with this setting. Otherwise, you will want to leave this checked to get maximum performance from your application.

The second setting in the Performance group helps Windows more than it helps the application. This setting allows Windows to retrieve some of the memory that the DOS application uses for graphics mode when it goes into character mode. This modicum of memory isn't much, but it could add up if you were running a lot of DOS sessions. As with so many other settings, giving Windows the flexibility it needs to fully control the memory on your system is usually a good idea. The only time you'd want to remove the checkmark from this setting is if your application spends all or most of its time in graphics mode.

Misc

The Misc (miscellaneous) page mainly provides settings that determine how Windows interacts with your application from a functional point of view. Figure 12.20 shows the settings you'll find here.

Figure 12.20.
The Misc page allows you to control a variety of settings that don't fit into the other categories we explored.

The Allow screen saver setting doesn't really have much of an effect when you're using windowed applications. It determines whether Windows can interrupt a full-screen session to run a screen saver. Some full-screen applications really get confused if you allow the screen saver to operate. This is especially true of graphics applications and those that use RAM fonts. (A RAM font provides the checkbox and radio button controls that you see in some character-mode applications.)

The Mouse group contains two settings. The QuickEdit checkbox allows you to use a mouse within a DOS window, just like you would with any Windows application. This means you can select, copy, and paste with a lot less trouble than you could before. The Exclusive mode checkbox gives a windowed application exclusive control over the mouse. The consequences of doing this on a permanent basis are pretty severe. This means that you can't use the mouse with your regular Windows applications as long as this application is active. It would probably be a better idea to run this application in a full-screen session if it has this much trouble sharing the mouse.

Some of the settings on this page can provide subtle performance control over your application. The Background and Idle sensitivity controls fall into this category. Checking the Always suspend checkbox does more than suspend the application when it's in the background. It frees resources for Windows 95 to use with other applications. If you're using a DOS application for data entry or some other task that requires continuous input, it pays to check this box and use those resources for other applications. The Idle sensitivity setting also controls how Windows allocates resources. Normally Windows tracks the amount of activity from an application. If it determines that the application is sitting there doing nothing while waiting for input from you, Windows 95 will reduce its CPU resources. This is fine in most cases, but sometimes Windows doesn't give the application enough resources to complete the task it's performing. If this is the case, lowering the Idle sensitivity setting will give the application the resources it needs at the expense of other applications that are running on the system at the time.

The Warn if still active checkbox in the Termination group displays a message if you try to terminate the DOS application window without ending the program first. Normally you'll want to keep this checked to prevent potential data loss from a premature application termination.

Another performance enhancement, albeit a small one, is the Fast pasting checkbox. You should normally keep this box checked so that Windows can use a high-speed method of pasting information into your DOS application. The only time you should change this is if data gets damaged during transition when you're using the fast paste mode.

The final group on our page controls the use of control key combinations under Windows 95. Checking a box in the Windows shortcut keys group allows Windows to use that key combination. Unchecking it allows the application to use the key combination. Obviously you'll want to keep as many key combinations checked as possible. The only time you really need to change these settings is if the application needs them for some purpose and you can't change the application's settings.

On Your Own

Find a DLL for one of the smaller applications installed on your machine. Use the procedure in Chapter 6 for viewing the contents of files to determine which DLLs and other system files this application needs in order to work. Once you make up the list, see if other applications require the same files. You might be surprised by what you find. Windows 95 reuses a lot of the same files.

Use the procedures outlined in this chapter to create an MS-DOS mode session for one of your ill-behaved applications. Does the application run any better in MS-DOS mode? Try this with an application that seems to work fine under Windows 95. Does the application run any faster in MS-DOS mode than it does under Windows 95? Can you see any difference in the way it runs?

13

Exploiting Your Hardware

In Chapter 12 we looked at some of the things you could do to exploit your software. Getting the most out of your software is really only part of the process, however. You have a large investment in hardware as well, so it pays to get the most you can out of it. A combination of optimum hardware and software usage will enable you to get your work done quickly, yet use the least number of resources. We'll use the same criteria in this chapter that we did in the preceding one to define exploiting your hardware. In short, this chapter will provide the information you need to get the job done fast and with few resources, without sacrificing any quality.

One of the problems with trying to come up with a set of definitive hardware guidelines is that not everyone has the same equipment. Your equipment is probably different from just about everyone else's. Unlike software, which must at least standardize to the hardware and follow the interface rules used by all Windows software in general, each piece of hardware seems to need a unique set of drivers. Sure, two SVGA display adapters use some of the same access methods, but hardware vendors differentiate their products by the things they don't do the same.

Another problem with hardware is that there are variances within the same model. My Pro Audio Spectrum 16+ Revision D has some subtle differences from Revision C that cause problems under Windows in some cases. In fact, I can't use the Revision C drivers with my Revision D device; they simply won't work. Obviously you can't provide a driver for every little variation a piece of hardware might have; that would require literally hundreds of drivers for each vendor. However, you can provide a driver that uses the common features of each variation and hope that the subtle differences won't cause any problems.

Problems aside, you'll find that Windows 95 does provide good support for most of the hardware on your machine and even takes a few quirks into account so you don't have to. In the following sections, we'll look at all the classes of hardware you can install. I'll provide you with general tips for optimizing your setup and give you some guidelines you can use to implement an effective strategy for nonstandard hardware.

Installing and Deleting Devices

Windows 95 normally detects all the hardware on your machine during setup. It goes through a checklist to see if it can figure out what kind of devices you have and then loads the appropriate drivers for you. We covered this entire process in Chapter 4. That chapter also covered some of the things you could do if Windows 95 doesn't detect your hardware, so we won't cover any of that ground again here. However, what happens if you install a new piece of hardware after installing Windows 95? What do you do with old devices that are no longer installed? These are the topics we'll cover in this section of the chapter. We'll also look at troubleshooting procedures you can follow if Windows doesn't act as expected.

Installing Hardware

Windows 95 normally conducts a check of your system during startup. It automatically searches for each device you're supposed to have installed and loads the appropriate drivers. Normally it also looks for new devices you don't have listed anywhere. If Windows 95 finds a new device, it performs the same kind of .INF file search that it did during initial installation to detect the kind of new device.

At least, this is the way things are supposed to work. Reality is very different. I tried installing and removing a variety of devices from several types of machines just to see how Windows 95 would react. It does a superb job on plug and play compatible machines. The better the manufacturer followed the plug and play guidelines, the better Windows 95 will detect new hardware.

The problem starts with older systems. Windows 95 can't always detect a new device with a non-plug and play system because the device might not even turn on until you load the device driver. We covered most of the reasons behind this in Chapter 4, so I won't bore you with the details again. Suffice it to say that Windows 95 won't detect every device installed in those older systems without help.

I did find a correlation between device type and Windows 95's ability to detect it. For example, I didn't experience too many problems getting Windows 95 to detect network adapters or name-brand hard drive controllers. It had a little more trouble detecting display adapters. Windows 95 normally could tell me that the display adapter was present, but it couldn't always accurately detect the type. The worst card on this list was the sound board. I found that even if Windows 95 did detect the sound board, it was usually wrong about the vendor. For example, it kept insisting that my Pro Audio Spectrum was an older Sound Blaster. I wasn't too surprised about the outcome of my tests. Without getting any real information from the device itself, Windows 95 does a good job of detecting the devices in your machine.

Automatic Installation

Now that you understand the problems, what do you do to get around them? I usually try to get Windows 95 to detect the device automatically using the following procedure. Always try this method first.

1. Open Control Panel and double-click on the Add New Hardware applet. You should see the Add New Hardware Wizard dialog, shown in Figure 13.1.

2. Click on Next. You should see the dialog shown in Figure 13.2. Notice that this dialog has two options. The first allows Windows 95 to automatically detect the hardware for you. Use this method first since it involves the least amount of effort on your part and reduces the chance that you'll install the wrong driver.

Figure 13.1.
The initial screen of the Add
New Hardware Wizard
dialog.

Figure 13.2.
Use this dialog to select the
automatic or manual
hardware installation
method.

3. After you've clicked on the Yes radio button, click on Next. Windows will display a dialog telling you what it will do. Essentially, it performs the same type of hardware search it did when you first installed Windows 95.

Note: The hardware detection phase can take quite a while, especially on older machines. The one constant I noticed is that when disk activity stops for more than five minutes, it's a pretty safe bet that the machine is frozen. As long as you hear disk activity during this phase, you're fairly safe in assuming that hardware detection is still taking place. (The hardware detection indicator doesn't move at a steady pace. It appears to take more time as it nears the end.)

4. Click on Next. Windows 95 will display a dialog showing you its hardware detection progress, as shown in Figure 13.3.

5. Once Windows 95 completes the hardware detection phase, it will display a dialog similar to the one shown in Figure 13.4 if it finds something new.

Figure 13.3.
The Add New Hardware Wizard keeps you informed of its progress using this dialog.

Figure 13.4.
Use this dialog to determine if Windows 95 detected your hardware correctly.

Note: If Windows 95 doesn't detect any new hardware, it will display a dialog telling you so. You'll then have the opportunity to perform the manual installation that I outline next. All you need to do is click on Next to start the process.

6. Click on the Details pushbutton to determine if Windows 95 successfully detected the new hardware (see Figure 13.5).

Figure 13.5.
The Add New Hardware Wizard will tell you exactly what hardware it detected.

7. If Windows 95 successfully detected the new hardware, click on the Finish pushbutton to complete the installation process. Windows 95 might ask you to supply some setting information if this is a non-plug and play device. In most cases, it will provide default settings that match your current real-mode setup. Windows 95 will copy all the required

drivers to disk. It will also display some messages about the new hardware it found and perhaps a message about building a driver database. In some cases, Windows 95 will ask you to reboot after you complete this step. If it doesn't ask you to reboot, you should do so anyway to make certain that all new drivers are loaded properly.

Note: If the Add New Hardware Wizard didn't correctly detect your device, click on Cancel. Check your hardware's settings to make sure that they won't conflict with any other devices using the initial steps of the manual process outlined next. If the hardware settings did conflict with something else, change them to an unused setting and try the automatic installation procedure again. Otherwise, proceed with the manual installation.

Manual Installation

Windows 95 might not detect some of your hardware using the Hardware Installation Wizard's automatic detection method. For example, some sound boards don't provide any kind of useful information until you install a device driver to turn them on. These devices relied on the older real-mode drivers you used under DOS. The vendor assumed you'd load the device drivers before using the device, so there was no reason to turn the device on before then. It was a good assumption in the days of DOS, but a real problem when using Windows 95. Now, instead of being a feature (devices that didn't turn themselves on until needed could actually prevent conflicts under DOS), it's a hindrance to installation.

Another problem could get in your way as well. What happens if two devices are currently set to use the same I/O (input/output) port address, DMA (direct memory access) address, or IRQ (interrupt request) setting? The active device would mask the inactive one. (We'll see in Chapter 23 what happens when both devices are active.) If an active device is masking the device you want to detect, there's no way for the automatic procedure to succeed. You'll need to correct the settings first. Of course, this applies only to hardware that uses jumpers for configuration purposes. Windows 95 will automatically reconfigure hardware that uses software configuration settings and plug and play-compatible hardware.

The following procedure starts by showing you where to look for the settings that your machine is currently using. Determining this information in advance will allow you to set the jumpers right the first time. If you're using this section to continue from an automatic installation, proceed to step 6. You can also proceed to step 6 if you have already installed your adapter and don't need to find a set of nonconflicting IRQ and I/O settings. Otherwise, make sure you check your hardware settings before you start the manual installation.

1. Right-click on the My Computer icon and select the Properties option.

2. Select the Device Manager page. You should see a dialog similar to the one shown in Figure 13.6. The dialog for your machine will look slightly different because your machine contains different equipment than mine does. Notice that this dialog displays a complete list of each category of equipment installed on your machine.

Figure 13.6.

The Device Manager will show you a list of all the equipment installed on your system.

3. Select the Computer entry, as shown in Figure 13.6, and click on the Properties push-button. Click on the View Resources tab and the Interrupt request (IRQ) radio button on that page. You should see a dialog similar to the one shown in Figure 13.7. This is a complete list of all the interrupts that are in use on your machine. What you'll need to do is select an interrupt for your new device that doesn't conflict with any of these current settings. If all 16 interrupts are in use and your new device requires one, you'll need to remove an old device before you can install the new one.

Figure 13.7.

The IRQ section of the Computer Properties dialog will show you all the interrupts that are in use on your machine.

Note: Some people used to place more than one device on an interrupt if needed. For example, if they had four serial ports, ports 1 and 3 would share one interrupt and ports 2 and 4 another. Although this setup might have worked if the user didn't accidentally try to access both devices at once, it was a source of conflict. Using one interrupt for two devices won't work under Windows 95. It will simply deactivate one of the conflicting devices.

4. Click on the Input/output (I/O) radio button. You'll see a dialog similar to the one shown in Figure 13.8. These are the port addresses I mentioned earlier. You'll need to select an unused port address range for your new card. Some adapters won't let you select a port address, which means that you might have to change the settings for another card to make this one fit. Fortunately, this is pretty rare.

Figure 13.8.
The I/O section of the Computer Properties dialog will show you all the port addresses that are in use on your machine.

5. You'll need to follow the same steps to find a DMA setting if your card uses one. Once you get all the required settings, close the dialog by clicking on Cancel twice. Shut down the machine and install your adapter according to manufacturer instructions. Restart Windows.

6. Use the Start | Settings | Control Panel command to open Control Panel. Double-click on the Add New Hardware applet and click on the Next pushbutton.

7. Click on the No radio button and then click on Next. Highlight the CD-ROM Controller entry in the Install Specific Hardware field and then click on the Next pushbutton. You should see the dialog box shown in Figure 13.9.

Figure 13.9.
The Manufacturers and Models lists in this dialog allow you to scroll through the list of devices supported by Windows 95 with ease.

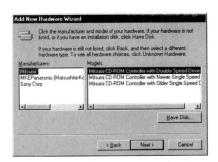

8. This dialog will appear every time you select a device from the previous dialog. The Manufacturers list will change to match the particular device type. If the device installed on the current machine doesn't appear on the list, the dialog gives you the opportunity to use a third-party disk. Normally you'd select the device connected to your machine. In this case, leave the default device highlighted and click on the Next pushbutton.

9. Click on the Details pushbutton. Windows 95 will display a dialog containing the interrupt and address settings for this particular device, as shown in Figure 13.10. Windows 95 chooses a device setting based on all available information. It chooses the best setting that won't interfere with other devices in the system (if possible).

Figure 13.10.
Windows 95 always tells the user what interrupts and addresses it uses for the devices it installs.

Tip: A special "unknown hardware" device type allows you to view all the devices supported by Windows 95 on one screen. This comes in handy for two purposes. First, Microsoft doesn't always place devices in the category where you expect them to be. Searching through this list will provide one final check if you don't find a device where you expect to see it. Second, you can use this list when researching a new product. It will allow you to choose a device that Windows 95 will definitely support. I'm not saying that other products are incompatible, just that these products received a little more attention than some of the others you might find.

10. Clicking on the Next pushbutton again will install the device drivers required for this device. You will normally take this action. Windows 95 might prompt you for a disk if the driver didn't appear on the hard drive and the appropriate disk didn't appear in the CD-ROM drive. It would display a dialog showing the progress of the file copy process. However, since we don't want to install this particular device, click on the Cancel pushbutton. Windows 95 will exit the Hardware Installation Wizard without installing the new device.

Removing Hardware

It's interesting to note that removing hardware—at least the driver—is easier than installing it. In most cases, you'll want to remove the drivers for a device first and then remove the device. Reversing the process could prevent Windows 95 from booting properly. Fortunately, Windows 95 will at least boot in safe mode (unlike Windows 3.x, which could cause significant problems in this regard). However, I always like to take the safest route possible when it comes to my machine's configuration. Removing the driver first is the safest route. The following procedure shows you the method for removing a driver from your machine.

> **Note:** You might want to use the Device Manager to obtain a list of the drivers for the device you plan to remove. Windows 95 usually does a good job of removing all the unneeded files from your system, but sometimes it doesn't. Making a list of drivers will help you find them in the \SYSTEM directory later.

1. Right-click on My Computer and select the Properties option. Click on the Device Manager tab. Select the device category you want to remove and click on the plus sign next to it. You should see a dialog similar to the one shown in Figure 13.11.

Figure 13.11.
Clicking on a device category shows you a list of installed devices.

2. Click on the device you want to remove. Click on the Properties pushbutton and select the Drivers tab. You should see a dialog similar to the one shown in Figure 13.12. Make a copy of the driver list so that you can later verify that Windows 95 removed them. Otherwise, you'll end up with a lot of additional disk clutter after installing and removing a few devices.

Figure 13.12.
Making a list of the drivers
needed by this device is
always a good idea.

Note: Some adapters contain more than one real device. For example, the Pro Audio Spectrum adapter in my machine contains a sound board, a joystick controller, and a SCSI adapter. Each device requires a separate entry in the Device Manager. To remove the device, you must find the main entry and remove it. Windows 95 will automatically remove all of the supporting entries. Make sure you record the drivers used by each entry, because the main entry won't provide you with a master list.

3. Once you finish recording the driver names, click on Cancel.

4. With the device that you want to remove highlighted, click on the Remove pushbutton. Windows 95 will remove the device and all supporting entries.

5. Shut down Windows and reboot your machine to allow the changes to take effect.

Tip: For some strange reason, Windows 95 occasionally forgets to remove all the required entries from the registry. If you get a message saying that Windows 95 can't find a specific device when you start the computer, there's a good chance it didn't delete all the required entries. You might need to use the procedure in the "Using Find to Change Strings" section in Chapter 6 to locate any entries for the device or its associated device drivers. Simply remove the unneeded keys using the Delete command. Be sure to make a copy of the registry before you delete any entries.

Configuring Ports

Ports provide the means for the processor and other devices to communicate with the peripheral hardware on your machine. Any data that a device requires to work goes through the port. Think of a port as the mailbox and the data as the mail. If everyone had the same address, the mail carrier would never know where to put the mail. The same idea holds true in your computer. If two devices were to use the same address, the computer wouldn't know where to send the data.

A port conflict does more than just annoy the user; it can cause system instability or a malfunction of some type. The user might not be able to use part of the system or might experience "the slows" as the system tries to figure out which device it's supposed to use. A system with fully exploited hardware lacks any kind of port conflict. Each device has its own port to use.

Fortunately, there's an easy way to get rid of port conflicts. Windows 95 provides three different port configuration methods, depending on the type of hardware you want to configure. Most hardware uses the first method, which I'll present in the next section. The second and third methods apply to your parallel and serial ports. The last two configuration methods provide more of a performance boost rather than a means of conflict resolution. They tune your ports for maximum application and network compatibility.

Standard Port Configuration

Communication is the name of the game in your computer. In order for communication to occur, there must be some way to exchange information. In the PC, the physical part of the communication path is called an I/O (input/output) port. If you want to send data from one area of the machine to another, your application must first tell the computer what I/O port (or address) to send it to. We looked at part of this process earlier in this chapter when we examined hardware installation. The Computer Properties dialog tells you the address of every port on your machine. Normally you'll never need to change these settings, but sometimes you do. For example, if you have a board in your system that allows more than one setting and it happens to occupy the same address as a board that doesn't, you can change the address of the flexible board as needed. The following procedure takes you through the process of changing an I/O port on your machine.

Note: This procedure changes the settings of the device driver. It won't change the settings of your adapter if it depends on jumpers. Make sure you change any required jumpers after you make changes to the driver configuration. Failure to do so will prevent the hardware from responding.

1. Right-click on My Computer and select the Properties option.
2. Select one of the device classes—like Sound, video and game controllers—and click on the plus sign to display the list of devices it contains.
3. Select one of the devices and click on the Properties pushbutton. Click on the Resources tab. You should see a dialog similar to the one shown in Figure 13.13. Notice that this dialog has the Use automatic settings checkbox checked. Letting Windows 95 manage the settings for your equipment is always a good idea.

Figure 13.13.
The Resources tab of the Device Properties dialog makes it easy to see what settings each peripheral uses.

Looking Ahead: This particular dialog also contains some diagnostic information that we'll cover in Chapter 23.

4. Uncheck the Use automatic settings checkbox. This should enable the Change Setting pushbutton and the Setting based on listbox.

5. Click on the Setting based on listbox. You'll see a list of basic configurations, as shown in Figure 13.14.

Figure 13.14.
The Setting based on listbox displays the standard configurations that Windows 95 provides for a particular device.

6. Try each setting in turn to see if one of the other settings will allow you to resolve the port conflict. Windows 95 will alert you to any conflicts with registered devices, as shown in Figure 13.15. Notice that the error message tells you exactly which device you're conflicting with. This allows you to change that device's settings if necessary to resolve the conflict. Obviously you'll want to keep the number of changes to the absolute minimum. The more you change the Windows 95 setup, the greater your chances of introducing unforeseen conflicts.

Figure 13.15.
Windows 95 will instantly alert you to any problems in the settings you choose.

7. If you try all the basic configurations offered and none of them work, reset the Settings based on listbox to its original setting. Otherwise, click on OK twice to save the setting and then shut down and reboot the machine to make it active.

8. To change a single port address, highlight it and click on the Change Setting pushbutton. You should see the dialog shown in Figure 13.16.

Figure 13.16.
This dialog allows you to change the setting of a single port.

Tip: Some revisions of a specific piece of hardware will provide more settings than Windows 95 will recognize. Modifying the .INF file using the procedure in Chapter 4 will often resolve this problem. All you need to do is add the settings that Windows 95 doesn't recognize and then shut down and reboot the machine. Be sure not to add unsupported settings to the .INF file, or you'll get unpredictable results.

9. Scroll through the list of acceptable settings. As before, Windows 95 will tell you if you select a conflicting setting by displaying a message in the Conflict information field.

10. Once you select a new port address, make it permanent by clicking on OK three times. Shut down your machine and reboot.

This procedure isn't limited to just port settings. You can use it to configure any hardware setting. Windows 95 won't allow you to change some settings. If you try to change one of these settings, Windows 95 will display the appropriate error message. In most cases, a hardware limitation rather than a problem with the driver will prevent you from changing a setting.

Serial Port Configuration

The serial port offers a variety of configuration options that go beyond address conflict resolution. Several options control both the speed of the port and its compatibility with software. Figure 13.17 shows the Port Settings page, where you would make changes of this nature. You access it through the System Properties dialog, which we saw in Figure 13.6. Notice that this page controls the actual port parameters such as communication speed and number of data bits. Normally you set a port's parameters to match those of your modem and any online service you wish to access.

Figure 13.17.

The Port Settings page of the Communications Port Properties dialog allows you to change some of the port's speed-enhancing features.

There's another way to set these parameters. When you're using the Direct Cable Connection program provided with Windows 95, you'll want to reset these settings to maximum. Some users will miss this particular bit of irony since the utility never asks you to set the port settings. They just assume that the Direct Cable Connection program uses the maximum settings available. However, experience says otherwise. You can actually slow data transfers from your notebook to a crawl by failing to observe this little "gotcha."

Windows 3.x provided all of these settings, as do most DOS applications. The one area where Windows 95 rises above its predecessors is in the way it handles advanced UART (universal asynchronous receiver transmitter) chips. A UART contains the intelligence of the serial port, and some of the newer models contain features that allow better performance in a multitasking environment. It is this support that lets Windows 95 provide a higher level of support for background communications than you might expect.

Clicking on the Advanced pushbutton displays the dialog shown in Figure 13.18. Notice that it contains only one checkbox and two sliders. Windows 95 automatically checks the Use FIFO buffers checkbox if it detects the proper port. This option is available only on the 16550 UART. Attempting to use it with an older 8250 UART will result in lost data.

Figure 13.18.
The Advanced Port Settings dialog is one place where you can tweak the performance of your communications program.

Note: MSD (Microsoft Diagnostics) can't reliably determine your UART type. In many cases, it will tell you that you have an 8250 UART even if your system contains the newer model. Microsoft claims that this is due to a bug in the UART that makes it difficult to detect, yet many third-party diagnostic programs can make the determination. If you're uncertain what kind of UART is installed in your system, either check the documentation that came with your machine or use one of the better third-party diagnostic aids to check your port type. You can also check the part number on the UART itself (it is conspicuously placed on most motherboard configurations) and ask your local computer store or direct-sale manufacturer to verify the type for you.

Tip: Some motherboards come equipped with emulations of the 16550. Unfortunately, some of these emulations work better than others. If the motherboard vendor states that the communication port supports the full 16550 capability, but Windows 95 doesn't automatically check the Use FIFO buffers option, you might want to test this capability anyway. In some cases, the option works even if Windows 95 doesn't detect the port properly. I usually check the box and then test the port by downloading a large file in the background while using a single application in the foreground. Something like a word processor or data entry program works best, but you should test the port using the same application you'd normally use while downloading a file. If the background transfer works without any data errors, you'll know that the port at least marginally supports the FIFO capability.

Before we go much further, let's talk about the differences between certain UARTs. Older UARTs could store only one character at a time. This meant that the CPU had to retrieve that character immediately, or the next character the UART received would overwrite it. This is what people mean when they say their port "dropped" a character. It means that the CPU couldn't respond fast enough and the UART overwrote a character in its buffer as a result. Forcing the CPU to attend to the needs of the UART is fine in a single-tasking system like DOS, but it isn't all that efficient in a multitasking environment like Windows. Once UART vendors realized that the older UARTs were a bottleneck when used in a multitasking environment, they started making new UARTs with a FIFO (first in, first out) buffer. The FIFO buffer can store up to 16 characters, giving the CPU time to complete whatever it was doing and then respond to the needs of the UART.

Once you select the Use FIFO buffers option in the Advanced Port Settings dialog, Windows 95 will enable the two sliders, which control the FIFO buffer. There are actually two buffers: one for data you want to send, and another for data you receive. The setting affects the number of buffer slots that the CPU can use. Setting a high number allows a longer time between CPU checks, making your system more efficient. However, using a large number also reduces the margin of error. You might find that your application no longer transmits or receives data accurately. The way to fix this is to reduce the number of buffers, giving the CPU a wider margin of error. Tuning your buffer for maximum performance will involve some trial and error, but it's well worth the effort.

> **Tip:** Your modem's transmission speed affects the buffer slider setting. A high-speed data transfer leaves less time between characters in which the CPU can respond. As a result, you might have to set the buffer setting lower. On the other hand, a high-speed CPU partially compensates for this problem. You might find that a Pentium can handle the load of a 9600 baud transfer better than an 80486 in some cases. Hand-tuning this setting is about the only way you can ensure optimum performance. The biggest mistake you can make, though, is tuning it in the foreground. Always test your settings with the communication program as a background application.

Parallel Port Configuration

The parallel port offers fewer, yet more customized, opportunities for tuning than the serial port does. You need to consider a few things when making changes to the printer port settings that you didn't need to consider with the serial port. The most important is that a device attaches to the serial port. In other words, the device must abide by the settings that the serial port provides. This is why you have one centralized dialog for tuning a serial port. On the other hand, the parallel port attaches to the device. You can hand-tune the parallel port settings for each device that will connect to it. When you think about it, this arrangement makes a lot of sense. Seldom will you see more than one device attached to a serial port, yet AB switches for parallel ports abound. People are always attaching multiple devices to their parallel ports.

Looking Ahead: Chapter 14 provides complete details of the Printer Properties dialog. I provide only an overview of it in this section.

With this first difference in mind, you'll probably figure out that we don't change the printer port settings in Device Manager. You use a simple four-step approach to opening the dialog shown in Figure 13.19: Open Control Panel, double-click on the Printers folder, right-click on the printer, and select Properties from the context menu. All the port settings appear on the Details page of the Properties dialog, as shown in Figure 13.19.

Figure 13.19.
A parallel port's configuration settings are attached to a particular printer.

Two different settings affect the efficiency of your printer connection to varying degrees: port and spool. The Port Settings pushbutton displays the dialog shown in Figure 13.20. The first checkbox, Spool MS-DOS print jobs, tells Windows 95 to place a copy of any DOS print jobs in the spooler so that they can print in the background. Using this setting will return control of the machine to you faster. The trade-off is that you'll experience reduced machine efficiency until the print job completes. The Check port state before printing option tells Windows to check the printer's status before it starts the print job. If the printer is offline or otherwise unable to print, Windows displays an error message. You'll get a chance to fix the problem and then retry the print job.

Figure 13.20.
This dialog allows you to set the method used to handle DOS print jobs.

The Spool Settings pushbutton opens the dialog shown in Figure 13.21. Of all the radio groups shown, only the first is always available. Spooling print jobs are a requirement if you use the printer as a network printer. Selecting the first suboption in this group tells the spooler to send data to the printer after it spools the last page of the print job. This will actually return machine control to you a lot faster. I normally use it for long print jobs since the machine will be tied up printing for a while anyway. At least I can get back to work quickly at a slightly reduced level of efficiency. The second suboption, Start printing after first page is spooled, allows the spooler to start printing immediately. If you normally print short jobs, this option makes more sense because it completes the overall print job faster.

Figure 13.21.
Use this dialog to change the way your printer handles spooling.

The Spool Settings dialog box also includes a listbox with two entries: RAW and EMF. EMF (enhanced metafile) is a new way of sending information to the printer in Windows 95. It uses a data-independent method that's much smaller than the RAW option and frees your program up faster. The downside to this format is that it takes longer for the print job to complete in the background, because Windows 95 still has to convert the metafile format to something printer-specific. The RAW format sends the data to the printer in a format it already understands. It will take your application longer to produce this output, but this could save substantially on the amount of time the spooler spends working in the background. Combining the EMF spool data format with the Start printing after last page is spooled setting provides the fastest method of sending data to your printer.

If this isn't a shared printer, you can choose to print directly to the printer. The advantage of this method is that you don't waste time spooling the job and then sending it to the printer. When the machine returns control to you, it's at full efficiency because the print job is finished. This particular feature comes in handy when I have one or two pages and I don't want to wait very long for them to print.

Peter's Principle: A Printer for Every Task

No law states that you can't create multiple copies of the same printer connected to the same port but configured in different ways. I do it to improve the flexibility of the Windows environment. I have one printer with spooling disabled, and I don't share it with anyone. It allows me to print small jobs very quickly.

A second copy of the same printer gets shared with everyone on the network. I enable spooling with it and allow it to start printing after the first page. This way, my machine doesn't get a lot of heavy jolts as someone else uses the printer attached to it. There's a constant, but barely noticeable, load. I also use this strategy for my medium-sized print jobs. It reduces the overall time that I wait for the print job to complete.

A third copy of the same printer isn't shared with anyone, but it does use spooling. I set this one up to wait until the last page of the print job appears in the spooler. This allows me to regain control of my machine in the minimum amount of time. I use this particular setting when I have a long print job that's going to reduce overall machine efficiency for a long time anyway.

There are numerous ways you can set a single printer on your machine to look like more, special-purpose, printers. Doing this might take a little time and thought, but it will enhance your overall efficiency and improve printer throughput. You can also use this same idea for control. For example, what if you don't want a particular group to use the font cartridge attached to the machine? You could create a special setup for them that allows full printer access but doesn't provide access to the fonts. (All you have to do is choose "none" when asked for fonts on the Font page.)

Normally you'll want to enable bidirectional printer support. This allows your printer to communicate with the computer and tell it when it needs maintenance. Bidirectional support also allows the computer to get better information about printer failures. However, bidirectional support also exacts a toll in speed. This isn't a problem with the printer or the computer, but with the amount of traffic flowing through the parallel port. The port has to support a lot more traffic in bidirectional mode than it does regularly. As a result, you might notice slightly better printer performance when you turn off bidirectional support. The speed gain is minimal, though, so think twice before you actually take this step. The loss of information could make a big difference in the computer's ability to help you diagnose problems.

Fonts and Printers

There are a number of ways to look at fonts under Windows 95. Some people look at them the wrong way and end up thrilling us all with "ransom note" presentations and letters. Aesthetics aside, fonts can create problems in a number of efficiency-related ways as well. For example, every font you load consumes disk space. If you have a lot of disk space, this isn't a problem. However, at an average size of 60 KB, each TrueType font you load can quickly start to consume space that your hard drive can't afford to provide.

Space considerations aside, too many fonts in your application list boxes can also present a dilemma. Which font do you choose for a given job? I find that using stylesheets helps a lot, but there are still times where I must choose a font manually.

When you get right down to it, just how many fonts does the average person really need? I find that I can usually get by with roman, bold, bold italic, and italic versions of three or four fonts just fine.

After a lot of fumbling around with a bunch of fonts I would never use, I decided on one serif, one sans serif, a fancy font, and a symbol font. These four fonts handle all my business correspondence and personal needs.

Of course, I'm not a graphic artist or someone who creates presentations on a daily basis. If you're in one of those lines of work, you'll need a wealth of fonts loaded on your machine. I'm equally certain that you'll have the real estate to deal with them as well. Still, sometimes even I need a special font to make that dramatic presentation. Windows 95 makes it easy to load and unload fonts as necessary. We'll cover all this in Chapter 14.

What do fonts and printers have to do with efficiency? Once you get past the font management issues, you encounter several speed-related issues. The following list provides some of the tips I've gathered while working with Windows 95:

- A laser printer can usually print with a native font much faster than it can with a downloaded font. Not only that, but the memory that you'll save using the built-in fonts will usually allow you to print larger pages.

- Dot matrix printers also benefit from the use of internal fonts. In this case, it's the difference between printing in character or graphics mode. You need to print using graphics mode when you select a Windows TrueType font. A native printer font allows you to print in character mode. The speed differential is quite noticeable.

- More fonts usually means longer print times. On a dot matrix printer, you have to wait for the machine to render each font. A laser printer needs to download each font before you can use it. Either way, it'll take longer to use more fonts. Discreet use of fonts normally produces a better effect and is more efficient from a printing perspective as well.

- Using raster fonts is usually faster but less flexible than using TrueType fonts. The computer doesn't have to create a raster font; it's already in pixel format. Unfortunately, this also means that the computer can't resize them without a loss in resolution. Overall, using TrueType fonts to gain the benefits of flexibility is a better idea. We'll cover the exact differences between raster and vector fonts in Chapter 14.

- Avoid using non-TrueType fonts if possible. Alternatives to TrueType were a good idea at one time. They allowed you to gain access to fonts you might never be able to use otherwise. However, the extra memory and system incompatibilities that the managers of these fonts introduce into Windows 95 make them relics.

- Printing at a lower resolution is faster than printing at a higher resolution. The printer requires more time to output text or graphics at a higher resolution. However, using a lower resolution will reduce the quality of the font output. Many fonts include a special form of high-resolution and size control known as hinting. We'll cover this in more detail later.

Depending on the printer you use, there might be even more ways to use fonts efficiently. Always match your font requirements to the job at hand. Never use more than you need, but always use enough to get your point across.

Miniport Driver Support

What exactly is a miniport driver? This was the first question that came to my mind. We touched on this particular topic in Chapter 8 when we looked at the file system architecture. A miniport driver is a device-independent way of moving data. It doesn't matter what form that data takes—it could be graphics, sound, or text. Windows 95 uses the miniport driver concept for every subsystem on your machine. The benefit of using the miniport driver for your applications is improved speed. The application only needs to worry about the data it wants to output, not the format that the data takes.

Not only does miniport driver support mean a better and easier-to-use interface for the user, it also means a lot to software vendors as well. Under DOS, you have to write code for every little function. If you want to provide a File menu, you have to write all the code that the File menu requires. The same thing holds true for every other function a program might perform. Windows 3.x started a process in which the programmer didn't have to write so much code. Using the common dialogs is just one example. You no longer have to write a File menu, because Microsoft provides one as part of the common dialog DLL.

Windows 95 takes this concept even further with the miniport driver support it provides. If you develop communication programs, you used to worry about the differences in control sequences for each modem type. Using Windows 95 Unimodem support (a miniport driver), the programmer opens each modem and writes to it like a file. The miniport driver takes care of details such as control codes.

There are other significant advantages to this approach. For one thing, you no longer need to worry as much about how well an application will handle the details. Since each vendor is writing to the same interface, any changes to that interface will come from Microsoft. Using a common interface also means that every application will provide the same level of support for the various devices on your system. If one application supports a device, they all do, and to the same level.

We'll look at the specifics of miniport driver support as we visit each subsystem. Chapter 8 already covered the miniport driver concept from the file system point of view. I also mentioned this form of support in the "Fonts and Printers" section of this chapter. Chapter 14 covers printer support in much more detail. Look in Chapter 15 for information about mouse miniport driver support and in Chapter 16 for the same information on the video subsystem. Details on network miniport driver support appear in Chapter 19. You'll get your last bit of miniport driver support information in Chapter 21, when we cover the mobile computing environment. In most cases, I've shortened "miniport driver" to "driver" in the rest of this book because a miniport driver is simply a special form of driver.

Faxes and Modems

Communication is a major part of the job these days. It used to be that you could take care of everything with the office fax and a few phone calls. Today, a lot of people can't take the time to use the office fax; they need one close by to take care of their needs. The amount of electronic "paper" passing hands these days is amazing. A lot of people are busier in other ways too. Playing telephone tag isn't fun, especially when you can leave a message for the person on e-mail and expect a response later that day. Online services are becoming a major source of information for many people. Sometimes I can actually get an answer to a networking or application-related question faster by getting online than I could if I called a vendor support line. The difference is the vast amount of knowledge that these online services represent.

Looking Ahead: We'll take a closer look at using your fax and modem under Windows 95 in Chapter 18. In Chapter 21 we'll look at the mobile computer user's point of view.

It's no wonder that people are always looking for better ways to use the communication features that their computers offer. Under Windows 3.x it was a foregone conclusion that you would find it difficult, it not impossible, to communicate in the background. Windows 95 is a totally different story. Communication isn't only possible, it's easy too.

Configuring your machine for optimum performance when using background communication isn't hard; it just takes a little time. You need to try a setting, communicate a little to see its effect, and then tune a little more as necessary. Unlike other tuning tips I've presented in this chapter, there's no quick and easy way to tune your communication programs. The problem is that every machine is slightly different, as is every modem and every communication program that uses the modem.

Tuning Your Modem

To tune your modem settings, Open Control Panel and double-click on the Modem applet. Select your modem and click on the Properties pushbutton. Select the Connection page. You'll see a dialog similar to the one we saw for the serial port. Figure 13.22 shows that this dialog contains those settings plus a few related to modem communications.

Note: These settings will affect your communication program only if it uses the Windows 95 miniport driver setup. Older 16-bit communication programs will maintain their own settings. Check the software vendor's manual for the procedure to tune these applications.

Figure 13.22.
The Modem Properties dialog looks similar to the serial port configuration dialog, but it has some modem-specific additions.

Click on the Advanced pushbutton. You'll see a dialog similar to the one in Figure 13.23. This is where you can modify your connection settings for added efficiency. The settings look straightforward, and they are. If your modem supports error correction, it's normally a good idea to select it. The same holds true for data compression, which boosts your effective transfer rate by as many as four times.

Figure 13.23.
The Advanced Connection Settings dialog allows you to configure your modem for maximum efficiency.

Tip: Sometimes, using error correction and data compression can actually hurt the efficiency of your transmission. Certain types of TelNet connections fall into this category, as do some BBS calls in which the host modem doesn't quite support your modem's protocols. If you're having trouble maintaining the connection, or the data transfer rate isn't as high as you expected, try turning off data compression first, then error correction, to see if there's any improvement.

I've found an interesting use for the Required to connect checkbox. Some BBSs have more than one connection. They use a switch to move you to the nearest unused connection when you call in. If this is a local call, the fact that you can't use error correction and data compression might not be a big deal. On the other hand, the cost of using such a connection during a long distance call can add up quickly. I use this checkbox when I don't want to make a connection that will disable the advanced features of my modem—the ones that will reduce my overall telephone bill.

The Modulation type list box allows you to select from the various forms of signal modulation that the modem provides. Using the standard modulation is usually more efficient than the alternatives. However, using the modulation that gives you the best connection is always the route to follow. I always try the standard connection first. If it proves reliable, I use that mode. I switch modes only when the connection doesn't work properly.

Some modems provide additional control sequences that you can use in specific situations for added speed. The Extra settings field allows you to enter these control sequences. You'll need to consult your modem manual for details.

Tuning Your Fax

The number of fax settings that Windows provides is fairly minimal. To access them, you need to open the MS Exchange Settings Properties dialog. I usually do this by right-clicking on the Inbox applet and selecting Properties. You can also access it by double-clicking on the Mail and Fax applet in Control Panel. After you open this dialog, select Microsoft Fax, click on the Properties pushbutton, and select the Modem tab. You'll see a dialog similar to the one shown in Figure 13.24.

Figure 13.24.
The Modem page of the Microsoft Fax Properties dialog allows you to configure your modem for optimum performance.

We'll cover this dialog's user-specific fields later. For now, select the modem you'll use to transmit faxes and then click on the Properties pushbutton. Once you see the Fax Modem Properties dialog, click on the Advanced pushbutton. You'll see the dialog shown in Figure 13.25.

Figure 13.25.
This dialog allows you to select the advanced properties for your fax modem.

The settings in this dialog allow you to change the way the modem works. In most cases, you can improve either usability or efficiency, but not both at the same time. Checking the first setting, Disable high speed transmission, will keep you from transmitting or receiving faxes above 9600 baud. This can actually improve your machine's multitasking capability. Receiving high-speed faxes in the background might improve transmission speed, but it also costs you processor cycles. Microsoft also mentions that you can check this box if you can't receive faxes without error. Normally, errors occur when the serial port starts dropping characters due to high traffic. (Incidentally, this situation has much more to do with the other background and foreground tasks that you're running than with which UART you have. If your CPU is heavily bogged down with other tasks, the CPU itself—not the UART—becomes the bottleneck, and you open yourself up to the danger of degraded performance or lost data.)

The Disable error correction mode setting also affects efficiency. In one way, working without error correction is faster. The additional processing time required for error correction slows down transmission speeds. However, without error correction, you might find yourself resending faxes. You'll normally want to leave error correction on unless the receiving modem uses a different protocol.

I can understand why Microsoft didn't default to checking the first two options. Using them does improve foreground fax transmission speeds. However, disabling data compression doesn't make a lot of sense unless you have a very noisy line. In most cases, you'll want to enable data compression to gain the additional transmission speed that it offers.

The Enable MR compression option allows you to use one of two advanced fax data compression techniques: MR and MMR. The actual technique used depends on the capabilities of the fax you call. Each of these techniques provides data compression as follows:

- Modified Huffman (MH): This is the standard compression technique used by all fax machines today. It can just about double the transmission speed of most fax machines. A fax scans each line of your original document and converts it into a series of 1s (black) and 0s (white). One line is equal to 1/200ths of an inch. (Fax machines normally transmit data at 200 dpi.) The Huffman coding technique takes these long strings and breaks them into characters of 8 bits. It then uses a "code word" to represent each character. Common characters use short code words, and rare characters use longer code words. For example, an e might be represented as a single-bit 1, while a z might require 16 bits. The end result is that the overall data stream requires less space. You might want to refer to a book that deals specifically with encoding techniques if you're interested in how this coding technique actually works. Chapter 17 also provides you with a list of the fax standards that tell exactly how a fax transmission works.

- Modified read (MR): Some of the newer fax modems provide this option. The first line of fax data is compressed using the MH technique that I described earlier. The second line begins with only the changed data. In other words, if at a specific point in the data stream the first line contains a 0 and the second line contains a 1, the fax would record the bit's location and difference. It then compresses this change data using MH. The third line is a full line of MH data, just like the first line, while the fourth line contains only change data. The fax machine alternates between sending full lines of data and changed lines of data until it has sent the entire page. This method of data compression provides an inherent level of protection. Even if you do lose a line of data during transmission, the next full line will restore the fax data stream to its original state. That way, even if you do lose one line of data, it will affect at most two lines of fax output. You will see a 15 to 20 percent increase in data transmission rate using this method of compression.

- Minimized modified read (MMR): Using this option gives up some of the security of MR and trades it for speed. The fax transmits only the first line of the fax as a full line of data. All remaining lines get transmitted as change data only. This means that an error anytime during transmission has the potential for destroying the rest of the fax. Of course, this means that you can use MMR only on a very clean (non-noisy) telephone line. MMR may include its own error correction method along with the transmission, but this will reduce some of the benefit of using the compression technique in the first place. Normally you can expect a near doubling of transmission speed when using this method.

The next option, Use Class 2 if available, prevents you from receiving Class 1 faxes. The only time you'll want to check this box is if the software you're using won't let you receive Class 1 faxes. Class 2 faxes are the standard graphic type. Class 1 faxes are editable and therefore easier to manipulate.

Finally, the Reject pages received with errors listbox/checkbox combination lets you do a couple of things. Removing the check from this box tells Windows that you don't want to receive any pages a second time, even if they're totally garbled. This usually isn't the best route to pursue. On the other hand, checking the box and selecting very low in the Tolerance listbox virtually guarantees you'll get at least one resend of each page. (Tolerance is the level of tolerance that Windows has for errors on a fax page.) I usually use the high setting unless I need better fax quality for some reason. For example, if I wanted to use the information in the fax for a presentation, I might select low or medium. The only time I would select very low is if I needed to use the pages as is, without any changes at all, for some type of presentation or formal document.

TAPI and MAPI support

Application programming interfaces (APIs) allow programmers to accomplish a lot of work with only a little effort. That's the first goal of every API. The second goal is to ensure a standardized form of access to specific system resources and capabilities. Using a standard interface allows the operating system vendor to change the implementation details without "breaking" too much code. Finally, an API also standardizes the results of using specific system resources and capabilities. For example, using the Windows API ensures that the user will see some of the standard types of interface components that we take for granted.

Windows 95 provides two new APIs. The Telephony API (TAPI) provides a standardized method of handling telephone services. The Messaging API (MAPI) provides a standardized method of handling online services and other forms of messaging. Both APIs provide standardized methods for utilizing your modem more efficiently to conduct business. We'll examine both APIs in depth later in this book. Right now, the important thing to remember is that both APIs exist under Windows 95 in the form of new utilities.

You'll see the effects of TAPI directly in the Modem applet in Control Panel. It allows you to configure your modem in one place. Any application that supports TAPI will use those settings. This includes Microsoft Exchange and Microsoft Network as native Windows 95 applications. It doesn't include older 16-bit Windows applications. If you want the benefits of TAPI, you'll need to upgrade those applications as the vendors come out with new versions.

Microsoft Exchange is an example of a MAPI application. It allows you to access Microsoft Mail using a MAPI driver. A different MAPI driver provides access to CompuServe. Still another driver allows you to send a fax. In fact, you could have a MAPI driver to access each online service you subscribe to. The presence of these drivers would allow you access them all using one application. The result is reduced training costs and the ability to move information from one service to another with the click of a button.

MAPI and TAPI aren't limited to Windows 95-specific applications. For example, Microsoft Word provides a Send option on the File menu. This option allows you to send all or part of a document using MAPI anywhere you can communicate. Using the native capabilities of Windows 95, this means you could send it as a fax or an e-mail or to an online service—all without leaving Word.

Multimedia

Multimedia is another big area of improvement under Windows 95. The CD-ROM ships with several samples of multimedia presentations. They don't fully exploit the potential of multimedia, but they do give you an idea of what's possible. I can foresee a lot of people using this media for interactive training. The instructor could appear in a corner of the screen and provide you with interactive instructions as you perform a task.

Multimedia will change the way we conduct business in other ways. Instead of flying a group of people to one place to see a presentation, you could send the presentation to the group of people using a CD-ROM. This same group could meet using conferencing software and discuss the presentation's impact and viability. Air travel might not become a thing of the past, but using the multimedia capabilities that Windows 95 is starting to provide will help reduce the need to travel.

Notice that I said Windows 95 is only starting to provide this capability. The cost of building a multimedia machine that will really do the job is still fairly high. Using something less than optimum almost always results in a presentation that lacks the pizzazz of a live presentation. We also have a long way to go before interactive training is a real option. It's getting closer, and the Windows 95 demonstration programs show this, but it's still not perfect. Multimedia still needs improvement in some areas before anyone can say that it's ready.

Warts aside, multimedia under Windows 95 is greatly improved. The sections that follow give you an overview of multimedia under Windows 95 and how it allows you to better exploit your hardware. Right now, its hard to say who's ahead in the game—hardware or software. Neither is to the level where I'd say that it gives you the kind of presentation you're looking for, but I'll leave it for you to decide just how far we need to go.

MPEG Support

Motion pictures revolutionized the world, and now they'll revolutionize your PC. MPEG (Motion Pictures Experts Group) is a method of compressing VHS video into a very small format that will fit on a CD-ROM. VHS is the same format your VCR uses.

The technical term for the type of functionality that MPEG provides is a codec (coder/decoder). Think of a codec in the same way you would think of a modem. It allows you to send and receive video data using a standard medium. Instead of a telephone wire, you're using a CD-ROM drive. In place of digital data, you're receiving video images.

Windows 95 currently provides the capability to display VHS-quality images in a 640 × 480 window at 30 frames per second. That's about the same rate that you see on television. You're supposed to get this level of performance from a double-speed CD-ROM drive, but I have a quadruple-speed unit connected to my system and just barely get what I would call acceptable performance. I'm sure part of Microsoft's assumption is that you won't be running anything else when using the multimedia capabilities, but that probably isn't very valid. Most people will want to use this capability for training, which means that they'll probably have another application open.

Suffice it to say that if you want to fully exploit your machine's hardware capabilities to perform training, this is one way to do it. Make sure you get more than a minimal system if you plan to use the multimedia capabilities Windows 95 provides on more than an occasional basis, though. Otherwise, you'll probably be disappointed with the acceptable performance that low-end hardware will provide.

Sound Boards

I've had sound for so long that I can't imagine using Windows without it. In fact, you've probably had it that long too. So why even mention it here? What does Windows 95 provide that Windows 3.x didn't?

There are all kinds of sound. You don't have to settle for the mediocre level of sound that Windows 3.x provided. Windows 95 provides the controls required to fully exploit the expanded capabilities that modern sound boards provide. All you need to do to start using these capabilities is to adjust the settings found in the Audio Properties dialog. To access this dialog, right-click on the Speaker icon on the Taskbar and select Adjust Audio Properties. You should see a dialog similar to the one shown in Figure 13.26.

Figure 13.26.
The Audio Properties dialog allows you to make full use of the audio capabilities your system provides.

Windows 95 will always play back any audio using the full capability of the sound board you select. However, there's a lot of room to customize the recording of sound. Microsoft thoughtfully provided three default recording selections. Each selection reflects the kind of sound recording quality these settings will give you: CD, radio, or telephone.

The actual level of quality you get has to do with the frequency, or the number of samples of sound that Windows takes per second. The more samples it takes, the better the quality of your sample. Using stereo and 16-bit samples also improves the sound quality, as does the recording format. Before we go much further, let's define a few terms.

- Sample rate: The number of times per second that Windows samples the microphone input line. A higher setting means that you get more samples. More samples always provide a better playback.

- Sample size: Windows supports two sample sizes: 8-bit and 16-bit. A 16-bit sample allows you to record a broader range of values. This means that you can better differentiate between various sounds, resulting in a higher-quality recording.

- Format: There are many ways to store a sound, just as there are many ways to store graphics. Some formats take more space but preserve image quality better. Likewise, some audio formats are better than others at preserving sounds. You'll have to experiment to see which one sounds the best to you. Most recordings use the PCM (pulse-code modulation) format. Since this is the most common format, you'll probably want to use it when you need to exchange the recording with someone else, unless there's an overriding reason to do otherwise.

- Number of channels (mono or stereo): You probably already know the implication of this setting. A stereo recording uses two microphones to record the sound from different perspectives. During playback, a stereo recording has much greater depth than a mono recording of the same quality.

Now that you have some ideas of the ways you can customize sound under Windows 95, let's look at the dialog you use to do it. Click on the Customize pushbutton to see the Customize dialog, shown in Figure 13.27.

Figure 13.27.
Use the Customize dialog to change the way you record sound under Windows 95.

Notice that there are two listboxes. One determines the recording format, and the other allows you to select from a variety of options, including the sample rate, sample size, and number of channels. Notice that this listbox also tells you the storage requirements for the sample in kilobytes per second. This is the number of kilobytes that the sample would consume for each second you recorded. Obviously, some formats can eat a lot of storage space quickly.

You can save any custom settings that you create using the Save As pushbutton. Windows will store the settings and present them later in the Preferred Quality listbox of the Audio Properties dialog.

So what's the best way to customize these settings? Remember that the better the quality, the higher the storage requirements. I tend to prefer stereo over mono recordings because the depth of sound can make up for a host of other problems. The trouble is if you have only one microphone. In that case, selecting stereo is a waste of disk space since you can record only one channel of information. Selecting 16-bit sound improves quality a great deal for a very small increase in storage size. You get a sample 2^{16} (65,536 possible combinations) versus 2^8 (256 possible combinations) for a mere doubling of disk space. Unless you're recording music, the highest sampling rate you need is 22,050 Hz. In fact, using 11,025 for simple voice recordings usually proves sufficient.

Virtualizing Your Hardware

To make the best use of your hardware under Windows 95, you must be able to access it. There are three different ways to do this, and I've mentioned them all before. You can use a real-mode driver if absolutely necessary to access an older device. DLLs allow you to access devices that provide

Windows 16-bit support but don't provide a Windows 95-specific driver. This is better than using a real-mode driver but shy of the real goal you want to achieve. The best driver to use is a Windows 95-specific virtual "anything" driver (VxD). We'll cover all three types of support from an efficiency and ease-of-use standpoint in the following sections.

Real-Mode Drivers for Older Devices

There are a lot of problems with using real-mode drivers under Windows 95. I've covered just about every problem you can experience in other areas of this book. Suffice it to say that a real-mode driver isn't the best choice you could make.

The first decision you'll need to make is whether the device is even needed all the time. You had to load a device you intended to use at boot up in the DOS and Windows 3.x environments because there was no way to load it later. If you need a device for a very special purpose under Windows 95, you can always load it later in an MS-DOS mode session. Simply set up a copy of the command processor with the CONFIG.SYS and AUTOEXEC.BAT settings required to load the device in its optimum environment. Of course, you won't be able to load Windows 95 when using MS-DOS mode—or access other applications, for that matter. It's a problem of balancing convenience with overall system performance and stability.

You'll need to make a few decisions when using such a driver under Windows 95. The first choice is the amount of DOS space you need in comparison to the flexibility you want to give Windows when it comes to managing your memory. Loading all your device drivers low will affect the amount of conventional memory you need. However, this choice also means that you won't have to load a memory manager and that Windows will be able to provide the maximum flexibility possible.

If you find that you have to load the driver high, you'll also have to load something other than the Windows memory manager. Try to optimize both the driver and memory manager settings to reduce their impact on the Windows environment. For example, use the least amount of memory possible for buffers.

Using 16-Bit Drivers

Using an older 16-bit Windows driver is a little bit better than using a real-mode driver. At least Windows still controls the memory environment. Unfortunately, using these older drivers will still have an effect on overall system efficiency. Remember that all 16-bit applications, including drivers, run in a single session. Using that session's resources for a driver doesn't seem like the best way to go.

The 32-bit drivers that come with Windows 95 also provide built-in safeguards to help protect your system environment. The older 16-bit drivers provide no such protection. They're more likely than a newer driver to crash, or at least destabilize, the system.

Finally, a 16-bit driver won't know how to interact with the miniport driver architecture used by Windows 95. This means that you'll lose all the user and programmer benefits of such an architecture for that specific device. I provided an overview of those benefits earlier in this chapter. We'll take a detailed look at them in the architecture-specific chapters. I provided a list of these chapters earlier.

Default 32-Bit Drivers

Using 32-bit Windows 95 drivers is the best solution if you want to get the most out of your hardware. Windows 95 isn't a perfect operating system, but it does provide enough advanced features that updating your hardware to use the new drivers is the best way to go. Exploiting your hardware always means getting the most out of it. Using old drivers is just another way to introduce inefficiencies and stability problems into your system.

On Your Own

Use the automatic installation technique in this chapter to determine if your machine has any undetected devices. Normally, Windows 95 will report that it didn't find anything. If so, click on Cancel to exit the detection routine.

Try changing the configuration settings of various devices listed on the Device page of the System Properties dialog. Make sure you save the settings in case you can't get Windows 95 back to its original configuration. Use settings that conflict with another device to see how Windows reacts. Make sure you change the setting back so that you can use the device again.

14

Fonts and Printing

Printing and fonts go hand in hand. You can't have one without the other. From the very first day that Gutenberg used moveable type to print a document, we've looked for ways to improve the process. It would be inaccurate to say that Gutenberg had much to worry about from early computers. Those green screens with monospaced type that you could barely read were an exercise in frustration for most people. Today we can put together a document that would've made Gutenberg green with envy in a fraction of the time that it would have taken him just to lay out the type.

Windows 95 improves on the process of printing a great deal. Even the simple act of installing a printer is easier now. Removing one is easier still. Managing your fonts has also taken a turn for the better. For one thing, you no longer have to dig through your \SYSTEM directory looking for them. Windows 95 places them in a separate directory and provides a utility that you can use to manage them.

The following sections take you on a tour of the complex world of printers. Windows 95 has taken some of the pain out of managing your printer; now there are more choices and more features than ever before. I'll show you how to use these features to your benefit and explain some of the more intriguing aspects of the new environment that Windows 95 provides.

Installing a Printer

Before you can use a printer, you have to install and configure it. I used to hate doing this under Windows 3.x because it seemed as if every printer was just different enough to make life difficult. It was a nice surprise to see how easy things are under Windows 95. We looked at the topics of installing and configuring your printer briefly in Chapters 10 and 13. Chapter 10 told you how to perform a special file installation. In Chapter 13, we looked at a few of the most efficient ways to use your printer's capabilities. This section provides the details required to install a printer. It also includes some productivity tips.

The Printer Folder

Even if you don't have any printers installed on your system, you'll have a Printer folder in Control Panel. At a minimum, this folder will contain an applet that allows you to install a new printer. This is the applet we'll use to add a new printer to your system. The following procedure takes you through a generic installation session. We'll take a look at some configuration details as well.

1. Use the Start | Settings | Printers command to open the Printers folder. You might see one or more printers already installed in the folder, along with the Add Printer applet.

2. Double-click the Add Printer applet. You'll see the dialog shown in Figure 14.1.

Figure 14.1.
The Add Printer Wizard provides an easy method of adding a new printer to your system.

Note: You might not see the dialog shown in Figure 14.2 if your machine doesn't have network support installed. If you don't see Figure 14.2, simply bypass the rest of step 3 and the first sentence of step 4. You should see the dialog in Figure 14.3, which allows you to select a printer type.

3. Click on Next. The dialog shown in Figure 14.2 will appear. This is where you determine whether this will be a network or local printer. Selecting the Network printer option allows you to share the printer with other people. Selecting the Local printer option won't allow sharing, but it will provide some advantages when it comes to the spooler. (See Chapter 13 for more details on this topic.)

Figure 14.2.
This dialog allows you to choose between a local and a network printer setup.

Tip: Windows doesn't restrict you from creating multiple installations for the same printer. In fact, doing so will allow you to create multiple setups that are optimized for specific types of jobs. I covered this topic in detail in Chapter 13.

4. Choose either Network printer or Local printer and click on Next. The Add Printer Wizard will ask you to select a printer using the dialog shown in Figure 14.3. Notice that there are two lists. The one on the left contains a list of printer manufacturers. Selecting a

vendor will change the list on the right to display printers manufactured by that vendor. Windows also allows you to install an unsupported printer by clicking on the Have Disk pushbutton. We covered this procedure in Chapter 10, so I won't talk about it again here.

Figure 14.3.
Use the entries in this dialog to select a printer vendor and model.

5. After you've selected a printer vendor and model, click on Next. The next dialog (see Figure 14.4) asks you to select a printer port. In most cases, you'll see only the local ports if you haven't used a network printer port before. I'll show you how to add a network printer port in the section "Configuration." We'll also look at a problem with using network ports with Windows 95.

Figure 14.4.
The port selection list might not include any network connections if you haven't used them before.

Tip: You can create multiple connections for one printer. I normally add a File connection as a minimum so that I can delay printing until later. A fax connection is also a good idea to support applications that don't provide a fax connection.

6. Select a port. You may configure the DOS options for the port by clicking on the Configure Port pushbutton. We covered these options in Chapter 13. Click on Next to continue. You'll see the dialog shown in Figure 14.5.

Figure 14.5.
*This dialog allows you to
select a printer name and
whether it is the default
printer.*

7. You have two important decisions to make in this dialog. The first is what to name the printer. The Add Printer Wizard will suggest something appropriate, and you can accept this name if you intend to create only one copy of the printer. However, you might want to use a more descriptive name if you plan to install multiple configurations of the same printer. The second decision is whether to make this the default printer. Windows applications use the default printer unless you specifically select something else. You should make the default printer the one you'll use the most often.

8. Click on Next to continue. You should see the dialog shown in Figure 14.6. I always send a test page to a local printer connected to an actual port. It makes little sense to print a test page for a file connection. Unless you already have your network connections configured, you'll need to test them later. Choose whether you want to print a test page and click on Next to complete the installation.

Figure 14.6.
*The final step in the
configuration process is to
print a test page to test your
printer connection and
configuration.*

9. Windows 95 will display a status dialog as it copies all the needed files to your drive. Once it completes this task, you will see the appropriate icon in the Printers folder. Double-clicking on this icon will allow you to view the current print jobs. Right-clicking will allow you to see the context menu.

As you can see, installing a printer isn't difficult. You'll probably need to configure the printer for your specific needs. I've found that Windows doesn't always choose the optimum settings for some items. For example, it chose the 180 × 180 resolution for my dot matrix printer instead of the higher-resolution 360 × 360 mode. The next section will take you through the process of adding a port. Then we'll look at the overall configuration procedure.

Adding a Port

Adding a network port is very easy under Windows 95. All you need to do is right-click on the Printer icon, select Properties, and click on the Details tab. You should see a dialog similar to the one shown in Figure 14.7. Windows 95 allows you to perform a variety of tasks in this dialog, including changing the printer by changing the driver you're using. The port-specific buttons allow you to add a new port or delete an existing one.

Figure 14.7.
The Details page of the Printer Properties dialog allows you to add, delete, and configure the ports your printer attaches to.

Clicking on the Add Port pushbutton displays the dialog shown in Figure 14.8. You can choose from two different types of ports using the radio buttons: local and network. The local (Other) options vary according to the utilities you have installed. They'll include a local port as a minimum. The options could include fax and Microsoft Network if you have them installed. The network connections will depend on the type of network you have installed and the devices that are shared on the network. You can use the Browse button to find a particular device. If you're using one of the networks that Windows 95 directly supports, a copy of Network Neighborhood will pop up.

Note: If your network isn't directly supported by Windows 95, its connections won't appear in Network Neighborhood. This means that you'll have to type the precise network connection information in by hand. Don't use any mapped names. Always use the fully qualified network path in this dialog.

Figure 14.8.

You can select from a variety of print connections in this dialog.

Clicking on OK at this point will store the new connection name and return you to the Details page. Windows 95 will automatically select the port as a destination. There's a problem with network connections, though: You can't configure them. You must capture the port first before you configure it. Capturing a port assigns it to a local connection. To capture a port, all you need to do is highlight it and click on the Capture Printer Port button. You'll see the dialog shown in Figure 14.9. Notice that it consists of three entries: a local port name, the network connection path, and a checkbox that asks if you want to reconnect to the port after each logon. I've noticed that Windows 95 still looks for the printer connection at each logon, even if you choose not to reconnect. The only difference that the reconnect checkbox makes is whether the connection is actually available for use.

Figure 14.9.

The Capture Printer Port dialog allows you to assign a network connection to a local port.

Tip: If you don't plan to use the network connection on a daily basis, use the End Capture pushbutton to remove the connection. This will save system resources and reduce boot time. It will also keep Windows 95 from displaying an error message if the connection isn't available the next time you boot the machine.

There's a final configuration issue for the ports you create on your machine. You need to decide what timeout settings to use. The first field, Not selected, determines how long Windows 95 will wait for a printer-ready signal. The only time that the printer provides this signal is when it's online and ready to go. The default value normally provides sufficient time. However, some specialty printers might require additional time if they perform some type of paper cycling or other maintenance procedure. The second setting, Transmission retry, determines how long Windows will try to send data to the printer. In some cases, the printer is online but is unable to print for some reason. Normally the default value works fine here as well. However, you might need to increase the value for network printers, especially on networks with print servers such as NetWare. Sometimes the print server is slow to respond because it's servicing another request.

Now we come to one of the problem areas associated with Windows 95 and ports. What happens when the network connection that you just created becomes invalid? Logic would dictate that you should be able to remove the network connection by using the Delete Port dialog. However, doing so will only net you an error message in some cases (see Figure 14.10). Windows 95 will refuse to delete the port.

Figure 14.10.
One of the potential problems that you'll face with a network connection is the inability to get rid of it.

There's a way around this problem. Simply open the registry to the key shown in Figure 14.11. Notice that this key contains subkeys, each one a network connection. In this particular case, LPT2 is assigned to the \\AUX\LABELS connection. You can delete the LPT2 key and remove the old network connection from your system. This technique is also more selective than simply deleting the old connection using the Delete Port dialog. In some situations, Windows will decide to delete all the network connections using the Delete Port method. Directly editing the registry is risky, but it can provide more control for the savvy network administrator.

Figure 14.11.
When Windows won't let you delete a port, use the Registry Editor to delete it instead.

Configuration

Configuring your printer should be the next step after you assign it to a port. Most of the settings control the appearance of the output and the features that the printer provides to the user. In some cases, a configuration option also affects the speed of printing. I'll let you know what kind of choices you'll be making as we go along.

Opening the Printer Properties dialog is as simple as right-clicking on the Printer icon and selecting the Properties option from the context menu. The first page you'll always see is the General page, shown in Figure 14.12. All this page contains is the printer name, a comment that other users can use to identify the printer, and a separator page entry. The comment can contain any information you want it to, such as the days and times that the printer is available for use. You shouldn't make any temporary comments since this field gets copied only once to other machines that need to use the printer. In other words, the comment is permanent and won't change as you change the comment on your machine. The Separator page option is useful when more than one person uses the printer. It sends a page containing your name and other identifying information to the printer before it actually prints your document. Using a separator page wastes a piece of paper for each print job, but it does make sorting through the printouts a lot easier. There's also a Print Test Page pushbutton at the bottom of the screen. You can use this to test the capabilities of your printer at any time.

Figure 14.12.
The General page of the Printer Properties dialog allows you to change the basic identification of the printer.

The Sharing page, shown in Figure 14.13, allows you to share the printer with other people. It contains two radio buttons. Selecting the Shared As button allows other people to use the printer. You must provide a share name. The comment and password are optional. I always recommend including a comment so that other people will know whether this printer's the one they're actually looking for. Doing so will reduce the number of inadvertent connections to your machine. Once you share a printer, Windows 95 adds a hand to its icon. This shows that the printer is shared and helps prevent any confusion over local and network resources.

Figure 14.13.
Use the Sharing page to
allow other people to use
your printer.

 Tip: Sharing reduces your spooling options. In addition, using a shared printer imposes other speed penalties on the local user. I always create a second printer for myself that isn't shared. This way, I get the best of both worlds: a shared printer for other people to use, and a nonshared printer that's configured specifically for my needs.

The Paper page, shown in Figure 14.14, allows you to select the paper you want to use. Windows 95 supports a much broader range of paper types than Windows 3.x did. I especially like all the envelope options. Although I don't use this particular feature, you might want to configure an envelope printer if you print envelopes a lot. The Orientation section allows you to choose the direction of printing: landscape or portrait. The Paper source listbox allows you to choose from the various paper bin options that the printer provides. The Copies field tells Windows how many copies of the printout to make. I usually find it easier to select the number of copies from within the application than to specify it here.

Figure 14.14.
The Paper page contains all
the entries required to select
your paper type and print
orientation.

Clicking on the Unprintable Area pushbutton will display the dialog shown in Figure 14.15. This dialog is especially important for laser printers, because they have a "dead zone" where the toner can't reach. The default settings are usually adequate unless you run into a special printing situation. For example, sometimes with my dot matrix I want to run the print almost to the edge of the page. The default settings won't allow me to do this, so I change them as required for the work I'm doing.

Figure 14.15.
You might need to change the defaults in the Unprintable Area dialog when printing to the edge of the page.

The name of the Graphics page is somewhat misleading. It also determines the print quality of the text you output using TrueType or other nonresident fonts when using some types of printers. For example, the settings on this page will affect a dot matrix or inkjet-type printer, but not a laser printer. The laser printer downloads its fonts, so the printer determines their quality level within the limitations of the resolution you set for it. Figure 14.16 shows the Graphics page.

Figure 14.16.
The Graphics page might affect more than just graphics, depending on the type of printer you use.

The Resolution field on this page has a significant effect on the output quality of your document. It also has an effect on print speed and could affect system memory. High-resolution printouts require more time, especially from a dot matrix printer, in which the output speed could drop to as little as one-tenth the normal level. In addition, managing these printouts will require more system resources such as CPU cycles and memory. Finally, any high-resolution printout that uses the spooler will need more temporary disk storage as well. Always consider all the factors before choosing a particular course of action with your printer. A lower-resolution printout might not look as appealing, but it will reduce the drain on system resources.

The various dithering options allow you to determine how Windows represents color on your printer output. It's especially important to use the correct settings for black-and-white printers, because Windows has fewer methods to provide aesthetically pleasing color differentiation. The None option forces Windows to use the printer's built-in capabilities rather than dither the image. This usually doesn't work very well with noncolor printers. As with the resolution settings we just talked about, the Coarse option takes less time to process but produces less pleasing results. Coarse dithering normally provides one-fourth the number of color combinations that the Fine option produces. I use the Fine option for final print output. It provides the best color differentiation your printer can support. The Line art option removes the colors and prints only the lines used to create a graphic. It comes in handy when you need to print an outlined graphic and don't want the colors to interfere with the quality of the output. Finally, Windows 95 provides an Error diffusion option. Have you ever seen a pattern in the dithering scheme used by some printers? This is called a moiré pattern. Most artists consider it a nuisance. The Error diffusion option trades a little additional processing time for a random dithering scheme. It reduces the chance that you'll see patterns in your printed output.

The Intensity slider allows you to change the darkness of your printout. It works like the slider on your toaster. The default value of 100 usually produces the crispest printout when you're using a new ribbon or cartridge.

> **Tip:** The Intensity slider can actually save you money. Simply set it lower when you first install a ribbon or cartridge. This will reduce the amount of ink or toner that you use per page. Of course, the quality of the printout will suffer slightly. Increasing the darkness as you near the end of the ribbon or cartridge's life will allow you to use it longer. Doing so might cause some graphics to look "muddy," but this setting won't adversely affect text.

Some printers include an additional setting like the one shown at the bottom of the page. In this case, the Printer Properties dialog is asking whether you want to output graphics in vector or raster mode. (I describe the difference between vector and raster graphics in the "Font Types" section.) Using vector graphics might provide a little more flexibility. This will also reduce the processing load on the machine at the expense of the printer. In addition, vector graphics require more printer memory, because you need to store both a vector graphic and its raster counterpart. Using raster graphics means a slower printout, but this could allow you to print pages that wouldn't otherwise fit in printer memory.

The Fonts page, shown in Figure 14.17, allows you to control how the printer handles fonts. Since the font capability of a printer varies from machine to machine, it's very likely that your Font page will look different than mine. However, there are some standard capabilities, and we'll cover them here.

Figure 14.17.
The contents of the Fonts page can vary greatly from machine to machine.

Most printers support cartridges these days. Even the lowliest dot matrix printer usually provides some type of cartridge support. The Cartridges listbox in this dialog allows you to tell Windows which cartridges the printer contains.

Note: Windows 95 still doesn't provide complete cartridge support for all printers. For example, Epson has sold a master cartridge for its LQ series printer for a number of years. This cartridge contains all of the fonts that the printer will support. Unfortunately, Windows 95 doesn't list this option in the Cartridges listbox, so you can't use the full potential of this feature. Always check the Cartridges listbox to determine which fonts Windows 95 supports before you make an investment.

Most laser printers provide the capability to manage TrueType fonts. There are three options in this case, but your printer might support only one or two of them. The first option allows you to download the fonts as an outline. This is the most flexible option and the one that I generally recommend. The advantage of this method is that the printer can create the full range of type sizes that TrueType allows. This method also saves memory, because the TrueType font will probably take less room than the bitmap equivalents. The negative side to this selection is that it will cost you some print time. The printer will have to render all the fonts that it needs for a print job rather than just use them. The second option allows you to download the fonts as bitmaps. You would use this option if you intended to use only a few fonts for your print jobs and speed were a critical factor. This option will probably use more memory, but it really depends on how many bitmaps you download and their size. The third option is for people who don't have much printer memory to spare. It keeps the TrueType fonts loaded on the local machine. The advantage is greatly reduced printer memory requirements. The disadvantage is greatly increased print times. Sending output to a printer in graphics rather than text mode takes at least twice as long under the best circumstances. Think twice before committing to this particular option.

The HP LaserJet (and other printers) come with a special utility that allows you to download fonts. You access the download utility by clicking on the Install Printer Fonts pushbutton near the bottom of the dialog. Figure 14.18 shows what this dialog looks like. Essentially, you tell the utility which fonts you want to download to the printer, and it takes care of the rest. Since each download utility is different, I won't go into further detail here.

Figure 14.18.

Some laser printers include a font download utility that you access from the Fonts page of the Printer Properties dialog.

The final page of the printer configuration dialog is Device Options (see Figure 14.19). As in so many other cases, the laser printer provides more options than other types of printers you might use. Just about every printer you use will include a Print quality listbox. This allows you to select from the various quality modes that the printer supplies. In most cases, the term is a little nebulous. A printer might provide a "letter quality" mode and a "draft" mode. Don't confuse this setting with resolution, because the two settings are completely different. The best course of action is to check out your printer manual to find out exactly what this term means to a particular vendor. In general, letter quality is always better than draft. However, as you can see from Figure 14.19, some vendors don't use easily recognized terms. In this case, there's nothing you can do but read the manual.

Figure 14.19.

The Device Options page can contain just about anything.

There are three other optional fields on this page. One that's common to most laser printers is the Printer memory field. The printer normally knows how much memory it has, but the Windows 95 driver doesn't. The LaserJet 4 also includes special features such as page protection and a printer memory manager. You'll want to spend some time reading your printer manual to determine precisely what these settings will do for you.

Point and Print

Point and print is a new Windows 95 feature. It allows you to do a few things you couldn't do with previous versions of Windows. The most significant thing it does is simplify remote printer installation. All you need to do to install a remote printer from a Windows 95, Windows NT, or NetWare network location is drag the icon from Network Neighborhood into the Printer folder. Windows 95 will take care of the rest. It might ask you to insert the CD-ROM so that it can load the proper drivers on your machine. Other than that, installation is as close to automatic as you can get.

Note: If you need access to a printer attached to a WFW workstation or a print server that doesn't support point and print, you can still load the printer driver using the standard technique we talked about at the beginning of this chapter. Dragging any icon from Network Neighborhood to your Printer folder should at least start the installation utility. Double-clicking on the Printer icon in Network Neighborhood will accomplish the same thing as Windows attempts to open the Printer Status dialog. (Whether it is successful or not depends on the limitations of your network, the printer driver, and whether the remote workstation responds.)

Quick Printing Techniques

Remember the context menu I've been talking about throughout the book? Well, you won't escape it in this chapter either. Windows 95 takes a proactive approach when it comes to printing. There are a lot of different ways you can get a document to the printer. I usually use the context menu shown in Figure 14.20, since most of my documents go to the same place if I don't have them open. Of course, you still have the usual Windows defaults for sending a document to the printer, including your application's Print menu.

Figure 14.20.
The context menu for a document usually offers the choice of sending the document to the default printer.

Tip: We've viewed DDE in a variety of ways throughout this book. The most recent was in Chapter 11, where we discussed some of the ways you can use DDE with a document. In Chapter 5, we looked at the way Explorer uses DDE. Here's one additional way to use DDE: Use Explorer to add another menu option to the context menu of your documents if you normally use more than one printer. This will allow you to select something other than the default printer with the context menu. Unfortunately, your application must support DDE in order for this option to work. Use the current Print entry as a basis for creating your advanced Print option.

Another method that people use to send documents to the printer is to place a shortcut to the printer on their Desktop. Then, all you need to do to print a document is drag it to the printer you want to use and drop it. Of course, using this technique consumes some valuable Desktop real estate, so you'll want to use it only when required.

32-Bit Printing

Now that you have a printer configured and ready for use, it might be a good time to look at the way Windows 95 handles this task. An understanding of how printing works will often help you discover new optimization techniques or track down an equipment failure with ease. Figure 14.21 gives you an overview of the Windows 95 print architecture. I describe each component in the following list.

- Graphics device interface (GDI): We've talked about this particular element of the printing picture in the past. The GDI is the API that an application uses to talk to the printer. An application doesn't directly access a printer like DOS did. It uses the Windows services. This allows for centralized scheduling and control of print jobs, a necessary requirement of a multitasking environment.

- Device-independent bitmap (DIB) engine: The DIB engine is normally associated with the display adapter. It works with the GDI to produce the bitmap you see on-screen. For example, when Windows displays wallpaper on the Desktop, it's the DIB engine that actually produces the bitmap under the instruction of the GDI. We'll talk about this topic more in Chapter 16. As far as a printer is concerned, the DIB engine provides a convenient method of manipulating graphics. For example, if you choose to print a file in graphics mode instead of text mode, the DIB engine helps prepare the print job for you.

- Printer driver: This is the third piece of the print page preparation. It interfaces with both the GDI and the DIB engine to produce printer-specific output in the form of journal records. Think of a journal record as the disassembled pieces of a puzzle. All the pieces will eventually be put together, but for right now, each record is just a piece of that puzzle. Just like with puzzle pieces, you can look at them individually and recognize what they will eventually become.

Figure 14.21.
Windows 95 uses an improved print architecture that depends on minidriver support.

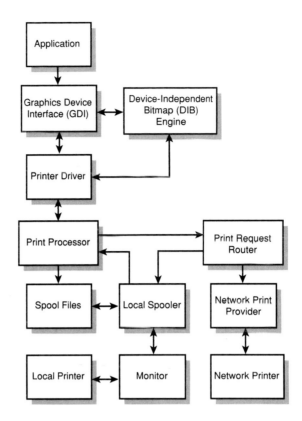

- Print processor: The print processor accepts the printer-ready data from the printer driver. Its only function at this point is to despool the data to the print request router. In other words, it sends the journal records out single file in an orderly manner. Later, the print processor takes care of spooling the data to the local hard drive (spool files) if this is a local print job. This means that it takes all the puzzle pieces (journal records) and connects them into a single document.

- Print request router: This component routes the formatted data to the appropriate location. It determines whether the job is for a local or remote printer. If it's for a remote printer, the print request router sends the data to the network print provider. Otherwise, it sends the data to the local spooler.

- Network print provider: The network print provider is network-specific. It's the interface between your machine and the beginning of the network data stream. Its job is to accept the journal records, connect them into a single document, convert the document into a network-specific format (if required), and transmit the converted data to the next component in the network data stream. If all goes according to plan, this data will eventually find its way to a network printer.

- Local spooler: The first job of this particular component is to hand off print jobs to the print processor. The print processor converts the journal records it receives into a document. The local spooler reads the data files that the print processor stores on disk and sends them to the monitor. It also accepts messages from the monitor regarding the status of the printer. We'll discuss the types of information it receives when we discuss the monitor.

- Spool files: These are the physical files that the print processor stores in the Spool folder under the main Windows folder. Each printer type has its own storage location in this folder.

- Monitor: The monitor handles all communication with the printer. It accepts data from the spooler and transmits it to the printer. The monitor is also responsible for providing the spooler with plug and play information about the printer. Finally, the monitor provides the spooler with printer error information. Instead of giving you a "printer not ready" message, printers that support a bidirectional port can supply an "out of paper" or "toner low" message.

This might look like a lot of work just to get your document from an application to the printer that's connected to your machine. You're right. If that's all the tasks that Windows 95 could handle, this architecture would be very inflated indeed. However, there's much more here than meets the eye. Using this kind of interface provides the user with a lot more freedom in regard to printer usage. It ensures that everyone gets equal access to the printer. Programmers benefit as well, because it's easier to write print drivers. The DIB engine improves the quality of your output. I could go on, but I think the point is made. The printing architecture might be complex, but it makes printing easier from a user perspective.

Managing Print Jobs

With so many new capabilities, it's no small wonder that your ability to manage print jobs under Windows 95 is improved as well. Gaining access to the print jobs you have running is no problem. Whenever you print, Windows adds a Printer icon to the control area of the Taskbar. Resting your mouse pointer over the Printer icon will tell you how many print jobs are pending (see Figure 14.22). This provides a quick method of monitoring your printer status without opening any new windows.

If multiple printers are in use on your workstation at one time, right-clicking on the Printer icon will display a menu of available printers (see Figure 14.23). You can choose to open one or all of them. The top menu item will open all active printers—those with print jobs. It doesn't matter if the print job is paused or not.

The following sections describe the management tools that Windows provides for printers. We'll look at both local and remote printers.

Figure 14.22.
The Printer icon tells you how many print jobs are pending. Right-clicking tells you which printer is being used.

Figure 14.23.
Right-clicking on the Printer icon on the Taskbar allows you to choose a new printer.

Local Printers

The first type of printer we'll look at is the local printer. All you need to do to open a printer is right-click on the Printer icon and select it from the list. As an alternative, double-clicking on this icon will display the current print jobs for the default printer. The printer management display is shown in Figure 14.24.

Figure 14.24.

Getting to the dialog needed to manage your print jobs under Windows 95 is easily accomplished from the Taskbar.

Note: Windows 95 will always default to a printer with an error. If you're having a printing problem, double-clicking on the Printer icon will display the problem printer. The Printer icon will also change in appearance to tell you there's a failure. This allows you to track the status of all your print jobs, even if the printer isn't in the same room as you.

Managing jobs is fairly simple. Once you open the printer management display, you can access all the print jobs on an individual basis. The Printer menu contains two options that allow you to control the printer itself: Pause Printing and Purge Print Jobs. The Pause Printing option allows you to stop the printer momentarily and restart it later. You could use this option to stop the printer for a quick ribbon change or to correct a paper jam. Purge Print Jobs clears all the print jobs from the spooler. Use this option with care, because you might accidentally remove something you didn't want to.

This menu has several other options as well. The Save as Default option allows you to maintain any configuration changes you make as permanent settings. The Properties option opens the Printer Properties dialog we discussed earlier.

You can access the Document menu in one of two ways. The first method is to select a document and access the menu directly. The second method is faster: Just right-click on the document you want to work with and select the option from the context menu. The Document menu has two options. You can pause print jobs using the Pause Printing option. The Cancel Printing option removes the print job from the spooler.

Tip: One thing that isn't apparent when you look at this display is the fact that you can select a print job and move it somewhere else in the list. This allows you to change the priority of print jobs by simply moving them around as needed. You can move groups of print jobs with equal ease.

Remote Printers

Managing a remote printer under Windows 95 is nearly as easy as managing a local one. The only caveat is that the print server must be a Windows 95, Windows NT, NetWare, or other network that supports point and print. Otherwise, remote print jobs won't show up on your display. Once you do establish a connection with the remote printer, you can exercise all the document management capabilities you have with a local printer. (All this assumes that you have the access rights required to perform the task.)

Remote printing does offer one opportunity that local printing doesn't. You can perform what is called an *offline* print. Essentially, this is a form of pause. The Printer menu contains a special option for remote printers called Work Offline. Figure 14.25 shows a remote printer in the Work Offline mode. Checking the Work Offline selection pauses the printer and stores the print jobs on disk. When you uncheck this entry, all the print jobs get sent to the remote printer.

Figure 14.25.
The Work Offline option allows you to work with a printer, even when it isn't connected.

Notice the Printer folder display in Figure 14.25. The printer that's in Work Offline mode is grayed out. Windows 95 provides this visual indicator to tell you that you can use the printer but that none of the print jobs will actually go anywhere. Another reminder is the Printer icon on the Taskbar. You'll see the Printer icon, but it will include the error indicator I mentioned earlier. Again, this tells you that one of the printers requires service. In this case, it isn't an unexpected error, merely a feature that Windows 95 provides.

Font Types

You'll need to learn about two different types of fonts when using Windows 95. The raster font provides you with a nonresizeable bitmap form of font that's quick to use. The vector font comes in a variety of forms, but all of them share one common feature: They all represent the font as a series of math equations rather than a bitmap. This makes the vector font easy to resize. The following sections detail the use of both font types under Windows 95.

Raster Fonts

Most people don't use raster fonts for printing purposes anymore. The biggest reason is that they're inconvenient. You can't resize a raster font. That means that you have to keep one copy of each font size you plan to use on disk. In addition, you also have to keep one copy of each style: roman, italic, bold italic, and bold. Since raster fonts represent each character as a bitmap, the size of the file used to hold them also increases in size as the point size of the font increases. A small 6-point font might consume only 4 KB, but a 12-point font will consume 8 KB or more. It doesn't take very many of these fonts to exceed the 60 KB storage that most TrueType fonts require.

Problems aside, raster fonts don't require any additional work to use; they are already bitmaps. It's this factor that keeps some forms of raster font around. A raster font is easy to display, so you'll often see it used as a display font. This is especially true for areas in which you need only one or two font sizes at a time, such as the DOS window.

Another advantage to raster fonts is that they tend to produce a better display when used at their specific size than a vector font does. The reason is simple: The vendor can hand-tune the appearance of each raster font for a specific size. A vector font has no such ability. Unless the vendor that created the font includes hinting (which I'll describe later), a raster font will produce the better result in most cases.

Vector Fonts

Vector fonts are stored as mathematical formulas. These formulas specify how to draw each character in the font. A vector font doesn't contain a bitmap that a device can use as output, so it must render (or draw) the font each time it's used. Windows 95 reduces the overhead of creating recently used fonts by storing them in the TTFCACHE file in your main Windows directory. However, this takes care of only one problem with using vector fonts.

A vector font's rigid mathematical representation of how the font should look also has problems. Many people have noticed that some vector fonts look good at one point size and others at a different point size. The problem is that even though the font is a perfect representation, the number of pixels used to represent it allow discrepancies to creep in. Normally, a font vendor would hand-tune this representation to get rid of the discrepancy or at least fool the eye into thinking that it was gone. Vector fonts have no such luxury.

TrueType and other font types introduced a new idea called *hinting*. A hint is a way to create an exact representation of the font and then modify that representation slightly to fool the human eye. What you see is a tuned version of the font. It's not as well-tuned in many cases as a raster equivalent would be, but it's close enough to create the right visual effect.

These problems aside, vector fonts have a great deal to recommend them. Their relatively small size allows you to keep many of them on your hard disk without filling it up. In addition, you can resize a vector font to just about any point size. It even allows you to create fractional-point-size fonts. You can't do this with a raster font.

Understanding TrueType

TrueType is a specific form of vector font. It comes with hinting and other features that mark an advanced font format. The important thing to remember is that TrueType is the native font format supplied with Windows 95 (and many previous versions of Windows, for that matter). If you want to use other font formats, you need to install a third-party manager. In most cases, you won't want to expend the memory to use a third-party manager. All the vendors who used to support alternatives to TrueType have now dropped that support because of the problems with supporting more than one font manager under Windows.

Note: There's a big difference between printer fonts and third-party fonts. Laser printers usually include a number of specialized printer fonts that you can download to the printer. You can still use these fonts with ease under Windows 95. In fact, Windows has actually made the process of downloading easier. Contrast this with third-party products such as Adobe Type Manager, which must load as an application under Windows. Trying to use two different font managers at the same time not only wastes time and effort, but also seems more than a little counterproductive. Even though such measures were warranted before TrueType font support became widespread, they are no longer necessary under Windows 95.

How can you differentiate between a TrueType font and any other font on your system? We'll see later that Windows 95 provides different icons for the two types. Another way to detect the difference is by their extensions. Windows 95 provides a number of files with the .FON extension. These are either raster or vector fonts originally supplied with Windows 3.x. TrueType fonts are far superior to these fonts in capability and appearance.

> **Tip:** Windows 3.x required that a TrueType font use two files. The first had a .FON extension and pointed to the second, which had a .TTF extension. Windows 95 no longer requires the first file. As a result, you can erase any .FON files on your hard drive without any loss of font data. Make certain, however, that the .FON file really is an older Windows 3.x font file. Normally these files appeared in the Windows \SYSTEM directory.

Hinting is one of the things that differentiates a TrueType font from a standard font. This normally affects the printed output by making characters appear "normal" to the human eye. As I explained in the discussion of vector fonts, storing fonts as a mathematical expression has the undesired effect of introducing small errors at some resolutions. The result is very unappealing. The fonts look normal, but your eye tells you that something isn't quite right.

Windows 95 also provides another font feature called *anti-aliasing*. This feature removes the jagged lines you normally see when a font becomes too large. It can also help small fonts become more readable. All this comes from the way that Windows 95 uses the hinting contained in TrueType fonts to display them.

The final benefit of using TrueType fonts is the fact that Windows uses the same font for both screen and printer. Older font technologies used one font for the screen and another for the printer. The reason is fairly obvious with raster fonts. The different resolutions of your display and printer would make the raster font appear much larger on one than the other. The same thing holds true for vector fonts, but to a much smaller degree. Using the same font for both screen and printer means that what you see on the screen is what you'll receive from the printer in the form of output.

Installing Fonts

Just about everyone needs a new font from time to time. Getting ready for a presentation, a new company policy, the need to differentiate your work from someone else's, or simply a need for change can all provide the motivation needed to install a new font. Under Windows 3.x it was fairly easy to install a font, but you were never quite sure what you were getting. In addition, you had to use a program that made the whole process seem a little more mysterious than it needed to be.

There are actually two ways to install a font in Windows 95. I'm going to show you both ways. The first method is the one that Microsoft recommends. The second method is the one that I use because it allows me to look before I leap.

The Standard Font Installation Method

The standard method of installing a font is pretty straightforward, but it does prevent you from really seeing the font before you install it. In this way, it shares some of the deficiencies of the older

Windows 3.x method. On the other hand, it's safer because it's guaranteed to work every time. With that in mind, let me show you the first method of font installation.

1. Open Control Panel and double-click on the Fonts icon. You should see the display shown in Figure 14.26.

Figure 14.26.
This Explorer-style display allows you to view all the fonts installed on your machine.

2. Use the File | Install New Fonts command to display the Add Fonts dialog, shown in Figure 14.27.

Figure 14.27.
The Add Fonts dialog allows you to select fonts to add to your Windows installation.

3. Browse your hard disk, floppy disk, or CD-ROM drive until you find the fonts that you want to install. Highlight the desired fonts and click on OK. You'll see the new fonts in your Font folder.

The Enhanced Font Installation Method

I prefer a little more control when I install fonts on my machine. For one thing, I like to have a good idea of what they look like. Installing a font so that you can view it seems a little counterintuitive to me, and it should to you as well. Windows 3.x didn't offer me much of a choice in this regard; I had to follow the Microsoft way of installing a font. Windows 95 does offer some choices. I found that this particular installation technique is both easy and flexible. Best of all, it allows me to view the fonts before I install them.

1. Open Explorer. Open the directory tree so that you can see the Fonts folder under the main Windows 95 directory, as shown in Figure 14.28.

Figure 14.28.
You can see the Fonts folder using Explorer; you just have to look in the right place.

2. Select the directory that contains the fonts you want to add. Double-click on the first font to see what it looks like. You should see a dialog similar to the one shown in Figure 14.29. Repeat this process until you find all the fonts you want to add to your font directory.

Figure 14.29.
Double-clicking on a font allows you to see what it looks like.

3. Use the scroll bar to move the Fonts folder into view, but don't select it. Select all the fonts you want to move in the right window, and then simply move them to the Fonts folder, as shown in Figure 14.30.

Figure 14.30.
Windows 95 allows you to simply move the fonts that you want into the Fonts folder.

That's all there is to it. See how easy that was? This technique works just as well as the more formal technique. I find that it's more flexible, it's faster, and I really know what I'm getting.

Removing Fonts

Removing fonts is very easy under Windows 95. All you do is open the Fonts folder—either through Explorer or by double-clicking on the Fonts applet in Control Panel—select the fonts you want to remove, and press the Delete key. It's that easy.

You need to observe a few precautions. First and foremost, don't erase any font that you're not sure of. Windows 95 requires some fonts for system use, and erasing them could cause problems. Second, if you do erase a font, make sure that you don't need it anymore or that you have a copy stored somewhere.

> **Tip:** Instead of deleting a font that you no longer require, archive it. All you need to do is move it from the Fonts folder to a floppy disk or a network drive. You can even use the Send To option on the context menu to do it. This technique will save you heartache later when you look for the font you deleted and it's no longer available.

Viewing and Printing Fonts

The interface in the Fonts folder might be Explorer, but the options are different. The View menu contains some unique features that you'll want to use to really see your fonts. I'm not talking about the files themselves, but the fonts. Let me show you what I mean.

Open Control Panel and double-click on the Fonts applet. (You can get to the same place using the Explorer technique that I talked about earlier.) Open the View menu. You'll notice that Explorer now sports some new View options, as shown in Figure 14.31.

Figure 14.31.
The Fonts folder provides font-related view options that will come in handy as you learn to use Windows 95.

The List Fonts By Similarity option is the one I like. It allows you to see which fonts you could use as a substitute for something else. For example, what if you really like the font you're using for a particular purpose but want a slightly different effect? You could use this option to find the closest match in your directory or on a CD-ROM full of fonts. Figure 14.32 shows this display. Notice the field at the top of the display. This is where you select the name of the font you want to use for comparison purposes.

Another handy view selection is the Hide Variations option. You can use it with any of the display formats to hide the different files required to create a complete font family. For example, if you turn this option on, you will see only one Arial font, even though there are four files in the directory. Variations typically include bold, italic, and bold italic versions of the font. Figure 14.33 shows what this display looks like if you use the large icons format.

Unlike with Windows 3.x, it is very easy to print a sample of a font. All you need to do is right-click and select Print from the context menu. As an alternative, you can always click on the Print pushbutton when viewing the font or use the File | Print command. The printout you get will look similar to Figure 14.29.

Figure 14.32.
You can quickly find font families on a disk full of fonts using the List Fonts By Similarity option.

Figure 14.33.
Use the Hide Variations option to clear some of the clutter that might otherwise obscure a specific font that you want to see.

How Windows Matches Fonts

Windows uses a specific set of criteria to find a replacement font if the one you request isn't available. To get an idea of how this works, use the List Fonts By Similarity option in the Font folder. The results will tell you a lot about how Windows 95 implements the rules in something called the font matching table.

The font matching table isn't actually a table; it's an algorithm that Windows 95 uses to match fonts. Windows uses the following criteria to find a matching font: the character set, variable versus fixed pitch, family, typeface name, height, width, weight, slant, underline, and strikethrough.

A TrueType font is always replaced with another TrueType font, even if a raster or vector font is a closer match. This enables your application to maintain the flexibility that TrueType provides. The negative aspect of this is that the output might not look even close to what you originally anticipated.

If the font you're trying to use is either a vector or raster font, Windows 95 will use some additional methods to obtain a good match. The following list shows, in order, the sources that Windows 95 will try to tap.

1. Printer ROM font
2. Printer cartridge slot font
3. Downloadable soft font
4. TrueType font

Note: Microsoft Plus! adds font smoothing to Windows 95 if you're running high-color video or better. Font smoothing gets rid of jagged edges you might see when the fonts are very large. To turn on font smoothing after installing Microsoft Plus!, right-click on the Desktop icon in Explorer and select Properties from the context menu. On the Plus! page of the Display Properties dialog box, check the Smooth edges of screen fonts checkbox. For more information on other Plus! features, see Chapter 24.

On Your Own

This chapter showed you two different ways to install fonts. Try both methods to see which works best for you. Many graphics programs include additional fonts. You can also download them from CompuServe and many BBSs. Use this exercise to install the set of fonts that will get the job done for you.

Look in your \FONTS folder to see if you can identify the various types of fonts that Windows 95 supports. How can you tell them apart? What purpose does each kind of font serve?

Install several versions of your printer, each with different settings. Try this new installation for several weeks and see if you notice the additional ease of use that several pseudo-printers can provide. Also try the various print settings to see if you notice the variations in print speed and output quality that I mentioned earlier.

Place a shortcut to your printer on the Desktop and try the drag and drop method of printing. Simply drag a file with your mouse pointer to the Printer icon and drop it. This is the easy way of sending output to the printer using the default setup. You might want to experiment to see which printer settings work best as a default setup for you.

15

Mice and Keyboards

The keyboard has been the mainstay of data input from the very beginning of computers. Even before people used displays—when everything was done using keypunch cards—they still sat at a keyboard to create input. It's somewhat amusing to see the strange arrangements of "ergonomically correct" keyboards on the market today. There was one keyboard, not too long ago, that looked like Chinese finger puzzles. You slipped the keyboard over your hands. Moving a finger forward would type one character, back another, right still another.

A little less strange are the permutations that the mouse has gone through. It started out looking like a bar of soap. Today's versions are all shaped to fit the palm of your hand. The fact that every vendor used a different human for measurement is reflected in the size and shape variations of this new breed of rodent. Every manufacturer seems to have at least settled on two or three mouse buttons. If you've been around long enough, you'll remember the multibutton monstrosities that some companies introduced. I still remember the 12-button mouse that one company tried to get everyone to buy. It allowed the user to basically replace the keyboard for command codes by using the mouse buttons. Unfortunately, it was nearly impossible to use, and the button combinations were even worse.

Aside from these physical manifestations, there are a variety of other ways that the keyboard and mouse have changed. Every mouse used to come with menuing software for your DOS applications; perhaps many of them still do. I haven't had to use my software for quite a while now; I might retire it permanently if things continue to go well with Windows 95. Still, this old software sits on my hard drive waiting to fulfill its destiny as an aid to DOS application enhancement.

Gone too are the keyboard enhancers that everyone bought into. They were well worth the money when introduced, but the benefits they provided seem a little weak in retrospect. Still, I don't know what I would have done without some of them when DOS was in its prime.

The more things change, the more they stay the same. My Logitech mouse came with some handy Windows utilities. For example, I can change the way that the buttons work within applications. I assigned one key combination to cut text and another to paste it. It's pretty handy to be able to grab some text, cut it, move the mouse, and then paste where needed. Of course, I don't even need this feature in applications such as Word, which provides full text movement features.

Windows 95 has also gotten in on the new and improved input device bandwagon. Some of these changes are very worthwhile, and others are sort of ho-hum unless you really need them. The following sections give you a tour of the great, and not so great, mouse and keyboard improvements that Windows 95 has made.

Multilingual Support

I partially covered this feature in past chapters. More of the world is using Windows today, so it's not too surprising to see Windows come in a variety of language options. I was a little surprised by the fact that this language support is at least partially built into every copy of Windows. No longer do you have to perform strange rituals and hand-edit your system files to get the proper level of language support. Windows 95 has it built right in using the code pages that we all learned to hate under DOS.

Installing a New Language

The convenience factor of using multilingual support under Windows 95 is compounded by the fact that you don't have to memorize code page numbers. Installing a new keyboard language is as simple as a few clicks. Let's take a look at what you'll need to do to install a new language on your machine.

1. Open Control Panel. Double-click on the Keyboard applet and select the Language tab. You should see a dialog similar to the one shown in Figure 15.1. Notice that English is the only language listed in the Language field. This field also provides other information that you can use to determine the installed language type. In this case, it tells you the type of English (United States) and the keyboard layout (United States).

Figure 15.1.
The Language page of the Keyboard Properties dialog allows you to select one or more languages for your computer.

2. Click on the Add pushbutton. You'll see the dialog shown in Figure 15.2. It's important to consider which version of a language to choose. The English example is a good one. I currently have United States English installed. There is also a selection for other forms of English that might require a different keyboard layout. For example, pressing Shift-4 could produce a pound symbol instead of a dollar sign. The choice of language also affects the way Windows makes assumptions about other setup needs. For example, it affects the default selection for monetary and numeric formats.

3. Click on OK to complete the process. You should see a new language added to the Language field. Completing this process also enables several other fields. For example, you can now choose which Ctrl-*key* combination to use to switch between languages. You can also choose whether or not to display the International icon on the Taskbar (I'll you show how to use this icon in a little while).

Figure 15.2.
*Make your choice of
language carefully, because
there are several variations of
some languages.*

4. Choose a default language by highlighting and then clicking on the Default Language pushbutton. You will see the new default displayed in the Default Language field.

5. You will probably want to check the layout for your new language. Highlight the new language and click on the Properties pushbutton. You should see the dialog shown in Figure 15.3. (This figure will also display the other changes you have made.) The dialog is a little deceptive. At first you might think that it's asking you to change the language again, but this isn't so. What it is asking you to change is your keyboard layout. Select a new layout to see for yourself.

Figure 15.3.
*This dialog will change your
keyboard layout, not the
language you're using.*

6. Click on OK to complete the process. In this case, I chose the Dvorak layout. Figure 15.4 shows the results. Notice that the language remains the same; only the keyboard layout has changed. I will use the Dvorak layout whenever I choose the German language from my list.

Figure 15.4.
*This dialog shows the results
of choosing another layout
using the Properties
pushbutton.*

Note: You might have noticed that this combination of language and layout provides the means to create a very customized keyboard layout. The folks at Microsoft call this *localization*. I call it a good idea for those of us who lived through the DOS code page nightmare. This elegant solution provides far greater flexibility than the user has ever had in the past. If you do need multilingual support, try the various options to see which setup is most comfortable.

7. Close the Keyboard Properties dialog to complete the process. Windows might ask you to insert a disk containing any files that it requires. You can accomplish the same thing using the Apply key if you don't want to close the Keyboard Properties dialog.

8. Close Windows and reboot your computer to make the change permanent.

Changing your keyboard layout and language won't display prompts in the language you select. It affects only the way your keyboard reacts and, to some extent, helps Windows 95 provide better input in regard to other configuration selections.

Removing a Language

You'll probably run into a situation in which you no longer require a specific keyboard layout. For example, you might have needed to use a German layout for a while to type letters to another office, but you don't need it any longer because that office closed. Whatever your reason for wanting to remove the language, Windows 95 makes it easy. The following procedure will show you how.

Tip: This would be a good time to use the procedures I showed you in Chapter 6 for checking the filenames of the drivers used to support the language you want to remove. Windows 95 won't remove these drivers, which means that they will clutter your hard drive until you decide to install Windows from scratch—hopefully, a long time from now. Recording the filenames now, before you remove the name from the Language page, means that you will be able to remove the driver files later on. Make certain you shut down and reboot your machine first, or Windows 95 will display an error message stating that the driver is in use.

1. Open Control Panel. Double-click on the Keyboard applet and select the Language page. You should see a dialog similar to the one shown in Figure 15.1.

2. You want to remove the German language support from your machine, so highlight that entry.

3. Click on the Remove pushbutton.

4. Close the Keyboard Properties dialog to complete the process. You can accomplish the same thing using the Apply key if you don't want to close the Keyboard Properties dialog. Windows might get confused and think that another application is using the keyboard layout if you activated it at any time during this session. All you need to do is click on OK to accept the error message. Windows will still remove the layout, but it won't do so until the next session.

5. Close Windows and reboot your computer to make the change permanent.

Note: Windows 95 will disable the Remove pushbutton if you have only one language installed. This makes sense, because you have to use a language in order to use the keyboard. It will also remove the International icon from the Taskbar if you have only one language.

Accessing a Language from the Taskbar

Whenever you have more than one language installed on your machine, Windows gives you the opportunity to automatically add the International icon to your Taskbar. Figure 15.5 shows what this icon looks like.

Figure 15.5.
The International icon provides quick access to multiple language selections.

The International icon

Peter's Principle: Easy Keyboard Access

Adding the International icon to your Taskbar is more than just a convenience that comes in handy when you need to change layouts from time to time. It provides a quick way to change all your keyboard settings whenever you need to. Of course, the number of keyboard settings is rather limited, but they are important. So, the question remains, why would I want easy keyboard access?

If you're like me, long hours at the keyboard really take their toll on your hands. The keyboard settings that you used this morning could make for a lot of mistakes this afternoon as you find yourself repeating more keystrokes than you intended. It's a pain to go through Control Panel every time you want to change something, so most people don't. That's where the trouble lies, in a lack of accessibility.

Having the International icon on your Taskbar provides quick access to the keyboard settings. However, it doesn't normally appear unless you install more than one language on your machine. You can manually add this icon to your Taskbar by adding the International Settings application—INTERNAT.EXE—to your Startup folder. You will find it in the SYSTEM folder, under the main Windows folder for your machine. (I don't know why Microsoft is so fond of placing the really neat utilities there, but if you ever need something, this is a good place to start looking.) This will give you access to the keyboard settings even if you have only one language installed.

There are several different ways to use this icon. The first is to determine which language you're currently using. Notice in Figure 15.4 that each language has a two-character abbreviation. The Taskbar is where this two-digit abbreviation gets used. For example, the icon shown in Figure 15.5 tells me that I have the United States English configuration installed.

A left-click on the International icon displays a list of languages currently installed on the machine, as shown in Figure 15.6. Notice that each entry is preceded by its two-digit abbreviation. This is one way to determine which language you're using if you forget what the abbreviation on the icon means. All you need to do to select a new language is click on it, just like you would with any other menu.

A right-click brings up the context menu shown in Figure 15.7. I was especially taken by the What's This? entry. It's apparent that no one at Microsoft thought the user would be able to figure this icon out for themselves. At least the associated help text is useful and could help someone who is just starting to learn to use Windows 95. I just wonder why Microsoft didn't include this help with the other icons for the sake of consistency, if for no other reason.

Figure 15.6.
*A left-click on the Interna-
tional icon allows you to
quickly switch between
installed languages.*

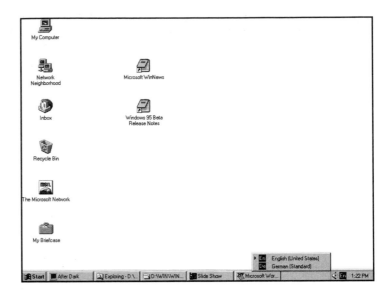

Figure 15.7.
*The context menu for the
International icon has a
somewhat strange entry in
it—What's This?*

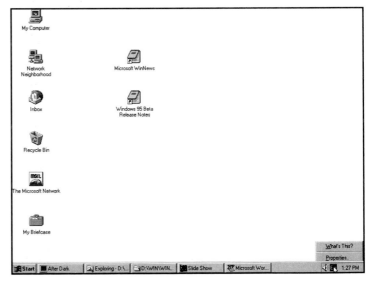

The Properties option of the context menu acts as you would expect. It takes you to the Keyboard Properties dialog that we looked at earlier. Even though it automatically displays the Language page, you can quickly switch to other pages as needed.

As with many of the other icons on the Taskbar, you can also momentarily hold your mouse cursor over the International icon to get more information. Doing so displays the full name of the language that you're currently using.

Configuring Your Keyboard

Languages aren't the only thing you can change about your keyboard. There are two more pages of selections that you can make regarding its setup. Figure 15.8 shows the first page. This is where you decide how the keyboard will react to your key presses.

Figure 15.8.
The Speed page contains the settings required to adjust the keyboard to your typing habits.

The Repeat delay setting adjusts how long the keyboard will wait before it starts repeating keys. Setting this value too short could force you to undo a lot of excess keystrokes. You will probably find this more of a problem at the end of the day. The Repeat rate setting adjusts how fast the characters repeat across the screen. Setting a slightly lower rate will enable you to control repeated keys better. Microsoft thoughtfully provided a test area that you can use to check the combination of settings. Make sure you actually try the keyboard settings for a while before you make big changes in the settings. I found that even small changes affect the way the keyboard reacts.

Use the Cursor blink rate setting to change how often the edit cursor blinks per second. Some people like a very fast rate, and other people like things a bit slower. You will want to use a slower rate on portables than you would on your Desktop machine, because it takes displays on these machines a little longer to react. A setting that works well on your Desktop machine might make the cursor disappear on your laptop.

The General page, shown in Figure 15.9, contains only one entry: the type of keyboard you're using. If you decide to use a different keyboard, click on the Change pushbutton to see a list of compatible devices. This list comes in handy when the driver you're currently using doesn't work as well as it should and you want to try a driver for a compatible device. In reality, you will seldom—if ever—need this option, because the keyboard driver setting is pretty straightforward. Clicking on the Show all devices radio button displays a complete list of keyboards that Windows 95 supports.

Figure 15.9.
Use the General page to
view the name of the
keyboard driver you're using
or to select a new one.

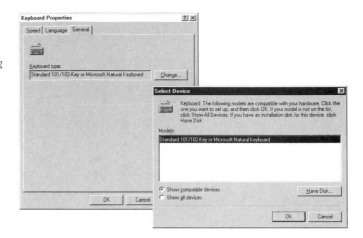

Configuring Your Mouse

Using a mouse started out as a nice feature in DOS. You really didn't have to use one, but some people viewed it as a productivity enhancer. By the time I started using Windows, the mouse had gone from being a nice feature to being a should-have feature. Early versions of Windows allowed you to get around pretty well without a mouse. Today a mouse is a must-have. To really use Windows, you have to have a mouse. Some tasks are difficult—if not impossible—to perform without one.

Just as you should configure your keyboard for optimum performance, you should configure your mouse as well. To do this, open the Mouse Properties dialog by double-clicking on the Mouse applet in Control Panel. Figure 15.10 shows what the first page, Buttons, looks like.

Figure 15.10.
The Buttons page of the
Mouse properties dialog
allows you to change the way
the mouse is configured and
reacts.

The first group of settings on this page allows you to reverse your mouse buttons for left-handed use. Windows 95 defaults to a right-handed installation. The second group allows you to change the double-click speed. I find that setting this during the middle of the workday seems to provide the best configuration for me. Your mouse's double-click speed is important. Setting it too low might mean that you'll double-click where you didn't intend to, especially in graphics programs, where you move the mouse and click a lot to select items. Setting this value too high is an exercise in frustration, because Windows won't wait long enough for you to double-click things. In some cases, this means that you'll get a menu in place of an action. In other cases, it will mean that you won't get anything done at all. The test area allows you to test this setting. A jack-in-the-box alternately appears and disappears when you double-click.

The Pointers page, shown in Figure 15.11, allows you to change the mouse pointers used to indicate specific events. Besides the standard cursors that Windows 3.x provided, Windows 95 provides a few "fancy" cursors, such as the 3-D versions displayed in the figure. In addition to the static cursors that you could use before, Windows 95 also provides some cursors that move.

Figure 15.11.
This page of the Mouse Properties dialog allows you to change the appearance of the mouse cursor.

The upper section of this page allows you to save and load various mouse schemes. Think of a mouse scheme in the same way that you would a color scheme under Windows 3.x, and you'll have the right idea. Use the listbox to select a previously saved scheme. Clicking on the Save As pushbutton displays a dialog that you can use to enter the name of a new scheme.

> **Tip:** Windows 95 provides a wealth of mouse pointers, including some extra-large ones. The extra-large pointers are actually designed for use with some of the Accessibility Options. However, they also come in handy on laptops, where seeing the cursor can be a real chore, and presentations, where a larger-than-normal cursor helps you make your point.

The lower section of the Pointers page contains the actual mouse pointers. The purpose of each pointer is self-explanatory. To change a cursor, highlight it and click on the Browse pushbutton. Windows will display a list of cursors in the CURSOR folder (found within the main Windows folder), as shown in Figure 15.12. All you need to do is double-click on the cursor you want. Windows will replace the current cursor with the one you selected. Notice that this dialog also displays a preview of the cursor. Any animated cursors will appear to move within the preview box. This is how they will look when you use them in an application or another area of Windows. If you ever select a cursor by accident and want to return it to the default setting, click on the Use Default pushbutton at the bottom of the Pointers page.

Figure 15.12.
Use the Browse dialog to select from the list of currently available cursors.

The Motion page, shown in Figure 15.13, affects how the mouse cursor tracks your hand movements. This is the slider at the top of the page. Setting the speed too high can cause jerky cursor movement and make it difficult to control some operations, such as drawing. Set the speed too low and you will need to make a large movement with the mouse to get a small movement on-screen.

Figure 15.13.
The Motion page allows you to set the pointer speed and whether Windows provides pointer trails.

The bottom half of this page controls whether Windows provides pointer trails. A pointer trail really isn't what most people think. Windows produces many copies of the pointer that track the movements you make with the mouse. These additional pointers are the pointer trail. The slider controls the length of the trail, and the checkbox turns it on or off. This feature is specially designed to make it easier for portable users to track the mouse's position. However, kids really like to see extra pointers on their display. Adding pointer trails can also help the visually impaired track the mouse.

The General page, shown in Figure 15.14, lets you change the type of mouse installed on your machine. The only time you would need to do this is if you replaced your mouse with a different type. Clicking on the Change pushbutton displays a dialog containing a list of supported mouse types. All you need to do is select the correct mouse type and click on OK to change the mouse driver.

Figure 15.14.

You use the General page to select a different mouse driver for your machine.

Access for Users with Disabilities

Windows 95 provides special access features for people with disabilities. I gave you an overview of these options in Chapter 1. We also looked at some of the speed keys that the Accessibility options provide in Chapter 5. I won't go over these details again here. What we will look at is the features themselves and how you can use them to enhance productivity. The first thing you'll need to do to look at these features is open Control Panel and double-click on the Accessibilities Options applet.

Special Keyboard Features

Windows provides three special keyboard features: StickyKeys, FilterKeys, and ToggleKeys. You'll find them on the Keyboard page of the Accessibility Properties dialog, as shown in Figure 15.15. You can turn any of them on by using the special key combinations that Microsoft provides.

All these features have one thing in common: They change the way that the keyboard works, independently of the keyboard driver. You must install the Accessibility Options feature to make them work. The option that intrigued me was the Show extra keyboard help in programs checkbox at the bottom of the page. It adds help information to applications that support this feature. Unfortunately, none of the applications that I tested, including the new Windows 95 utilities, supports it. Hopefully some vendors will pick up on this option later.

Figure 15.15.
You can turn on any of the keyboard accessibility-related functions from this page.

Using StickyKeys

The StickyKeys feature comes in handy for a variety of purposes. It makes the Shift, Ctrl, and Alt keys act as a toggle switch. Press the key once and it becomes active. Press it a second time and it's turned off. I don't really need this feature a lot, but it does come in handy for a couple of purposes.

One of the ways I use it is in graphics programs that require you to hold down the Ctrl key to select a group of items. It's kind of inconvenient to hold down the Ctrl key while you look around for objects to select. The StickyKeys feature alleviates this problem.

I also find that it's pretty handy when I want to type a lot of Alt-*key* combinations—for example, when I want to use the extended ASCII line-draw characters in a document. It's true that I could use the Character Map utility to do the same thing, but Character Map isn't always easy to access, and I might need only one or two characters.

Let's take a look at some of the options you can select. Click on the Settings pushbutton to open the Settings for StickyKeys dialog, shown in Figure 15.16.

Figure 15.16.
The Settings for StickyKeys dialog allows you to change how this feature works.

There are several groups of settings for StickyKeys. The first option, Keyboard shortcut, allows you to enable StickyKeys using the shortcut key. There really isn't any good reason to turn this off, since it's very unlikely that any application would use the same control key sequence.

The Options group contains two settings. Normally the StickyKeys option works like a toggle. Checking the first box tells Windows to wait until you press the same control key twice before making it active. The second checkbox is designed to allow two people to use the same keyboard. Pressing a control key and a noncontrol key at the same time will turn StickyKeys off.

The Notification group also contains two settings. The first setting tells Windows to play a different sound for each unique control key that it makes active. This can keep you from activating a control key by accident. The second option displays an icon on the Taskbar so that you can control StickyKeys more easily. I normally select this option to make it easier for me to turn StickyKeys on and off.

Using FilterKeys

Do you ever find yourself making a lot of extra keystrokes at the end of a long day? I do. There are times where some words come out like "tthis" instead of "this." FilterKeys is a perfect solution to the problem of tired hands. I use it all the time near the end of the workday to filter out those extra keystrokes.

As with StickyKeys, you can adjust the way FilterKeys works by clicking on the Settings pushbutton. The Settings for FilterKeys dialog appears in Figure 15.17. Notice that the first option in this dialog allows you to turn the shortcut key on and off. It works just like the same feature in StickyKeys. The Notification group at the bottom of the page should look familiar. The only difference is that instead of playing a sound, FilterKeys will beep when you activate it.

Figure 15.17.
*The Settings for FilterKeys
dialog allows you to change
how this feature works.*

The Filter options group allows you to select between two ways of filtering keystrokes. The first option filters keys that get pressed in rapid succession. For example, this feature would filter the rapid typing of the extra "t" in the example just mentioned. The Settings pushbutton displays a dialog that allows you to select how long an interval must pass between the first and second times you press the same key. It also provides a field where you can test the setting. The second option in this group filters accidental key presses. You might press a key for a moment, not really meaning to. As with the StickyKeys option, the Settings pushbutton will take you to a dialog where you select how long you have to press a key before Windows will accept it.

Using ToggleKeys

Ever start typing an e-mail message to someone, only to see later that you left the Caps Lock key on? It's time-consuming to fix such a mistake, but you have to do it for formal documents or memos. A better solution would be to be alerted each time you turned on one of the Lock keys. That's precisely what ToggleKeys does. It emits a tone every time you turn on the Caps Lock, Scroll Lock, or Num Lock keys.

Figure 15.18 shows the Settings for ToggleKeys dialog. Notice that it has only a single option. This option allows you to turn the shortcut key on or off.

Figure 15.18.
The Settings for ToggleKeys dialog allows you to change how this feature works.

Special Mouse Settings

Have you ever gotten to the point of screaming as you try to precisely position an object on a drawing screen using the mouse? It's difficult to do after a full day of drawing—especially if you aren't a graphic artist with the training and tools required to get the job done right. That's one of the reasons why I really like the MouseKeys feature. It allows you to use the arrow keys as a mouse. Instead of moving the mouse cursor with the mouse, you can move it with the arrow keys. Of course, this doesn't disable your mouse; it merely augments it. Figure 15.19 shows the Mouse page of the Accessibility Properties dialog.

MouseKeys has only one dialog of settings. You access it by clicking on the Settings pushbutton on this page. Figure 15.20 shows the features that this dialog provides. The first option, Keyboard shortcut, allows you to enable MouseKeys using the shortcut key. There really isn't any good reason to turn this off, since it's very unlikely that any application would use the same control key sequence.

Figure 15.19.
MouseKeys can put the control back into your mouse cursor.

Figure 15.20.
The Settings for MouseKeys dialog allows you to change how this feature works.

The second group, Pointer speed, is where you can optimize the performance of this particular feature. The first option allows you to set the fastest speed at which you can move the mouse cursor using the arrow keys. Set it to a slower speed to gain better control of the mouse cursor. Using a higher speed allows you to move around the display faster. The Acceleration setting determines how fast the cursor reaches full speed after you press it. Windows doesn't start the cursor off at full speed; it brings it there gradually. This allows you to make a small change without seeing the cursor take off for the other side of the screen if you set the speed fairly high. The combination of these two settings will determine just how much added control MouseKeys gives you over the cursor. Notice the checkbox in this group. Checking it gives you another option. Pressing the Ctrl key will speed the mouse cursor up; pressing the Shift key will slow it down. You can use this option when you need a variety of speeds to get the job done.

The final group contains two settings. The radio button controls when MouseKeys is active. You must specify whether the Num Lock key should be on or off when you use MouseKeys. The choice you make depends on how you normally use the numeric keypad. The second option determines whether the MouseKeys icon appears on the Taskbar. As with most of the special features that Windows provides, I keep this icon on the Taskbar for quick access to this feature. It's a lot more efficient to do so.

On Your Own

Try all the different Accessibility options to see if any of them provide features you can use. I provided suggestions on how you could use each feature in this chapter.

Install and try using the Dvorak keyboard layout. Once you learn how to use this setup, you'll find that you can type faster and with a lot less fatigue. This particular setup can also help you fight repetitive stress injuries such as carpal tunnel. Of course, nothing will provide 100 percent protection. The Dvorak keyboard layout can't reverse years of abuse, but learning this new setup could help keep any problems you have now from getting worse.

Go back to earlier chapters—especially Chapter 5—and practice using the various shortcuts I discussed with the Accessibility Options turned on. Does using this feature with your standard shortcuts make a difference? Try a variety of combinations to create the fastest keyboard interface possible.

16

Video
Configurations

Video is the most noticeable architectural component of Windows 95. It's the underlying combination of hardware and software that allows you to see the graphics, dialog boxes, icons, and other elements that make Windows 95 worth using. It's little wonder, then, that this is also one of the more complex parts of the computing picture.

The problem isn't simply one of displaying a picture on-screen; that would be easy to manage. The problem is one of communication between the various elements that create and manage the picture in the first place. The following list illustrates some of Windows 95's communication problems.

- Application level: Three different kinds of applications use Windows 95. DOS applications normally think they are alone in the world, so they violate just about every imaginable rule for displaying information. Game programs are the worst in this area. You can count on them to change the display adapter registers in unusual ways and write directly to video memory with nary a thought that anyone else might be using the system. Although 16-bit Windows applications are a bit more conscientious than their DOS counterparts, they still use an older interface to draw to the display. Finally, newer 32-bit Windows might offer the ultimate in available features right now, but they're often hampered by other applications running on the machine.

- Device driver: I own an older display adapter that drives me crazy when I use Word for Windows. It's not really a problem with the adapter; it's a problem with the drivers that support the adapter. If the display driver doesn't correctly interpret the commands issued by applications running under Windows, or if those applications use undocumented command features, there's a good chance of miscommunication. In the case of my faulty setup, the adapter misinterpreted some of the commands that Word and a few other applications used, resulting in an unreadable screen.

- Adapter: In the beginning, IBM set the tone and the baseline for all display adapters. Its leadership was responsible for the somewhat standard way in which the CGA and EGA display adapters worked. By the time VGA came around, IBM was starting to lose its leadership position. Then came SVGA (super VGA), and there was no IBM standard to follow. For a while there was a lack of any kind of standardization for the extended modes that vendors built into their display adapters. The result was total chaos. How do you build a set of standardized drivers for an operating system when there's no standard to follow? We'll look at how this problem finally got resolved a little later in this chapter.

- Monitor: There's less of a standardization problem with monitors, but it's still present. This problem manifests itself in setups in which one monitor works fine but another doesn't. The problem is in the signals coming from the display adapter. With today's ergonomic concerns, such as the 70 Hz refresh rate needed to reduce eyestrain, frequency ranges have expanded dramatically. Some monitors just can't handle the increased frequency requirements. Add to that some level of ambiguity on the part of vendors. I'll never get over the fine-print problem with several monitors I looked at. A monitor supposedly supports 1024 × 768 mode. When you look at the fine print, though, it becomes obvious that this support is good only in interlaced mode. This led to a problem with one monitor when I installed Windows NT. I got the upper half of the picture just fine, but the lower half disappeared. The problem was some combination of adapter, driver, and monitor. If the monitor had supported 1024 × 768 noninterlaced mode, there wouldn't have been a problem.

- Operating system requirements: Normally, the operating system itself is the least of your worries with the display. However, sometimes it can actually be the source of your problems. Take icons, for example. We all take them for granted because they generally work without any difficulty. But what happens if some file that the operating system needs gets changed by an application or gets corrupted somehow? On one machine I had to completely install everything from scratch. One of the system files had suffered some type of damage, and all the icons disappeared. No amount of work would bring them back, so I finally ended up reinstalling everything from scratch to get them back.

Now that you have a better idea of the communication problems that Windows suffers from, you might wonder why it works at all. Windows uses something known as an *event loop* to talk with applications. Think of an event loop as a bulletin board where Windows and applications post messages. A message could ask for a service such as opening a file or telling an application that it needs to perform some maintenance task. Windows notifies the application that it has a message waiting. The application picks up its messages and acts on them. The event loop allows Windows to send "paint" messages to any application that might require them. The combination of an event loop and constant redrawing allows Windows to keep your display up-to-date, even if small amounts of miscommunication do occur.

You can usually tell when Windows is going through a repaint cycle. You can actually see each application quickly flash as it redraws itself. Of course, the cycle becomes a lot more prominent if each application uses a conflicting palette, because then you can also see the color changes.

This chapter talks about video under Windows 95. However, more than that, it talks about communication. Without the required level of communication between all the system elements, you would never see anything when using Windows 95. I'll refer to this idea of communication whenever necessary. Look for the communication requirements, though, as we discuss each of the following topics.

Graphics Standards

Many different standards organizations help keep things running smoothly on your computer. Several competing standards affect how your modem works. One of these organizations, the CCITT, has become a major contributor as of late. Another organization, EIA, defines specifications for the various port connectors, serial and parallel, that attach your machine to the outside world and peripheral devices. The standards organization you want to keep your eye on for display adapters and monitors, though, is the Video Electronics Standards Association (VESA).

Tip: VESA can provide you with detailed specifications for a number of display adapter and monitor standards. You can usually get copies of these standards from online sources such as CompuServe. They also often appear in the manuals that come with your adapter or monitor. You can contact VESA directly using the following information:

Video Electronics Standards Association
2150 North First Street, Suite 440
San Jose, CA 95131-2029
Voice: (408) 435-0333
Fax: (408) 435-8225

I first ran into this organization in 1989, but they were probably around a while before that. IBM had dropped VGA in favor of its proprietary 8514/A display adapter. Without a leader in the field to dictate a standard, the entire display adapter arena fell into a state of disarray. At the time I first heard about VESA, they were working on a standard to fix the SVGA problem. Of course, the resolutions and number of colors were severely limited in comparison with what you can get today. They were also working on defining the 8514 ports that IBM wouldn't talk about at the time.

The main difficulty that the graphics community was facing was communication. Before this time, every display adapter used the same programming interface, in the form of a BIOS call, to change display settings and otherwise control the display adapter. All the old display methods worked, but vendors chose to differentiate their products by implementing the VGA "extended" modes differently. The resulting chaos made it impossible for any programmer to write an application that used SVGA modes without writing a different driver for each adapter.

VESA stepped in to make sense of all this chaos. The result of these initial efforts were several VESA standards and some additional software for each display adapter. That VESA driver that you load for some applications is actually a BIOS extension that allows display adapters to use a standardized SVGA interface. The extension translates VESA standard BIOS calls into something adapter-specific. As a result, an application can use one set of BIOS calls to configure and control the display adapter. Newer display adapters no longer require you to load a special driver; their BIOS chips come with VESA support installed. Table 16.1 shows many of the common standards that VESA has produced. There are also older standards that will shed some light on some issues that these newer standards don't cover. A representative at VESA will be more than happy to answer any questions you might have.

Table 16.1. VESA standards for display adapters and monitors.

Standard	Title	Purpose
VS911020	Super VGA protected-mode interface	This document provides informationtion on a standardized method of accessing the BIOS routines from a protected-mode program.
VS911021	Video cursor interface	Use this standard to learn how to build an interface between a pointing device and the display adapter.
VS911022	Super VGA BIOS extension	This is the document you'll need in order to learn about VESA standard display modes for the SVGA.
VXE 1.0	XGA extensions standard	This document tells you about some of the standardization efforts under way for the XGA.
VS910810	Monitor timing standard for 1024 × 768 with 70 Hz refresh rate	This standard helped provide a consistent method of providing ergonomically correct displays. It allows a vendor to create a display adapter and monitor that will work together at the 70 Hz refresh rate, which greatly reduces eyestrain.
VS900601	Standard 8514/A register bit fields	A programmer needs to know the details of how a register works. This standard provides that information.
VS890803	Standard VGA passthrough connector	There was a lot of confusion as to how to get a high-resolution display adapter to work with a standard one. The passthrough connector seemed an ideal way to do it, but the connections for it weren't standardized. That's what this standard does: It defines the passthrough connector and allows you to use multiple adapters in one machine.

continues

Table 16.1. continued

Standard	Title	Purpose
VS890804	Standard 8514/A registers	Before you can program a register, you need to know what to call it. This standard defines what registers an 8514/A contains. Remember that IBM didn't want to share this information with anyone.

Of course, this selection of standards is by no means complete. VESA works on a whole array of other standardization efforts, such as industrial guidelines for the manufacture of computer components. Its most famous nondisplay-related standard is probably the VL bus. This was such an important standard at one time that in 1993, Dell wanted to take VESA to court over the matter of who owned the standard.

The Windows 95 Graphics Architecture

Now that you have some idea of the problems that Microsoft (and any other vendor) faces when it comes to providing something for you to look at, it's time to discuss how they do it. Display adapters and monitors have both moved beyond the simpler requirements of the time when IBM was at the helm. In the interim, we've seen the emergence of even higher resolutions and a new adapter called the XGA. The SVGA is also improving on an almost daily basis. It used to be that 640 × 480 resolution and 256 colors were something to whistle about. Today an adapter is considered almost inadequate at 1024 × 768 resolution and 24-bit (16.7 million) colors. Windows 95 endeavors to handle this wide range of capabilities using the same centralized control mechanism that it uses for printing—a combination of the minidriver and DIB engine.

One of the main architectural components is the GDI. The GDI has been tuned and retuned throughout the various incarnations of Windows. It's no surprise that Microsoft has spent so much time in this area, since many benchmark tests focus on graphics performance. In fact, from a user perspective, the thing they notice most is the way the graphics engine performs. Microsoft did some more tuning of the GDI for Windows 95, but I would term this tuning more incremental than major. The following list provides details on some of the more significant changes.

- DIB engine: The new DIB engine is handcrafted assembly language. Not only is this area heavily used in rendering graphic images, but it's used for the printer as well. The GDI and DIB engine work together with the display device driver to produce the picture you will eventually see on-screen. Unlike previous versions of Windows, though, Windows 95 doesn't force every graphics instruction to go through the DIB engine. If a display adapter provides a coprocessor that can handle the operation more efficiently, Windows uses it in place of the DIB engine.

- TrueType rasterizer: This is the component responsible for changing the font descriptions in your .TTF files to a bitmap that Windows can display on-screen. Microsoft moved the data for this part of the GDI out of the 64 KB heap area to a 32-bit area. They also rewrote the rasterizer code in 32-bit format to improve overall performance.

- GDI component duplication: We talked about the use of a thunk to convert 16-bit data to 32-bit format in Chapter 6. Thunks cost time. This isn't a big deal in most cases, because a thunk can be a lot less expensive than a transition to real mode to handle a device need. However, some operations are performed so often that Microsoft decided to provide both a 16-bit and a 32-bit version in Windows 95. This allows for a small but noticeable speed improvement over Windows NT.

- Path support: A Windows application used to create complex objects using lots of standard objects such as squares, triangles, and circles. All these little calls could eat up a lot of processor time if the program needed to create something really complicated. Using paths allows a Windows 95 application to describe a complex shape in one function call. The GDI can then figure out the most efficient way to present it. The result is that the programmer spends less time describing the object, and the user sees a performance improvement.

- Metafile support: A metafile contains drawing commands that describe the drawing instead of actually providing a bitmap for it. Each command is called a *record*. The GDI processes records to reconstruct the image. The advantage of a metafile is that you can make it any size you want and adapt it to any device resolution. Windows 3.x didn't provide metafile support as part of the operating system. Windows 95 improves on this by providing partial metafile support. It doesn't include the full range of metafile commands that Windows NT does, but it does provide some. The result is that you gain the advantages of using a metafile, but Windows 95 won't completely understand some Windows NT metafiles. Fortunately, if the GDI doesn't understand a particular command, it ignores it and goes on to the next one.

- Bézier curve drawing: A Bézier curve is drawn using a set of points. A curved freeform line connects the points. The idea isn't to necessarily touch all the points, but to draw a line that most nearly defines a shape that flows from point to point. Many advanced graphics applications such as CorelDRAW! support this feature right out of the box. Windows 95 adds this feature so that an application can describe a curve using points and allow the GDI to figure out how to draw it.

- Image color matching (ICM): It wasn't long ago that everyone used green screens and black-and-white printers. Today the cost of a color printer is dropping rapidly, and color displays are standard on every machine. There's a problem in trying to get the color on your screen to match the color on your printer, however. For one thing, the two devices use different methods to create colors. Another reason is that it's nearly impossible to create some colors on certain devices. The technical details of all this are keeping several standards groups talking right now, so it's impossible to say how the problem occurs or what to do about it. Still, the problem remains. With the emergence of color as a major new component of computing, Microsoft saw the need to provide color matching between devices. Although it's not a perfect solution, ICM is a good start for people who can't afford professional publishing equipment.

Improvements in the GDI aren't the only change in Windows 95. There are some pretty big architectural changes as well. Let's take a look at the overall architecture. I won't get into bits and bytes here, but I will tell you about the basic components required to display something on-screen. Figure 16.1 is an overview of the Windows 95 architecture. The following paragraphs tell you what task each of the components performs.

Figure 16.1.
An overview of the Windows 95 graphics architecture.

- WINOLDAP: This is a module that senses when a DOS application is about to take control of the display area. It notifies USER and the screen grabber so that they can preserve the graphics system status information. You'll find this module listed as WINOA386.MOD in your \SYSTEM directory.

- Screen grabber: I always think of this as a camera. In essence, that's what it is. The screen grabber takes a picture of the screen and preserves it for later. This allows Windows to restore the screen to its former appearance after you exit a DOS session. Any file with a .2GR or .3GR extension in your \SYSTEM directory is a screen grabber. You don't need the .2GR files for Windows 95, because it doesn't support standard mode. In addition, you need only one .3GR file—the one designed for your display adapter.

- User: We've already discussed the uses for this module extensively. This module tracks the state of all the display elements, such as icons and dialog boxes, in addition to drawing them. That's why it needs to be informed before a DOS session comes to the foreground—so that it can take a snapshot of the current state of these components. As I stated earlier, there are actually two User-related files on disk—a 16-bit and a 32-bit version.

- GDI: This is another module that we have spent a lot of time discussing. Like the User module, there are two physical files—one for 16-bit and another for 32-bit needs. The GDI module works with the display driver and the DIB engine to produce the graphic components of a Windows display.

- Display minidriver: With Windows 3.x, every video signal went through the Virtual Display Driver (VDD). The VDD would process the signal and send it to the display adapter. Windows 95 can use a combination of the display minidriver and the DIB engine for adapters that can support them. Using this driver combination results in a speed increase from 32-bit code. The name of this file varies, depending on the type of display you're using. On my system, it's named SUPERVGA.DRV. Unlike the VDD, which performs all video processing, the display minidriver takes care of only device-specific details. The DIB engine takes care of graphics rendering. A minidriver contains a lot less code than a full-fledged VDD, reducing the amount of code that a vendor must write.

- Device-independent bitmap (DIB) engine: The DIB engine takes the graphics instructions provided by the GDI and renders them into an image. Unlike printing, in which the DIB engine doesn't do the whole job, it actually draws the rendered image on the frame buffer. A *frame buffer* is a piece of system memory set aside to represent video memory. When the drawing on the buffer is complete, the entire buffer gets sent to video memory at one time. Anything sent to video memory usually ends up on the display. This process is known as *virtualization*. The DIB engine itself is found in DIBENG.DLL. There's also a compatibility module for Windows 3.x applications called DISPDIB.DLL, which was the predecessor to the DIB engine. This second DLL allowed Windows 3.x to use a DIB for small objects instead of the entire display. You might also find several DIB*.DRV files in your \SYSTEM directory. Each one of these files provides some type of expanded display or memory management function for Windows 3.x DIBs. In almost all cases, these drivers are designed to work on individual objects rather than the entire display. The frame buffer management routines are found in FRAMEBUF.DRV.

- Color profile: This is a data file that contains the color capabilities for your output device. It doesn't matter whether the device is a printer or a display adapter; the type of information is the same. The purpose of a color profile is to provide the ICM with the information it needs to keep the display and other color devices in sync. That way, when you select dark red on the display, you get the same dark red on your printer. We talked about some of the problems with color matching earlier, so I won't go into them again here. You'll find all the color profile files in the COLOR folder in the SYSTEM folder. All these files have an .ICM extension. The Properties dialog associated with each one will give you many more technical details about the actual profile.

- Image color matcher (ICM): The whole process of matching the output of your printer to what you see on the display is complex—much too complex to really cover here. We discussed the problem of color matching earlier in this chapter. The ICM is the module that actually performs the work. It subtly changes the output of your printer and display so that they match. The GDI, display minidriver, and ICM work together to compare the current color set and translate it into something that will work on both devices. It's not a perfect solution, but it works for the most part. Let's just say that the results are very close, but not absolutely the same. Most of us wouldn't notice, but a professional artist might. Of course, this solution can't take into account the many details that a professional would, such as temperature, humidity, and other environmental aspects beyond Windows' control. The files that contain the ICM include ICM32.DLL and ICMUI.DLL; both appear in the SYSTEM folder.

- VFLATD.VXD: This module gets used only for bank-switched video adapters. Its main purpose is to manage the video memory window that these devices provide. The easiest way to think about this is using the explanation I provided for expanded memory in Chapter 7. The display adapter on your machine could contain a very large amount of memory. Unfortunately, there's only a 64 KB window set aside to access that memory. Depending on your adapter's configuration, Windows might not be able to get around this limitation. VFLATD.VXD can manage up to a 1 MB frame buffer. It reads this buffer into video memory as required in 64 KB chunks.

- Virtual display driver (VDD): Windows 3.x used this module as its sole source of communication with the display adapter. Windows 95 provides it for compatibility purposes and for DOS applications. In most cases, the name of this file contains some part of the name of the display adapter vendor. For example, the name of the VxD for my system is VIDEO7.VXD. You'll find it in the SYSTEM folder. This driver converts drawing commands into signals that the display adapter can use. It also manages the display adapter and performs a variety of other tasks related to the way that all the applications on your machine share the display adapter. In essence, it's a 16-bit version of the display minidriver and DIB engine combination.

- Display adapter: This is the physical piece of hardware in your machine.

- Video memory and screen: Video memory is where the electronic form of the image that you see on-screen is stored.

Keep in mind that this was a quick tour of the video subsystem. The actual inner workings of this part of Windows are a lot more complex than you might think. To give you a better idea of the way things work, think of Windows as having three video paths (it's more complex than that, but let's not get mired in too much detail at this point): one 16-bit DOS, one 16-bit Windows, and one 32-bit Windows. The path that Windows uses depends on what applications you're using, the type of adapter you have, and the video performance settings you select in the System Properties dialog. The 16-bit DOS path consists of the VDD, display adapter, and video memory. It also might include VFLATD.VXD if required. The 16-bit Windows path adds WINOLDAP, the screen grabber, User, and the GDI. The 32-bit path includes User, the GDI, the display minidriver, the DIB engine, and video memory. It also includes VFLATD.VXD if your display adapter uses bank-switched memory. Both Windows paths could include the ICM and the associated color profiles. It depends on your setup, the drivers that Microsoft eventually includes, and the capabilities of the devices you're using.

Video Boards

While I have your attention focused on the complexities of the video subsystem, let's take a quick look at video boards. You might have missed a few performance clues tucked away in the discussion of architecture. Did you notice that VFLATD.VXD supports only a 1 MB address space? What happens if your display adapter contains 2 MB or more of memory? Don't worry. Windows 95 will completely support the entire range of memory provided by your display adapter. However, it might have to rely on the display minidriver more to do it. This means a lot more calls and perhaps a few more thunks between various display components. The end result is a slight loss in performance from a purely display subsystem point of view.

It's not all bad news, of course. You'll gain from having more video memory in several ways. First, more memory means more colors. A higher number of colors could result in better font anti-aliasing and other aesthetic qualities of your display. Second, more memory means higher resolution. A higher level of resolution could help you position graphic elements more accurately and result in reduced eye fatigue.

No matter which way you look at it, though, more colors and high resolution spell decreased performance. Moving the video window around takes a little time; allowing the frame buffer to manage more than 1 MB of video memory takes even more. Each layer of management that you add to the video subsystem will chew up processor cycles. So, how do you get around these problems?

- Dual-ported video RAM (VRAM): Many display adapters come with this feature, but some do not. VRAM is a Texas Instruments innovation. They first introduced it with their TMS340x0 series of processors, such as the one used in the Artist TI12 display adapter.

The reason that it's called dual-ported is that it actually contains two ports. A serial buffer allows the display to read the contents of video memory. A parallel buffer allows Windows to simultaneously write to video memory. Dual-ported memory gets rid of one of the constraints that an application had with the display adapter: You could write to video memory only during part of the display cycle.

- Display coprocessor: Quite a few display adapters also come with a coprocessor. Windows 3.x didn't make use of this feature; it sort of ignored that it was there. Windows 95, on the other hand, has coprocessor support built right in. It will offload as much of the display processing as possible to the display coprocessor instead of using the DIB engine. There are two ways that this speeds performance. First, since offloading part of the graphics processing responsibility frees processor cycles, you'll notice an overall improvement in system speed. Second, the display processor is usually a special-purpose state machine. It will process the graphics instructions much faster than the DIB engine could. Think of it this way: The math coprocessor in your machine is a state machine. It can't replace the general processor for most purposes. However, it is incredibly fast when it comes to performing some types of math calculations.

- 32-bit display adapter: Graphics routines process a lot of data. There's no way around it. To display an image, you have to move data, and that requires time. However, you can reduce the amount of time by using a wider data path. Some display adapters come with a 32-bit path. Just the increase in data width will improve graphics performance. Add to that the fact that the 32-bit bus on a computer normally operates at a higher clock speed than its 16-bit counterpart, and you have an opportunity for a significant increase in performance.

Tip: Look through the list of devices that Windows 95 supports with native drivers before you buy a new display adapter. The hand-tuned Microsoft drivers will almost always work better than those you get from the vendor because they are tested more extensively. They'll definitely work better than a 16-bit driver, which some older display adapters come with. Buying a new adapter that sports a Windows 95 logo will probably cost you more but won't buy you that much, other than a label. Looking through the supported hardware list will probably net you a great display adapter at lower prices, yet retain all the capabilities that Windows 95 provides.

There are other things that you need to look for in a Windows 95 display adapter. One of the biggest convenience items is plug and play. You will gain a lot from having both a plug and play-compatible monitor and display adapter. Not only are these devices self-configuring, but they allow a greater level of flexibility as well. One of the ways that Windows 95 limits you with a non-plug and play device is color selection. I can change the resolution of my Video 7 display adapter without rebooting, but I can't change the number of colors.

Peter's Principle: More Than Enough Graphics

You'll probably be very tempted to go out and buy the first display adapter that offers 16.7 million colors and 2048 × 2048 resolution. That might be a good way to build for the future, but it might be a little too much for today unless you're an artist or work in a graphics-oriented field. Go ahead and get the tomorrow solution today; that only makes sense from a financial perspective. However, once you do get a high-performance display, think about the way you'll actually use it. In most cases, a 256-color display provides more than enough color. A 17-inch monitor supports a resolution of 1024 × 768 just fine too. Once you start going beyond this color and resolution level, your machine will take a performance hit because of the way Windows 95 handles video memory.

Using the higher level of display capability is fine if you don't mind giving up performance as well. I'd rather squeeze every ounce of performance from my machine and use settings that are a little more in line with what I can actually use. Of course, that shouldn't stop you from getting a high-performance display adapter, but it should change the way you configure it. Always consider when you have "enough" graphics to meet the need.

Installing Video Display Adapters

We covered the physical process of installing your display adapter as part of the hardware installation process in Chapter 13. The process for installing a new display adapter isn't all that much different. However, I'd like to show you an alternative to that process.

Of course, installing a new display adapter or monitor isn't the end of the process—it's the beginning. Chapter 9 contains a complete description of the four pages of configuration settings for the Display Properties dialog, so I won't go through them again here. Suffice it to say that Windows 95 provides all the settings you had under Windows 3.x, plus a few pleasant surprises.

Installing a Display Adapter

Installing a new display adapter can be very easy. You can use the standard hardware installation procedure, but the one I'll show you here is shorter and a little more straightforward. However, it skips the automatic detection method I described in Chapter 13. You might want to use that procedure if you have a plug and play display adapter.

1. Right-click on the Desktop and choose the Properties option. You should see the Display Properties dialog.

2. Select the Settings page. Click on the Change Display Type pushbutton to see the Change Display Type dialog, shown in Figure 16.2. Notice that this dialog has two settings. You use the same dialog box (but different fields) to install a monitor or a display adapter. There are several other features that you should notice in this dialog. First is the fact that it tells you which drivers the display adapter required. Note that this is the adapter itself, not the video subsystem as a whole. The video subsystem also contains a number of files that are either generic or specific to certain conditions. Second, notice that this dialog tells you the current display adapter type and its version number. This could provide important information when you're troubleshooting.

Figure 16.2.
The Change Display Type dialog allows you to reconfigure your display adapter or monitor.

3. Click on the Change button in the Adapter Type group. You'll see the dialog shown in Figure 16.3. Notice that only one display adapter type is listed. If there were other display adapters that were compatible with this one, this listbox would contain those as well.

Figure 16.3.
The initial Select Device dialog shows only compatible display adapters.

Note: If you have a vendor disk containing drivers for your display adapter, you would click on the Have Disk pushbutton here to look at it. The Have Disk dialog works just like any other browser under Windows 95.

4. Click on the Show all devices radio button. Windows will change the list to show all the display adapters it supports by vendor, as shown in Figure 16.4. You could use this screen when selecting a new display adapter. Clicking on Cancel here would take you back to the initial screen without changing your display type.

Figure 16.4.
Clicking on the Show all devices radio button will show every display adapter that Windows 95 supports.

Tip: If your display adapter vendor doesn't appear in the list and you don't have a special disk for it, you can always use the Standard Display Adapter category at the very beginning of the Manufacturers list. It might be a good idea to use this category anyway if your special driver disk contains only older 16-bit drivers. You won't get the same number of features that you might with the special disk, but using the standard drivers will provide a performance boost.

5. After you select the correct manufacturer and display adapter model from the list, click on OK. Windows will take you back to the Change Display Type dialog.

6. Click on Cancel, and then click on Apply. Windows might ask you to insert disks as it installs the new adapter. It will also ask if you want to restart your machine to make the changes permanent. Click on Yes to restart your machine.

Installing a Monitor

It might not seem like a very big deal to tell Windows 95 which monitor you're using, especially if that monitor doesn't provide any special capabilities. However, the monitor you use will determine which display adapter features you can use. Selecting the right monitor type will help Windows 95 provide you with better information regarding your display choices.

1. Right-click on the Desktop and choose the Properties option. You should see the Display Properties dialog.

2. Select the Settings page. Click on the Change Display Type pushbutton to see the Change Display Type dialog, shown in Figure 16.2. Notice that this dialog has two settings. You use the same dialog box to install a monitor or a display adapter. Monitors provide only one additional setting. You can check the Monitor is Energy Star compliant checkbox if this feature is provided. The Monitor Type group tells you which monitor you currently have installed.

3. Click on the Change button in the Monitor Type group. Click on the Show all devices radio button. You'll see the dialog shown in Figure 16.5.

Figure 16.5.

The Select Device dialog allows you to choose from a list of monitors.

4. After you select the correct manufacturer and monitor model from the list, click on OK. Windows will take you back to the Change Display Type dialog.

5. Click on Cancel. Notice that Windows doesn't enable the Apply button this time. It doesn't ask if you want to restart your machine either. I usually restart the machine anyway, just to make sure that the change is permanent and that every part of Windows knows about it. This is especially important when you're installing an Energy Star-compliant monitor.

6. Click on OK to close the Display Properties dialog. Use the Start | Shutdown command to restart Windows 95.

On Your Own

Some people find that an underpowered machine might not provide all the speed they need to get their work done fast. Try a variety of display resolutions and color-level settings to find a compromise between system performance and the aesthetic value of the display. You'll find these settings on the Settings page of the Display Properties dialog. Also try the various font-size settings. Perhaps a custom setting will provide that perfect balance between readability and the number of icons you can fit on the Desktop or within an Explorer pane.

Check your SYSTEM folder and see if you can find all the files that make up the video subsystem. Use the video subsystem discussion in this chapter as the basis for your search.

17

Connecting and Communicating

Connections and communications are what makes using the computer worthwhile for some people. It's not being able to do something faster that drives these people; it's a matter of being able to obtain and present information. Exchanging information with others means that you'll have to spend a little more time thinking about how you'll do it. Windows 95 provides a lot of different types of connections, and each of them will help you communicate in some way.

I'm not going to tell you that every type of connection works well under Windows 95. You'll need to address some real problem areas in order to make things work properly. Communications aren't always as clear as they could be. You'll find that not only do you need to learn new computing skills, but you need to learn a new way of talking with other people as well. This chapter will take you through the pitfalls you could experience and help you avoid them.

This chapter has two distinctly separate parts. Both of them build on information that we've talked about in previous chapters. The first part spends some time with physical details we haven't covered yet. Hardware connections are a necessary step in getting your machine ready for information exchange of all types. I'm not going to spend any time talking about troubleshooting or network specifics here, but I will spend some time talking about common connections—the devices you use every day.

The second topic we'll talk about is software connections. Anyone who works out of his or her home knows the problems involved in keeping up with what's going on at the office. Sharing files and any other type of communication is a problem as well. Previous versions of Windows left the user out in the cold when it came to these very necessary concerns. Windows 95 takes care of that discrepancy by providing some very real assistance for the remote user.

Looking Ahead: I'm not going to cover the particulars of online communication here. We'll cover that issue in Chapter 18. Network connections begin in Chapter 19. Make sure you look there for the ins and outs of that type of connection. If you're a mobile computer user, be sure to read Chapter 21. We'll also cover troubleshooting in Chapter 23. Of course, these other chapters cover a lot more than just connections; they cover many user issues as well.

When you combine the software and hardware connections that Windows 95 provides, you'll find a somewhat complete level of coverage. However, I was appalled at some of the areas where Microsoft skimped when it came to this important subject. I was equally pleased at some of the new features they decided to include. Overall, Windows 95 is an improvement, but perhaps not as big an improvement as you might expect. It's not time to throw away that third-party remote connection package yet, but perhaps in another few versions it will be.

Making Hardware Attachments

As advanced as some users are when it comes to software, they're handicapped when it comes to hardware. Perhaps you've heard the story of the guy who placed a floppy in the space between the two drives because his machine lacked a 5 1/4-inch floppy drive. It's funny to think about someone actually doing something that silly. Of course, there's also the joke about people who use Witeout to cover up on-screen mistakes. Everyone has a favorite joke about someone who did something harebrained on their computer.

Making the wrong connection in real life is another story. Finding that your printer or modem doesn't work when there is a critical deadline isn't funny at all. Frantic workers trying to figure out why their external SCSI drive or another device won't work without a terminator is enough to send chills up anyone's spine. That's the kind of serious connection work we'll talk about here. I won't bore you with stories of the oddball; I'm going to tell you about real-life connection problems and how to avoid them.

Any Port in a Storm

The first thing we need to talk about are the external ports on your machine. The problem for many people is not knowing where these ports connect or what they do. Some very different ports even look alike. For example, there's the distinct possibility that you could confuse a game port with a thick Ethernet port, because they look exactly the same. Even though most ports are easy to identify given certain clues, just grabbing any port on the back of your machine isn't such a good idea. It's always better to mark the ports and know exactly what they do before you try to use them. You might end up costing yourself a lot of time if you don't. For example, what if you have two 9-pin serial ports on your machine? Which one is COM1? Just knowing what function the port serves might not be enough.

Fortunately, some types of ports are tough to confuse. For example, a 25-pin port with male pins is a serial port. Nothing else on your system uses that configuration. Some external SCSI ports are pretty difficult to confuse. They contain so many pins that they fill the entire width of the expansion slot. But those are the only really easy ports—the ones you can identify just by looking at them. The other ports require closer identification before you know what they do.

In particular, you must be careful not to confuse a printer port (which uses a 25-pin female connector) with a Macintosh-compatible SCSI port (which uses the exact same connector). Plugging a printer into a Mac-SCSI port can cause actual physical damage to the printer or the port card or both.

You can make several generalizations by looking at the back of your PC. Table 17.1 contains a partial list of the clues I used to identify the ports on the back of my machine. You too can use these clues if there's some reason that you can't open your machine up. (Some warranty policies don't let you open the machine because the vendor is concerned about user tampering. I strongly suggest that you not give your money to such companies. A lease is one thing; a purchase is another. No vendor should put you in the position of having to call them—or physically return your system to them—every time you want to insert or remove a card or some other device.)

Table 17.1. Adapters and their associated ports.

Adapter	Port Description
Ethernet	This adapter frequently has a 15-pin thick Ethernet port and a coaxial cable thin Ethernet connector. The round coaxial connector is the same width as the slot and has two knobs on it for connecting the cable. The adapter might also provide DIP switches. Another version of Ethernet card has the 15-pin connector and an RJ-45 jack (which looks like an oversized telephone jack). Similar-looking cards include ArcNet adapters. However, these always lack the 15-pin port. ArcNet adapters usually provide an active indicator LED as well.
I/O port combo	The combination port card usually provides a 25-pin parallel port and a 9-pin serial port on the back of the adapter. The serial port is usually COM1 and the parallel port LPT1. Be warned that the installer could have changed these default settings using the jumpers on the card or software setup. An I/O port combo adapter might also include a 9- or 25-pin serial port or a 15-pin game port that attaches through the back of the machine. If your case doesn't provide the extra cable connector holes, these ports might appear in one of the expansion slot openings. Some older multifunction cards such as the Intel Above Board used this port layout as well. Fortunately, the ports served the same purpose.
SVGA display	Some older versions of these cards provide both a 9-pin digital and a 15-pin analog port. Note that this 15-pin port is the same size as the 9-pin port. The pins are arranged in three rows of five rather than the two-row arrangement used by the game port. They're also a little smaller than the ones used by the game port. The display adapter might include a mouse port for a PS/2-style mouse. Some adapters provide only the 15-pin port (a requirement for SVGA).

Adapter	Port Description
	Other features on the back of this card might include DIP switches or three high-frequency connectors to connect to a high-resolution monitor.
Game	This adapter usually contains two 15-pin game ports, although only one is present on some very popular models. The one nearest the top of the machine is usually the one you want to use. Game adapters sometimes include a submini plug used for a variable-speed controller. This controller matches the speed of the game port to the speed of the machine. If you see a connector with 15 pins in two rows plus an RJ-45 connector (similar to a telephone jack), you're probably looking at an Ethernet card. If you see a connector with 15 holes in three rows, it is for (S)VGA video output.
Sound board	You'll usually see a 15-pin game port that doubles as a MIDI port when you select the right jumper or software settings. This adapter also includes three submini jacks that look the same as the earphone jacks on a portable radio. The precise arrangement of these jacks varies by vendor, but they serve the following purposes: output, microphone, and line input from an external source, such as a CD-ROM drive. Some older sound boards also include a volume level thumbwheel.
External SCSI	You might also see a number of large connectors on the back of a machine. One type of external SCSI connector has 50 lines and looks like a larger version of the Centronics connector that is on your printer. Unlike the Macintosh-compatible version (which has only 25 pins and is exactly like a printer port connector), this type of external SCSI connector doesn't use the same type of pins that the more familiar serial or parallel connector does. The newer SCSI-II connectors are miniaturized versions of the large 50-pin SCSI. Again, they are quite unlike anything else you're likely to find on a PC.
External drive	A number of older CD-ROM drives used a 37-pin plug. It looks like a huge version of the parallel port. You might see this with other types of drives as well. It's never safe to assume anything about this plug. Always check it against the vendor documentation.

continues

Table 17.1. continued

Adapter	Port Description
Fax/modem	A fax or modem card will usually provide two RJ-11 jacks (they look like the ones on your telephone). One jack allows you to connect the incoming cable, and the other jack is for your telephone. This adapter usually provides some DIP switches as well.

Besides all these combinations, there are a multitude of third-party adapters that might look like one of the adapters in Table 17.1 but won't provide the same functionality. Fortunately, you'll probably know if you have one of them installed, because you'll need it to perform some special task on your machine. The general rule to follow is this: If you see a port that you don't recognize and it isn't marked, open the machine to identify it. The second rule I always follow is that you shouldn't always believe the markings on the back your machine. If you look back there and see that all the ports you do recognize are correctly marked, you can probably assume that the rest are correct too. However, if you see a serial port identified as a parallel port, you should question whether any of the markers are correct.

Tip: Always mark the ports on the back of the machines you maintain after you identify the ports. Also, don't simply write down that something is a serial port. Specify COM1 or COM2 as part of the marking. Performing this little extra step can save you a lot of time later. You might want to follow this same procedure with cables, especially if the machine is connected to a workstation setup in which the cable source might become hidden. Trying to identify the correct cable when there are several possibilities is never a welcome task. It's easier to mark everything at the outset.

Printers

We covered the topic of printers in great detail in Chapter 14. I'd like to cover printer connections in this chapter. Some people think there's only one way to connect a printer: through a parallel port. And for some printers, that is correct. A few older printers used only a serial port connection. Some other, newer printers provide two or three connection types. These printers might have a serial port connector in addition to the standard Centronics parallel port connector, and they might have a network connector (Appletalk or Ethernet) in addition to the serial and/or parallel port connectors.

Tip: Some printers don't provide a serial port as standard equipment; you have to buy it as a separate piece. Your vendor manual should provide details on buying the serial port option. Look to see if the vendor also supports other connection options that might help in some situations. Many vendors now support a network connection as standard equipment; others support it as an optional module.

Choosing between these two connections isn't always easy, even though it seems like a no-brainer. A parallel port delivers the data 8 bits at a time and at a faster rate than a serial port. Choosing the parallel port doesn't take too much thought if your machine has only one printer attached to it. But what if your machine acts as a print server for many different printers? You could easily run out of parallel ports in this situation. Just about everyone resorts to an AB switch to increase the number of available connections, but there might be a better solution. Connecting your printer to the machine through an unused serial port will allow better access to it. No one will have to flip an AB switch to use it. (Some electronic AB switches provide an automatic switching scheme when you send certain commands through the printer cable, but this means training the user to send those commands and a lot of frustration when the user forgets to do so.) The problem is that the access is slower—a lot slower than with a parallel port.

Warning: If you're thinking about using a mechanical AB switch with a laser printer, be sure its use won't void the printer's warranty. Check with the printer's manufacturer to be sure.

Categorizing how people will use the printers attached to your machine is the next step. Placing a printer that the user is less likely to use or a printer that normally experiences a lower level of activity on a serial port shouldn't cause any problems. Just make sure that you warn people that their print job could take a little longer in the new configuration. I find that this allows me to connect at least four different printers to most machines. Of course, when you get to this level, you need to question whether you should dedicate a machine to act as a print server instead of trying to get by using a workstation on a peer-to-peer network.

Tip: There's a point where it becomes difficult to support too many printers on a peer-to-peer network. I usually start to look at other solutions once the number of workstations reaches 10 people or the number of printers exceeds four. After that limit, the performance of a peer-to-peer setup diminishes to the point where it's doubtful that you can get any useful work accomplished. There are always exceptions to the rule, but observing these limits usually provides the best measure of when it's time to upgrade.

These days, some printers come with a built-in NIC. You can attach them directly to the network without using a workstation connection. The two most popular connection types are Ethernet and AppleTalk. Of course, the appropriate selection depends on the network you're running. Whether this solution will work for you depends not on the NIC so much as it depends on the software included with the printer. The printer actually boots as a workstation or a self-contained print server on the network. You see it just as you would see any other workstation. The only difference is that this workstation is dedicated to a single task—printing. You need to find out which networks the vendor supports. Unfortunately, the very nature of this type of connection excludes it from consideration until more vendors come out with Windows 95-specific products. This really is a great solution for a peer-to-peer network, because it allows you to use the printer without loading the workstation down. Adding a printer this way will also preserve precious workstation resources such as interrupts and I/O port addresses.

Printers also support some of the more exotic network connections these days, but you might be hard-pressed to find them. One solution that I see gaining in popularity is the wireless LAN. Just think, using this type of connection you could unwrap the printer, plug it in, and perform a few configuration steps to get it up and running. In the future, adding a printer to the network might be even easier than adding it to your local workstation.

Modems

There are two different kinds of modems: internal and external. I prefer an external modem for several reasons. The biggest reason is portability. I can move a modem in a matter of minutes by disconnecting it from the current machine, moving it, and reconnecting it to the new machine. It's a lot faster and easier than opening the machine to get at the modem. I also find that external modems provide better visual feedback, although some software is taking care of this now by displaying all the indicators that you normally see on the modem. An external modem still has the edge when it comes to troubleshooting, though, because the light indicators you get from your software might not always reflect reality. In addition, most of the software out there doesn't accurately report the modem's connection speed, an important piece of troubleshooting information.

Yet another advantage of the external modem is that you can turn it off without turning off your computer. This can come in handy when you must reset the modem manually and you don't want to reboot your computer. It also provides some people with added peace of mind, because when the modem is turned off, no one can call into their computer. (You can keep people from calling into a computer with an internal modem simply by setting up the modem so that it won't answer the phone line. Seeing the modem power light off is a way to know for sure that this has been done.)

Note: The old 8250 UART chip won't provide a good connection beyond 9600 bps. You must use a 16450 or 16550 UART with a 14.4 Kbps or above modem to ensure an error-free connection. Although there's nothing wrong with the UART itself, the lack of a buffer in the 8250 will cause data overflows. These overflows will in turn cause failures in the connection protocols.

Once you get past the physical location of a modem, you get to the connections. The first connection is the telephone cable required to contact the outside world. Most offices don't have the RJ-11 jacks that a modem uses as standard equipment. They might use a six-wire jack that looks like a larger version of the RJ-11. You can plug an RJ-11 jack into this plug, but I can guarantee that it won't work. Or they might use a long multipin connector that carries many phone lines to the instrument. Normally you have to get an office wired for a modem before you can actually use it. Some recent phone instruments in offices and, increasingly, in hotel rooms sport a standard RJ-11 jack labeled a "data port." This is a fine place to plug in the cable from your modem. Of course, home users won't run into this problem because a modem uses a standard home telephone jack.

The second connection for a modem, if yours is external, is between the modem and the computer. This cable normally is a standard serial port cable (not a null modem cable) and might have either a 9- or 25-wire connector at each end. (A few external modems differ in this area. They are designed to connect to your computer's parallel port.)

Finally, there might be a second RJ-11 connector on your modem where you can plug in a standard single-line telephone. Doing so will enable you to make and receive voice calls on the same line you use for modem calls at other times. It also lets you use the modem to dial outgoing voice calls. When the dialing is complete, you just pick up the handset and then press the Esc key to make the communications program let go of the line.

Modems are also rated by speed and capability. The speed that a modem can communicate at is increasing all the time. It seems that just a short time ago a 14.4 Kbps (kilobits per second) connection was considered the fastest around. Now some vendors have introduced 28.8 Kbps modems. Of course, the reigning champ is still the 9600 baud modem. Some online services still top out at this transfer rate, as do many BBSs. This will change with time. Some of the bigger online services such as CompuServe already offer 14.4 lines in the larger cities (and a very few 28.8 lines as well). You'll also find that more than a few Internet providers offer access at the 28.8 rate. Since a modem can usually communicate with any modem at its speed or lower, there never is a good reason to buy a low-speed modem unless the cost for a higher speed becomes prohibitive.

There are a ton of modem standards, most of which won't make a lot of difference to you as a user. However, there are some standards that you should know about. A lot of standardization has to do with the modem's speed, the way it corrects errors, or the method it uses to compress data. Knowing about these standards could mean the difference between getting a good buy on a modem or getting one that's almost useless. Table 17.2 provides a list of the more common modem standards, but you should also be aware of any new standards that develop around higher-speed modems.

Table 17.2. **Common modem standards.**

Standard	Description
Bell 103	The American standard for 300 baud communication. It's pretty much outdated now, but when PCs first arrived on the scene, it was the rate that everyone used.
Bell 212A	The 1200 baud modem included both this standard and the Bell 103 standard if you bought an American model. The European standards included just enough differences to require a separate modem in most cases. Fortunately, we're well beyond this requirement now.
CCITT V.21	Defines the European standard for 300 baud communications. Like its counterpart, this standard is very much out of date.
CCITT V.22	The European version of the 1200 baud modem standard. It also includes the V.21 standard.
CCITT V.22bis	You might wonder what the "bis" in this standard number means. Just think of it as revision B. In this case, it refers to the general standard for 2400 baud modems.
CCITT V.23	A specialty 1200/75 bps standard for the European market. The slash indicates that the modem sends at one speed and receives at another. Many modems don't support it unless they're specifically designed for overseas use. You might want to check your requirements before getting a modem that supports this standard.
CCITT V.25bis	Defines an alternative command set for modems. In most cases, you won't need these alternative commands unless your modem also supports an X.25 interface.
CCITT V.32	Defines the 4800 bps, 9600 bps, 14.4 Kbps, 19.2 Kbps, and 28.8 Kbps standards.

Standard	Description
CCITT V.34	Defines the data compression specifics for the 28.8 Kbps standard.
CCITT V.42	Defines a data compression method for modems. It allows the modem to transfer data at apparent rates of up to 19.2 Kbps. This standard also requires the modem to provide MNP levels 2 through 4.
CCITT V.42bis	The second revision of a standard that defines how data gets compressed on a modem. It allows up to a four times compression factor or an apparent transfer rate of 38.4 Kbps from a 9600 bps modem. Of course, some of this speed gets eaten up in control characters and the like.
CCITT V.FAST	This was a proprietary method of defining data compression for the 28.8 Kbps standard. It's been replaced by the CCITT V.34 standard, but some vendors still adhere to this older standard. Always look for a V.34-compatible modem for maximum compatibility.
CCITT X.25	Some asynchronous modems also support this synchronous data transfer standard. You won't need it if your only goal is to communicate with online services or to access your local BBS. It does come in handy if your company plans to send interoffice data using a leased line.
MNP 2-4, 5, 10	Microm Networking Protocol, a standard method of error correcting for modems. The precise differences between levels aren't important from a user prospective. A higher level is generally better. Essentially, MNP provides a method of sending data in larger blocks, eliminating some of the control characters that usually impede data transmission.

Knowing about these standards should help you choose a modem. It's vitally important that your modem adhere to all the standards for speed and other capabilities. Otherwise, the modem might not be able to make a good connection at a lower speed. Also make sure that the modem manual outlines just how the modem adheres to the standards. It should include information on FCC rules Parts 15 and 68 or the equivalent for the country you're in. The manual should also state what kind of serial port it can connect to. The current standard is RS-232C. Some modems require that standard; others can use older ports. In most cases, you won't need to worry unless you have an older machine.

Here's the bottom line: You want a modem that will work with as many other modems as possible, over phone line connections that might be anything from superb to horrible. The more standards your modem supports, the more likely it is to work when you need it to. (Also look for support for fax/modem standards if you'd like to be able to send or receive faxes as well—a point discussed in more detail in the next section.)

Fax Boards

The section "Modems" introduced you to modem connections. Fax boards characteristically appear on the same board as the modem does, or perhaps on a daughter card. They usually use the same telephone connector as the modem does too.

After looking at the section on modems, you might wonder what's in store for you in this section. You should follow some general rules of thumb when selecting a fax board. The most important of these is to be sure your modem will communicate correctly with whatever is at the other end of the line. For normal faxing to standard fax machines, support for Group 3 faxes is sufficient. Supporting various error correction protocols can help ensure that your faxes arrive ungarbled.

If you use an application that requires DCA/Intel CAS (communicating applications specification) compatibility, you must be sure to get a fax board that supports that standard. For example, many database applications require a fax board with this capability before they'll recognize it. You'll also want to make sure that the fax follows the same version of the standard that the application requires, because there are some variances between versions of the specification.

Some vendors decided to follow the CAS standard because it provided a simplified method of accessing the fax. Before this time, every fax used its own set of port addresses and usually required a special application to access it. Using the CAS standard still allows for that flexibility, but it provides an API that allows a program to determine what that interface is and how to use it.

The only problem with CAS is cost. It's very expensive to buy a CAS-compatible fax. Invariably, the modem part of the equation is an extra cost. Fortunately, Windows 95 appears to support a wide range of fax/modems, even those that don't support CAS. If all you plan to do is fax documents using Exchange, you might be able to do so without buying a lot of fancy hardware.

Every fax/modem transfer consists of five phases. The ITU (formerly CCITT) defines these phases in several standards, which we'll examine later. These five phases aren't cast in concrete, and each one could repeat during any given session. It all depends on the capabilities of your fax/modem, the software you're using, and the environment conditions at the time.

- Phase 1, call establishment: Your computer calls another computer or a standard fax machine.

- Phase 2, pre-message procedure: The sending and receiving machines select parameters that will allow them to transfer data at the fastest possible rate. These parameters also take into account the resolution, modulation, and other factors.

- Phase 3, message transmission: This is the phase in which the actual data transfer takes place. If the initial group of parameters set in Phase 2 results in less than optimal results, the fax/modem will perform Phase 2 and Phase 3 again as required.

- Phase 4, post-message procedure: Some software considers each page as a separate message. In fact, that's the way your fax machine works as well. Phase 4 allows the sending and receiving machine to evaluate the results of each message and then raise or lower the transmission speed as required. This is also the phase in which the sending machine transmits a page break marker. This is the same thing as a form feed on a printer, except that the fax might simply print a line across the page or might actually cut the page off at that point. Remember that faxes can be either long or short, depending on the message needs.

- Phase 5, call clear down: This is the easiest part of the conversion. The two machines hang up the phone after the sending machine transmits an end-of-transmission signal.

As with modems, there are several fax/modem specifications. You'll want a fax/modem that adheres to the following ITU standards. Table 17.3 lists these various standards.

Table 17.3. Common fax/modem standards.

Standard	Description
ITU T.4	Defines the image transfer portion of the session used in Phase 3.
ITU T.30	Defines the negotiation and interpage phases (2, 3, 4, and 5). A normal multipage transfer uses T.30 only at the beginning of the call, between pages, and after the last page.
CCITT V.17	Defines the specifications for the 4800/1200 bps speed. The slash shows that the fax receives at one speed and sends at another. If the fax portion of a fax/modem is the sender, the data gets sent at 4800, but the fax receives acknowledgment at 1200. Some vendors reduce the complexity of this rating by giving only the first number (the higher of the two speeds), but this can be misleading.
CCITT V.27	Defines the specifications for the 9600/7200 bps speed.
CCITT V.29	Defines the specifications for the 14400/12000 bps speed.

Microsoft also provides for two different classes of fax communication between fax/modems. Here's the user view of what these different classes mean. Class 1 communications send an editable fax to the other party. This means that the fax appears as actual text that the other party can edit. Class 2 communications are more like the fax you usually receive. They are graphic representations of the text and graphics in the document. This is the same format as Group 3 faxes, like the one you're used to seeing in the office.

The real-world difference between Class 1 and Class 2 fax/modems is really quite different. A Class 1 fax performs both the T.4 and T.30 protocols in software. This allows the additional flexibility that Windows 95 needs in order to create editable faxes. All data translation is performed by Windows 95 drivers. A Class 2 fax performs the T.4 protocol in firmware—an EEPROM in the modem that does part of the work for the processor. This is a faster solution, because it removes part of the processing burden from the processor. A Class 2 fax/modem should also be able to create editable faxes. However, this is where the plot thickens. Because the Class 2 standard isn't defined very well, Microsoft didn't have any dependable information on what to expect from a Class 2 fax/modem. They made the decision to restrict Class 2 faxes to the Group 3 graphics format.

Note: The Electronic Industries Association (EIA) recently approved a new Class 2 standard that stringently defines what vendors need to provide in firmware. As a result, you might see software that uses Class 2 fax/modems more efficiently in the next 6 months to a year. Look for software vendors to make a big deal out of the new "high-speed" fax transmission capabilities offered by their product sometime in the future. This fax/modem software will use this new Class 2 fax/modem specification.

CD-ROM Players

CD-ROMs usually have two connections that you need to worry about. The first is the bus connector that allows data transfer between the computer and the CD-ROM. Generally this is a SCSI connector or an IDE or EIDE connection. The principle is the same; the data transfer rate might be a lot slower, depending on the method of connection. SCSI will always beat IDE hands-down, but SCSI and EIDE offer comparable performance. The bus connector for a CD-ROM serves the same purpose as the equivalent connector for your hard drive. It allows you to transfer data from the CD-ROM to your machine.

Tip: The price of CD-ROM recorders has dropped significantly in recent months. In the near future, it might become possible to buy a CD-ROM recorder for about three times the price of a player. There are two advantages to buying a CD-ROM recorder instead of a player. First, you can use it to make archive copies of CDs. Despite popular folklore, CDs are resistant, not impervious, to damage. Considering the cost of some CDs and the less-than-thrilling replacement policy some vendors have, an archive copy could make a big difference when the inevitable does occur. Second, you could use a CD-ROM recorder in place of a backup tape. The permanent nature of the backup makes it a medium of choice in cases where long-term storage is desired, such as with law firms and the medical community. A CD-ROM backup is also faster than some types of tape backup, although I won't say that you can't get better performance out of some DAT tapes. One thing is certain: The random-access feature of a CD makes it a lot faster than a tape for data retrieval.

Some people don't really think about the second connection. They'll try to use the CD-ROM with a game or another application that plays sound right off the CD—just like you would with a music CD—and discover that the game doesn't appear to work with their machine. The problem is that they don't have the RCA plugs in the back of the CD-ROM drive connected to anything. External CD-ROM drives use the RCA connectors (the ones that look like the speaker connectors on your stereo). Internal CD-ROM drives usually require some type of special connector for your sound card. This is a proprietary connector in some cases; in other cases, the vendor will try to make you believe that their common cable really is proprietary. Check with your local computer store to see if they have an inexpensive alternative to the expensive cable that the vendors normally offer.

Peter's Principle: How Much Speed Do You Need?

Once you get the connectors in place, your CD-ROM drive is ready to go. However, the speed at which it goes is cause for concern for many people. Although a single-speed CD-ROM drive might be adequate for data transfer, it won't work for multimedia applications at all. I recently bought a CD game. The sound was great on my 4X (four-speed) CD-ROM drive, but the same CD sounded very jerky and hesitated a lot on my 1X drive.

There's a gray area when it comes to other drive speeds. A 2X drive will probably work for the majority of games because game vendors try to get every ounce of speed from them that they can. On the other hand, you'll probably get very poor results for many multimedia education products. And don't even think about using a 2X drive for full-motion video. A 3X drive is marginal for full-motion video. Plan on missing some frames. It'll work perfectly with the vast majority of educational multimedia applications and just about every game out there.

Of course, there are other performance factors as well. The same factors that affect the performance of your hard drive also affect CDs. Things such as bus width and hardware caches can make a big difference in the actual performance you'll see. Even the controller you choose will make a big difference in the performance you'll get from your CD. It hardly pays to use a 16-bit controller with a 4X CD drive. You'll want to maximize performance by using a 32-bit controller instead.

Buying the best CD-ROM player available is probably a good idea when you consider the small price differential between them. However, if you're on a tight budget and need to get the best value for your money, try to match the speed of your drive with the type of use it will get. A drive that is too slow for the job will only frustrate you and make it impossible to actually do the required work. Just imagine the effect of a multimedia presentation in which a slow drive, rather than your stunning graphics and sound, grabs the audience's attention.

Beside the other connections on your CD-ROM drive, there's a headphone connector on the front of it. Imagine my surprise when I plugged some headphones in and heard sound out of my speakers and headset at the same time. Some vendors disable the speaker output when you plug in the headset; others don't. You'll want to check out this feature if this is an important consideration for your application.

Making Software Attachments

Once you get your hardware up and running, you have to get some software to talk to it in order to do any useful work. That's where some of the utilities you get with Windows 95 come in. They don't necessarily provide the best capabilities, but they do provide enough for you to get going. In fact, you might be surprised at just how well they meet some of your needs.

The following sections describe several of the utilities that come with Windows 95. These utilities won't help you "surf the net" or download the latest industry gossip. We'll cover those in the next chapter when we look at online services. These utilities help you make the necessary connections.

Peter's Principle: The Right Kind of Connection

It might be very tempting to use a single type of connection to meet all your computing needs, but that wouldn't be the most efficient way to do things. You might view a direct cable connection as the panacea for all your portable data-transfer woes, but the direct cable connection is really designed for occasional, not daily, use. A direct cable connection (using either serial or parallel ports to link two computers in conjunction with Windows 95's "Direct Connection" program, or the roughly equivalent DOS Interlink program or Laplink or a similar third-party program) works fine for those quick transfers from one machine to another when you have a fairly large amount of data to move. For example, it works very well when you initially set up the portable.

If you use a portable on a daily basis, using such an Interlink-style connection is a waste of time. You'll want to find some other method of creating your connection to the Desktop. If you have a docking station that can accept a standard network card, or if you plug in a PCMCIA network card, you will be able to use this much faster Ethernet connection to make your data transfers. However, this works only if you have a network and a PCMCIA card. Alternatively, you could get an external Ethernet adapter that plugs into your portable's parallel port. This solution works fine, but it isn't quite as speedy as the standard network interface cards that plug into the computer's bus or the PCMCIA network adapters.

We briefly covered the Briefcase in Chapter 2. We'll cover it in more detail in Chapter 21. This isn't a physical connection to your Desktop machine, but it does do the job for smaller amounts of data. In fact, you'll find out that a Briefcase can hold a substantial amount of data if you use it correctly.

OK, so the network and Briefcase options are out of the question because you're out of town. You can still make a connection to your Desktop using Dial-Up Networking. It won't be as fast as some of the other techniques, but it will allow you to get the data you require while on the road or when working from home.

Windows 95 provides a lot of different connections. You need to use the right one for the job, and that means taking the time to learn about the various options available to you. A connection that works well in one instance could be a time killer in another. Don't succumb to the one-connection way of computing; use every tool that Windows 95 provides.

Making a Direct Cable Connection

Portable users will love the direct cable connection feature that Windows 95 provides. You can make a direct connection using either the serial or parallel port. Of course, the parallel port is a lot faster than the serial port, but either connection will net good results. Direct Cable Connection is a much better version of a similar utility offered with DOS version 5.0 and above. The older version tied up the host machine as the client looked around for the files it needed. This new version allows you to make the connection in the background, effectively freeing the host for use while the client makes the required transactions.

Windows 95 won't automatically install this utility as part of a default package. It isn't part of a standard application such as Dial-Up Networking, either. You need to load the separate Direct Cable Connection utility using the Add/Remove Programs applet. We've visited this procedure in the past, so I won't go through it again here.

Once you get Direct Cable Connection installed, you have to get the host set up. This means that you'll define the port that your machine will use and its mode. Let's look at this procedure first.

Tip: You can create the required data transfer serial cable using a standard serial cable, a null modem, and a gender changer. This will provide all the components you need to make a data transfer cable using a standard modem cable. Your local electronics or computer store can usually provide the null modem and gender changer.

1. Use a special serial or parallel cable to connect the two computers. You can normally get one of these at your local computer store. Be sure to tell them that you plan to connect two computers for the purpose of data transfer. The parallel cable uses a very special crossover wiring, and the serial cable must be wired with the required wires cross-connected, or else you will need to use a null modem as well in order for the connection to work.

2. Open the Direct Cable Connection utility on the host computer. You should see a dialog similar to the one shown in Figure 17.1. Notice the Listen pushbutton. This allows you to start listening for the client computer immediately after opening the program if you already have it configured. The dialog displays the current settings so that you know if you can use them.

Figure 17.1.
The initial Direct Cable Connection dialog allows you to go directly to listen mode.

3. Click on Change to display the dialog shown in Figure 17.2. Notice that there are two radio buttons, one for each mode of operation. One computer must provide host services; the other must act as a client. Normally, the computer supplying resources is the host. You can't create a dual connection using Direct Cable Connection. In other words, you can't make it act as a pseudo-peer-to-peer network with both machines acting as servers.

Figure 17.2.
This dialog allows you to select the operating mode.

4. Select the service type—in this case, Host— and click on Next. You'll see a dialog similar to the one shown in Figure 17.3. Notice that the local ports are automatically listed. You can add other ports using the Install New Ports pushbutton.

Figure 17.3.
This dialog allows you to select the port used for data transfer.

5. Select the port you want. Make sure you use the same type of port on both machines. Click on Next. You'll see the dialog shown in Figure 17.4.

Figure 17.4.
Use this dialog to set a password if necessary.

Tip: The password option in this dialog comes in handy when more than one person needs to use the direct cable connection to a machine. You could leave the host running in the background and then connect other machines as necessary—even remote machines. However, this feature is limited, especially when you consider that the Dial-Up Networking utility allows remote users to call into a machine using a better interface. Microsoft doesn't provide the Dial-Up Networking host software with Windows 95. Connecting your serial cable to a modem will allow you to use a Desktop machine as a rudimentary remote server, but it would probably be better to invest in software designed for remote access if you make this type of connection very often.

6. Check the Use password protection checkbox if you want to password-protect your connection. Use the Set Password pushbutton to change the password from a blank if you select this option.

7. Click on Finish. Direct Cable Connection will wait for the client machine to log in, as shown in Figure 17.5. If the client doesn't respond in a few seconds, Direct Cable Connection will ask if it is properly connected. Ignore the message until you get the other machine running.

Figure 17.5.
Once you complete the Direct Cable Connection setup, it will wait patiently in the background for a connection.

The procedure for setting up a guest computer is exactly the same as for a host computer. The only difference is that you don't need to set a password. Once the two computers establish a connection, the client computer will be able to use the resources of the host.

Using Dial-Up Networking

Dial-Up Networking under Windows 95 is limited to calling into a server. Microsoft decided not to provide the host software required to turn your Windows 95 workstation into a host. (Microsoft does include the host software as part of Microsoft Plus!, an add-on package for Windows 95 that's described in Chapter 24.) Most of the time, this means that you'll need to call into a Windows NT server—at least until third-party software vendors create solutions for other network servers.

Before you can use Dial-Up Networking, you'll need to install it using the Add/Remove Programs applet in Control Panel. We covered that procedure earlier in this book, so I won't discuss it again here. The following paragraphs assume that you've already installed Dial-Up Networking.

The procedure for setting up to call a host remotely is simple. As with the Printers folder that we visited earlier in this book, Dial-Up Networking has its own folder. You'll always see at least one component in that folder: the Make New Connection applet. Let's look at this part of the service first.

1. Open the Dial-Up Networking folder. Double-click on the Make New Connection applet. You should see the dialog shown in Figure 17.6. Note that the utility suggests a default name of My Connection. Make sure you provide a descriptive name here if you plan to create more than one connection. Notice that this dialog also provides a Configure pushbutton, which brings up the same set of dialogs we looked at in Chapter 13 for the Modems applet.

Figure 17.6.
The initial Make New Connection dialog allows you to specify the name of the computer you are calling and the modem type.

2. Once you select a connection name, choose a modem model, configure the connection, and click on Next. The next dialog, shown in Figure 17.7, allows you to input the area code and telephone number for your connection. Notice the Country code listbox, which allows you to create connections even if you aren't currently at home.

Figure 17.7.
You'll need to provide an area code and telephone number at a minimum for the new connection.

3. Click on Next to see the dialog shown in Figure 17.8. This is the final screen. The Make New Connection applet gives you one more chance to change the connection name before it saves it. Of course, you can always change the name later if you need to.

Figure 17.8.
The Make New Connection dialog gives you one last chance to change the connection name before it saves it.

Creating a connection is the first part of the equation. Using the connection after you create it is simple. Just double-click on the Connection icon to see the dialog shown in Figure 17.9. Notice that your name and the telephone number you need to call are automatically added to the dialog. The only thing you need to add is the password for the machine you want to call.

Figure 17.9.
Using a connection after you define it is easy. Just a double-click and a password are all you need.

What happens, though, if you need to call from another location? You can select any predefined location from the Dialing from listbox. But let's say that you're dialing from another location, perhaps outside the country. The following procedure shows you how to quickly add a new location to the Dialing from listbox.

1. Click on the Dial Properties pushbutton. You'll see the dialog shown in Figure 17.10. Notice that this dialog contains everything you need to define a local connection.

Figure 17.10.
The Dialing Properties dialog contains a complete description of your current location.

2. Click on the New pushbutton. You'll see the dialog shown in Figure 17.11.

Figure 17.11.
The Create New Location dialog allows you to specify a new location.

3. Type a descriptive location name and click on OK. You will see the Dialing Properties dialog shown in Figure 17.10. Notice that it contains all the settings I described for the Default Location.

4. Change the area code and country fields to match your current location. Don't worry about any long distance considerations. Windows 95 will take care of that for you automatically. All you need to know is your current location.

5. The How I dial from this location group contains settings that describe the telephone connection. Most of the fields are self-explanatory. The one field that might require a little explanation is the Calling Card field. You'll need to work with your local calling card company to completely fill this out. Windows 95 will present the dialog shown in Figure 17.12. You'll need to supply a calling card type and perhaps a calling card number.

Figure 17.12.
Setting your calling card parameters correctly is very important.

6. Once you complete the Location dialog, click on OK to save it. Notice how the telephone number automatically changes to reflect your location. Figure 17.13 shows an example of dialing from another country instead of within your current country. Windows 95 automatically includes all the required codes for you.

Figure 17.13.
Windows 95 automatically tracks details like the country code for you.

Of course, the last thing you need to do is click on Connect to actually make the connection. When you do so, Windows 95 will send the server your name and password. It will also take care of details such as using your phone card if you supply that information. Configuring the connection the first time might take a little time, but once you get it done, everything is pretty automatic from that point on.

Using Phone Dialer

I didn't think that Phone Dialer would come in very handy for me. After all, I've got an autodialer built right in to my phone. It's a pretty fancy autodialer, too. I press just one button to call my most common numbers.

Phone Dialer comes in handy not for your most common calls but for those that you make infrequently. Have you ever tried to call a government agency? I used to spend a lot of time just trying to get through, only to find that I had reached the wrong number. Phone Dialer might not fix the wrong number part of the equation, but I've found that it works very well for the first part. I can have it call in the background while I continue to work in the foreground—a very handy, time-saving feature.

Let's look at what Phone Dialer has to offer. Open Phone Dialer. You'll see a display similar to the one in Figure 17.14. Notice that there's a keypad on the left side of the dialog, a list of speed dial numbers on the right, and the current number at the top.

Figure 17.14.

The Phone Dialer dialog looks like a telephone keypad with an autodialer.

There are several ways to dial a number. You could just cut it out of your database manager and paste it into the blank at the top. This is one of the methods I use for infrequently called numbers. It has the advantage of allowing you to call a lot of numbers quickly without giving yourself a case of carpal tunnel syndrome in the process.

Before you make any real connections, you should look at the Tools menu to see what configuration options you have. This menu has three options; each one addresses a different need. If you select the Connect Using option, you'll see the dialog shown in Figure 17.15. This dialog has only three fields. The first field, Line, asks which modem you want to use. Only modems that you've set up using the Modems applet in Control Panel are listed. The second field, Address, asks which telephone line you want to use to dial out. It's active only if you have more than one available. The Use Phone Dialer checkbox tells Windows 95 to use Phone Dialer for all application requests. Here's the real story on that one: It services only Windows 95 applications that know how to request outgoing phone services from the autodialer. It wasn't too surprising to see that even Access doesn't use this capability yet. Clicking on the Line Properties pushbutton brings up the Modem Properties dialog we talked about in Chapter 13.

Figure 17.15.

The Connect Using dialog allows you to select from more than one modem if you have more than one attached to your machine.

We saw how to use the Dialing Properties option of the Tools menu earlier. Essentially, it allows you to specify the location you're dialing from so that Phone Dialer can automatically compensate as needed for long distance calls.

The Show Log option of the Tools menu displays the Call Log dialog, shown in Figure 17.16. There isn't too much to say about this particular dialog except that it maintains a record of the calls you make, including the number, the person's name, and how long you were on the phone. The nicest feature of this particular dialog is that you can double-click on an entry to call it again. With this feature, I can save some time when calling a number I don't have memorized, because I don't have to look it up.

Figure 17.16.

The Call Log dialog not only keeps track of the calls you make, but it also allows you to dial them again with ease.

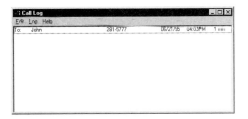

There are two convenient methods for adding new numbers to your Speed dial group. The first method is to simply click on a blank spot. (The only problem with this technique is that it works only for blank buttons. Clicking on a filled-in blank will dial the number.) You'll see the dialog shown in Figure 17.17. This dialog contains only two entries: the name of the person you want to call and the number to reach him or her. The pushbuttons on the side are pretty self-explanatory.

Figure 17.17.

Adding a new speed dial number is as easy as clicking on a blank button.

You can also use the Edit | Speed Dial command to display the dialog shown in Figure 17.18. This dialog allows you to access any of the buttons. All you need to do is click on the one you want to edit. Erasing the contents of both the name and number fields will blank that button for future use.

Figure 17.18.
The Edit Speed Dial dialog allows you to change the single-button connections provided by the Phone Dialer.

On Your Own

Look through the vendor manual that came with your printer. See if the vendor provides any accessories for your printer that might make it more flexible to use. Especially important is the availability of alternative port options. You also might want to check for third-party solutions for your printer. Some third-party vendors provide port accessories for some of the more prominent printers, such as the HP LaserJet.

Identify the five phases of a fax transaction if you have a fax/modem attached to your machine. This is especially easy when using an external model. The lights on the front of the device help you detect when the various phases occur. Tracking this type of information can help you troubleshoot a faulty connection.

If you have a notebook computer, and both a network and a direct cable connection are available for it, try both methods of transferring a file. Most people have a serial connection available, so try that first. You should find that the network connection is a lot faster, but it's interesting to see how much faster. Try the same thing with a parallel connection (if possible).

Install and set up Phone Dialer. Try it out for a few days to see if its additional features make phone calling a little easier for your harder-to-reach numbers. Also try the log feature to see how well it meets your needs.

18

Talking to the Outside World

In the preceding chapter we looked at some of the intricacies of making connections within Windows 95. In this chapter we'll look at some of the things you can do with those connections after you make them. Unlike its predecessor, Windows 95 provides a combination of communication options that should meet the majority of your needs.

As of this writing, Microsoft has already withdrawn some Internet support from the main Windows product. There are also rumors that they'll pull CompuServe support, but that hasn't been confirmed. You might find that the actual support you get is a little less than I talk about in this chapter, but the total communications package for Windows 95 will still surpass what you got in either Windows NT or Windows 3.x. The Microsoft Plus! add-on product, discussed in Chapter 24, provides most features you'll want that aren't in the main product.

Note: If you're going to do a lot of Internet surfing, you should take a serious look at Microsoft Plus!. Microsoft Plus! includes the Internet Setup Wizard, which takes you through the necessary steps to get online through direct connections or through Microsoft Network or any other Internet access provider using PPP connections. Microsoft Plus! also provides tools to access SLIP accounts, and it supplies you with Scripter, a tool for writing scripts to access Internet access providers with special login needs, such as CompuServe.

Note: In addition to all the tools for getting connected, Microsoft Plus! includes the World Wide Web browser Microsoft Internet Explorer. It also upgrades Microsoft Exchange so that it can read POP/SMTP Internet e-mail so that you can use the Internet effectively from Windows 95. You'll learn more about these features in Chapter 24.

Before we get into the actual communications packages, let's look at the communication subsystem architecture. Actually, we won't get the total picture in this chapter. Figure 18.1 reflects only the local part of the communication structure. We'll look at the remote network architecture in Chapter 21. However, if you look carefully, you'll see all three of the main connections we discussed in Chapter 17: Dial-Up Networking, Phone Dialer, and direct cable connection. The following list provides details about all the components of the communication subsystem.

- Telephony API (TAPI): All the new modem-specific services are clustered under this API. It provides command translation for the new Windows 95 applications that make use of it. When an application asks about the modem setup or status, this module provides the information translation required for a seamless interface. TAPI might configure the modem from a virtual point of view, but VCOMM still manages the actual port. Modem commands flow through the port from TAPI. A good analogy of this arrangement is that VCOMM provides the pipe, but TAPI provides the water.

Figure 18.1.

An overview of the Windows 95 local communications architecture.

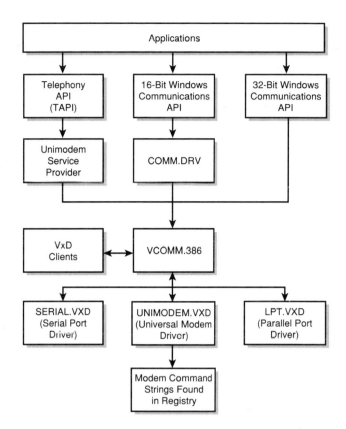

- Windows 16-bit communications API: The API is the module that accepts instructions from an application and translates them into something that Windows 95 can understand. One API instruction might actually require an entire module's worth of detailed instructions in order to perform. Windows 95 doesn't really use the 16-bit version of the Windows communication instructions. The old instructions didn't provide the robust environment that the rest of Windows 95 provides. However, instead of writing a new 16-bit module, Microsoft provides access to the new 32-bit interface through these instructions and the COMM.DRV module that I'll describe in a moment.

- Windows 32-bit communications API: This is the enhanced 32-bit instruction set for Windows 95. Like its 16-bit counterpart, the 32-bit API translates application requests into commands that Windows can actually implement.

- Unimodem service provider: This is the specific driver for your modem. It takes the generic commands provided by the TAPI module and translates them into something your modem will understand.

- COMM.DRV: Under Windows 3.x, this module actually carried out the communication tasks ordered by the API. The Windows 95 version is a thunk layer to the 32-bit instructions held in the 32-bit communications API and VCOMM.386. The positive aspect of this is that you'll see a definite boost in the speed of communication programs, even if you use an older 16-bit application. For example, I noticed that background downloads go well, even using my older copy of Procomm for Windows, which never worked in the background under Windows 3.x. It's unfortunate that Microsoft decided to maintain the old 16-bit instruction set rather than upgrade it to the fuller 32-bit set. This decision will probably solve more problems than it creates.

- VxD clients: VCOMM.386 provides services to more than just the communications subsystem. Every time any other Windows subsystem requires port access, it must go through VCOMM.386 as well. These requests are fielded through APIs that act as clients to this module. This is an internal Windows 95 function that you'll never really notice, but you should know that there are interactions between subsystems. A port failure might not always be the result of a communications or print-specific problem; it could be related to some interaction from another, unrelated, subsystem.

- VCOMM.386: Calling this a part of the communication subsystem is almost inaccurate. VCOMM.386 is a static device VxD that Windows 95 always loads during the boot process. Part of the job that VCOMM.386 performs is to load all the port drivers shown in Figure 18.1. Other parts of Windows also call VCOMM.386 through their respective APIs to perform a variety of port-specific services. You'll probably see VCOMM.386 in other parts of this book in other formats.

- SERIAL.VXD: This is the serial port driver. It's the actual serial port engine. Another driver is associated with the serial port as well. SERIALUI.DLL provides the interface you use while setting the serial ports up.

- UNIMODEM.VXD: The modem setup is a little more complex than the other port drivers supported by VCOMM.386. This one actually works with either a serial or parallel port to provide modem services for the rest of Windows. It's also responsible for making any modem-specific registry changes. Every time you change the modem strings, this module records them in the registry. As with the serial port driver, the VxD doesn't provide any interface elements. It relies on MODEMUI.DLL to provide these services. There's also a Control Panel element to worry about in this case. You'll find that MODEM.CPL manages this aspect of the interface.

- LPT.VXD: This is the parallel port driver. Unlike the serial port, the parallel port is usually managed by the printer subsystem. As a result, it relies on MSPRINT.DLL for user interface services.

- Modem command strings found in registry: Actually, this is the completion of a circle. Many of the upper modules rely on the registry entries to know how to interact with the modem. These strings provide those instructions. Each string defines some aspect of modem behavior. In most cases, it affects the modem's setup or the way it communicates with another machine. You'll need to refer to your modem manual to get a better idea of exactly how these strings work.

Unlike many other subsystems, the communication subsystem looks fairly straightforward, and it is—to a point. There is a risk of underestimating the effect of this subsystem on the rest of Windows if you don't account for the number of ways it interacts with other subsystems. The centerpiece of this whole subsystem is VCOMM.386. This module loads the port drivers, provides access to them during system operation, and generally manages the way Windows interacts with the outside world. It's an important role that you might take for granted until it stops working. We'll look at some things that can go wrong with this subsystem in Chapter 23.

Using Microsoft Exchange

Microsoft Exchange is central command as far as communications go. You can perform almost any kind of communication that Windows 95 will support just by opening Microsoft Exchange. We'll see, as time goes on, that, like Explorer, Microsoft Exchange pops up in the strangest places. Even if you think that each communication module under Windows 95 is a separate entity, they aren't. They all rely on Exchange for a user interface. The details differ from service to service, but the part that the user sees remains fairly constant.

Before we begin looking at specific communication services provided by Windows 95, I want to take you on a quick tour of Microsoft Exchange. I'm not talking about working through the intricacies of every service it provides; we'll cover that in the individual service descriptions that follow. What we'll cover now is the generic core that you should know about. Once you get this part of the interface down, the little differences between components will seem a lot less intimidating.

Understanding the User Interface

The following discussion assumes that you have Microsoft Exchange installed. We'll look at how you can install individual components later. You'll use Microsoft Exchange to perform that work. What you want to do now is look at the user interface itself.

Figure 18.2 shows a typical Microsoft Exchange display. Of course, your display will probably vary from this one a bit, but you get the idea. The main thing to remember is that your interface will vary a little because of the settings you choose and the options you install.

Figure 18.2.
The Inbox folder not only provides access to your messages, but it also helps you organize them in a variety of ways.

Microsoft Exchange always defaults to your Inbox as the first location it shows. After it opens the Inbox, it updates any e-mail messages you have on the network (assuming that you're attached). You'll need to go online to update your other messages, but they all appear in this single Inbox (unless you change the settings that we'll discuss later).

Let's quickly look at how Microsoft Exchange presents your Inbox messages. This is the default setup of columns; I'll tell you how to change this setup later. We'll start at the very first column of the message header and work our way across. The first column can contain nothing, a red exclamation mark, or a blue down arrow. Medium-priority messages receive no symbol. A red exclamation mark tells you that this message is high-priority, and a blue down arrow says that the message is low-priority. The second column tells you what type of item is stored there. In most cases it will be a message, as shown by the envelope symbol. The little paper clip symbol in the third column tells you that a message has attachments. You can either attach files outright or add OLE objects to your messages. I was surprised to find that you can add objects in such a way that they'll actually start an online session. You can also create an object that will access a file on the network. In the fourth column you'll find the name of the person who sent the message or item. The fifth column contains the message's subject line. The sixth column tells you when the message was received. Finally, the seventh column tells you how big the file is.

Tip: It almost always pays to change this default setup. Exchange provides a wealth of column headings that old versions of Microsoft Mail didn't. You'll at least want to see what's available and consider how you can use it to optimize your setup.

Sorting the messages in any given folder is easy. You'll notice that the column headings are actually pushbuttons. Clicking on a column heading sorts by that column. You can change the sort order by clicking a second time. Exchange displays an arrow in the heading that the messages are sorted by (if there's room in the heading). It uses an up arrow for ascending order and a down arrow for descending order. If you prefer a dialog interface for changing the sort order, you can always use the View | Sort command to display the dialog shown in Figure 18.3. It offers the same column selections that you see on the display. All you need to do is select one from the listbox, click on the order you want to sort in, and click on OK to complete the action.

Figure 18.3.
The Sort dialog box allows you to select a sort order, but clicking on the column headings is a lot faster.

Notice the use of bold text on the display. Whenever you see either a folder or a message name in bold, it means that you haven't read that message or completely viewed the contents of the folder. I find that this is the fastest way to see new messages on my system. Of course, this is a little less valuable when you use the default folder setup, but it can be quite valuable as you expand your system. Along with this use of bold text are two Edit menu options. You can mark a message as read or unread using the two options on this menu.

> **Tip:** It's important to use all the Exchange features to your benefit. For example, some people might view the Edit | Read and Edit | Unread commands as superfluous, but they're really quite useful. I don't often mark a message as read, but I do mark messages as unread from time to time. This is handy for times when you read a message, realize you don't have time to take care of it now, and mark it as unread so that you'll remember to look at it again later.

Looking at the default display, you can see a relationship between Exchange and Explorer. Certainly the hierarchy of folders is the same, and the messages equate to files in your postoffice. There are other similarities as well. For example, you can add folders to the default hierarchy to better organize your messages. I find that moving messages around into various project areas is a great way to make Exchange a lot easier to use. Use the File | New Folder command to display the dialog shown in Figure 18.4. All you need to do is type in a name and click on OK to complete the process. Moving messages from place to place is also as easy as using Explorer. Each entry has a context menu containing Exchange-specific functions that work the same as the Explorer equivalent. The bottom line is that if you know how to use Explorer, learning Exchange shouldn't be very difficult.

Figure 18.4.
Adding folders to the default
Exchange hierarchy will let
you organize your messages
more easily.

Note: Exchange will let you remove folders you create by using the Delete command or by pressing the Delete key, just like Explorer. However, it stops short of allowing you to delete the default folders in the hierarchy. These folders have to remain in place to support the mail structure.

You might notice that the Recycle Bin doesn't change if you delete a message. That's because Exchange provides its own delete area in the Deleted Items folder. If you delete a message from any area of Exchange, it ends up in this folder. If you delete a message in the Deleted Items folder, you'll remove it from the system permanently. I usually disable this option to keep myself from removing old messages that I'll need later. You can't place Exchange messages in the Recycle Bin. We'll see later that you can make the process of removing old messages a little more automatic by changing the Exchange options.

Exchange also provides a fairly complete toolbar right under the menu bar. You'll notice some standard icons here, but most of them are unique to Exchange. We discussed all these icons in Chapter 2, so I won't go through them again.

Using the Address Book

Microsoft Exchange provides an address book that helps you maintain a list of the people you normally contact. Before you send a message to anyone, it's usually a good idea to add his or her name to the address book, even if you intend to use the address only once. The reason is simple. I've often been in a situation where I think I'll use an address only once, but then I have to look all over the place for it later when I need to send a second message.

Figure 18.5 shows the initial Address Book dialog. Exchange defaults to using the Microsoft Mail postoffice address book, but you can reset this default to any address book you like. It also adds all the names of people on your local network or workgroup, allowing you to send messages immediately without a lot of typing. The display normally provides the person's name as a minimum. Any other information it provides is format-specific (we'll cover that in detail later).

The toolbar below the menu bar provides access to the majority of the Address Book functions. In fact, I don't think I've ever had to use the menu itself. The following list provides an overview of each toolbar pushbutton.

Figure 18.5.
*The initial Address Book
dialog shows the addresses
that you select as a default.*

- New entry: This allows you to add new names to the address book.

- Find: You can use this pushbutton to filter the names displayed in the dialog. It actually creates a new address book called Search Results.

- Properties: Use this to change the properties of the address book. You right-click on a specific name to change its properties. The postoffice address book doesn't provide any overall properties for you to change, so Exchange displays an error message if you select this pushbutton.

Note: As of this writing, the actual function of the Properties pushbutton tends to change with the address book you're using. In some cases it works, but in others it doesn't. In some cases it changes the properties of the address book itself, and in others it brings up the Properties dialog for the individual entry. The definition provided here is consistent with the current Microsoft documentation.

- Delete: This pushbutton allows you to remove an entry from the address book. Unfortunately, there's no recovery area if you accidentally erase a name you needed.

- Add to personal address book: Use this button to add a name from a public or other address book to your personal address book. Exchange always creates a personal address book for you. Of course, that doesn't restrict you from creating other personal address books, but this button will work only with the default set up by Exchange.

- New message: You can click on one or more names in your address book and then click on this button to send a message to the people you selected. The message creation dialog will automatically display the selected list of names when you open it.

- Help: As with every Windows application, you can request help using a variety of methods. Clicking on this button will display the help cursor. Point to whatever you need help with and click. Windows will provide context-sensitive help that will aid you in using the Address Book dialog.

Adding a New Address

Adding a new address is fairly easy. The only challenge is figuring out exactly what you need to provide. Each of the MAPI clients that Exchange supports uses a different address format because their methods of sending messages are different. However, besides a few vagaries in the way an address gets stored for a specific type of MAPI client, there are a lot of similarities. The first step in adding a new address book entry is deciding what type of address it is (see Figure 18.6). Once you decide what type of address to add and where to add it, click on OK to view the format-specific address page. Let's take a look at one or two of specialty pages in the Address Book dialog. Then I'll describe the pages that are common to all formats.

Figure 18.6.
You need to decide what kind of address to add before you can add it.

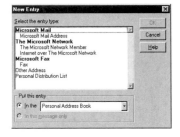

Figure 18.7 shows a new address book entry for Microsoft Mail. You'll need to add new entries using this page only for users who are part of other workgroups. All the local workgroup names get entered automatically. This page has four blanks. Each one provides part of the routing information needed to send your message to its destination. The first field, Alias, is the person's login name. This might or might not be his full name. It could be a nickname or a shortened version of his full name if there is more than one person on the network with the same name. Type whatever name he uses to log into the network. The Mailbox field contains the person's nickname, the name that the Postoffice Administrator used when entering his name in the postoffice. This field usually contains the same information as the Alias field. The Postoffice field contains the name of the postoffice. This might or might not be the name of the machine that actually contains the postoffice. Finally, the Network field contains the name of the network, workgroup, domain, or other identifying information. It's the name you'll see at the root of a network entry in Network Neighborhood.

A new fax address book entry probably contains less information than you would expect. Figure 18.8 shows an example of this entry. Notice that you need to supply only a name and some telephone information. We covered this particular dialog in Chapter 17, so I won't go over the specific fields again. Note the Mailbox field. It's not a functional routing entry, but it could help the person at the other end direct the fax to the correct person.

You see a new Microsoft Network address entry in Figure 18.9. This is typical of most online service entries. It consists of a member name and an online identification number.

Figure 18.7.
A Microsoft Mail address entry requires just a few simple pieces of information about the network routing needed to reach a recipient.

Figure 18.8.
A fax address entry requires the person's name and a telephone number.

Figure 18.9.
The Microsoft Network address entry is the easiest to fill out so far. All you need is a name and identification number.

Figure 8.10 shows the last type of new address entry we'll cover. A new Internet entry contains three fields. The first contains the person's e-mail address. This is the same address that he would normally use if he were on that service. The second field contains the domain name. This might require a little explanation. It would be easy to think of the Internet as an entity. It really isn't. The Internet is composed of literally thousands of smaller networks, each providing common access. When you see an Internet address, it usually looks similar to this one: 71570.641@compuserve.com. The @, or "at" symbol, separates the e-mail address from the domain name. In this particular case, you would send a message to someone on CompuServe. If you wanted to send a message to America Online, you would use aol.com as the domain name. Every server has a unique domain name that allows it to receive messages. The third field contains the person's name.

Figure 18.10.
A new Internet address page might look a bit strange at first.

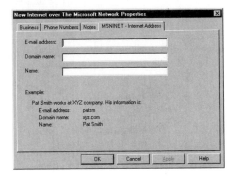

Now that we've seen all the format-specific pages, let's look at the common pages that the Address Book provides. Figure 18.11 shows the Business page. It allows you to record all the specifics that you're likely to need about contacting that person. All of the fields are self-explanatory; you'll find them in any contact manager. One of the nice features of this particular page is the Phone number field. You can select the location you want from the listbox and then enter a number. I'll describe all the locations in the next paragraph, but it's nice to know that you can record more than one. Another nice feature is the ability to dial that phone number right from this page using the Phone Dialer utility that we discussed in Chapter 17.

Figure 18.11.
The Business page provides a fast way of recording all the pertinent contact information you need in order to reach someone.

The Phone Numbers page, shown in Figure 18.12, provides a quick list of all the phone numbers you can use to contact the person. I felt that adding the assistant's phone number was an especially nice touch. Unfortunately, you can't record any more than the eight phone numbers shown here. In most cases, this is enough unless the person you're trying to contact travels a lot or normally works in more than one location.

The final page, Notes, is a big notepad. You can enter previous contact information or any other freeform information here. I often use it to track the last date I contacted someone and a brief note on what we talked about. This note taker won't replace a contact manager, though. If you spend most of your time on the phone, and keeping track of all those contacts is important, I recommend a full-fledged contact manager in place of this solution. The notepad provided with Address Book is more for the occasional user than anything else. You could, however, store a customer ID or another number here to make it easier to find this person's record in your contact manager.

Figure 18.12.

The Phone Numbers page allows you to enter up to eight contact numbers for each person in your address book.

Note: Some services might include an additional page. For example, Figure 18.12 shows an additional page for the Internet service. You can be certain that this page will become prominent as third-party developers add their own MAPI drivers. Make sure you follow the vendor-supplied instructions when filling out this page's information.

Finding Names in Your Address Book

Finding names in your address book is very easy. All you need to do is click on the Find icon on the toolbar. Address Book will display the dialog shown in Figure 18.13. All you need to do is fill in a name or even part of a name. Clicking on OK will display the list of names in a new address book called Search Results. You can switch between this address book and your original one using the listbox below the toolbar.

Figure 18.13.

You can use Find to whittle down a large address book into one containing just the names you need.

Changing the Address Book Properties

You can make a few configuration changes to each address book on your system except the public postoffice address book. You access the Address Book Properties dialog shown in Figure 18.14 by clicking on the Properties icon on the toolbar.

Figure 18.14.
The Address Book Properties dialog allows you to change the way your address book works.

The first page contains three fields. The Name field allows you to change the name of the address book. In most cases, you'll want to retain the name of the default personal address book that Exchange sets up for you so that you can automatically add names to it. The second field contains the location of the actual address book file on disk. This too normally stays the same unless you move the address book to a new location. The group of radio buttons changes the way the address book lists names. I find this feature quite handy when I'm looking for a specific name. Changing the order makes it easier to find an entry for someone when I forget his last name.

Tip: You can create new address books with specific names using the Find button. Use the Properties dialog to change the name of that address book to something else so that Windows won't overwrite it the next time you need to create a special address book.

The Notes page of this dialog contains a miniature notebook. You can use it to track the address book and anything you do with it. It might come in handy for writing a reminder of why you started this particular address book.

Adding and Configuring Address Books

One Address Book feature isn't covered by the toolbar. The Tools | Options command brings up the dialog shown in Figure 18.15. This dialog actually performs two different functions. The first is to configure Exchange to use your address books. The second is to create new address books as you need them.

Figure 18.15.
Use this dialog to configure
Exchange to use your address
books and to create new
ones.

Let's examine the first purpose. The Show this address list first field determines which address book Exchange shows first whenever you create a new message. If most of your messages go to the company e-mail, using the default setting of Postoffice Address List makes sense. However, if you're like me, you send messages to a variety of places, including the company e-mail. In this case, you might want to select your Personal Address List as the first location instead. The second field contains the name of your personal address list. Unless you want to personalize this setting for some reason, you'll want to keep the default setting. Exchange automatically creates this address list for you, so there's no real reason to change it later.

The second purpose is to add new address lists to your address book. The listbox will always show a complete list of the current address lists that you have, except for any recent searches. You can add a new address list by clicking on the Add pushbutton. Simply follow the prompts to create the new address list. In most cases, you'll find that the default address books provide more than sufficient flexibility.

Finding Specific Messages

Ever find yourself buried in a mound of messages with no real way to organize them and even less opportunity to find the one you need fast? Exchange provides a handy search dialog that looks similar to Explorer's Find dialog (see Figure 18.16). This dialog contains quite a few mail-specific features. Of course, it won't help you find any files on your drive.

Most of the fields in this dialog are pretty self-explanatory, but using some of them might not be. For example, if you want to search through all your mail, you select the Personal Information Store folder. You can't search from the Exchange level. Of course, you can always go lower than this top level by looking through the folder hierarchy.

The Sent directly to me and the Copied (Cc) to me checkboxes aren't mutually exclusive. However, if you select the first one, you won't be able to ask for a specific person in the Sent to field even though Exchange doesn't blank it out. You can combine the Copied (Cc) to me checkbox and a specific Sent to name, though.

Figure 18.16.
Exchange's Find dialog looks similar to the one found in Explorer, with some important exceptions.

Using the various fields in tandem is the key to finding precisely the message you want. The Advanced pushbutton will show you some additional criteria you can use to search for messages. It uses the dialog shown in Figure 18.17 to allow you to perform a more stringent search.

Figure 18.17.
You can perform a very detailed search of the message base using the criteria in the Advanced dialog.

Some of these options have interesting uses. For example, when it comes time to make room on the server containing the postoffice, you can get rid of the bigger messages using the Size group. I use this option from time to time just to see how many large files I have accumulated. You'd be surprised how fast they can build up.

Getting back from vacation usually means you have a lot more work to do than time to get it done. I start by categorizing the various things I need to do by placing them in separate folders. Then I use a high-priority search to find the items I need to get done right away.

You can also use the entries in this dialog to search for messages you haven't read yet or messages received during a certain time span. The time span option is nice when you know you received a message during a specific time period but you can't remember much else about it. Any attempt to look through the entire message base will likely prove frustrating.

Once you select all the search criteria, clicking on the Find Now pushbutton will display a list of matching messages in the listbox at the bottom of the Find dialog. This list will respond to all the usual actions, such as right-clicking and double-clicking. You can also delete messages in this list and respond to them in the normal way. The one item in this dialog that surprised me a bit was the ability to create new messages. It certainly makes life a lot easier when you remember to write an important message in the middle of or as a result of looking for something else.

Working with the Exchange Services

Windows 95 comes with a limited number of MAPI servers. (We covered MAPI in Chapter 13. A MAPI server simply provides access to a particular online service.) Each server uses Exchange as a front end. In other words, once you learn how to use Exchange, you pretty much know how to use all the generic pieces of each MAPI server as well. The big difference between servers and the interface that you get is the medium in which they operate. The medium will determine some of the differences that you see in how the various MAPI servers operate.

Exchange might come with some or all of the servers added. The default servers are pretty much self-installing. But it's quite likely that you'll need to add new MAPI servers as third-party products arrive on the scene. For example, you might choose to use a MAPI server to access your local BBS instead of buying a full-fledged communication program. Not only would you ease the learning curve that such a product requires, but the software vendor will be able to provide similar functionality in a much smaller package.

Use the Tools | Services command to display the dialing Services dialog, shown in Figure 18.18. The top of the dialog contains a list of the current servers you have installed. In most cases, you won't need to install the Windows 95 servers individually unless Microsoft comes out with an update or the original server gets contaminated in some way. The five pushbuttons below this list describe various actions that you can perform when adding, removing, or modifying a MAPI server.

Figure 18.18.
The Services dialog is where you manage the MAPI servers attached to your machine.

Adding a New Service

Adding a new Service to Exchange is very easy. All you need to do is click on the Add pushbutton in the Services dialog. Exchange will display a list of default services available for Windows 95, as shown in Figure 18.19. However, you can add third-party MAPI services by clicking on the Have Disk pushbutton.

Figure 18.19.
The Add Service to Profile
dialog allows you to add new
MAPI servers to Exchange
with little effort.

Normally the procedure would involve selecting the service you want to install and clicking on OK. That's what you should do to install the service. However, I found an interesting piece of information in this dialog. Clicking on the About pushbutton displays a dialog similar to the one shown in Figure 18.20. Notice that it lists all the files required to make this service operate. You can use this dialog later if you need to know the names of the files to remove from your hard drive when a service is no longer needed. This dialog also provides helpful diagnostic information if you have problems later. For example, you could use it to determine the size of the various files, the version number of each component, and who to call for help with a particular service.

Figure 18.20.
The About Information
Service dialog tells you a lot
more than the usual About
dialog.

After Exchange completes the installation of a new service, it usually asks if you want to configure it. This usually involves providing routing information or perhaps some specifics about the equipment you plan to use. You don't necessarily have to configure the service right away if you don't have the required information. Clicking on the Properties pushbutton later will allow you to configure the service to meet your needs. However, if the service does require some type of routing or equipment-specific information, you'll need to perform the configuration before you can use the service.

Customizing Exchange

Exchange provides a great deal of flexibility in the way you access information. We've already seen much of that flexibility in this chapter. As third-party vendors create more MAPI servers, we'll only see that flexibility increase. However, Exchange's flexibility goes beyond that. You can also configure just about every aspect of the interface itself. The Tools | Options command displays an Options dialog like the one shown in Figure 18.21. This dialog allows you to change the way Exchange interacts with you.

Figure 18.21.
The Options dialog allows you to change the way Exchange interacts with the user.

The General page contains four main sections. The first tells Exchange how to notify you about new mail—if you do in fact want to be notified. The checkboxes in this group are fairly easy to figure out. You can have Exchange play a sound, change the mouse pointer, or display a message to notify you of new mail. Of course, you can select combinations of all three if you like. The second section tells Exchange what to do with deleted items. The first selection tells Exchange to warn you before it permanently deletes anything, just in case you really want to keep something. You can automatically remove any deleted messages from the hard drive when you exit Exchange by checking the second selection. The first setting in the third section allows you to choose the profile (list of services) that you'll use each time you start Exchange. You can keep more than one profile if needed, but I usually find that centralized control of my messages is far more valuable than the flexibility of using additional profiles. The default setting is to use the standard Microsoft Exchange Settings profile.

The final two checkboxes on this page are miscellaneous settings. The first setting affects ToolTips. Those are the little dialogs that appear under each control if you rest your mouse cursor there long enough. They provide a quick description of that control's purpose. The second setting affects how the editor works. Checking this box means that Exchange will select an entire word at a time instead of single characters. It comes in handy for block deletes, but I personally find that the editor works better without this option turned on.

The Read page, shown in Figure 18.22, contains two main sections. The first tells Exchange how to move the cursor after you read and either move or delete a message. The default setting moves the cursor to the next item in the list. This is very convenient when your message base is sorted by date, because you waste a lot less time positioning the cursor this way. Of course, you might organize your list in reverse order to see the older messages first. In this case, the second setting would work better. Whichever way you organize your messages, selecting the right radio button can add a measure of convenience to the process of selecting, then reading, your messages.

Figure 18.22.
Use the Read page of the
Options dialog to change the
way Exchange reacts when
you read messages.

The second section of this page allows you to change the tasks that Exchange automatically performs when you answer a message. The first option allows you to include the original message in your response. The second option indents the original text to make it clearer that you are including the original text. If you use the first option, always include the second for the sake of clarity. The third option closes the original item after you respond to it. This allows you to move to the next message without wasting time. Finally, the Font pushbutton displays a list of fonts and font sizes in a dialog. You should normally select a typeface and font size that will help the other person see your response clearly.

Peter's Principle: Quoting: A Waste of Money or a Friendly Gesture?

Exchange offers you the chance to include the text of the original message when you make a reply. This process is called *quoting* when you use it with an online service such as CompuServe. Other services might use different names, but the effect is the same. When you include part of the original message in your response, you're quoting the other person.

This particular policy generates a lot of controversy in some online services. Some people think quoting is a waste of time because the other person should know what you're talking about. Time spells money on some online services, because they charge you for every minute that you spend actively using it. To the people who oppose this practice, downloading quoted material means wasting money. Other people—those who spend a lot of time online—really like this practice because it allows them to keep individual conversations separate. They believe that the small amount of additional text is the cost of maintaining a clear dialog.

You can compromise to keep both parties happy. Simply enclose the significant part of the original text in angle brackets, like this: `<<Some part of an original message.>>` Make sure you place the quoted text on a separate line so that it's clear you're quoting the other person. I usually use this measure if I'm not sure whether the other party likes quoting or not. My responses usually include quoted questions or perhaps a comment that caught my attention. I never include more than absolutely necessary to get my point across or to clarify my response.

What about your company e-mail? Quoting is always a good idea when you're carrying on a lot of conversations with one person. I find that it helps me remember the exact nature of a particular discussion as I go from topic to topic. Whether or not you use quoting when you access an online service is a matter of personal preference. Using it with the people you work with is a matter of necessity and company policy.

The Send page shown in Figure 18.23 contains settings that change the way you send messages to other people. This dialog has five main areas. The first setting allows you to change the font that you use to create messages. Clicking on this pushbutton displays a list of typefaces available on your machine. Always select a typeface and font size that will allow the other person to read your message with a minimum of squinting. The second item allows you to determine if the other party received and/or read your message. I almost never use the receipt feature unless I've been having communication problems. It tends to make the other person think you don't trust him. The Set sensitivity listbox tells the other person how much secrecy to attach to your message. I usually include a lot more than just a sensitivity setting, though, if the information is very important or if it's critical that the other person guard the contents of the message. The next setting allows you to adjust the standard importance associated with a particular message. Unless you're the president of the company, you'll probably want to keep it at the Normal setting. Fortunately, you can easily adjust this setting on an individual basis when needed. I'll tell you how later in this chapter. The final setting on this page places a copy of your message in the Sent Items folder. I always use this feature because people often lose the messages I send. Most people have this problem. Keeping a copy of the message where you can grab it quickly changes a major headache into a minor nuisance.

Figure 18.23.
The Send page of the Options dialog allows you to change the way Exchange sends messages you create.

The Spelling page, shown in Figure 18.24, can save you more than time. It can save you the embarrassment of making a major spelling error on a message you planned to use to impress someone. I often wonder what the other person was thinking when he wrote a message because of the number of spelling errors. In fact, such a problem is almost inexcusable today, because just about every product that works with Windows also includes a spelling checker of some type.

Figure 18.24.
The Spelling page determines when and how the spelling checker will keep your messages free of spelling errors.

We looked at both the Addressing and Services pages in the preceding section. The Addressing page is where you add new address lists and define the default address list to use when creating a message. The Services page allows you to add new services to Exchange.

The Delivery page appears in Figure 18.25. The first two fields allow you to define a primary and secondary mail delivery location. All you need to do is select the desired location from the listbox. The third listbox defines which address lists Exchange will use to process recipient addresses. You can change the order by highlighting the desired entry and using the arrows to move it up or down the list.

Figure 18.25.
The Delivery page allows you to define the delivery location for your mail.

Customizing the Toolbar

I like the way the Exchange toolbar is arranged. It seems to contain everything I need without getting cluttered with things I don't normally use. However, you might need to use different Exchange features to get your work done. That's one reason I was so happy to see the customization feature.

Use the Tools | Customize Toolbar command to display the dialog shown in Figure 18.26. This is where you customize the toolbar. There are two lists. The one on the left includes all the commands and other features you can include on the toolbar. The list on the right contains all the commands and other features that are on the toolbar right now. To add a new feature to the toolbar, simply highlight the position on the right list where you want it to appear, and then highlight the item on the left list that you want to add. Click on the Add pushbutton to add the new item. Likewise, if you want to remove an item from the toolbar, simply highlight it and click on Remove.

Figure 18.26.
Customizing the toolbar is as easy as a few clicks using this dialog.

You can also move things around on the toolbar. Simply select the item you want to move and click on the Move Up or Move Down pushbutton to make the change. If you decide that all the changes you made were in error, a click on the Reset button will return them to their previous state. Finally, click on the Close pushbutton to make your changes permanent.

Customizing the Column Headings

Exchange even allows you to modify the amount and type of data it displays. You can easily change the column widths by moving the mouse cursor between two columns, waiting for the pointer to change to a line with two arrows (one pointing each direction), and dragging the column line wherever you want it. Once you get past the point where you can adjust column widths using the mouse, though, you'll need to use the View | Column command to modify other column features. Figure 18.27 shows what this dialog looks like.

Figure 18.27.
There's no reason to keep data around that you don't need. Get rid of it using the Columns dialog box.

There's no reason to keep specific columns around when you no longer need them. Likewise, you might find that Exchange provides some type of information you would really like to see. I usually err in favor of too much data if I have the screen real estate to support additional columns. It's better to have too much data than to miss something important because you don't have enough.

This dialog works much like the toolbar dialog I discussed in the preceding section. To add a column to the display, simply select where you want it to appear in the right list, highlight the data you want to appear there in the left list, and click on Add. Removing unneeded data is just as easy. Highlight the entry you want to get rid of in the right column and click on Remove.

If you find that you added or removed too many columns, click on Reset to restore things to their unedited state. Moving columns around is easy, too. Just select the desired column in the right list and use the Move Up and Move Down pushbuttons to change its position.

This dialog has one additional field. The Width field allows you to set the size of the columns in pixels. Personally, I find this a little counterintuitive. I prefer to use the mouse to change the column size using the technique I described at the beginning of this section.

Understanding the Online Services

Now that you have a better understanding of Microsoft Exchange, it's time to look at some of the things you can do with it. Exchange comes with three different MAPI servers: Mail, Fax, and Microsoft Network. Each of these servers uses Exchange as its front end to varying degrees.

Tip: The original version of Microsoft Exchange came with four MAPI servers, but Microsoft dropped the CompuServe service at the very end of the test cycle. There are rumors that CompuServe will pick up support for this particular server sometime in the near future. You'll probably want to keep your eyes peeled for it if Exchange is your medium of choice for online communications.

The following sections explore the MAPI servers that come with Windows 95. These servers can interact with each other through Exchange. All the messages you receive will appear in one place, regardless of which server you used to retrieve them. In fact, from a user perspective, you might even be tempted to think that you're using a single product for all your communication needs. Of course, it's just the level of front-end integration that makes it appear that way.

Note: Microsoft Plus!, the add-on product for Windows 95, includes additional MAPI servers. One of the servers provides complete access to the Internet. If Internet access is important to you, you might want to see what Microsoft Plus! has to offer by looking at Chapter 24.

Microsoft Mail

Microsoft Mail is the easiest of the MAPI servers to describe. We've already looked at all the interface elements in this chapter. The only thing you'll notice as far as Mail is concerned is that any changes to your local postoffice automatically appear in your setup as well. I find that Mail is probably the most integrated of all the MAPI servers.

Sending a Mail message is very easy. All you have to do is click on the New Message icon on the Exchange toolbar to display the dialog shown in Figure 18.28. Your dialog might not have all the fields that mine does. I selected all the options in the View menu so that I could show you what they look like. As with every new Windows application, this one has a toolbar that provides access to just about every feature that Mail supports. The following list provides an overview of what the features can do for you.

Figure 18.28.
The New Message dialog provides the basic tools for creating any kind of new message in Exchange.

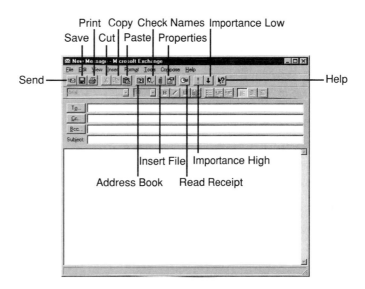

- Send: As soon as you get everything filled out in your message, click on this button to send your message to the recipient.
- Save: Exchange allows you to save a copy of the message in an external file. You use this button to display the Save dialog. You can use the File | Save As command to save this message under a different filename.
- Print: Clicking on this button allows you to print the current message. It uses the default print setup.
- Cut: This button removes the selected data and places it on the Clipboard.
- Copy: Use this button to copy the desired data to the Clipboard.
- Paste: This button places the data on the Clipboard at the selected position.

- Address book: Use this command to open the Address Book and find any addressees for your message. You can perform the same thing by clicking on any of the buttons next to the address fields on the message itself.

- Check names: As soon as you come up with a list of people you want to send a message to, you can click on this button to make sure that they're all correct. If Exchange finds that a name doesn't appear in one of your address lists, it displays a dialog asking if you want to add the name to an address list or correct it. Exchange usually supplies a list of substitutes for you. Of course, the size of this list depends on how many names in your Address Book are close matches to the one incorrect entry.

- Insert file: You can send someone a file as a message attachment using this button. It displays a dialog that allows you to browse your local and network hard drives. Any inserted files appear as icons within the message. Exchange doesn't actually place a copy of the file in the message; it uses an OLE link instead. You can link or embed objects in a message using the other techniques we discussed in Chapter 11 as well.

- Properties: The Properties dialog tells you the basics about a message. It also allows you to select the sensitivity and importance levels. Three checkboxes allow you to select receipt types and whether Exchange saves a copy of the message in the Sent Items folder.

- Read receipt: Clicking on this button automatically requests a read receipt for this message. You'll get an acknowledgment from Exchange as soon as the recipient opens the message for reading.

- Importance high/importance low: You may select either of these buttons to send a message with other than a normal importance level. Exchange displays high-importance messages with a red exclamation point and low-importance messages with a blue down arrow.

- Help: Use this button to receive context-sensitive help about any items you don't understand.

Besides all these toolbar options, there are other configuration options on the menu. All of the configuration options you saw in the Exchange section also appear here. For example, you can configure the New Message dialog toolbar to meet your needs. The service configuration option appears here as well.

Below the toolbar is a formatting toolbar. It includes everything you might expect. You can select a typeface, font size, bold, italics, underline, and font color. This toolbar also allows you to format the paragraph by adding bullets and indentation. It also allows you to determine if the paragraph is right-, center-, or left-justified.

Microsoft Fax

Microsoft Fax operates essentially the same way as Microsoft Mail. You even use the same type of message editing box. However, the initial screens are somewhat different, so I'll cover them here.

You create a new fax using the Compose | New Fax command in Exchange. Figure 18.29 shows the initial Fax Wizard dialog. The first thing you need to do to create a new fax is describe your location. We visited this issue in Chapter 17 (and even looked at it again in this chapter), so I won't go though the details again.

Figure 18.29.
Use the Compose New Fax dialog to format the address portion of any fax you want to send.

After you describe your location, click on Next to proceed to the next step of creating a fax. You'll see the dialog shown in Figure 18.30. This is where you tell the Fax Wizard where you want the message sent. You can use the Address Book pushbutton to display any of your address lists and select a recipient from them. I use this method because it ensures that the address is correct and saves me time typing the required information. Notice the Add to List pushbutton. Clicking it will add the current name and telephone number to the Recipient list field. Use this option when you want to send the same fax to more than one person.

Figure 18.30.
You create a recipient list using this dialog.

Click on Next when you complete this information to display the dialog shown in Figure 18.31. It allows you to select a cover page. It also contains an Options pushbutton that displays a configuration dialog. Optional items include the message format and when you want to send the fax.

Figure 18.31.
Use this dialog to describe
some of the optional features
for your fax.

Click on Next one more time to display the dialog shown in Figure 18.32. This is where you'll define the subject and message content of this fax. It doesn't look very much like the Exchange format, but the finished fax will include all the same elements. In fact, if you had selected the Create New Fax option from the Create New Message dialog, this display would look exactly like its Exchange counterpart. The Start note on cover page checkbox allows you to place the beginning of your note on the cover page. If the entire note fits there, you'll save paper, because you'll need to send only a single page. Removing the check from this checkbox causes the note to always be sent on a separate page.

Figure 18.32.
This dialog allows you to add
a subject line and message to
your fax.

Click on Next to reach the next dialog, shown in Figure 18.33. This dialog allows you to attach a file to your fax. Of course, it won't appear as an OLE object this time. The attached file will get sent to the recipient as a file or an attached set of pages. The listbox will contain a list of files that you want to send. Clicking on the Add File button will display a browse dialog that you can use to select another file. Highlighting an entry in the listbox and clicking on Remove will remove that file from the list.

The next time you click on Next, you'll see a dialog saying that your fax is ready to send. All you need to do now is click on Finish to send it. If everything goes well, you should either see a new entry in the Outgoing Faxes dialog or hear the fax/modem as it whisks your message off to the recipient.

Figure 18.33.
Use this dialog to attach files to your fax.

Note: One of the advantages of using Microsoft Fax instead of a standard fax machine is that you can send a fax late at night when the telephone rates are low. Unlike a standard fax machine, there are no pages to jam or other mechanical problems to overcome. Of course, problems at the other end can still prevent the recipient from actually receiving your fax.

Microsoft Network

The Microsoft Network (MSN) is Microsoft's attempt at creating an online service similar to CompuServe or America Online. Whether it will be successful or not remains to be seen. As of this writing, much of Microsoft Network is still in a beta status, so you'll probably see a lot more than I describe here once it does become active.

You can access MSN in a variety of ways. If you're currently using Exchange, use the Tools | Remote Mail option to display the dialog shown in Figure 18.34. This is where all your MSN-specific messages get stored after you connect to the network. Notice that the indicator in the lower-right corner shows when you're connected or disconnected.

Figure 18.34.
The Remote Mail dialog is where MSN stores any messages you receive on the network.

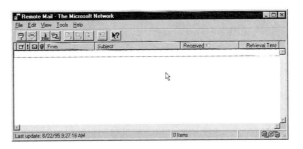

Clicking on the connect icon on the toolbar will display the dialog shown in Figure 18.35. Notice that this dialog contains three fields. The first field contains your name. The second contains the password for your MSN account. The checkbox tells Exchange to remember your MSN password between sessions. Clicking on the Settings pushbutton (not visible in Figure 18.35) brings up a centralized dialog for changing your modem and dialing properties. We've seen both of these dialogs before, so I won't describe them again. The only other setting that this dialog changes is your access number—a single setting that allows you to access the Microsoft Network. You change this setting by selecting the city with an access number nearest your own.

Figure 18.35.
The MSN Sign In dialog is where you enter your name and password prior to going online.

Note: Exchange will remember your MSN password between sessions only if you have some other form of Windows 95-specific password protection for your machine. If you use Windows 95 without enabling passwords, you'll have to enter your MSN password each time you use it. The reason for this safeguard is simple: It protects your account from misuse by other people.

Once you enter your name and password and change any required settings, click on Connect to proceed. (This pushbutton isn't visible in Figure 18.35.) You'll hear your modem attempt to make access with MSN. The dialog also displays messages during this process in case your modem speaker is turned off.

This method of access doesn't show the full MSN display that we'll see in a few moments. All it does is allow you to access your e-mail. When you do finally make a connection, Exchange displays the Remote Mail dialog again. Use the Update Headers button to collect all your message headers (this doesn't actually retrieve them). You'll use three buttons on the toolbar to mark the various message headers as you read them. The first retrieves the message and erases it online. The second retrieves a copy of the message but leaves the original in your online e-mail box. The third deletes the message without reading it. After you decide the fate of all your message headers, use the Transfer Mail button to retrieve any messages you decide to keep. This will download them from MSN and place them in your Inbox.

Getting e-mail isn't the only reason to use MSN. Now that we've looked at the speedy way to get your mail, let's look at what you can do to browse through the features that MSN offers. You should see an MSN icon on your Desktop. Double-clicking on it will display the same Sign In dialog that we saw before. However, instead of simply getting logged on and seeing the Remote Mail dialog, you'll see a different display this time. Figure 18.36 gives you an idea of what you might see.

Figure 18.36.
The first thing you'll normally see when you sign in to MSN is MSN Today.

This is a brief description of the various events taking place on MSN Today. You'll also get a quick summary of important news events and other information of this sort. When you get done looking at this page, you can use the MSN icon in the control area of the Taskbar to get back to MSN Central, shown in Figure 18.37. This is the starting point for all your adventures on MSN. From here you can check your e-mail, get some assistance with using MSN, or check out the categories of other places you can visit on MSN. Notice the Favorite Places option. You can store the locations of places you visit frequently so that you can find them quickly.

Figure 18.37.
MSN Central is the starting point for any online time on MSN.

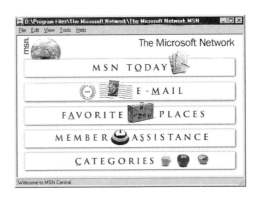

Categories is where all the action is on MSN, so let's take a look there. Figure 18.38 shows an example of what you might see. However, Microsoft is constantly changing the features that MSN offers, so this view will change often. What's the first thing you noticed about this display? It should look just like an Explorer single-pane view with a little window dressing, because that's exactly what it is. You'll navigate MSN using an Explorer-type interface. Of course, this means that it will be easy to use, but it also means that you'll spend some time boring down through the various folders to find what you want. That's why setting up some Favorite Places is so important.

Figure 18.38.
It's no surprise that MSN uses a single-pane Explorer view to help you get around.

I don't want to spoil all the fun of exploring MSN, but let's look at one of the categories you probably will want to see immediately. Suppose you wanted to check the Internet listings for a new job. Double-clicking on The Internet Center, then on The Most Popular Newsgroups, then on misc.jobs.offered would take you to a place where you could learn about new job possibilities. Figure 18.39 shows how the messages appear in a typical MSN forum. I've pulled down the folder listbox here to show you that you can move through MSN using the same techniques that you use with Explorer.

You can use the File | Add to Favorite Places command to add this location to Favorite Places. That way, the next time you wanted to view the listing of available jobs, it would be easy to get to this particular forum. Instead of "drilling down" through all those folders, you would gain direct access.

As with every other aspect of Exchange, you can retrieve messages from MSN and place them in your Inbox. Once you respond to them offline, you can upload the responses to the forum. Everything for MSN works the same as any other Exchange MAPI server.

Now that we have the basics of using MSN out of the way, let's talk about a few things that you'll need to really use this product. The following list tells you about the language of using an online product like MSN.

Figure 18.39.

A typical MSN forum contains a list of messages available for reading.

- Forum: This is a gathering place for people of like interests. One person will leave a message and someone else will respond to it. You can look at the message header to determine what a particular discussion is about. In essence, you can think of a forum as a room in a house where people of like interests get together to talk. Finding the right forum can provide you with a wealth of information that you might not find elsewhere. It can also help you solve problems related to your software, your machine, or even your business.

- Message: A single note on a particular subject is a message. You use messages in e-mail and other places already, so the concept of a message shouldn't be new to you.

- Thread: A group of connected messages on the same topic. As each person responds to a message, he makes the list of messages about a given topic longer. You can read an entire list of messages (or a thread) to discover the conversation that took place on a specific topic. The fact that the messages are written rather than spoken is an advantage, because you can read the messages when it's convenient. Threads are also a key way to store information for future use. Many people archive message threads about specific topics because that information can't be easily found anywhere else.

I don't want to make this a book about using online services; there are plenty of those on the market already. I suggest that you buy one or two of them to build your knowledge of online services. It's important to learn the rules of the road when it comes to reacting to other people's messages. You will also need to learn rules of etiquette for forums. I've presented some of these ideas already. For example, many people frown on the practice of quoting on a forum.

Body language is a missing element of any online conversation. You can't really tell someone that a comment is tongue-in-cheek using a wry smile, because he won't see it. To help avoid conflict whenever possible, people have come up with something called an *emoticon*. It's a little text icon that tells the other person what you mean by a certain comment. Table 18.1 lists common emoticons that you can use to dress up any written communication. In fact, you could even use them on your company e-mail.

Table 18.1. Standard emoticons.

Emoticon	Description
:-)	A happy face
:->	An alternative happy face
:-D	Said with a smile
:<)	Humor for those with hairy lips
:<)=	Humor for those with beards too
B-)	Smiling and wearing glasses or sunglasses (or a message from Batman)
8-)	Smiling and wearing glasses or sunglasses. Also used to denote a wide-eyed look.
:-1 or :-,	A smirk
;-)	A wink
:-(	Unhappy
:-c	Very unhappy
(:-(	Very unhappy
:/)	Not funny: The receiver of a message sends this emoticon to show that a particular comment wasn't received as the sender intended.
(:-&	Angry
:-))-:	Theatrical comments: Use this for comments that are either theatrical in nature or used for emphasis.
(@ @)	You're kidding!
:-"	Pursed lips
:-C	Incredulous (jaw dropped)
:-<	Forlorn
:-B	Drooling (or overbite)
:-|	Disgusted
:-v	Speaking
:-V	Shouting
:-o or :-O	More versions of shouting
:-w	Speaking with a forked tongue: You're lying to the other person in a whimsical sort of way. In other words, you're making a point sarcastically.
:-W	Shouting with a forked tongue
:-b	Bleahhh! (tongue sticking out)

Emoticon	Description
<:-O	Eek! You can use this for a number of purposes. You can even use it to tell the network administrator that your equipment is down and you can't do anything without it.
:-*	Oops! (covering mouth with hand)
:-T	Keeping a straight face (tight-lipped): Use this emoticon when you mean something in a serious way that the receiver could interpret as a humorous comment.
:-#	Censored: You'd love to use a little profanity but resisted the urge.
:-x	Kiss, kiss
:-?	Licking your lips
:~i	Smoking
:~j	Smoking and smiling
:/i	No smoking
:-) :-) :-)	A guffaw
:-J	A tongue-in-cheek comment
:*)	Clowning around
:-8	Talking out of both sides of your mouth
<:-)	For dumb questions: Everyone knows that the only dumb question is the one you failed to ask before trashing the network. However, some people might feel that they have a dumb question they want someone to answer.
OO	Headlights on: Use this emoticon to show someone that you want him to pay special attention to a comment.
:-o or #:-o	"Oh, nooooooo!" (a la Mr. Bill)
|-(	A late-night message
(:-$	Ill
#:-)	Matted hair
:^)	A big nose
:-{#}	Braces
(:^(	A broken nose
:-(=)	Big teeth
&:-)	Curly hair
@:-)	Wavy hair

continues

Table 18.1. continued

Emoticon	Description
?-(	A black eye
%-)	Broken glasses
:	A fuzzy person
*:**	A fuzzy person with a fuzzy mustache
(:<)	A blabbermouth
+<:-|	A monk or nun
(:-|K-	A formal message
||*(	A handshake is offered
||*)	A handshake is accepted
<:>==	A turkey
@>--->----	A rose
(-_-)	A secret smile
<{:-)}	A message in a bottle
<:-)<<|	A message from a spaceship
(:-...	A heartbreaking message
(:>-<	A message from a thief: Hands up!
...---...	SOS
:-I	It's something, but I don't know what...: You can't figure out what the other person is trying to say or reference.
@%&$#*	Profanity

Hopefully you'll come to enjoy using online services as much as I have. MSN is just starting out, but you can use other online services as well. CompuServe seems to be one of the favorite places for businesspeople to congregate, although there are forums to attract just about anyone's attention. America Online is extremely popular as well. Of course, the trick to selecting any online service is to find the one that meets your needs. Obviously, no one can determine that but you.

On Your Own

Set Microsoft Exchange up to handle your faxing, online communication, and mail needs. See if you can tell any difference between the messages you receive from the three sources. In most cases, you won't unless the sender provides some kind of clue.

Check your \SYSTEM folder to see if you can identify the various pieces of the communication subsystem. This chapter provides you with a list of the major files and many hints on how you can find the other, special files that pertain to your system.

I provided you with a list of standard emoticons in this chapter. One of the fun elements of online computing is coming up with your own set of special emoticons (of course, this means you'll have to explain them to everyone). Try creating a few emoticons of your own. For example, one person recently created an emoticon that resembles Berkley Breathed's Bill the Cat character.

19

Networks

Just about every business, large or small, has a network these days. The benefits of linking a group of computers to share peripherals and some data are just too great to ignore. Even two- and three-person shops commonly have a network installed—if for no other reason than to share a laser printer and a few documents. I'm often surprised at the number of home networks that I see as well. It doesn't come as too much of a shock, though. Just think about the benefits to mom and dad of having a modern home workstation with a large hard drive, fast processor, and other new machine features. Using a peer-to-peer network allows the parents to give that old machine to the kids. Even if the kids' workstation has a hard drive only large enough for the Windows system files, their application files can reside on the larger hard drive of the machine used by their parents. Keeping the parents' machine separate from the kids' machine is a good way to keep your work separate from their play.

No matter the size of your network, there's bound to be some native support for it in Windows 95. You can even install limited support for some of those older real-mode peer-to-peer networks on the market. A few of these older networks don't provide the same level of features that they did under Windows 3.x, but at least they work well enough to get the job done.

This chapter talks about the networking capabilities that Windows 95 provides. For the most part, I purposely avoid talking about networks in general or even comparing the various options you have. The reason is simple: A single chapter can't possibly contain everything you'll need to ever know about networking. There are literally volumes of information about this topic—and some people think that these are just barely adequate.

I'll provide you with some insights into the way Windows 95 provides network services—and that's something you'd be hard-pressed to find in one of those networking tomes. That's the whole reason for this chapter—to give you the Windows 95 view of networking. I strongly suggest that you also spend some time learning about networks in general before you actually install one.

The discussion in this chapter also assumes a certain level of knowledge on your part. I'm going to assume that you've already spent some time on a network and know some of the basics. You don't need to be a networking guru to understand this chapter, but you will need to know what logging in is all about and know some of the easier terms such as network interface card (NIC).

The Client Module

This section of the chapter looks at the how of network support under Windows 95. What can you expect, and why do things work the way they do? These are just some of the questions I'll answer here. Before we become too embroiled in some of the details of actually using Windows 95's network capabilities, I'd like to spend a little time looking at its architecture. Figure 19.1 shows the Windows 95 network architecture. Notice that a request can follow two discrete paths. Windows 95 provides a 32-bit protected-mode path for any networks that it supports directly. It will use a real-mode path for drivers that it doesn't support. Both paths end up at the NIC driver. The following list describes the individual components.

Figure 19.1.
An overview of the Windows 95 network architecture.

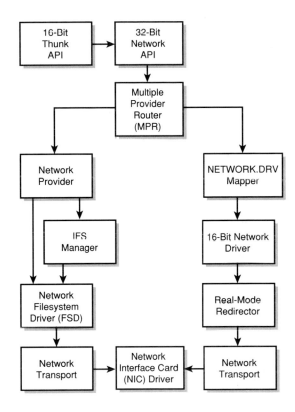

- 16-bit thunk API: Windows 95 provides full network support using 32-bit code. However, there are a lot of 16-bit applications to support out there as well. This module replaces the standard 16-bit API with calls to the 32-bit API. It has to provide thunk support in order to do this. We've looked at the thunk process before (in Chapter 6), so I won't go into it again here.

- 32-bit API: All application requests start at this module. I won't go into details about the API, but Microsoft has gone to great lengths to reorganize and simplify it. A user won't notice these details—except in the way that they affect network performance—but they'll make a definite impact on the effort required to program. The API translates one application request into one or more standardized network requests. Quite a few files are involved in creating the network API under Windows 95. The two most prominent are NETAPI.DLL and NETAPI32.DLL. Loading NETAPI32.DLL also loads NETBIOS.DLL, which provides most of the low-level functionality that the API requires.

- Multiple provider router (MPR): You can use more than one protocol with Windows 95. In fact—theoretically, at least—you should be able to mix and match protected-mode and real-mode drivers on the same network. The current Windows 95 implementation will always allow you to perform the first function. For example, you can mix NetBEUI and IPX/SPX on the same network. However, it usually won't allow you to do the second without some restrictions. For example, you can't mix LANtastic with a Microsoft network, but you can mix it with other systems in some cases. All network protocols require a network provider. The whole function of the MPR is to accept network requests from the API and send them to the appropriate network provider (NP). Part of each request states which NP to use. This is how the MPR knows which one it should send the request to. However, some requests are generic. For example, a request for the status of the entire network falls into this category. In that case, the MPR calls each NP in turn to fulfill the application request. In still other cases, a request might not include enough information for the MPR to know which NP to use to fulfill the application requirement. In this case, the MPR will "poll" the NPs to see if one of them can fulfill the request. If none of the installed NPs can, the MPR returns an error message. You'll find that the MPR functions appear in the \SYSTEM folder in MPR.DLL. This DLL gets loaded when Windows 95 executes MPREXE.EXE during startup. An intermediate file, MPRSERV.DLL, performs the actual loading process. Interestingly enough, loading this set of DLLs also loads ADVAPI32.DLL. The MPR uses the functions in this DLL to view the contents of the registry to determine which NPs and other network resources are available. The MPR also loads MSPWL.DLL. This module checks for your password and performs other security-related activities. There is also a path from the MPR to NETWORK.DRV. This path becomes active when you use a real-mode driver in place of a Windows 95-specific NP. The MPR can't poll the real-mode driver or perform any of the other NP-specific tasks that I described earlier. NETWORK.DRV provides the NP services that Windows 95 requires. I'll describe this particular part of the network a little later in this chapter.

- Network Provider (NP): The Network Provider performs all the protocol-specific functions that an application requires. It will make or break connections, return network status information, and provide a consistent interface for the MPR to use. An application will never call the NP; only the MPR performs this function. Even though the internal structure of NPs varies, the interface that they provide doesn't. This mechanism allows Windows 95 to provide support for more than a single protocol. The code used by the MPR can remain small and fast because none of the NPs require special calls. If an NP can't fulfill a request because of a limitation in the network protocol, it simply tells the MPR that the required service is unavailable. The NP also keeps the IFS Manager up-to-date on the current connection status. This is how Explorer knows when you've made a new drive connection.

- IFS Manager: When the IFS Manager obtains new status information from the NP, it calls the Network Filesystem Driver (FSD) to update file and other resource information. For example, when the NP tells the IFS Manager that it has made a new drive connection, the IFS Manager calls on the Network FSD to provide a directory listing. The same holds true for other resource types, such as printers. Besides this function, the IFS Manager performs its normal duties of opening files and making other file system requests. The MPR doesn't know what to do with a pathname, so it passes such requests through the NP to the IFS

Manager to fulfill. Of course, applications also access the IFS Manager in other ways. The only time that the MPR becomes involved is if a network-specific request also requires its intervention.

- Network Filesystem Driver (FSD): Each server on the network could use a unique file system. For example, if you make a connection to an OS/2 server, you could require access to an HPFS drive. NetWare and other client-server networks all use special file systems that the vendor feels will enhance performance, security, reliability, and storage capacity. Since Windows 95 understands nothing about HPFS or any other special storage system, it needs a translator. The Network FSD performs this task. It translates the intricacies of a foreign file system into something that Windows 95 can understand. A Network FSD is usually composed of a file system-specific driver and VREDIR.VXD. The second file provides the Windows 95 interpretation of the file system specifics. Normally there is only one Network FSD for each NP. However, there is nothing to enforce this limit. An NP might require access to both a FAT and an NTFS Network FSD for a Windows NT Server. If so, both drivers will get installed when you install network support. The IFS Manager will also call on the Network FSD for support. While the NP usually makes requests for network status or connection information, the IFS Manager takes care of application needs such as opening files and reading their contents. These two modules—NP and IFS Manager—work in tandem, each fulfilling completely different roles.

Note: You might wonder why Microsoft didn't combine the NP and the IFS Manager into one module. After all, from this discussion it appears that the IFS Manager is simply part of an access strategy for network drives. Remember to take the whole picture into account. The IFS Manager also works with local drives. In addition, combining the modules would have produced a lot of replicated code. In essence, using two separate modules to access the drive status information and contents is the only way to get the level of flexibility that network requests require with the minimum amount of code.

- Network transport (NT): I placed a single module called Network Transport (NT) in Figure 19.1. Actually, this module is made up of many smaller modules and drivers. The number of pieces in an NT is determined by the complexity of your setup and the requirements of the protocol. The smallest NT could consist of a mere four drivers. For example, you could create an NT for the NetBEUI protocol using the following files: VNETBIOS.VXD, NETBEUI.VXD, NDIS.VXD, and NE2000.SYS. These are just the drivers, but let's take a quick look at them.

VNETBIOS.VXD virtualizes access to the protocol. This is the reason that more than one virtual machine running on your system can access the network drives at the same time. NETBEUI.VXD performs the task of talking with the NDIS (network driver interface specification) module. It takes protocol-specific requests and translates them into smaller, standardized network requests. NDIS.VXD translates each Windows 95-specific request into a call that the NIC driver can understand. Finally, the NIC driver talks to the NIC itself. The driver can take things such as port addresses and interrupts into account—everything needed to talk to the NIC. Of course, the NIC converts your request into an electrical signal that appears on the network.

NT requires other files as well. For example, NDIS30.DLL provides the actual API support for NDIS.VXD. You will find that NETBIOS.DLL performs the same function for VNETBIOS.VXD. In essence, it takes a lot of different modules to create one transport. The reason for all these files is fairly easy to understand. For example, what if you wanted to use a different NIC? All you need to do is change the NIC driver, not any of the protocol-specific files. What if you wanted to use two different levels of NDIS support (Windows 95 does support two)? You would add an additional driver and its support files to the equation. Rather than going into too much additional detail, let's close the book on the NT for now. All you need to know is that the NT takes care of the "transportation" details for your network installation.

- Network interface card (NIC) driver: I make special mention of this part of the NT here for a reason. This particular driver is hardware-specific. It has to communicate with the NIC on a level it can understand. That's the first problem—trying to find a driver that provides a standard Windows 95 interface yet talks with the NIC installed in your machine. The second problem is that there can be only one driver. I mentioned earlier that there was a chance that a real-mode and a protected-mode network could coexist, but that it wouldn't happen in a lot of cases. Here's the reason why. If you can't load a Windows 95-specific NIC driver because it interferes with a driver that the real-mode product requires, you're faced with a decision of which network to use.

Tip: Even if you've invested in a real-mode networking product such as LANtastic, the performance and reliability increase that you'll get from a Microsoft Network running under Windows 95 might make it worth the effort to switch. Of course, you have to consider the trade-offs of making that decision versus the loss of features. Windows 95 doesn't provide many of the features that people switched to other networks to get. For example, Artisoft provides a DDE Link Book that helps you make OLE links to other machines. You will also find that the Windows 95 mail and scheduling features are inadequate when compared to products such as Artisoft Exchange. In addition, there's a very good chance that vendors such as Artisoft will eventually provide Windows 95-specific solutions to replace their current product. Even if you decide not to switch, it might be beneficial to see if the real-mode network vendor can provide the required Windows 95 NIC driver to allow you to use multiple networks.

- NETWORK.DRV: The reason for this file is simple. You need to have an NP to gain access to a network under Windows 95. When you install the LANtastic client in the Network applet, this is one of the files that gets installed. It provides the interface to your real-mode network that Windows 95 requires in order to use the network. In this case, the NP also acts as a mapper—a module that maps the Windows 95-specific calls to something that the 16-bit driver will understand. It also provides a thunk layer to translate the 32-bit requests into their 16-bit equivalents. Remember that you still need to install the old 16-bit Windows version of the network drivers. In the case of LANtastic, you'll need the LANTASTI.386 and LANTNET.DRV files from your distribution disks.

- 16-bit network driver: As I mentioned in the preceding paragraph, you'll still need a Windows driver for your real-mode network. Otherwise, there's no magical way that Windows 95 will be able to talk to it. There has to be a framework for discussion before a discussion can take place. The 16-bit network drivers typically translate any requests into something that the real-mode redirector can understand. They then ask Windows 95 to make the transition to real mode so that the redirector can do its job.

Tip: In some cases it's nearly impossible to get a good real-mode network installation under Windows 95. Some of the problems include the real-mode network setup program over-writing Windows 95-specific files, and the use of undocumented Windows 3.x features. A few setup programs also require Program Manager to complete their installation, so you might want to start a copy of Program Manager before you begin. I've found that the best way to get a good real-mode network installation under Windows 95 is to install a copy of Windows 3.x first, install the real-mode network there, and then install the copy of Windows 95 over the Windows 3.x installation. It seems like a roundabout way of doing things, but it will ensure that you'll have a minimum of problems.

- Real-mode redirector: This network component translates your requests into network calls. It works with the real-mode network transport to create an interface with the NIC. Essentially, it performs about the same function in real mode that the IFS Manager and Network FSD do in protected mode.

This might seem like a lot of work just to create a workstation, but that's only half the picture on many peer-to-peer installations. Once you get past being a workstation, you have to take care of network requests as well. I'd like to show you how Windows 95 provides peer-to-peer network services. The next section does just that. We'll look at Windows 95's peer-to-peer support from a server level. We'll also look at a lot of the implementation details. For example, how do you share your printer or local hard drive with someone?

Peer-to-Peer Support

Peer-to-peer networks represent the easiest and least expensive way to get started in networking. Everyone starts with a workstation, just like you would normally need in any business environment. However, you can't share resources on stand-alone workstations; you need to connect them in order to do that. In the past, the standard method for sharing resources was to buy additional machines (called servers) and place the common components there. The investment in hardware and software for a full-fledged network can run into tens of thousands of dollars—prohibitively expensive for many companies and out of reach for others. Peer-to-peer networks take a different route. One or more workstations also act as servers. In fact, if you work things right and the network is small enough, everyone will probably have access to everyone else's machine in some form. This means that, except for the NICs and cabling you'll need, a peer-to-peer solution under Windows 95 is free for the asking.

Windows 95 provides peer-to-peer networking capabilities right out of the package. All you need to do is install a NIC in each machine, run some cable, and add a few drivers to your setup. Of course, once you get everyone set up, you'll want to install a few extra utilities, such as a centralized calendar and e-mail.

I was actually a little disappointed with the network utility feature set that Microsoft decided to provide for Windows 95. Exchange is a wonderful e-mail system. However, past versions of WFW (Windows for Workgroups) came with Schedule+. Windows 95 doesn't provide this feature, and almost everyone will notice. Microsoft plans to introduce a Windows 95-specific version of Schedule+ as part of Office 95. Of course, this brings up another problem—that of incompatibility between the old and the new version of Schedule+. No matter which way you look at it, Schedule+ will become a thing of the past unless you're willing to perform a major upgrade of all your PCs at the same time—something I doubt that most businesses could do even if they wanted to and had the required resources. I see a definite third-party opportunity here. People will still need a centralized calendar for planning meetings, and with Schedule+ gone, some third-party vendor will fill the gap.

Peter's Principle: Grabbing a Piece of the Past

You don't have to do without Schedule+ in your new Windows 95 installation if you still have the files from your old version of WFW lying around. Even though that version of Schedule+ won't work with Exchange, you can still share information with other people on the network by copying the required files to your drive. Here are the files you should copy to your \WIN95 folder:

*.CAL
DEMILAYR.DLL

MSCHED.DLL
MSMAIL.INI
MSREMIND.EXE
SCHDPLUS.EXE
SCHDPLUS.HLP
SCHDPLUS.INI
TRNSCHED.DLL

You'll also need to copy the following files to your \SYSTEM folder:

AB.DLL
FRAMEWRK.DLL
MAILMGR.DLL
MAILSPL.EXE
MSSFS.DLL
STORE.DLL

If the new version of Microsoft Mail doesn't exactly meet your specifications, you can still use the old version under Windows 95. Simply copy these files to your \WIN95 folder:

MSMAIL.EXE
MSMAIL.HLP
MSMAIL.PRG

You will also need to copy VFORMS.DLL to your \SYSTEM folder.

Once you copy all these files, make any required changes to the .INI files. For example, you'll want to change the directory names so that they match the new location. The only problem I've detected with this arrangement so far is that Schedule+ won't remember your password. This is a small price to pay for using an old and familiar utility program.

A Little History

Before we delve into all the details of how Windows 95 supports peer-to-peer networking, let's take a brief look at the history of this networking system. Apple actually introduced peer-to-peer networking in a covert manner in 1985. They included AppleTalk in every Macintosh sold. Most people didn't realize that they were actually using a network when they printed a document using the LaserWriter.

Peer-to-peer networking continued to be a cult classic in the years that followed. Many companies wouldn't recognize peer-to-peer networking as much more than a kludge or a poor man's network. Novell's NetWare used a client-server model that mimicked the big iron that corporations were used to using. It was comfortable using a network operating system that provided the look and feel of something substantial. In the PC world, many people thought it was client-server or nothing at all.

Note: Don't get me wrong. I'm not saying that peer-to-peer networking is the end-all solution for everyone. However, it's a very good solution for those on a limited networking budget who need to connect anywhere from two to 10 workstations. You might even want to look at it for workgroup connections (the very reason that Microsoft came out with Windows for Workgroups). You can combine the benefits of a client-server network with those of a peer-to-peer network under Windows 95. Although I would probably set an upper limit of 10 workstations for a peer-to-peer network, it might also work for larger numbers of workstations if the network load were very light.

A group of companies began distributing peer-to-peer networking solutions for the PC. One of the bigger contributors to this ground swell of alternative networking technology was Artisoft, which still sells LANtastic today. Other vendors contributed products such as 10Net and TOPS. The Software Link even marketed a processor-sharing operating system for the 80386 called PC-MOS/386. This solution and others allowed people to share system resources without having to purchase a file server to do it. In addition, the cost of a peer-to-peer network operating system was a lot lower because these vendors faced stiff competition from Novell.

I'm not sure whether Novell helped or hindered the expansion of peer-to-peer networking with its introduction of NetWare Lite in 1991. This product was designed not to interfere with Novell's client-server product. As a result, NetWare Lite wasn't well-designed or implemented. It couldn't even compete with other peer-to-peer products such as LANtastic. However, the introduction of a peer-to-peer networking product by a major vendor such as Novell at least put this type of networking on some people's agenda for the first time.

Things started to change for the better in the peer-to-peer market when Microsoft introduced Windows for Workgroups at the 1992 fall COMDEX trade show. This show of support by Microsoft legitimized the use of peer-to-peer networking for some corporate applications. Of course, Microsoft didn't go so far as to say that you could use it for more than a few people. Still, it was a step in the right direction.

So, has everyone bought into the peer-to-peer networking technology? Not by a long shot, and I doubt that peer-to-peer networking will ever take over the market. However, using a solution such as Windows for Workgroups or Windows 95 in the right place could make a big difference for a very small cost. Windows 95 goes a long way toward making dual solutions—a combination of client-server and peer-to-peer networking—a viable solution.

A Look at the Architecture

We've already taken a detailed look at what it takes to provide workstation support under Windows 95. However, what happens if you also want to act as a server? Providing server support means that your machine must accept requests from other workstations, process those requests, and return the requested information. Figure 19.2 shows the Windows 95 peer-to-peer network server support. The following list describes each component in detail.

Figure 19.2.
An overview of the Windows 95 server architecture.

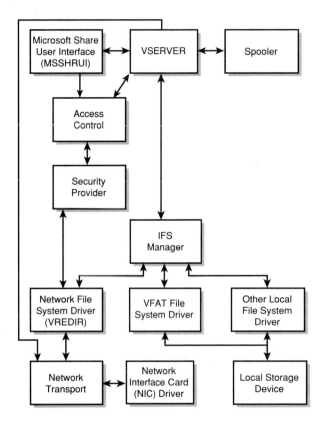

- Microsoft Share User Interface (MSSHRUI): This module responds to external requests from the user for network resource configuration. Every time you right-click on a resource and tell Windows 95 that you want to share it, this module fields that request. It works with the access control module to set password protection. An interface to the MPR and ADVAPI32.DLL allows the MSSHRUI to set the proper entries in the registry. You'll find it in the MSSHRUI.DLL file in your \SYSTEM folder.

- VSERVER: The central point of all activity for the server is the virtual server driver, VSERVER.VXD. As with all the other drivers in this chapter, you'll find it in your \SYSTEM folder. This component provides direct access of all local resources to network requesters through the Network Transport. It works with the IFS Manager and access control modules to limit access to shared resources and to ensure that any access is performed properly. Each access to shared system resources is maintained in a separate thread. This means that access by one requester need not interfere with any other request. In addition, a single requester can make multiple requests. Of course, the number of actual requests is usually limited by the protocol settings you provide.

- Spooler: If you grant someone access to your printer, VSERVER will send any requests for print services to the spooler module. This module works just like it would for a local print request. As far as it's concerned, the request originated locally. There are three spooler-specific files in your \SYSTEM folder: SPOOLSS.DLL, SPOOL32.EXE, and WINSPOOL.DRV.

- Access control: Windows 95 uses this module for a variety of purposes, not just network access control. For example, Windows calls on this module to verify your initial logon password, even if you don't request access to a network afterward. Unlike the other modules discussed so far, the access control module makes use of .PWL files on your drive as well as registry entries to verify and set security. You'll find access control in the SVRAPI.DLL file in the \SYSTEM folder.

Tip: You can get around a potential security problem by removing user access to all of the .PWL files on your drive. If a user erases one of these files, it becomes a lot easier for him to override any security you provided. In addition, you can erase a user's .PWL file to give him access to Windows 95 if he forgets his password. Unfortunately, this means that you'll also have to perform the setup required to re-create that .PWL file.

- Security provider: There are a number of sources for this module. In fact, even if you choose to install a Microsoft Network, you can still choose between the Microsoft Network client and the Windows 95 Login module as a security provider. The Microsoft Network client is a network-specific security provider that might include features that the Windows 95 Login module (a generic dialog box) might not provide. You can always access the Windows 95 Login module, even if the network isn't running. The advantage of using it is that the Login module will always be available, even if you change the network setup or remove it altogether. The security provider performs two tasks. First, it's the module that asks you for a password. Second, it combines the user's login name and the password she provides to verify any network requests.

- VFAT file system driver (FSD) and other local file system driver: I covered both of these modules in detail in Chapter 8.

- IFS Manager, Network FSD, Network Transport, and NIC driver: I talked about these modules at the beginning of this chapter.

Understanding the server capabilities that Windows 95 provides is pretty straightforward from a conceptual point of view. However, once you get past theory, implementation becomes another story altogether. The problem isn't due to a poor plan, but due to all the compatibility issues that come into play. Fortunately for the user, the design of the server capabilities makes all these details fairly seamless.

Sharing Files and Printers

Sharing is the main reason to install a network. The very concept of networks came from the need to share expensive peripheral devices and files. Windows 95 provides an easy-to-use interface that allows you to share just about everything on your network with a few clicks of the mouse. Let's take a look at what you'll need to do to share files and other resources located on your machine.

The first thing you'll need to do is install support for file and printer sharing. Right-click on the Network Neighborhood icon and select Properties. If you have a peer-to-peer network installed, the File and Print Sharing pushbutton will be enabled. Click on it to display the dialog shown in Figure 19.3. Notice that you can select file and printer sharing individually. Of course, installing support doesn't give everyone access to your system. You still have to select the specific items you plan to share.

Figure 19.3.
The File and Print Sharing dialog allows you to determine what level of sharing support Windows 95 will install.

> **Tip:** The NETCPL.CPL file in your \SYSTEM folder provides the actual interface that you use to configure the network. Some real-mode or older 16-bit Windows network installation programs will insist on changing this file. If you ever lose your Network icon (as I once did), check to make sure that this file didn't get overwritten or otherwise corrupted. In fact, you might want to make a copy of this file before you install any real-mode network on your machine.

After Windows 95 enables file and print sharing, you'll need to select the items to share. Right-clicking on any of your drive or printer icons and clicking on Properties (depending on what support you installed) will display an additional Sharing page like the one shown in Figure 19.4. (The context menu also includes a Sharing option that will take you directly to this page.)

The first two radio buttons on this page allow you to determine whether the resource is shared or not. Selecting Not Shared means that no one can see the resource, even if they have other access to your machine. If you do select shared access, some additional blanks become available.

You'll need to provide a resource name in the Shared Name field. This is how Windows 95 will present the resource in dialog boxes, such as with the Drives field of the File Open dialog. The optional Comment field allows you to provide a little more information to someone who wants to share the resource. I normally include the precise resource name and my name as part of the comment. This reduces the chance that someone will accidentally try to use a resource on my system.

Figure 19.4.
The Sharing page of the Print
or Drive Properties dialog lets
you define the level and type
of sharing for that device.

Use the Access Type group to define the level of access to a particular resource. You can provide two actual levels of access: read-only and full. The third option allows you to assign two different access passwords. This would allow one person full access, while another could only read the contents of the drive or other resource. The two password fields allow you to define the password required to access that resource.

Windows 95 doesn't limit you to providing access to an entire drive or printer. You can define access to an individual directory as well. I find it very convenient to set aside a temporary directory on my machine for file sharing. People can upload their files to a specific directory and avoid changing the contents of the rest of my drive. You can use the same principle for other resources. The key is to maintain control of your system.

Peter's Principle: Maintaining Control of Your System

Sharing doesn't always mean that you allow everyone to access every resource on your machine. It's easier to simply provide access to an entire drive than it is to set the required level of security folder by folder, but the drive strategy might not be the best way to go when it comes to your company's health.

Many of us work with confidential information that we must keep safe, but we also work with other people who need to see some of the things we work with. For example, someone working in the accounting department might need to share analysis files with a workgroup. However, can you imagine what would happen if she also shared access to the payroll files? What about the new plans that your company might be working on? Even though you need to share access to the current project, you'll want to keep that new project a secret. A little bit of discretion can save you a lot of headaches later.

It's important that you provide the right level of access to everyone in your workgroup. I won't cover every bit of security in this chapter (we'll look at this in detail in the next chapter), but you might want to put your thinking cap on now. Where are the potential security leaks in your company? It's a well-known fact that people complain when they don't have enough access to the network. Have you ever heard anyone complain about having too much access?

Finding the areas where people have too much access will give you the most trouble. Audits and other forms of security checking are just as important as the sharing itself on your network. Performing an audit takes time and resources that might be very difficult to defend using when management asks for an accounting. Of course, having a security breach is even more difficult to defend. Allow others to use the resources you have available, but don't allow misuse of those resources. It's up to you to do your part in maintaining the proper level of security on your network.

Login Scripts

Windows 95 provides several support mechanisms for login scripts. The best support is for most versions of Novell's NetWare, but the same principles hold true (for the most part) with any other NOS (network operating system) that Windows 95 supports. This support doesn't extend to real-mode networks such as LANtastic. You'll need to perform any login script requirements as a call from AUTOEXEC.BAT before you enter Windows 95. In most cases, this means running STARTNET.BAT for LANtastic. Check the vendor documentation for any requirements for using a login script with your real-mode network. In most cases, you'll follow the same procedure that you did prior to installing Windows 95.

Now that we have the real-mode networks out of the way, let's look at the kind of support you can expect for supported networks such as NetWare. The first thing you'll need to do is disable any AUTOEXEC.BAT or other batch files that you used to use under Windows 3.x. You don't need to log into the network before entering Windows 95. Any workstations that use NetWare must have an account on the server before you try to install Client for NetWare.

Note: I was surprised to find that the protected-mode Client for NetWare Networks isn't under the Novell entry of the clients listing. You'll find it in the Microsoft list of clients. Novell didn't supply the protected-mode client NetWare—Microsoft did. If you install either of the entries from the Novell listing, you'll be using real-mode drivers. Not only will this reduce performance and cause some level of system instability, but it will also remove many of the positive benefits of using an integrated approach to networking. For example, you won't be able to use a single login screen for both NetWare and Microsoft; you'll have to enter them separately. Always try the protected-mode drivers first, just to see if they'll work with your system setup.

Once you get Client for NetWare installed, select it in the Primary Network Logon field of the Network Properties dialog. You access this dialog by right-clicking on the Network Neighborhood icon and selecting the Properties option. The first time you run Client for NetWare, you will see two login dialogs. The first dialog will log you into a preferred server. The second login dialog will take care of the Windows 95 security requirement. As long as the user name and password for NetWare and Windows 95 are the same, you'll see this dual login dialog only once. The next time you log in, you'll see only one dialog that will take care of both login needs.

To enable login script processing on the NetWare server, you need to check the Client for NetWare Networks Properties dialog, shown in Figure 19.5. This dialog has three fields. The one that you're interested in is a checkbox that will enable login script processing. You'll also see fields for the preferred server and the first network drive.

Figure 19.5.
The Client for NetWare Networks Properties dialog allows you to enable login script processing.

Tip: You can reduce your need to use the MAP command (or anything similar) by using the persistent mapping capability available using Explorer or the context menu of Network Neighborhood. We covered the Explorer part of the equation in Chapter 2. You'll find the Network Neighborhood described in this chapter. Using the native Windows 95 capability means less chance of error if an individual workstation's configuration changes.

Enabling login script processing allows an administrator to maintain the pre-Windows 95 security policy on the server. It also provides a means for creating automatic drive mapping and other NOS-specific features. You'll need to check the documentation that came with your network to see exactly what types of script file processing you can perform.

Note: Windows 95 doesn't currently support the NetWare 4.x NDS style of login script processing. You must use the bindery-style login scripts provided by NetWare 3.x and below. This means placing your NetWare 4.x server in bindery emulation mode. The system login script for a NetWare server is stored in NET$LOG.DAT. You'll find it in the \PUBLIC directory. The individual user scripts will appear in their \MAIL directory. Keep in mind that NetWare 4.x utilities will run only under true NDS.

Warning: The Windows 95 protected-mode script processor can't run TSRs. The TSR will start in a separate virtual machine, which will terminate with an error when the script file processing completes. This lack of TSR processing in your script files means that you'll have to come up with a different way to install backup agents and other files that you normally install using the login script. In most cases, you'll need to install such files as part of the AUTOEXEC.BAT or within a DOS session after you start Windows 95.

TCP/IP and PPP—It's in There!

Windows 95 provides a fairly complex and complete set of Transmission Control Protocol/Internet Protocol- (TCP/IP) related features. Think of a protocol as a set of rules for a game. The rules tell you how to play the game and give you a basis for playing it with someone else. A protocol performs the same task on a network. It establishes rules that allow two nodes—workstations, mainframes, minicomputers, or other network elements such as printers—to talk to each other. TCP/IP is one of the more popular sets of network communication rules. Windows 95 also provides support for Point-to-Point Protocol (PPP). Just like TCP/IP, PPP is a set of communication rules. However, in this case the rules provide a method of conducting online (from one point to another) communications. Both of these features allow you to connect to a UNIX host or the Internet or enhance your Dial-Up Networking capability. In almost all cases, the support that Windows 95 provides deals with remote communications, but there are exceptions. For example, the monitoring capability provided by SNMP could work in a local server setup. There are two reasons that it's important to include this support as part of the operating system. First, adding TCP/IP and PPP to the operating system makes it easier for software developers to write agents (special drivers or applications that use the rules that these protocols establish to perform useful work). If you added either protocol as a third-party product, there wouldn't be any standardization, making it nearly impossible for other third-party vendors to write standard agents. Second, adding this level of protocol support to the operating system means that Microsoft can incorporate an additional level of support as part of its utility program offerings. For example, you'll find that both protocols are important when it comes to communicating with the Internet through Microsoft Network (MSN). Before you can use TCP/IP, you have to install it. Let's quickly go through a few of the things you'll need to do to install TCP/IP support.

Tip: Installing TCP/IP support before you install Dial-Up Networking will save some extra steps later. The Dial-Up Networking installation routine will automatically install the required protocols for you if you install TCP/IP support first.

1. Right-click on the Network Neighborhood icon and select Properties.

2. On the Configuration page, click on the Add pushbutton. You'll see the dialog shown in Figure 19.6.

Figure 19.6.
The Select Network Component Type dialog allows you to choose the type of network component to install.

3. Select Protocol and click on Add. Scroll through the list of vendors and select Microsoft. Then select TCP/IP in the listing on the right side. You'll see the dialog shown in Figure 19.7.

Figure 19.7.
Use the Select Network Protocol dialog to select TCP/IP as the protocol you want to install.

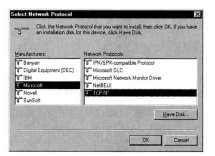

4. Click on OK to complete the selection. Click on OK again to close the Network Properties dialog. Windows 95 will prompt you for installation floppies or the CD-ROM as needed. After it installs the required files, it will ask if you want to restart the system. Click on OK to complete the installation process.

Configuring the TCP/IP support once you get it installed is easy. All you need to do is select the TCP/IP entry in the Network Properties dialog and click on the Properties button. You will see a dialog similar to the one shown in Figure 19.8. (I discussed the various TCP/IP setup options in Table 4.1.) Essentially, all the pages in this dialog allow you to set the addresses and other TCP/IP properties for your machine. All the setup options available for automatic setup are present when you use this manual technique.

Figure 19.8.
*The TCP/IP Properties
dialog allows you to
configure TCP/IP support
under Windows 95.*

Once you complete this initial installation process, you'll need to perform other installations to provide specific levels of support. For example, you'll need to install Dial-Up Networking, then the TCP/IP support that Windows provides, before you can access that support for a remote connection. The following sections show you how to configure Windows 95 to use both TCP/IP and PPP. I'll also cover a few of the usage issues you need to know about.

SNMP Support

Windows 95 provides remote monitoring agent support for agents that use the Simple Network Management Protocol (SNMP). SNMP was originally designed for the Internet. It allows an application to remotely manage devices from a variety of vendors, even if that device doesn't normally work with the managing device. For example, a mainframe could use SNMP to send updated sales statistics to a group of satellite offices in a large company. You can use an SNMP console to monitor a Windows 95 workstation once this support is installed. SNMP support under Windows 95 conforms to the version 1 specification. Microsoft implements SNMP support for both TCP/IP and IPX/SPX using WinSock (which I'll describe later). The following procedure will allow you to install SNMP support under Windows 95.

1. Right-click on the Network Neighborhood icon and select the Properties option.
2. From within the Network Properties dialog, click on Add and then double-click on Services. You should see the dialog shown in Figure 19.9.
3. Click on Have Disk and then click on Browse. Search for the \ADMIN\NETTOOLS\SNMP folder, as shown in Figure 19.10. Notice that the dialog automatically finds the .INF file required to install this service.
4. Click on OK twice. You should see the dialog shown in Figure 19.11. It allows you to select from the list of network components that the .INF file will install. In this case, there's only one on the list—SNMP support.

Figure 19.9.
You'll find a list of the common network services in the Select Network Service dialog.

Figure 19.10.
Browsing is the easy way to find the network component you need to install.

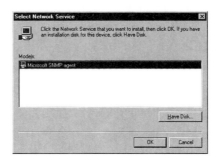

Figure 19.11.
This second Select Network Service dialog presents a list of services supported by the .INF file you selected.

5. Select the new service and click on OK. You'll see that SNMP support is part of the installed component list of the Network Properties dialog.

6. Click on OK to close the dialog. Windows 95 will install the required files from the CD. When it completes this task, Windows 95 will ask if you want to shut down and restart the operating system. You'll need to do this before SNMP support will take effect.

Unlike just about every other feature in Windows 95, there is no Properties dialog for SNMP support. You'll need to edit the various properties using the System Policy Editor. Simply open the System Policy editor and use the File | Registry command to open the registry. You can install the System Policy Editor using the procedure found in the section "Special Utility Installation" in Chapter 10. The System Policy Editor appears in the \ADMIN\APPTOOLS\POLEDIT folder of the CD-ROM. Double-click on the Local Computer icon and select the SNMP option of the Network policy, as shown in Figure 19.12. There you can change all the SNMP policies for your machine. Notice that there are two change areas. The first is where you check the property that you want to enable. If this property has other settings, they will appear in the box at the bottom of the dialog. All you need to do is click on the pushbutton you find there to display a dialog containing any options for that property.

Figure 19.12.
The System Policy Editor provides the only method for changing your SNMP configuration.

As you can see from the figure, you can change four different settings. The following list tells you which setting each item affects.

- Communities: Defines the hosts that your computer can connect to for administration purposes. You must belong to a community before you can use SNMP services on it. Even though they aren't exactly the same, you could look at a community as a NetWare group or a Windows NT domain.

- Permitted managers: This setting defines a list of IP or IPX addresses that can query the SNMP agent installed on your machine. If you don't provide a value here, any IP or IPX address can query the agent.

- Traps for 'Public' community: Use this setting to define a list of host IP or IPX addresses that you want to send SNMP traps to. In essence, a trap is an automatic monitoring method. It automatically updates the host when specific events occur on your machine.

- Internet MIB (RFC1156): Determines a point of contact and location if you're using the Internet MIB.

The System Policy Editor configuration procedure comes in handy for more than just SNMP installation and configuration. I'll refer to it several times in this chapter. You can also use the System Policy Editor to affect the condition of other network settings. However, I normally find that the Properties dialog that comes with this feature usually provides an easier-to-use interface.

Using the FTP Utility

Using the Internet requires some form of browser support if you want to download files or upload messages. FTP is actually a utility program that Windows 95 installs for you along with TCP/IP support. It's a DOS application that uses a standard character-mode interface. The syntax for FTP is as follows: FTP [-V] [-N] [-I] [-D] [-G] [<Host>] [-S:<Filename>]. The following list defines each option.

Tip: Once you get more familiar with the Internet, you'll find that the FTP and TelNet utilities provided with Windows 95 are pretty limited as far as browsers go. For example, some of the page links didn't work properly, and I didn't see the same level of graphics that Mosaic provides. A lot of other browsers, such as Mosaic, Gopher, Archie, and WAIS, will make your life a lot easier. You can get any of them commercially or as shareware from Internet servers. You can also get the WWW (World Wide Web) Browser from a variety of sources. The Plus! pack also provides an enhanced browser specially designed for the Windows 95 interface from Spyglass. The bottom line is that you need an easy-to-use browser that meets your particular needs to make best use of the resources that the Internet makes available.

- -V: This switch disables the display of remote server responses. It comes in handy if you want the download to progress in the background without disturbing your foreground task.

- -N: Use this switch to disable autologon upon initial connection.

- -I: You can use this switch to remove interactive prompting during multiple file transfers. This allows you to automate the file transfer process.

- -D: Use this switch to display all FTP commands passed between the client and server. This allows you to debug script files.

- -G: This switch disables filename globbing, which permits the use of wildcard characters in local filenames and pathnames.

- <Host>: Replace this parameter with the name or address of the host that you want to connect to for a file download.

- -S:<Filename>: Replace <Filename> with the name of a text file containing FTP commands. In essence, this switch allows you to create a script for your FTP download. Use this switch instead of redirection (>).

The FTP utility provides a surprising array of commands that you can use once you run it. There really are too many to list here, but you can get a list easily enough. All you need to remember is one command, the question mark (?). If you type a question mark, you will see a list of all the things you can do with FTP.

SLIP Support

Windows 95 provides both SLIP (Serial Line Internet Protocol) and CSLIP (Compressed Serial Line Internet Protocol) support for remote network connections. This is the type of connection supported by older UNIX remote servers. The operator of the host machine will let you know if you require this level of support, so don't install it unless you need to. You access both types of connections using the Dial-Up Networking utility, which I described in Chapter 17. Before you can use either level of support, you have to install it. Unfortunately, like most of the features in this chapter, it's not one of the things on the standard Windows installation menu. You'll have to use the following procedure to install SLIP and CSLIP support (they both get installed at the same time).

> **Note:** Make sure you install the Dial-Up Networking utility before you install SLIP support. Otherwise, the SLIP and CSLIP options won't appear in the Connection Properties dialog when you need to configure the connection. You'll also need to reinstall SLIP support if you update or otherwise change the Dial-Up Networking utility.

1. Open Control Panel and double-click on the Add/Remove Programs applet.
2. Select the Windows Setup page and click on the Have Disk pushbutton.
3. Use the Browse button to display an Open dialog like the one shown in Figure 19.13. Find the \ADMIN\APPTOOLS\SLIP folder and select the RNAPLUS.INF file. Notice that it's the only file shown in this dialog.

Figure 19.13.
Use the Open dialog to find the .INF file needed to install SLIP support.

4. Click on OK twice to select the .INF file. You'll see the Have Disk dialog, shown in Figure 19.14. Notice that it contains only one entry. There would normally be one entry for each installation option that the .INF file supports.
5. Click on the option you want to install, and then click on the Install pushbutton. Windows 95 will copy the required files from the CD and list the new option on the Windows Setup page of the Add/Remove Programs Properties page.
6. Click on OK to exit the dialog. You'll probably want to shut Windows down and reboot the machine so that any registry changes take effect.

Figure 19.14.
The Have Disk dialog shows
you which installation
options the .INF file
provides.

You don't configure SLIP support like most of the Windows 95 features either. The first thing you'll need to do is open Dial-Up Networking and create a new connection. We covered this procedure in Chapter 17, so I won't go over it again here. Once you get this done, right-click on the new connection and select the Properties option. Click on the Server Types pushbutton. You'll see the dialog shown in Figure 19.15. Notice that the list of available server types includes both SLIP and CSLIP support.

Figure 19.15.
You add SLIP and CSLIP
support to a connection
through the Server Types
dialog.

After you select a SLIP or CSLIP server, it's time to configure it by clicking on the TCP/IP Settings pushbutton. You should see the dialog shown in Figure 19.16. Notice that it contains all the familiar TCP/IP address information required by the host computer. We covered all the options listed here in Chapter 4.

Using the TelNet Utility

This is another browser utility program that Windows 95 installs automatically when you install TCP/IP support. The strange thing is that Windows 95 doesn't automatically install it in your Start menu. You'll need to add it manually. The TelNet utility always appears in your \WIN95 folder.

Figure 19.16.
After adding a SLIP or
CSLIP server to your
connection, you need to
configure it using the TCP/
IP Settings dialog.

When you open the TelNet utility, you'll see a dialog similar to the one shown in Figure 19.17. It's fairly simple to operate this application. The four menus provide a very basic set of features for logging onto a host and keeping track of your session.

Figure 19.17.
TelNet provides a very basic
terminal-like front end for a
host connection.

The Connect | Remote System command displays the Connect dialog, shown in Figure 19.18. This dialog has three fields. The first contains the name or address of the host you want to connect to. The second field contains the host type. The third field specifies a terminal type. In most cases you won't have much of a choice about terminal types, but I find that the ANSI terminal is usually a bit easier to use if you can gain access to a host that supports it. Disconnecting from the host is very easy. Just use the Connect | Disconnect command.

Figure 19.18.
The Connect dialog is where
you tell TelNet how and
where to make a connection.

The Edit menu contains the normal Copy and Paste commands, so I won't spend any time discussing it here. The Terminal menu provides a few options you should know about. For example, you can use the Start Logging and Stop Logging options to keep track of your session. The Start Logging option displays a File Open dialog that you can use to find or create a log file.

Figure 19.19 shows the dialog that appears when you select the Terminal | Preferences command. The Terminal Options and Emulation groups are pretty self-explanatory. They configure the way the host machine interacts with the terminal emulation program. The Fonts pushbutton allows you to select a different font than the default Fixedsys. You can also add a little color to the display by clicking on the Background Color button. I normally keep it set as is since you can't change the foreground color. The Buffer Size field allows you to change the number of lines of text you'll see in the terminal window. TelNet uses a default setting of 25, which seems to work well with most hosts.

Figure 19.19.
Use the Terminal Preferences dialog to configure TelNet to the host that you plan to connect with.

Desktop Management Interface (DMI) Support

Have you ever wondered how you were going to figure out which computers on the network required new hardware before you could make an upgrade? For example, will your current hardware run Windows 95? You might ask just that question in the next few months after you've had time to evaluate Windows 95. Desktop Management Interface (DMI) is part of Systems Management Server. It's the hardware auditing component of this utility.

A vendor will write a Management Information File (MIF) that contains all the particulars about a piece of equipment. When the System Management Server looks at a workstation and finds this file, it will add its contents to an SQL database that you can open with any number of products. Besides the hardware information, System Management Server will add the software auditing information that it finds to the database. The combined software and hardware information will give you the data required to know whether a particular workstation can run a piece of software without an upgrade.

Unfortunate as it might seem, none of this is fully implemented in Windows 95 as of this writing. DMI support is present, but you won't find System Management Server anywhere on your CD. This is a future upgrade that Microsoft might make to Windows 95. Although it might not help you much right this second, it's good to know that help is on the way. However, if you have the following equipment, you can implement System Management Server today:

- Windows NT Server version 3.5 or later
- Microsoft SQL Server version 4.21 or later

- A 486/66 or better processor
- 32 MB of memory (recommended)
- A hard disk with at least 100 MB available
- A network-accessible CD-ROM drive
- A network adapter
- A Microsoft mouse or compatible pointing device (a mouse is recommended but optional)

Remote Procedure Calls (RPC) Support

Remember near the beginning of this chapter when we talked about network transports and the way Microsoft implements them? I mentioned then just how complex a network transport could get if you added a few features. Remote procedure calls (RPCs) are a somewhat new concept for Windows 95. They're implemented as a network transport mechanism using named pipes, NetBIOS, or WinSock to create a connection between a client and a server. RPC is compatible with the Open Software Foundation (OSF) Data Communication Exchange (DCE) specification.

So what does RPC do for you? OLE uses it, for one. Actually, OLE uses a subset of RPC called light RPC (LRPC) to allow you to make connections that you couldn't normally make. We discussed this whole issue in detail in Chapter 11, so I won't talk about it again here. However, OLE is only the tip of the iceberg. There are other ways in which RPC can help you as a user.

Think about it this way. You're using an application that requires any number of resources in the form of DLLs, VxDs, and other forms of executable code. Right now, all that code has to appear on your machine or in a place where Windows will be certain to find it. What this means is that every time a network administrator wants to update software, he has to search every machine on the network to make sure the job gets done completely. What if you could "borrow" the DLL from someone else's machine? That's what RPCs are all about. An RPC lets your application grab what it needs in the form of executable code from wherever it happens to be.

You won't find a lot of RPC support in Windows 95 right now, but there's one way to see how it works. If you're running a Windows NT network, Microsoft provides a remote print provider utility in the \ADMIN\APPTOOLS\RPCPP folder. Installing this utility will allow a Windows 95 client to administer printer queues on Windows NT Servers. Using this print provider, a Windows 95 client can obtain complete accounting and job status information from the Windows NT Server.

Windows Sockets (WinSock) Support

Windows sockets (WinSock) started out as an effort by a group of vendors to make sense out of the conglomeration of TCP/IP protocol-based socket interfaces. Various vendors had originally ported their implementation of this protocol to Windows. The result was that nothing worked with anything else. The socket interface was originally implemented as a networked interprocess communication mechanism for version 4.2 of the Berkeley UNIX system. Windows 95 will require all non-NetBIOS applications to use WinSock if they need to access any TCP/IP services. Vendors may optionally write IPX/SPX applications to this standard as well. Microsoft includes two WinSock applications with Windows 95: SNMP and FTP.

Before I go much further, let me quickly define a couple of terms used in the preceding paragraph. We looked at what a protocol is earlier. It's a set of rules. TCP/IP is one common implementation of a set of rules. Think of a socket as one of the tube holders found in old televisions and radios. An application can plug a request (a tube) for some type of service into a socket and send it to a host of some kind. That host could be a file server, a minicomputer, a mainframe, or even another PC. An application can also use a socket to make a query of a database server. For example, it could ask for last year's sales statistics. If every host uses a different size of socket, every application will require a different set of tubes to fit those sockets. WinSock gets rid of this problem by standardizing the socket used to request services and make queries.

Besides making the interface easier to use, WinSock provides another advantage. Normally, an application has to add a NetBIOS header to every packet that leaves the workstation. The workstation at the other end doesn't really need the header, but it's there anyway. This additional processing overhead reduces network efficiency. Using WinSock eliminates the need for the header, and the user sees better performance as a result.

Sockets are an age-old principle (at least in the computer world), but they are far from out-of-date. The WinSock project proved so successful that Microsoft began to move it to other transports. For example, Windows 95 includes a WinSock module for both the IPX/SPX and NetBEUI transports.

Of course, WinSock is really a stopgap measure for today. In the long term, companies will want to move from the client-server model for some applications and use a distributed approach. This will require the use of a remote procedure call (RPC) interface instead of WinSock. We've already looked at the implications of RPC in this chapter.

 So what does it take to implement WinSock on your system? A group of five files in your \SYSTEM folder are used to implement WinSock. The following list tells you what they are and what tasks they perform.

- WINSOCK.DLL: This 16-bit application provides backward compatibility for older applications that need it. For example, an application such as Ping would use this DLL.

- WSOCK32.DLL: 32-bit applications use this DLL to access the WinSock API. It provides support for newer socket applications such as TelNet.

- VSOCK.VXD: Windows uses this driver to provide both 16-bit and 32-bit TCP/IP and IPX/SPX WinSock support. It provides virtualized support for each virtual machine, enabling Windows to perform more than one WinSock operation at a time. This is the general driver used for both protocols. If Microsoft added more WinSock interfaces later, they would all require this file for interface purposes.

- WSTCP.VXD: TCP/IP requires a protocol-specific driver. This file provides that support.
- WSIPX.VXD: IPX/SPX requires a protocol-specific driver. This file provides that support.

On Your Own

Use the information in this chapter to determine which of your system resources are shared and which are not. You might want to create a written list of who has access and where for future reference. This allows you to plug any security leaks whenever someone leaves the company.

Once you determine who has access to your machine, look for any security leaks. Make sure you change passwords on a regular basis, especially after someone leaves the company. Check to see how the use of your system resources by others affects system performance and overall usability.

We discussed the network subsystem architecture in this chapter. Go through your \SYSTEM folder and see if you can identify the components that comprise it. See if your network needs any specialty components because it uses a different protocol than normal. You might also want to take this opportunity to look for any real-mode drivers that are still lurking around your hard drive.

20

Setting Up Security

Network security is a major thorn in most network administrators' sides. Even a small network requires some level of planning, and many managers fail to see the value of implementing the type of security they really need. Of course, I've seen the opposite side of the coin as well. Some administrators wrap the people who use the network in a tight cocoon of regulations and passwords. The choke hold that these people create inhibits any kind of creative resource management and often impedes work as well.

It's difficult to create a bullet-proof network setup that offers the level of flexibility that most users require. Adding a bit of flexibility normally means that you also open a security hole. I find that a network administrator must reach an important balance. The first thing you need to realize is that there's no such thing as a bullet-proof security system. Any security system you design can be breached by someone else.

So what do you do? Just leave the network open to whoever might want to access it? That's not the way to go either. The real goal is to put reasonable security restraints in place. You need to assess your security risks and do whatever it takes to reduce your risk to an acceptable level.

More important than physical security and password protection is the cooperation of those around you. I recently went into a client's office to check on his network setup. He let me use one of his employee's desks to get the work done. Right in front of me was one of those yellow reminder pads. It contained not only the employee's password, but the superior's password as well. Names were all over the desk. Anyone could have simply walked into the office and gained access to the network because of this security breach.

This incident reminded me of the importance of the "human" factor in any security plan. To really implement a good security system, you need to consider the following elements:

- Physical security: Place your file server in a locked room. I can easily break the security for a NetWare setup (or most other networks, for that matter) if I have access to a running file server. If you lock the file server up, I can't access it unless I have a key.

- Software protection: Using passwords and other forms of software protection is your next line of defense. Make sure that all the right kinds of security measures are in place. I'll cover this particular topic in greater detail later, but this is one area where Windows 95 can really help. It contains all the right features; all you need to do is implement them.

- Cooperative security: You can't secure the network by yourself. The larger your network, the more you'll need every user's cooperation. If you expect the user to cooperate with you, you'll need to actually talk to him and find out what's reasonable. No one will use an unreasonable security plan. This cooperative strategy also extends to management. If you don't talk to management and tell them what your security problems are, they won't be able to help. You also need to make sure that management knows what kinds of security risks are present in the current setup. This reduces the chance of someone getting surprised later.

- Training: It's never a good idea to assume that users know how to use the security features that Windows 95 provides. You can implement a lot of the physical security, but it's the user who will use the software part of the equation. An untrained user might not use a particular security feature correctly or might not even know that it exists.

- A written security plan: I don't find this particular step necessary on small networks. However, as your network becomes larger, it becomes vitally important to get the rules put down in writing. Otherwise, how will a user know what's expected or how to react in a crisis? Writing everything down will also make management aware of the security you have put in place.

This might seem like a lot of work to implement security, but it isn't when you consider the loss that a single security breach can cause. A pirate isn't going to steal last week's letter to the general public; he's going to steal something valuable. The more secret something is, the better the pirate likes it. Just think about what a competitor could do with your new marketing plan or the design for that new widget you plan to produce. Even if a pirate doesn't take anything, he could leave something behind. What would a virus do to your network? It doesn't take too much thought to imagine your entire setup crumbling as a virus infects it.

The next section of this chapter addresses network security in the broad scheme of things. In other words, it actually goes a little beyond what you would need to implement in Windows 95 itself. The reason I'm including it is because security needs to be cohesive. You can't create little security groups in a network. The entire network must use a consolidated plan to ensure that your security net is consistent and that there aren't any holes in it. Anything less is an open invitation to whoever would like to circumvent your security to gain access to sensitive information.

Once we get past these general guidelines, I'll show you the features that Windows 95 provides to help you implement a company-wide plan. We've looked at many of these features already, so I won't go into a lot of detail in some areas. (I'll tell you where the detailed information does appear in this book, though.) Even if you're running a small network, you'll want to read both sections. The first section tells you what to implement, and the second tells you how to do it.

Creating a Security Plan

To run a network efficiently, you need to have a plan. Ad hoc solutions to any problem are simply that—ad hoc. They won't go very far in helping you plug a security leak or tell someone why he needs to observe a particular rule. Without a plan, you won't know what your security goals are or what steps you need to take to meet them. The problem that most administrators face is that they really aren't sure what goals a security plan helps them achieve. Figuring out what a security plan does for you is almost as important as creating it. A security plan will help you achieve at least five goals:

1. A security plan helps you define and organize your security system into manageable pieces. "Divide and conquer" is the technique used by many generals to win a war. Instead of trying to fight an entire army of problems by working on them all at the same time, take them on one at a time. You can win the war against security leaks by using this tried-and-true strategy. A network security plan is the map you need to see where to break the problem into smaller pieces.

2. Most networks have security problems from time to time. An old employee leaves and a new one takes her place, creating a potential gap in your security net. Someone gets promoted and you need to extend his rights on the network. Will he know how to handle these new responsibilities if you don't train him? What if someone gets transferred from one department to another? Do you really want him to have access to both departments' data? The network administrator might not even know that these problems exist. What if a manager inadvertently gives someone rights to a sensitive directory? One way to find problem areas quickly is to compare the current network state with a baseline condition. A network security plan can provide that baseline. It captures the network's ideal state rather than its current state.

3. If you're like most administrators, users constantly ask why you implement one procedure over another. They might want to legitimately ferret out ways to increase their freedom on the network. (Some users equate increased freedom with increased productivity, an inaccurate assumption on a properly designed network.) So how do you answer these questions? A network security plan can provide a historical context that tells why you implemented a specific procedure or network rule. Recording a rule and why you implemented it often helps you keep the network security plan up-to-date. Keeping old rules without apparent reason is counterproductive. On the other hand, too much freedom is an invitation to security problems.

4. You might find that the goals of management and the network's users don't reflect the goals of the network administrator. A network security plan provides an opportunity for you to express these differences. It also provides the means to discuss reasonable alternatives and compromises. Arguing a particular course of action once you study the ramifications of that action is the only way to create a network that everyone will enjoy using. Rules based on knowledge rather than personal feelings is the best way to later ensure that you know why the rule is in place.

5. Evenhanded administration of the network means that you enforce the network rules the same way each time someone breaks them. (Some NOS even provide you with the tools required to detect security breaches in your system. For example, NetWare provides the SECURITY utility for this purpose.) It also means that you explain the rule the same way to everyone who uses the network. Unless you write the rules down, someone could legitimately say that you show a bias toward certain network users or that you make arbitrary decisions regarding some infractions. Clearly written rules alleviate this problem by making the rule, the implementation, any penalties, and its historical context clear to everyone.

Tip: A small company doesn't necessarily need a written security plan. However, you should at least think these issues through before you start setting Windows 95 up. A peer-to-peer network needs some type of security plan too. Trying to implement a security plan after installation is fine, but it will probably cost you extra time to do things this way. Just as you plan your installation in advance, take the time to consider the security needs of your network too.

As you can see, a properly designed and implemented security plan can change the way everyone views the network. There's always a group of people who fail to understand that a security problem on the network costs everyone money. A security plan can handle this situation as well. Even if a user doesn't agree with the implementation of a security feature, he won't want to face any penalties that management assigns for failure to follow the rules. Of course, this is the last course of action you want to take. Assigning a penalty might show that a user failed to follow the rules, but it also shows that your plan failed to work in this instance. It's unlikely that you'll ever create a plan that everyone agrees with and no one disobeys, but getting as close as possible to this ideal is the goal you should seek to attain. The following paragraphs provide you with more details about designing and implementing a security plan for your company.

Breaking the Company into Groups

Many companies use a combination of workgroups and a client-server architecture. The workgroup might use Windows 95 to implement a small peer-to-peer network just for the people in that section. The client-server network might use NetWare or some other NOS. It allows the company to communicate as a whole.

Tip: It's easy to get confused about the ways you need to split your company's various security needs into manageable pieces. Think of workgroups in terms of a group of people working together on a single project. This is a key concept, because they don't necessarily have to come from the same department to be in the same workgroup. Think of security groups as people with similar security needs. You can assign a person to more than one group. For example, they could be part of the engineering workgroup but also be part of the managerial security group. These ideas are separate, and you need to consider them separately.

Whether your company uses several small networks or simply has everyone log into one file server, you'll need to break a large network into smaller pieces before you create a security plan. This helps you organize your company into functional security areas. By breaking the security task into smaller pieces, you can reduce the overall complexity of making your system secure. There are many different ways to break the problem into smaller pieces, and you'll probably need to employ more than one of them. The following paragraphs provide you with some ideas on how to accomplish this task.

- Department/workgroup: Since users who work together are apt to require similar access to the network, you can easily break the company into groups along this natural line. For example, people working in personnel are unlikely to require access to financial records. Likewise, the company's accountants won't require access to the personnel records. This is the best way to go if your company already uses peer-to-peer networks to connect small workgroups.

Tip: Always assign someone to manage every workgroup on the network if you have more than one. Let this person take care of some security details by allowing him to assign access for the local workgroup resources. It might also be a good idea to assign someone from the group to manage the print server if the group has one with more than one printer attached. You can't take the time to see to every networking detail, especially when a network starts to grow beyond 100 or so workstations. It'll take a lot of time just to keep the network applications current, keep the workstations up and running, and attend to the myriad of other details that a network administrator needs to worry about. Making someone in the local workgroup responsible not only reduces your work load, but also helps keep any security measures in place.

- Seniority/longevity: Some companies assign tasks based on a person's seniority. For example, when a manager leaves town for a few days to attend a convention, he might assign the senior employee in that section to act in his stead. You might need to give that employee access to certain managerial areas of the network to allow him to perform these duties. Even though the person doesn't need to have access to these areas as a result of department or workgroup affiliation, he needs to have them as a substitute manager. As with many security considerations, this scenario is definitely an exception to the rule.

- Job function: Another natural way to break the company into groups is by job function. For example, management might have one area set aside on the network for managers. Another area might contain information of vital importance to people who maintain print servers on the network. A foreman might require access to an area set aside for all the foremen in the company. As you can see, some of these job function areas cross department and workgroup lines.

- Special designation: Some companies give individuals special designations. For example, you might have a person on staff who wears more than one hat. She might require access to records from more than one department. You might need to accommodate the needs of a consultant from time to time as well. All these people fall outside the normal security boundaries. You need to list these special considerations.

Security Plan Considerations

Once you break a company into functional groups, it's a good idea to figure out the security needs for each group. Accounting will need much more stringent security than someone who takes care of the company's correspondence. Sometimes you might be able to get by with read-only access for this group. For example, no one would need to edit last year's accounting records, but they might need to refer to them. You might need extra flexibility in an engineering section to promote the flow of ideas from one person to another without giving away new ideas to a competitor. One engineer might have one piece of the puzzle, and that piece could trigger someone else's creative abilities to come up with yet another piece. Inhibiting an engineer with a straitjacket of rules is never a good idea. A management group will need very tight security but will also need the maximum level of access within the group. You can provide management with a straitjacket and actually expect that they'll use it. Hopefully, a manager will understand the need for tight security when discussing the company's future plans.

Besides these considerations, you need to think about special security items within your company. You'll also want to start implementing your security plan. The following steps will help you with both processes. They help you complete a security plan and present some additional ideas that you should consider as you implement it.

1. Assessing company tasks: Even if you do a perfect job of identifying all the groups in your company, you might find that there are still a few tasks that the company must perform that fall outside the purview of a group. In many cases, more than one group performs these tasks. For example, creating the end-of-year report might require the efforts of several departments in the company. Since this isn't a task the company performs every day, there's no need to create a special group to do it. However, you do need to consider this type of task when you create your security plan. Other examples of task-related groups include special committees and research groups. In this case, several specialists get together to work on a specific problem or idea.

2. Appointing each person to one or more groups: Once you break the company into groups and decide what major additional tasks the company needs to perform, it's time to assign people to them. For example, the finance group maintains accounting records, and the personnel group maintains employee records. In many cases, the assignments you need to make are very straightforward. It's easy to see that everyone in the accounting department will easily fit within the financial group. However, there are some assignments you might not think about at first. For example, you might have someone in personnel who needs assignment to both the financial and the personnel groups. She might need to make entries into the financial program regarding employee raises or terminations.

3. Brainstorming special user needs: There are other ways to look at your company's security needs, not just from an organizational point of view. Breaking the company into physical and logical units is fine for most security needs. Doing so allows the network administrator

to work with both management and network users to make reasonable security assignments based on fact. In some situations, a lack of information prevents you from making reasonable assignments. For example, what if a user is just starting a new project? He certainly won't know what types of access he'll require on the network since he's never tried to perform that task before. The manager might have a reasonable idea of what type of access the user requires, but this is mere conjecture. You will find yourself at a loss to make a reasonable assignment without more information. Unless you want to spend a lot of time retuning your network to compensate for these situations, you might want to take the time to brainstorm the user's needs.

I'd like to look at that third step in more detail. It's the last one you need to complete your security plan. Once you do figure out special user needs, you have all the information required to make the plan work. Brainstorming is a think-tank approach to network management. It's a tried-and-true method used in many other ventures. Essentially, you define a task based on past knowledge of similar tasks and on future goals. You answer questions such as "What do we plan to achieve?" and "How do we plan to achieve these goals?" You must consider what tools you have available on your network to get the job done. This includes both hardware and software resources. You also throw out ideas for consideration. Someone might need to play the part of devil's advocate to make sure you consider both the positive and negative aspects of a particular decision. Of course, you want to use this approach only if there's insufficient information on which to base a decision using standard techniques. You can take a number of steps to make this process work properly:

1. Break the user's task into logical elements. For example, what types of applications does the user need to use? Each application involves a different set of security rights. Perhaps one or more groups already provide these rights on the network. (Whenever possible, try to avoid making nongroup assignments.)

2. Create a list of equipment that the user needs to access. For example, does the user need to use a fax or a special printer? If the security system on the network limits access to these items, you might need to provide the user with the special access required to use them.

3. Write down a list of tasks the user needs to perform. Sometimes you'll see a special application or a piece of equipment that the user will need to use to accomplish a task. Make sure you don't just list these tasks. Describe the tasks so that everyone is talking about the same task.

4. Look for areas where the user might have too much access. Once you figure out where the user might need access, trim your list to areas where the user must have access to get the job done. There's no reason to give someone too much network access simply because he's starting a new project.

As you can see, brainstorming a task can really help in a situation where you lack the information needed to make a good decision using just the available facts. What you need to realize is that your group bases such decisions on conjecture and derived information. Keep in touch with the user as he gets further into his project. You might find that you can reduce his access in some areas and that he requires additional access in other areas. (The user normally will tell you when he doesn't have enough access, but seldom will he tell you if he has too much access.) Remember that it's your responsibility to make sure that the user has enough access but not too much. Some users will try to convince you that they need additional rights to certain areas when they really don't.

Peter's Principle: Delegating Network Administration Tasks

You've gotten your network installed, and all the Windows 95 workgroups are in place. So why are you still running around like the proverbial headless chicken? Windows 95 provides a lot of tools to help the administrator manage a network. We learned in Chapter 19 that these tools pertain not only to Windows 95 peer-to-peer installations, but to other types of networks as well. You can install agents to monitor the status of a workstation remotely or through a local host. You can use all kinds of connections to get a bird's-eye view of your network. Yet even with all these aids, you feel out-of-touch and barely able to maintain the system.

Some network administrators are under the impression that they can maintain the entire network themselves given enough time and tools to do the job. The truth of the matter is that only Superman can fulfill all the needs of some networks. This includes the area of network security. Although you don't want to give anyone rights he doesn't need, you might find that you need someone to help you maintain a large network—and you'll have to decide what kind of rights to give that person. How much help you need and what size of network can be defined as large is primarily a matter of network complexity and whether you are a full-time network administrator. If management gives you a few hours each day to perform network duties and you wear another hat for the rest of the day, a large network could be as few as 20 users. Even a full-time administrator will begin to feel the pinch at around 100 users, especially if your company performs a wide variety of tasks with a conglomeration of equipment.

There are a few problems in allowing other people to help you maintain network security. Centralized control of the network for security purposes is a real advantage. If one person is responsible to management for ensuring that network security remains high, there's little possibility that he'll do a halfhearted job. In addition, centralized control means that fewer problems will slip through the cracks. Users will never wonder whom to ask for more rights on the network. They'll always know the one person who can help them out.

I always follow a simple principle when it comes to network security. Always maintain control. When you can't maintain control, find out why. You might find that it's a problem with a network administrator who's overwhelmed with requests for service and little time to really take care of the network. Don't kill the security plan that you worked so hard to create. Give the network administrator sufficient help to get the job done.

Local Security

Now that we've gotten a bird's-eye view of security, let's look at what Windows 95 can do to help. I was pleasantly surprised by some features but a bit dismayed at others. For example, the ability to assign two levels of password protection to every resource is nice and will probably work fine for a peer-to-peer network. The inability to assign a password to a specific file didn't sit well with me. Sometimes you need to protect one file in a directory but not another. For example, some older applications really need to have their configuration files in the same directory as the rest of the executables. I usually like to make my executable files read-only so that the user doesn't erase them.

However, putting these inconveniences aside, you can still implement a significant security strategy using Windows 95's built-in capabilities. The following sections describe these features. In most cases, I've described how to use and implement these features in other chapters, so I won't cover that aspect again here. I'll show you how to use the features that Windows 95 provides to implement the security plan that I talked about in the preceding section.

Logon

The best way to prevent a security breach is to keep someone from getting onto the network in the first place. The dialog that you see when you start Windows 95 is your first line of defense against someone who would try to break into your system. I've talked about the logon feature of Windows 95 in several places. We looked at it as part of the Control Panel applets in Chapter 10 and again in Chapter 19. We also looked at how you can change the source of the network logon using the Network Properties dialog in Chapter 19. Let's take a look at how you can actually use the Logon dialog to help implement a security strategy.

Stand-Alone Security

It always amazes me when someone asks why it's important to take the time to protect a stand-alone workstation. Does the fact that a workstation doesn't connect to the network reduce the quality of the data it contains? The only part of the security picture that has changed is that a stand-alone workstation will at least keep someone from accessing your data on the network. The fact that many stand-alone workstations contain valuable data is still very important. In fact, I think you'll find that most stand-alone machines at your company are either relics that no one wants to use or engineering workstations that no one wants to expose to the security risks of network use. Either way, if your stand-alone machine has Windows 95 on it, it's pretty certain that the data it contains is valuable. The initial strategy to follow for a stand-alone workstation is to enable password protection using the Password Properties dialog, shown in Figure 20.1. Simply open Control Panel and double-click on the Password applet.

Figure 20.1.
Protecting a stand-alone machine might require you to enable the multiple Desktops feature, which requires each user to log in.

Tip: If security for a specific workstation is so important that software alone won't take care of the problem, consider one of several alternative solutions. For example, you could add a locking bolt to the back of the machine to prevent people from opening it up and use the BIOS password feature to prevent access by any means until the user provides the correct password. Physical locking mechanisms are also available. One of them goes over the floppy disk drive to prevent the user from accessing it. You can also add a lock to a standard PC on switch. Unfortunately, most of these solutions are either expensive or inconvenient or both. It's almost always worth your while to seek other solutions to the problem.

Note: You'll need to install the System Policy Editor using the Special Utility Installation procedure in Chapter 10. The required .INF file appears in the \ADMIN\APPTOOLS\ POLEDIT folder. Once you get the System Policy Editor installed, you can access it from the \Programs\Accessories\System Tools folder of the Start menu.

Of course, just enabling passwords doesn't help you very much. What would prevent someone from coming along and turning the settings off? I always back up my configuration changes with a policy change to go with the password setting. This means opening the System Policy Editor and turning off various types of access. For example, you can turn the Control Panel settings off using the options shown in Figure 20.2. Notice that one of the settings in this list is the Passwords applet. Use the File | Registry command to load the current settings from the registry. The File | Save command will save any changes you make in the registry before you exit the System Policy Editor. You'll see two icons after loading the registry—one for the user and one for the machine. It's the user settings that you'll want to modify. You'll need an administrator account to use the System Policy Editor this way. The following paragraphs explain each Control Panel restriction in detail.

Figure 20.2.
*The System Policy Editor
can help you protect Control
Panel.*

- **Restrict Display Control Panel:** You can choose to disable the entire Display applet, or you can select which pages in the Display Properties dialog get disabled. The first option in the list disables the entire applet. Every other option disables a single page at a time. This particular setting comes in handy for setting a screen saver password and then shutting off the page so that the user can't disable it.

- **Restrict Network Control Panel:** As with the Display applet, you can choose to disable the entire applet or individual pages. The Access Control page is the one to check here, but it really only applies when you have a network setup on the machine.

- **Restrict Passwords Control Panel:** This is one of the few applets I would consider disabling completely. Every page on this one could produce potentially harmful effects for your setup. Of course, the big ones in a stand-alone setting are the User Profiles and Password pages.

- **Restrict Printers Settings:** The only good reason to implement this policy is if you're afraid that the user will add a nonexistent printer or delete one installed on the machine. This particular policy affects only the General and Details pages.

- **Restrict System Control Panel:** This policy affects the Device Manager and Hardware Profiles pages. It also removes the Virtual Memory and File System buttons. Whether you disable these settings or not depends largely on the user's expertise. In most cases, you'll probably gain more than you'll lose by leaving these settings alone, because the user will be able to help you troubleshoot many system problems if he can access the information that these pages provide.

I mentioned in Chapter 19 that a user could circumvent the password by erasing the .PWL file. You can keep this from happening by taking another preventative measure. Figure 20.3 shows the System Restrictions policy. Checking all four of these items will prevent the user from accessing the hard drive in any manner other than the one you allow. You could restrict access to applications to only those required to complete the user's work. Disabling the DOS prompt will also prevent the user from erasing the .PWL files that way. Of course, the user who has to live with these restrictions might see them as very constricting. Even though this strategy gives the network administrator the tools needed to prevent user meddling, it could backfire somewhere along the way.

Figure 20.3.

The System Restrictions policy allows you to control user access to potentially harmful applications.

> **Tip:** Disabling the user's access to the hard drive after he starts Windows 95 won't prevent other forms of access. For example, a user could boot his system using a floppy and remove both the .PWL and .POL files. (The System Policy Editor stores its data in the .POL file, and the system passwords appear in the .PWL file.) This would effectively disable any restrictions you placed on the user. Removing the floppy would disable this form of access but would make it very difficult to troubleshoot the machine or add new applications. You'll also need to set specific MSDOS.SYS settings to prevent the user from exiting the boot sequence. See Table 6.3 for a complete list of MSDOS.SYS switches.

Using a combination of these settings will allow you to restrict user access to most of the "harmful" features that Windows 95 provides. It would be a lot better, though, if you could participate in a cooperative form of security rather than resorting to these very harsh measures that will likely cause a lot of user unhappiness.

You can impose a final level of restrictions on the user of a stand-alone machine. Figure 20.4 shows the Shell Restrictions policy options. As you can see, most of these options will effectively prevent a user from exercising any form of control over the shell itself. Notice that these policies also provide some network settings. I'll refer to them again in the next section.

Of all the policies presented here, disabling the Run command is probably the most reasonable. It allows you to restrict the user from starting applications on the hard drive. This is especially important if you maintain a set of diagnostic tools locally. For example, it's fairly likely that you wouldn't want the user to access the Registry Editor or the System Policy Editor. Most of these settings are pretty self-explanatory. The one that really caught my attention, though, was the Hide all items on

Desktop policy. About the only use I can think of for this setting is when you create the general system policy. You could disable access to everything, including the Desktop. That way, if someone did manage to bypass the Logon dialog, he wouldn't see much of value when Windows 95 did start.

Figure 20.4.

The Shell Restrictions policy allows you to control user access to the shell itself.

Peer-to-Peer Security

All the policies I covered in the "Stand-Alone Security" section apply here as well, but there are several important differences. First, you'll probably load the system policies from a .POL file instead of directly from the registry. Second, you'll probably see more than just one user; this dialog will include groups as well. We covered the details of creating a policy file for a peer-to-peer network in Chapter 4.

Whether you set policies by groups or by the individual (or even a combination of both), the settings that we covered in the preceding section are the same. You can restrict the user from doing just about anything by implementing the right set of policies. The problem is that the more you restrict the user, the harder it is for him to get anything done. As I mentioned at the beginning of this chapter, creating a security plan is often more a matter of considering an acceptable risk rather than trying to seal all the holes.

I'd like to again direct your attention to the Shell Restrictions policy shown in Figure 20.4. I wanted to talk about quite a few network restrictions in this section since they don't really apply to stand-alone machines. There are three Network Neighborhood-specific settings here. The problem with implementing these policies is that they restrict the user from exploring the network. This could be a good policy if you're working with a computer novice who has managed to damage network files "by accident" in the past. However, restricting a user from exploring his computer only removes any reason for him to really learn about it. Training a user is almost always a matter of sparking his interest in what the computer can do. Inhibiting that interest is about the most counterproductive thing you can do. That said, you'll probably want to think twice about implementing these policies for most users.

There's one set of policies you should probably consider implementing on a structured network, especially if you manage a lot of machines. Figure 20.5 shows the Network Sharing policies. There are two of them—one for printers and one for drives. Disabling the user's ability to share (or not share) resources on his machine could save you a lot of trouble in the long run. A user might not always understand why you granted someone else access to his hard drive. Unless you want to explain each and every setting on every machine on the network to every user, you'll probably want to disable these settings.

Figure 20.5.
The network administrator, not the user, should set the policy regarding drive and printer sharing.

Peer-to-peer networks also need to consider the machine settings. For example, how do you want the various machines to talk to each other, and which protocols will they use? We covered many of these issues in Chapter 19. Other settings will be discussed in the following sections. The important thing to see right now is the overall picture. Figure 20.6 shows the overall settings picture for the machine network settings.

Figure 20.6.
Machine-specific settings become important in a peer-to-peer networking environment.

The Access Control setting performs the same function as that page in the Network Properties dialog. It's included here so that you can set that policy using a remote terminal. (In fact, every important setting that you can change with a Properties dialog also appears somewhere in the System Policy Editor so that you can change it remotely.)

The System policies for a machine can provide some additional security as well. Figure 20.7 shows the various settings you can change. One of the settings I use quite a bit is Network path for Windows setup. This particular policy allows you to place a copy of Windows 95 on a file server and then prevent the user from accessing it. The network administrator can update a system with ease, but the user is restricted from adding new Windows 95 features.

Figure 20.7.

Although it's not immediately apparent, the System policy can help you implement a security strategy.

The three Run policies provide an opportunity to load network monitors and other applications. A monitor can help you keep track of how the user interacts with the network and keep track of the current status of the workstation itself. Of course, you can also use this policy to add default applications to the user's setup. For example, company policy might dictate that everyone use a specific contact manager or e-mail program. You could add either to the Run policy in order to load them automatically for the user.

Client-Server Security

As I mentioned earlier, you can use the same settings that I described in the "Stand-Alone Security" section with a client-server security setup for a NOS such as NetWare or Windows NT. You can also add the peer-to-peer networking security that I described in the preceding section. Windows 95 provides some additional capabilities for client-server setups that I didn't describe earlier. Some of these settings appear in Chapter 19. For example, you can implement a remote monitor using SNMP.

The major addition to security that Windows 95 provides for client-server networks is the ability to download system policies from the file server. You must install the Group Policy features using the same procedure that I provided in Chapter 4 for installing the System Policy Editor. Placing the GROUPPOL.DLL file in your SYSTEM folder enables Windows 95 to download group policies included in your .POL file to the local workstation.

You need to know some things about group policies. First, Windows 95 won't override an individual user policy with a group policy. If you want to use groups, don't define any individual policies for that particular user.

Second, Windows 95 processes the groups in the order of precedence that you set using the Options | Group Priority command. The Group Priority dialog, shown in Figure 20.8, allows you to change the way Windows 95 views each group policy. A policy in a high-priority group will always override a policy in a low-priority group. This means that you'll have to set the priorities to reflect the security requirements of the network. Otherwise, you could accidentally give a user access to something he would normally not require access to.

Figure 20.8.
Use the Group Priority dialog to change the order in which Windows 95 interprets each group policy.

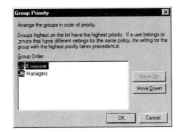

The Password Cache

Windows 95 implements something called a *password cache*. The .PWL or password list file in either the main Windows 95 or your individual profile folder contains more than just the password for your system. This file also remembers the password for Microsoft Network (MSN) or any of the resources that you need to access. Your password unlocks this file, which in turn contains the passwords that unlock all the other resources you can access.

Setup normally provides password caching as a default. (This means that Windows 95 remembers your password when you use programs such as Microsoft Network.) In fact, there isn't any place to turn it off in a Properties dialog. However, if you open the Network Passwords property of the Local Computer Properties dialog using the System Policy Editor (see Figure 20.9), you'll see an option for disabling password caching.

The other three policies here are pretty self-explanatory. Notice the Minimum Windows password length policy. It can help you make it more difficult for a hacker to break into the network. It's a proven fact that some people use a single-character password—or none at all. This isn't just under Windows 95; it's everywhere. Setting a minimum password length of five characters greatly reduces the chance that a hacker will guess a user's password and break into the system. In fact, the longer the password, the harder it is to break in. Of course, there's a point where you'll spend a lot of time bailing the user out because he forgot his password. Setting a reasonable length between five and 10 characters is usually sufficient. You should also set a policy of using a combination of letters and numbers that don't form birth dates or other combinations that a hacker who knows the user could easily guess.

Figure 20.9.
Normally you will want to keep password caching on to make life a little easier for the user.

 What happens, though, if the .PWL file becomes corrupted? Windows 95 also provides a Password List Editor, shown in Figure 20.10, to remove corrupted passwords from the file. As you can see, there's no way for the administrator to know the user's password, but he can remove a specific password from the list. In this case, the .PWL file contains two Microsoft Mail passwords and one for MSN. You'll find the Password List Editor in the \ADMIN\APPTOOLS\PWLEDIT folder.

Figure 20.10.
The Password List Editor is a simple utility for removing old or corrupted passwords from the user's .PWL file.

 Warning: There are a few caveats about using the .PWL editor. First, the user needs to log in to "unlock" the file. This means that you can't edit a .PWL file remotely. You must do it at the user's machine. Second, the Password List Editor might corrupt a .PWL file if an application adds a password in an unknown format. Make sure you create a backup of the .PWL file before you edit it.

Network Security

Let's get back to peer-to-peer networking for a while. Windows 95 provides several levels of security that fit different kinds of networking needs. You can select only one level at a time, so it's important to select the correct one. Changing your policy later will prove time-consuming at the least.

The following sections provide you with the details of Windows 95 security. This information is very peer-to-peer-network-oriented, but I do throw in a few bits of information that you can use with client-server networks as well.

Share-Level Versus User-Level Security

The first level of security that Windows 95 provides is share-level access control. You get to this setting using the Access Control page of the Network dialog, shown in Figure 20.11. The other security level is user-level access control. Each of these security levels provides a different set of features, and each has different qualities that make it useful in a given situation.

Figure 20.11.
Windows 95 provides two levels of security: share and user.

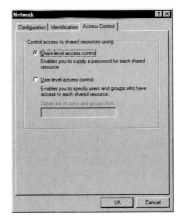

Share-level access control allows you to assign a password to each resource on the network. You can use the same password for each resource or a variety of passwords. Share-level access control also allows you to determine whether a user gets read-only or full access based on a password. This is my favorite form of access on a small network. I normally use three different levels of security:

- No password: Since the user has to log into the network in the first place, you can assume that she already has a certain level of security. I don't assign an additional password to low-priority resources. The user has already proven that she is supposed to be on the network, so why ask her to prove it gain?

- Read-only: When I do assign a password to a resource, I give it both a read-only and a full-access password. The read-only password allows me to give people quick access to documents that they can either copy to their hard drive or simply read online. This works well with applications that don't provide a revision marks feature, because I can see who made what comments. Of course, I still have to go to the trouble of consolidating the comments later.

- Full: Anyone who is working on a sensitive project with me usually gets full access to the resource. This allows us to work together on a single document. I normally use Word for Windows for group projects. (Of course, if you're working on a financial projection, you'll probably use something like Lotus 1-2-3 instead.) Turning on the revision marks feature allows me to see who made what changes. It also allows all of us to interact without actually setting up a meeting.

User-level access control allows you to set resource access by user name or group. This is the same type of access that client-server products such as NetWare use. I use this form of access control when the user will also interact with a larger network. The advantage is obvious. I don't have to spend a lot of time retraining the user to use the peer-to-peer setup. He already knows how to use it based on his previous experience with NetWare.

There is a more important reason to use user-level access control. This is the method that allows you to use a policy file created using the System Policy Editor. We covered this topic pretty well in Chapter 4, so I won't cover it here again.

Master Key

What do I mean by a master key? This is a policy more than a feature. Suppose your company uses a combination of client-server and peer-to-peer networks. It's important to keep things as simple as possible for the user yet make maximum use of company resources and still provide the needed level of flexibility.

Trying to get any user to remember more than one login password is difficult. It also wastes time in some respects because the user will spend a lot of time logging in to the various networks he needs to access. Also, there's a frustration factor to consider as the user goes from login screen to login screen. Do you really want to frustrate a user who is trying to help you implement a security strategy?

Windows 95 provides the capability to use one "master key" to get to all the networks that a user can access. A master key allows users to enter one password to access all the resources they need. The old system was to use a different password for each resource. If you needed to log into the workgroup network, you needed one password. Another password would give you access to the company network. You needed another password for your mail program and yet another for your communication program. Even if you used the same password for every access, it was inconvenient to say the least to enter a password every time you required access to something. Windows 95 remembers all the user's passwords and enters them automatically as needed. All the user needs to do is enter the initial password when starting Windows 95. Implementing a master key strategy is simple.

All you need to do is have the user provide precisely the same password to every login screen the first time she goes through them. I stress the word "precisely" here because capitalization makes a difference on some networks.

After you do this the first time, Windows 95 will remember the master key and use it to log the user into every network that she has access to. Instead of going through a long, frustrating procedure, the user will see one consolidated Logon dialog at the beginning of her Windows 95 session. This one password is all she'll need to use the full flexibility of the network.

On Your Own

Take this opportunity to design your own security plan. Work with the network users and management to come up with a plan that is both fair and reasonably secure.

Analyze the plan you created for leaks and potential security risks. Make sure that you tell management about these risks and their effect on the network. Also come up with contingency plans to plug the leaks if management decides the risk is too great.

Spend some time training the users on your network about security. It's very important that you also take the time to explain what types of passwords are acceptable. Spend a little time with each user who has problems understanding the security plan.

If you're a home user, try setting up a variety of security options on your machine. For example, you might want to create a security profile for young users that gives them access to programs they can use but removes access to programs that could damage your machine. Try using the System Policy Editor and the other tools I described in this chapter to make the process of creating a home security plan easy.

21

Mobile Computing

Few people who travel can get by without their constant companion, the notebook computer. In this chapter, I use the term *notebook* to refer to every kind of mobile computer. Of course, mobile computers actually range in size from the smallest PDA (personal digital assistant) to some of the luggable dinosaurs I still see from time to time.

Fortunately, most people use something that provides enough flexibility to get the job done, but without all the weight. It's the transition from klunky and archaic to sleek and feature-packed that has brought on another change that Windows 95 addresses. No longer does everyone regard notebooks as second computers. They contain most, if not all, of the features of desktop computers. The only difference is the display and keyboard, both of which are easily taken care of by a docking station.

Yet, before Windows 95 came along, many notebook computer users were still strapped to a desktop. The reason was simple: The operating system wasn't up to the task of working with a notebook. Consider the following scenario. You're working on a report and decide to take it home with you. Since you're in a car pool and not driving today, you figure that you can work on the report on the way home. To do that, you have to completely close all your applications, undock your machine, reboot your computer, and set everything up again. That's not too bad, but you have to go through the same process all over again when you get home.

The inconvenience of using a notebook can be illustrated in a number of ways. The "taking work home" scenario was just one example. What happens when you need to change a card in your machine? Say that you no longer need the modem card and want to replace it with a NIC to access the network. Unless you have some special setup software, you'll actually have to turn the machine off and reconfigure it to make the switch. It's time-wasting events like this that really frustrate people who use a notebook from time to time. Windows has a fix for this problem that you'll really like— I know I like it.

Before we go much further, let's define this "notebook" computer a little. First, Windows 95 won't take your PDA and make it into a desktop equivalent. We're looking at machines that are really capable of running Windows 95. This means that they have to meet all the installation criteria I discussed earlier. I'm also talking about something that's a bit newer than the Model T. A notebook has to provide a PCMCIA (Personal Computer Memory Card International Association) slot or its equivalent in order to use some of the features that Windows 95 provides. You'll also want a computer that can use a docking station. In other words, I really don't care how heavy or large the computer is, but it has to provide enough features to take the place of a desktop.

We'll also revisit plug and play (PNP) in this chapter. We took a look at how every computer can use PNP in Chapter 2. There are some new capabilities that will really make a difference for notebook computer users. If you're at all intrigued, read on.

PCMCIA Devices on Your Notebook Computer

The first topic on our agenda is the PCMCIA bus. This is a "little" bus that is specially designed to meet the needs of the notebook computer market, but it's found in a growing number of desktop machines as well. The PCMCIA bus uses credit card-sized cards that connect to external slots on the machine. This is perfect for a notebook, because notebooks are notorious for providing few, if any, expansion slots. A PCMCIA bus makes it very easy for the user to change a machine's hardware configuration without opening it up. For example, you could take out a memory card to make room for a modem card.

This bus also supports solid-state disk drives in the form of flash ROM or SRAM boards. The flash ROM boards are especially interesting, because they provide the same access speeds as regular memory with the permanence of other long-term storage media such as hard drives. Unlike SRAM boards, flash ROM boards don't require battery backup. Many people use solid-state drives to store applications or databases that change infrequently. This frees up precious space on the internal hard disk for data and applications that the user needs to access on a continuous basis.

Unfortunately, the PCMCIA bus also creates a problem for people who use it. Imagine, if you will, the reaction of Windows 3.x to the user taking a card out of the system and replacing it with another. The user will definitely see the difference right after rebooting the machine. Every time you plug in a new card type, you need to reconfigure your system to accept it. (Of course, this doesn't necessarily apply to exchanging one hard disk, or another like card, for another.) Configuration programs make this really neat feature a real pain to implement under Windows 3.x. Of course, some vendors provide utility programs to make the change easier, but this still doesn't change the way Windows itself operates. It also can't make up for deficiencies in DOS. The operating system must provide dynamic loading and unloading of device drivers to make the system as user-friendly as possible.

PNP changes all this. No longer do PCMCIA bus users need to reconfigure their systems when a component changes. Windows 95 is designed to detect system changes and make the appropriate modifications to its setup. However, this flexibility comes at a price. Users must disable their PCMCIA-specific utilities and allow Windows to manage the bus. The bus vendor must also provide the 32-bit drivers needed under Windows 95 (unless your bus already appears in the Windows 95 support list). Doing this enables the PCMCIA enhanced mode. So, what does enhanced support buy you? The following list provides an overview of enhanced support features.

- Friendly device names: This feature provides users with device names they can recognize. Instead of the more familiar XYZ.VXD, the user will see something like Flash ROM Driver. It also helps the user determine which devices are actually present and which ones are disconnected.

- Automatic installation: The automatic installation feature allows the user to hot swap various devices in and out of the PCMCIA slot without worrying about reconfiguring the machine.

- Drive change detection: In some situations, the user will have to unmount and then mount a PCMCIA drive before Windows 95 will recognize the change if enhanced support is disabled.

- Other device-specific mode and configuration information: Each PCMCIA card vendor implements special features for their device. Check the documentation that comes with the device for further details.

In most cases, Windows 95 automatically enables enhanced mode, but it won't do so if you have any real-mode PCMCIA drivers loaded. Fortunately, it's very easy to see if Windows 95 enabled enhanced mode on your machine. Right-click on My Computer and select the Properties option to open the System dialog. Click on the Performance tab to display the dialog shown in Figure 21.1.

Figure 21.1.
The Performance tab helps
you optimize system
performance. It displays all
performance bottlenecks,
including PCMCIA status.

If your dialog box looks like the one in Figure 21.1, Windows 95 hasn't enabled enhanced support. The first method you should use to try to correct the problem is to click on the Details pushbutton. This displays the help dialog shown in Figure 21.2.

Figure 21.2.
This help dialog provides a
button that enables
PCMCIA 32-bit support.

Notice the button that enables 32-bit PCMCIA support. If you click on it, you'll see PCMCIA Wizard, shown in Figure 21.3. Windows 95 will attempt to help you enable 32-bit support. All you need to do is follow the prompts to diagnose any problems that Windows can detect. However, sometimes this attempt will fail. The following paragraphs provide some troubleshooting tips.

Figure 21.3.
Use the PCMCIA Wizard to help you diagnose problems with your installation or with the bus itself.

- The most common problem associated with enabling enhanced support is that there are PCMCIA device drivers in CONFIG.SYS or TSRs in AUTOEXEC.BAT. Removing these entries should fix the problem.
- Windows 95 normally tells you if there is an I/O port address or interrupt conflict, but you should check the settings under the Resources tab of the PCIC (peripheral connect interface card) or compatible PCMCIA controller Properties dialog, shown in Figure 21.4, to make sure. (To open this dialog, simply right-click on My Computer, select the Properties option from the context menu, and select the Device Manager tab of the System Properties dialog.) Any conflicting devices appear in the Conflicting device list field near the bottom of the dialog.

Figure 21.4.
The Resources tab of the PCIC or compatible PCMCIA controller Properties dialog box alerts you to any conflicting devices.

- Always install a card in the slot while booting. Failure to do so could prevent Windows 95 from detecting the PCMCIA card slot.
- Make sure Windows 95 supports your card by checking it with the Hardware Installation Wizard in Control Panel. (You can browse through the list of hardware presented on the second screen and then click on Cancel to exit the utility without installing anything.)

Even if Windows 95 doesn't support your PCMCIA slot, you can still use it by installing real-mode drivers. Of course, using real-mode drivers means that you won't gain any benefit from the PNP features. It always makes sense to contact the bus vendor to see if a 32-bit driver is available.

Hot Docking

Remember at the beginning of this chapter when I mentioned that Windows 95 had a solution to your docking problems? A PNP feature called hot docking allows you to remove a portable computer from its docking station without turning it off. The portable will automatically reconfigure itself to reflect the loss of docking station capability. Plug that portable back into the original docking station, or a new one somewhere else, and it will automatically reconfigure itself to take advantage of the new capabilities that the docking station provides.

> **Tip:** It isn't always the best idea to move your computer with the power on. Sure, it can save you a little time when you perform a setup, but unless you're right in the middle of something that you spent hours setting up, it's usually better to shut down and turn the power off before you remove the computer from its docking station. There are a number of ways you could create surges or other electrical interference that could shorten the life of your machine by moving it with the power on. For example, you could accidentally short something out when removing the notebook from its docking station. Moving your machine from place to place without turning it off is OK—it's a supported feature—but you need to consider the cost of exercising that option.

Hot Swapping

Another problem that we talked about at the beginning of this chapter was the ability to take one card out of the PCMCIA slot and plug another in its place. PNP answers the call here as well. A PNP-compatible system will reconfigure itself dynamically. You might have seen advertisements for portables that provide a capability called hot swapping. This is really a component of the PNP specification. Hot swapping allows you to remove components from a machine without rebooting it. For example, what if you had a modem card in your PCMCIA slot and needed to exchange it for a network card? Currently, you would need to turn the machine off, exchange the cards, and reboot. Of course, you'd also need to remove any modem-specific device drivers or TSRs and add the network card software.

> **Warning:** Never touch the contacts of your PCMCIA cards when you remove them from the bus. Doing so could give the card a static electric shock that will damage it or shorten its life.

Hot swapping allows you to take the card out and put the new one in without turning the machine off. The computer automatically recognizes that it can no longer communicate with your favorite BBS, but that the network lines are now open. The PNP component of Windows 95 even installs the required drivers and configures them for you in the background. This means that users no longer need to worry about how a device works; they only need to think about what work they need the device to perform. (The only exception to this rule is when Windows 95 can't find the required drivers on your hard disk. It will ask you to supply a disk containing the required drivers.)

Windows 95 Mobile Computing Services

What PCMCIA doesn't do to make life for a notebook user easier, some of the new utility programs provided with Windows 95 do. Microsoft went a long way toward meeting the needs of notebook computer users with the release of Windows 95. I'd like to say that they went all the way, but that wouldn't quite be true. Windows 95 started out with a lot fuller feature set, but some features got dropped and others moved to the Microsoft Plus! offering. Still, Windows 95 is miles ahead of where Windows 3.x was. It provides what I would call the very basics needed to make Windows 95 notebook-computer-friendly. Communication is the key feature that Windows 95 provides for the notebook computer user. We discussed most of these features in Chapter 19. However, you'll find other features equally impressive.

So, what are these features I keep talking about? One of them is the Briefcase, which I'll describe next. I wouldn't call this a feature exclusive to mobile computer users, though. I've even used it to send files to other people across the network. You don't always have to follow to the letter Microsoft's suggested uses for a utility; there is a lot of potential in a utility like Briefcase. Experiment to see where it will work best. Sometimes I use Briefcase in place of folders because of its ability to update files for you (something else that we'll look at later). Other times this feature gets in the way, so I use folders to move data around instead.

I'll also take another look at Dial-Up Networking in this section, but from a notebook computer user's point of view. We'll take a look at some of the ways you can get around potential problems using this new feature to communicate on the road. Fortunately, we already covered all the usage basics in Chapter 19, so you can skip this section if you really don't foresee a need to use Dial-Up Networking on your next business trip.

Briefcase

Windows 95 includes a Briefcase. Like its physical counterpart, you use the Windows Briefcase to store files that you need to move from place to place. Of course, a physical briefcase uses paper as its storage media, while the Windows Briefcase uses electronic media. The Briefcase sits on the Desktop, along with the Recycle Bin and My Computer.

Setting your Briefcase up is very easy. All you need to do is install the Windows software (it's optional), and a Briefcase icon will appear on the Desktop. Stuff the Briefcase with files that you plan to move from place to place. What you should get is a centralized storage location for all the files you work on, even if those files appear in different areas of your hard drive. (For that matter, they could appear on a network drive.)

Working with Briefcase files is no different from working with any other file. Windows 95 monitors the status of the files and presents a display of their status when you open the Briefcase icon, as shown in Figure 21.5. Notice that it tells you when your Briefcase requires an update to keep it up-to-date with the files on your machine. All you need to do is select the Briefcase | Update All command if the files are out of date. Once the files are up-to-date, you can move the briefcase from your machine to a network drive or floppy.

Figure 21.5.
Briefcase offers a fast and convenient method of centralizing your files. It also provides the means to move those files from work to home and back with a minimum of fuss.

Briefcase also provides a context menu for each of its files, just like the context menus you're used to seeing in Explorer. It also provides a Document Properties dialog, shown in Figure 21.6. The General, Summary, and Statistics pages all look like the ones that you'd see in a standard document.

The one change you'll notice is the addition of an Update Status page (see Figure 21.7). This page provides you with quite a bit of information about the document in your Briefcase versus the one on your drive. It also provides some options that you wouldn't normally get from the menu. The middle of the page shows the current document status—which document has been updated and when you made the changes.

There's an interesting feature in the information box. It looks like an ordinary information box. All it tells you is that the original document has a newer date than the one in the Briefcase. However, if you click on the Replace icon in the middle of these two entries, you'll see the context menu shown in Figure 21.8. The interesting thing about this menu is that you can choose to replace your updated document with the original in your Briefcase.

Figure 21.6.
A Briefcase file provides a standard Document Properties dialog that looks similar to the ones in Explorer.

Figure 21.7.
The Update Status page shows you the current document status and gives you the ability to update the file.

Figure 21.8.
The Replace context menu item is a hidden extra that Briefcase provides.

How many times have you wished that you had a copy of your original file when the changes you made didn't quite fit? Wouldn't it be nice if you could restore the document to its original form without resorting to a backup tape? Using this feature will help. If you keep your Briefcase up to date, you can always restore an original copy of a document after you change it. This safety feature comes in handy when a few hours of editing just don't turn out as you anticipated. Notice that this list has a third entry. You can choose to skip an update. Just select the Skip option and close the dialog. This allows you to use automatic updating for all your other files and still retain the original version of this particular file.

Tip: You can use Briefcase as a rudimentary version control system. Here's how it works. Create a new Briefcase as you reach each new milestone in a project. Change the name of the Briefcase to match the milestone's name or date. Place a copy of all the files in the Briefcase, but never update it. What you should end up with is a bunch of Briefcases, each one representing a stage of your project. Even though this technique does consume a lot of hard drive space, it could also save you a lot of rework time later.

The three buttons in the Document Properties dialog allow you to manipulate the link you've created. The Update button updates your linked copy to match the original document (or just the opposite). The direction of the update depends on which way the Replace arrow is pointing in the information box. Briefcase uses a default of updating whichever document is older than the original. The Split From Original pushbutton allows you to separate the copy from the original. This comes in handy if you decide to make a new document out of the original in your briefcase. The Find Original button opens a copy of Explorer with the original document highlighted. You can use this button to quickly find a document in the Briefcase. I found it strange that this particular button doesn't appear on the context menu; you must access it using the Properties dialog.

Moving your Briefcase from work to home is just as easy as using it. Just stick a floppy in one of your drives and right-click on the Briefcase icon. You should see a display similar to the one in Figure 21.9. Notice that you can update the Briefcase from here as well; you don't have to open it up if you don't want to. To move the Briefcase from your machine to a floppy, just select the Send To menu option and choose a location. The Briefcase icon will disappear from the Desktop and reappear on the floppy. Moving it back to your Desktop the next day is just as easy. Just select the floppy drive in Explorer so that you can see the Briefcase icon. Then right-click on it and drag it to the Desktop. When Windows displays a menu asking what you want to do, click on Move. That's all there is to it! So what happens if you lose your Briefcase? You can create a new Briefcase by right-clicking on the Desktop and selecting New from the context menu. One of the new items you can create is the Briefcase.

Figure 21.9.
*The Briefcase context menu
provides access to some, but
not all, of Briefcase's
features.*

Tip: Here's a tip for you if you have a bulging Briefcase. You can compress the floppies used to transport information from one machine to another. Use the Drivespace utility to do this. Compressing the floppy will nearly double its carrying capacity, especially when you consider that most people carry data files, not the executable files required to edit them. Data files normally contain a lot of empty space that compression programs can squeeze out.

Synchronizing Files

Keeping the files on your notebook computer in sync with your desktop system isn't just a nicety, it's a necessity. Taking work home is one thing, but making sure those changes get into the final document is something else. The easiest way to keep your files in sync is to use the same machine as both notebook and desktop machine. Of course, that isn't always practical. Your desktop machine might provide features that you can't get from the notebook, or maybe you simply like using the Desktop better.

Before Windows 95, the notebook user had only two choices when keeping the files in two or more machines in sync. One method was to keep all the mobile data on a floppy. All you needed to do was pass the floppy around as needed to keep the files in sync. This easy solution also had a pretty significant problem. A floppy's access speed isn't very good, and its storage capacity is very limited when compared to a hard drive. Suffice it to say that this wasn't the best way to go.

Another solution was to copy the files from your hard drive to a floppy and then back again. This had the advantage of using the best possible speed for opening and using the files. The big disadvantage was that it relied on the person's memory to make sure the files were kept in sync.

Using the Briefcase option in Windows 95 is a big step forward for notebook users. It has one of the characteristics of floppy-based synchronization. You just move the Briefcase around as needed. It also provides the advantage of the file copying method. Every application makes use of the hard drive's enhanced access speed when you open and edit files.

Is Briefcase the only Windows 95 solution? Probably not. I've also used the folder concept that I've talked about in various places in this book. It allows a group to keep one set of files on a central machine in sync. But how do you use this feature if you're working on a document at home? That's where Dial-Up Networking comes into play. Instead of simply moving a Briefcase around, you can use Dial-Up Networking to call into the network and edit the files remotely. That way, even though you're working on the file from another location, your team can continue updating it as well.

Tip: Using the combination of folders and Dial-Up Networking is ideal if you're a team supervisor. It allows you to continue your work on the documentation that the team is preparing while you're on the road without resorting to the Briefcase. Even if you're currently working on the documents alone, there could be an occasion in which a team member needs them as well. Using the Briefcase means that the folks at home won't know if they're using the current documents. There's never a good reason to slow the team's progress on a project because you need to work on it while on the road. Using this combination also allows you to monitor the team's progress. Checking in each day to see the work they've accomplished will help you keep an eye on things back home while you're on the road.

 # Remote Dial-Up (Dial-Up Networking)

We talked about the mechanics of using Dial-Up Networking in Chapter 19, so I won't go through that process here. However, once you do get the software installed and configured, where do you go from there? If you're a notebook user, there are plenty of reasons to use this particular Windows 95 feature.

- Document access: I've already mentioned how you can use Dial-Up Networking to enable an entire group of people to work together. All you need to do is place a folder with shortcuts to the team's documents in a folder on the network. When a person calls into the network, he can open the folder and see all the pieces of the project without looking very hard for them. I often place this folder in the user's home directory on the network. That way, I can personalize each folder as required, and the user doesn't need to memorize yet another location on the network.

- Application access: You won't need to access applications such as word processors or spreadsheets from a remote location (at least not very often). But what about the custom database that your company uses as a contact manager? Unless you plan to either print the entire database or create a copy of it on your notebook's hard drive, you'll need to access it remotely. In fact, this is probably the only way you could use this centralized application if it contains sales or inventory information that you'll need to update later.

- E-mail: It's surprising just how much a company depends on e-mail to keep employees apprised of events. Think about the e-mail messages that you receive that talk about marriages and new babies—as well as company-specific events such as getting a new access code for the security system or updating your W-2 form. Losing this communication means that you'll be out-of-touch when you return from your trip. A few minutes of online time could keep you up-to-date on current situations in your company and reduce that "vacation" syndrome that many people feel after a road trip.

- Emergency decisions: What if you're traveling in Europe and your company's in California? How do you find a good time to call them up and make a decision that requires a 24-hour turnaround? The old way of doing things was waiting up until the wee hours of the morning and calling your company during normal business hours. Either that or waking someone up at home. Using the company or an online service e-mail to leave a message, then checking for responses later, could give you those few extra hours of sleep at night. After all, who wants to fight politics and sleepiness at the same time?

- Missing-file syndrome: Notebooks almost always need at least twice as much hard disk space as they really have. How often have you cleared a bunch of files off your notebook only to find that you really needed them after all? If you're on the road, it's usually too late to regain access to those files, and you have to figure out a way to do without them. Or do you? A remote connection can let you grab some files that you didn't think you'd need. Placing a copy of your Desktop machine's hard drive—or at least the data—where you can access it using a remote connection will save you a lot of trouble later. Make sure you ask the network administrator's permission before you do this, though.

These are just some of the common ways you can use Dial-Up Networking with a notebook. You'll need to find the specialty technique that applies to your specific situation. For example, in my particular case, I find it handy to use Dial-Up Networking to grab presentations. I have room for only one or two on my notebook at a time, but I might need several during the time I'm on the road. Using this feature allows me to call in and grab the next presentation in line. The result is that each presentation is fresh and specifically designed for the group I'm talking with, yet I don't have to lug around a monster-sized hard drive or other storage.

Remote Network Users

Networking is an essential part of any business today. I've already talked about Dial-Up Networking to an extent, but let's take a look at some of the communication and other considerations you'll need to make. Using Dial-Up Networking is one thing; using it efficiently is another.

I'd like to begin by providing a little insight into one of the problems with using Dial-Up Networking. Most people know that the telephone company charges more for the first three minutes of a long distance call than they do for the time that follows. People try to keep their long distance calls short and to the point. The telephone company capitalizes on this by charging you more when you make several short calls instead of one long one.

Given this set of circumstances, imagine the cost differential of making one long computer call as compared to a whole bunch of short ones. It's very easy to get into the habit of dialing the company every time you need a bit of information. Consolidating all your information needs into one call is better than making several short ones. In Chapter 20 we covered the method of dialing after hours using Exchange. You can save a lot of money by delivering all your mail during off-peak hours.

There are still times where it's impossible to take care of all your communication needs at one time. You'll still find the need to make a few short calls during the day to gather information. However, you don't have to do that for message delivery. Delivering responses to e-mail and performing other chores can always wait for off-peak hours, especially when you're overseas and the people who wrote the message won't see it until after you're in bed anyway.

The following sections describe some of the other methods you can use to reduce the cost of Dial-Up Networking. Although these techniques won't always work because your need for data exchange with another party is immediate, they'll work in the majority of cases.

Local Communications

There are many forms of long distance communication, and some of them are local. Here's one scenario. You're in Detroit and your company is in Los Angeles. It's important that you send a file containing some new information about your client to an assistant for processing. You also need some additional information about another client that's stored in your company database. You have access to both Dial-Up Networking and CompuServe. Which do you use? Some people would use Dial-Up Networking because it's faster and more convenient, but the low-cost solution would be CompuServe in this case.

Note: Even though I talk specifically about CompuServe in this section, the same principle applies to other online services. You can use many of them by making a local call and paying a small fee for transferring large files. Make sure you compare the rates of the various online services if you subscribe to more than one. Some services might charge less than others for specific types of file transfer.

Making a local phone call to CompuServe is just as fast as transferring that file over the company e-mail, and it'll cost you a lot less. CompuServe requires only a local call and perhaps a few cents for an upload charge. For example, I recently uploaded a 600 KB file for about $1.80. That's a lot less than a long distance call would have been.

However, sometimes the obvious choice isn't the one you should use. For example, suppose you need to transfer the same files and get the same information. The difference is that this time you're in another part of the state instead of another part of the country. It'll only cost about 40 cents to make the toll call to your company, so using Dial-Up Networking is the right choice. CompuServe adds a surcharge to some types of billing systems, but not to others. You should check the CompuServe rate against the toll charge to see which one is better.

Tip: Once you determine a local rate, write it down for future reference. Keeping a rate sheet for the places you frequent will save you from having to look up the information more than once. Most communication programs provide some method of determining your CompuServe rate. All you need to do is look at the long distance rate versus the CompuServe rate.

If your company has its own Internet address, you might be able to use it to transfer information using a local call. Of course, you'll need an account with a local provider to make this work. As with the other suggestions in this section, you'll want to check the cost of using an Internet solution against that of making a long distance call.

Dynamic Networking

Despite your best efforts, you'll run into times when you need to work with the company database or other applications live. You can't solve every problem with e-mail or a file upload. There are times when working with live applications or data is the only way to get the job done. You'll want to keep these times to a minimum, but keeping a local database management system (DBMS) current might override other cost considerations. Even if this is the situation your company is in, you don't need to pay through the nose to get the kind of service you need. Your notebook still has a few tricks up its sleeve to solve the problem. The following list provides some of the ideas I've come up with, but you can probably think of others based on your unique set of circumstances.

> **Tip:** If you're using a custom DBMS, it might be possible to add batch updating capability to it. This would allow you to use a smaller version of the application on the road, create new records, modify existing ones, and make all the changes in batch mode when you returned from your trip or as part of an upload to the company database. This is a less expensive solution for inventory control or other types of sales databases than making the changes live in many cases. There are two criteria for using a batch system: You need a fairly large outside sales force to make the change cost efficient, and the company must be able to get by with daily or weekly database updates instead of real-time data. This would work in most situations, but you couldn't use it for something like an airline ticket database.

- Internet access: Using the Internet still might provide the best means of working with live data. You'll need to overcome two problems. The first is gaining access to a local server that allows live connections. The second is that you'll have to make a TCP/IP connection and use a special modem to make this work. Both problems can be solved given enough resources.

- Using a local office's PBX connection: Sometimes a local office will provide the long distance call solution you need. It might mean a little wrangling with the local boss and perhaps a short drive, but this solution could save your company some money.

- Keeping notes: Even if your database doesn't support batch mode processing, you could still keep notes and make all the updates at one time. This would allow you to make one phone call instead of many to record the required information. Of course, this solution still won't work with "live" data such as ticket sales and the like.

- Off-hour calling: This is probably the least likely solution. If your data needs are so time-critical that you can't afford to wait even a few minutes, off-hour calling won't work. However, you could combine this technique with batch mode or note-taking methods to work with live data on the network. You could even use this off-hour calling technique when using a local office's PBX connection. This would reduce the local boss's objection to tying up the line in order to service your needs.

Offline Printing

Remember in Chapter 14 when I covered printing? I talked about two techniques that the notebook computer user will love. The first is the idea of creating a printer for every purpose. You can create printers for all the local offices you will visit during a trip. That way, you can print any notes or documents you need without worrying about whether you have the proper print driver to get the job done. You can also use this technique to print at client sites that are amenable to your doing so.

However, that isn't the only way you can print. You can also print to your hard drive using the offline printing technique we looked at in Chapter 14. All you need to do is set the printer to work offline. Everything you send to disk will wait on the hard drive until you send it to the printer.

What I didn't include in that chapter was something notebook-specific. Whenever you disconnect your notebook from the network printer or docking station, Windows 95 detects the loss of printing capability and sets the printer to work offline automatically. Unfortunately, this doesn't work all the time. I experienced a few situations in which the printer disconnection wasn't detected. Either way, detection was consistent. Check your printer the first time, and you should be able to rely on the connection being consistent from that point on.

On Your Own

This chapter presented a lot of different ideas on how a notebook user can use the capabilities provided by Windows 95 to improve productivity. Of course, one of the big things we covered was the use of the PCMCIA interface. If you have a PCMCIA bus on your notebook computer, right-click on My Computer and select the Properties option. Click on the Performance tab to see if your system is fully optimized. Make sure you double-check the bus.

Another productivity enhancement is the combination of Briefcase and Dial-Up Networking. Try splitting your projects into two categories: those that you're working on alone, and those that you're working on with a group. Try using the Briefcase method with the projects that you're working on alone. Use the folder and Dial-Up Networking combination for projects that you're working on in a group.

Make a list of the ways you can use Dial-Up Networking to improve your productivity. I mentioned the most common ways in this chapter, but your company might have special needs that I didn't cover. It's important to use a little creativity when thinking about the ways Windows 95 can help you. This is one way to do it. Keep the list handy for later and refer to it when you're looking for ways to solve a particular mobile computing problem.

V

Troubleshooting Windows 95

22

Software Problems

It would be nice to say that Windows 95 takes care of every problem and that you'll never experience any kind of software error ever again, but that wouldn't be reality. Windows 95 does provide a level of safety you've probably never seen before. It certainly isn't as safe as Windows NT, but it's a lot better than Windows 3.x.

When you look at Windows 95, you're seeing a middle ground of reliability, not the best there is. Microsoft had to make some concessions to allow all the products you used under Windows 3.x to run under Windows 95 as well. In addition, there was a problem with getting enough security in a package that also runs under 4 MB of RAM. (Of course, even though Windows 95 will probably start with 4 MB, we've already discussed the practical recommendations for RAM.)

So how do these limitations affect you? First, you'll still have problems with GPFs. Windows NT provides a very strict environment for sensing programs that make illegal calls and recovers from them by terminating the offending application. This won't quite work with some applications that depend on those illegal calls to run. The result is that you'll experience some GPFs because Windows 95 relaxes the rules to allow more applications to run—even those that aren't necessarily good citizens.

Another problem occurs with DOS support. Just like any Windows environment, when your application switches to real mode to run, the operating system is vulnerable to attack. Windows NT handles this problem for the most part by implementing a strict set of rules. As with the Windows applications, Windows 95 relaxes these rules so that more applications can run. The result is that an errant application can crash the system.

Fortunately, you'll still notice a superior level of support from Windows 95. It recovers from a great many more problems than Windows 3.x will. In addition, the more 32-bit applications you use, the less your chance of having the system crash.

I've been testing Windows 95 pretty thoroughly over the course of writing this book. I've changed the registry and tested what will and won't work. Setup has also gotten a good workout as I've added and removed applications. I even changed the network setup quite a few times to test different configurations. If Windows 95 ever had a good reason to crash, it was while I kept changing its configuration. During this time I've experienced less than one system crash per day. That's pretty good considering what I put Windows 95 through. Of course, it would have been better if the record were perfect, but you'd need something a little more robust in the protection area, such as Windows NT, to accomplish that.

The bottom line? You don't get anything for free. That applies to operating systems as well. People don't want an operating system that places their applications in a straitjacket and forces them to buy new ones. They want something that will run their old stuff well and their new stuff even better. That's what Windows 95 provides, but it comes at the cost of system stability.

This chapter covers from a software perspective some of the problems you'll experience. I'll also tell you about some of the fixes Microsoft provides to alleviate them. Will these fixes always work?

Probably not. During one incident I had to actually reinstall Windows 95 and all the applications I use because the registry got trashed beyond recognition. An application decided to overwrite some files that would have been fine under Windows 3.x but not under Windows 95. Suffice it to say that you'll experience fewer problems under Windows 95 and that the cures Microsoft provides work most of the time, but thinking that they'll cure every problem just isn't realistic.

Startup and Configuration Errors

Configuration problems normally manifest themselves in several ways. The most devastating is during system startup. Have you ever seen the infamous blue screen? If you reconfigure your machine as often as I do, you're definitely going to see it.

The other types of configuration problems are a lot more devious. They usually rob your system of its flexibility or make some of its components unusable. You might find yourself running in circles trying to identify the culprit, only to find that it wasn't any of the things you suspected at all. One of the problems I found in this category was my sound board. I couldn't figure out what was wrong. The Midi Balance setting kept getting out of whack. I looked at the driver—no luck. The same held true with the hardware itself. I thought there might be a problem in the way that the CD software was working, so I disabled it. No luck there either. After several days of searching, I found that the problem occurred only when I ran a specific version of After Dark. Problems such as these can really make you want to pull your hair out.

Don't get the idea that configuration problems are always obvious. It's pretty easy to figure out when your sound board isn't working correctly—especially with my previous problems. Even my neighbors knew I had a problem with my sound board. But what about the problem I was having with another application? It would work just fine—at least just fine on most days. What would happen on the other days is almost indescribable. My machine would make a strange noise, the screen would look funny, and then the system would reboot. I couldn't figure out what was going on. The solution to this problem turned out to be a Control Panel setup problem. One of my applications had overwritten the standard ODBC files. The new files were incompatible with this application in certain low-memory situations. I discovered that the problem always occurred when I had my word processor or any other large application open.

Tip: I could've had a lot less grief fixing the ODBC file problem if I'd recorded the time stamp for the files in that section or at least made note of the time stamp for my Windows 95 files. You can do the same thing. Throughout this book I've made every effort to tell you which files affect what functions. You can use this information when you're troubleshooting. It also comes in handy when you're recording information for a setup that works. When you get into a situation where the setup no longer works properly, one of the things you can do is go back to your notes to find a potential source of trouble.

If you have plenty of disk space, you can give yourself a measure of security against this sort of problem. Just before you install a new program or a piece of hardware, make a zip file (a compressed archive) of all the files in your Windows and Windows system directories. If anything goes wrong, you can compare the files in those directories with what they used to be back when your system was working OK. If you can't afford to use that much disk space, zip up just your .INI files (and also your CONFIG.SYS and AUTOEXEC.BAT files) and then use the DIR command redirected to a file (DIR > *filename*) to save at least that much information about how things were. This won't prevent the problems or even give you copies of the files as they used to be, but at least you'll know which ones were changed. Sometimes that helps point you toward the proper steps to recover from a problem.

As you can tell, I've had lots of fun digging up these real-life problems for you to learn about. The next few sections describe some of the types of problems that you'll run into when your machine's configuration gets out of whack. I'll also provide you with some ideas on how to fix these problems.

Startup Problems

Startup problems are the very worst kind of configuration problem to fix because you can't use the tools that Windows 95 provides to find them very easily. What usually happens is that the settings for one or more devices conflict, get lost, or are somehow incompatible with the device you're using. When a device conflict affects the display adapter or your hard drive, you see a blue screen. This blue screen means that Windows 95 can't recover from this sort of problem.

So how do you get around this? The best way is to start the machine in fail safe mode. This mode starts your machine with the bare minimum of devices installed. That should get rid of the majority of your problems. The only two devices that you really must have in order to start Windows 95 are the display adapter and the hard drive. It's extremely unlikely that these two devices will have any conflicts. Windows also uses a generic VGA display driver. This will get rid of the rest of your problems. Even if your display driver is somehow corrupted or you've used the wrong settings, the generic VGA display driver will work. Figure 22.1 shows a machine in fail safe mode. Notice that you'll always know when you're in this mode because "Safe mode" appears in all four corners of the screen.

There are two ways to get into this mode. The first is automatic. When Windows 95 detects a problem in booting, it automatically sets the machine up to reboot in fail safe mode. Of course, that depends on Windows 95's actually detecting the problem. Sometimes it doesn't. For example, if you make it most of the way through the boot process, Windows 95 might not detect a startup problem. The most difficult situation to detect is a sound board problem. The system is most or all of the way through the boot sequence before a sound board problem occurs. If Windows fails to detect the startup problem, use the manual startup method. You can force a manual fail safe mode boot by pressing the F8 key when you boot your machine. Normally, pressing F8 displays a menu. This menu will have one or more entries for fail safe mode. The following is a complete list of the items you can expect to find on the boot menu.

Figure 22.1.
It's easy to see when you're in fail safe mode.

- Normal: Allows you to boot the machine normally. The only reason you would need this entry is if you pressed F8 by accident during the boot process.

- Logged (\BOOTLOG.TXT): We've discussed this particular feature before. You can use the contents of BOOTLOG.TXT to determine precisely where the boot sequence is failing. Of course, it takes a little time to analyze the contents of the files, so you should rely on this as one of the later troubleshooting methods. The advantage of this method is that it gives you the best picture of exactly what's going on during the boot process.

- Safe mode: This is the entry you would normally select to find boot problems. It starts your machine with the minimum number of devices enabled. Windows 95 doesn't process the contents of CONFIG.SYS or AUTOEXEC.BAT. None of your Startup folder entries will get processed either.

- Safe mode with network support: Use this entry if safe mode startup doesn't really tell you where the problem is and you suspect your network card. Always use this startup after you try safe mode; otherwise, you can't be certain that the failure isn't being hidden by something else. For example, I had a conflict with my COM port. The fault showed up as a mouse not responding. The COM port didn't show any errors at all. If I hadn't taken the time to really look at what was going on, I could have missed the conflict and replaced my mouse, thinking it had finally bitten the dust.

- Step-by-step confirmation: If you must use real-mode drivers, this option will allow you to find a real-mode driver conflict. You can restart your machine several times, excluding a different driver each time, until you find the one that's causing problems with your Windows setup. Of course, the best way to get rid of these types of conflicts is to get rid of the real-mode drivers so that Windows can help configure your machine.

- Command prompt only: Use this option if you need to get to the command prompt to check something out. It does process your CONFIG.SYS and AUTOEXEC.BAT entries, so any real-mode drivers you need will get loaded. This is a great setting to use if you need to install an older DOS application that insists on not having anything else loaded. I also found it handy when installing the NetWare client software.

- Safe mode command prompt only: I find this setting handy if I need to get to the DOS 7.0 prompt for some reason. For example, if a CONFIG.SYS or AUTOEXEC.BAT entry is causing problems, I can get to the DOS prompt, make any required modifications, and reboot the machine. Windows 95 boots to a DOS prompt without processing either CONFIG.SYS or AUTOEXEC.BAT when you select this option.

- Previous version of MS-DOS: You'll see this option only if you include the `BootMulti=1` setting in MSDOS.SYS. It allows you to boot the previous version of DOS. Of course, this assumes that your previous version of DOS is still available. Removing the previous version should disable this feature. Also remember that some types of installations will also remove your ability to boot your old version of DOS.

Note: Some MSDOS.SYS settings disable the user's ability to use the F8 key. A network administrator could use this setting to prevent users from circumventing network security. If this happens, you'll need to use your startup disk to start the machine from a floppy. Go to the hard drive and edit the MSDOS.SYS file using the settings I described in Table 6.3.

Tip: Several other boot modes are available on the F8 boot menu. One of them allows you to boot into MS-DOS mode. This comes in handy if you need to access a diagnostic program to locate a problem. You can also select which CONFIG.SYS and AUTOEXEC.BAT entries get executed (this works the same as the F8 feature under DOS). You can use this feature to find a real-mode driver or a TSR that might be preventing your system from booting.

Once you get your machine booted in fail safe mode, start looking for hardware or software conflicts. You might want to begin by removing all the applications and data files from your Startup folder. Also check WIN.INI to make sure that there are no LOAD= or RUN= lines in it. Go ahead and comment out any lines you do find so that the application won't run the next time you start Windows. After you make sure all the conflicts are resolved, start your machine again.

Hardware Configuration Problems

Hardware-specific configuration problems are fairly easy to find because Windows makes most of them pretty obvious. All you need to do is right-click on the My Computer icon. Look at the Device Manager page of the System Properties dialog to see if there are any conflicts. We covered the ways of using this dialog in Chapter 13. You'll need to look for conflicting devices and change their settings as required. Windows 95 will display the conflicting device, as shown in Figure 22.2.

Figure 22.2.

Hardware conflicts that Windows 95 can detect are pretty easy to find.

In most cases you can figure out the cause of the conflict by looking at the Resources page, shown in Figure 22.3. Notice that this particular page lists two conflicts, but there could just as easily be three or even four conflicting devices. You'll need to clear the ones that Windows 95 detected the first time around to see if there are others.

Figure 22.3.

IRQ conflicts are the most common hardware configuration problem.

The problem with some hardware conflicts is that you might not see them immediately. For example, if Windows 95 doesn't manage a particular device, it might not know that a conflict exists. Any device that requires a real-mode device driver to operate generally falls into this category. What this means is that you'll need to find the configuration problem by scanning through the documentation that came with all the pieces of hardware in your system, looking for what DMA channels, IRQ lines, and port addresses they use. Then you'll have to manually set them to nonconflicting values.

Another problem could occur if Windows 95 provides a generic driver for a specific device and the vendor introduces a version of that device that conflicts with the driver. For example, there's only one driver for the Pro Audio Spectrum 16 Plus sound card, but there are four revisions of that board and even more of that driver. The revision that you use could make a difference in how compatible the device driver and board really are.

Even more problematic is if you think you disabled a device feature but really didn't. Take another look at that Pro Audio Spectrum sound board. It includes a game port that really doesn't work all that well on high-speed machines. You might disable the game port and use those same settings for an adjustable game port. What happens, though, if the driver fails to do its job properly? I actually ran into this problem. The only solution was to reinstall the driver, but I was probably lucky in this case. Even if Windows thinks it has disabled a specific feature, you might want to view it as a potential area of conflict.

Windows Software Configuration Problems

There are many ways that a Windows application configuration can go wrong. For example, I recently installed an older 16-bit application that required Program Manager in order to install properly. For whatever reason, the Setup application didn't signal its need for Program Manager, and I thought the installation was a success.

Quite the contrary. The setup program had actually quit before it completed the installation, so I was missing an important .INI file. The result was a piece of software that kept freezing my machine. I fixed the problem by reinstalling the software with Program Manager running. The moral of the story is to always install 16-bit Windows applications with Program Manager running. That way, you'll avoid any problems. Even if the application doesn't actually need Program Manager, you won't lose anything by running it.

There are other Windows application problems as well. For example, have you ever noticed that many applications want to modify your path statement in AUTOEXEC.BAT? If you let every application have its way, you'd probably have a mile-long path. Unfortunately, there is a definite limit to how long the path can be and still work. Many applications run just fine without a path statement. However, there are two different ways in which an application can fail.

I ran across the first problem area by accident. I added the file association required for a new application I installed. Whenever I double-clicked on a data file, though, I got a message that the application couldn't find the data file. The application started just fine, but it wouldn't load the data file. After a few hours of troubleshooting, I found that I could get rid of the problem by adding the application's location to my path.

Some applications fail in a big way if you don't add them to the path statement. CA-Visual Objects and some other large applications fall into this category. They usually provide some nebulous error message and quit before you can get them going. Either that, or the application will load and then refuse to load any add-ons because it can't find them. You might see symptoms of this problem when an application refuses to maintain the settings you save from session to session. Whenever you're in doubt, try adding the application to your path statement to see if the problem goes away.

DLL, or other shared-file corruption, is another problem area. The DLL might not actually contain any bad data. It might work just fine with several other applications. However, one application might require an older version of the DLL because it uses an undocumented feature of that DLL or makes use of some bug to its advantage. Sometimes you'll need to keep the old version of a DLL on disk to satisfy the needs of a particular application.

However, what happens if one application needs the new version of the DLL and another application requires the old version? Unless one or both applications keep their own version of the shared DLL in their own separate directory (which is a regrettably uncommon practice), you must make a decision about which application to keep. In most cases, I use this situation as an excuse to upgrade my software. There usually isn't any reason to keep an old application around if it refuses to work with all your newer applications. In fact, an incompatibility of this type usually means that it really is time to retire that old application and get the newer version.

I ran into a really strange problem with one application on my machine. It was a communication program, but I imagine the same thing could happen with any application. Every time I tried to open this application, it would fill the screen and then some. I had recently lowered my screen resolution in order to capture some screen shots, but I needed to run this application quickly to download a needed file from CompuServe. No matter what I did, as soon as the main application window appeared, the machine would freeze and I'd have to reboot. This was yet another example of an application that failed because its environment wasn't set up correctly. The point I'm trying to make is that the cause of failure isn't always obvious. You usually need to spend some time looking for the potential cause of a problem. Some of these causes can lead you down blind alleys into places you thought would never fail.

DOS Software Configuration Problems

If you thought Windows software had a lot of failure points, you haven't worked with enough DOS software recently. There are some applications that you'll never get to run under any version of Windows. Most of these applications fall into the game category, but I've seen others in this situation as well.

An application that assumes it has the machine to itself, combined with users who keep asking for better performance, equals a situation in which the programmer is going to access the hardware directly in ways that the programming community as a whole would never recommend. This is precisely the situation that some game and utility program vendors get into. Users are always demanding faster games with better graphics and sound, yet they want to run these programs on very outdated hardware. The game programmers usually have to resort to register-level programming to get the speed that the user wants. Of course, this usually means that any mistake in programming, even a small one, will result in a frozen machine or worse.

Applications that fall into this category can be fixed in only one way: You have to run them in MS-DOS mode. We covered MS-DOS mode earlier, so I won't cover it again here. The thing to remember is that running an application in MS-DOS mode means that you can't allow it to interact with any of your other applications. Using MS-DOS mode is the very last alternative you should try.

If MS-DOS mode is the last resort, what should you try first? I usually look at the application settings to see if I can find and fix any potential problems. Here's one scenario. You have a game program that always freezes when you run it in Windows, but it works fine from the DOS prompt. What's the problem? I found several setting-related problems that can wreak havoc with a game. One of them is that you can't assume that the sound board settings that you use in DOS are the same ones that Windows will use. Checking all your settings is an important part of getting a DOS application to run.

There are other setting-related problems as well. For example, many of my games require that I add a Sound Blaster setting to my AUTOEXEC.BAT. They read this setting and configure themselves appropriately. If you don't include the SET statement, the game freezes because it doesn't know what settings to use.

Speaking of settings, most DOS applications are very sensitive to the environment settings. I find that compilers are the worst culprits in this area, but other applications can be quite challenging as well. It's usually a good idea to run every application that requires a complex environment setup from a batch file. Add all the required environment settings to the beginning of the batch file and make running the application the last step. You might have to change the program's environment size setting to make this work. See Chapter 12 for more details on the DOS application memory settings.

Once you get past settings and strange hardware access problems, you might face a few other problems. One of the big problems, especially when talking about games, is a lack of conventional memory. We covered this issue fairly well in Chapter 12, but it pays to mention it again. Using a memory manager probably isn't the solution you're looking for. Getting rid of unneeded TSRs and device drivers is. You can save a lot of memory by getting rid of TSRs such as DOSKey. Installing it as part of a batch file from any DOS sessions you start makes more sense. It also makes sense to get rid of ANSI.SYS since you no longer need it. Windows 95 provides this functionality for you automatically, so loading an additional device driver doesn't make sense.

Memory-Related Problems

You could have quite a few memory-related problems under Windows 95. They fall into several different categories. It's important to know which one you're dealing with before you attempt to fix it. The following list categorizes the various memory-related problems you could have when using Windows 95. Go through the list to see if you can find the symptoms that match your particular problem.

- Real-mode memory manager conflict: Some memory managers such as 386MAX and QEMM could cause problems when you're using Windows 95. The benefit of using them is a few additional kilobytes of conventional memory. Admittedly, they do a better job in this area than Windows 95 does. The problem is that you now have two very different memory managers fighting for control of the machine. The loser will always be the user. Some of the symptoms of this type of problem are a failure of Windows 95 to boot at all, a sudden freeze-up of the machine, or abnormal device problems such as errors in displaying data. If you experience this problem and your application really needs the additional conventional memory, consider creating an MS-DOS mode setup for using the memory manager with that particular application.

- Memory leaks: A few Windows applications don't manage memory properly. They grab a lot of memory from Windows, then don't release all of it when they terminate. The result is a gradual loss of memory capacity that you can actually track using the memory field of the application's Help About dialog box. You'll also notice that your other applications start to slow down after a while as the system starts using a larger swap file to make up for the memory loss. If you have an application that shows a gradual loss of memory, the best way to use it is to start it once and leave it open the entire time you need to use it. Such an application will still gradually bleed memory from the system, but the loss is more gradual if you don't open and close it very much. Eventually you will need to reboot the system.

Note: Selecting the Reboot the computer option is not sufficient. You actually need to restart the system from scratch either by using the reset button or by powering the system down and then back up again.

- Too many frills: Some types of memory problems are created when you have too many frills on your machine. For example, you might find that Access or another large application is running very slowly or could even GPF a lot after you add a screen saver or another frill to the system. Most people associate utilities with small memory requirements, but this isn't necessarily true. You'll find that many DOS applications had to stay small to keep their conventional memory requirements to a minimum. Windows utilities have no such limitation. Their designers have fewer reasons to keep their applications small because Windows is designed to allow for better memory management. As a result, I have one screen saver that actually grabs an entire megabyte on my system and more than a few percentage points of system resources as well.

- Windows system space corruption: I find it incredible that some vendors put so little effort into testing their product that this type of problem could actually go unnoticed. What usually happens is that an errant pointer in their application starts overwriting the Windows system area. Most of the time, Windows 95 detects this problem and displays an appropriate dialog. It recovers by terminating the application. On a few occasions Windows 95 won't detect the problem and will simply freeze. In most cases, you'll want to contact the vendor about this kind of problem and see if a work-around or fix is available.

- Disk thrashing: If you try to use an application that your system can't really support, you might experience something called disk thrashing. This actually happens more under Windows 95 than it did under Windows 3.x. You'll know your system is thrashing if the hard disk light stays on for abnormally long periods of time and the application runs really slowly. The only way to fix this problem is to add more memory. Of course, you could also look at some of the memory-saving techniques I discussed in Chapter 3.

- Display memory corruption: Some older Windows applications might experience problems when writing to the display. Even though they use a different method than DOS, there are situations in which a Windows application can cause problems with the entire display. One of these situations is when it changes the palette (the display colors) without regard for any other applications running on the system. You can't do much about this problem. What you'll see is that the application window will probably look fine, but everything else around it will use really strange color combinations that might produce unreadable text. The big problem occurs when an application leaves the display in this state, even after it exits. You might see other forms of display corruption as well. For example, it's possible for an application to corrupt the icon cache. What you'll see on the display is either icons that no longer match the function associated with them, or your icons might disappear altogether. The fix is to exit the application and reboot the system. Sometimes that doesn't work. If you find that the problem persists, you might have to erase the ShellIconCache file in your main Windows 95 folder and reboot the machine again. The ShellIconCache file contains an archive of the most recently used icons. Windows 95 loads this file when it starts to reduce the time it spends reading the icons from disk. Some types of corruption become embedded in this file when Windows exits with a corrupted icon cache in memory.

There are probably other ways to corrupt memory as well. For example, Windows 95 uses other cache files. Any of these caches could become corrupted and cause problems for your system. You'll need to spend some time looking for the particular cache files on your system. Besides the ShellIconCache,

I also had a ttfCache and a frmCache.dat file on my system. ttfCache affects the fonts listed in the Fonts folder. You might find that the fonts listed no longer match the fonts actually in the directory if certain types of memory corruption occur. The same holds true for the frmCache.dat file. Any type of cache corruption is easily cured by erasing the corrupted file and allowing Windows 95 to rebuild it during the next boot cycle.

Once you identify and clean up a memory corruption problem, it's usually a good idea to find the application responsible. Most memory corruption problems won't simply go away. You'll find that the corruption occurs over and over again at the very worst possible moment. After you identify the culprit, you usually have to contact the vendor to find out if a fix is available. If one isn't, you need to decide whether to live with the corruption problem or get a new application—one that hopefully doesn't exhibit the same memory corruption problem that you're trying to get rid of.

So how do you find the culprit? You can't simply assume that the culprit is the foreground application; it could be a background application. For that matter, it doesn't have to be an application at all. A device driver could be causing the memory corruption as you use a specific device. A third class of problem is some type of interaction between two applications or an application and a device driver. However, you have to start somewhere, and looking at the applications you have running is a good place to start. You can follow this simple procedure to find many, but not all, of the memory corruption problems on your system:

1. Start a list of potential problem applications. I usually make note of all the applications I had running when a memory corruption problem occurred. It's also important to make notes on any devices you had running. Of course, some devices are always running. It doesn't pay to list those.

2. Run the suspected applications one at a time to see if you can get the problem to repeat. Make sure you start Windows with a clean Startup folder and no applications loaded using WIN.INI. It's also important to reboot after each test to make sure you're starting with a clean memory environment.

3. If you still don't find the culprit, go back to your normal setup and try various combinations of applications. You could be seeing some type of interaction problem.

4. Test the various devices on your machine one at a time to eliminate any device drivers.

5. Keep a running list of active applications each time the memory problem appears. Eventually you'll see a pattern of one or more applications that are always present when the problem occurs. Try loading just this group of applications and see if you can get the problem to happen again. Keep whittling the list down until you end up with one or two applications that won't work together. The solution is to avoid running them at the same time.

6. If you don't see an application pattern emerge, the problem is definitely device-driver-oriented. Try disabling one peripheral device at a time to see if you can find the problem. Don't discount the effects of real-mode drivers on Windows; make sure you check those first.

This kind of testing is time-consuming, but if you do it right you can usually track a stubborn prob- lem down in a matter of days. Unfortunately, memory problems are incredibly difficult to locate in an environment like Windows 95 because so many different things are happening at once. Each application and device driver interact. You'll find that the hardest problems to find are those that result from three or four applications or device drivers working against each other. It always pays to take your time and do a thorough job of testing each potential problem area.

Of course, once you come to a conclusion, finding a permanent fix could prove to be the most dif- ficult part of the journey. You've probably gone through this before—the waiting on the phone as each vendor points the finger at someone else. The reality of the situation is that there might not be an easy fix for some types of memory problems. You might just have to avoid the situations that cause them in the first place, get a newer version of the same application, or even go so far as to update your hardware.

On Your Own

Reboot your machine and press F8. See which of the menu settings that we discussed in this chapter are present. If you don't see all eight options, find out why. Check your MSDOS.SYS file to make sure you can access this important feature when needed if the F8 key doesn't work. You might want to check with your network administrator regarding company policy for this particular setting.

Look at the Device Manager page of the System Properties dialog box to familiarize yourself with its contents. We discussed this feature in Chapter 13, but it's a good idea to know what this particular display can do for you. It's one of the major troubleshooting aids that Windows 95 provides.

If you have an application that you currently run in MS-DOS mode, try to find out if you could make it run under Windows. You might find that the sound board or other device settings you're using don't match those used by Windows. If there's a conflict, try changing the DOS application settings to those used by Windows to see if that will allow you to run the application normally. Also check for environment settings that could affect your ability to use the application from within Windows.

23

Hardware Problems

Hardware problems usually are less of an issue under Windows 95 (or any operating system, for that matter) than software problems. The reason is fairly easy to understand. Hardware problems usually fall into two easily recognized groups: compatibility and catastrophic.

Catastrophic errors can include subtle problems such as loss of functionality. By and large, though, you can quickly determine that a catastrophic failure has occurred because the device no longer works. You try to access a hard or floppy drive and nothing happens. Trying to use a faulty modem might mean that it picks up the phone line but refuses to dial. Figuring out the sources of these kinds of problems is easy; fixing them is even easier (albeit expensive, for the most part).

Even compatibility problems are fairly easy to fix under Windows 95. You'll probably get a symptom in which a device looks as if it failed, but later testing shows that it hasn't. We've already looked at some of the fixes for this type of problem. For the most part, you'll find they're easy to trace and fix.

A Quick Look at Catastrophic Failures

Figuring out a catastrophic error usually takes a little time and a few hardware and software tools. You also need the knowledge required to use these tools. Here's a typical scenario. You start your machine in the morning and Windows 95 comes up fine, but you can't use the mouse. After a little looking around, you find that there aren't any conflicts and you haven't installed anything new recently. The most probable cause of your problem is some type of hardware failure. At least, that's a good place to start searching for a problem that doesn't appear on the Device Manager page of the System Properties dialog box as some type of conflict or other problem.

All kinds of problems fall into the catastrophic category. For example, severely crimping a cable (putting an obvious dent in it) will normally cause some type of hardware failure. It might be as simple as a device that won't respond or a network connection that seems to work intermittently. Port failures don't happen often, but they do happen. You'll also find that NICs fail from time to time. Everyone knows that hard drives fail.

Part of the problem for a network administrator or a home user is figuring out how to find the problem for certain. "Easter-egging" is the solution that some people use. They just try replacing one component at a time until they locate the problem. Unfortunately, that's really not the best way to do things. Using diagnostic aids and other troubleshooting tools will save you a lot more time than they cost. It's also a lot less expensive to find the right component the first time and replace it.

Tip: Never discount the usefulness of hardware-specific diagnostic aids. Most sound board and display adapter vendors include a complete diagnostic for their product as part of the package. Some hardware vendors are starting to include this feature as well. I even found one motherboard vendor—Hauppauge—that provides a diagnostic disk with its products. The diagnostic tests basic motherboard functionality and any installed memory.

Let's look at some of the diagnostic aids I've found helpful in the past. The following sections aren't designed to be an inclusive list of every tool that you'll ever need, but you might find that they provide just enough help so that you can get through a repair with a minimum of effort.

Peter's Principle: Using DOS Versus a Windows Diagnostic Program

Windows applications provide an ease of use that makes most DOS applications look totally unusable. That's the point in their favor. You can rely on most Windows diagnostics to provide very useful and easy-to-read information. They find a great majority of the hardware problems you could experience as well. Early entries in this field were unsuited to this task, but I could probably feel comfortable using a Windows diagnostic aid for many types of troubleshooting today.

However, there isn't any reliable way to completely test your hardware from within Windows. The multitasking nature of the operating system makes this impossible. Some diagnostic programs need total access to the hardware as well, and Windows won't allow this kind of access. In fact, getting rid of the operating system altogether is probably the best way to go. Some software tools out there do just that. Others run from the DOS prompt, where they have better control over the hardware.

There's another problem with Windows diagnostic programs as well—something that won't occur to most people until it's too late. What happens if you can get DOS up and running, but a hardware conflict or failure prevents Windows from starting? I've had this particular problem more than a few times. Using a DOS diagnostic means that if the system will boot at all, you can at least figure out what's going on.

Here's the bottom line: If you're going to rely on only one diagnostic program, choose a DOS-based one rather than a Windows-based one. Use the latter only if it's a supplement to the DOS-based one.

Note: Although you could probably run at least the DOS diagnostic products from within Windows, the results you'll get are inaccurate at best. Always run your diagnostic programs in MS-DOS mode, preferably from the DOS prompt before Windows 95 starts. You can access the DOS 7.0 prompt by pressing the F8 key and selecting the Safe mode command prompt only option. Chapter 22 covers this topic in greater detail.

Microsoft Diagnostic (MSD)

Microsoft Diagnostic (MSD) has been around for a long time. Microsoft includes it with both DOS and Windows but doesn't install it to your hard drive with Windows 95. The current product version shipping with Windows 95 is 2.13. That's the same version that's been around for quite some time now.

Tip: Windows NT includes a Windows version of MSD called WinMSD that appears to work just fine with Windows 95. You might want to consider using this product versus MSD if your system is running a Windows NT file server. This version of MSD won't work with your Windows 3.x workstations, because it uses the Win32 interface.

The original purpose of creating MSD was to provide Microsoft technicians and beta support staff with a full accounting of the capabilities that your machine provides. Figure 23.1 shows that this is still the main purpose of this program. It helps detect any hardware you have installed on your machine. It also has command-line parameters for compiling this information to a file that you can use for future reference, as shown in Table 23.1.

Figure 23.1.
The opening MSD display shows the types of hardware it will detect for you.

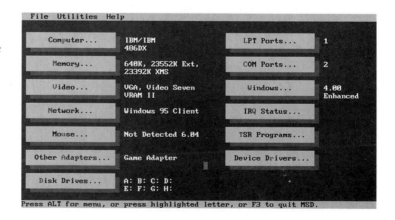

Table 23.1. MSD command-line switches.

Switch	Description
/B	Switches MSD to a white-on-black display mode. This comes in handy for running MSD on LCD displays.
/I	Tells MSD to bypass initial hardware detection. Use this setting if your hardware seems to freeze every time you enter MSD. Some detection phases interfere with normal hardware operations on some machines.
/F <d>:<p><f>	This is one of the automated report settings. It asks the user to provide a name, address, and telephone number before it produces the report. MSD inserts these items into the report. I find it handy to use this feature to insert a machine name and location instead of the intended information. You also need to supply the following report information: d is the drive letter, p is the path, and f is the filename. Notice the space between the /F and the drive letter. MSD won't recognize the switch if you don't include the space.
/P <d>:<p><f>	The /P switch does the same thing as the /F switch, except it doesn't ask for the user's name and address first.
/S <d>:<p><f>	Use this switch to produce a summary instead of a full-length report. The summary report contains only the very basics about your computer: processor type, memory types and sizes, video type, network type and vendor name, operating system version numbers, mouse type and vendor, other adapter type, drive listing, and port listing. Omitting the filename sends this report to the screen.

The main reason for using MSD is that it will detect all your functional hardware. The key word, of course, is functional. If you run MSD and find that it doesn't detect something, there's a pretty good chance that one of two things occurred. Either the driver required to turn the device on isn't present, or the device has failed. If you can eliminate the first cause, you will have found the cause of a hardware failure.

MSD really is pretty limited as far as diagnostic aids go, but you can use it in a pinch. I'd recommend that you use MSD for its intended purpose—hardware inventory—and go with a diagnostic aid that provides just a little more input.

Touchstone CheckIt

Finding an inexpensive troubleshooting aid can be quite difficult. At about $45 for the DOS or Windows version, CheckIt is quite a deal for someone who needs to find simple workstation problems quickly. It's much more than a hardware inventory program. It also includes a variety of diagnostics, a virus scanner, a hard disk formatter, and a floppy disk alignment checker. This is essentially a total workstation diagnostic on a disk. In fact, you can place both of the DOS version CheckIt 360 KB floppies on one 1.2 MB or 1.44 MB disk and have plenty of room left over for the DOS boot file and your network drivers.

Touchstone now also sells a couple of newer versions of this program—CheckIt Pro and WinCheckIt. But the original CheckIt (version 3.0) is good enough for most purposes.

CheckIt provides three important pieces of machine configuration information. All three of them appear on the System Configuration menu. First, the configuration display, shown in Figure 23.2, helps you see exactly how much memory the workstation has installed and an gives you an overview of how the memory is used. This same display provides you with basic workstation configuration information. For example, it tells you whether the workstation has a mouse installed.

Figure 23.2.
CheckIt version 3.0 provides a variety of information about the devices installed on your machine.

The memory display shown in Figure 23.3 gives you a detailed look at how the workstation uses the memory it has installed. You can use this display to find the location in the CPU's memory address space of ROM chips and to help you optimize the workstation's environment. More importantly, it might alert you to special hardware needs that you should consider when configuring Windows 95. For example, are there any hidden BIOS areas that you'll need to worry about if you decide to use a third-party memory manager?

The final display, shown in Figure 23.4, depicts interrupt usage. This is another factor you should take into consideration when you need to make an update to the system. You need to know if the machine has a free interrupt to use as required by the new hardware. Notice that this display also includes DMA channel usage. Few products provide you with this information, but it's essential to the PC user of today. For example, many multimedia cards rely on one or more IRQ lines and one or more DMA channels to perform their work. Fortunately, Windows 95 provides you with a detailed listing of port addresses, interrupts, and DMA addresses. However, this display could help you find out about devices that still use real-mode drivers—an important consideration when you're experiencing some type of hardware conflict.

Figure 23.3.
You can use CheckIt to determine your current memory settings, but this display is a little out-of-date.

Figure 23.4.
Windows 95 provides a very complete picture of your system, but this CheckIt display could help with devices that use real-mode drivers.

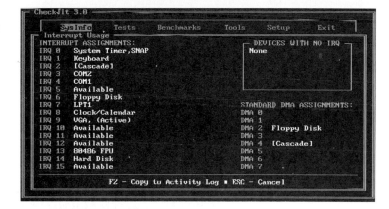

The System Configuration menu has two other items of interest. The most important one allows you to see the current CMOS setup. A much less generally useful item is the device driver listing. Keeping a record of the settings in your CMOS will make it much easier to recover when the battery that maintains that information dies, or if your PC loses the information in some other way (this happens from time to time). The device driver list, on the other hand, provides additional information, but none that is essential to completing the inventory.

The Test menu includes the ability to run tests alone or as part of a batch process. Figure 23.5 shows the batch test display. As you can see, it includes all the tests that CheckIt will run. The memory test provided with this particular product is exceptional. The only test that I've found more complete is the one included with the KickStart2 card, which I'll discuss later.

One of the other features that you'll see on this test screen is the batch mode feature. You can run a set of tests over and over again until you find a particular error. Some types of hardware faults are intermittent in nature or occur only after the machine has been running for a while. CheckIt helps you find both types of errors.

Figure 23.5.
CheckIt provides a complete suite of diagnostic programs.

```
┌─ Select Batch ──────────────────────────────────────────────────────────┐
│   Serial Ports:          COM1 Y          COM2 Y          COM3 N          COM4 N │
│                      Loopback N      Loopback N      Loopback N      Loopback N │
│ Parallel Ports:          LPT1 Y          LPT2 N          LPT3 N                 │
│                      Loopback N      Loopback N      Loopback N                 │
│   Floppy Disks:   Drive 0(A:) N   Drive 1(B:) N   Drive 2(NA) N   Drive 3(NA) N │
│                    Write Test N    Write Test N    Write Test N    Write Test N │
│     Hard Disks:   Drive 0(C:) Y             Drive 1(D:) Y                       │
│    Motherboard: System Board Y          Real Time Clock Y                       │
│         Memory:          Base Y     0K to   640K  (0000000h to 009FFFFh)        │
│                      Extended Y  1.000M to 16.000M  (0100000h to 0FFFFFFh)      │
│                       EXPANDed N     0K to     0K  (        h to        h)      │
│                     Quick Test N          Memory Test Passes:   1               │
│          Video:        Memory Y          Text N          Graphics N             │
│ Output Devices:       Printer N  Type: IBM/Epson       Port: LPT1               │
│  Input Devices:      Keyboard N  Type: Enhanced Keyboard (101 Key)              │
│                        Mouse N          Joysticks N                             │
│  Error Logging: Display Only          Batch Passes:   1    Pause on Errors: N   │
│                                                                                 │
│  The tests selected above will be run for this batch.                          │
│ ─────────────────────────────────────────────────────────────────────────────│
│ Run batch? Y                                                                    │
│ Y-Yes  N-No  C-Change Setup  S-Save  R-Restore Defaults          ESC-Cancel    │
└─────────────────────────────────────────────────────────────────────────────┘
```

I was also impressed by some of the other features you'll find under the Tools menu, shown in Figure 23.6. The Locate RAM Chips option helps you find a bad set of RAM chips on the motherboard. All you need to do is enter the motherboard chip configuration; the locater takes care of the rest. The virus checker and other options are nice touches as well. (Just don't forget to get updated virus signature files frequently.)

Figure 23.6.
The Locate RAM Chips features help you find a bad RAM chip fast.

Windsor Technologies, Inc.'s PC-Technician

Running a diagnostic using any operating system is risky business. The problem is that the operating system can actually interfere with your ability to find a problem. This is less of a problem under DOS than Windows, because the diagnostic can simply bypass the operating system, but the problem is real.

PC-Technician seemed a little expensive when I first looked at it. Expect to pay at least $200 for this comprehensive diagnostic. The thing that sets it apart from CheckIt isn't the tests it runs, but the fact that it runs them without an operating system like DOS. All you do is place the floppy in a drive and boot the machine. The next thing you'll see is the PC-Technician display.

The fact that PC-Technician doesn't need an operating system is a big advantage in several ways. First, you can use PC-Technician on any machine, even if your company uses several different operating systems. Second, using this product means that you don't have to have a functional hard drive to test the machine. Of course, CheckIt can say the same thing if you use the DOS version of the product. Third, you don't need to worry as much about viruses affecting the results of your tests. The non-DOS format of the PC-Technician disk makes it more difficult for a virus to infect it. Still, Windsor Technologies does provide some information on virus prevention that you should follow.

Landmark Research International's KickStart1

What do you do when your machine won't boot at all? You can't use a diagnostic aid such as PC-Technician because it needs a functional floppy drive system and a machine that will at least marginally boot to do its work. Easter-egging the problem might seem like the only way to go in this situation. After all, only a few things can keep a PC from booting at all, and it wouldn't take very long to replace them. However, there is a better way.

There are many different ways to monitor a PC. One of them is by checking the POST (power-on startup test) results by intercepting the contents of port 80h. Using this port is a well-documented method of monitoring the progress of your system startup tests. As your system tests itself, it sends the number of each test to an output port, usually port 80h. All you need to do to find a particular system fault is see which test number the machine stops at. You'll also need a listing of the test numbers from the vendor or the test card manufacturer. Fortunately, Landmark provides a book that contains the POST codes for most of the common BIOS chips. You can refer to this book whenever you need to test a machine that won't boot.

The KickStart1 card is an unimposing diagnostic aid. It contains only 12 LEDs and three chips. The first four LEDs monitor the power supply to within 10 percent of its specified rating. If one of the lights is out, it's time to replace the power supply.

The other eight LEDs provide output from port 80h. They read as a binary counter. The first four LEDs form the first number, and the second set of four LEDs forms the second number. For example, if lights 1, 2, and 4 are lit, the first number is Bh. This decoding process is somewhat error-prone, however. You could easily see the POST code as 1Ah when in reality it is 1Bh. This difference of 1 can make all the difference in the world in finding the problem.

Some BIOS chips don't provide a port 80h output. In that case, you'll need a special test BIOS that Landmark sells to go with its KickStart cards. The advantage of using this special BIOS is that it's fully documented—better documented, in fact, than just about any other vendor's BIOS that you'll find. It's unfortunate that you have to buy it as a separate item. Landmark currently sells one test BIOS for each major type of PC. Just plug in the appropriate test BIOS ROM chip in place of the regular BIOS chip on an ailing motherboard, and it will subject all the hardware to a much more thorough Power On Self Test. (Another option for PCs that report their POST codes to a different port than 80h is to use a card like the PocketPost card, which includes jumpers to select the correct port for almost any brand or model of PC.)

The advantage of this model of KickStart card is price. You can get a KickStart1 card for less than $100. The disadvantage is that it provides only the bare bones of diagnostic aid. It won't help you find anything beyond power supply failures and clues that the POST codes can supply.

Landmark Research International's KickStart2

The KickStart2 card is the younger brother of the KickStart1 card. This diagnostic aid also monitors port 80h and provides you with four LEDs for monitoring the power supply. However, instead of using LEDs for the port 80h output, this card outputs the actual numbers, making it less likely that you'll misinterpret the POST results. (Two alphanumeric LEDs are mounted on the board.) The power supply LEDs also provide a little more flexibility. A switch allows you to select between monitoring power of 2.5 percent or 5 percent of the rated voltage. This means that you can monitor a power supply to a closer tolerance than with the KickStart1 board.

Besides these enhanced features, the KickStart2 board provides an assortment of additional features. For example, the diagnostic aid doesn't end with monitoring port 80h and checking the power supply levels. This card also provides a set of intense diagnostics in ROM. One of the reasons to use a ROM-based diagnostic is that these diagnostics are unaffected by the operating system or other software problems. The ROM-based diagnostics on the KickStart2 card initialize before the system loads the operating system—a handy feature for times when you need to decide whether the hardware or software is the source of the problem with the workstation.

The diagnostics on the KickStart2 board do a lot more and less than standard software diagnostics. The memory tests are much more intense. For example, you can find a problem in the memory support chips, a problem that most software solutions can't locate. Some of the video and input device tests are less powerful than those provided by software aids, but this is a minor problem considering the purpose of buying such a card.

If you want to communicate with the outside world, the KickStart2 card provides the means. It comes equipped with both a parallel and a serial port. The parallel port allows you to troubleshoot a motherboard even if no other peripheral cards are attached. By default, the KickStart2 card sends the results of every test it runs to both the display and the seven-segment LEDs on the card. This provides you two ways of viewing test results. Unfortunately, you can't obtain detailed test results by viewing the LEDs. However, you can choose to send the test results to the printer. Even though this might waste a little paper, it does allow you to see what's happening with the faulty workstation. You can use the serial port to connect the test machine to another machine. This allows you to use the other machine's display and input devices to troubleshoot a nonfunctional workstation. In fact, you could even use this technique to have your PC call a PC that has an intermittent problem via modem. To catch such an error, simply tell the remote user to let you know when the problem appears, and then place the call. Rebooting the failed machine will take you directly to the KickStart diagnostic program.

As you can see, the KickStart2 board is a formidable aid in diagnosing difficult workstation failures. It can save you a lot of time and effort finding problems that software solutions can't handle. In addition, it might provide one of the best ways to separate the hardware from the software so that you can see which component is causing your problem.

Serial and Parallel Port Loopback Plugs

You can't fully test the serial and parallel ports in a workstation without loopback plugs. These plugs pass the signal from the port's output back to its input. To create a loopback plug, you use a blank connector without wires and then connect wires between specific pins. Most of the high-end diagnostic programs you buy (such as PC-Technician, AMI Diags, or the Norton Utilities) provide these plugs. Others, such as CheckIt, don't provide them. However, Touchstone tells you how to build them, and it will sell them to you as a separate product.

Table 23.2 provides you with the pin connections for a parallel port. Every parallel port uses a 25-pin male connector. Another designation for this type of connector is DB25P. You need to create two connectors to test serial ports. There are 9-pin and 25-pin serial ports. Every serial port uses a female connector. The designation for a 9-pin serial port is DB9S. Table 23.3 lists the pin connections for a 9-pin serial port. The designation for a 25-pin serial port is DB25S. Table 23.4 gives you the pin connections for a 25-pin serial port. You can find the blank connectors and wire you need at most electronics stores.

Table 23.2. Parallel port (DB25P) loopback plug connections.

First Pin	Connected to Second Pin
11 (Busy +)	17 (Select Input −)
10 (Acknowledge −)	16 (Initialize Printer −)
12 (Paper Out +)	14 (Autofeed −)
13 (Select +)	01 (Strobe −)
02 (Data 0 +)	15 (Error −)

Table 23.3. 9-pin serial port (DB9S) loopback plug connections.

First Pin	Connected to Second Pin
02 (RD: Received Data)	03 (TD: Transmitted Data)
07 (RTS: Request to Send)	08 (CTS: Clear to Send)
06 (DSR: Data Set Ready)	01 (CD: Carrier Direct)
01 (CD: Carrier Detect)	04 (DTR: Data Terminal Ready)
04 (DTR: Data Terminal Ready)	09 (RI: Ring Indicator)

Table 23.4. 25-pin serial port (DB25S) loopback plug connections.

First Pin	Connected to Second Pin
03 (RD: Received Data)	02 (TD: Transmitted Data)
04 (RTS: Request to Send)	05 (CTS: Clear to Send)
06 (DSR: Data Set Ready)	08 (CD: Carrier Direct)
08 (CD: Carrier Detect)	20 (DTR: Data Terminal Ready)
20 (DTR: Data Terminal Ready)	22 (RI: Ring Indicator)

As you can see, the pin connections are relatively easy to make. Whether you buy premade loopback plugs or make your own, this is an essential tool for your tool kit. Without loopback plugs, you will never know if the serial or parallel port you tested really works.

Cable Scanner

Network administrators, especially those managing large networks, can spend a lot of time tracing cables. People are forever abusing cables in ways that would seem impossible unless you actually looked at the damage. If you're in this position, a cable scanner is the most important tool you can get for your tool kit. An average cable scanner costs about $1,000, although you can usually find them a little cheaper. Alternatively, you could build your own cable scanner using plans in some electronics magazines for about $200. For example, *Circuit Cellar INK*'s October/November 1992 issue contains a set of plans on page 22.

One of the better cable scanners on the market is the Cable Scanner from Microtest. (Microtest provides many other cable scanners with more features, but the Cable Scanner model provides the minimum feature set you need to maintain a network.) This product tests for opens, shorts, and improper terminations. It tells you the distance from your current location to the cable fault. In most cases, all you need to do is track the cable for the required distance and you'll find the problem. To help you trace the signal, the main unit outputs a signal that you can pick up on a remote unit. Instead of taking down every ceiling tile in your office, you simply use the remote unit to trace the cable.

You can send the data collected by the Cable Scanner to a serial printer. The unit collects the data, stores it, and allows you to output it later. The Cable Scanner provides both text and graphic output. This is a handy feature for maintaining records on your system. All you need to do is print the results of the cable check and add it to the network documentation.

The Cable Scanner provides a few other unique functions that you might not use very often. For example, it can detect the noise level of the cable on your system. This means that you can reduce the number of packet errors by simply reducing the noise that the packet signal must overcome. You can also interface the Cable Scanner with an oscilloscope. This allows you to actually monitor the signal that flows across the network. An experienced network administrator could use this information to troubleshoot problem installations.

Incompatible Hardware

For the most part, any hardware that runs under the DOS and Windows 3.x environment will also run under Windows 95. Even if you have to use a real-mode driver (which I'll talk about in the next section), you should be able to use that old device if you really want to. The problems start when you mix that old hardware with new hardware or when the old device uses some of the undocumented features provided by previous versions of DOS.

Windows 95 really does try its best to figure out which interrupts and port addresses are in use, but it doesn't always succeed if you have an eclectic mix of old and new. Older devices often require real-mode device drivers to work at all; that's not a problem. Unfortunately, some of these devices don't register themselves properly. A device driver is supposed to register itself in a device chain and provide certain types of information as part of that registration process. If they don't provide the right level of information, Windows 95 can't detect them. What happens next is inevitable, given such circumstances. If Windows 95 doesn't see the device driver, it might assume that the interrupts and port addresses it uses are free. The result is that you might find two devices trying to share the same interrupt or port address.

Of course, one of the best ways to eliminate some of the problems is to make a checklist of all your hardware and the settings that each device uses. You need to include port addresses, interrupts, and DMA addresses. Physically check the settings on cards that use jumpers. You might want to take this opportunity to physically check your card's BIOS revision. An undocumented update could make a big difference in the settings you'll need to use with Windows 95. Make sure that you double-check any settings included in CONFIG.SYS or AUTOEXEC.BAT. A software-configurable device always includes the current settings as part of the command line. All you really need to do is get out the vendor manual and determine what the settings mean. Since some device drivers provide a default setting, you'll need to check for the default if the entry in CONFIG.SYS or AUTOEXEC.BAT doesn't contain a complete list of settings.

Once you get all the settings written down, check your list for potential conflicts. Windows 95 might tell you that there aren't any, but it's possible that you'll find some anyway. For example, someone I know recently tried to install Windows 95 but found he couldn't. The machine he was using included two SCSI adapters. Windows 95 recognized one adapter but not the other. As a result, Windows 95 didn't recognize the CD-ROM drive attached to the second adapter and therefore couldn't install itself properly. Removing the second SCSI adapter and connecting the CD-ROM drive to the first one cleared up part of the problem. At least Windows 95 would install. However, performance on the network was very slow, and the user still experienced some problems. A check of Windows didn't show any device conflicts. However, a physical check of the remaining SCSI adapter showed that it was using the same interrupt as the NIC. (Windows 95 had claimed that the NIC was using interrupt 5 and that the SCSI adapter was using interrupt 3.) Physically changing the SCSI adapter's interrupt setting cleared up the remaining problem.

Sometimes you might not be sure you got all the settings right during the first check. You can determine the equipment settings by viewing the port and interrupt addresses that a device uses with MSD or a diagnostic program such as CheckIt. In fact, using this technique coupled with physical inspection of your CONFIG.SYS and AUTOEXEC.BAT will ensure that you have all the settings for each device. Even if there aren't any conflicts, you'll still want to maintain a complete record of your hardware and any real-mode drivers you need to use. Avoiding problems with real-mode drivers starts with the detective work you perform during this phase of the installation. Record real-mode driver settings and then avoid using the address and interrupt, even though Windows 95 says it's free. This also means that you'll have to manually configure your setup rather than relying on Windows 95's automatic configuration features.

Tip: Watch out for older plug-in cards and some of the cheaper "no-name" ones. In the early days of PCs, no one used any port addresses above 3FFh, and most cards decoded only the low-order 10 bits of a port address to find out if a command was intended for that card. Now many cards use higher addresses (all the way up to FFFFh). If you have one of these newer cards and an older one in the same PC, you could run into a very subtle sort of problem. If the addresses used by the newer card are the same in the low-order 10 bits as those used by the older card, both cards will think that commands meant for the newer card were meant for it. There's no telling what will happen in this case, but it might not be pretty!

Some devices simply won't work with Windows 95. Unlike your old DOS setup, Windows 95 is a lot less forgiving about adapters that try to share the same address or interrupt. You simply can't do this under Windows 95 and expect the device to work. If that device happens to be a hard disk drive controller, you might find it impossible to boot all the way into Windows 95.

Some of those real-mode device drivers will cause problems too. A well-behaved device driver makes direct access only to the hardware it controls. It calls on the ROM BIOS routines for other types of service. An older device might use direct hardware access to other devices as well as the device it controls in order to make the driver faster. Windows 95 normally ignores the device if you try to use a device driver of this type. Sometimes a device driver of this type can actually cause the system to freeze when Windows switches to running a real-mode interrupt service routine. We covered many of the architectural aspects of this problem in previous chapters.

Unfortunate as it might seem, an ill-behaved device driver normally looks like a malfunctioning device rather than a piece of software that Windows 95 won't work with. I was surprised when I found myself in this position with an old CD-ROM drive. Fortunately, I was able to get a newer driver that did work from the vendor. This is the solution you should try as well. Many vendors will even allow you to download the upgrade directly from their own BBS for the price of a phone call. They also might make the upgrade available through a commercial information service such as CompuServe or America Online. Some even make it available on an Internet FTP site.

Some older devices include their own BIOS. Sometimes the BIOS routines conflict with Windows 95 and cause various types of system failures. Most vendors upgrade their BIOSes as time goes on. They fix bugs and perform some types of optimizations. I've never been able to understand why, but hardware vendors are notoriously reluctant to tell anyone about these fixes. If you have an older piece of hardware with a BIOS that is causing problems with Windows 95, see if the vendor has some type of BIOS upgrade that might fix the problem. Installing a new chip is usually cheaper than buying a new peripheral.

By now it should be apparent that hardware incompatibility can cover a lot of ground. Everything from misinterpreted settings to a poorly designed device driver can make it appear that your hardware is incompatible with Windows 95. Let's take a look at the hardware compatibility problem from a procedural point of view:

1. Get into MS DOS mode and test the hardware to ensure that there's no problem with the device itself. It's important to test the hardware with the same device driver that you plan to use with Windows 95 if you intend to use a real-mode driver for it under Windows 95.

2. Check the device settings to see if there is a conflict with any of the devices that Windows supports directly. This is especially important when you try to mix older hardware with new plug and play-compatible hardware. If Windows insists on using a specific setting for a plug and play-compatible board, see if your old board can use a different set of unused settings.

3. Once you determine that the hardware is working and that it doesn't conflict with anything, see if the vendor documentation provides any insights as to the requirements for using the device driver. For example, you'll probably find that device drivers written to work with versions of DOS prior to 3.3 will have some level of problem with Windows 95. These older device drivers often wrote directly to the hardware and definitely didn't use all the features that newer versions of DOS provide to support device drivers. See if the vendor can provide a new set of drivers.

4. Check your BIOS revision level. Many adapter cards that have a BIOS extension ROM on them display a version number on the screen during the boot process. With other pieces of add-in or connected hardware, you will have to determine the revision level some other way. Vendors provide a variety of ways to detect this information, so you'll have to check your documentation for details about your particular device. My modem uses a Hayes-compatible AT command to display the BIOS revision number. A display adapter that I own has an actual program that I run to display the BIOS and setup information. Check with the vendor to see if a newer version of the BIOS is available. You might have to send the device to the vendor's repair facility to get the BIOS replaced. It depends on the vendor's policy concerning sending BIOS updates to customers.

5. If all else fails, see if replacing the board with a similar board from another vendor helps. You might find that a software or other conflict is disguising itself as a hardware problem this way. For instance, my mouse example at the beginning of this chapter was an example of a problem with a serial port that disguised itself as a faulty mouse. You might find that other types of problems disguise themselves.

Tip: Actually, there is a very easy way to distinguish a serial mouse problem from a serial port problem. To do so, first run a diagnostic on the serial port with a loopback plug installed. If the port passes the test, then test the mouse.

Incompatible hardware rarely is. There is usually some problem that you can define, given enough time and resources. The question you have to ask yourself is whether that old hardware is really worth the effort. In my case, I replaced the hardware that was giving me problems, which probably saved me time and frustration. Some types of expensive hardware might be worth the effort involved in looking for the cause of incompatibility, but make sure you'll get some type of payback.

Using Real-Mode Device Drivers

I never use real-mode device drivers under Windows 95 if I can help it. We've discussed this topic several times throughout this book. I've shown you that real-mode device drivers are less reliable and a lot slower than their 32-bit protected-mode counterparts.

Still, you really don't want to get rid of those drivers, and here's why. What happens if you experience some type of failure on your machine? Say that Windows 95 can't start because of a corrupted file. You could restore it using Backup, but Backup needs Windows 95 to run. So what do you do now?

Getting a new copy of the corrupted file from a floppy setup of Windows 95 wouldn't be too hard, but you're using the CD version and you need Windows 95 to gain access to that, too. Now you're really in trouble—or are you? You really need a boot disk that contains all the drivers needed to activate your hardware. Make sure you include all the real-mode driver equivalents for your CD-ROM drive and sound board. In fact, you'll want to include everything needed to make your computer fully functional on this disk.

You'll also want to keep a copy of those real-mode drivers around if you test your system using a DOS-based diagnostic program such as CheckIt. Of course, you can't use a memory manager to load the devices high. Memory managers and diagnostic programs usually don't get along very well. Just load the drivers in low memory to get your testing done. A diagnostic program is usually fairly easy on memory anyway, since the vendor wants it to run on the maximum number of machines possible.

Device Conflicts Under Plug and Play

As I mentioned earlier, Windows 95 does an outstanding job of managing a system if it can see all the devices. When nothing is hidden, Windows 95 will do the best job it can to find alternative settings for every device. It will provide a set of port addresses, DMA addresses, and interrupts that will meet the device's needs and yet avoid conflict with everything else on the system. Unfortunately, there are limits to what Windows 95 can do. That's where you come in.

What if you have one too many devices installed on your machine and there isn't a free interrupt for one of the devices? Windows 95 will try to come up with the best solution possible and then leave one device turned off because it can't find an interrupt to service it. There is one exception to this rule. Printers might not need an interrupt. In this case, Windows 95 will let that device operate without an interrupt if one isn't available for its use. You have only 16 interrupts on your machine, and many of them are used before you install the first device.

That's where looking at the Device Manager page of the System Properties dialog comes into play. We've seen this dialog many times throughout this book, and you'll probably use it a lot when you're configuring your system for the first time. Windows 95 will display the device it chose to leave out of the computing picture using the same technique that it uses to display any conflict. You'll see the device name with either a yellow exclamation point or a red "not" sign through it.

It's quite likely that you'll want all the devices installed on your machine to work, but that might not be possible due to a shortage of interrupts. What you'll need to do is decide which device to get rid of, remove it, and reboot Windows 95. Check the Device Manager page again to make sure that Windows has reconfigured itself and that the remaining devices are functional.

There are alternatives to getting rid of an important device. For example, most sound cards come with a game port. If you don't use that game port, you might have an additional port address free that you really hadn't thought about. If you normally use a network printer instead of a local printer, you might consider disabling your printer port so that you can use its interrupt. The same holds true for any other unused port. Look for something you don't need before you remove something you do need.

Windows 95 provides a special device view for just this purpose. Figure 23.7 shows the interrupt version of this special view. (There are three other views as well.) To see it, highlight Computer on the Device Manager page of the System Properties dialog and click on Properties.

Figure 23.7.
Windows 95 gives you an easy way to find open interrupts, DMA addresses, and port addresses.

This dialog has a second page. I strongly recommend that you not use it unless you absolutely have to, although it could help you resolve some types of conflicts. Figure 23.8 shows the Reserve Resources page of the Computer Properties dialog. This is where you can reserve various system resources. The problem with this solution is that it interferes with the normal arbitration process that Windows 95 uses and might make the situation even worse than before. I've tried this particular feature quite a few times and have found that it's in the "still needs work" category for most situations.

Figure 23.8.
You can use the Reserve Resources page of the Computer Properties dialog to reserve interrupts, DMA addresses, or port addresses used by real-mode devices.

Warning: Never reserve a resource used by a system device. In general, this includes the real-time clock, system timer, system CMOS, keyboard, and programmable interrupt controller. Doing so will cause the machine to freeze, and you'll find it difficult at best to correct the problem. In some cases, you can fix the error by starting the machine in safe mode, but there's no guarantee that this will work. If the safe mode method doesn't work, the only way to fix the problem is to install a new copy of Windows 95 over your current copy. Sometimes even that measure doesn't work, because the setting got saved in the registry. When this happens, you'll have to start your Windows 95 installation from scratch.

To add a new reservation to the list, simply click on the Add button. This displays a dialog similar to the one shown in Figure 23.9. This is the interrupt-specific Edit Resource Setting dialog, but the other ones look about the same. All you need to do is tell Windows 95 which resource you need to save and then click on OK. You'll get an error dialog if the resource you want to save is already in use. Saving the setting anyway could stop your machine from running. The best course of action is to find out which device is using the resource, manually change it, reboot the machine, save the resource, put the device back into automatic, and reboot again. This whole procedure ensures that the arbitration process will continue to function smoothly.

Figure 23.9.
Adding or modifying a saved
resource is easy using the
Edit Resource Setting dialog.

Clicking on the Modify pushbutton displays the same dialog you got when you clicked on the Add pushbutton. The only difference is that you'll modify the current setting rather than add a new one. If you decide later to remove a saved setting, all you need to do is highlight it and click on the Remove pushbutton.

EISA Configuration Requirements

Under DOS, an EISA machine will run fine even if you don't run the EISA configuration utility. Running it could help you resolve some resource conflicts, but it isn't essential. You really should run it in order for Windows 95 to function properly. Part of the plug and play functionality of Windows 95 depends on being able to poll the EISA configuration to find out what kind of devices you have installed.

What does the EISA configuration utility do? It places information about each adapter in your machine in an area of CMOS. When you run the configuration utility, you see one blank for each slot that your EISA bus provides. The EISA configuration utility comes with a list of adapters it supports. All you need to do is select a slot and then select a device from the list of available devices. This tells your motherboard the specifics of the adapter installed in that slot. The configuration utility automatically displays a device name in each slot that you define. After you tell the configuration utility the contents of each slot, you have to supply it with the interrupt, port address, DMA address, and any other configuration information for that device. Windows 95 will use this information to configure your machine even if the real-mode device drivers or the adapter itself can't supply the required information. This information will also help Windows 95 locate some types of problems. For example, if Windows 95 can't detect a device that the EISA bus says is present, it will display an error message telling you so instead of simply ignoring the device. The configuration utility also allows you to enable or disable some types of motherboard features, such as installed ports. You'll need to consult the manual that came with your motherboard for full details on how to use the configuration utility.

Will anything terrible happen if you don't run the configuration utility? It won't be terrible, but it will hinder you from making full use of your machine. Without this information, Windows 95 won't be able to perform some types of optimizations that it would normally provide for your system, and it could end up running slower as a result.

The problem for most people is that their EISA configuration utilities are out of date, and some peripheral device vendors don't provide the files needed to configure the bus. For example, it's unlikely that you'll find a configuration file for your modem. To solve the first problem, you'll need to contact the vendor to get a new set of configuration files and perhaps a new utility program as well. The second problem might prove a little more difficult. In some cases, your motherboard vendor will be able to help you with a generic file that will take care of the peripheral. In other cases, the vendor who designed the peripheral might have a configuration file that you can use; they just didn't include it with the device. In some situations, though, despite your best efforts, you won't be able to find a configuration file. The thing to do in these cases is to configure everything else and leave that particular spot blank. Windows 95 will still pick it up during its scan of the system.

PCMCIA Conflicts

The last kind of hardware I'll address in this chapter is the PCMCIA bus. There's been a problem with this bus since the day it came out. Some cards won't work with your bus. You might plug a card into the slot and it won't work at all. Of course, when you take it back to the place you bought it, they'll show you that it does work. (This is one of the reasons you should take your machine with you if at all possible when you suspect some type of compatibility problem.) Even worse, some cards will work with your bus, but only in a certain slot or only with certain other cards. You might find that a modem card works fine in the first slot but not in any of the others.

Most people have heard about the problems with getting PCMCIA cards to work properly. Finally there are some standards for making the cards compatible, but only the new cards adhere to these standards. Unfortunately, many cards have already gone out that won't work together, so you'll need to choose your cards with care. The best piece of advice I can offer is to buy new cards from a vendor that will actually allow you to test them with the other cards in your machine.

Make sure you run a thorough test, using several different combinations of cards to check the new one for compatibility problems. The test should include checking the card in several different slots. I usually test the card under both DOS and Windows. You never know when you'll need to access that card outside of the normal Windows environment to take care of some kind of diagnostic.

On Your Own

Use MSD to find out about the components installed in your machine. The following procedure will guide you through the process:

1. Copy MSD from the \OTHER\MSD folder on your CD-ROM drive to the COMMAND folder within your main Windows 95 folder.

2. Shut down Windows and reboot your machine. Press F8 when you see the starting Windows 95 message.

3. Select Safe mode command prompt only from the boot menu.

4. Change directories to the \WIN95\COMMAND directory. Type MSD and press Enter.

5. Look through the various options that MSD provides. For example, what type of serial ports do you have? Do they use an 8250 UART or a 16550 UART? How many cylinders, heads, and sectors per track are listed for your hard drives? Check your system to see what features it provides.

6. Use the File | Exit command to exit MSD.

7. Reboot your machine into the standard Windows 95 setup.

Buy a diagnostic program and completely test your system, especially the hard drives. Make sure you get a diagnostic that's easy to use and that tests everything your machine has to offer. Use the loopback plugs provided with the diagnostic program to test your ports, or create your own loopback plugs using the procedure in this chapter.

Check any real-mode device drivers installed on your system. Make sure they are the most current drivers that the vendor has to offer. Do the same with any peripherals that provide their own BIOS. This includes both modems and display adapters. You'll also find a BIOS on most hard disk controllers and many other devices installed on your machine. Using the most current BIOS not only ensures that you'll have the least number of bugs to contend with, it could also mean a slight speed boost because of optimizations that the vendor made to it.

Don't wait until you have a problem to make this detailed checklist of all the device drivers in your system. This can be much easier to do when your PC is working normally. Then, when it fails in some way, you will already be a good ways down the path toward a solution to the problem.

VI

Microsoft
Plus!

24

Microsoft Plus!

Microsoft calls its Plus! package a companion to Windows 95 for computers with 486 or Pentium processors. Plus! makes a good companion indeed. With Microsoft Plus! added to your machine, you can do the following:

- Keep your Desktop lively and interesting through visual and other multimedia enhancements.

- Automatically perform system maintenance in the background while you work or even while you sleep.

- Add powerful enhancements to the standard disk compression facilities provided by Windows 95.

- Bring data and information from around the world to your Desktop through its network and Internet features.

- Sit back and relax with a game of 3D pinball.

This chapter discusses each of these features in detail.

Installing Microsoft Plus!

Installing Microsoft Plus! couldn't be easier, but you must have a computer with a 486 or Pentium processor. The features are simply too powerful to run on lesser machines. To take advantage of many of the features, your computer must have a graphics card that can support at least 256 colors.

Tip: The number of colors displayed by a graphics card usually depends on the display resolution it's set at. The resolution is the number of pixels, or the smallest unit of light, displayed across your monitor from left to right and from top to bottom. For instance, some cards can display only 16 colors at a resolution of 1024 × 756 pixels but can display 256 colors at a resolution of 640 × 480 pixels.

It's desirable to have a high-color graphics card so that you can have dazzling graphics on your Desktop. You also deprive yourself if you don't have a sound card and speakers (which would result in pinball without a lot of noise).

Installing Microsoft Plus! from CD-ROM

To install Microsoft Plus!, put the CD in your CD-ROM drive. You'll hear a soothing jingle (if you have a sound card) as the Microsoft Plus! for Windows 95 window automatically launches. The window displays three buttons floating in clouds. Click on the Install Plus! button at the top right, as shown in Figure 24.1, and follow the instructions.

Figure 24.1.
From the Microsoft Plus!
splash screen, you can click
on a button to install Plus!,
get information on other
Microsoft products, or
browse the Plus! CD.

CD auto-launch doesn't work on some computers. In this case, simply run SETUP.EXE from the Plus! CD. For instance, if your CD-ROM drive is drive D:, you would do the following:

1. Click on the Taskbar's Start button and select Run from the Start menu.
2. Type `d:\setup` in the Run dialog box's Open text box.
3. Click on the OK button.

Alternatively, you can double-click on the My Computer icon on your Desktop and then double-click on CD-ROM Drive, which should show up as a Plus! icon. Double-click on the setup.exe icon to start the Plus! setup.

Installing Microsoft Plus! from Diskettes

To install Microsoft Plus! from diskettes, insert disk 1, the setup disk, into a disk drive and run SETUP.EXE from that disk. For instance, if you inserted disk 1 into drive A:, you would then do the following:

1. Click on the Taskbar's Start button and select Run from the Start menu.
2. Type `a:\setup` in the Run dialog box's Open text box.
3. Click on the OK button.

Alternatively, you can double-click on the My Computer icon on your Desktop and then double-click on A: Drive, which should show up as a 3.5" Floppy icon. Double-click on the setup.exe icon to start the Plus! setup.

Using the Typical or Custom Installation

The Microsoft Plus! for Windows 95 Setup will ask you to select the typical or custom installation. The typical installation, the choice for most people, simply installs all components. There are a few instances in which you might want to use the custom installation.

If there's a specific option you know you won't use and you don't want it to take up space on your Desktop or disk drive, use the custom installation so that you can deselect it. In the Microsoft Plus! for Windows 95 - Custom dialog box, shown in Figure 24.2, click on the check box to the left of each option in the Options list that you want to deselect. If you're running low on disk space, you might need to do this so that you can load only the facilities that you need the most.

Figure 24.2.

All options in the Options list are selected by default. To deselect an option, click on the check box to the left of the option.

Table 24.1 lists all the Plus! options you can you select or deselect during the Plus! custom installation.

Table 24.1. Microsoft Plus! options available during custom installation.

Option	Disk Space Required	Description
DriveSpace 3	2,497 KB	Provides enhanced disk compression, including Compression Agent, to create more hard disk space.
System Agent	1,033 KB	Runs system maintenance tasks and other programs at regularly scheduled times or when your system is idle.

Option	Disk Space Required	Description
Internet Jumpstart Kit	16,135 KB	Makes configuring access to the Microsoft Network, the Internet, and Internet Mail quick and easy.
Desktop Themes	25,637 KB	Customizes your Windows 95 Desktop around a central theme.
Dial-Up Networking Server	320 KB	Configures your computer server so that you can dial into it from another location.
3D Pinball	3,713 KB	The classic arcade game, including great graphics and sound.
Visual Enhancements	1,193 KB	Enhancements for high-end systems to maximize graphics capabilities.

When you select the Desktop Themes or the Visual Enhancements options, you're given the opportunity to see additional options by clicking on the Change Option button. When you click the Change Option button while Desktop Themes is selected, the list of options shown in Figure 24.3 appears.

Figure 24.3.
You might want to deselect some of the Desktop Themes options if you have limited disk space or if your video driver can display only 256 colors.

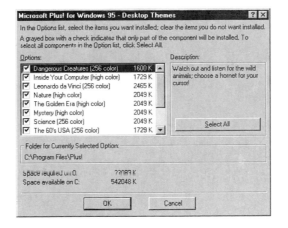

Table 24.2 lists all the Desktop Themes options.

Table 24.2. Microsoft Plus! Desktop Themes you can install during custom installation.

Desktop Theme	Disk Space Required	Description
Dangerous Creatures (256 color)	1,600 KB	This wild-animal motif focuses on mountain lions, poisonous frogs, hornets, and so on.
Inside Your Computer (high color)	1,729 KB	This theme revolves around motherboards, chips, and other computer guts.
Leonardo da Vinci (256 color)	2,465 KB	The Master's work becomes part of your Desktop, animated cursors, and an animated screen saver.
Nature (high color)	2,049 KB	This theme includes docile animated caterpillars crawling around in leaves.
The Golden Era (high color)	2,049 KB	This theme is set in the 1940's industrial, art deco "Golden Age of Radio."
Mystery (high color)	2,049 KB	Microsoft writes "Col. Batwing did in your computer's haunted library with the knife!" What does it mean?
Science (256 color)	2,049 KB	This theme covers the physical sciences. You'll find atoms, stars, and beakers.
The 60's USA (256 color)	1,729 KB	This theme features tie-dyed wallpaper, love bugs, and revolving peace signs. What would the hippies think if they saw this?
Sports (256 color)	2,602 KB	Every time you click the mouse button, you return a serve. When your screen saver appears, football strategy is scrawled on the blackboard.
Travel (high color)	2,272 KB	Trains, planes, and cars move around to take you virtually anywhere.
Windows 95 (256 color)	2,908 KB	This theme is full of Windows 95 images.
More Windows (high color)	3,018 KB	The high-color Windows 95 Desktop.

When you click on the Change Option button while Visual Enhancement Options is selected, the list of options shown in Figure 24.4 appears.

Table 24.3 lists all the Visual Enhancement options. You'll probably pick and choose items in these lists if you need to conserve disk space or if you don't have video hardware that can handle high-color graphics.

Figure 24.4.

Some Visual Enhancement objects require high-color capacity, but none use much disk space. Deselect an option if you can't use it.

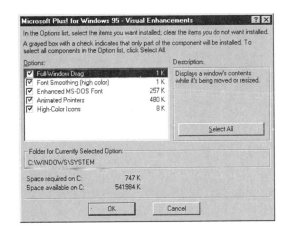

Table 24.3. Microsoft Plus! visual enhancements you can install during custom installation.

Visual Enhancement	Disk Space Required	Description
Full Window Drag	1 KB	Displays a window's contents while it's being moved or resized.
Font Smoothing (high color)	1 KB	Smoothes jagged screen fonts to improve their appearance and legibility.
Enhanced MS-DOS Font	257 KB	Uses the more-legible Lucida font for the MS-DOS Command Prompt window.
Animated Pointers	480 KB	Additional animated mouse pointers.
High-Color Icons	8 KB	Replaces the standard Windows 95 icons with high-color icons.

You might have hardware limitations that make some Plus! features irrelevant to your system. For instance, my laptop displays only 256 colors; therefore, it makes no sense to load the high-color Desktop Themes provided by Plus!. In this instance, I selected custom installation and deselected all high-color themes from setup, thus saving about 18 MB in disk space.

Note: As this book was going to press, I received the following new, undocumented information directly from Microsoft about high-color themes. If your video handles only 256 colors, high-color images in high-color Desktop Themes are dithered down to 256 colors. When images are dithered, they are filled in with fewer colors by using the closest matching colors available. However, icons can't be dithered. So, under 256-color video, you'll get 16-color icons and 256-color dithered versions of the 16-bit (high-color) bitmaps.

Running System Maintenance Tasks at Night

The next thing Microsoft Plus! setup asks is whether you want to run system maintenance tasks at night (see Figure 24.5). Plus! comes with a tool, System Agent, that will run system maintenance tasks at preset times. If you usually leave your computer on overnight, you should answer Yes when setup asks if you want to run system maintenance tasks at night so that maintenance programs will be run while you're not using the computer. This avoids any computer slowdown during your work-day. Otherwise, if you shut your computer down at night, answer No, and system maintenance will be scheduled during the day. Of course, you can specify your own times to run each system mainte-nance utility. See the section "System Agent."

Figure 24.5.

If you leave your computer on all the time, you'll like the option of having Microsoft Plus! set up preset nighttime system maintenance for you.

If There's Not Enough Disk Space

Setup then checks for the necessary disk space. If there's not enough space, the Microsoft Plus! for Windows 95 dialog box will show you a listbox of the options selected and will let you change them. The first options to consider deselecting are those that you know you'll never use. For instance, if you know you'll never use disk compression, deselect DriveSpace 3, and you'll save nearly 2.5 MB of disk space. However, if you're tight on disk space, disk compression might be just the ticket. You might want to exit the Plus! setup and compress your drive (see the section "Disk Compression with DriveSpace 3"). Now, with all your new drive space, you can run the Plus! setup again without de-selecting anything.

The Internet Setup Wizard

If you told Plus! setup to install Internet facilities, you'll be taken through the Internet Setup Wiz-ard at this time during the initial installation process. The first page of the Internet Setup Wizard will appear, as shown in Figure 24.6. For details on using the Internet Setup Wizard, see the section "Internet Setup Wizard."

Figure 24.6.
The first page of the Internet Setup Wizard greets you after Microsoft Plus! setup copies most of the Plus! files to your disk.

Choosing a Desktop Theme

Your final task while installing Plus! is to choose a Desktop Theme. Use the Themes drop-down list in the upper-left corner of the Desktop Theme dialog box, shown in Figure 24.7, to select a theme. Be sure to select high-color themes only if you have your display set to 16-bit color (high color).

Figure 24.7.
The Desktop Themes dialog box.

When you select a theme, you'll see a preview of how your Desktop will look in a large area under the Theme drop-down list. Figure 24.7 shows a preview of the 256-color theme The 60's USA. When you find a theme you like, click on the OK button to complete the setup. Don't worry if you're not sure that the theme you chose is your favorite. It's easy to change themes later or even create your own themes.

The Desktop Environment

The new Desktop environment in Windows 95 is considerably improved, both functionally and aesthetically. Plus! adds many features that allow you to customize almost every aspect of your Desktop environment to match your mood, your interests, and your artistic tastes.

Desktop Themes

Desktop themes are complete, prepackaged Desktop environments designed with a particular theme, or subject, in mind. Plus! gives you 12 Desktop themes (listed in Table 24.2) plus a Windows default.

Naturally, you must have the right hardware on your computer to use a theme. If you have a graphics card capable of high color (16-bit color), you can use any of the 12 themes. Otherwise, you must have a card capable of 256 colors (8-bit color) to run the six 256-color themes and the Windows default.

Each theme is more than just a background image. If you've used previous versions of Windows, you're familiar with wallpaper. To spruce up the old Windows Desktop, you would find a bitmap that you liked and add it to the Desktop, the whole screen area behind all the windows. If you were especially determined to customize the look of your Desktop environment, you might have added custom icons to certain programs. In Windows 95, virtually every aspect of your Desktop environment can be modified, and each theme does just that.

A theme changes the entire look and sound of your Desktop. (Yes, even sound, if you have a sound card.) Each theme has its own Desktop wallpaper and icons, but it goes much further than that. Each theme also has a custom screen saver, sound events, mouse pointers, colors, font names and styles, and font and window sizes. Many of the pointers are animated, and all the screen savers have animation and sound.

If you feel that your creativity is stifled by prepackaged themes, never fear. You can customize every aspect of your Desktop. Creating a Desktop that's completely your own takes a bit of work, but once you've designed it, you can save it as your very own Desktop Theme.

Selecting a Theme

Plus! setup asks you to select a Desktop Theme. If you canceled theme selection during setup or if you want to change your Desktop Theme, you must open Control Panel. Select the Taskbar's Start menu, select Settings, and select Control Panel. Double-click on the Desktop Themes icon in Control Panel. The Desktop Themes dialog box, shown in Figure 24.8, opens and shows what the current theme looks like.

Figure 24.8.
*Current Windows settings is
listed in the Theme drop-
down list. Beneath this list is
a window showing what the
current theme looks like.*

You can select from the themes listed in the Themes drop-down list at the upper-left of the Desktop
Themes dialog box. When you select a new theme, it's loaded into the preview window, as shown in
Figure 24.9. The Sports theme is selected.

Figure 24.9.
*Sports is selected in the
Theme drop-down list. A
preview of this theme is
shown in the area below the
Theme drop-down list.*

If you like what you see in the preview, click on the OK button to apply this theme to your Desktop
and to close the Desktop Themes dialog box. If you prefer to keep the Desktop Themes dialog box
open after you apply the theme, click on the Apply button. Otherwise, try another theme or, if you
decide that you don't want to change your Desktop Theme, click on the Cancel button.

Customizing Desktop Themes

There are two ways you can create your own customized Desktop theme. Relatively minor adjustments to existing themes can be done inside the Desktop Themes dialog box. For more ambitious customization jobs, you'll want to work with most of the tabs in the Display Properties dialog box and perhaps use the Desktop Themes dialog box to give your new Desktop Theme a name. Using either method, you can customize virtually every aspect of your Desktop environment.

Note: To open the Display Properties dialog box, right-click on the Desktop icon and select Properties from the context menu.

Using the Desktop Themes Dialog Box

The Desktop's current settings are always listed in the Desktop Themes dialog box as Current Windows settings in the Theme drop-down list. After you select and apply a theme such as Dangerous Creatures to your Desktop, all your settings will reflect those specified by the Dangerous Creatures theme and will be saved as the Current Windows settings. You'll see in a moment why this is an important step.

Suppose that you like the Dangerous Creatures theme that you've applied to your Desktop, but the colors are just too dark for your laptop computer (see Figure 24.10).

Figure 24.10.
*The Dangerous Creatures
Desktop Theme uses dark
colors.*

In contrast, the color scheme in the Leonardo da Vinci theme looks just right (see Figure 24.11).

Figure 24.11.
The Leonardo da Vinci
Desktop Theme uses
relatively light colors.

You can remedy this problem easily. Assuming that your current Desktop Theme is Dangerous Creatures, open the Desktop Themes dialog box. Notice that the Theme drop-down list says Current Windows settings (see Figure 24.12). Notice also that the preview window shows the same Desktop configuration as the Dangerous Creatures theme would if you had selected it.

Figure 24.12.
The Current Windows
settings are now the same as
if you had selected the
Dangerous Creatures theme.

To change the color scheme in your Current Windows settings to the color scheme in the Leonardo da Vinci theme, select the Leonardo da Vinci theme in the listbox, as shown in Figure 24.13.

Figure 24.13.
The Leonardo da Vinci theme.

Notice that the preview window shows the full Leonardo da Vinci theme. Your Current Windows settings would change to reflect all the settings in the Leonardo da Vinci theme if you were to click on the Apply button or the OK button now. However, all you want to change in the Current Windows settings is the color scheme. Notice the Settings checkboxes on the right side of the dialog box. All of them are checked. Click on the check box to the left of Desktop wallpaper. The Leonardo da Vinci wallpaper disappears, and the wallpaper specified in your Current Windows settings, the picture of a mountain lion, appears (see Figure 24.14).

Figure 24.14.
The Leonardo da Vinci theme with wallpaper deselected.

Only the selected settings, the settings with check marks next to them, are applied to your Current Windows settings. Since you want to change only the color scheme, remove the check marks next to all of the settings except Colors, as shown in Figure 24.15.

Figure 24.15.
The Leonardo da Vinci theme with every setting deselected except Colors.

The preview window should now look a lot like the Dangerous Creatures theme, except that the colors are from the Leonardo da Vinci theme. Click on the Apply button, and your Current Windows settings now include the new, lighter colors.

You might be very happy with your new creation, but you're also eager to try other combinations. If you simply apply new settings to your Current Windows settings, you'll lose any particular combination that previously existed unless it's saved as a Desktop Theme. You can create a new theme from the Current Windows settings at any time. Select Current Windows settings in the Theme drop-down list. Notice that the Save As button to the right of the Theme drop down list is now activated, as shown in Figure 24.16.

To save the Current Windows settings as a Desktop Theme, click on the Save As button. The Save Theme dialog box appears, as shown in Figure 24.17. Give the theme a name—Dangerous Creatures Light (256 color), for instance—and click on the Save button.

Figure 24.16.
Click on the Save As button to save the Current Windows settings.

Figure 24.17.
The Save Theme dialog box.

  Tip: It's a good idea to continue the naming conventions that Microsoft started and include the color requirements in parentheses after the theme's name.

When you save the new theme, it becomes the selected theme in the Theme drop-down list. Notice that the Save As button is now deactivated, but the Delete button is activated. If you don't like a theme, you can delete it by clicking on the Delete button. You can save only the Current Windows settings.

Using the Display Properties Dialog Box

You can completely customize your Desktop environment using the Desktop Themes dialog box. However, combining settings sprinkled across many or all of the existing themes can become clumsy. Also, maybe you'd like to use settings that aren't included in any existing theme. In either case, you'll want to change your Current Windows settings using the Display Properties dialog box.

Windows 95 allows nearly complete customization of its Desktop environment without Plus!. However, there is no way to save multiple Desktop environment configurations under the same user profile, and there is no way to customize the standard Desktop icons without Plus!.

Note: You can create multiple Desktop configurations without Microsoft Plus! by creating multiple user profiles. On a machine used by more than one person, each person can set up his Desktop just the way he wants it. However, a single user must use only one Desktop configuration or log on using different user IDs to save different Desktop configurations. Using Microsoft Plus! allows a single user to save multiple Desktop configurations using a single user profile.

Plus! adds a Plus! tab to the Display Properties dialog box, shown in Figure 24.18. This tab lets you change the standard Desktop icons to anything you'd like.

Figure 24.18.
The Display Properties dialog box lets you change the standard Desktop icons and other visual enhancement options.

Note: There are other features on the Plus! tab of the Display Properties dialog box. These will be discussed later.

The four standard Desktop icons are

    My Computer
    Network Neighborhood
    Recycle Bin (full)
    Recycle Bin (empty)

Changing the Background, Screen Saver, and Appearance tab settings in the Display Properties dialog box was discussed earlier in this book. There's one major drawback to using the Background tab: You can't select from the different Plus! Desktop theme wallpapers. You can select Plus! from the Background tab's Wallpaper list and use the wallpaper from the last Desktop Theme you selected, as shown in Figure 24.19.

Figure 24.19.
Selecting Plus! from the Background tab's Wallpaper list selects wallpaper from the last Desktop Theme you used.

The reason for this is that Microsoft has set up the Plus! Desktop Themes in a way that saves disk space. Wallpaper for all of the themes is stored in the Program Files | Plus! | Themes folder as JPEG (.JPG) files. You'll find wallpaper listed as the theme name followed by the word "wallpaper." For instance, the Dangerous Creatures theme wallpaper is listed as "Dangerous Creatures wallpaper." When you select a Desktop Theme, the theme's JPEG wallpaper file is converted to a bitmap (.BMP) file in the Windows folder (see Figure 24.20). You can find a bitmap of the last Desktop Themes wallpaper you used as the Plus! bitmap (.BMP) file in your Windows folder.

Figure 24.20.
When you switch to a new Desktop Theme in the Desktop Themes dialog box, the new wallpaper is con-verted from a JPEG file to a bitmap file.

Bitmap files are larger than JPEG files, but you can work with bitmap files only from the Background tab of the Display Properties dialog box. The Dangerous Creatures wallpaper JPEG file in the Pro-gram Files | Plus! | Themes folder is 97 KB. The same wallpaper as the Plus! bitmap file in the Windows folder is 301 KB. This saves disk space, but you'll either need to use the Desktop Themes dialog box to change between different Desktop Theme wallpapers or convert the Desktop Theme wallpaper JPEG files to bitmap files using an image conversion program.

Create a new Desktop Theme when you've finished making your Current Windows settings just the way you want them using the Display Properties dialog box. Open the Desktop Themes dialog box and, with the Current Windows settings selected in the Themes list, click on the Save As button to save your new Desktop Theme.

Animated Mouse Pointers

Plus! gives you several animated mouse pointers. As I noted earlier, it provides several animated pointers with its Desktop Themes. Plus! also places several other animated pointers in the Windows | Cursors folder. You can access animated mouse pointers by doing the following. Open Control Panel and double-click on the Mouse applet to open the Mouse Properties dialog box. Select the Pointers tab, as shown in Figure 24.21. Select the type of mouse pointer you want to change. The Busy pointer is selected in Figure 24.21.

Figure 24.21.
Select the Pointers tab in the Mouse Properties dialog box to customize your mouse cursor.

Click on the Browse button to open the Browse dialog box, shown in Figure 24.22.

The Browse dialog box opens to the Windows | Cursors folder by default. If you want to use the animated mouse cursors included in the Desktop Themes, go to the Program Files | Plus! | Themes folder in the Browse dialog box. Select a cursor. The Banana cursor is selected in Figure 24.22.

The Files of Type drop-down list says Cursors (*.ani, *.cur). You might recognize the "cur" type as the typical cursor type. The "ani" type is the animated cursor type. When you select a cursor, it is displayed in the Preview area at the lower-left of the Browse dialog box. If it's an animated cursor, it will be animated in the Preview area, as shown in Figure 24.22.

Figure 24.22.
The Browse dialog box opens
to the Windows | Cursors
folder. The animated
Banana cursor is selected.

Click on the Open button. You should be back in the Mouse Properties dialog box with the new cursor added to the cursor type you selected earlier (see Figure 24.23).

Figure 24.23.
The animated Banana cursor
is now the Busy cursor.

Click on the Apply button to add the cursor to your current list of cursors and to leave the dialog box open so that you can modify other cursor types. Otherwise, click on the OK button to add the cursor to your list and exit the dialog box.

Full-Window Drag

With Plus! installed, you can set your Desktop environment so that it shows a window's contents rather than just an outline when you drag or resize it. You can find the Show window contents while dragging option on the Plus! tab of the Display Properties dialog box inside the Visual Setting frame.

Font Smoothing

Font smoothing gets rid of any jagged edges that large fonts sometimes display. You must be running your video at 16-bit color (high color) or better to take advantage of font smoothing. You can find the Smooth edges of screen fonts option on the Plus! tab of the Display Properties dialog box inside the Visual Setting frame.

Wallpaper Stretching

Have you ever found an ideal wallpaper image, only to discover that it's either too small or too large for your Desktop? Plus! gives you the ability to stretch the image to fit your Desktop. This setting also shrinks images to fit your Desktop. You can find the Stretch desktop wallpaper to fit the screen option on the Plus! tab of the Display Properties dialog box inside the Visual Setting frame.

Fun with 3D Pinball

I felt compelled to do extensive research on this Plus! feature, and I'm happy to report that 3D Pinball is fun. Start the program, select Options | Full Screen to hide all of that pesky work, and launch the ball using the Spacebar (see Figure 24.24).

Figure 24.24.
3D Pinball in action. Just imagine all the bells, clangs, and flashing lights! You can start your copy by choosing Accessories | Games.

The left flipper is the Z key, and the right flipper is the / key. If someone tries to interrupt your game, ignore them. If they break your concentration, press the F3 key to pause the game and regroup, and then press F3 again to resume playing. If it's your boss, however, you can press the Esc key to quickly minimize and pause the game. Remember the work you hid beneath the game? It's prominently displayed until your boss disappears. Click on the 3D Pinball button on the Taskbar, press F3, and resume playing.

What good is a game of pinball if you can't knock the machine around a bit to persuade the ball to go to the right location? The X key knocks the machine to the right, the . key knocks it to the left, and the up arrow pushes it. Be careful, though! You can tilt the machine.

Program Scheduling and Monitoring Disks

If you're like me, you probably fire up a disk defragmenting program once a day and maybe test the disk for any errors while you're at it. These tasks typically take a long time to run and often make the computer unusable while they operate. Why not perform them automatically while you eat lunch or sleep? System Agent, a new program included in the Plus! package, does just that and more.

System Agent

System Agent is probably already installed and running on your machine if you've installed Plus! (unless you specifically deselected it during a custom installation). Plus! installation automatically installs System Agent preset to run the ScanDisk for Windows, Disk Defragmenter, and low disk space notification programs at times that are generally best for most people. During installation, you're asked if you'd like to run system maintenance tasks at night (see Figure 24.5). If you click on Yes, ScanDisk for Windows and Disk Defragmenter will be set to run at night. Otherwise, they'll be set to run during the workday at times when you're least likely to be using the computer. Just to be sure that the system maintenance tasks don't interrupt anything, System Agent runs them only after the computer hasn't been used for a set amount of time. The low disk space notification program runs in the background once an hour to check on your disk space. You'll never notice that it's running unless it finds that your drive has less than the preset amount of space left on it. Then it will notify you of the space squeeze. Finally, if you compressed a drive to alleviate disk space squeeze, Plus! will automatically schedule Compression Agent to run once a week. We'll look at each of these programs in detail later. First, let's see how System Agent does its job and how you can use it to schedule other software to run repetitive jobs.

Scheduling Backups Using System Agent

Backing up hundreds of megabytes of hard disks is something that no one enjoys doing even once, let alone on a regular schedule. How many times have you wished that you could back up everything the way you should? Do you? Of course not! This is a perfect task for the System Agent to perform.

Backing up files to floppy disks requires someone to remove filled disks and enter fresh, empty disks into the drive, so a mass storage device is the one special hardware requirement for automated backups. These include tapes and WORM drives. (A WORM drive writes once and reads many times from its storage medium.)

Using Backup was covered in detail in Chapter 8. You'll need to define backup sets and how often you want to run each backup set. You'll also need to set a time and day or days on which you want to run the backup. Simply build a backup set for each type of scheduled backup you want.

Scheduling a New Program in System Agent

Once you've defined your backup sets, you can automate the backup process using System Agent. Open System Agent by double-clicking on the System Agent icon on the right side of the Taskbar. Open the Program menu and click on Schedule a New Program in order to open the Schedule a New Program dialog box, shown in Figure 24.25.

Figure 24.25.
Add a program to System Agent using the New Program dialog box.

In the Cmd line box, type

```
"C:\Program Files\Accessories\Backup.exe" C:\Program Files\Accessories\setname.set
```

where *setname*.set is the name you assigned to the backup set. Be sure to include the quotation marks.

Fill in the Description box with an easy-to-understand description of your backup set, as shown in Figure 24.25. Click on the When to Run button on the right to schedule the backup. The Change schedule dialog box, shown in Figure 24.26, will appear.

Tip: "Wait until I haven't used my computer for *x* minutes" is a handy feature supplied in the Change schedule dialog box. Click on the checkbox next to this feature and fill in the amount of time. System Agent will run the program at the scheduled time. However, if you're using the computer when the program was scheduled to run, System Agent waits until you stop using it for the amount of time you specify before it starts the scheduled program.

Figure 24.26.

Select the times and days that you want Backup to run a particular backup set in the Change Schedule dialog box.

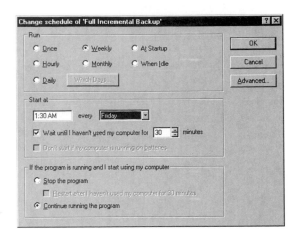

Click on the OK button. Repeat these steps for every backup set that you want to schedule.

> **Tip:** Making sure that you have a complete backup of each drive is important. However, you probably won't want to back up every file repeatedly. I find that the best approach is to do a complete backup of a drive and then have System Agent periodically run an incremental backup of the entire drive. How often will depend on how quickly changes accumulate on your drives.

The Low Disk Space Notification Program

System Agent runs the low disk space notification program in the background while you work to alert you to any drive that might be getting full. Its default setting upon installation is to run once an hour.

Using Your Computer as a Dial-Up Server

Windows 95 wasn't built to be a powerful dedicated server. If that's what you want, you need Windows NT Server. Nevertheless, there might be times when you'd like to access data on your computer while in another town or country, especially if you're on the road with your laptop. Alternatively, you might want to give friends or colleagues access to certain files or directories on your machine. The Plus! pack provides a program that allows telephone access to your computer. Of course, you must have a modem.

Setting Up Dial-Up Server

You can find the Dial-Up Server settings by opening the Dial-Up Networking window. Double-click on the My Computer Desktop icon, and then double-click on the Dial-Up Networking folder or on the Start menu go to Programs | Accessories, and select Dial-Up Networking. In the Dial-Up Networking window, open the Connections menu and select Dial-Up Server to open the Dial-Up Server dialog box. To allow dial-up access, select the Allow Caller Access radio button. You must share any folders that you want to give dial-up access to (see Chapter 20), and don't forget to leave the computer on!

Disk Compression with DriveSpace 3

Unlike with some previous versions of Windows, disk compression in Windows 95 is very reliable and is an excellent option to use when you need more disk space—and who doesn't? I especially like to use disk compression on my laptop computer. My 0.5 GB drive gives me nearly 1.5 gigabytes of space when I use the compression facilities that come with Windows 95 and the Plus! pack. Windows 95 comes with the disk compression program DriveSpace. Plus! upgrades the standard DriveSpace to DriveSpace 3. Additionally, it adds the compression utility Compression Agent, which is run by System Agent when you're not using your computer to optimize disk space and performance.

There are several advantages to using DriveSpace 3 disk compression instead of the standard DriveSpace. Perhaps the most important advantage is that you can create compressed drives larger than 512 MB. DriveSpace 3 supports compressed drives of up to two gigabytes. With the ever-growing size of programs, this is a welcome capability. DriveSpace 3 uses all the free space on your drive, even if it's fragmented. The standard DriveSpace can use only contiguous, unfragmented disk space to compress files. DriveSpace 3 allows you to achieve maximum compression, called UltraPack compression, on files you don't use often, further increasing storage efficiency. Finally, DriveSpace 3 is built to work together with Compression Agent to maximize your storage efficiency and performance.

Compressing a Drive with DriveSpace 3

Compressing a drive with DriveSpace 3 is essentially the same as compressing it with the standard DriveSpace, except that you get the advantages of the extra features just discussed. If you want to create a compressed drive larger than 512 MB, you must use DriveSpace 3. This substantial increase in capacity is welcome, but, sadly, there is still a limit—2 GB. This means that you can compress up to between half a gigabyte and one gigabyte of uncompressed drive space. This number is sure to be closer to half a gigabyte since, in my experience, DriveSpace 3 really gives you about three times your original disk space.

Upgrading a Compressed Drive with DriveSpace 3

Like compressing an uncompressed drive with DriveSpace 3, upgrading a compressed drive using DriveSpace 3 is essentially the same as upgrading it with the standard DriveSpace. The exception is that you must also upgrade drives compressed with the standard DriveSpace to get the added features of DriveSpace 3.

Balancing Disk Space and Speed with DriveSpace 3

DriveSpace 3 allows you to fine-tune how your drive is compressed, giving you control over trade-offs between disk space and operation speed. Three compression types used by DriveSpace 3 form the basis of these adjustments: Standard compression, HiPack compression, and no compression at all.

Standard Compression

With Standard compression, DriveSpace 3 typically compresses files to just over half of their uncompressed size. A special Plus! feature of Standard compression is that more of the disk drive is searched for repetitive data. This results in better compression ratios and relatively fast disk reads and writes.

HiPack Compression

With HiPack compression, files are typically compressed to just under half their uncompressed size. Reading data from HiPack compressed files is relatively fast. However, writing data to HiPack compressed files is relatively slow.

Tip: You get the highest compression ratios from something called UltraPack compression. Only Compression Agent can pack your files using UltraPack. See the section "Compression Agent."

Balancing Optimization and Compression Using DriveSpace 3

Nearly everyone will want to optimize their compressed drive for a balance between speed and drive space. Nevertheless, it's possible to fully optimize your compressed drive for either speed or space. We'll consider these extreme optimizations first, because they're easy to understand and they demonstrate the principles behind disk compression optimization well.

Compression Optimized for Speed

If you want your machine to run at the maximum speed possible, you want your programs to load files from disk as rapidly as they can, and you want to optimize your compressed drive for speed. That's silly, you say. Everyone wants that! Right you are. The "gotcha" is that, in this extreme example, you don't care at all about disk space. Presumably, you have plenty of it. To maximize speed, configure DriveSpace 3 to save files uncompressed. That's right—compress your drives with DriveSpace 3 set so that it doesn't compress your files! Naturally, this is the fastest compression option. It also seems a bit silly. However, we'll see later that there are times when this setting can be useful.

To compress a drive for maximum speed, open DriveSpace 3. Select Advanced | Settings to open the Disk Compression Settings dialog box, shown in Figure 24.27. Select the No Compression (fastest) radio button. Click on the OK button and compress the drive in the usual way.

Figure 24.27.
*Select DriveSpace 3
compression features in the
Disk Compression Settings
dialog box.*

Compression Optimized for Drive Space

If you're trying to squeeze a lot of program and data bytes onto a small disk drive, you'll want to maximize your disk compression with drive space. You can set DriveSpace 3 to maximize drive space while, for the most part, ignoring performance considerations. Of course, you'll take a performance hit if you do this, but it might be worth it if you need the space. Actually, the default DriveSpace 3 compression method compresses every file. However, it compresses them using Standard compression, which should show a small, if even noticeable, performance hit. You can squeeze even more space onto your drive if you select the HiPack compression method. You should compress your entire drive with HiPack compression only if you desperately need the space, because this setting causes a substantial slowdown in writing data to the drive. You might find HiPack tolerable if your machine has a Pentium or faster central processing unit.

To compress a drive for maximum space with very little degradation in performance, open DriveSpace 3. Select Advanced | Settings to open the Disk Compression Settings dialog box, shown in Figure 24.27. Select the Standard compression radio button. Click on the OK button and compress the drive in the usual way.

To compress a drive for maximum space while throwing performance concerns to the wind, select the HiPack compression radio button instead.

Compression Optimized for a Balance Between Speed and Drive Space

I like this option. Balance always seems to be a good option. Extremes often get us into trouble. DriveSpace 3 lets you have a balance between speed and drive space that best suits you and your computer hardware. It works like this: You tell DriveSpace 3 to use the uncompressed method on files until a specified percentage of the drive, predefined by you, fills up. Then DriveSpace 3 begins compressing files using Standard compression. The default is set so that when 90 percent of the compressed drive is filled, DriveSpace 3 begins compressing files. However, you can fill in your own percentage. At the 90 percent setting, DriveSpace 3 is optimized to favor speed over space until it's absolutely necessary to have more room. In contrast, if you set it to 10 percent, you'd be optimizing DriveSpace 3 in favor of drive space over speed.

To compress a drive for a balance between space and performance, open DriveSpace 3. Select Advanced | Settings. In the Disk Compression Settings dialog box, shown in Figure 24.27, select the No compression, unless drive is at least 90% full radio button. Modify the percentage if you wish. Click on the OK button and compress the drive in the usual way.

Compression Agent

Using Compression Agent can significantly increase the storage efficiency and performance of your drive compressed by DriveSpace 3. As we've seen, DriveSpace 3 compresses uncompressed drives, upgrades drives previously compressed using DoubleSpace or DriveSpace, and sets the compression method of saving new files to disk, allowing you to specify some optimizations for drive space and performance. Compression Agent picks up where DriveSpace 3 leaves off and works with DriveSpace 3 to optimize drive space and performance better than DriveSpace 3 can on its own.

In particular, Compression Agent scans your compressed drive and looks at each file for the time it was last accessed and how it is compressed. If the file is seldom accessed, Compression Agent will compress it at the highest compression ratio—UltraPack compression. Only Compression Agent can compress files using UltraPack. If the file is used often but has been compressed, Compression Agent will probably uncompress it to increase system performance.

DriveSpace 3 sets the standard compression method, as discussed earlier. Compression Agent optimizes the compression method set through DriveSpace 3 by checking individual file usage against compression type.

The Compression Tab

Plus! adds a Compression tab to your disk drive Properties dialog box. The Compression tab contains different information, depending on if the drive is compressed or not. If your drive isn't compressed, the Compression tab shows you the amount of used and free space currently on your drive and how much you would have of each if you compressed the drive. See Figure 24.28.

Figure 24.28.

The Compression tab in the disk drive Properties dialog box of an uncompressed drive.

It also tells you the approximate size of a new drive that could be built by compressing your drive's remaining free space. This is the perfect option if you want to compress files on your boot drive but don't want to risk having your whole boot drive compressed. Buttons on this tab allow you to compress the drive or make a new compressed drive. If your drive is compressed, the Compression tab is filled with statistics on the percentage of files compressed, with various compression types and the amount of disk space you've gained.

When you select the Compression tab from the Properties dialog box of a compressed disk drive, all sorts of drive statistics are calculated, as shown in Figure 24.29. Beware that this can take a while. You can, however, cancel the operation if you want.

Figure 24.29.
You can obtain information about your compressed drive in the Compression tab of the Properties dialog box.

The Compression tab will tell you how many megabytes of files are taken up by each compression type on your drive. It will also tell you the compression ratio achieved for each compression type and the number of megabytes you've gained by compressing the files.

In the disk drive Properties dialog box, you have the option of clicking on the Run Agent button to run Compression Agent to optimize disk compression. You can also click on the Advanced button to open the Advanced Properties dialog box, shown in Figure 24.30, where you can elect to hide the host drive or click on the Run DriveSpace button to reset various parameters inside DriveSpace 3.

Figure 24.30.
You can hide the host drive using the Advanced Properties dialog box.

The Internet

You've no doubt heard about the Internet—the Information Superhighway. Microsoft Plus! makes it easy for you to use the Internet. Microsoft built in everything you need to connect to the Internet, over a telephone or through a local area network (LAN), in Windows 95. However, knowing how to set up and use these resources can be difficult for most people. All it takes is one trip to the bookstore to see all the Internet titles to realize that this is true. Microsoft's Plus! package includes tools that make both setting up Internet access and using the Internet a breeze.

The Internet Setup Wizard is the principal tool that Plus! provides to take the pain out of setting up Internet access on your computer. Once you've run the Internet Setup Wizard, you can perform adjustments to your Internet connection settings using the Internet Control Panel applet provided by Plus!.

The Internet Setup Wizard

The Internet Setup Wizard is typically run during Microsoft Plus! setup. Using the Internet Setup Wizard can be anything from a "no brainer" to a bit more involved, depending on the Internet service provider you decide on. An Internet service provider is a person, business, company, or even a university that provides you with Internet access, either through a LAN or through the telephone using PPP (point-to-point protocol). The Internet Setup Wizard doesn't support the Serial Line Internet Protocol (SLIP). You can set up a SLIP connection using Windows 95, but you'll need to do that without the help of the Internet Setup Wizard.

> **Note:** SLIP is a simple dial-up protocol that turns your telephone line into a serial connection to the Internet. With SLIP, you must have an IP address and DNS addresses before you can connect to the Internet. PPP is a newer dial-up protocol that builds in several advanced features that allow the automatic setting of your IP address and DNS addresses by your Internet access provider.

If you're running Microsoft Plus! setup and have selected the Internet Jumpstart Kit, you'll get to the first page of the Internet Setup Wizard after Setup copies most of the Plus! files to your hard disk (see Figure 24.6). Otherwise, you can start Internet Setup Wizard by clicking on the Taskbar's Start button and selecting Programs | Accessories | Internet Tools | Internet Setup Wizard. When Internet Setup Wizard starts, it opens to the same first page that it does during Microsoft Plus! setup, shown in Figure 24.6.

Click on the Next button. If you have both a modem and a networking card installed on your computer, an Internet Setup Wizard page will appear, asking if you want to connect using your phone line or by using a direct networking connection. If you have only a modem installed on your machine, select Connect using my phone line and go to the next section of this chapter, "Dial-Up Networking." If you have only a networking card installed on your machine, select Connect using a LAN or CERN-compliant proxy server and go to the section "Local Area Network Access."

Dial-Up Networking

If you have a modem installed but not a network card, the Internet Setup Wizard's second page will be the How to Connect page, shown in Figure 24.31. If you choose to use a dial-up connection on the second page of the Internet Setup Wizard, this same page will be displayed even if you have both a modem and a network card installed. At this point, you need to make a decision about who you want to use as an Internet access provider. The next three sections cover your options.

Figure 24.31.

You can use either the Microsoft Network or another Internet access provider to connect with the Internet over the telephone.

Accessing the Microsoft Network and the Internet at the Same Time

The easiest way to set up access to the Internet is to use Microsoft Network's Internet access. Of course, Microsoft hopes you'll use this method. Microsoft Network offers excellent Internet connections through 28.8 Kbps modems. However, at the time of this writing, the number of cities with Internet access was limited.

> **Note:** Microsoft has promised to eventually offer 28.8 Kbps Internet access as a local call from anywhere in the continental U.S. But they're far from achieving this goal.

A unique feature of the Microsoft Network is that you can surf the Internet and the Microsoft Network at the same time. Suppose you hear about a particular page on the Internet's World Wide Web during a chat session on the Microsoft Network. While you continue chatting, you can fire up Microsoft's Internet Explorer and check out the Web page. Microsoft Network is the first online commercial network to allow simultaneous access to its online services and the Internet.

To set up an Internet account on the Microsoft Network, select the Use The Microsoft Network radio button on the How to Connect page of the Internet Setup Wizard (see Figure 24.31) and click on the Next button. The rest is easy!

Dialing Up Other Internet Access Providers

The Internet Setup Wizard lets you set up dial-up Internet access with providers other than Microsoft. The only stipulation is that the provider must allow point-to-point protocol (PPP) connections. Internet Setup Wizard doesn't support Serial Line Internet Protocol (SLIP). The procedure for setting up Internet access through providers other than Microsoft is a bit more involved, but not exceedingly so.

> **Note:** Your Internet access provider will give you specific instructions on how to connect to their service. Be sure to follow to the letter your provider's instructions for a Windows 95 connection.

You'll need four pieces of information before running Internet Setup Wizard to set up dial-up PPP access to an Internet access provider other than Microsoft. First, you'll need the provider's name—CompuServe, for instance. Then you'll need the number of the provider's modems through which you'll access the Internet. You can get access numbers from your provider. Be sure to check the speed of the modem. Surfing the Internet gets unbearably slow at less than 14.4 Kbps. 28.8 Kbps is ideal. Third, you'll need your user name and password. Finally, you'll need the Internet Protocol (IP) address of the access provider's Domain Name Server (DNS). Again, your Internet access provider should give you this information.

Your Internet service provider might provide POP/SMTP mailboxes. You can use Microsoft Exchange for your Internet e-mail. If you do, you'll need your e-mail name and password and the address of your e-mail server.

To set up an Internet account using an Internet Service Provider other than Microsoft, select the I already have an account with a different service provider radio button on the How to Connect page of the Internet Setup Wizard (see Figure 24.31) and click on the Next button.

On the Service Provider Information page, type the name of your service provider, as shown in Figure 24.32, and click on the Next button.

Type the telephone number of the modem you'll be dialing up on the Phone Number page, as shown in Figure 24.33.

Figure 24.32.
*Type the name of your
Internet access provider in
the Name of Service Provider
drop-down list box.*

Figure 24.33.
*Be sure to include the area
code of the Internet access
provider's modem.*

Local Area Network Access to the Internet

If your computer is part of a LAN, and if it's already connected to the Internet, there's no need for you to connect to the Internet over the phone. In fact, direct connections are much faster and therefore more desirable than phone connections. Plus! also supports using a CERN-compliant proxy server to connect your LAN to the Internet.

A Direct LAN-to-Internet Connection

To use the Internet Setup Wizard to make a direct LAN-to-Internet connection, you'll need at least two pieces of information. First, you'll need the Internet Protocol (IP) address of your Domain Name Server (DNS). You might have more than one DNS address. In that case, you can specify a main and an alternate server. Second, you'll need the IP address of the Internet gateway computer on your network. If you have a POP/SMTP mailbox on your LAN, you can use Microsoft Exchange for your Internet e-mail. You'll need your e-mail name and password and the address of your e-mail server. You might also need an IP address and Subnet Mask for your computer. Ask your network administrator if you need one or if your network supports automatically assigned IP addresses. Once you have this information, start the Internet Setup Wizard and click on the Next button to go to the second page.

If you have only a networking card installed on your machine, select Connect using a LAN or CERN-compliant proxy server and go to the Local Area Network Access section. If you have both a modem and a network interface card installed on your machine, select the Connect using my Local Area Network radio button on the How to Connect page. Click on the Next button to open the IP Address page.

If your network supports automatically assigned IP addresses, leave the Use DHCP to choose one automatically (recommended) radio button selected. Otherwise, select the Always use the following radio button and fill in your IP Address and Subnet Mask in the proper fields. Click on the Next button to go to the DNS Server Address page.

Fill in the DNS Server field with the address of the DNS server given to you by your network administrator. If you have an address for a second DNS server, type it into the Alternate DNS Server field. This field is optional. Click on the Next button to go to the Internet Gateway page.

Fill in the Gateway Address field on the Internet Gateway page with the gateway address given to you by your network administrator. Click on the Next button to go to the Internet Mail page.

If you've been given an e-mail account on a machine with a POP server, click on the Use Internet Mail checkbox and enter your complete e-mail address in the Your Email Address field. Enter your server's address in the Internet mail server field. Click on the Next button.

If you checked the Use Internet Mail checkbox, skip this paragraph. After filling in your e-mail address and your mail server's address and clicking on the Next button, you should be at the Exchange Profile page. You can either use an existing profile or create a new Internet mail profile by clicking on the New button. If you click on the New button, the default Internet Mail Settings will be in the Profile name field of the Profile Name dialog box. Click on the OK button and then click on the Next button on the Exchange Profile page.

You should be on the Finished Setup! page of the Internet Setup Wizard. Click on the Finish button, and your direct Internet connection is ready.

A LAN-to-Internet Connection Through a CERN-Compliant Proxy Server

Configure proxy support by opening the Internet Control Panel after running the Internet Setup Wizard, and choose the Advanced tab on the Internet Properties dialog box.

If you have a POP/SMTP mailbox on your LAN, you can use Microsoft Exchange for your Internet e-mail. You'll need your e-mail name and password and the address of your e-mail server.

Adjusting Connection Settings with the Internet Applet

Plus! installs the new Internet icon in your Control Panel. You'll use the Internet Control Panel if you want to change settings or add connections to other Internet providers after you've installed Plus! and used the Internet Setup Wizard.

Double-clicking on the Internet icon in Control Panel opens the Internet Properties dialog box. The tabs contained in this dialog box depend on the type or types of Internet connections you've specified.

The AutoDial Tab

If you're accessing the Internet over the phone, you'll see an AutoDial tab in your Internet Properties dialog box, as shown in Figure 24.34. When AutoDial is on, whenever you launch an application that tries to access the Internet, AutoDial is alerted and automatically launches Microsoft Network's Sign On dialog box or Connect To dialog box, depending on your Internet access provider. You select the provider that you want AutoDial to call in the Settings section. To dial up your Internet provider's modem, you simply click on the Connect button.

Note: Not all Internet applications are compatible with the AutoDial feature. As of this writing, the Microsoft Internet Explorer, Netscape 1.2, Windows 95 Telnet & FTP, and Microsoft Exchange definitely support it.

Figure 24.34.
The AutoDial tab in the Internet Properties dialog box.

The Advanced Tab

The Advanced tab, shown in Figure 24.35, is used to set up a connection through a proxy server. You'll use this if you're connecting to the Internet from a LAN through a CERN-compliant proxy server.

Figure 24.35.

The Advanced tab in the Internet Properties dialog box.

Surfing the Internet with the Internet Explorer

Now that your Internet access is set up, you can have fun. Microsoft has carried its concept of "information at your fingertips" to the Internet. The idea is that you focus on the information, not the gritty details of the technology used to retrieve it. For example, sometimes you arrive at a point where you need more information in order to continue. If you were writing a document on mountain gorillas, you would simply ask your computer how many mountain gorillas were left in the world. The data would show up on your document, and you would continue working, incorporating the data into your discussion. Unfortunately, technology isn't that far along. Nevertheless, Windows 95 goes a long way toward this goal, and the way Microsoft integrated its Internet tools, especially the Internet Explorer, with your Desktop environment is no less innovative.

Introducing the World Wide Web

The World Wide Web (WWW for acronym lovers and the Web to the rest of us) is an interactive way to visually move through the huge virtual space of the Internet. The Web is visual because each piece is similar to a page in a glossy picture book, but it's much more than that. Each page almost always contains text and graphics, but often you can also play movies or listen to sound. The Web creates a multimedia environment that extends to your Windows 95 Desktop environment and to your room through your monitor and speakers.

The Web is interactive. Each page usually has icons, graphics, and text that you can point to in order to get to other pages on the Web, see a picture, play a sound, or retrieve a file. When you point and click on something and end up on another page, you're experiencing the fundamental interaction that the Web was named for. Whatever you click on is linked to another page. If you visualize each page as a dot sitting somewhere in virtual space and a link as a string that connects one dot to another, you'll understand why it's called the World Wide Web. Literally millions of pages (or dots) are connected through an unimaginable number of links or strings that form a virtual web spanning the globe.

The Web is always changing. The *Wall Street Journal* has daily Money and Investing pages. There are several continuously updated weather pages. Most Web pages update or change their contents to remain interesting.

If my definition of the Web still doesn't seem that precise, perhaps it's because the World Wide Web can be precisely defined only by the protocols and other technical underpinnings that go into building each part of it, each page, and the interactions between its many millions of pages around the world. However, the sum of the Web is greater than its parts. You don't need to know a lot of technical jargon to effectively use the Web.

Web Browsers

Web browser is the nontechnical term applied to programs used primarily to browse pages in the Web. Browsing the Web is sort of like browsing through pages in a book or magazine. Microsoft Plus! includes a very good Web browser, aptly named the Internet Explorer, that provides all the features you need to explore the Internet thoroughly.

Addresses on the Web

Just as each house is associated with a unique address so that a mail carrier can deliver a letter there no matter where it's from, each Web page is associated with a unique address, called its Universal Resource Locator, or URL. If you know a Web page's URL, you can find it. If you don't know any URLs or Web pages, you can still use the Web. You can usually find what you're looking for, but you'll be much more efficient and far more confident during your navigations if you understand something about URLs.

A good place to start learning about URLs is to look at one, and a good URL to start with is the address of Yahoo. Yahoo is a comprehensive compilation of Web sites around the world, grouped into hierarchical categories according to subject matter. You'll find Yahoo at http://www.yahoo.com/. We'll talk more about Yahoo later. First, let's take a closer look at this URL.

We'll look at Yahoo using the Microsoft Internet Explorer. We'll also see how the Internet Explorer uses URLs. Take a peek at Figure 24.43 to see the Yahoo home page. Notice Yahoo's URL listed just below the Internet Explorer's toolbar in the Address field.

At the highest level, an URL can be divided into two parts by a pair of backslashes (//). Information to the left of the backslashes identifies the protocol name (in this case, HTTP), and the information on the right is the address of the computer where the Web page that you want is stored.

First, let's find out what HTTP means and why the URL must identify a protocol. HTTP stands for Hypertext Transfer Protocol, the name given to the technical specifications behind the mechanisms that make the World Wide Web work. It's not important for you to know these specifications in order to use the Web. The only thing that's really important is that when you see HTTP, you know you're using the Web.

Since the first part of the URL specifies a protocol, maybe you've theorized that a Web browser can use more than one protocol—and you're right. Protocols define how computers talk to each other and the computer user. The Web protocol is a newcomer to the Internet community. When the Web started, popular protocols such as the e-mail protocol SMTP (Simple Mail Transfer Protocol) were already in use. If Web browsers (such as the Microsoft Internet Explorer) supported only the new Web protocol and ignored the others, they couldn't use much of the existing Internet. This would severely limit the usefulness of a Web browser. Luckily, the designers of Web browsers thought of this and included the ability to use many existing Internet facilities by defining protocols.

HTTP will probably be the most common protocol that you'll use, especially if you stick to looking at Web pages. However, you can use six other protocols (see Table 24.4). Of these, the most common are ftp and gopher. We'll return to these, and others, later in this chapter.

Table 24.4. Protocols used by a Web browser.

Protocol	Description
ftp://	Takes you to a File Transfer Protocol site, a site set up so that you can transfer files back to your computer.
gopher://	Takes you to a gopher menu system.
http://	Loads Web pages.
mailto:	Used to send e-mail.
news:	Used to read UseNet news groups.
telnet://	Starts a Telnet session, in which you can log onto another computer on the Internet.

Let's look again at that URL for Yahoo, http://www.yahoo.com/. Again, the part of the URL to the right of the two backslashes specifies the address of the computer where the Web page that you want is stored. The computer, usually called the server, is found on the Internet at www.yahoo.com. This address is actually a human-friendly form of what is technically an Internet Protocol, or IP, address that consists of a string of four numbers separated by periods. The IP address for www.yahoo.com is 205.217.231.67. For our purposes, we never need to look at a string of numbers again. The human-readable address, like the string of numbers, is broken up by periods. Each part of the address specifies a computer's Internet site, starting with the most specific information on the left through the most general on the right. In general terms, the part of the address before the first period usually gives the name of a specific computer; the next one or two parts usually gives the name of a subnet or institution; and the final part of the name, the suffix, identifies the kind of institution that maintains the site. Common suffixes are listed in Table 24.5.

Table 24.5. Common Internet address suffixes.

Suffix	Host
com	A commercial site
edu	An educational site
gov	A government site
mil	A military site
org	An organization such as the United Nations

You might see other information in an URL. Most of this information will be to the right of the Internet address. For instance, as you move through Web pages at a particular Internet address, you'll see directory information appear in the URL. You're also likely to see a file listed on the far-right side of an URL after a list of directories. Often this will be an HTML file—a Hypertext Markup Language file. HTML is the language that Web pages are programmed in. It's not important for you to know HTML in order to use the Web, but if you see an URL ending with .html or .htm, you know it's an HTML file. You don't need to know every last thing about an URL to surf the Web effectively, so I'll point out some of these subtleties later when we surf.

 To see what an URL with a directory listed looks like, take a look at the URL in the Address box in Figure 24.46. Here we're in the Science directory. Figure 24.48 shows an URL with the HTML file alife.html listed at the end of the directory cb. Notice also that this page is at a new address, www.fusebox.com.

Browsing the Web with the Microsoft Internet Explorer

Let's look at the premier Internet tool that's provided in Plus!—the Microsoft Internet Explorer. While we're at it, let's go surfing!

If you installed the Internet Jumpstart Kit during the Microsoft Plus! setup, you should see the Internet Desktop icon on your Desktop. See Figure 24.36.

Figure 24.36.
You'll find a quick way into the Internet by double-clicking on the Internet icon on the left side of the screen. (This figure shows the Science Desktop Theme.)

Double-click on the Internet icon to launch Microsoft Internet Explorer. If you're using a dial-up connection to the Internet but you're not connected when you launch Internet Explorer, a Sign In dialog box, shown in Figure 24.37, will appear.

Figure 24.37.
When the Microsoft Internet Explorer is launched from the Desktop, a Sign In dialog box appears. In this case, the dial-up Internet access provider is Microsoft Network.

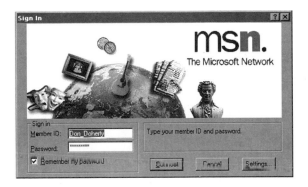

Click on the Connect button. Otherwise, if you're connecting directly to the Internet or through a LAN, you must already be communicating properly with the Internet before launching Internet Explorer. When the Internet Explorer opens, it automatically loads the Microsoft Network's home page on the Internet, as shown in Figure 24.38.

Let's take a closer look at the Microsoft Network's home page. It shows several general features that are common or even ubiquitous on the Web, using different Web browsers and some features that are specific to the Internet Explorer.

Figure 24.38.
The Microsoft Network's home page is loaded when you launch the Microsoft Internet Explorer.

A central feature of browsing the Web is something called the link. Text objects and graphic objects on a Web page can be linked to other Web pages or files in such a way that when you point and click on the text object or graphic object, they either take you to the other Web page or load the file to your computer.

The Microsoft Network's home page has 10 links. You can tell when something on a Web page is linked by passing the mouse pointer over it. If the pointer icon turns into a hand, the object is linked. You can see in Figure 24.38 that the Explore the Internet: Searches, Links and Tools graphic in the middle of the Microsoft Network home page is linked because the hand pointer is pointing to it. Notice also that the status bar at the bottom-left shows the message `Shortcut to access.htm`. When you point to a linked object, Internet Explorer's status bar tells you where the object is linked to—in this case, an HTML page named "access." Can you find the nine other links on this page?

Tip: If you don't see a status bar when you open Internet Explorer, select View | Status Bar. The status bar is displayed when there's a check mark next to this option on the View menu. Notice that Toolbar and Address Bar are also on the View menu. Each is displayed according to whether it's checked on the View menu.

A couple of other general features of the Web browser are worth mentioning. Notice that the title bar displays the name of the Web page you're viewing. You can see Microsoft Welcomes You To The Internet! displayed at the top left in the title bar in Figure 24.38. I'll point out items of interest in the menu bar and toolbar as we go along. Below the toolbar you should see the address bar, which displays the address or URL of the current page. You can also type in a page in the Address field if you know it. All of the typical text editing features are available in the Address field. Just right-click inside the Address field to highlight the URL and display a shortcut menu that lists familiar editing commands. If you find a great new Web page that you must share with a friend, simply right-click in the Address field; select Copy, as shown in Figure 24.39; paste it into an e-mail message; and send it off. Likewise, you can paste an URL you receive in e-mail by using the e-mail's Copy command, the same shortcut menu in Microsoft Exchange, and the Paste command in the address bar.

Figure 24.39.
You can use familiar editing commands with a click of the right mouse button in the address bar's Address field.

Tip: You can also use Microsoft Internet Explorer's Edit menu while editing the address bar's Address field.

Some features make the Internet Explorer special. The most important of these is its OLE support. We'll look at all of the Internet Explorer's special features as we move through the Web. For now, let's take a break from surfing to look at what OLE support will do for you.

To see what OLE can do, make sure that the Internet Explorer's window takes up only a portion of your Desktop, and point to the Explore the Internet: Searches, Links and Tools graphic object in the center of the Microsoft Network's home page (see Figure 24.38). Hold down the left mouse button while you move the mouse pointer to anywhere over your Desktop where no Desktop icon is showing. Release the left mouse button. You should now have a .GIF image icon sitting on your Desktop with the name "internet" under it, as shown in Figure 24.40.

You can do this with any graphic object on the Web page. Just don't release the left button before you get to the Desktop, or you'll go to the place that the Explore button is linked to.

Figure 24.40.

Dropping a graphic object from a Web page onto the upper-right corner of the Windows 95 Desktop results in a .GIF file named "internet" being placed on the Desktop and shown as an icon.

You can also drag and drop text from a Web page. Open an OLE-enabled word processor, such as Microsoft Word 6, to test this. When you move the mouse pointer over text in a Web page while using the Internet Explorer, the pointer changes into the Bar cursor. Highlight the text you want to drag and drop, and then point the mouse cursor at the highlighted text. Hold the left mouse button down and drag the text to a page in your OLE-enabled word processor. Let go of the left mouse button. Now the text is included in your document. OLE lets you grab just about anything from a Web page and drop it into any OLE-enabled container. Just think how handy this will be when you need to grab the latest weather statistics from a Web page and add them to your report. Microsoft Exchange is also an OLE application.

Note: WordPad, the OLE-enabled word processor included with Windows 95, should be able to handle text dragged from the Internet Explorer. However, I got a blank page when I tried this. On the other hand, dragging and dropping text from the Internet Explorer worked perfectly when I dropped it into a Microsoft Word or a Microsoft Excel document. If you want to use WordPad, you can use the shortcut menu by pointing to the highlighted text in the Internet Explorer, right-clicking, and selecting Copy. Now activate your WordPad document and select Paste from the Edit menu or WordPad's shortcut menu.

I was recently reading the online version of the *Wall Street Journal* when I saw a quote that I thought a friend would appreciate. I simply highlighted the quote on the Web page, dragged and dropped it into a note I was composing under Microsoft Exchange, and sent the message to her. OLE is a key feature in integrating the Internet with your Desktop.

> **Tip:** As an alternative, you could have selected File | Save to save the whole Web page on your PC as an HTML or a text file, then dragged and dropped or cut and pasted your text later offline.

> **Note:** You can find the online version of the *Wall Street Journal* at http://update.wuj.com.

OK, we've taken our first step into the Web and looked at some features of our Web browser. Now let's get into some serious surfing. Back on the Microsoft Network's home page, click on Explore the Internet: Searches, Links and Tools at the center of the page to get started. This should take you to the Microsoft Network's Explore the Internet page, shown in Figure 24.41.

Figure 24.41.
The Microsoft Network's Explore the Internet page scrolled down a bit to view Microsoft's Top Ten (favorite) sites.

Click on the linked text that says Microsoft's Top Ten or click on the linked Our Favorites graphic. You should now see the Microsoft Network's Our Favorite Websites page, shown in Figure 24.42. Right under the listing for ESPNET Sports Zone is our old friend Yahoo, listed as the Yahoo Search Server.

Click on Yahoo Search Server to load Yahoo, as shown in Figure 24.43. Yahoo is a good place to start browsing the Web because from here you can find Web pages on nearly any subject. This is a good time to look at the Internet Explorer's favorite places facilities.

Figure 24.42.
Find out Microsoft's favorite Web sites from the Microsoft Network's Our Favorite Websites page.

Figure 24.43.
From this Yahoo Web page you can find Web pages on nearly any subject.

Wouldn't it be handy to be able to jump to the Yahoo page wherever you were on the Web and whenever you needed to find a page by subject? You could do this by saving the Yahoo page address or URL. The Internet Explorer makes this easy with its favorite places facilities. While you're viewing Yahoo, either click on the Add To Favorites button on the toolbar or select Favorites | Add To Favorites. The Add To Favorites dialog box, shown in Figure 24.44, will appear.

Figure 24.44.
Add to your list of favorite places using the Add To Favorites dialog box.

In the Name text box, accept the default name of the Web page or change it to something that makes sense to you, and then click on the Add button. Now, when you open the Favorites menu, the favorite page you just added—in this case, Yahoo— will be listed at the bottom, as shown in Figure 24.45. When you want to go to Yahoo, simply open the Favorites menu and select Yahoo.

Figure 24.45.
All the pages you add as favorites will be listed at the bottom of the Favorites menu.

Tip: Your favorites are saved in the Windows | Favorites folder. Each time you save a favorite, a .URL file is created in the Favorites folder. You can open your Favorites folder from the Internet Explorer either by clicking on the Open Favorites button on the toolbar or by selecting Favorites | Open Favorites. Each .URL file is given the name of the Web page it's associated with. You can manipulate these files in the normal way. Right-click on the file and select Properties from the context menu to see the URL. Drag and drop an .URL file to your Desktop. Then, when you want to go directly to that page, double-click on the .URL file. You can also send an .URL file to friends so that they can drag and drop it into their Favorites folder. Finally, you can organize your favorite files by creating folders inside your Favorites folder and dropping .URL files into them. These folders will show up as submenus in your Favorites menu. Any .URL files that you drop inside a folder will be listed under the submenu named after that folder.

Now we'll continue browsing until we get to an interesting page. Suppose we want to find out what science resources are listed at Yahoo. Scroll down the list on the Yahoo Web page until you see Science, and then click on the listing to go to the Yahoo Science page, shown in Figure 24.46.

Figure 24.46.
Yahoo's Science page.

Artificial Life looks interesting. Click on the Artificial Life link. Now you should see the Yahoo - Science:Artificial Life page, shown in Figure 24.47.

The Live Alife page looks interesting. Click on Live Alife.

Note: Alife is short for artificial life. Therefore, the page we're going to has live artificial life!?

You should now be in the Live Artificial Life Page, shown in Figure 24.48.

Figure 24.47.
Yahoo's Science:Artificial Life page.

Figure 24.48.
The Live Artificial Life page.

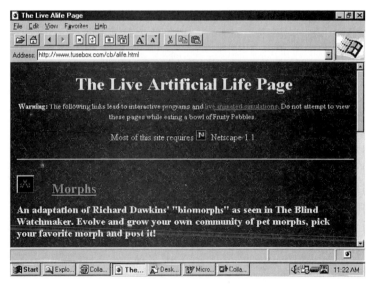

You can learn a lot about artificial life here and, better yet, you can do real experiments in artificial life at this site. For instance, you can click on Morphs and then click on Morphs Lab to evolve your own Morphs. But wait! Why is there a red dot with an X in it on the Morphs Instructions page, shown in Figure 24.49?

Figure 24.49.
The Morphs Instructions page demonstrates a limitation of the Microsoft Internet Explorer.

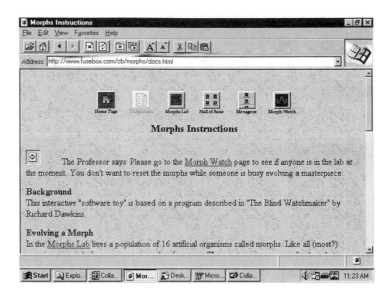

Perhaps you noticed a warning on the Live Artificial Life Page in Figure 24.48, which said "Most of this site requires Netscape 1.1." Every Web browser has common features, but, as we've already seen, each browser can have special features not found on other browsers. The Internet Explorer is the only OLE browser that I know of to date. A browser called Netscape has typically been an innovative leader. In my experience, the Internet Explorer does almost everything that Netscape can do. However, one thing the Internet Explorer can't deal with is a kind of real-time animation used at this Web site. Netscape also has security features that the Internet Explorer doesn't.

Tip: If you're now set on seeing all the animated features at the Live Artificial Life Page site, don't despair. You can download the latest Netscape browser from the Internet and evaluate it at no charge. Netscape is shareware, so if you decide to keep it, be sure to register it and pay the shareware fees. Currently, a Windows 95 version is available. Go to http://home.netscape.com/comprod/netscape_nav.html to find out more about it, and go to http://home.netscape.com/comprod/mirror/index.html to find a site to download the file. You'll see how to download a file later in this chapter. Figure 24.50 shows the Morphs Instructions page using Netscape.

Tip: When possible, always use 32-bit applications under Windows 95. Netscape is available in both 16-bit and 32-bit formats. Either of them will run under Windows 95, but 16-bit applications actually cripple Windows 95. For instance, multitasking is far less efficient when you run a 16-bit program. The bottom line is that you'll get your best performance when using 32-bit programs under Windows 95.

Figure 24.50.

The Morphs Instructions page using the 32-bit version of Netscape 1.2b5. Notice that the icon on the far left is different from the one in Figure 24.49.

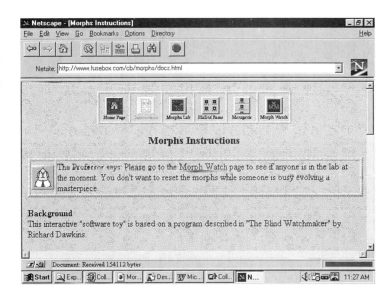

Now that you've surfed through a small portion of the Internet, you can look at the Internet Explorer's history feature at the bottom of the File menu. You should see the previous Web pages you've visited at the bottom of the File menu. Number 1 is the most recent. At the end of the list you'll see the menu selection More History. When you select it, the History folder opens. (Your History folder can be found under Program Files | Plus! | Microsoft Internet when you use Explorer.) Your History folder contains .URL files from the Web sites you've visited. You can drag and drop files from your History folder into your Favorites folder, your Desktop, or anywhere else that's OLE-enabled.

Tip: You can set the number of Web pages that are saved in your History folder in the Options dialog box. From the Microsoft Internet Explorer, select View | Options to open the Options dialog box. Select the Advanced tab, shown in Figure 24.51. Within the History frame, the default setting of Remember the last *x* places visited is 300. Reset this number to the number of sites you want remembered. You can also change the History folder from the default using the Change button, and you can empty the History folder by clicking on the Empty button.

You're now ready to step out into cyberspace on your own. If you're interested in artificial life, you can connect to other pages on the subject through links from the Live Artificial Life Page, or you can hunt for pages centered on your own favorite subject. Just select Favorites | Yahoo.

Figure 24.51.
*You change history settings
using the Options dialog box
in the Microsoft Internet
Explorer.*

FTP and Gopher Using the Microsoft Internet Explorer

Web browsers were built to utilize not only the World Wide Web but also various Internet facilities that were already in place when the Web was first conceived.

Using FTP

FTP, or File Transfer Protocol, is a set of technical specifications that define a protocol that allows you to transfer files from one computer to another over the Internet. Luckily, you don't need to understand these specifications to use FTP. The Microsoft Internet Explorer makes it easy to gather files using FTP.

To use FTP from the Internet Explorer you'll need to either click on a link from a Web page to an FTP site or enter an URL into the address bar's Address field with the FTP protocol type (see Table 24.4) and the address of an FTP server.

Let's say you want to try out the Netscape browser to compare it with the Internet Explorer. Type

```
ftp://ftp.netscape.com/pub
```

into the Address field and press Enter.

Note: Netscape is a shareware program. This means that you can download the program and evaluate it for free, but if you decide to keep it, you must pay for it.

If the site isn't too busy, you should see a page with the words "pub Folder" in bold at the top left, as shown in Figure 24.52.

Figure 24.52.
The pub folder at one of Netscape's FTP sites.

As of this writing, the most recent release of Netscape is version 1.2b5 (1.2 beta 5). "Beta" means that this version of Netscape is still under development and that the program is bound to have some glitches. New betas are coming out fast and furious, so when you access this page, just look for the highest-numbered release. Click on netscape1.2b5 (or the most recent release). You should see a page that looks like the one shown in Figure 24.53.

Figure 24.53.
This folder at Netscape's FTP site contains only 16-bit and 32-bit versions of Netscape 1.2b5.

You're now in a bottom folder at Netscape's FTP site that contains only files. Click on .message, license, or readme.txt to read the contents of these files. Files that contain text are loaded directly into the browser. This can get annoying when you want to read a text file but you also want to stay in the same page. The Internet Browser solves this problem by letting you open as many windows as you want. For example, if you hold down the Shift key and click on readme.txt, another Internet Explorer window will open with readme.txt loaded, as shown in Figure 24.54.

Figure 24.54.
You can open as many Internet Explorer windows as you want. You can do this anywhere on the Internet, not just at an FTP site.

You can do the same thing by right-clicking while pointing to readme.txt and selecting the Open In New Window command from the shortcut menu. This command is available for any link you find on the Internet. You can save the text loaded into an Internet Explorer window by selecting File | Save As.

The other two links in the netscape1.2b5 Folder shown in Figure 24.53 are links to the executable files n1612b5.exe and n3212b5.exe. The n stands for Netscape, the 16 and 32 tell you the bits your operating system must be able to handle in order to use the program, and the 12b5 stands for version 1.2b5. Since you're running Windows 95, you definitely want the 32-bit version, so click on n3212b5.exe. The Internet Explorer doesn't load executable files. When you click on a link to an executable file or other binary files that the Internet Explorer doesn't open, a Confirm File Open dialog box appears, as shown in Figure 24.55.

Figure 24.55.
The Confirm File Open dialog box opens for files that the Internet Explorer doesn't normally open.

Since you want to load this file to your local disk drive, click on the Save As button. The Save As dialog box opens. Go through the usual procedures to save a file. When you click on the OK button, the Internet Explorer downloads the file to your computer. You should see a Copying file message in the status bar, telling you the filename and size of the file being transferred. Also, on the right side of the status bar, you should see a progress bar indicating the relative percentage of the file downloaded.

> **Tip:** If you want to continue browsing the Web while downloading a file, try opening a new window by holding down the Shift key while clicking on the link to the file you're going to download. A new Internet Explorer window opens, and the Confirm File Open dialog box appears. Go through the usual procedures and then, while the file downloads, continue browsing the Web in the other Internet Explorer window.

You've now used Internet Explorer's built-in FTP capabilities. If you want to try out the program you just downloaded, follow the installation instructions provided by Netscape in its readme.txt file.

Using Gopher

Gopher space is something like the Web without the graphical interface. Gopher predated the World Wide Web and was built mainly for easy text-based Internet navigation using links. Microsoft Internet Explorer provides access to Gopher space when you click on a link to a Gopher server or if you enter an URL into the address bar's Address field using the Gopher protocol identifier "gopher" (see Table 24.4) and a Gopher server's address. One major advantage of using Gopher is its speed. Without the graphics overhead, you'll find moving around Gopher space noticeably faster than on the Web.

Maybe after hearing so much about the United Nations in the news, you decide that you want to learn more about what they do in troubled areas around the world. Enter the URL gopher:// nywork1.undp.org/11/ into the Address field and press Enter. You should see the Gopher page shown in Figure 24.56.

The link to The United Nations, what it is and what it does looks promising. When you click on the link, the Gopher page shown in Figure 24.57 appears.

At the bottom of the list is a link to information about United Nations Peace-Keeping Operations. When you click on it, the Gopher page shown in Figure 24.58 appears.

This page lists a collection of links to files describing UN peace-keeping missions around the world and files that describe current situations in various trouble spots. Click on Information notes on Yugoslavia (July 95), for instance, and you see the document shown in Figure 24.59.

Figure 24.58.
This Gopher page lists a collection of links to files describing United Nations peace-keeping missions and situation reports from around the world.

Figure 24.59.
Recently updated information on Yugoslavia from the United Nations Gopher server.

Note: Due to the nature of the reports shown in Figure 24.58, you're likely to see a different screen. The world situation is constantly changing. This Gopher page reflects those changes through constant updates.

Using Helper Applications with the Microsoft Internet Explorer

Because the Internet's content is constantly changing, Web browsers need to be flexible in the way they handle files found on the Internet. For instance, initially the most common audio file on the Web had a low-fidelity 8-bit mono format and an .AU extension. This form of audio file had the advantage that the files remained relatively small, but has the disadvantage that they had poor sound quality. Other formats began to proliferate for various reasons. When the Windows 3.x multimedia extensions were released, wave files began showing up on the Web. Wave files, with the .WAV extension, had the advantage of very good sound quality, but their disadvantage was that they could be very large. You could compare advantages and disadvantages between half a dozen formats. The Internet Explorer is configured at setup time to run most audio formats you'll encounter, including .AU, .AIFF, and .WAV. Additionally, it's preconfigured to run RealAudio files with the .RAM extension. All the other sound file formats mentioned force you to download the whole file before listening to it. A couple of minutes of sound can form a file of several megabytes. If you're using a dial-up network to connect to the Internet, it could take a huge amount of time to download. RealAudio feeds the sound file to your player through the Internet in real time, even over a 14.4 Kbps connection! Sites that use RealAudio are often radio-show-style talk shows that might last an hour or more!

The way that the Web browser built in flexibility to take advantage of the tremendous changes and growth in technology was to use what are often called helper applications. When you try to link to a file that the Internet Explorer can't display or play directly, it looks at the Windows 95 file registration list to see if there's another application that can. If there is, the Internet Explorer launches that application and displays or plays the file with it. Otherwise, the Internet Explorer displays the Unknown File Type dialog box. Usually, if you don't have a helper application that will play a file, you can find a helper application on the Internet that will.

To see the list of registered files from within the Internet Explorer, select View | Options and then click on the File Types tab in the Options dialog box, shown in Figure 24.60.

Reading Newsgroups with the Microsoft Internet Explorer

Perhaps you've heard of Internet newsgroups or UseNet. If you use the Microsoft Internet Explorer with the Microsoft Network, you can access newsgroups through links in the Web. The Internet Explorer has been integrated with the newsgroup services offered through MSN itself. When you click on a link to a newsgroup—bionet.neuroscience, for instance—a window for the newsgroup pops up. It contains a list of all of the newsgroup's messages.

Figure 24.60.
The File Types tab in the Options dialog box lists registered file types from within Internet Explorer.

Note: Where did I come up with bionet.neuroscience? It's one of the newsgroups blocked by MSN until you give MSN a release for full newsgroup access. For more information, go to MSN's Internet forum.

Internet Mail and Microsoft Exchange

When you install the Internet Jumpstart Kit, the Internet mail service is added to Microsoft Exchange.

When you want to send or receive Internet mail through a POP/SMTP server, open Microsoft Exchange. When the Choose Profile dialog box appears, select the Internet Mail Settings profile in the Profile Name list box.

Note: You don't need the Internet mail service to send or receive Internet mail through the Microsoft Network. It's provided for your SMTP (Simple Mail Transfer Protocol) accounts that you might have with other Internet access providers.

When you use the Microsoft Network, Microsoft Exchange is closely integrated with Microsoft Internet Explorer. Remember the mailto: protocol in Table 24.4? When you click on a link to an e-mail address on a Web page, Exchange's New Message window opens, and the To field is filled in with the e-mail address you clicked on. After you fill in the Subject field, fill in the body of the message, and click on Send, the person will receive your e-mail message.

Summary

The Microsoft Plus! package is greater than the sum of its parts. There are endless ways that you can use different features of Microsoft Plus! with standard Windows 95 features to enhance your productivity and pleasure. Like Microsoft Windows 95 itself, you'll be mining Microsoft Plus! for new ways to do things long after your introduction to it.

VII

Appendixes

A

Online Resources

User groups provide a valuable source of information for the average user, but they can be a little limited. There's only so much information that you can expect to get from the members of your user group. Even if it's a larger group, you'll see a lot less than the literally thousands of people on CompuServe who work specifically with Windows 95. The Internet and other online services also provide a wealth of resources for the typical user. The types of information that each online service provides vary, but in the long run you'll find that most of them provide a level of information superior to that found in a local users' group.

I won't say that every person you run into when using an online service will be an expert. Most of them are just average users like you. However, I've had the pleasure of running into some truly remarkable people from time to time while browsing through the messages. In fact, some people are constantly looking for ways to make Windows better in their spare time. You'll usually find them in a forum somewhere, just waiting to share this information with you.

Online services offer other things of value as well. For example, if you talk with your local users' group, you're getting the local view of Windows 95. On the other hand, talking with someone on an online service such as CompuServe or the Internet might give you the English, Australian, or Japanese view of Windows 95. This international flavor will give you a better appreciation of features you might not have considered important before. In addition, the cultural differences actually work together to help you see new ways of using features you might not have seen before.

Aside from all the talking you'll do with other users, an online forum also gives you access to vendor representatives. There have been times when I've started a conversation with three, or even four, people who work for the company whose product I'm using. You'll find that the expert knowledge that the vendor representative provides often gets mixed in with the real-world view of the other users. The result is that you actually get better information from the online service than you could have gotten from the vendor's technical support line.

Is this all there is? Not by a long shot. Online services provide many of the features you've come to expect from a vendor BBS. For example, you can go online to CompuServe, the Internet, or MSN (the Microsoft Network) and download the latest patches for just about any Microsoft product. The same holds true for other vendors as well. However, many of them provide only CompuServe or Internet access, so you'll have to check to make sure you'll find the vendor you need on the service you subscribe to. I've often found a needed NetWare patch on the NetWire forum on CompuServe.

If you think CompuServe or any other online forum is all software, think again. Practical Peripherals, AST, Hewlett-Packard, IBM, and other hardware vendors provide valuable services here too. I think you'll find this hardware presence useful each time you need to download a new driver or ask a configuration question regarding Windows 95. You'll find the same level of expertise in these areas that you find in the software areas.

CompuServe and other online forums aren't all work. You'll also find several areas that deal specifically with the fun end of life. For example, some CompuServe forums deal with travel and hobbies.

Some online services, such as the Sierra Network, specialize in games or other forms of entertainment. The list goes on and on. I dare say that if you get online, you'll never visit every forum there is or even scratch the surface of the knowledge you could use. An online forum can provide a wealth of information and enhance the way you work. If you're really interested in all these other activities, I suggest that you get one of the many books on the market that deal specifically with online computing.

The Microsoft Network

Windows 95 comes with the ability to use Microsoft Network (MSN) as part of the installed features. We took an initial look at what you could expect to find here in Chapter 19. Actually, that chapter covered more of the usage end of the product—how to get something done. Let's take a look at MSN from another perspective.

I don't want to tour every nook and cranny of MSN, but I'd like to give you an idea of what's available. The problem is that even the look I give you right now won't be quite complete. Microsoft is still working on getting vendors together for their new online service, and it looks as though it might open without the full complement they originally hoped to have. With that in mind, let's take a look at what you'll find today. At least you'll know what features are available right now. It's important to remember that these are preliminary features and that you'll most likely see many more features later.

The top menu is the place to begin with MSN. Like any online service, it uses a hierarchical format to allow you to "drill down" to the specific areas you want to find. Unlike many other services, though, using the hierarchical format is easy with MSN. In fact, you really can't get away from it because of the Explorer interface that MSN uses. Figure A.1 shows what this top-level folder grouping looks like. The following list tells you a little about each entry.

Figure A.1.
The top level of the MSN Explorer interface tells you about the major features you'll find here.

- Arts and Entertainment: You'll find much of what you'd expect here. There are forums devoted to writers, musicians, artists, comedians, and a variety of other fields. In fact, here you'll find just about any artistic endeavor that also deals with entertainment. I was a bit surprised to see an interactive book available online. The one I looked at was called "The Big Chip." It was about everyone's desire to get their hands on a new computer chip. It was fun looking at this online book. There's also a section devoted to movies. It includes not only a forum for aspiring filmmakers, but a movie review BBS and other movie-related features. You'll also find sections for various types of films. Some of the sections include Ultraviolent Movies and another named Sex and Movies. I was happy to see a section specifically devoted to kids. You can also find out about television, radio, and the theater here.

- Business and Finance: My first thought about this area was that it would offer access to the *Wall Street Journal* and other sources of financial information. Actually, it contains quite a few different forums, all of which deal with a different aspect of financial planning. For example, if you run a small business out of your home, you'll find a forum specially designed to meet that need. A folder in the Small Office/Home Office area contained all kinds of business services. (You can find the same Business Services folders in the main Business and Finance folder.) For example, you'll find an Ask a Lawyer forum here, as well as access to TRW. I was also very pleased to see a UPS forum. You can schedule packages for pickup or check on the status of a package while online. One of the more unusual offerings was access to the PhotoDisk service. Another folder in the Small Office/Home Office area is called Starting Up. Here you'll find access to the Small Business Administration (SBA) and a variety of forums specially designed to meet the needs of those just starting a business. Once I got out of the Small Office/Home Office folder, I found that the Business and Finance folder includes an area where professionals of various persuasions could meet to discuss their trade. It includes 17 different professions as diverse as airline pilots, doctors, and the fashion industry. Overall, the Business and Finance folder seems tuned to the needs of a small business or a home user. However, this area needs a lot of work if you plan to find anything of a high-end or serious nature.

- Computers and Software: This forum contains the sections that you'd expect: hardware, software, computer games, and access to at least one magazine vendor (*PC Magazine* in this case). It's the other forums that you'll find interesting. For example, there's a section devoted to multimedia and another to telephony. You'll also find sections for desktop publishing and MIDI. I was happy to see a computer classified ad section where you could look for a piece of used hardware or software or get rid of one that's been cluttering up your closet. The Altair Pavilion is a good place to go if you have questions about your computer or the computer industry in general. It appears that they have an online chat section where you can ask questions during a live session, but it wasn't active when I checked. You'll see announcements in MSN Today regarding the various seminars and other services provided at the Altair Pavilion. Overall, you'll find everything that a home user will need here if all you're looking for is help from other users. On the other hand, if you need help from a vendor, you'll probably have to use an online service such as CompuServe, at least in the interim until Microsoft garners the support it needs. There were only two hardware vendors and 16 software vendors as MSN neared its opening date of August 24th.

- Education and Reference: I hope this area eventually takes off, because it already shows some promise. To begin with, you'll find editions of both Microsoft Bookshelf and Microsoft Encarta online. You'll also find sections devoted to colleges and universities, fields of study, and computer education. There was also a section specifically designed with educators in mind. It offers a forum in which they can discuss important issues and a BBS that they can use to download files. Parents can talk with primary and secondary educators here. I was intrigued by the section for home schooling as well. International students will find a section specifically designed for their needs. It includes the usual files and chat sections. The international exchange program folder looked pretty interesting too. This folder has many things an international student would need. For example, there is a forum dealing with student housing and another for pen pals. The International Language Learning forum will certainly come in handy for those who don't know how to speak the language of the country they're going to. I also thought the Phone Home Tips and Tools forum was a nice idea since it's difficult to know the best way to contact those at home after you make the move.

- Home and Family: The potpourri of subjects offered here should keep just about anyone happy. There were sections for teenagers and children and a lot of different hobby-specific areas. The pet forum looked like it was the most active when I visited. Besides the usual cat and dog sections, I found sections for fish, birds, reptiles, and something called "wee furry folk." These forums contained the usual chat and file sections. I found it interesting that they also included special sections for the care and feeding of your pet and another for pet pictures. Besides the pet areas, you'll find sections on home improvement, gardening, and genealogy in the Home and Family area. The Home and Garden folder contains a wealth of information. For example, you'll find separate forums for improving, building, and buying a home. There's even a gardening for kids forum. The '90s-specific forums included topics such as work-at-home dads and working mothers. I thought these added just the right "updated" touch that might separate MSN from other online offerings—at least in this area. The Home and Family Town Hall folder provides an area where you can talk with others about home- and family-related topics. This is also the area where special guests—as listed in MSN Today—appear to talk about home and family.

- Interests, Leisure, and Hobbies: Would you like to find out about the latest paranormal activities in the world? This is where you would go. I expected to find some of the more mundane hobbies here, such as gardening and crafts, and they were present, but there were some unusual offerings as well. Besides the other interesting forums such as Games and Gaming, you'll find a forum devoted to magazines. It wasn't very active when I looked, but it will probably contain the usual chat and file sections along with a magazine review area. The Travel forum also contained an unusual entry—Theme Parks. Here you can find out about your favorite theme park. Disney had its own special section. Perhaps the most helpful feature of this entire area was all the pictures of the various theme parks. Some of them numbered in the hundreds when I checked. By the time you read this book, you should be able to download a picture for just about every aspect of the major theme parks. The pictures are usually followed by a description of what you're seeing. This is one way to find out in advance what you'll see. Some of the other folders in this area include Automotive Interests (where you can talk about a variety of car-related topics), Holidays and Special Occasions (you can find American Greetings here in addition to the normal chat and file areas), Models and Radio Control (an area for discussions about scale and radio-controlled models), and Science and Electronics. (Remember that because this is a hobbiest area, you'll see topics related to modest home-type science and electronics projects.)

- People and Communities: It was almost a disappointment to get to this section. MSN currently supports only a few of the items that you would see on other online services. There's a section for men, another for women, and one if you want to discuss religion. The Culture forum turned out to be one of the highlights here. It contains a European and a Chinese section. It isn't clear why MSN doesn't provide sections for other cultural groups, but they definitely should. The Pop Culture forum turned out to be rather interesting because the people there express a lot of avant-garde ideas. For example, an entire thread is devoted to the meaning of the word "culture." The History and Archeology section is brewing with the results of modern archeological research. If you like plays and first-run productions, you might want to look at the Cultural Events forum. There is even a forum for Politics and Culture. It wasn't very active when I looked, but it seemed to focus on how politics is affecting our world culture. For example, one of the current topics in this forum is about a United Ireland. There are also forums for Holidays and Special Occasions (where you can discuss the holidays or other events practiced by your culture or a culture in another country) and Genealogy (which contains the usual chat and file download sections, coupled with a genealogy library you can use to research your background). Missing from this area are some of the '90s topics you'll find on other online services. For example, I didn't see anything for people with alternative lifestyles. Also missing are the special kid sections that I found so prevalent in other areas of MSN.

- Public Affairs: You'll find a lot of forums relating to government and world affairs here. I found the same types of access to the White House, Senate, and House of Representatives here that I've found in other online services. There are also forums for the armed forces and one for the United Nations. The Local Politics area allows you to access information about your community, but it wasn't very active when I looked at it. There's one folder for every state in the Union here. All you need to do is select your state to see what's going on. The GoverNet Game: Virtual President folder looked pretty interesting. The goal of this game is to "Collect the most votes and become Virtual President". If you've ever thought about running for president, here's your chance. Three folders allow you to react to the current political situation in the United States: Voter Report (an area devoted to reporting the latest government happenings), Voter Alert (an area where special-interest groups can tell you about the government's misdeeds), and Weekly Survey (an area where you can respond to a survey about current issues that the government is considering). For people who really like researching our government by looking at what well-known politicians had to say, there is a Famous Speeches and Text forum. You can download any speech from the 18th, 19th, or 20th century. For example, I found the Monroe Doctrine and the Gettysburg Address in the 19th century area.

Two special areas are Inferno (under the Consumer Services and Information folder) and Journalism World (under the Media Affairs folder). The Inferno forum contained everything from home emergencies to living in the wild. If there's a disaster or emergency topic, you'll find it here. The Journalism World forum contained sections for just about every topic imaginable. There were separate sections for radio, television, and newspaper journalists. You could also find jobs or items for sale in two other sections of this forum. If you're a journalist or aspiring to become one, this is the place to go to meet your colleagues.

- Science and Technology: The science and technology area held very few surprises for me. It included all the forums you would expect, such as biology and astronomy. You'll also find sections on electronics, chemistry, communications technology, medicine (the scientific end of it, not the practical end), physics, transportation, engineering, geology, geography, and the social sciences. The one forum I didn't expect was one specifically devoted to math. It seems as though each math discipline has its own set of equations to memorize, so I expected to find math discussions in those forums, but I didn't expect to find the wealth of other information that I found there. For example, there was one thread on how to create your own 3D graphing calculator and another that dealt with solutions to Rubik's Cube. The Edison Pavilion is another question-and-answer forum. All you do is leave your science or technology question and then return for the live session in order to get your answer. I was very happy to see a specific forum on the environment. The only section present at the time I looked (besides the usual chat and library sections) was one on environmental chemistry. Hopefully Microsoft will get this forum built up so that you can find the entire host of environmental issues represented here. Of all the forums, the Astronomy and Space forum seemed the most active. There were several libraries here, including one for astronomy pictures (those taken from a telescope) and space pictures (those taken from a spacecraft or the Hubble Telescope). You'll also find a library devoted to NASA press releases and another for Astro Magazine. Of course, this folder also contains the usual chat and user library sections.

- Special Events: This is where you would look for real-time discussions of any events listed in MSN Today. It includes an area for Babbage Auditorium and a forum where you can test your communication skills. (Babbage Auditorium is a general question-and-answer chat section. It gets used for special guests—some of which you'll see listed in MSN Today.) At the time I looked, there were also special forums for the Americas Cup, the British Grand Prix, and golf's U.S. Open. The United Nations had a forum here, and there was a special forum for the Runner's World Prefontaine Classic (a running competition). You'll find that the contents of this area will change as the topics in MSN Today change.

- Sports, Health, and Fitness: If you like sports of any kind, this is the forum for you. I found areas for water, winter, indoor, outdoor, field, court, and motor sports. This forum is also appropriate for people who want to stay in shape but don't necessarily want to become the next boxing champion of the world. You'll also find forums designed to inform you of health and fitness issues. There's also a separate sports medicine area where you can find out how to get rid of the leg cramps you get after running or other types of sports injuries.

- The Internet Center: We had already looked at this in Chapter 18, but let me give you a quick rundown of it. The Internet Center allows you to access the Internet. It also provides quick access to many of the news services that the Internet provides. It's especially important to look at the Read Me! icon in this folder, because it provides special news and information regarding the Internet. The document you download will also contain an icon that requests full access to the Internet resources that MSN provides—including adult material that you won't normally see. Not surprisingly, this was the most active area on MSN during my visits there.

- The MSN Member Lobby: This area will help you get started using MSN and provide some vital services that members need in order to use MSN effectively. The main folder you'll need to look at is the Reception Desk. It provides the tips and guidelines that you'll need in order to learn how to use MSN. There is an area for practicing your online communication skills. You can also find out about the various rules you should follow when communicating online. One of the nice touches in this folder was the Welcome Committee folder. It contains pictures of some of the support people you'll meet online, and it will help you get acquainted with MSN faster. Once you leave the Reception Desk folder, you'll probably want to look at the Maps and Information folder. It contains a map of MSN's organization and even provides a tour of MSN. (The tour takes you through the various features that MSN offers.) One of the tip folders here shows you how to find things fast. A separate folder contained a user activity guide. It contained four folders: Windows 95

Stories (a place where you can get help with Windows 95), The Toybox (a place where you can get help with other Microsoft products or get help of a general nature), Chat World (where you can have discussions of a general nature with other members in real time), and Log On Sweepstakes (an MSN contest; you'll need to download the rules for a complete description of this option). Other items that you'll find in the Member Lobby folder include Member Directory (you can find a friend), Member Support (find help using MSN), Accounts and Billing (find out about your accumulated charges), and MSN Gift Shop (online shopping for MSN-specific items such as T-shirts and hats).

- The Microsoft Network Beta: I wasn't sure if you would see this one or not, but I decided to include it anyway. As long as MSN is still in the construction stages, you'll be able to find information about new features and future plans here. Microsoft is also asking for input from everyone who uses the service, so this is a good place to visit if you have a great idea for something new.

It's not too difficult to see that MSN is a work in progress. There are still a lot of features to add before this will provide nearly the same level of service that other online products provide for large-business users. Home and small-business users will find a wealth of information here that should make computing with Windows 95 a lot easier. To its credit, MSN does offer something for everyone. The fact that you have such easy access to it through Windows 95 is a real plus. You'll likely find that the level of support you'll receive will get a lot better if this product matures. However, that's a big if right now, because Microsoft seems to be having more than its share of troubles garnering support for MSN. For example, look at the extreme lack of software and hardware vendor participation. You'll probably want to take a good hard look at MSN before you commit to it.

WUGNET

Windows Users Group Network (WUGNET) isn't an online service, but it's an important group to get to know. They have a forum on CompuServe and many users' groups throughout the United States. WUGNET also has its own newsletter, *Windows Journal*. They encourage people to contribute articles. If you're interested, contact Howard Sobel at 76702,1356 or at sobel@libertynet.org. Sobel will also be your contact on CompuServe for many forum-related activities.

WUGNET was founded in 1988 as an independent organization devoted to providing technical resources for Windows users. Their main goal is to communicate trends and developments in Windows programming and usage to the user community on an international level. They also get involved in some standardization efforts, but their actual participation is not as easy to see here as it is elsewhere.

What will working with WUGNET buy you? They provide presentations about Windows in general through CompuServe, conferences, trade shows, publications, trade books, and various membership interactions. You can access their forum using GO WUGNET. You'll also find that their members are very active on the WinNews forum. This is a special forum that Microsoft developed just for the Windows 95 beta prerelease program.

Note: Joining WUGNET is easy. All you need to do is fill out a membership form that you can download from the CompuServe forum. They offer a range of membership levels, including both personal and corporate rates. WUGNET also provides a few points of contact outside of CompuServe. Here is the information for their main membership contact:

Jim Herndon
Windows Users Group Network
126 E. State St.
Media, PA 19063

E-mail: CompuServe 76702,1356
Internet e-mail: sobel@libertynet.org

Telephone: (215) 565-1861
Fax: (215) 565-7106

Direct membership enrollment: 800-WIN-USER (1-800-946-8737)

When you become a member of WUGNET, you'll receive a toolkit. It contains a variety of things, including online Windows help versions of the Microsoft Windows 3.1 and Windows for Workgroups resource kits, WUGNET System Engineer (available soon), and a support-oriented CompuServe forum with a private library for members. System Engineer is the most interesting tool of the group. It allows you to decipher the myriad of entries in the SYSTEM.INI and WIN.INI files on your machine. System Engineer also provides a variety of performance and resource monitoring tools. Overall, you'll find this a helpful tool for any version of Windows, but it is admittedly Windows 3.x-specific for the moment. Hopefully they will come up with a version of this valuable tool for Windows 95. Of course, this toolkit also includes *Windows Journal*, which I mentioned earlier.

Besides the direct benefits you get from being a WUGNET member, there are additional bonuses as well. The one that most people will really appreciate is reduced prices for software and hardware from a variety of vendors. Some of these vendors include Lotus, Artisoft, Knowledge Garden, hDC, and Micrografx. This is just a short list, but it shows the wide variety of vendors who provide support for WUGNET.

There is also a CD offering for Windows 95 users in the works. It contains a wealth of shareware and freeware utilities. These are demo versions of programs from people you don't know. In addition to shareware and freeware, you'll also find some fully functional utilities from name-brand vendors. Some of the companies who provide software for this CD include Attachmate, American Megatrends Inc. (AMI), Micrografx, and yours truly. Yes, that's right: You'll see a Personal Training Systems Product—*Peter Norton Presents Windows 95 Made Easy Tutorial*—as part of the WUGNET Windows 95 CD.

Microsoft Knowledge Base

Before I get into a full-fledged look at CompuServe in general and the Microsoft offerings in detail, I'd like to look at one special Microsoft forum called the Microsoft Knowledge Base. This isn't a standard forum like the others you'll find on CompuServe. Rather, it's a library of articles, white papers, and other sources of information that you'll need in order to use specific Microsoft products. We'll see later how this special forum fits into the overall scheme of things.

Right now, I'd like to cover why it's important and how you use it. I often look at the Microsoft Knowledge Base for information about the future direction of Microsoft products. For example, I found a white paper dealing with "Program Manager issues in Windows 95." You can also find out a lot about problems people are having—people just like you—and Microsoft's suggested solutions. One white paper informed me of "Windows 95 and After Dark 2.0 Issues" that I could expect. Finally, you can find out the technical details of a product. I found a white paper that provided an "Explanation of System Resources in Windows 95" while browsing through the Knowledge Base. It's not too difficult to figure out that the Knowledge Base is more like a fax support line than anything else. However, the method you use to interact with it is a lot different.

The problem with using automated support in most cases is that unless you really know what you're looking for, it's not very likely that you'll find it. I've been through some fax support lines that are so unfriendly you won't get any information at all unless you know a specific article name or its number. Microsoft Knowledge Base is different. It provides a search engine that you can use to actually find the information you're looking for.

So how do you use this nifty Microsoft offering? The first thing you need is a CompuServe account. You'll have to follow the specific guidelines from your software vendor for getting an account set up and your communications software installed. Once you get all that done, you need to get online in terminal mode. (Products such as CompuServe Information Manager use this mode as a default. Other products, such as TapCIS and OzWin, require you to enter a special command to get into terminal mode.) After you get online, use whatever command your communication package provides to GO MSKB. When you get there, you'll see a menu with the following options:

- What's New in the Knowledge Base: This option displays a help screen that tells you about the features provided by Microsoft Knowledge Base and any new articles you need to know about. It also keeps you up-to-date on future article additions. You can download this help screen by typing DOWN at the prompt.

- Description of Database: Use this option to display a general help screen telling you what kinds of information Microsoft Knowledge Base will provide. As with the preceding selection, you can download it to your hard drive for future reference by typing DOWN at the prompt.

- Online User's Guide: You can use this option to get detailed information about the various search engine features and how to use them. It's a lot more detailed than the first menu option and goes through every menu entry that you'll see. Downloading this help screen also means typing DOWN at the prompt.

- Search the Knowledge Base: This is the option that most people will use. It displays a menu-driven method of obtaining the name and number of various articles. You can choose to download the article immediately or save the number for future reference. We'll discuss the search criteria that this option provides a little later in this section.

- Search Using Expert Mode: Some people hate menus. Once you gain a little experience with Microsoft Knowledge Base, you can use the expert mode to search for articles without using the menu. I don't find this particular method any faster than using the menu-driven approach, but you can use it to automate your searches using script files.

- Quick Search by Document ID Number: Sometimes a support person on one of Microsoft's forums will tell you to download a specific Knowledge Base article for more information about a particular problem. Some questions get asked so often that it's easier to provide a complete answer in an article and allow the user to download it as needed. In addition, some problems are a little more complex than others. This method allows a support person to provide a complete answer even when the question is very complicated. A message on one of the forums just wouldn't provide the same level of information.

- Microsoft Software Library: Sometimes you need a new driver or patch to take care of a problem. The Knowledge Base articles you download might contain an "S" number. You can use this number to download the correct software. All you need to do is select this option and provide the number when asked.

The Search the Knowledge Base selection is probably the most likely choice unless someone from Microsoft directs you to a specific article or you use the search engine quite a bit. Once you choose this option, you'll see a menu of choices for limiting the number of articles that Microsoft Knowledge Base will display. This menu allows you to choose the following criteria: product name, product version, publication date, operating environment, document type, document text, and title text. The last two options allow you to display all the articles that Microsoft Knowledge Base found and start a new search.

CompuServe Forums

CompuServe is absolutely huge. I don't think I've ever really seen everything it has to offer. There's something here for everyone, no matter what your occupation, hobbies, or interests. Seeing really is believing. In fact, it's so large that most people seem to stick to one or two areas because of the number of features that CompuServe has to offer. Beside news, weather, and the stock market, you can shop online and access other services such as Delphi. I even use CompuServe to access the Internet and look for reference materials in Books in Print.

One of the biggest areas that CompuServe offers is software. I've seen vendors here that you would never expect to see online. Just about every game and utility vendor that has any market share at all is here. Many shareware vendors are here as well. You'll also find big companies such as Borland, Computer Associates, and Lotus. Some companies have more than one forum to offer. For example, both Computer Associates and Novell occupy more than one forum area.

It would be difficult to describe in an appendix what some entire books have a problem describing. Some of these books are as large as or even larger than this one and still can't provide a complete listing of all the features that CompuServe provides. With that in mind, I want to concentrate on one area. Since this book is about Windows 95, I'll tell you what kinds of services Microsoft has to offer.

Microsoft offers a wide range of services to all its product users and support technicians. Besides the standard publication of magazines and books, Microsoft offers electronic online services as well. There are two basic services: Microsoft Online and Microsoft's forums on CompuServe. (You can also gain access to some Microsoft information through the Internet.) With these services you can use your computer to stay in touch with Microsoft. The Microsoft Online service is by subscription only, so I won't cover it here. This section does cover Microsoft's CompuServe forums, a vast array of places you can use to get answers for every conceivable question. These forums also offer download services that provide you free updates to your Microsoft products. (Of course, you'll see this service only when the update is free of charge.) Figures A.2 through A.4 provide an overview of Microsoft's CompuServe forums.

As you can see from these figures, Microsoft's CompuServe offering is huge—and this doesn't even include all the beta forums that Microsoft supports. If you feel a little overwhelmed by the number of services that Microsoft offers, you're not alone. You could spend days just trying to find the right forum for your particular needs. For that matter, unless you use a product such as WinCIM (a Windows-based communication program specifically designed for use with CompuServe) to maneuver through the labyrinth of CompuServe menus, you might not even reach your destination. Using Figures A.2 through A.4 should make your job easier and allow you to use more cost-conscious tools such as TapCIS to find your way through CompuServe. Microsoft also offers some special forms of WinCIM that include all the required GO words as part of the Favorite Places listing. One of these appears on the Microsoft Developer Network (MSDN).

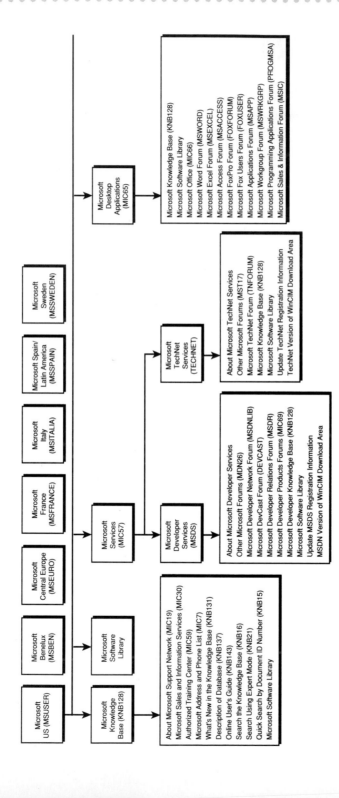

Figure A.2.
A hierarchical view of Microsoft's CompuServe offering.

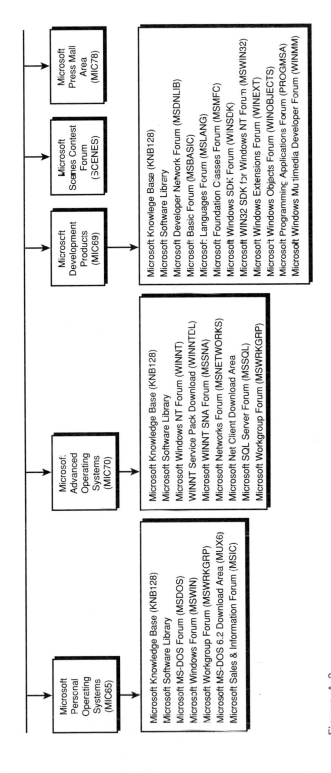

Figure A.3.
Microsoft's CompuServe offering continued.

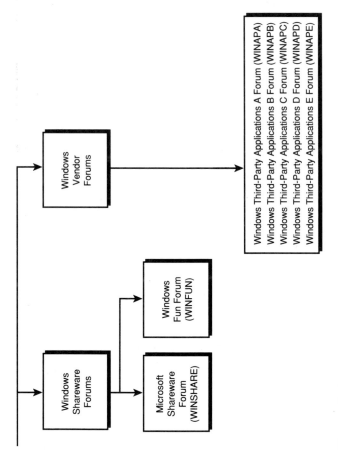

Figure A.4.
Microsoft's CompuServe offering continued.

Figures A.2 through A.4 are arranged in a hierarchical format. This means that the upper-level menus appear first. The actual forums appear at the bottom of the hierarchical tree. Notice the GO words in parentheses beside each menu or forum name. A GO word provides a shortcut on CompuServe. If you know the GO word, you can go directly to the menu or forum that you want to see. Not every menu entry has a GO word, but enough are provided in Figures A.2 through A.4 to greatly decrease your search time. Every forum has a GO word, making it easy to get to any forum you want to visit. You type GO *Forum Name* to get to your destination. Some software, such as WinCIM, OzWin, and TapCIS, automates the GO part of the command for you, but you still need to provide the forum name. Most CompuServe-specific communication software lets you add the forum name to a list so that you don't have to remember it each time you want to access the forum.

Notice that the upper-level menu doesn't list product areas or forums. What this level does provide is access to Microsoft forums in various languages. This allows you to communicate with Microsoft even if you don't understand English. Unfortunately, not every language provides all the services that the Microsoft US section does, so you might need to use this section in some cases.

There is one special GO word that these figures don't contain. You can use GO MSP to get to the Microsoft Press section of the mall. Think of the CompuServe mall as an electronic form of a mall that you shop in. You'll find a wide variety of stores here besides Microsoft Press. You can use the Microsoft Press forum in the CompuServe mall to order books or a catalog. Using it will save you a trip to the bookstore by providing you with a complete list of the books you can order. Even the best-stocked bookstore in the world might miss a selection or two out of Microsoft Press' vast array of books. The following text describes the sections you'll find in the Microsoft US section.

Information on Microsoft

This section offers four services. The About Microsoft Support Network service tells you all about Microsoft's service support offerings. It specifically looks at what the Microsoft Support Network offers. Use the Microsoft Sales and Information Services selection to obtain sales and service information. The Authorized Training Center service provides information about Microsoft's authorized training center program. It also provides a phone number you can use to obtain further information. Finally, the Microsoft Address and Phone List service provides a complete list of telephone numbers and addresses. It includes individual product service numbers as well as numbers for various Microsoft subsidiaries.

You can download any of these four services for future reference. Each one tells you about a different component of Microsoft. Unfortunately, this section doesn't provide any interactive capability. Microsoft provides these services through the plethora of forums described in the following section. Overall, this section provides you with quick references. Essentially, it contains the telephone numbers you need to obtain further information.

Microsoft Knowledge Base and Microsoft Software Library

We covered both of these selections earlier in this appendix. I'd like to provide a couple of additional paragraphs about the Microsoft Software Library since it appears by itself in some areas. It provides some additional features when it appears by itself that it doesn't provide when shown as part of the Microsoft Knowledge Base. You'll see what I mean when you actually start using Figures A.2 through A.4 to find various areas of interest on CompuServe.

The Microsoft Software Library provides access to a wide assortment of Microsoft tested and approved software. This is differentiated from the software you normally download from forums, which Microsoft might not have tested. The Software Library uses a search engine similar to that used by the Knowledge Base. Of course, there are a few differences due to the differences in the tasks performed by these two services.

Once you find the software you need, the Software Library gives you the opportunity to download it. There's no real difference between the download procedure for the software library and any other service on CompuServe. All you need to do is provide a filename for your computer and specify the download protocol. In most cases, your communication software will take care of the rest.

Microsoft Services

The Microsoft Services menu entry contains two submenus: Microsoft Developer Services and Microsoft TechNet Services. The Microsoft Developer Services entry provides access to all the developer-related services, such as the Microsoft Developer Network forum. A developer is someone who writes applications using any number of tools, including compilers and debuggers. This particular forum is heavily tied to the Microsoft Developer Library (formerly the Microsoft Developer Network) subscription service. This is a CD-ROM packed with information, Knowledge Base articles, books, and even some software. You can even download a special version of WinCIM in this area. This version provides special menu entries that relate to the Microsoft developer services.

Like the Developer Services area, the Microsoft TechNet Services area revolves around a CD-ROM subscription service. In this case, the subscription is called the Microsoft TechNet CD-ROM-based information service. This service is designed for people who require in-depth information on Microsoft products and how to support them. This differs from the programming language and operating system support provided by the Developer Network. The TechNet forum allows users to exchange ideas and provide feedback to Microsoft. It also provides access to TechEd information. (TechEd, which is short for "technical education," refers to Microsoft's educational services outside of the programming and operating system arenas.) As with the Developer Services area, you can download a special version of WinCIM for this area. This version provides special menu entries that relate to the Microsoft TechNet services.

Microsoft Desktop Applications

This area of Microsoft CompuServe support provides access to all the user-oriented tools, such as Word, Excel, Access, and FoxPro. In fact, these four products have their own special forums. FoxPro rates two forums: one for developers and the other for users. You can usually obtain information about the other Microsoft applications by going to the Microsoft Applications forum.

Four special menu entries allow you to access the Knowledge Base, Software Library, sales, and Programming Applications forum. All four entries work just like their counterparts in other areas.

Microsoft Personal Operating Systems

Microsoft differentiates between single-user and multiuser operating systems. This area deals with single-user or personal operating systems. There are three operating systems in this category: MS-DOS, Windows, and Windows for Workgroups. The menu entries for each area are pretty self-explanatory.

Notice the special entry for the Microsoft MS-DOS 6.22 Download Area. Going to this entry allows you to download the MS-DOS 6.22 step-up software free of charge (except for connect time). As with the other areas described in this appendix, Microsoft provides access to its Knowledge Base and Software Library in this area as well.

Microsoft Advanced Operating Systems

Microsoft set aside a special area for users of advanced operating systems. Currently only one operating system, Windows NT, falls into this category. However, you can see from the figures that a lot is going on with this one product. Notice the special areas for SNA and SQL Server. Like the other areas described in this appendix, this one also contains access to the Knowledge Base and the Software Library.

If you're a developer, you'll probably want to visit more than one of these forums. For example, if you develop Windows NT applications, you'll probably need to visit the Windows NT and Networks forums.

An application user can probably get by with just one forum. In most cases, a visit to the Windows NT forum will give you all the information you need. Unlike the developer, you work with the operating system to a greater extent in getting applications to work together properly. As a result, you'll probably want to download all the messages in this forum. Check the section titles carefully; you might find that you can eliminate one or two of them from your list. Remember, you'll probably want to visit this forum in addition to application-specific forums.

Microsoft Development Products

There is a special area besides the Developer Network section for application developers. The Development Products area is much more general in nature. It gives you access to all the language products that Microsoft provides. Note the special forums for Basic users and multimedia developers.

If you're a developer, you'll probably want to visit more than one of these forums. For example, if you develop Windows applications, you'll probably need to visit the Languages forum and the Windows SDK forum. Sometimes you might want to visit three or four forums. Talk about information overload! If you don't monitor your time carefully, you could easily spend all your time gathering information instead of performing useful work. Fortunately, you'll probably find that you won't need to read all the messages on the forum, just the few related to your specific areas of interest.

Microsoft Scenes Contest Forum

This is a temporary forum (just how temporary remains to be seen) that allows you to submit your photographs to the Microsoft Scenes contest. There are a few limitations and some rules that you must follow in order to enter.

Microsoft Press Mall Area

This is a special area for the computer press. You won't need to go here in most cases unless you're interested in press releases and so forth.

Windows Shareware Forums

Many people discount the value of shareware software, but Microsoft doesn't. Shareware can provide the same or better quality than an off-the-shelf commercial product, and at a greatly reduced price. It always pays to check this area for special needs. You never know when you'll find something that a client has asked for in the past but you couldn't find.

The Windows Shareware Forums area is split into two forums: Windows Shareware Forum and Windows Fun Forum. Both forums are designed to provide a venue for you to talk with shareware authors who create Windows products. The main difference between the two forums is that one is for application products you can use for serious work and the other provides items such as screen savers that you can use for fun.

Windows Vendor Forums

This group of five forums is a place for smaller commercial product vendors to provide their services. Each vendor occupies one section of the forum. (There are 18 sections in each forum, but at least one section is private in most cases.) This includes one message and one library area. They all share the conference rooms. You might want to check each area to see if a vendor of a product you use is present.

Windows BBSs

Some people will find the cost of using an online service such as CompuServe just a bit too high for what they get out of it. They like to frequent local BBSs and find information that way. Not only is this information free, but the cost of calling isn't too high, either.

Trying to find a Windows-specific BBS in your area won't be hard at all. The best place to start looking is your local user group. Most larger cities also have a local computer magazine or two. You'll find these free magazines in your local software stores and some of the larger technical bookstores. Near the back of such a magazine, you'll usually find a listing of all the local BBSs. Although these listings usually don't provide a lot of information, the BBS name usually implies its orientation.

If these methods of finding a local BBS fail, you can always try to call the Association of Personal Computer User Groups (APCUG) at (914) 876-6678. This number will at least help you find a user group in your area. Many of them run their own BBSs as well. Finding a BBS this way could actually double the benefit you receive, because then you'll know how to contact the user group as well.

A local BBS will have limitations that an online service won't, but I mentioned most of them in the early part of this appendix. I usually tell businesses that they'll make back the cost of using an online service with increased employee productivity and better sources of information for problem resolutions. However, the payback for a home user isn't as easy to see. You'll probably want to at least try both an online service and a BBS for a while to see which one meets your needs better.

B

Glossary

American Standard Code for Information Interchange   See ASCII.

API (Application Programming Interface)   A method of defining a standard set of function calls and other interface elements. It usually defines the interface between a high-level language and the lower-level elements used by a device driver or operating system. The ultimate goal is to provide some type of service to an application that requires access to the operating system or device feature set.

application independence   A method of writing applications so that they don't depend on the specific features of an operating system or hardware interface. It normally requires the use of a high-level language and an API. The programmer also needs to write the application in such a way as to avoid specific hardware or operating system references. All user and device interface elements must use the generic functions provided by the API.

application programming interface   See API.

ASCII (American Standard Code for Information Interchange)   A standard method of equating the numeric representations available in a computer to human-readable form. For example, the number 32 represents a space. There are 128 characters (7 bits) in the standard ASCII code. The extended ASCII code uses 8 bits for 256 characters. Display adapters from the same machine type usually use the same upper 128 characters. Printers, however, might reserve these upper 128 characters for nonstandard characters. For example, many Epson printers use them for the italic representations of the lower 128 characters.

B-step processor   An older 80386 processor type that incorporated elements that are incompatible with Windows 95. The normal reason for using this processor type was to provide additional system functionality or improved speed characteristics.

bidirectional support   Defines a printer's ability to transfer information both ways on a printer cable. Input usually contains data or printer control codes. Output usually contains printer status information or error codes.

binary value   Refers to a base 2 data representation in the Windows registry. Normally used to hold status flags or other information that lends itself to a binary format.

.BMP files   Windows standard bitmap graphics data format. This is a raster graphic data format that doesn't include any form of compression. OS/2 can also use this data format to hold graphics of various types.

CDFS (Compact Disc File System)   The portion of the file subsystem specifically designed to interact with compact disc drives. It also provides the user interface elements required to tune this part of the subsystem. The CDFS takes the place of an FSD for CD-ROM drives.

class ID   See CLSID.

client   The recipient of data, services, or resources from a file or other server. This term can refer to a workstation or an application. The server can be another PC or an application.

CLSID (class ID) A method of assigning a unique identifier to each object in the registry. Also refers to various high-level language constructs.

CMOS (Complimentary Metal Oxide Semiconductor) Normally refers to a construction method for low-power, battery-backed memory. When used in the context of a PC, this term usually refers to the memory used to store system configuration information and the real-time clock status. The configuration information normally includes the amount of system memory, the type and size of floppy drives, the hard drive parameters, and the video display type. Some vendors include other configuration information as part of this chip as well.

compact disc file system See CDFS.

Complimentary Metal Oxide Semiconductor See CMOS.

container Part of the object-oriented terminology that has become part of OLE. A container is a drive, file, or other resource used to hold objects. The container is normally referenced as an object itself.

DAT (Digital Audio Tape) drive A tape drive that uses a cassette to store data. The cassette and the drive use the same technology as the audio version of the DAT drive. However, the internal circuitry of the drive formats the tape for use with a computer system. The vendor must also design the interface circuitry with computer needs in mind. DAT tapes allow you to store large amounts of information in a relatively small amount of space. Typical drive capacities range from 1.2 GB to 8 GB.

data-centric The method used by modern operating systems to view the user interface from a data perspective rather than from the perspective of the applications used to create the data. Using this view allows users to worry more about manipulating the data on their machines than the applications required to perform a specific task.

DDE (Dynamic Data Exchange) The ability to cut data from one application and paste it into another application. For example, you could cut a graphic image created with a paint program and paste it into a word processing document. Once pasted, the data doesn't reflect changes made to it by the originating application. DDE also provides a method of communicating with an application that supports it and requesting data. For example, you could use an Excel macro to call Microsoft Word and request the contents of a document file. Some applications also use DDE to implement file association strategies. For example, Microsoft Word uses DDE in place of command-line switches to gain added flexibility when a user needs to open or print a file.

device-independent bitmap See DIB.

DIB (Device-Independent Bitmap) A method of representing graphic information that doesn't reflect a particular device's requirements. This has the advantage of allowing the same graphic to appear on any device in precisely the same way, despite differences in resolution or other factors that normally change the graphic's appearance.

digital audio tape drive   See DAT.

direct memory access   See DMA.

disk defragmenter   An application used to reorder the data on a long-term storage device such as a hard or floppy disk drive. Reordering the data so that it appears in sequential order—file by file—reduces the time required to access and read it. Sequential order allows you to read an entire file without moving the disk head at all in some cases and only a little in others. This reduction in access time normally improves overall system throughput and therefore enhances system efficiency.

DLL (Dynamic Link Library)   A special form of application code loaded into memory by request. It is not executable by itself. A DLL does contain one or more discrete routines that an application may use to provide specific features. For example, a DLL could provide a common set of file dialogs used to access information on the hard drive. More than one application may use the functions provided by a DLL, reducing overall memory requirements when more than one application is running.

DMA (Direct Memory Access)   A memory addressing technique in which the processor doesn't perform the actual data transfer. This method of memory access is faster than any other technique.

DOS protected-mode interface   See DPMI.

DPMI (DOS Protected-Mode Interface)   A method of accessing extended memory from a DOS application using the Windows extended memory manager.

drag and drop   A technique used in object-oriented operating systems to access data without actually opening the file using conventional methods. For example, this system allows the user to pick up a document file, drag it to the printer, and drop it. The printer will print the document using its default settings.

dual-ported video RAM   See VRAM.

Dvorak layout   An alternative method of laying out the keyboard so that stress is reduced and typing speed is increased. It's different from the more familiar "QWERTY" layout used by most keyboards and typewriters.

dynamic data exchange   See DDE.

dynamic link library   See DLL.

embedded systems   A combination of processor, operating system, and device-specific applications used in concert with a special-purpose device. For example, the control used to set the time and temperature on a microwave is an embedded system. Another form of embedded system is the computer that controls engine efficiency in a car.

EMF (Enhanced Metafile)   Used as an alternative storage format by some graphics applications. This is a vector graphic format, so it provides a certain level of device independence and other features that a vector graphic normally provides.

EMM (Expanded Memory Manager)   A device driver like EMM386.EXE that provides expanded memory services on an 80386 and above machine. (Special drivers work with 80286 and a few 8088/8086 machines.) An application accesses expanded memory using a page frame or other memory-mapping techniques from within the conventional or upper memory area (0 to 124 KB). The EMM usually emulates expanded memory using extended memory managed by an extended memory manager (XMM) like HIMEM.SYS. An application must change the processor's mode to protected mode in order to use XMS. Some products, such as 386MAX.SYS and QEMM.SYS, provide both EMM and XMM services in one driver.

EMS (Expanded Memory Specification)   Several versions of this specification are in current use. The most popular version is 3.2, even though a newer 4.0 specification is available. This specification defines one method of extending the amount of memory that a processor can address from the conventional memory area. It uses an area outside of system memory to store information. An EMM provides a window view into this larger data area. The old 3.2 specification requires a 64 KB window in the UMB. The newer 4.0 specification can create this window anywhere in conventional or UMB memory.

enhanced metafile   See EMF.

expanded memory manager   See EMM.

expanded memory specification   See EMS.

FAT (File Allocation Table)   The method of formatting a hard disk drive used by DOS and other operating systems. This technique is one of the oldest formatting methods available.

file allocation table disk format   See FAT.

file system driver   See FSD.

FSD (File System Driver)   A file subsystem component responsible for defining the interface between Windows and long-term storage. The FSD also defines features such as long filenames and what types of interaction the device supports. For example, the CD-ROM FSD wouldn't support file writes unless you provided a device that could perform that sort of task.

GDI (Graphics Device Interface)   One of the main Windows root components. It controls the way that artistic graphic elements are presented on-screen. Every application must use the API provided by this component to draw or perform other graphics-related tasks.

GDT (Global Descriptor Table)   A memory construct that contains the information required to control all the extended memory in an 80386 or above processor. The GDT normally passes control of smaller memory segments to the LDTs used by an individual application.

general protection fault   See GPF.

global descriptor table   See GDT.

GPF (General Protection Fault)   A processor or memory error that occurs when an application makes a request that the system can't honor. This type of error results in some type of severe action on the part of the operating system. Normally, the operating system terminates the offending application.

graphical user interface   See GUI.

graphics device interface   See GDI.

GUI (Graphical User Interface)   A system of icons and graphic images that replaces the character-mode menu system used by many machines. The GUI can ride on top of another operating system (such as DOS or UNIX) or reside as part of the operating system itself (such as Windows or OS/2). Advantages of a GUI are ease of use and high-resolution graphics. Disadvantages are higher workstation hardware requirements and lower performance over a similar system using a character-mode interface.

high memory area   See HMA.

high-performance file system   See HPFS.

HMA (High Memory Area)   The 64 KB area of memory beyond the 1 MB boundary that the processor can access in real mode on an 80286 or above processor.

HPFS (High-Performance File System)   The method of formatting a hard disk drive used by OS/2. Although it provides significant speed advantages over other formatting techniques, only the OS/2 operating system and applications designed to work with that operating system can access a drive formatted using this technique.

ICM (Image Color Matcher)   A special component of the graphics subsystem that allows Windows to match the colors produced by one device with those available on another device. The result is that the output of both devices doesn't show the normal variations in color that Windows applications currently produce.

icon   A symbol used to graphically represent the purpose and/or function of an application or file. For example, a text file might appear as a sheet of paper with the filename below the icon. Applications designed for the environment or operating system usually appear with a special icon depicting the vendor's or product's logo. Icons normally are part of a GUI environment or operating system such as Windows or OS/2.

IFS (Installable File System) manager   The API component of the file subsystem. It provides a consistent interface that applications can use to access a variety of devices, local and remote. This component also provides a standard interface that device drivers can use to provide services such as file opening and drive status.

image color matcher   See ICM.

.INF file A special form of device or application configuration file. It contains all the parameters that Windows requires to install or configure the device or application. For example, an application .INF file might contain the location of data files and the interdependencies of DLLs. Both application and device .INF files contain the registry and .INI file entries required to make Windows recognize the application or device.

installable file system helper A special real-mode component of the IFS manager used to allow access of Windows drive functions by DOS applications. It uses the same DOS interface as before, but all processing is performed by the protected-mode manager.

installable file system manager See IFS manager.

interrupt request See IRQ.

IRQ (Interrupt Request) The set of special address lines that connect a peripheral to the processor. Think of an IRQ as an office telephone with multiple incoming lines. Every time a device calls, its entry lights up on the front of the phone. The processor selects the desired line and picks up the receiver to find out what the device wants. Everything works fine as long as there is one line for each device that needs to call the processor. If more than one device were to try to call in on the same line, the processor wouldn't know who was at the other end. This is the source of IRQ conflicts that you hear about from various sources. Older PC class machines provided eight interrupt lines. The newer AT class machines provide 16. However, only 15 of those are usable since one of them is used for internal purposes.

LAN (Local Area Network) A combination of hardware and software used to connect a group of PCs to each other and/or a mini or mainframe computer. There are two main networking models in use: peer-to-peer and client-server. The peer-to-peer model doesn't require a dedicated server. In addition, all the workstations in the group can share resources. The client-server model uses a central server for resource sharing, but some special methods are provided for using local resources in a limited fashion.

LDT (Local Descriptor Table) A memory construct that controls access to the memory used by a single application or a group of applications that share the same memory. The LDT is subservient to the GDT that manages system memory overall.

listbox A windowing construct that contains a list of items. Normally the user selects one or more of these items in order to respond to an application or operating system query.

local area network See LAN.

local descriptor table See LDT.

MAPI (Messaging API) The set of functions and other resources that Windows provides to communication programs. It allows the application to access a variety of communication channels using a single set of calls and without regard to media. This is the component of Windows 95 that allows Exchange to process information from e-mail and online services using the same interface.

MCA (Microchannel Architecture)   A specialized bus introduced by IBM. It's faster than the old ISA bus and gives the operating system information about the peripheral devices connected to the bus. It also provides the means for devices to become self-configuring.

messaging API   See MAPI.

microchannel architecture   See MCA.

miniport driver   A specialized Windows component that provides access to a resource, normally a peripheral device of some type. It's also used to access pseudo-devices and network resources.

Motion Picture Experts Group   See MPEG.

MPEG (Motion Picture Experts Group)   A standards group that provides file formats and other specifications in regard to full-motion video and other types of graphic displays.

multiple-boot configuration   A method of creating a configurable environment that was first introduced with DOS 5.0. The user simply selects the operating environment from a list of environments presented prior to the boot sequence. This technique provides an additional layer of flexibility and allows the user to optimize the operating environment to perform specific tasks.

multitasking   The ability of some processor and environment/system combinations to perform more than one task at a time. The applications appear to run simultaneously. For example, you can download messages from an online service, print from a word processor, and recalculate a spreadsheet all at the same time. Each application receives a slice of time before the processor moves to the next application. Because the time slices are fairly small, it appears to the user that these actions are occurring simultaneously.

national language support   See NLS.

nested objects   Two or more objects that are coupled in some fashion. The objects normally appear within the confines of a container object. Object nesting allows multiple objects to define the properties of a higher-level object. It also allows the user to associate different types of objects with each other.

network interface card   See NIC.

NIC (Network Interface Card)   The device responsible for allowing a workstation to communicate with the file server and other workstations. It provides the physical means of creating the connection. The card plugs into an expansion slot in the computer. A cable that attaches to the back of the card completes the communication path.

NLS (National Language Support)   A method of reconfiguring the keyboard and other system components to support more than one language through the use of code pages. Each code page defines a different language configuration. Unfortunately, this technique doesn't change the language used for display purposes. In other words, NLS won't cause your English-language version of Windows to suddenly display prompts and other text in German.

NTFS (Windows NT File System)   The method of formatting a hard disk drive used by Windows NT. Although it provides significant speed advantages over other formatting techniques, only the Windows NT operating system and applications designed to work with that operating system can access a drive formatted using this technique.

object conversion   A method of changing the format and properties of an object created by one application to the format and properties used by another. Conversion moves the data from one application to another, usually without a loss in formatting, but always without a loss of content.

object linking and embedding   See OLE.

OLE (Object Linking and Embedding)   The process of packaging a filename and any required parameters into an object and then pasting this object into the file created by another application. For example, you could place a graphic object within a word processing document or spreadsheet. When you look at the object, it appears as if you simply pasted the data from the originating application into the current application (similar to DDE). When linked, the data provided by the object automatically changes as you change the data in the original object. When embedded, the data doesn't change unless you specifically edit it, but the data still retains its original format and you still use the original application to edit the data. Often you can start the originating application and automatically load the required data by double-clicking on the object. The newer OLE 2 specification allows for in-place data editing as well as editing in a separate application window.

password caching   A method of saving the passwords for resources that a user might need to access. The user still needs to enter the main password required to access Windows, but Windows remembers the passwords required to access other resources, such as a network or an online service that directly supports the Windows password caching capability.

.PCX file   A raster graphic data format originally used by ZSoft Paintbrush. This format has gone through many nonstandard transitions and occasionally presents problems when accessed by applications other than the original. It provides for various levels of color and includes data compression.

PD (Port Driver)   Performs the task of communicating with the device through an adapter. It's the last stage before a message leaves Windows and the first stage when a message arrives from the device. The PD is usually adapter-specific. For example, you would have one VxD for each hard drive and one PD for each hard drive adapter.

PIF (Program Information File)   A special configuration file that Windows and OS/2 use to define the environment for a DOS application. The PIF usually includes various memory settings along with the application's command path and working directory.

plug and play   The combination of BIOS, operating system, and peripheral device components that provides a self-configuring environment. This self-configuring feature allows the operating system to avoid potential hardware conflicts by polling the peripheral devices, assessing their requirements, and determining and implementing optimal settings for each device.

port driver   See PD.

POST (Power-On Self Test)   The set of diagnostic and configuration routines that the BIOS runs during system initialization. For example, the memory counter you see during the boot sequence is part of this process.

power-on self test   See POST.

program information file   See PIF.

protected mode   The processor mode in which the processor can access all of extended memory. This mode also provides a better level of application error detection as part of the processing cycle.

protected-mode mapper   A special application that converts real-mode device driver calls into those used by a protected-mode counterpart. It enables you to use your DOS drivers under Windows. Without the support of this VxD, Windows couldn't support legacy devices that lack Windows-specific drivers.

real mode   A Windows operating mode that supports the capabilities of the 8088/8086 processor. This essentially limits you to loading one application within the confines of conventional memory. Windows versions after 3.0 don't support this mode. You must use these versions with workstations containing an 80286 or higher processor.

.REG file   A special file used by the registry to hold a text version of the keys and values it contains. Some applications provide .REG files that you can use to incorporate their file associations and OLE capabilities into Windows.

registry key   This is a registry heading. It provides the structure required to hold configuration values and other information required by both Windows and the applications it runs.

registry value   Each value provides some type of Windows configuration information. There are three types of registry value: string, DWORD, and binary. Of the three, the only human-readable form is string.

remote access   The ability to use a remote resource as you would a local resource. In some cases, this also means downloading the remote resource to use as a local resource.

remote procedure call   See RPC.

RPC (Remote Procedure Call)   The ability to use code or data on a remote machine as if it were local. This is an advanced capability that will eventually pave the way for decentralized applications.

SCSI manager   Windows NT introduced something called the miniport driver. With Windows 95, you can use the Windows NT miniport binaries. However, before you can actually do this, Windows 95 must translate its commands to a format that the miniport driver will understand. The SCSI manager performs this service.

SCSIzer This is a file subsystem component that deals with the SCSI command language. Think of the command language as the method that the computer uses to tell a SCSI device to perform a task. The command language isn't the data the SCSI device handles; rather, it's the act the SCSI device will perform. There's one SCSIzer for each SCSI device.

server An application or workstation that provides services, resources, or data to a client application or workstation. The client usually makes requests in the form of OLE, DDE, or other command formats.

shell extension A special application that gives some type of added value to the operating system interface. In most cases, the application must register itself with the registry before the operating system will recognize it.

system resource Data, peripheral devices, or other system components used to create, delete, or manipulate documents and produce output.

system VM (Virtual Machine) The component of the Windows operating system tasked to create virtual machines and manage DOS applications.

TAPI (Telephony API) An interface used by applications to interface with various types of communication equipment. This currently includes both modems and fax devices.

task switching The ability of an operating system to support more than one application or thread of execution at a time. The foreground application or task is the only one that executes. All other threads of execution are suspended in the background. Contrast this with multitasking, in which all threads—background and foreground—execute.

Telephony API See TAPI.

terminate and stay resident program See TSR.

thunk The programming interface that translates 32-bit data and system calls to their 16-bit counterpart. The opposite translation takes place going from a 16-bit application to its 32-bit counterpart.

TrueType A special form of vector font originally provided with Windows but used with other operating systems as well. This vector font provides hinting and other features that give it a smoother appearance on-screen.

TSD (Type-Specific Driver) Part of the file subsystem, this layer deals with logical device types rather than specific devices. For example, one TSD handles all the hard drives on your system, and another TSD handles all the floppy drives. A third TSD would handle all network drives.

TSR (Terminate and Stay Resident) An application that loads itself into memory and stays there after you execute it. The program usually returns you directly to the DOS prompt after loading. Pressing a hot key combination activates the application, allowing you to use the application. In most cases, TSRs provide some type of utility, print spooling, or other short-term function.

type-specific driver   See TSD.

UAE (Unrecoverable Application Error)   A processor or memory error that occurs when an application makes a request that the system can't honor. The operating system normally doesn't detect an error of this type. The result is that the system freezes or becomes unstable to the point of being unusable. Also see GPF.

UMB (Upper Memory Block)   The area of memory between 640 KB and the 1 MB boundary. IBM originally set aside this area of memory for device ROMs and special device memory areas. Use of various memory managers allows you to load applications and device drivers in this area.

unrecoverable application error   See UAE.

upper memory block   See UMB.

VCPI (Virtual Control Program Interface)   A method of accessing extended memory from a DOS application using a third-party XMM. Also see DPMI.

VDD (Virtual Display Driver)   Windows 3.x used this module as its sole source of communication with the display adapter. Windows 95 provides it for compatibility purposes and for DOS applications. It translates application requests into graphics commands and draws the result in video memory.

vector font   A type of font that uses mathematical expressions instead of a bitmap to define its characteristics.

vector table   The place in lower memory where ROM and DOS store pointers to operating system-specific routines. Most of these routines allow an application to access a device or perform some specific task, such as opening a file.

VESA (Video Electronics Standards Association)   A standards group responsible for creating display adapter and monitor specifications. This group has also worked on other standards, such as the VL bus used in some PCs.

VFAT (Virtual File Allocation Table)   An enhanced method of disk formatting based on the FAT system. It allows for additional functionality such as long filenames.

Video Electronics Standards Association   See VESA.

virtual anything driver   See VxD.

virtual control program interface   See VCPI.

virtual display driver   See VDD.

virtual file allocation table   See VFAT.

volume tracking driver   See VTD.

VRAM (Dual-Ported Video RAM)   A special form of memory that allows simultaneous reads and writes. It provides a serial read interface and a parallel write interface. The advantage of using VRAM is that it's much faster and doesn't require as much detection code on the part of the application or device driver.

VTD (Volume Tracking Driver)   This file subsystem component handles any removable devices attached to your system.

VxD (Virtual Anything Driver)   A special form of DLL that provides low-level system support.

Windows NT file system   See NTFS.

Wizard   A specialized application that reduces the complexity of using or configuring your system. For example, the Printer Wizard makes it easier to install a new printer.

Index

Add to Your Sams Library Today with the Best Books for Programming, Operating Systems, and New Technologies

The easiest way to order is to pick up the phone and call
1-800-428-5331
between 9:00 a.m. and 5:00 p.m. EST.
For faster service please have your credit card available.

ISBN	Quantity	Description of Item	Unit Cost	Total Cost
0-672-30624-7		Peter Norton's Inside the PC, Sixth Edition	$35.00	
0-672-30614-X		Peter Norton's Complete Guide to DOS 6.22, Premier Edition	$29.99	
0-672-30615-8		Peter Norton's Visual Basic 4 Programming, Fourth Edition	$39.99	
0-672-30670-0		The Winn L. Rosch Multimedia Bible (book/CD-ROM)	$39.99	
0-672-30504-6		Teach Yourself Windows 95 in 24 Hours	$25.00	
0-672-30531-3		Teach Yourself Windows 95 Programming in 21 Days, Second Edition	$39.99	
0-672-30474-0		Windows 95 Unleashed (book/CD-ROM)	$35.00	
0-672-30685-9		Windows NT 3.5 Unleashed, Second Edition	$39.99	
0-672-30620-4		Teach Yourself Visual Basic 4 in 21 Days, Third Edition	$29.99	
0-672-30684-0		Teach Yourself OS/2 Warp in a Week, Second Edition	$25.00	
0-672-30735-9		Teach Yourself the Internet in a Week, Second Edition	$25.00	
0-672-30765-0		Navigating the Internet with Windows 95	$25.00	
❑ 3 ½" Disk		Shipping and Handling: See information below.		
❑ 5 ¼" Disk		TOTAL		

Shipping and Handling: $4.00 for the first book, and $1.75 for each additional book. Floppy disk: add $1.75 for shipping and handling. If you need to have it NOW, we can ship product to you in 24 hours for an additional charge of approximately $18.00, and you will receive your item overnight or in two days. Overseas shipping and handling adds $2.00 per book and $8.00 for up to three disks. Prices subject to change. Call for availability and pricing information on latest editions.

201 W. 103rd Street, Indianapolis, Indiana 46290

1-800-428-5331 — Orders   1-800-835-3202 — FAX   1-800-858-7674 — Customer Service

Book ISBN 0-672-30791-X